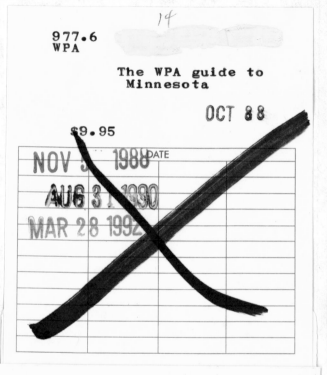

977.6
WPA

14

The WPA guide to
Minnesota

OCT 88

$9.95

NOV 5 1988 DATE		
AUG 31 1990		
MAR 28 1992		

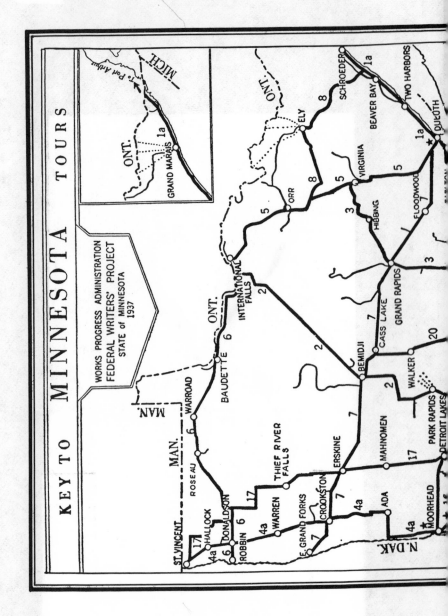

KEY TO MINNESOTA TOURS

WORKS PROGRESS ADMINISTRATION
FEDERAL WRITERS' PROJECT
STATE of MINNESOTA
1937

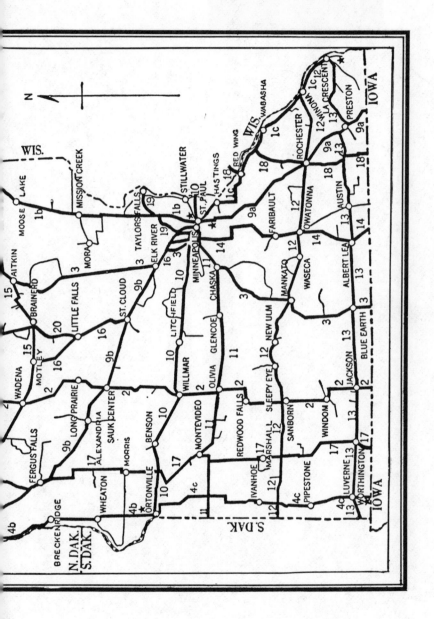

The WPA Guide to
MINNESOTA

The WPA Guide to
MINNESOTA

*Compiled and Written
by the Federal Writers' Project of the
Works Progress Administration*

With a New Introduction by
FREDERICK MANFRED

MINNESOTA HISTORICAL SOCIETY PRESS
St. Paul • 1985

MINNESOTA HISTORICAL SOCIETY PRESS, St. Paul 55101
Manufactured in the United States of America
Copyright © 1938 by the Executive Council, State of Minnesota
New material © 1985 by Minnesota Historical Society
All rights reserved
International Standard Book Number 0-87351-185-9
10 9 8 7 6 5 4 3 2

LIBRARY OF CONGRESS CATALOGING IN PUBLICATION DATA

Main entry under title:

The WPA guide to Minnesota.

  Reprint. Originally published: Minnesota, a state
guide. New York : Viking, 1938. With a new bibliography.
  Bibliography: p.
  Includes index.
  1. Minnesota. 2. Minnesota—Description and travel—
1858–1950—Guide-books. I. Minnesota Federal Writers'
Project. II. Minnesota, a state guide.
P606.W86   1985   977.6   84-29475

Contents

Part II. Minnesota: Cities and Towns

Part III. Minnesota: Tours

Part IV. *Appendices*

List of Illustrations

*Page numbers listed here refer to the illustration pages,
all of which are grouped in a section preceding Part I.*

Photographs marked * are by courtesy of Farm Security Administration; those marked
† are by courtesy of the University of Minnesota; those not otherwise credited are the
work of the Works Progress Administration staff. The drawings are by George Wallace of
the Federal Art Project of Minnesota.

List of Maps

Introduction

IF there ever was an argument for state support of the arts, it came about in 1935 when the federal government initiated the Federal Writers' Project as part of the Works Progress Administration (WPA) to produce, among other things, the American Guide Series. That act compares favorably with the state support the Greeks gave their dramatists and poets, Aeschylus, Sophocles, Euripides, and Menander, some twenty-four centuries earlier. It kept alive the hopes of many fledgling writers — as well as those of established authors — that perhaps they could survive at writing long enough to make a go of it later on their own. It kept them from giving up in those dark depression days. For the rest of the country, the series provided, for the first time, a detailed study of the people, resources, and traditions of each state in the union.[1]

The WPA Guide to Minnesota (originally entitled *Minnesota: A State Guide*) was published in 1938, three years after Mabel S. Ulrich, a physician and former bookstore owner, became director of the new Minnesota Writers' Project. She later wrote that when she accepted the job, she was asked: Could she find 250 writers in the state in ten days? She said that at the time she was not sure there were any "mute inglorious authors" in Minnesota. She put out the call, and soon she was interviewing men and women, "all of them genteelly shabby and obviously — almost too obviously — 'educated' "; all of them bearing "some earmarks of defeat, the younger ones defiantly, the older ones with bleak, downcast eyes or propitiatory smiles." In the group were unemployed preachers, lawyers, executives, editors of country newspapers, publicity men, salesmen, even "a gentleman farmer." She finally accepted 120 "from the neediest and most promising."[2]

All had "written a little." Among the group was Meridel Le Sueur, already well known as a storyteller and teacher of creative writing. She has since become a writer of national stature and still lives in Minnesota. Another young writer who applied was Earl Guy, who went on to write an acclaimed

---

[1]For more on the Federal Writers' Project and the production of the state guides, see Jerre Mangione, *The Dream and the Deal: The Federal Writers' Project, 1935–1943* (New York: Little, Brown and Company, 1972).

[2]Ulrich, "Salvaging Culture for the WPA," *Harper's Monthly* 178 (May, 1939): 653–664. This article is a fascinating insider's view of the Minnesota Writers' Project.

novel, *Heaven Is a Sunswept Hill*. Earl Guy later told me that he had much
to do with smoothing out the varied writings that came in to give the Minnesota guide a consistent style and emphasis.

Some of the WPA state guides are still talked about as first-rate pieces of
writing, in part because some states could draw from larger pools of available
first-rate writers or because a qualified writer wrote or re-wrote the final draft
of each. Vardis Fisher wrote the Idaho state guide almost singlehandedly. He
visited every little burg as well as all the big cities in his state, alone investigated lumbering camps, mines, irrigated farms. Fisher had a clear style that
often leapt into spare poetry. Wallace Stegner did much of the final draft
of the Utah state guide, and his sure, masterful hand shows on every page.

Speaking for myself as a writer, I found the various American state guides
to be a mine of many treasures.

One evening in February of 1939, while visiting Hugh McAllister, an
employee of the Minnesota state government, I happened to see on his sofa
table a copy of *Minnesota: A State Guide*. The dark blue jacket, showing
several men loading gear into a boat on a lake shore, caught my eye. After
dinner, while Hugh listened to a favorite radio program, I began to browse
through the book. I saw right away that it was loaded with information I had
never seen before.

I looked up two tours, numbers 4 and 13 (p. 342 and p. 417), to see what
the guide had to say about Luverne, Minnesota, where some of my relatives
lived. (My grandfather, who worked during the winter months for the old
Bonnie Doon railroad, had once taken me there and back on a handcar from
Doon, Iowa.) From tour 13 I learned why Luverne had so many red stone
buildings. The stone came from Sioux quartzite quarries up on the Blue
Mounds two miles north of town. (The guide incorrectly calls this stone
"granite.") The stone gave the town an old, settled look, as if it had been
there for centuries.

Tour 4 mentions that the Blue Mounds in what was then known as Mound
Springs State Park made up "a massive bluff of quartzite about 3 miles long."
Massive it is. From a distance the Blue Mounds ridge looks like an ordinary
height of land, a good-sized hogback, but when one stands on its highest
point one discovers that the land on all sides slopes gradually up to it. I had
seen the mounds when I was a boy and my father took me with him to trade
a Poland China boar with a farmer living near Edgerton, Minnesota. When
we started to climb the south slope of the Blue Mounds, the radiator of our
chain-drive Maxwell boiled over. My father pulled off to the side of the road.
With a little smile he said, "Boy, while the engine cools, how would you like
to see the mountains?"

Thinking he was joking, I said, "Sure, Pa."

"C'mon then, follow me."

We walked east along the Sioux quartzite crest of the Blue Mounds, and with every step we rose higher and higher, until on the southeast corner we reached its highest point. "How do you like them potatoes?" my father said.

I was stunned. To the east we could see the water tower of Worthington thirty miles away; to the south the water tower of Rock Rapids, Iowa, some twenty-five miles away; to the west the Cactus Heights near Sioux Falls, South Dakota, also twenty-five miles away; and to the north the water tower of Pipestone, twenty-three miles away (see the picture on page 5).

Checking the section called "geology" in the guide, I discovered that my father's remark about "mountains" was not all that far off. Geologists say that millions of years ago a mountain range once did exist in southwestern Minnesota. (I later read that scientists who examined the depth of the sediments that had eroded from this mountain range theorize that it had peaks higher than Mt. Everest, some 30,000 feet above sea level. The remainder of that mountain range was carried away by glaciers.)

I looked up the section on Indians next. As a boy living on the old King's Trail running from Winnipeg to New Orleans, or the K. T. Trail as it was then known (now U.S. Highway 75), I had often seen Indians coming south from Pipestone in caravans on their way to visit relatives and friends in Santee, Nebraska. Those dusky people always fascinated me, and I sensed at that time that some kind of injustice had been done them. I found the section on the Dakota (or Sioux) and the Ojibwa (or Chippewa) to be as good an introduction to them as could be found anywhere.

Hugh McAllister noticed that whenever I visited him I seemed to be more interested in looking into the guide than in visiting with him and his family, so he bought me a copy as a gift. "Now," he said, "this is for you to read at home. So that when you're here, you can pay attention to the ladies." (He was referring to his strong-minded wife and to his two bright daughters, one of whom he wanted me to marry.)

It was not until 1943, when I decided to try writing *This Is the Year* for the third time, that I began looking through the Minnesota guide again for farm detail. I had left the farm for college in 1930, when I was eighteen, and I had sworn then never to go back to the country (where I now live outside Luverne). In books, and by way of the radio, I had learned about "the gentle graces" of the cities. I wanted to be near libraries, symphony halls, playhouses; meet brilliant people who read and created; live along a lovely street with stately trees. At that time I hated the smell of hogyards and chicken coops. I hated the long hours of labor: picking corn by hand, plowing, shocking grain, putting up the hay. Thus by the time I started writing about the countryside, I discovered I had forgotten important detail. The guide was loaded with the very material I needed. Especially nostalgic were the pictures on pages 13–19 showing a field of grain shocks, strip farming, a huge close-up of a grasshopper, a grain seeder, grain stacks, a threshing scene, a hay rig, and a pasture with cattle.

The Minnesota guide was just the beginning for me. I checked out the red copy of the South Dakota guide from the University of Minnesota library late in 1943. I found that it had more good information. The best story was illustrated by a woodcut showing a man wrestling with a grizzly bear. It was the first time I had run into the great story of mountain man Hugh Glass. The picture and the account running with it were riveting. It flashed through my mind that here was a story to match the exploits of Achilles the Greek on the plains of Troy. Later on, in August of 1944, I bought the red book for myself so I could mark it up as I pleased. That same year I bought the guides for Iowa and Nebraska. All were packed with fine detail about farm life as well as with stories, legends, and myths.

In the next years, every time I went on a trip I took with me one or another of the guides. It was my usual practice to study beforehand the proposed route on a map, memorizing the numbers of the various highways and the names of the towns and cities so that I always knew exactly where I was without having to stop to look it up. I also checked what the guides had to say about the towns so I could better appreciate the country I was traveling through.

It was fun to know, for example, as I drove into Pipestone, Minnesota, that here was the place where Indians quarried for their peace pipes and where, on that holy ground, all Indians—Cheyenne, Ojibwa, Omaha, Iowa, Dakota—set aside their differences. As I drove into Fairmont, Minnesota, or into Le Mars, Iowa, I knew from the guides that both communities had been the home of British aristocracy, second sons of lords, who established beautiful mansions on the wild prairies, where in their red coats they hunted native fox with British hounds, played polo and cricket and tennis, always dressed for dinner, and carried walking sticks on their strolls; when they went to their favorite tavern they wore top hats and cutaway coats. It fired my imagination, and made me laugh out loud, to learn that a Minnesota legend says the *real* source of the Mississippi "was none other than Babe, Paul Bunyan's Blue Ox, who inadvertently capsized a water tank and started the long flow of waters to the Gulf."

Sometimes at night in a strange town, after eating the "dish of the place," I would get out the guide of whatever state I was in and pour over it to see what I might have missed during the day. Again and again it happened that I missed looking up something important: the Ionia Volcano in Nebraska; the 450 Blood Run mounds near Granite, Iowa (Granite is now gone); the highest point in Iowa, the Ocheyedan ("place where they weep") Mound near Ocheyedan, where the Indians went to mourn their dead; the monument at Minnesota's Lake Shetek commemorating a group of settlers who were massacred in the Dakota War of 1862. And always I swore that the next time around I would look them up — only to discover that once again, after having seen them, I had missed something else that was important. So rich were these books.

Having practically memorized the state guides of the Upper Midlands, I have gradually come to realize that the gathering, the writing, and the publication of the forty-eight volumes was one of the truly great cultural events of our American civilization. There they are, standing in a row, packed with information that, had they not been put together in the late 1930s, might have been lost forever. Today, it would not be possible to write those books with the same "infinite variety of detail" described by Federal Writers' project director Henry Alsberg.[3] The old-timers, trappers, mountain men, pioneers, printers, lumbermen of the 1930s have long ago died. Since then many records, diaries, and letters have also disappeared.

To see a book in print, published by a prestigious New York publisher, which told the story of Minnesota's cultural coming of age, meant much to me as a fledgling writer in those dark days of the 1930s. Other writers of those days have told me the same thing. To have in hand a beautifully bound book, full of the wonderful lore and learning of our state, was like having a Bible to take one's stand on, to take forth and proclaim the news by way of poems and stories and essays.

To travel with the guide today remains a fascinating experience. Take, for example, the description given on pages 416–417 of Worthington and Luverne of the late 1930s, and then have a look at those two towns today. Both now have their own liquor stores. The main east-west highway, Interstate 90, bypasses both towns; in the old days, U.S. Highway 16 went through a part of each. Baseball has been replaced by softball. Worthington no longer has a polo team. Winter basketball for the high school teams, boys and girls, has become *the* event of the week, and on the nights when those teams play you will find your friend at the game, not at home. The 1938 guide does not mention the mysterious row of stones on top of the Blue Mounds, but today they are featured in the Blue Mounds State Park brochure

[3]Quoted in Mangione, *The Dream and the Deal*, 353.

as something of great antiquity. The sun rises exactly above the east end of the row of stones and sets on the west end of it during the equinox — indicating to archaeologists that someone a long time ago knew what was true east and true west. When the guide was published not much was known about the local history before white settlers arrived, but today we know through archaeological digs that a people lived on the shores of Lake Benton more than 6,000 years ago.

Yet for me *The WPA Guide to Minnesota* remains, perhaps even more than a monument to the places it describes, an enduring monument to the writers of its time — and an inspiration to those who have followed.

Frederick Manfred

⪻⪻⪻⪻⪻⪻⪻⪻⪻⪻⪻⪻⪻⪻⪻⪻⪻⪻❁⪼⪼⪼⪼⪼⪼⪼⪼⪼⪼⪼⪼⪼⪼⪼⪼⪼⪼

Using the Guide

FREDERICK MANFRED'S description of his first encounter with this
book in 1939 gives clear examples of the joys and dangers of using the guide
in the 1980s. Its descriptions of "modern" Minnesota are now almost fifty
years out of date (Mound Springs State Park is now Blue Mound State Park,
for example), but the book remains a useful and enjoyable survey of the
state's early years. Manfred had to look elsewhere to learn more of the state's
geology, because the writers did not have space for all the information
available — a shortcoming common to guidebooks. Readers who use the book
as a traveling companion are encouraged to take along a current highway
map and to watch for the changes that have occurred in the countryside since
the late 1930s.

More difficult to spot are the text's minor errors of fact, like its mistaking
Luverne's quartzite for granite. Considering the pressure on the Minnesota
Writers' Project to produce quickly, and the difficulty of coordinating the
efforts of so many authors, the flaws are not surprising. There are too many
of them to list, but they are not so major as to misinform seriously.

Although this volume is not recognized as a scholarly reference work on
Minnesota history, it is recommended to readers who will delight in its
literary style and colorful evocation of the past. To help the reader overcome
its problems, the publisher has revised the book's original bibliography to
reflect recent scholarship (see p. 498). Users of the guide who are interested
in learning more about the state are encouraged to check these sources for
more information.

THE MINNESOTA STATE RELIEF AGENCY
STATE CAPITOL
ST. PAUL, MINNESOTA

OFFICE OF THE ADMINISTRATOR
HERMAN J. AUFDERHEIDE

Through funds allocated by the Executive Council, State of Minnesota, to the State Relief Agency, the publication of this volume, the first major work of the Federal Writers' Project of Minnesota, has been made possible. In *Minnesota: A State Guide* there is presented for the first time a full-length portrait of our State. From countless persons and sources the details of our rich heritage have been compiled for residents who wish to know their own community more intimately, and for the visitor who seeks the colorful history that lies behind these prairie cities and villages, these forests and "ten thousand lakes." Here is a book that takes us from the long-forgotten English fur traders, French *coureurs de bois,* and warring Indians to a highly complex present in which great industries and cooperatives have crowded out the last traces of the frontier. The results of these dramatic changes have been recorded on the physical horizons of the State. How best to see them by canoe, by automobile, and on foot, as well as how best to understand their significance, has been the purpose in the compilation of this book.

THE MINNESOTA STATE RELIEF AGENCY

HERMAN J. AUFDERHEIDE
Administrator

St. Paul, Minnesota
October 1, 1938

Preface

THE Minnesota unit of the Federal Writers' Project offers its contribution to the American Guide Series in a spirit of deep humility. We frankly admit that the net result of our work falls far short of the book we visualized in November 1935 when we started out so enthusiastically on its preparation. At that time we had little conception of the complexities of our task. Even less did we realize the extravagance of our hope of compressing between two covers a State 84,000 square miles in area, whose interests and resources were as varied as its topography.

An avalanche of facts, actual and near, began to pour into the State office. Even after each had been tested we still had enough to make a series rather than one volume. The weeding out was a long and often painful process. Had not Dr. Folwell required four large volumes for the history of Minnesota? We must tell the story, and tell it fairly, in a single essay. Communities that merited a chapter at least, must be squeezed into a few lines. Local pride, however justified, must be sternly repressed. From sins of commission we hope to have guarded ourselves fairly well with the help of consulting authorities. But for our sins of omission we have no defense other than the imposed space limitations.

If, despite its shortcomings, the book has merit—and we may as well admit we think it has some—credit is due largely to the generous cooperation we have received on all sides. To the many volunteers who sent us local stories and photographs we offer our profound thanks, and beg their forgiveness and leniency for our enforced treatment of their material.

Outstanding was the help given us by the University of Minnesota, whose department heads not only read our manuscripts and proffered invaluable suggestions, but permitted us to turn to them again and again as our court of last appeal; by the Minnesota Historical Society, its head and staff, who gave so generously of their knowledge and records; by the State Department of Education, whose commissioner rescued us in one of our darkest moments; by all those librarians to whom we fear we were a persistent trial; by the unfailing confidence and support we received from our State Administrator. We hope that in the Minnesota Guide they will find something to justify the time and sympathy they gave so freely.

The Minnesota Federal Writers' Project
MABEL S. ULRICH, *State Director*

WORKS PROGRESS ADMINISTRATION

HARRY L. HOPKINS, *Administrator*

ELLEN S. WOODWARD, *Assistant Administrator*

HENRY G. ALSBERG, *Director of Federal Writers' Project*

General Information

(State map showing highways, and maps giving routes of railroads, air lines, bus lines, and water transportation routes in pocket inside of back cover)

Railroads: Chicago & North Western Ry. (Northwestern); Canadian Northern Ry. (CN); Chicago, Burlington & Quincy R.R. (Burlington); Chicago Great Western R.R. (Great Western); Chicago, Milwaukee, St. Paul & Pacific R.R. (Milwaukee); Chicago, Rock Island & Pacific Ry. (Rock Island); Chicago, St. Paul, Minneapolis & Omaha Ry. (Omaha); Duluth & Northeastern R.R. (D&NE); Duluth, Missabe & Northern Ry. (DM&N); Duluth, Winnipeg & Pacific Ry. (Canadian National); Great Northern Ry. (GN); Illinois Central R.R. (IC); Minneapolis & St. Louis R.R. (M&STL); Minneapolis, Northfield & Southern Ry. (Dan Patch); Minneapolis, Red Lake & Manitoba Ry. (Manitoba); Minneapolis, St. Paul & Sault Ste. Marie Ry. (Soo Line); Minnesota & International Ry. (M&I); Minnesota & Northern Pacific Ry. (NP). All main roads in southern two-thirds of the State radiate from the Twin Cities; in the northeastern part, from Duluth, a Great Lakes terminus. Five railroads make connections with Canada; the Canadian National is the only foreign railway to enter the State. There are 14 intrastate steam, electric, and terminal and transfer railways, and 18 interstate lines.

Highways: Nine E.-W. and nine N.-S. Federal highways. Inspection only at International Boundary. State highway patrol on all main routes. In the sparsely settled northern part of the State filling stations are scarce and gasoline prices slightly higher. Gasoline tax, 4¢.

Bus Lines: Twenty-five bus lines. Interstate: Duluth-Superior Bus Line; Duluth-Superior Transit Co.; Interstate Transit Lines; Jefferson Transportation Co.; Minnesota Jack Rabbit Transportation Co.; Northland Transportation Co. (Canadian connections); Northland-Greyhound Lines, Inc.; Steward Bus Line; Triangle Transportation Co. Nine intrastate and seven local lines.

Air Lines: Northwest Airlines (Chicago to Seattle) stop at Rochester, Minneapolis, St. Paul, and Moorhead-Fargo airport; (Twin Cities to Chicago) stop at Minneapolis, St. Paul, and Rochester. Hanford Airlines (Twin Cities, Omaha, and Kansas City) stop at Minneapolis and St. Paul.

Waterways: Minneapolis-St. Paul, on the Mississippi River, at headwaters of the Federal barge line operated by the Inland Waterways Corporation (Twin Cities to New Orleans); Stillwater, on the St. Croix River, secondary headwaters of the Federal barge line. No passenger service on river except short excursions. Duluth on Lake Superior, headwaters of the Great Lakes navigation system. Great Lakes Transit Corporation, freight only, service every 48 hrs., May 1-Dec. 1 (Duluth-Port Arthur-Sault Ste. Marie, Michigan-Detroit-Cleveland-Buffalo); Northern Navigation Co. (Canadian), passenger service only, every Tuesday and Friday, last week of June to Sept. 1 (Duluth-Port Arthur-Sault Ste. Marie, Ontario-Windsor, Ont.) (passengers for Detroit disembark at Windsor); H. Christiansen & Sons, steamer *Winyah,* passenger and freight service, three sailings per week (Duluth-Port Arthur-Fort William-Isle Royale); Minnesota Atlantic Transportation Co., freight only, every 48 hrs., May 1-Dec. 1 (Duluth-Detroit-Buffalo). All passenger boats transport tourists' cars; automobiles must be at docks 1 hr. before sailing.

Accommodations: Good hotel accommodations only in larger cities. *(For tourist camps and resorts see Recreation section of General Information.)* Adequate resorts throughout the State in season. Resort accommodations vary from those offering board and room to those with housekeeping or sleeping cabins only. Many public tourist camps have cabins with housekeeping facilities as well as camping grounds. Resorts in southern and north-central Minnesota usually feature water sports, golf, tennis, and occasionally archery and riding, as well as hunting and fishing in season. The extreme northern resorts cater to canoeists, hunters, and fishermen. Though there is a lack of public tourist camps in the State parks and forest reserves, there are private resorts bordering these areas at which guides and complete equipment are available. Guides and complete equipment, including food, for canoeing, hunting, and fishing trips are also available throughout the lake and forest area, at resorts and towns.

Hunting and Fishing: The following information is a digest of the 1937 regulations, which are subject to yearly change.
The State is divided into northern and southern zones for the purpose of establishing open seasons of varying periods to conform to the seasonal variations in different parts of the State, or to the abundance of game. Limits of zones for fishing follow roughly along a line from Cambridge in the E. to Morris in the W. The hunting zone line zigzags from Pine City on the E. to St. Vincent in the extreme NE. Open season for pheasants as well as other game is frequently restricted to certain counties.

Fishing Laws: Game fish include wall-eyed pike, pickerel, great northern pike, yellow perch, sand pike (or saugers) ; muskellunge, crappie, bass, sunfish, trout, landlocked salmon. Rough fish include bullheads, catfish, garfish, whitefish (over 16 in.), carp, dogfish, redhorse, sheepshead, sucker, eelpout, buffalo-fish, and inland herring. All game fish, regardless of size, must be retained and counted. Brook trout cannot be taken between 9 p.m. and 1 hr. before sunrise.

Open Season: Wall-eyed pike, pickerel, great northern pike, yellow perch, May 15-March 1. Sand pike (saugers) and muskellunge, May 15-Feb. 1. Bass and sunfish, southern zone, May 29-Dec. 1; northern zone, June 21-Dec. 1. Trout (except lake trout), May 1-Sept. 1, except Lake, St. Louis, Itasca, Carlton, Cook, and Koochiching Counties, where season is May 15-Sept. 1. Lake trout and salmon, Nov. 15-Sept. 15. Angling for rough fish permitted during all months except March and April.

Licenses: Nonresident, 16 yrs. of age and over, $3.00. Resident, 18 yrs. of age and over, 50¢; $1.00 for immediate family (husband and wife, or guardian). Nonresident may ship to himself, at home station, 24 lbs. of game fish or a single fish above 24 lbs.

Limits: Wall-eyed pike, 8 per day, 16 in possession; sand pike (saugers), 8 per day, 16 in possession; pickerel, or great northern pike, 10, or 20 in possession; perch (yellow), no limit; muskellunge, 2; crappie, 15, or 25 in possession; bass, 6, or 12 in possession; trout, except lake trout, 15, or 25 trout (or 20 lb.) in possession; lake trout and salmon, 5, or 10 in possession; rough fish, no limit; bullheads, 20, or 30 in possession; sunfish, rock bass, and all unnamed kinds, aggregate of 15 per day, 30 in possession; two or more of any limited groups (but not exceeding fixed limits of each group), 15 per day, 20 in possession.

St. Croix and Mississippi Rivers-Open Seasons and Limits: Large- and small-mouth black bass, June 20-Dec. 1; 6 daily, minimum 10 in. White bass, June 20-Dec. 1, 10 daily, minimum 7 in. Sunfish and rock bass, June 20-Dec. 1; 15 daily, minimum 5 in. Pike, May 15-Feb. 1; 8 daily, minimum 13 in. Pickerel, May 15-Feb. 1; 10 daily, minimum 16 in. Perch, May 15-Feb. 1; no limit. Catfish, June 20-Feb. 1; 40 daily, minimum 7 in. in length. Daily aggregate and possession limit (excluding perch, catfish, and bullheads), 30. No open season for sturgeon.

Prohibited: Use of drugs, lime, fish berries, explosives, medicated bait, or other illegal substances; nets, tip-ups, trot lines, wire strings, ropes, and cables. Fish nets in possession (except minnow nets, landing nets, and dip nets). Fishing with more than one line or bait, except three artificial flies. Fishing within 50 ft. of fishway; depositing sawdust, refuse, or poisonous substance in waters containing fish; buying or selling game fish; possessing rock or lake sturgeon; taking shovel-nosed or hackleback sturgeon, spoonbill, or paddlefish from inland waters; taking fish in any manner than by angling with hook and line, except spearing or netting of certain kinds; taking fish from public water closed by director's order.

Hunting-Open Season: Deer (bucks), northern zone only, Nov. 15-Nov. 25, in even-numbered years. Raccoon, defined area, Nov. 10-Dec. 1. Squirrel, Oct. 15-Jan. 1. Skunk, Oct. 20-May 1. Mink, Nov. 1-Feb. 15. Pheasant and quail, opens about Oct. 24, areas and length of season defined yearly. Usually no open season for prairie chicken, white-breasted grouse, ruffed grouse, upland plover, and woodcock. Migratory birds, usually during October, 7 a.m. to 4 p.m. Noon, on opening day. No open season for wood duck, ruddy duck, bufflehead, redhead, canvasback, swans, greater and lesser yellow-legs.

Licenses: Nonresident, big-game, $50; small-game, $25. Resident (16 yrs. of age or over), big-game, $2; small-game, $1.

Limits: Deer, 1 buck per person each season. (Deer may be possessed 90 days after close of season if properly tagged.) Pheasants, 3 daily, only 1 female; 5 birds including 1 female in possession; season limit, 10 birds but only 2 females. Quail, 6 daily, 12 in possession. Migratory birds, daily aggregate of 10 of which not more than 4 are geese or brant; not more than 15 game birds of all kinds in one day.

Unlawful: Use of another person's license. Taking waterfowl with rifle or pistol or with other than shotgun larger than 10-gauge, fired from shoulder; taking migratory birds with automatic or hand-operated repeating shotgun holding more than three shells; baiting hunting grounds for taking ducks; using live decoys for migratory waterfowl; shipping game birds without attached coupon or to any county other than the one in which the license is issued; shipping more than three upland game birds on one shipping coupon or retaining untagged game more than 5 days after close of season.

Climate: Temperature variations are often great in both summer and winter. Summer travelers should be prepared for extremely warm weather and for cool evenings, especially in the northern sections. Campers in the extreme north need extra bedding and heavy clothing even in summer. In the spring and fall the nights may be extremely cold. Travelers should be prepared for zero weather from late November to early March throughout the northern half of the State and from December to March in the southern section. Because of the possibility of sudden temperature drops and blizzard conditions following even light flurries of snow, winter travelers should heed weather reports especially in the northwest area. Towns and farms in the rural districts of the extreme north are far apart and winter travelers should proceed with caution. Main highways are kept open throughout the year except immediately following heavy storms.

Motor Vehicle Laws: Maximum speed, 60 m.p.h., 50 m. when lights are required; 15 m.p.h. on curves and at intersections; speed zones in and near all municipalities. Nonresidents may operate vehicles 3 months, but register within 10 days; no nonresident license required. Minimum age for drivers, 15 yrs. Left turn only from lane nearest center line. A person involved in an accident resulting in injury, death, or damage to property, must immediately identify himself, render reasonable assistance, and report to some civil authority. Drivers must come to full stop while streetcars are loading or unloading passengers, unless at safety zones. Cars must have rear-view mirrors, windshield wipers, adequate headlights, rear lights, and brakes. Residents must carry license when driving. The usual laws regarding signaling, driving in proper lane, stopping for fire-trucks, police cars, and ambulances, and at stops and signal lights, apply throughout the State.

Prohibited: Coasting, parking on highways, or within 15 ft. of fire hydrant and "Stop" markers; use of a muffler cut-out; passing streetcars on L. within cities or towns, hitchhiking. *(Local traffic regulations under General Information for larger cities.)*

Trailer Regulations: Trailers permitted throughout State. Facilities provided in most State parks and many cities. Local time restrictions. Any new motor vehicle, trailer, or semitrailer sold and operated after Jan. 1, 1938, must have rear lamp and reflector within 20 in. from left edge, 24 to 60 in. from ground, and visible 300 ft. Every new motor vehicle or trailer exceeding 1,000 lb. gross weight must be equipped with service brakes on all wheels. Unladen weight of all except house trailers shall not exceed 2,000 lbs.; house trailers shall not exceed 6,000 lb. gross weight. Tow-cable, chain, or rope between vehicles shall display white flag 12 in. square. Separate towing device in addition to the regular hitch shall be securely attached to the rear axle or frame of the traction vehicle and the trailer or semitrailer.

Unlawful: To refuse to fight fire when summoned by a forest officer; to cut timber except for fuel or when clearing land without posting notices and notifying the forester; to leave fires unextinguished or unattended; to build campfires without clearing debris for a radius of 5 ft; to have fire except for domestic purposes; to carry naked torch, firebrand, or exposed light in or near forest land; to drop or throw in or near woodlands burning matches, cigars, cigarettes, ashes, or other burning substance; to destroy, deface, or remove notices posted for forest protection; to cut, remove, or transport living trees, bushes, or shrubs for decorative purposes without securing written consent from the owner of the land. No person within the State shall buy or sell the State flower *(Cypripedium reginae)* or any other species of the ladyslipper *(Cypripedae)*, or trillium lotus *(Nelumbo lutea)*, gentian *(Gentiana)*, arbutus *(Epigaea repens)*, or any species of lily *(Lillium)* taken from public land, or from privately owned land without the written consent of the owner.

Border Regulations: United States Customs offices are open 8 a.m.–8 p.m., April 1–Oct. 1; 8 a.m.–6 p.m., Oct. 1–April 1. Canadian Customs offices are open 9 a.m.–9 p.m. No passports required. Tourists must submit cars for inspection when entering either country, and should have State registration cards for identification. Health of pets and plants must be certified by a reputable authority before entry. Imports for personal use to the amount of $100 duty-free. Excluded from these regulations are tobacco and alcoholic beverages, 50 cigars, 300 cigarettes, and 3 lbs. of tobacco duty-free. Canada allows 1 qt. of alcoholic beverage, 40 cigars and 100 cigarettes per person duty-free. No guns are allowed to cross the border in either direction without permit.

Obnoxious Plants, Reptiles, and Insects: Wild parsnip (musquash root, water hemlock) is found throughout the State in swamps and moist meadows. It looks, smells, and tastes like parsnip; no antidote is known. Children especially should be warned against eating it. Poison-ivy, a shrub 1 to 3 ft. high (in the SE. a vine), has a leaf comprising three leaflets with ragged edges; the flowers are in a green cluster, the berries waxy greenish. Poison-sumac, also called poison-oak, grows in the area near the St. Croix River northward from Twin Cities and westward to Anoka County; especially prevalent in tamarack swamps. It resembles the harmless sumac, but has long drooping green berries and smooth-edge leaf. A fair preventive against contact poisoning is to allow thick laundry soapsuds to dry on the skin. After contact, skin should be washed immediately with strong laundry soap and hot running water, care being taken to avoid breaking skin. A

5-percent solution of potassium permanganate may give relief. Pure alcohol may be useful but clean swabs must be used to prevent spreading the poison. A strong epsom salts solution will relieve itching; medical care is often necessary.

Only one poisonous snake, the timber rattler, confined to the vicinity of the Wisconsin-Minnesota border below Taylors Falls. The small swamp rattlesnake may become a resident for it is found across the river in Wisconsin. All other Minnesota snakes are harmless and most are decidedly beneficial.

Black flies, usually numerous in early spring, become less frequent by the latter part of June. Mosquitoes also are most severe in early summer. Deer flies are present over most of the area, but the chiggers, widespread in more southerly States, are absent from the north woods.

Information Service: Minnesota Tourist Bureau, 9 State Capitol, St. Paul. There are 12 A.A.A. Clubs in Minnesota; all have official directories of hotels, tourist camps, and homes in addition to A.A.A. national detour maps and State highway bulletins; (Aitkin, Washington Blk., open 9-3; Austin, Austin State Bank Bldg., 9-5; Breckenridge, N. 5th St., 9-5; Chaska, City Hall, 8-9:30; Jackson, 606 2nd St., 8-6; Mankato, 119 E. Jackson St.; Moorhead, City Hall, 8-5. *(See CITIES.)*

Annual Events

(Only events of general interest listed; for descriptions consult index. Many opening dates vary with the years, and are placed in the week in which they usually occur. The abbreviation "nfd" signifies event occurs during the month but has no fixed date.)

Jan.	3d wk.	Duluth	Winter Sports Week
	4th wk.	International Falls	Winter Carnival and Dog Derby
	4th wk. (or early Feb.)	Minneapolis	N. W. Golden Gloves Amateur Boxing Tournament
	nfd	Red Wing	Ski Meet
	nfd	Duluth	Ski Meet
	nfd	Minneapolis	Snow Modeling (Winter Sports Play Week)
	nfd	Minneapolis	10,000 Lakes Speed-Skating Meet
	nfd	Minneapolis	John S. Johnson Memorial Skating Meet
	nfd	Bush Lake	N. W. Ski Meet
	nfd	Duluth	15-mile Ice Boat Races
Feb.	nfd	Hibbing	Winter Sports Frolic
	nfd	Detroit Lakes	Winter Carnival
	nfd	Virginia	Winter Fair
	nfd	Brainerd	Winter Carnival
	nfd	Cass Lake	Mid-Winter Indian Fair
	nfd	Bemidji	Winter Carnival
	nfd	Fergus Falls	Winter Carnival
	nfd	St. Paul	North American Indoor Skating Championship
Mar.	nfd	Duluth	Curling Bonspiel
	nfd	Chisholm	Winter Sports Frolic
	nfd	Eveleth	Winter Sports Frolic
Apr.	1st wk.	Minneapolis	N. W. Sportsman's Show
	nfd	Minneapolis	Bach Society Concert
	nfd	St. Paul	State Gallery Rifle Matches
	nfd	Hibbing	Exhibit of Easter Lilies
May	1st	Winona	May Day Class Ceremonies of Teachers' College and St. Teresa College
	1st wk.	Minneapolis	Lilacs in Bloom
	3d wk.	Northfield	May Fete (Carleton College)

May	3d wk.	Northfield	Music Festival (St. Olaf College)
	nfd	Mountain Lake	Festival of Mennonite Choirs
June	14	White Earth	Indian Pow-wow and Carnival
	28	Itasca State Park	Minnesota Historical Society Pageants (every 2 wks. to Sept. 1.)
	2d wk.	Faribault	Mid-June Peony Show
	2d wk.	Minneapolis	N. W. Air Pageant
	2d wk.	Minneapolis	Peonies in Bloom
	2d wk.	Brainerd	Paul Bunyan Carnival
	nfd	Ft. Snelling	Minnesota Trap Shooting Championship
	nfd	Ft. Snelling	Polo Matches (continue to late Aug.)
	nfd	Duluth	"Kitchi Gammi" Golf Tournament
	nfd	Rochester	S. E. Minnesota Peony Show
July	4	Bena	Indian Pow-wow
	4	International Falls	Lumber Festival and Paul Bunyan Parade
	17	Detroit Lakes	Summer Festival
	21	Hopkins	Raspberry Festival
	4th wk.	Minneapolis	Playground Pageant
	nfd	Marshall	Zinnia Day
	nfd	Deephaven	N. W. Sectional Doubles and N. W. Lawn Tennis Tournament
	nfd	Fergus Falls	Summer Carnival (Lake Alice)
	nfd	Ft. Snelling	Minnesota Rifle and Revolver Championship Matches
	nfd	St. Paul	St. Paul Open Golf Tournament
Aug.	4-5	Atwater	Melon Festival
	1st wk.	Alexandria	Annual Resorters' Golf Tournament
	4th wk.	St. Paul	Minnesota State Fair
	nfd	Ortonville	Sweet Corn Festival
	nfd	Milan	Lefse Fete
Sept.	27	Montgomery	Kolacky Day
	1st wk.	Milaca	Indian Rice Dance
	1st wk.	Tracy	Boxcar Day
	nfd	Springfield	Sauerkraut Day
	nfd	Ft. Snelling	State Rifle Championship
Oct.	nfd	Stillwater	Lumberjack Day
	31	Anoka	Halloween Celebration
Nov.	4th wk.	St. Paul	'Mum Show (Como Park)
	nfd	Hibbing	'Mum Show (Bennet Park)
	nfd	Minneapolis	Diamond Belt Amateur Boxing Tournament
	nfd	Minneapolis	Twin City Art Exhibit
Dec.	nfd	Hibbing	Christmas Flower Show (Bennet Park)

Minnesota in Pictures

The three ice sheets that crossed Minnesota molded a country of lakes and rivers, deep valleys and rolling plains. Now much of the timber has been felled and the plains have been cultivated; but there are still lakes ringed with virgin forest, lonely prairies, and islands crossed by Indian trails, that hold the atmosphere of that wilderness the first explorers found.

NORTHWOODS LAKE—KABETOGAMA

SOURCE OF THE MISSISSIPPI, LAKE ITASCA

4]

OLD MILL DAM, LANESBORO

SUGAR LOAF, INDIAN WATCH TOWER, WINONA

ROCK OUTCROPPING, SOUTHWESTERN MINNESOTA

UNLOADING AT THE PORTAGE, SUPERIOR NATIONAL FOREST

LAKE SAGANAGA

GUNFLINT TRAIL, GRAND MARAIS

HIGH FALLS OF PIGEON RIVER

LILY PADS

10]

INDIAN PIPE

From handsome stock-breeding farms like the first one shown, to forlorn holdings in cutover timber, or dust-ridden farms in the western portion, Minnesota is very much an agricultural state, concerned with the preservation of its resources. Attempts are being made to curb soil erosion by strip and terrace farming and to control the grasshopper and other insect pests. The farmers of Minnesota are constantly trying to raise the standard of rural life; the modern co-operative creamery represents an effort in this direction.

A MINNESOTA FARM

RED RIVER WHEAT

STRIP FARMING

GANGSTER OF THE PRAIRIE

STRIP AND TERRACE FARMING

LEGUMES STOP EROSION

SEEDING THE PRAIRIE

16]

IN THE RED RIVER VALLEY

AWAITING THE THRESHERS

THRESHING ALFALFA FOR SEED

HAY RIG

DAIRY COUNTRY

ON A DAIRY FARM

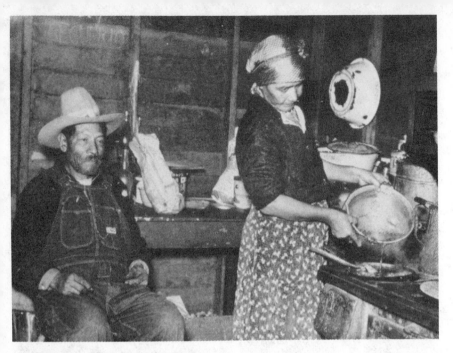

MEXICAN SUGAR BEET WORKERS

20]

FARM FAMILY

PULLING BEETS

DIGGING POTATOES

CUTOVER LAND IN NORTHERN MINNESOTA

FARM HOUSE, CUTOVER AREA

CREAM TESTING IN A CO-OPERATIVE

Mining, milling, quarrying, logging, shipping, fishing—these pictures give only glimpses of the industrial life of Minnesota. Iron ore in barges out of Duluth destined for all the ports of the Great Lakes; flour going down the Mississippi or by rail across the western plains; trees converted into lumber; pulp wood into paper; the solid hills cut into building stone—Minnesota products contribute to the wealth and well being of the Nation.

GRAIN ELEVATORS, MINNEAPOLIS

ST. PAUL RIVER FRONT

MINNEAPOLIS MILLING DISTRICT

ST. PAUL

[27

MINNEAPOLIS

WINONA

ELEVATORS AND MINNESOTA POINT, DULUTH

AERIAL BRIDGE, DULUTH

MENDOTA BRIDGE ACROSS THE MINNESOTA RIVER

HIGHWAY NEAR LANESBORO

WINTER ROAD

STRIP MINING IN THE IRON COUNTRY

FREIGHTER AT DOCK, DULUTH

FREIGHTER ENTERING DULUTH HARBOR

AWAITING THE SPRING THAW, LITTLE FORK RIVER

WHITE PINE LOGS ON LITTLE ROCK RIVER

LUMBER CAMP

FISH NETS, TWO HARBORS

QUARRYING

MINING PROSPECTOR

LOGGING DAYS ARE OVER

SUGAR BEETS FOR PROCESSING

38]

SUGAR BEET FACTORY, EAST GRAND FORKS

SAWMILL SMOKESTACK, STILLWATER RELIC

The settler's first thought after land and bread was education. Schools were held in one-room cabins, built in limitless forests, and on lonely prairies. Education is still a major interest to Minnesotans, and its institutions stand today commemorative of the pioneer's thirst for knowledge. Here today also stand the cities with their streamlined buildings, modern, well-equipped homes, the museums, city halls and other public buildings—each in its way symbolizing man's attainment.

PEACE MEMORIAL, CITY HALL, ST. PAUL

WOMEN'S CITY CLUB, ST. PAUL

AIRVIEW OF UNIVERSITY OF MINNESOTA CAMPUS AND MISSISSIPPI RIVER

[43

THE CAPITOL, ST. PAUL

SHATTUCK MILITARY SCHOOL, FARIBAULT

DORMITORY, ST. OLAF COLLEGE, NORTHFIELD

SKINNER MEMORIAL CHAPEL, CARLETON COLLEGE, NORTHFIELD

Minnesota's growth has been rapid. Only recently it was Indian territory. Extensive exploration came comparatively late and it was not until the exploitation of timber began that the State saw a substantial rise in its population and in the number and size of its cities. Recent years have seen another development of State-wide importance, appreciation of the great Northwoods as a recreation area.

ST. PAUL'S CHAPEL (1841)

LOG CABIN

SIBLEY HOUSE (1835), MENDOTA

CHIPPEWA HOUSEHOLD, RED LAKE

ROUND TOWER, FORT SNELLING

JIM HILL'S STONE BRIDGE

PIONEER

OLD RESIDENT

TOWN HALL, MARINE-ON-THE-ST. CROIX

OLD HOUSE, TOWER

MINNEHAHA FALLS, MINNEAPOLIS

CANOEING, NORTH WOODS

LAKE TROUT

CAMPING, SUPERIOR NATIONAL FOREST

GOLFING IN THE PINES

BEFORE THE RACE, LAKE MINNETONKA

PART I

Minnesota: Past and Present

Minnesota Today

WHEN the tourist from the eastern coast or from the South walks into the marble and bronze Memorial Hall of St. Paul's "functional" courthouse, when he listens with 4,000 others to the Minneapolis Symphony Orchestra, or suddenly comes upon a view of Duluth-Superior Harbor with its great freighters moving along the miles of ore docks and grain elevators, it is hard for him to believe that some Minnesotans clearly recall the terror of Indian massacres, the sight of browsing buffalo herds, and the creaking of thong-tied Red River carts. Yet if he is to understand the Minnesota of today, he must keep always in mind the fact that within the span of a single lifetime 54 million acres of forests, lakes, rivers, and untouched prairies have been converted into an organized area of industrial cities and rich farms, of colleges, art centers, golf clubs, and parks. The men and women who accomplished this were for the most part New Englanders, Germans, and Scandinavians—probably as hardy as the world has produced—and it is their children and their grandchildren who determine today the pattern of the contemporary scene.

To understand Minnesota it is necessary then that one respond to youth, forgiving its occasional awkwardness and egoism for the sake of its healthy vigor, its color, its alternating self-confidence and self-distrust, its eagerness for experiment. One will not expect to find here the mellowness of cities, villages, and countrysides in the older States. With the exception of a few villages, mostly in the southeastern section, the towns can claim little charm; the unbeautiful brick stores and banks of Main Street testify to grim physical work. Not many of the New England settlers had leisure to indulge their esthetic tastes, and the immigrants who poured into the State in the 1850's were only too glad to exchange the picturesqueness and discomfort of their Old World stone cottages and thatched barns for a plenitude of lumber. When prosperity came to the farmers, their children built larger models of their parents' boxlike frame houses, and it is not surprising that they should have been more preoccupied with a bathroom, electric lights, or telephone, than with the line of a roof. But with greater economic security has come a new kind of pride, and today every town of any size boasts its park, playgrounds, and scenic drives. Fortunately, the builders of the large cities remembered early in their planning the elm-lined streets of New England, and today the profusion of trees in these cities is a joy to citizens and visitors alike.

To rapidity of growth must be ascribed many of the incongruities one meets constantly in Minnesota. Its largest city boasts of one of the finest park systems in the world, yet endures philosophically the dangers and irritations imposed by many railroad grade crossings. While remaining Republican in theory, county, city, or State will cheerfully try almost any variety of politics, whether Populist, Non-Partisan League, Farmer-Labor, or Socialist. At a single meeting the State may raise a fortune to build an art institute or found a great orchestra, yet it offers little support to local art talent, and discourages all attempts of conductors to introduce into their concert programs the works of modern American composers. It has built one of the great universities of the country, yet permits such inadequate legislative appropriations that many of its best teachers are lost to more generous States.

But in spite of these and other adolescent vestiges, the thoughtful observer will find many signs that the State is growing up. In cities this is perhaps most evident in the arts; in country districts the widespread interest in farm bureaus, 4-H Clubs, and co-operatives tells the same story in different terms. Today if Beethoven, Brahms, and Bach are still unvaryingly demanded by large musical audiences (as well they may be), yet in small groups in private houses, in little halls, the younger musicians gather freely to experiment with new forms and to try out their own compositions. Young painters hold their group exhibits and, although they may receive small financial support, at least they have demonstrated the excellence of their work and their creative impatience with conventional patterns. Others, interested in the drama, are bending all their efforts to a revival of that art, in the past decade almost lost to Minnesota. In politics, too, there are signs of a changing order. Boys and girls no longer docilely accept the dicta of their fathers, but are found crowding the forums to weigh every theory of politics and economics before casting their first ballots.

The population of Minnesota is divided almost equally between the cities and country. This numerical balance prevents urban domination, while increased facilities of transportation and communication in one generation have diminished appreciably not only the physical but the spiritual, economic, and social distances between city dweller and farmer. The farmer of thirty years ago who went to town perhaps once a month may now go several times a week, and his family often goes with him—to shop, to attend church, the movies, parents' and teachers' meetings, farm bureau lectures, or even garden clubs. When he can afford it, his children go to the city to the State university; at home they make their "dates" for roadhouse and barn dances over the telephone, and, thanks to the radio, are fully as familiar with the latest swing music as their city contemporaries. Only in the remote and poorest sections of Minnesota is the dull and drudging farmwife of thirty years ago met today.

Automobiles and good roads, the wide use of improved machinery and motor power on the farm, have not only raised the material standards of living for the rural family, but they have changed markedly the economic characteristics of agriculture in Minnesota. Once agriculture was self-sufficing, but within recent years there has occurred a rapid change in the amount of buying and selling carried on by the average farm family. This tendency has resulted in the increasing importance of trade centers, in a rapid rise in the number of chain stores and specialized shops, and in the gradual disappearance of the crossroads or general store. With the mounting significance of trade centers as a factor in agriculture, there has come also a declining population in the smaller villages, the collapse of a large number of country newspapers when advertisers shifted their accounts to the trade centers, and a steady weakening of the village church. But despite the increase in town merchandising, the trade catalogs of the mail-order houses are still read diligently and are coming to be used for a kind of window shopping. In some localities they are spoken of as "wish books."

The farm bureau and other agricultural societies are, in most communities, the hub about which rural social life revolves. All members of the family attend their lectures, dinners, picnics, and entertainments. Women take an active part, and indeed often hold office in such organizations as the grange, or the co-operatives. Every organization is likely to have its annual picnic, a jolly affair in which contests play a leading part. Hog calling, husband calling, nail driving, rolling-pin throwing, cow milking, wood chopping, as well as the usual three-legged, potato, and other races, all have their champions and their boobies.

Parent-Teacher Associations have generally proved of practical assistance to the rural school and its teacher. If the community is too small to support such an organization, women often join P.T.A. groups in the nearest town and bring back suggestions of use to their own schools. Rural women often not only arrange hot luncheons for the children during the winter months but even go to the school and help serve them. To raise money for the purchase of books and equipment, they sponsor special programs and "box socials." The latter constitute a popular money-raising expedient in many parts of the State. To these gatherings, girls and women bring boxed luncheons, carefully prepared and elaborately wrapped, which an auctioneer sells to the highest bidders. They usually bring from fifty cents to a dollar or two, but occasions have been known when a single box brought as much as ten dollars.

With the depression, the barn dance came into general popularity. Farmers with large barns hang a few lanterns about, wax the floor, secure a dance band from a neighboring town, and for a small fee (ladies free) open their doors for dancing. These dances, however, bear little relation to the old-time barn dance. They are often patronized largely by motoring townfolk, and are acquiring more and more a night club atmosphere.

After the farm bureaus and the co-operatives, the 4-H clubs have unquestionably the strongest influence on rural life. In Minnesota, 43,000 boys and girls are enrolled in 2,600 of these clubs. They have not only developed a clean and friendly rivalry in the raising of cattle, hogs, sheep, and chickens, but through their annual parades and fair exhibits they have also demonstrated to even the more conservative of their parents the value of scientific farming and animal husbandry. Their work in home economics and manual arts has raised the standard of taste and attractiveness in farm homes.

Social life in Minnesota cities, large and small, is for the most part less formal than in most eastern centers, as might be expected from the nearness to pioneer days. "Western hospitality" is by no means an outgrown term. Country clubs flourish, women's clubs regard their civic and cultural intentions with solemn conscience, while the great number of men's clubs proves that the average male Minnesotan is a "joiner" indeed. Churches still play an active part in social life—particularly those of the Scandinavians.

As prosperity came to the early settlers it became more and more the custom of the wealthy to send their children away to school and college, yet many continue to educate their children in their own public schools, retaining an active faith in the democracy of these institutions. The University of Minnesota is second largest in full-time enrollment among State universities. The campus of the university is separated from the main section of Minneapolis by the river, and it fairly encompasses the social life of students. Lectures and entertainments attract large numbers outside the school circles.

Industrially, Minnesota was having a hard time long before the depression. The Northwest never shared fully in the prosperity of the 1920's. The opening of the Panama Canal, adverse rulings by the Interstate Commerce Commission, repeated crop failures all through the twenties, caused Minnesota to lag far behind States less dependent on agriculture and nearer to the great distributing centers. An important section of the milling industry moved to Buffalo. Chain stores cut great swaths in the jobbing business. Nevertheless, statistics show that wholesale business in the Twin Cities has survived the depression far better than in most communities of their size; and today that faith in its own destiny which has played so large a part in the State's precocious growth is again everywhere manifest.

Perhaps the most attractive feature of the State, after its rare natural beauty, is its refreshing attitude toward adventurous experiment. In groups and in individuals alike, the inhibiting forces of tradition have little place here. One sees this spirit operating in the State's co-operatives, the largest in number in America, in its lively political contests in both State and city government, in its schisms within political parties. Years ago, when medical schools were rife in the American scene, Minnesota decided that one medical school alone, and that a department of the State university, should be permitted to train its doctors; and then proceeded to require standards for students and teachers alike so far beyond the powers of the lesser schools that the latter were obliged to close. The university's department of medicine leapt almost at one stride to a place among the best, and made of the Twin Cities a great medical center for the entire Northwest.

Natural Setting

THE State of Minnesota lies in the center of the North American Continent, and includes the most northerly projection of the United States.

The northern boundary, for the greater part of its length, is formed by the watercourse of the Rainy River with its historic portages and interspersed lakes; the Red River along the North Dakota border forms two-thirds of the western boundary; South Dakota bounds the lower third; eastern Minnesota is separated from Wisconsin by the St. Croix and the Mississippi Rivers. The center of the State is crossed from west to east by the slow-flowing Minnesota in a tremendous valley remnant of the old glacial River Warren. At the Twin Cities it meets the glacier-shunted Mississippi, whose upper course from its headwaters in Itasca Park wanders over much of the upper middle of the State to be joined finally by the broad St. Croix.

In spite of the fact that most of its boundaries follow watercourses, Minnesota's shape is fairly rectangular; it is 406 miles long from north to south, and although 357 miles from east to west along the northern border, its average width is only 240 miles. Within its area of 84,682 square miles originate three great river systems: the Red River, which flows north to the Hudson Bay; the Minnesota and St. Croix, which join the Mississippi and flow to the Gulf of Mexico; the St. Louis and other North Shore streams that find their way to the Gulf of St. Lawrence through the Great Lakes.

Although water flows away from the State in all directions, the altitude is relatively low, reaching an extreme slightly above 2,000 feet only in the occasional hills of the rocky ridges north of Lake Superior. The Red River leaves the State at an elevation of 750 feet, the Mississippi has a fall of 620 feet between Minnesota and the Gulf, Lake Superior lies only 602 feet above sea level.

The surface of the State presents a great variety of topographic features. To the upper west are the flat prairies, merging into the rolling hills and valleys of the forest and lake region which attain, in the upper northeast, the semblance of mountain ridges; in the southeast the closed valleys and lakes are replaced by the unglaciated hills and deep cuts made by swift-flowing streams.

The types of hills are many and varied. There are hills formed by running water, others have been left by glacial deposit; some were made by an irresistible shove of the glacial ice; others, whose outlines are constantly changing, have been piled up by the persistent sand-moving power of the wind; while earth movements or volcanic expulsions have forced up the rougher elevations.

The floral covering of these hills varies greatly from southwest to northeast. Most of the western area, with the exception of the narrow, wooded margin along the Red River, is a treeless prairie, sometimes flat, often rolling, with acres of grain displacing the original prairie grass. This broad sweep is separated from the great coniferous forest of the upper east by a wide belt of deciduous hardwoods known to early explorers as the "Big Woods."

Climate

The areas of greater rainfall conform roughly with these forested areas. Along the eastern boundary the rainfall reaches an average of 32 inches; in the northwest it may not exceed 20 inches.

Minnesota's temperature is likewise varied. Lacking the tempering effect of ocean bodies it is subject to great fluctuations. The State lies in the path of the low-pressure areas that move across the continent from west to east at an average speed of 600 miles in 24 hours. The average frequency of these cyclonic air movements is twice a week. They are characterized by fair weather and warm temperatures followed by periods of rainy and cooler weather. The average annual temperature is about 41°. The winters are severe and reach extremes far below zero. The summers are characterized by rapid changes and occasional intense heat waves.

Temperatures in many counties range from 40° below zero to 100° F. Frost, although rare from the last half of May to the first half of September, has been recorded for every month of the year. The longest growing season, 160 days, occurs in the region between the Twin Cities and Winona; in the north it is considerably shorter, in some places less than 90 days. Near Lake Superior the temperature is influenced in all seasons by the lake, but is consistently cooler than in the Twin Cities area. The prevailing winds are northwest for most of the State.

The average relative humidity at 7 a.m. is 83 percent; at 7 p.m. it is 72 percent. The largest number of rainy days (132) in one year was recorded at Duluth; Lyon County has had as few as 64. The sunshine averages between 43 and 53 percent. The long hours of summer daylight in the northern counties help to compensate for the short growing season.

Geology

The familiar clock method of illustrating geological periods might well serve to give a quick view of Minnesota's physical history. If the entire period, from the time of the oldest known formations to the most recent geological events, be envisaged as having taken place in the 12 hours from noon to midnight, the period in which modern man inhabited the region will seem but a small fraction of a second. Ancient seas, volcanoes, and ice sheets preceded his coming by many thousands of years.

So long ago as to make the ice sheets that gave the State its present character seem modern, what is now Minnesota was a series of barren uneven bulges in the ancient granitic foundation of the earth. Some of this oldest known rock is still exposed. One of the most familiar exposures is Jasper Peak near Soudan and Ely in northern Minnesota (see Tour 8). In many places it is buried under hundreds of feet of more recent rock and soil.

At noon (by the geologic clock), in the beginning of this troubled history, Minnesota was torn by great volcanic flows. The fierce lava broke through the surface to cover the land and replace seas where sediments had been slowly accumulating. (It was in these early Archean waters that the ore of the Vermilion Range was deposited.)

Some 3 hours later according to the clock—much more than a hundred million years in actual time—the earth bulged and thrust up a mountain range reaching from southwestern Minnesota northeast into Canada and on into the region of Quebec.

For an hour or more the slow process of erosion wore down the mountains, exposing knobs of harder granite and gneiss that had not been able to reach the surface. In the Minnesota Valley near Ortonville and Big Stone City, and near Saganaga Lake in the extreme northeastern part of the State, these can still be seen. (The green schists of St. Louis and Itasca Counties are lava flows changed by the mountain-building processes.)

By late afternoon, on this same shrunken scale, another mountain range was formed, extending north from the Mesabi to Canada. (Outcrops of these stones are apparent north of the Giants Range.) Upon these old lavas, granites, and altered sediments, the present surface of the State has been laid.

Still later the seas had invaded north-central Minnesota. In their sediments the valuable Mesabi formations were deposited; probably the quartzite, with its now famous pipestone or catlinite deposit, formed at this period also. Volcanic masses again broke through cracks to cover much of the northeastern area and to spread as far as the Mesabi Range and Taylors Falls. Their remains are still plainly visible along the North Shore of Lake Superior. Close upon this vulcanism came a tremendous movement that folded the surface and made the dip that was destined to be the bed of Lake Superior.

By this time the formations had become so jumbled that scientists who sought to differentiate them were forced to devote years of research to their study. The most intensely studied region of the State comprises the iron ranges. It has been said that if iron were as precious as gold and silver, every farm in Minnesota would be a mine; but iron is one of the most common elements of the entire earth, and is found not only in rocks, but in most living things.

Many common minerals that appear insoluble are in time dissolved. Some of the richest iron ore is the residue after a gradual removal by solution of silica and other minerals. Again, water laden with dissolved iron has seeped through iron-bearing rocks and given up its metal. In a great many places throughout the State are to be found scattered residuary and enriched iron deposits, rich enough for smelting, but as a rule too small to warrant mining and shipping.

In the area known as the Lake Superior Region, covering much of upper Minnesota, Wisconsin, and Michigan, occur large concentrated deposits of some of the richest iron ore found anywhere on the earth. These concentrations appear in geological folds of rock known as the iron ranges. Not in any sense mountains, these ranges are rather the roots of very ancient and tremendous ridges worn down and now almost covered by the tons of drift or soil brought by the glaciers. Part of this rocky mass is exposed as far west as the Minnesota River valley and it extends far beyond the borders of the State.

Even though several of these rock masses are called iron ranges they are not uniformly ore bearing, but rather punctuated with pockets and sheets of iron ore. The total area of the ore-bearing soil is but a fraction of the entire formation. In the ancient rocks of the Vermilion Range the ores, which are of the hard type, are found in deep-pitched troughs so complex that in spite of extensive exploration it is not certain that all of the pockets have been found. This Vermilion district is from 5 to 10 miles broad and 100 miles long; the highest spots, which rise not more than a few hundred feet above the surface, are usually oblong in outline. The valleys and lakes also are attenuated in the northeast-southwest direction.

Mesabi, variously spelled, is from the Indian word for giant. In this range, as in the older Vermilion area, is a slight ridge merging on the southwest with the level country, but rising roughly a few hundred feet at its eastern end. It too lies in the general northeast-southwest direction, but its south slope is quite abrupt. The length of the ridge is about 110 miles, the width from 2 to 10 miles. Along its foothills are the ore deposits, usually of the soft variety, lying in broad stretches, more horizontal than in the Vermilion Range.

The Cuyuna Range differs from the other two in that it has no surface ridge or mark, but is entirely covered with glacial drift whose depth varies from 80 to 350 feet. The discovery of iron here was made by means of the dip needle. The ore consists of both the hard and soft varieties.

The United States Geological Survey describes the iron ranges thus:

"The iron-bearing formations of the Lake Superior region consist essentially of interbanded layers, in widely varying proportions, of iron oxide, silica, and combinations of the two, variously called jasper or jaspilite. These rocks become ore by local enrichment, largely by the leaching out of silica and to a less extent by the introduction of oxide. There are accordingly complete gradations between them and iron ores. Many of the intermediate phases are mined as lean siliceous ores."

Returning to the story of geologic time—Minnesota's evening was a quiet one, far removed from the mountain-making thrusts. The hills wore away to fill the sea; a great arm from the Atlantic reached the southern part of the State and the sediments formed the sandstone, limestone, and shale observable in the river ledges from Taylors Falls to Iowa. The receding sea left the sediment exposed to erosive processes, returned again, and once more receded. Sometime within the next few hours by the clock, while land animals were developing and reptiles were being displaced by smaller, more highly developed forms, the sea made its final thrust in the direction of Minnesota, this time from the Pacific. Thwarted by the Rockies this effort was of brief duration, and marked the end of the State's marine history.

During the few seconds preceding the era of recent time, occurred the activity that has given the landscape its familiar characteristics. From out of Canada came the ice to cover much of the continent and all of Minnesota except its small southeast triangle. During those thousands of years, only the few final seconds on the clock, the ice made four incursions and retreats. Down the valleys moved this huge load, slowly but irresistibly scouring rock ridges, polishing knolls, breaking off and shoving boulders about, unloading tons of soil, and, as it finally melted, leaving heaped-up debris in the form of innumerable moraines to dam up ten thousand lakes.

The earliest of the invasions, sometimes called the Nebraskan, covered almost the entire State and left a gray layer of soil or drift. After an ice-less interval this invasion was followed by another less extensive, and this too deposited a gray covering of soil. Then came the Illinois tongue entering from the East. (Its remnant is a bright red layer of soil, in some places covered only by its own weathered topsoil, in others protected by subsequent drift.) The final invasion came in three lobes: the Keewatin tongue came down from the northwest along the Red River and Minnesota Valley to Iowa and thrust broad lobes eastward; the Labrador pushed through the Lake Superior basin westward to deposit its load of pinkish drift; the Patrician, from the north of Lake Superior, brought a gray or lavender film but picked up on the Iron Range a mixture of iron rust which was scattered to its southern tip below the Twin Cities. This middle lobe came a bit earlier than its eastern and western collaborators and had receded before they deposited their own distinctive soil.

To these glaciers Minnesota owes its fertile pulverized limestone that has made wheat raising lucrative, and to them also it owes its undulating surface, its thousands of shallow water-filled depressions, its gravel beds, and, less fortunately, its boulder-strewn fields.

The retreating ice left the huge Lake Agassiz. Until the ice barring the northern Red River exit had melted away, this great body of water, larger than the combined Great Lakes, occupied the northwestern part of the State and extended well into the Dakotas and Canada, draining southward through the huge River Warren, in whose bed the Minnesota now flows.

Lake Superior is a remnant of the much larger and higher Lake Duluth. Barred by the melting glacier from draining through the present Great Lakes channel, Lake Duluth forced an outlet southward and sent its waters coursing down an ancient St. Croix.

Paleontology

During this long history the rocks themselves underwent so many changes that their original structure became almost unrecognizable, and it is indeed surprising to find that so fragile a structure as a marine animal could have left its imbedded imprint for thousands of centuries. Nevertheless many of the remains have been found, studied, and identified, even of those animals living as long ago as the period represented by the evening of the geological clock.

To one who has never seen a fossil or cracked open a stone to find within it the perfect outline of a strange crustacean or a familiar shell, such a search may seem complicated by technicalities. Most fossil layers in Minnesota are deeply buried, but their edges are often sufficiently exposed for examination along the rivers and streams in the southern part of the State. Many of the fossils found, as well as those collected from other States and foreign countries, are on display with accompanying explanations in museums in the Twin Cities and elsewhere.

Although scientists agree that plants and animals must have appeared in the long ages before the period known as the Cambrian, such forms have only rarely been preserved. But in the later cycles of Minnesota's geological history, when the seas submerged much of the midcontinent, myriads of mollusk-like animals—trilobites similar to the crustaceans of today and other forerunners of modern ocean life—lived, died, and were preserved in the rock layers that underlie the soil. The gray shales and sandstones of the earliest and thus deepest of the fossil layers—the Dresbach—contain several kinds of trilobites, shelled brachiopods, strange forms called pteropods, and cystoids, together with numerous trails and borings of worms. This layer can be seen today at Taylors Falls and along the Mississippi River near Winona. Immediately above it, and in many cases undifferentiated from it, is the Franconia, visible near the town of the same name along the St. Croix. A later Cambrian deposit, the oldest of the State's limestone layers, is the St. Lawrence, exposed at a former village in Scott County for which it was named. These hard layers are spotted with the stony remains of ocean forms. Nearer the surface, although in most places far beneath the topsoil, is a thick layer of Jordan sandstone, named also for a town in Scott County where the layer is uncovered in the quarry beds. This layer can be seen in many places but is especially well exposed along the St. Croix at Stillwater. Here, at Boom Hollow, is a highly fossilized stretch, although as a rule this layer is a poor fossil carrier.

Between the Cambrian period, whose separate layers are often more than 150 feet thick, and the succeeding layers of the Ordovician period, there is no sharply defined distinction, although the sea is believed to have receded and returned again. Where the waters were quiet and deep, the lime-carbonate shells of the myriads of marine animals were gradually changed to the familiar limestone, through the slow filtering of sea water followed by centuries of drying and pressure. The interlarding of these lime layers with sandstone is evidence of the changing levels and character of the seas.

The deepest of the Ordovician layers is the Oneota, observable from Garden City north to Chaska, from the river level at Hastings to the bluff top at Red Wing, and from there southward where it forms the tops of the bluffs. Although scientists have differentiated this layer from the preceding ones, the uninitiated will find them very similar. But new animals constantly appear and others, rare in the older rocks, here become more numerous. Cephalopods (related to the nautilus), gastropods, and trilobites were common and widely varied. The New Richmond sandstone and the Shakopee dolomite intervene between the Oneota and the next layer, the St. Peter, in whose porous structure the fossils are more difficult to find. It is in the St. Peter sandstone that numerous sewer and cable channels, mushroom and cheese caves have been cut. Carver's Cave and many less well known but much more extensive natural caverns also occur in this layer.

In the succeeding muddy depositions countless microscopic animals were buried, among them marine worms, primitive fish, and chaetopods (worms with bristle-like legs). The deepening seas then deposited the shales of the Glenwood beds, which are often erroneously called soapstone.

The succeeding limestone beds of the Platteville period (exposed along the Mississippi between the Robert Street Bridge and St. Anthony Falls) contain millions of sea-living animals, corals, graptolites (colonial water animals with no living representatives), and many other successors of earlier seas. Above the Platteville is the most highly fossilized of any Minnesota stone—the Decorah shale—which is exposed in many places, notably below Cherokee Park. Scores of species of animals have been identified from a single piece of this stone. In addition to the usual forms there are new sponge-like animals—bryozoans and many others. One cephalopod fossil from this layer, now on display in the geology museum of the University of Minnesota, is more than 5 feet long, and specimens are known to have reached 15 feet. The cephalopod was truly the giant of the Ordovician period, exceeding in size any animal of its time.

The Devonian seas are represented in Minnesota only in the Cedar Valley limestone which is exposed from a few miles west of Granger northward across Spring Valley into Mower County. Minnesota had become dry land while Iowa still lay at the bottom of the sea. Although the Cretaceous seas covered a good deal of Minnesota, their animal deposits are scarce; they include the oyster beds of the Mesabi. Exposures along the Minnesota River valley above Mankato are, however, a rich and valuable source of plant remains. Tulip trees, magnolias, laurels, pomegranates, and even giant sequoias made a luxuriant cover over prehistoric Minnesota, and were intermixed with many trees, such as willows and poplars, typical of a temperate climate. They were replaced by primeval evergreens, the well preserved remains of which are constantly coming to light.

With the receding seas the life record for Minnesota becomes obscured. Land forms are much more rarely preserved. No evidence has been found that dinosaurs wandered over Minnesota as elsewhere—though doubtless they did. Huge tusks, joints, jawbones, and teeth of elephant-like animals found in the glacial drift, bones preserved in peat-bogs, plants from the deep muck of ancient swamps, all point to a strange Minnesota. But those ages during which the coal beds of the eastern States and other famous deposits were being formed, and the modern living forms evolving, have left here only scattered and incomplete traces.

Natural processes, though slow, are never ending, and the contour of the land changes constantly. In Minnesota, lakes are disappearing, the lime of rich calcareous drift is being used up rapidly in the forested area; the prairies, more exposed to erosive elements, are becoming more uniform in texture.

Flora

Geological formation, altitude, soil, and climate have contrived to give Minnesota its varied plant cover. Three major types of vegetation are found in the State. In the upper north and east is the great coniferous forest; the western and southwestern area is covered by prairie grass and its plant associates; and betwen these two regions but with intrusions from both is a transition zone, a long diagonal strip varying from a few miles to almost a hundred miles in width.

Once the most characteristic feature of the transition area was its heavy cover of hardwoods, a not inconsiderable part of the timber that covered more than 70 percent of the State. A part of this hardwood belt, in regions where the soil was rich with lime and the rainfall sufficient, became known very early as the "Big Woods." The region so-named extended from Mankato to about 110 miles north from the Twin Cities and was in places 40 miles wide. The trees were principally sugar maple, basswood, and white elm, with some slippery elm, red and green ash, butternut, and bur oak. Beneath the undergrowth of ironwood, maple seedlings, dogwood, and other shrubs, bloomed hepaticas, anemones, bellwort, dutchmans-breeches, bloodroot, and trillium. Little of this beautiful forest remains; its trees have been cut and its undercover grazed.

Adjoining the "Big Woods" on the east and on the north, where the less fertile red drift covered the surface, the white oak thrived, and on the sand plains grew the still smaller scrub oak. In these less dense forests was an underbrush of many plants including wild roses, blackberries, and New Jersey tea. Flowers were more abundant than in the heavy forest— rue anemone, wild geranium, lily-of-the-valley, Canada anemone, and sweet pea in the spring; aster, goldenrod, and other plants in autumn. Here, as in the "Big Woods," man has modified the picture, leaving few of the forests in natural condition.

In many places the hardwood is invaded by both conifers and prairies. Near Anoka is a black spruce and tamarack swamp, a short distance away, an exile growth of cedar, a little farther are desert-like dunes and intermixtures of prairies. South of the Twin Cities, where the tamarack is found occasionally, it is without its most constant northern companion, the black spruce, although its smaller associates—the pitcherplant, twinflower, bunchberry, and the rare pink-and-white ladyslipper—are able to survive the warmer weather. All of these flowers flourished forty years ago within the city limits of Minneapolis. Now, however, few of these transition swamps remain in the original condition. Most of them have been drained or their trees cut for firewood.

In the extreme southeastern tip of the State and almost isolated from the more northern belt, the hardwood forest exists in its most varied form. Mixed with the species from the north are the more characteristically southern trees such as black oak, black walnut, river birch, and Kentucky coffee. Topping a bluff at Winona are red cedar or juniper, familiar to north woodsmen. Here the white pine lives precariously, far removed from its preferred colder environment.

More highly valued by the early fortune hunters than the hardwood

groves were the great coniferous forests that covered the entire northeastern third of the State and extended southward to within 50 miles of
the Twin Cities and west almost to the Red River Valley.

This timbered expanse comprised most of Minnesota's virgin forest of
38 million acres. Of this entire area less than half remains, and only in
isolated spots are there remnants of the virgin timber—white, jack, and
red or Norway pine—which grew in almost pure stands on the higher
areas or were intermixed with white spruce and balsam fir. White birch
is the only deciduous tree to grow abundantly with the evergreens, but
poplar and aspen, black and mountain ash, red maple, pin cherry, and
yellow birch are scattered throughout the area. Here, where farming is not
intensive, many of the swamps still exist in original form, their black
spruce and tamarack often accompanied by white cedar. Since the hardwoods require a rich soil, and cannot survive late frost, they are restricted,
in the evergreen belt, to lake shores and protective ridges such as are found
in the vicinity of Mille Lacs.

Trailing-arbutus, wintergreen, Labrador-tea, and dwarf kalmia are widespread in the forest openings. Blueberries and cranberries are sufficiently
abundant to be economically valuable. Familiar shrubs are white-flowered
thimbleberry, mountain maple, dwarf birch, sweetfern, elder, and several
varieties of honeysuckle.

Fire and lumbering have changed the ratio of evergreen and deciduous
trees. Poplar and birch spring up quickly when the evergreens are destroyed, to be replaced by conifers only after years of undisturbed growth.
If the seed has been destroyed, or if burning is frequent, the plant cover
of the area changes from evergreen to brush forest and finally, with the
depletion of the soil, to unproductive thicket.

Since the first commercial cutting of the white pine at Franconia on the
St. Croix, waste and carelessness have characterized the lumbering process.
Fires, greatly augmented by the neglected piles of slash, have destroyed
millions of additional acres.

Not until most of the timber reserves had been invaded and many of
them destroyed did Minnesotans realize how great and lasting a loss would
result from their heedlessness. Many areas suitable only for forests had
been sold to farmers whose lives were spent in trying to produce crops on
an unproductive soil. Their consistently meager returns, poor even in the
best years, left them desperate when the depression came. The problem of
reallocating farmers and reforesting their farmsteads is one of the most
difficult of Minnesota's conservation problems.

Early farmers cut the trees in order to plant crops, erroneously believing that the prairies were not fertile. Their supposition ultimately was disproved and the prairies now are the most intensively cultivated lands of the entire State.

From Canada to Iowa they extend, a great almost unbroken expanse covered over all but a southeastern tip by the rich glacial drift. Along the margins of the hardwoods they intrude to associate in many places with the true coniferous forest. Along this wooded border bur oaks and small trees push into the prairies where, as their struggle with arid land becomes greater, they are dwarfed into mere shrubs.

Intermixed with the prairie grasses, blossoming herbs and low shrubs flourish. In the spring, puccoons, birdsfoot violet, prairie phlox, and wild roses bloom. Blazing-stars, goldenrod, and asters flower in the autumn. These, since intensive cultivation has removed them from large areas, can be found only in isolated spots on steep hillsides and in the barren sandy stretches. Not even the forests are so quickly and permanently modified as is the virgin prairie.

The aquatic vegetation of each of the three vegetational regions is distinctive. Although the swamp trees are rare in the prairie area, the lakes are bordered by trees even in the more arid sections. Along the larger streams and bottom lands, the willows and cottonwoods grow. Far out on the prairies the species are limited, although boxelder and maple are quite sure to thrive on any of the higher river banks. Most lakes and ponds have heavy growths of aquatic and subaquatic plants. The surfaces of many shallow ponds are covered with yellow and white waterlilies, nearly all of the lakes have submerged waterweeds; bulrushes and cattails crowd along the shores. All of these plants tend to fill the lake and finally, when a drought comes and the water level falls, another lake has been obliterated.

So gradual is this transition that only the most observant realize that it is the fate of all these lakes to disappear as have those of the older glacial-drift area of the southern part of the State. During its transition a lake may survive as a swamp filled with tamarack, or become a sedge-covered meadow, and eventually a wet prairie.

Fauna

As a result of its diverse plant covering and varied climate, Minnesota's animal life has unusual variety. Many species of the north woods are absent in the southern area where distinctly different biological representatives are found. In some cases species that usually differ noticeably merge in this transition zone and are indistinguishable.

Long before its mineral wealth was dreamed of, Indians and adventurers were feasting on Minnesota's game birds, mammals, and fish; indeed no explorer could have survived without their aid. Since that day when Radisson wrote: "We killed several other beasts as Oriniacks (moose), stagg (elk), wild cows (buffalo), Carriboucks, fallow does and bucks, Catts of the mountains, child of the Devill, in a word we lead a good life," Minnesotans have looked upon their game as public property. But furriers and firearms have so changed the game picture that to the hunter of today Radisson's account sounds like a fabulous dream.

After 1830 the once common buffalo came rarely and soon disappeared; the elk, too rare to be regarded as a resident, is perhaps even now extinct; the prongbuck or antelope, although at one time found in western counties, no longer inhabits the State.

The only large mammals commonly found within its borders are the white-tailed deer, the bear, and the moose. The deer, whose population in 1930 was estimated at one hundred thousand, has been forced into the northern half of the State by the extension of cultivated areas, although previously it roamed throughout the forested regions. The moose, much more exclusive than the deer, restricts its wanderings to the extreme northern border area where it is increasing in numbers. Its population in 1930 was estimated at four thousand, but since it has little regard for international boundaries, its numbers are widely fluctuant. Traditional enemy of the deer is the bear, of which one species abounds in Minnesota woods to the exasperation of campers and rangers whose food stores are never safe from its maraudings. Its food habits are, however, much less sanguinary than commonly believed, for weeds, fish, insects, acorns, and berries are important in its omnivorous diet. The Minnesota representative is the black bear, but it varies considerably in color; one familiar variation is the cinnamon bear. The grizzly, now confined to the Rocky Mountain area, once hunted along the western Minnesota boundary.

One of the last and possibly the only herd of woodland caribou to be found within the United States grazes in the border area of Upper Red Lake. This relative of the European reindeer is distinguished from the deer family by the fact that the female carries rudimentary antlers. The Minnesota herd probably does not exceed thirty or forty animals.

The cougar, known as mountain lion or panther, never common in the State, has been exterminated, but its two smaller relatives, the Canada lynx and the bay lynx, or bobcat, are present. The Canada lynx, which may attain a weight of thirty pounds, is rarely seen except in the northern woods, but the smaller bobcat occasionally appears throughout the wooded areas.

The timber or brush wolf is rare; but the smaller coyote is common in the wooded north, persisting in the southern area only with great difficulty, for its natural cover is rapidly disappearing.

The red fox, progenitor of the valuable and often domesticated silver and black, is abundant in much of the region. Together with its highly bred captive descendants it provides the State with the largest single income from pelts. (Licensed breeders in the State keep approximately 10,000 foxes on their farms.) The more agile gray fox borders the Wisconsin boundary and is apparently extending its range, but, although a beautiful animal, it has little commercial value. Mink breeders have increased the mink population tremendously, but trappers still catch thousands of these animals each year. Next in value of the hunted furbearers are the muskrat, skunk, weasel, and raccoon.

A gnawing animal with undeniable distinction is the porcupine. Not the most attractive of the woods animals he is nevertheless friendly and deliberate. He does not, as commonly supposed, shoot his spines at an enemy; strangely enough, however, he is born with a full supply. He gleans his food from trees and roots; forest fires are his constant enemy, although his indifference to danger leaves him a victim of many other hazards.

More wary of man is the beaver, once the most lucrative to fur traders of all the western animals. Its skillfully built but conspicuous home is doomed to constant depredations in spite of stringent laws. The beaver is most frequently seen in the northern forests where the numerous lakes provide its aquatic habitat, but it is increasing in numbers, and is extending its range far into the prairie.

By far the most familiar of the entire rodent group are the gray squirrels whose two varieties are found in almost every wood. Occasional black and even white squirrels are variations from the normal color, not different species, as many believe. There are northern and southern species of red squirrels but they are not easily identified.

More restricted geographically is the large fox squirrel whose normal color is decidedly brownish. It is quickly recognized by its large rusty-colored tail. Its habitat extends from the southeastern border well into the State. Two flying squirrels, a northern and a smaller southern variety, live in the eastern border woods, but since both varieties are nocturnal, only the most inquisitive naturalists find them.

Many other small mammals are abundant. The ubiquitous house rat and mouse, introduced by man, are responsible for the calumny heaped upon their shy woods and prairie relatives. Most of the wild Minnesota forms are harmless, or only locally a nuisance. In addition to the common meadow mice, the observant may see the long-legged deer mouse, the rare grasshopper mouse, the tiny harvest mouse, or the queer stump-tailed bog lemming. None of these animals hibernates, unlike the incredible and more distantly related jumping mice.

The birds of Minnesota, like the animals, include a great variety. In the hardwood belt, birds of both evergreen forest and prairie may nest near the same locality.

Typical birds of the western prairies are the western meadowlark and Brewer's blackbird which, in the transition zone, sometime meets the Arctic three-toed woodpecker, which ventures south as far as the Twin Cities, or the eastern cardinal, once thought to be restricted to the regions south and east of the Minnesota border. Only in the western part of the State, however, can one see the lark bunting, the western burrowing owl, and other of their associates.

Occasional southern species such as the eastern mockingbird, the Carolina wren, and the Louisiana water thrush, may stray to the Twin Cities, but usually are found only in the extreme south. Many inhabitants of the coniferous forests, such as the Canada spruce grouse, the Canada jay, the northern raven, and the southern pine siskin, are rare or absent in the rest of the State.

The bottom lands and the thousands of lakes and ponds afford congenial haunts for immense numbers of water birds. But the cultivation of extensive areas has caused great changes in bird life. Many species once abundant have become rare or extinct; constant hunting and the advent of the stray domestic cat have helped to reduce the avian population.

The total number of species of birds known to occur regularly in Minnesota is 268. There are 22 additional subspecies and more than 50 rare or accidental visitors. Of the total population 218 nest regularly within the borders of the State. Of the three introduced species, the English sparrow is most obvious, the ring-necked pheasant most valued, and the starling the most frequently unrecognized.

Although migration begins in April, the bird student at the latitude of the Twin Cities usually sees the largest number of species in May. Since the flight of migratory birds often follows the great river courses, the Mississippi Valley and its branches are rich in bird visitors.

The hunting season varies from year to year as does the bag limit (see GENERAL INFORMATION, and SPORTS and RECREATION).

Waterfowl, other migratory species, and the now naturalized pheasant are favorite game birds, but the State protects several species once favorites of the sportsmen.

Minnesota's lakes and streams contain abundant fish populations; nevertheless they require continual restocking to insure a constant supply. Although some of the large varieties, like the spoon-billed catfish and sturgeon, have become rare or restricted in their range, the game fish have not so suffered.

Contrary to general belief the present population of brook trout is derived from imported stock. The native trout of north shore streams was completely fished out before conservation measures were adopted. This popular trout now thrives in all parts of the State where the water is clear and sufficiently cool. The steelhead and rainbow trout have become naturalized and furnish good sport to the angler in the Lake Superior region. The German brown trout thrives in warmer waters. Lake trout are abundant in Lake Superior and in certain other northern lakes. Minnesota's pike-like fish, the muskellunge, the northern pike or pickerel, and walleye are usually abundant. The muskellunge is the rarest and is restricted to lakes in the region of Park Rapids and Lake of the Woods. Small-mouth, striped, and large-mouth bass are but three of the many varieties of popular game fish. *(See SPORTS and RECREATION.)* There are many other species of importance to commercial fishermen *(see INDUSTRIAL DEVELOPMENT)*. Carp, unfortunately introduced about 1883, receives universal condemnation from anglers, but is used commercially to some extent.

The number of reptiles and amphibians in Minnesota is small, in comparison with more southern States. Only 17 amphibians occur here; of the salamanders only the tiger is common. The common toad is found over the entire State. Four of the nine species of frogs are diminutive tree varieties.

Of the 27 reptile species, 3 are lizards, 9 are turtles, and 15 are snakes. Only the rattler is poisonous and it is confined to the southeastern border. The timber rattler is fairly common but the smaller massasauga rattler has been found along the Mississippi in Minnesota, although occurrence records are extremely rare. All the other snakes are not only harmless, but decidedly beneficial by reason of their food habits. The only reptile of possible commercial use is the turtle, of which several species are used as food.

The clam, not usually considered an edible variety, is a source of considerable income in supplying shells to button manufacturers.

Conservation

As early as 1876 a forestry association was established to protect the State's timber resources. But the boom years, marked by heedlessness and lack of public interest and support, doomed many well-meaning but desultory efforts to save Minnesota's natural wealth. A land commission established in 1885 had jurisdiction only over public lands; later commissions from time to time attempted control of minerals, erosion, and water resources, besides performing a variety of related functions. Not until the establishment of the department of conservation by the 1931 legislature were the many conservation efforts united under a single commission.

To the original divisions—drainage and waters, forestry, game and fish, lands and minerals—have been added a division of State parks and a tourist bureau.

Within two years of its establishment the department faced a severe emergency in the drought of 1933. Its usefulness in co-ordinating drainage and erosion projects, drought relief, forest, game, and fish conservation at that critical time justified the hopes of its enthusiastic sponsors.

The problem of conservation is still, however, a portentous one. Large areas, once forested, are now tax-delinquent farmlands unfit for private use. The committee on land utilization, appointed by Governor Olson in 1932, reported (1934) that "inefficiency and incompetency, a palpable neglect of public welfare, a careless and unsympathetic conduct of the business of the State, unpardonable ignorance, and sometimes downright dishonesty are revealed in the manner that the land has been disposed of or exploited in the past."

The area with which they were most concerned, the northeastern counties, includes 37.3 percent of the total area of the State, a region larger than the State of Maine. From areas of unproductive cut-over land many farmers have eked out a precarious living. Many inhabitants have been moved to more productive lands, others continue only with public aid, unable to pay any taxes. It is in this region that the greatest conservation and rehabilitation projects of the State are being undertaken.

Several agencies are engaged in the attempt to recoup the wasted forests. The State divisions of forestry and parks have co-operated with Federal authorities in an aggressive campaign to reduce forest fires which, as recently as the years 1930 to 1935, destroyed 13,791 acres of Minnesota's timber valued at five million dollars. Ambitious reforestation projects involve replanting of many acres of forests each year. Technical advisers aid in such varied projects as silviculture, insect and plant-disease control, drainage, and park management, all of which affect the conservation of the forest lands.

The extensive peat beds that underlie many acres of soil have received relatively little consideration and many acres have been burned. Conservationists believe that in addition to their potential fuel value, they may eventually be important commercially as fertilizer.

The drought has focused attention on a wasteful, but controllable process —soil erosion—which is greatly accentuated when plant covering is lost. By far the most destructive erosion occurs in the loamy cultivated soils of the southern part of the State. Here drainage gullies form rapidly and the rolling hills are soon marred by denuded banks. Demonstration plots built by Government experts are showing farmers how to save their valuable soil; for the larger areas more extensive methods must be devised.

Inadequate investigation has prevented the maximum conservation of Minnesota's lakes. Their use for water storage, for fish propagation, recreational development, protection, and food production depends upon further careful study. The State maintains seven hatcheries with several field stations and substations. *(See SPORTS and RECREATION.)* A number of lakes are periodically closed to fishermen as a conservation measure. Prohibition of fishing during the spawning periods and the limitation of daily catches, help to insure a continuous fish supply. A large area in the Superior National Forest is permanently closed to hunters, but open to fishermen and canoeists. Other smaller refuges are scattered throughout the State, usually in the vicinity of large lakes or cities.

Water conservation, since it affects timber and other crops, recreation areas, and wildlife habitats, is of great importance in the State. An adequate control of water requires storage near the headwaters of the great river systems, prevention of drainage from the multitudinous lakes, and controlled drainage of the rocky region of Lake Superior whose scenic and recreational needs demand constantly flowing streams. Since Minnesota provides headwaters for the Hudson Bay, the St. Lawrence, and the Mississippi, its water conservation policy affects many other States and has even international significance.

Water power near industrial centers has been extensively developed; but in isolated regions it is still not utilized. The State's estimated undeveloped water resources total approximately 200,000 horsepower; 300,000 horsepower is now utilized (1938).

Associated with the wet lands and bogs are enormous deposits of marl or bog lime, a valuable soil replenisher which is widely distributed in the central part of the State. It occurs in layers sometimes many feet thick, is easily obtained, and, being soft and chalklike, requires little preparation. The marl deposits are supplemented by inexhaustible supplies of limestone. The latter is in layers sometimes 100 feet thick in the ledges exposed by the down-cutting of the Mississippi River. It must, however, be crushed and ground before it can be used on the land. Since the cost of transporting these minerals may be prohibitive, it is important that sources of supply be found close to the place of their use.

It is estimated that one and a quarter billion tons of merchantable ores remain in Minnesota; in addition there are more than 50 billion tons of poorer grades which may at some time prove usable. More than a billion tons of iron ore have been removed in a little more than fifty years, and at the present rate the richest ore supply soon will be exhausted. Conservation of this resource demands the complete extraction of ore from all mines before they are abandoned and become water-filled. With the hope of finding profitable use of the low grade ores, processing experiments are now being conducted at the State University.

First Americans

Archeology

WHO were the first inhabitants of the territory now called Minnesota? Today the mystery seems only a little nearer solution than in the first exciting days of archeological exploration when every rounded knoll was torn open in the hope of finding clues. Recent discoveries, far from clarifying the picture, tend to render it more complex. Amateur and professional explorers continually search here for relics of prehistoric man. Scattered clues, jumbled by the glaciers, nevertheless provide a working calendar for the dating of discoveries. It is possible that one small unglaciated region of the State may have provided prehistoric man with refuge from the encroaching ice.

Minnesota's Indian mounds have long attracted archeologists, but it was not until the discovery of a skeleton of obvious antiquity that investigators found what they had long sought—remains of Pleistocene man in North America.

As recently as 1929 the well-known archeologist, Sir Arthur Keith, expressed his surprise that in America no fossil form of prehistoric man had come to light, despite the conjectured existence of an unsubmerged land bridge at Bering Strait over which he might have crossed from Asia. "He almost certainly did take it," said Sir Arthur, "and his fossil remains will yet be found in America."

Only three years after this statement a crew of road builders near Pelican Rapids dug into the silt of a lake bed, known to be even older than the extensive glacial Lake Agassiz, and found there the well-preserved fossilized remains of a young girl. The fossil skeleton, found in layers that had been studied previously, was adjudged to be about twenty thousand years old. This much-discussed young woman has come to be known as the "Minnesota Man" and has been minutely measured and studied in order that her racial origin and age may be surmised. Measurements indicate that she is an ancient *Homo sapiens,* a more primitive Mongoloid than the Indian or Eskimo, being long-headed whereas finds of later groups are more or less round-headed.

The Browns Valley Man, another famous Minnesota skeleton, found a few years later than the Minnesota Man, is of a more recent time. He belonged to that early Indian race which made what are by some regarded as the oldest flint artifacts. His features must have resembled those of the Greenland Eskimo, and his jawbone, much wider than that of the mound builder, exceeds in width even that of the Heidelberg Man. Buried with this early Indian, whose age is estimated at twelve thousand years, were artifacts of a transition period between the Yuma and the Folsom types.

The great majority of Minnesota's archeological relics have come from the thousands of Indian mounds and habitation sites that dot the State. Although the mounds are more obvious than the village sites, the latter are particularly rich in relics. On many of them successive generations lived and worked, dropping broken tools and dishes, discarding bones of the animals that supplied their food, chipping the implements they used for the hunt, and sewing the skins they used for clothes. Some of these villages were on open ground, others were in rock shelters or caves. One cave home site on the St. Croix River has been thoroughly explored and its relics identified. Here successive families lived in one place so long that the debris accumulated around the "doorstep" to a depth of 4 feet. The first inhabitants chose the site perhaps as much as a thousand years ago. They chipped arrows, scraped skins, built fires, and prepared food. Along with their discarded fishhooks were found the bones of the fish they caught— sheepshead, pike, catfish, and the like. That their hunters were skillful is attested by the many bones of deer, bear, and smaller animals. Dogs and turtles seem to have added variety to the diet.

The hunting and household implements are of varied design and material. Many of the excavated tools are of bone, but a few have been found on the shores of old Lake Agassiz which point to probable prehistoric use of ivory. Ivory beads, pipes, and even imitations of animal teeth had apparently been carved from tusks, but whether from fossil or living ivory is undetermined.

Pottery vessels have been uncovered in many places. The prehistoric pottery from the State is of two distinct types. Those from the northern areas are usually of fire clay with elaborate impressed decorations and with a capacity as great as 3 to 5 gallons. The clay, mixed with sand or grit temper, was molded into a fragile vessel often less than one-eighth inch thick. Among those displaying the best craftsmanship are the Blackduck vessels named for the vicinity of their discovery in Beltrami County. To the south of the Twin Cities crushed shell was mixed with clay, and the pots were decorated in a very different style. Despite their differences both types are believed to have been made by Siouan tribes. Charred bits of broken vessels indicate that although extremely fragile these vessels were actually used for cooking.

Suggestive of the ingenuity of these early races are the numerous hammered copper implements—spearheads and knives—and even beads which frequently are found. Although it seems likely that the natives used copper nuggets scattered in the glacial drift, legend and some evidence bear out the opinion that prehistoric races actually mined this workable metal in the region of Lake Superior.

Many of these relics are found along portages traversed for no one knows how many generations or even centuries before the white men came. Well-worn prairie and woodland trails were noted by the very first explorers, who also saw maple trees gashed for drawing sugar sap, and often used for landmarks the ancient pictographs they found on the rocks.

But exciting as are these scattered and isolated discoveries it is not so much they as the ten thousand or more Indian mounds that have interested the population at large in the State's prehistory. Two early Minnesotans, Alfred J. Hill and Theodore Lewis, located almost eight thousand before 1895. Many other mounds have since been charted.

Although usually knob-like and symmetrical, there are in localized areas a few mounds whose pattern is so different as to have attracted keen attention. These are often shaped to resemble birds, and less frequently turtles, fish, or other animals. In some of them human remains have been found at the presumed position of the effigy's heart or head. This type of mound is present chiefly in a restricted area in southeastern Minnesota and is much less common than in Wisconsin. Although the explanation of these effigies has not been established, many people believe they have a religious or tribal significance.

Typical burial mounds are scattered throughout the State, although weathering, farming, road building, and relic hunting have reduced their number. Many seem to be empty, but may have contained decomposed human remains. A sufficient number contain preserved skeletal remains to make it clear that their primary use was for burial. Although there is some indication that they were still in use when the first explorers arrived, it is thought that most were built in the centuries immediately preceding the coming of the white man.

Examination of their contents has resulted in an interesting reconstruction of early customs. The presence in some mounds of only the long bones of the body is explained by the early practice of disposing of the dead in shallow graves, in trees, or on scaffolds, until the flesh decomposed, after which the large bones were gathered and given permanent burial in the traditional mound. Frequently tools, decorative beads, and utensils were buried with the bones, and some mounds have yielded relics identical with those from habitation sites.

Gruesome indications of early tribal culture are the human skulls with sections broken away (probably to facilitate brain removal), and human bones fractured in such fashion as to permit the removal of marrow by roasting.

It is impossible now to determine the period during which these mounds were built, or the specific tribe that made them, but continued investigations substantiate the opinion that they are not extremely old. Romantic tales of their construction by a strange giant race have been discarded. All the evidence seems to bear out the belief that the builders were Indians of ordinary size, much like the Indians of today, whose ancestors probably came thousands of years earlier from some primitive Asiatic stock.

‹‹‹‹‹‹‹‹‹‹‹‹‹‹‹‹‹ ☼ ›››››››››››››››››››››

Indians

The history of Minnesota's Indians is but a page in the world-wide story of the conquest of simple peoples and their homelands by the civilization, arms, and diseases of a more dominant race. The local story differs but little from that of most other States; the outcome has been, however, quite different. For while many States have banished practically their entire Indian population and others have segregated their native tribes on reservations, in Minnesota the prehistoric Siouan tribes have been displaced almost entirely by Indians of Algonquian stock.

In the stories of Minnesota's Indian tribes four names occur repeatedly and are often used with no clear implication of their differences. Dakota, Sioux, Ojibwa, Chippewa—these are met in almost every frontier tale, often to the confusion of the uninitiated. They are intelligible only when it is remembered that the Minnesota Sioux are more properly called Dakotas, and were only one group of the great Siouan family that once occupied almost the whole of what we now call the Midwest, and which claimed many tribes, among them the Omaha, the Osage, the Crow, and the Winnebago.

The Chippewa, or more properly, the Ojibwa, spring from another Indian line, the Algonquian family, who, with most of the Iroquoian peoples, occupied a region near the upper Atlantic Coast. Likewise of Algonquian stock were the Ottawa, Cree, Blackfeet, and Kickapoo.

Many factors contributed to the early ethnological confusion. It was customary for several Indian tribes to hunt together, exchange weapons and patterns for clothing, and even borrow embroidery designs, much as women today exchange crochet patterns. Intermarriage helped still more to mix tribal customs. Another factor was the custom of the whites of coining tribal names so that they could discuss Indian problems without arousing suspicion if overheard. In this fashion many tribes came to be known by disparaging or flattering names, several by their geographic locations, others for characteristic activities. Thus the Potawatami were council fire makers, the Kemisteno were killers, the Menominee were wild rice gatherers, the Nopeming were inlanders (located farther from the Lakes), the Muskego were swamp dwellers, the Mukkundwa were pillagers, or more literally takers.

This last band had established itself in Minnesota near Leech Lake, when one day a sick trader, one of the first whites in the area, stopped at their encampment with a huge load of pelts. They gave the suffering man a night's lodging but took from him his valuable cargo because he had sold firearms to the Sioux. Thenceforth they were known as pillagers. The cause given for the thievery typifies the enmity that existed for two centuries between the Chippewa and Sioux.

The Minnesota Sioux were forest dwellers and thus differed in many ways from the prairie Sioux farther southwest. Their food included wild rice and swamp roots—staples scarcely known to the Plains people. (More than a century before the Revolution, Father Allouez had been given "marsh rye"—wildrice—by men "toward the great river Messipi," but there is no evidence that he valued that delicacy, so highly regarded today and still gathered by many Indians precisely as it was then.) They had to travel far to hunt bison, but almost in their dooryards were bear, deer, moose, and many smaller animals. They, of all the great Indian tribes, were most like the Wild West Indian of the American boy. Their deer-skin shirts and leggings, fringes and embroidered trimmings, leather moccasins and elaborate headdress, became the almost classic Indian costume. They rode horses, hunted with bows and arrows or spears, covered their dome-shaped wigwams with skins, and crossed the lakes in awkward round boats. Their craft were shaped like washtubs, with a wood framework covered by skins.

The Minnesota Sioux had customs and habits common to both forest and prairie. They cultivated crops, but were skilled hunters; their arrows resembled those of the West; their bows, those of the East. Many of them were in more or less permanent association with tribes unrelated by language to them, but with whom they doubtless trafficked more freely than with their own distant kinsmen. They had large permanent villages on many of Minnesota's thousands of lakes. They used the rivers for highways as did the fur traders. They even attempted cultivation of the rice crop, although their simple methods of harvesting usually scattered sufficient kernels for the repeated seeding of the swamps.

Earliest explorers reported the Chippewa, or Ojibwa, at Sault Ste. Marie, and frequently referred to them as Saulteurs. Tradition indicates that long before they had been pushed westward, they ranged the St. Lawrence Basin.

In their westward hegira the Algonquian stock dispersed in various directions, the Ottawa (traders) to Canada, the Sauk and Fox to Wisconsin and later a few to Minnesota, while the Chippewa chose the shores of the Great Lakes and became the most important, if not the first, of the Algonquians in Minnesota.

It is true that the Cheyenne, kinsmen of the Chippewa, seem to have lived in southern Minnesota, but by 1700, when Le Sueur arrived at the Blue Earth River, they were no longer there and the Sioux assured him that their own people, the Oto and Iowa, owned all the surrounding country.

The great contest between the Ojibwa and the Sioux for the lands of

Minnesota began in the seventeenth century and was not concluded until after the historic Sioux outbreak against the whites in 1862.

When Du Luth, in 1679, came to Mille Lacs and at the flourishing Sioux village at Izatys (corrupted to Kathio) planted the French flag, the Ojibwa were claiming, by right of conquest, the hunting grounds to the north and east of the Mississippi headwaters.

The two centuries that followed were unhappy ones for the Sioux. The French came and were followed by the British; the Revolution of the eastern colonists was fought and settled. But to the Sioux the white man's struggle meant chiefly that the furs, whose values he had learned to appreciate, were increasingly difficult to get. In 1805 Lieutenant Pike bought for liquor and a handful of pin money the huge tracts near the present Twin Cities, and boasted their value at $200,000, but the Sioux evidenced no realization that the white man's regard for the land was in any wise different from his own—a place to hunt and camp. He was far more concerned with the steady encroachment of the Chippewa armed with the white man's guns.

As settlers spread westward, the question of the Indian became urgent and after 1825 the leaders of the new United States were gradually framing the policy which would place all Indians on the Plains west of the Mississippi, on which, most statesmen then agreed, the white man could never live.

In the meantime the settlers, constantly annoyed as they were by the natives, could scarcely be expected to see the Indian brave as the romantic and symbolic figure Rousseau had pictured, nor his squaw as the tragic lady that Schiller immortalized in his *Nadowessian Lament*. It was all very well for Longfellow to grow enthusiastic over Mrs. Eastman's descriptions of Indian legends, or to seize upon Schoolcraft's tales for his Hiawatha saga, but settlers saw little poetry in the red man. Far more heartily they agreed with Cotton Mather when he called the Indians "the devil driven race." During the same years in which poets sang of the natural man, settlers struggled to eliminate him, pushing the Chippewa back from their newly won hunting grounds into undisturbed lands of the north, thrusting the Sioux westward into the Great Plains. "I wandered about, after you first arrived at the falls," said a Chippewa chief to Schoolcraft, "like a bird not knowing where to alight."

The kidnaping of a young Ohio boy by a family of Indians late in the eighteenth century, and his sale to a kindly, bereaved woman chief of the Ottawas, was responsible for one of the earliest and most authentic tales we have of Minnesota Indian life. This story, published in 1830, tells of the wanderings of young John Tanner back and forth across the hunting lands of the upper Minnesota border country. Equally interesting is its preface in which the editor made a strong plea for a consistent American policy toward Indian problems. Let the Indians alone, he urged, or at least let the white man cease to treat them as if they had deliberately disobeyed the white man's laws of which actually they had no knowledge.

Such pleas were of small avail; little by little the Indians' lands were reduced, their activities restricted. By 1835 President Jackson could boast that the movement of tribes to the western prairies approached consummation, and that this great area could be forever "secured and guaranteed them."

Two treaties in 1837, one with the Sioux and another with the Chippewa, opened the triangle between the Mississippi and the St. Croix. The payment to the Sioux was $500,000, of which $200,000 went to the traders and half-breeds, the usual reward for influence. When on June 15, 1838, the waiting settlers heard that the treaties were ratified, they rushed to spots they had already selected and by morning were staking claims.

Only the first comers were satisfied with so small a share of the unbounded West, and when in 1849 Alexander Ramsey left the East to head the newly organized Minnesota Territory the war cry was "Get the Suland." Scarcely had Ramsey reached the little fort on the Mississippi when he dispatched runners to call in the chieftains. The Bureau of Indian Affairs had fixed the price, with only $6,000 allowed for presents, but St. Paul boosters, fearful that the opening of the western country would detract from their own land boom, discouraged the plan. An 1850 bill increased the gift to $15,000, but the red men were away on their autumn hunt and the delay permitted rival fur companies to fight for treaty committee appointments until members of the Indian bureau itself were placed on the committee. The new members, freed from restriction, were permitted to bargain with all who had influence, to clear the Indian throat with liquor, and to make a tacit agreement for payment of the Indian debts to the traders. That strange legal procedure, the Indian treaty, was at last at work in Minnesota.

Traders had to be placated outright or with promises of debt payments; chiefs had to be convinced, and firearms and firewater were found to carry conviction. Most difficult to handle were the half- or mixed-bloods among whom were numbered some of the most heroic of the frontiersmen as well as many of the most dissolute characters the settlers were to face. Mothered by Indians, fathered by lonely French traders, these children of the wilds (*bois brûlés* as they were called because of their burnt-wood complexion) were free from the tribal inhibitions and without the discipline of life in a crowded community. They were received both at the tribal fire and at the trading post, they could pass either as white or red, and were in truth go-betweens with a price.

To all of these avid participants, the bargainers made representations. They trekked long distances to the conclaves, and rationed out beef, pork, and flour, often to hundreds of Indians and for weeks at a time before the land cessions were signed. But oftener than not the money they paid out preceded their return to the Twin Cities via the groggeries, which were a constant temptation to the native, or through the hands of the trader whose overdue bills were provided for handsomely by the Government. By such methods in a series of treaties before 1863, the Sioux parted with their entire holdings with the single exception of a narrow strip along the Minnesota River; the Chippewa ceded almost the entire upper half of the State. One farsighted chief complained at the low price saying: "You forget that the land will be yours as long as the world lasts." But land acquisition by a method best described as one of food, flattery, and fraud was the order of the day; cynically, the historians of that time called the Minnesota treaties "as honest as any."

Unsavory as are the details of these Indian treaties, their questionable character dwindles by comparison with the "Half-Breed Treaties."

The Chippewa treaty of 1854 appeased the half-breeds of that tribe by giving to each grown person title to an 80-acre tract. Within two years 312 "bloods" had been satisfied. Ten years later a prominent Minnesota family with Indian blood but no tribal connection received two tracts. The Indian Bureau supported the claim with the ruling that a relative of any Chippewa tribe was eligible. Shrewd "altruists" immediately set about to search for beneficiaries who might otherwise have been overlooked. Twelve hundred were soon discovered, their applications in some cases duplicated, some of men no longer living. The certificates were legally non-transferable, but two power-of-attorney contracts circumvented the law, and permitted the lucky purchaser to look over the pine land and choose at will. Soon Chippewa bloods were rounded up, paid off with a small fee, and the bundles of applications forwarded to Washington.

The practice was stopped during Lincoln's administration only to be resumed in 1868 when a prominent citizen succeeded in having 310 applications approved, although an investigating committee believed not one to be valid. In 1869 the applications were again refused, but Minnesota speculators pushed the search for half-breeds, and found more than seven hundred and fifty. The Neal Commission, finding less than two dozen of these valid, ruled that only Congressional action could approve further awards. But optimistic lumber speculators continued to value the applications, bankers accepted them as valuable investments, and in 1872 Congress was prevailed upon to pass an "Act to quiet certain land titles." Persons who had bought the scrip in "good faith" should be allowed to make good their claims and purchase lands at not less than $1.25 per acre. In a short time "the innocent parties," whom Congress termed victims of a fraudulent system, had acquired for about $2.00 per acre almost 20,000 acres of Minnesota's richest timber, worth at that time about $150,000.

The Sioux "half-breed" tract on the Mississippi had been guarded until 1840 by the incorruptible agent Taliaferro, but in 1854 the President was given power to issue certificates to the mixed-blood Sioux who owned it, whereby they could take up land in any unappropriated territory. Four hundred and eighty acres was the share for each. Like the Chippewa scrip these certificates became negotiable by the power-of-attorney method, speculators fought for them, white men who had married squaws rejoiced, and since ten children were worth 4,800 acres, their delight is easily understood. Land speculators hastened to prospected town sites, took up the choice lots before the surveys were made, reaped a quick fortune, and hunted for new bonanzas. The more adventurous hastened to California with a pocketful of paper to grab rich mineral and timber lands.

But the end had not yet arrived. Lumbermen, not satisfied with obtaining a small fortune for a barrel of whisky, a dog or a cat, invented the "floating" scrip system. They located on a stretch of land, removed the pine, and then obtained a cancellation on the ground that they had not "done right" by the Indian client, moved to another stretch and repeated the process. When ore was discovered on Minnesota's Iron Range, the scrip came into undreamed-of demand. The Secretary of Interior denied the title to ore lands acquired by the Sioux scrip method, but the years of litigation were concluded in 1902 by a Supreme Court decision which accorded validity to the strange procedure, and assured the owners of their right to millions of dollars' worth of the richest iron land in the world.

Throughout this long series of unappetizing affairs, few but the religious or philanthropic sided with the Indians. Even the devout were handicapped by the difficult language, and by the white man's examples, which spoke to the Indians more loudly than words.

More practical than the missionaries was the farsighted Taliaferro. He hoped to teach agriculture to the red men who already had a working acquaintance with agricultural methods. Although Connecticut realists like Samuel and Gideon Pond could always spare a few hours from prose-lyting for mundane labor, later missionaries gave less time to practical matters.

A much more successful agriculturist was Joseph Renville, a half-breed Sioux who had held a captaincy in the British Army, but returned after numerous adventures to marry an Indian woman, and establish, at Lac qui Parle, a baronial estate with herds of cattle and sheep, acres of cultivated land, and a large Indian following. In his leisure he translated the French Bible of his trader father directly into Sioux, dictating to Gideon Pond.

In spite of occasional petty quarrels, the ministers were, as a group, the stanchest supporters of the Indians. But even the influential Bishop Whipple was able to do no more than mitigate the hate that consumed the Minnesota settlers when warfare broke out (see HISTORICAL SURVEY).

The horror of the Sioux uprising so infuriated the whites that with one sweep the standing debts to this tribe were abrogated, those under arrest were driven onto barges, and after great hardship were unloaded far beyond the existing boundaries of the white man's land. Not content with banishment, Minnesota officials, with the aid of the War Department, carried out punitive expeditions against the escaped bands far out in the Dakotas. Sibley's expedition of 1863 to the region of Devils Lake, and the winter skirmish of Hatch's Battalion at Pembina the following winter, were highly publicized drives that did little to correct the depredations within the State itself. But not until still more troops had been sent to join Sully's expedition in 1864–65 did Minnesota lose interest in wholesale acts of vengeance and turn to the less spectacular business of bartering with the Chippewa.

Visitors, who may travel through the State with never a glimpse of an Indian, are surprised to learn that Minnesota's Chippewa population exceeds fourteen thousand. Of these, 12,680 are members of the consolidated Chippewa agency which was established in 1919 to take over the work of five reservations. More than eight thousand live on the White Earth Reservation area (see Tour 17), the remainder in villages or on nearby farm or timber land on the various reservations (most of whose lands have been alloted) located in the region lying betwen Mille Lacs in the center of the State, and Grand Portage far up on the north shore of Lake Superior. Almost two thousand are found on the unallotted land of the Red Lake Reservation (see Tour 7). In addition to the Chippewa there are more than five hundred Sioux at Pipestone and a number of mixed families scattered throughout the southern counties. Many of the last have been partially or completely assimilated, and exercise all legal rights of citizenship, attending schools and churches and sharing generally in the activities of community life.

Yet the average Chippewa today lives at a bare subsistence level, and Government funds alone assure him his necessities. With the exception of the Red Lake Reservation, his lands have been allotted, and such work as he can obtain consists of mere seasonal or odd jobs. Harvesting the wild-rice and blueberry crop (see Tour 5), picking pine cones for the forest nurseries (see Tour 20), and fishing and lumbering are only temporary re-munerative tasks. Repeated attempts to re-educate the Indian in his native crafts have met with only partial success, although the tourist trade provides a lucrative market for products of his skill even when they include only the usual birchbark baskets, bird houses, and toy canoes. A few of the more intelligent craftsmen, however, make salable willow furniture. The birch canoe is now only rarely seen in Minnesota, for although its construction requires many weeks, it brings the maker less than $25, and must compete with the modern canvas or ply-wood product. Despite the fact that for years all the pipestone of the famous quarries has been reserved for the use of Indians, they have permitted whites to purchase the raw stone and to fabricate and sell the curios made from it.

Perhaps the most hopeful indication of the possible economic redemption of the Chippewa is their growing awareness of the advantages of group effort. Today many sell their products through the recently founded Chippewa Co-operative Marketing Association, which began with a capital of $100,000 from the tribal treasury. It not only insures the craftsman a better price for his wares, but also sponsors a wildrice cleaning and packaging factory designed to replace the primitive harvesting and cleaning methods still used by Indians in the north woods. Eventually the making and marketing of maple sugar will be added to the co-operative's undertakings.

A somewhat similar organization is the Red Lake Fisheries Association at Redby. Here the Indians have sole fishing rights in a prescribed area, and their product is prepared and marketed exclusively through the organization which, in this instance, is a lessee of the Minnesota State Fisheries.

The Red Lake Reservation (see Tour 7) includes those Minnesota Indians least modified in language and custom. Of all the Indians in the State they are regarded as having maintained most nearly the pure Indian strain, and to them ethnologists continue to go for what little can be observed of tribal lore and custom. Even there the new generation is giving up the parent tongue, although many families are still bilingual.

The educational training of the Indian has been as unsatisfactory in Minnesota as elsewhere, but educators are at last recognizing the need of training the Indian youth in skills and crafts rather than the conventional studies of the white school. Recent years have seen a marked improvement in pedagogical methods.

Public health work among the tribes by State agencies has received Federal commendation, and conditions have recently been greatly improved; but tuberculosis and trachoma are still appallingly frequent and a vast amount of both money and effort must be expended before the State will have met its obligations to its dispossessed.

Indian songs, legends, and customs have attracted many students of art and science. The most comprehensive collection of Chippewa lore is that made by Frances Densmore, a Minnesota woman. Her several volumes of Smithsonian publications contain invaluable material made available through her personal acquaintance with numerous older Indians, and through long residence among them.

Chippewa songs, according to Miss Densmore, are alive with the warm red blood of human nature. Music is so much a part of their daily lives that if an Indian visits another reservation one of the first questions asked on his return is: "What new songs did you learn?"

Every phase of Chippewa life is expressed in music. Many of the songs are so ancient that the idiom is archaic; others celebrate the latest events. There are "dream songs," revealed to the singers in the half-hypnotic state verging on slumber; songs of the Midé, representing the musical expression of members of the Midewiwin, a "medicine" society; hunting songs; songs for obtaining a good supply of maple sugar; love-charm songs; healing songs; and songs recalling battles, deaths, and personal losses.

What could be simpler or more poignant than this "Farewell to the Warriors"?

> Come
> It is time for you to depart
> We are going a long journey.

"It was the custom for the women to accompany the warriors a short distance, all singing this song; later the song would be heard again, faintly at first, then coming nearer as the women returned alone, singing still, but taking up the burden of loneliness which is woman's share in war." *

* *Chippewa Music,* Frances Densmore, Bulletin 45, Bureau of American Ethnology.

A "Woman's-Dance Song" suggests an age-old invitation to one of the male participants:

> My sweetheart
> A long time
> I have been waiting for you
> To come over
> Where I am.

The simple response of primitive man to nature is found in the two phrases of the "Friendly Song":

> The sky
> Loves to hear me.

That the Indians were not wholly stoical about death is evident in the lament of the Sioux women:

> The Sioux women
>   pass to and fro waiting
>   as they gather up
>   their wounded men
> The voice of their weeping comes
>   back to us.

Personal relations also called for the attention of the singer. There is fine scorn in "The Man Who Stayed Home":

> Although
> Jinwábe
>   considers himself
>   a man,
>   his wife
>   certainly
>   takes all his attention.

One of our modern vers-librists might well envy the delicate sensitivity of "Love-Charm":

> What are you saying to me?
> I am arrayed like the roses
>   and beautiful as they.

No white poet has better expressed the indefinable passage of a season than the unknown Indian author of "A Song of Spring":

> As my eyes
>   search
>   the prairie
> I feel the summer in the spring.

But the appetites of material man are not gainsaid in "Maple Sugar":

> Maple sugar
>   is the only thing
>   that satisfies me.

The complex structure of Indian music, the varying rhythms of drum, rattle, voice, and dancing feet, and the tonal and melodic peculiarities of the songs cannot be discussed in a brief space. It is sufficient to say that Indian music is not subject to white standards; it is a fully developed art with a wide range expressing every physical and emotional aspect of primitive man in America.

Historical Survey

From Wilderness to Commonwealth

ALTHOUGH the drama of Minnesota spans three centuries, the actual transition from wilderness to Commonwealth has been crowded into less than a hundred years. Two and a half million people today spend their lives in the State, and few recall the aborigines and pioneer settlements. Yet the grandfathers of these few were of the generation that shot buffalo and built stockades, and the fathers were of the time that brought forth homesteads and towns. The shadow of a priest in his martyrdom seems hardly to have melted away before the figures of miners, loggers, artisans, and farmers strained across the land. The tumult of construction had scarcely been stilled before the baton rap of a symphony conductor brought an audience to attention in Minneapolis.

The prologue of the story and its link with the legendary Vineland of viking sagas may have been written on the unearthed and oft-disputed Kensington Rune Stone. Some believe that the stone recounts the visits in 1362, of a company of thirty Norsemen *(see Tour 9)*. Three centuries of silence, and then recorded history takes up the tale. The French explorations of the Northwest began, and with the echo of civilized voices on the watercourses, the curtain rose on the picturesque company who were to enact the first scene in the Minnesota drama.

They came from the stockades and settlements on the St. Lawrence, and pushed boldly westward by the Great Lakes until their paddles dipped at last into the narrow reaches of the upper Mississippi. Royalty across the seas listened covetously to stories of vast and rich domains that promised salvation to their impoverished empires. The land of the Sioux and Chippewa, for centuries safeguarded by obscurity, was suddenly thrust into the glare of European politics.

Bidding for the favor of their monarchs, the soldiers and titled adventurers braved discomfort and death, appropriated lands, and established forts to support their claims. Traders made their hazardous way over lake and stream, carrying firearms, cutlery, and trinkets to exchange with the Indians for the prized peltries for which courtiers abroad were clamoring. Explorers, attracted by the mirage of a Northwest passage, pushed through the wilderness to draft the first crude maps. Catholic missionaries, fired by proselyting zeal, exulted in their opportunity.

With explorer, trader, soldier, and priest came the *voyageur,* and woven in and out of the pattern is the glowing story of the *coureurs de bois.* Unlicensed and outside the law, the *coureurs* penetrated the great woods on foot or in canoes, with the sure knowledge of Indians. Theirs was a knowledge hard-won. It was their stock in trade, and they prudently kept secret what they had learned, even while they saw their dashing countrymen from beyond the Atlantic risk their lives and fortunes in its quest.

Radisson and Groseilliers, Du Luth (his name, variously spelled, was probably Du Lhut), Father Hennepin and his companions Accault and Auguelle, De Noyon, Perrot, Le Sueur, La Vérendrye with his sons and nephew—all strode the stage in leading parts, while in the background raged European wars, dissensions between the Canadian and Louisiana Governments, conflicting ambitions of patrons, rivalries between traders, and perennial troubles among and with the Indians.

Radisson and Groseilliers, returning to Montreal in 1660 with a fleet of canoes, which they had loaded with rich furs on their second voyage to the west, gave to the civilized world its earliest authentic news of the native tribes of the Great Lakes region, and demonstrated the potentialities of a vast wealth lurking in the forests. The adventurous Du Luth appeared on the scene in 1679. One of his first acts, when he had sufficiently impressed the Indians with the glory and loving kindness of the King of France, was to lay claim to the whole area in the name of his ruler. For 11 years he traveled up and down the shores of Lake Superior and explored the triangle between the Mississippi and St. Croix Rivers.

Hennepin and his companions, Auguelle and Accault, all sent by La Salle, ascended the upper Mississippi from the Illinois country in 1680, and, although taken captive by a band of Sioux, got as far as Mille Lacs. After turning southward Hennepin and Auguelle discovered and named the Falls of St. Anthony, which they had barely missed on the upward journey (see MINNEAPOLIS). (The meeting between Du Luth and Hennepin downstream from the mouth of the St. Croix where Du Luth had gone, drawn by rumors of white "spirits," must surely have been one of the most dramatic encounters in Northwest history.)

Perrot, for some twenty years a leading fur trader in the region, established himself for a while near the foot of Lake Pepin, and in 1689 claimed the area in the name of his monarch. Le Sueur, a companion of Perrot, built a fort on Prairie Island, near Red Wing, in 1695. Five years later he erected another near the site of Mankato, to which he came not by the usual Great Lakes route but by boldly ascending the Mississippi from the Gulf. It was from this post that he transported to France two tons of blue-colored earth, supposing it to be copper ore, only to discover that it was worthless clay.

Stockades occupied intermittently at Fort Beauharnois, later called Frontenac (see Tour 1), from 1727 to 1754, brought De Gonnor and Guignas, who opened the first mission in the upper Mississippi Basin, and Captain St. Pierre, long prominent as a leader in New France. (School books tell of the meeting of this gallant officer with Washington at French Creek, Pennsylvania, in 1753, when the young Virginia surveyor brought a letter from Governor Dinwiddie, protesting the encroachments of the French.) In the north, De Noyon discovered the Lake of the Woods about 1688, and between 1731 and 1749 La Vérendrye and his sons established the canoe route from Lake Superior to Lake Winnipeg, built a line of forts reaching as far as the present site of Calgary on the upper Saskatchewan in Alberta, crossed the upper Missouri, and probably sighted the Black Hills.

By this time, however, French influence was beginning to wane. Traders and Indians were negotiating with English buyers on Hudson Bay and with merchants in Albany and New York. With the outbreak of the French and Indian War, loyal Frenchmen withdrew from the region and hurried east to the scene of conflict. They had explored and opened the way to the Minnesota area; they had quieted the suspicions of the Indians and taught them the uses of firearms and whisky; they had established the beginnings of the fur trade. There remained, as evidence of their passing, hundreds of colorful place names and a scattered host of half-breed progeny.

French claim to the North American Continent was relinquished in 1763. (By a secret pact signed the previous year, New Orleans island and all French land west of the river had become the nominal possession of Spain, although that nation made no attempt to occupy or explore the upper river country.) English and Scotch proprietors, whose headquarters were in Canada, now took over the French and half-breed traders, who continued to act as intermediaries with the Indians. A half century of British domination of the fur trade followed, and with it a series of bitter conflicts between rival interests. Three great concerns operated here: the Hudson's Bay Company, chartered in 1670; the Northwest Company, which developed from a partnership formed in 1783; and the XY Company, organized in 1798. (The Northwest Company gradually absorbed the business of the Hudson's Bay Company south of the international boundary, and in 1804 took over the XY Company.)

In charge of the posts were factors and clerks whose powers were almost absolute over the *voyageurs* and Indians alike, for already many tribes were beginning to lose the arts of their ancestors and depend more and more on the whites for their subsistence.

The area between the Great Lakes and the Mississippi passed into the possession of the newly established United States in 1783. Twenty years later, through the Louisiana Purchase, the young Nation acquired the land west of the river. British companies, however, continued to occupy their posts and Indians to follow their leadership well into the next century.

It was during the period of British trade dominance that Jonathan Carver, a New Englander approved by British officials, and Zebulon M. Pike, a young officer of the United States Army, made their famous journeys.

Carver spent the winter of 1766–67 with the Indians of the Minnesota country. During that time he ascended the Mississippi a short distance above the Falls of St. Anthony and made one trip up the Minnesota River. In the spring he visited an Indian burial ground, now the site of St. Paul, and entered the cavern since known as Carver's Cave *(see ST. PAUL)*. Carver published the book of his travels in 1778, when Europe's attention was drawn to the revolt of the American Colonies. Much of it was plagiarized from earlier accounts, yet it became a best seller. The book was translated into several languages and aroused widespread interest in England's Minnesota domains. (A lasting reminder of his visit is the perennial appearance of claimants in St. Paul with "Carver Script," by which they hope to gain title to rich areas in the heart of the most populous region of the State. This scrip, secured from speculators who succeeded to the interests of Carver's heirs, is based on an assumed agreement between Carver and the Indians. According to its terms the Sioux chiefs ceded to him a vast tract of Minnesota and Wisconsin territory. Congress argued the matter for twenty years before it finally repudiated the alleged treaty.)

To Pike was entrusted the duty of extending Federal authority over the newly acquired United States territory. From St. Louis he set out in 1805 with twenty soldiers and spent the winter on the upper river. He explored the banks as far north as Leech and Cass Lakes. For 60 gallons of whisky and $200 worth of baubles, he acquired military sites at the mouths of the St. Croix and the Minnesota Rivers. (The latter site embraced most of the area now occupied by the Twin Cities.) But he had no sooner departed than the fur traders hauled down his American flags and resumed their illegal activities, which were to be a factor in fomenting the War of 1812. The Indians, whom he thought he had reconciled to American rule, continued their allegiance to the British and, with a few exceptions, fought for the Canadians again as they had in 1776.

The final vestige of British authority was swept away with the treaty of Ghent in 1814, and the last British soldiers left Prairie du Chien a few months later. Congress passed a law denying fur-trading privileges to all but United States citizens. After 1816 the Northwest Company was entirely replaced in the area by John Jacob Astor's American Fur Company. The rank and file of the fur trade personnel again transferred its allegiance. Minnesota had become part of the United States.

The westward surge of settlers that followed the peace treaty necessitated the policing of the borders. Col. Henry Leavenworth arrived in 1819 and camped his troops on the site of the future Mendota. An additional $2,000 and a generous supply of rum were given to the Indians. The post was moved across the Minnesota River and in 1820 Colonel Josiah Snelling started the construction of the fort which now bears his name (see Tour 9), but which until 1825, was called Fort St. Anthony.

Soon after the soldiers arrived, the superintendent of farming from Lord Selkirk's ill-fated colony at Pembina stopped at Fort St. Anthony on the way to Prairie du Chien for supplies. In 1821 an agent for the American Fur Company whose post was near the fort drove a herd of cattle to the colony and brought back with him five Swiss families who squatted on the military reservation. These five familes are significant as being the first strictly agricultural settlers in the State. In succeeding years many more of the colonists were driven down by Indian troubles, fur company rivalries, severe weather, and flood. They lived on the fort lands until 1840 when, expelled from the reservation, they moved a few miles down the Mississippi and founded St. Paul. In May 1823 the *Virginia,* first steamboat to navigate the Mississippi from St. Louis, reached the fort. Here, on the first steamboat to come to the community of St. Anthony Falls, in 1823, Major Lawrence Taliaferro brought the first group of Negro slaves to come to Minnesota for which satisfactory records can be found. Later freeing all of his slaves, Major Taliaferro for 20 years exercised a wise supervision over the Indians and performed the ceremony which united one of his former slave girls to Dred Scott, whose status later was to become a national issue. Between 1821 and 1823 the garrison at Fort St. Anthony built the grist mill and the sawmill which formed the nucleus of the future Minneapolis.

To Mendota (until about 1837, called indiscriminately St. Peter's and Mendota) came Henry H. Sibley in 1834 as resident partner and manager of the American Fur Company. He was destined to be one of Minnesota's most distinguished citizens. His post was the river terminus for the tonnage of furs brought from the Red River country in the slow and cumbersome Red River oxcarts. These carts played a picturesque part in Minnesota's history. First used as early as the twenties, by the middle of the forties they were made up in long trains of 50 to 100. They bumped along the trail at the rate of 20 miles a day, their ungreased wooden wheels screeching a cacophony that could be heard for miles. Within the next 15 years about 500 of these carts were in constant use, making regular scheduled trips.

The fort, with the Indian agency and fur trading post opposite at Mendota, became the hub of Northwestern civilization. Here were entertained the explorers who added to the geographic knowledge of the country, among them Henry R. Schoolcraft, who in 1832 visited the headwaters of the Mississippi and named Lake Itasca.

Negroes figured in the early history of the fur trade. Among them were Pierre Bonza, or Bonga, servant to Alexander Henry when the latter in 1800 had charge of the Northwest Company's Red River brigade, and Bonza's son, George, *voyageur* for the American Fur Company. Having served satisfactorily as personal servant and joint keeper of a fur trading post, Pierre Bonza in 1804 became an interpreter for the Northwest Company on the lower Red River. In 1820 George Bonza acted as interpreter for Governor Lewis Cass at Fond du Lac, later achieving wealth and prominence as an independent trader at Leech Lake.

Catholic missionaries continued their efforts among the Indians but also administered to the white settlers. Protestant missionaries visited the Mendota fort as early as 1829 and laid plans for work among the natives. Soon thereafter many bands of Sioux and Chippewa had their resident Protestant missionaries and agricultural teachers. The Chippewa tongue had already been reduced to print, and in 1834 the Pond brothers came to the fort and later evolved a phonetic transcription of the Sioux language. They succeeded in preparing a dictionary, making a Sioux version of a portion of the Gospels, and establishing a school with 6 Indian pupils who were later joined by 15 more. The territory's first Christian church for whites was organized for the Presbyterians of Fort Snelling in 1835. Downstream the first church building for the settlers was completed by the Rev. Father Lucian Galtier in 1841 and dedicated to St. Paul. From the church the future capital city which grew up there took its name.

With the cession of the triangle between the St. Croix and the Mississippi in 1837, lumber towns sprang up along the St. Croix. The first post office was opened at Point Douglas at the mouth of the St. Croix in 1841, and in 1846 offices were opened at St. Paul and Stillwater. The first school to be regarded as public was started in a blacksmith shop in St. Paul in 1847. The first parochial school also started in St. Paul in a log hut four years later.

In 1847 settlement began on the east side of the Falls of St. Anthony. Two years later the first of a group of dwellings on the west side was erected. Bridges were to spring from these two hamlets and merge them into the city of Minneapolis.

In the closing days of the pre-Territorial period, the Sioux and the Chippewa still claimed and occupied the vast tract westward from the Mississippi to the Missouri River. (The only excepted territories were those of the military reservation of Fort Snelling, and the Indian reservation of Long Prairie to which the Winnebagos were transplanted under the protection of the soldiers of Fort Gaines, afterward Fort Ripley.) St. Paul, the river town, St. Anthony, the sawmill town, and the smaller trading settlement, Mendota, were grouped within a few miles of the Minnesota-Mississippi junction. The majority of the other settlers were living at isolated points along the lower St. Croix River, where the biggest town was Stillwater, only 15 miles downstream from the sawmill village of Marine. French-Canadian *voyageurs* lived at Wabasha and Traverse des Sioux; at Lac qui Parle the half-breed Joseph Renville lived on an almost feudal scale with his relatives and friends.

A few fur traders maintained scattered posts in the wilderness, with the families of their employees as more or less permanent residents. (The more populous were at Fond du Lac [Duluth], Crow Wing, Sauk Rapids, Elk River, Swan River, Long Prairie, and Lake Traverse.) Missionaries and agents were still living with the Indian bands. Far to the northward at Pembina the *bois brûlés* were engaged in trapping and trading furs. The only strictly agricultural life was at Red Rock, Cottage Grove, Lakeland, and Afton in the Mississippi-St. Croix delta, and in the nearby settlement stretching northward from St. Paul to Little Canada.

In this period none of the points of settlement was self-sustaining. Aside from wild game and fruits, and the little produce raised on the few small farms and in family gardens, everything required by the whites—even most of the fodder for their livestock—was brought from the outside by steamboat. The dwellings were mostly of logs, some surrounded with stockades. Fallen trees provided the bridges, roads were mere trails, stores were housed in one-room buildings, schools and churches had made scarcely a beginning. From December to April the hamlets were often without mail for weeks at a time, and isolated settlers received none at all. (News of the national election of November 1848 did not reach St. Paul until January of the following year.)

The opening of the land office at St. Croix Falls in 1848 brought the first great wave of settlers. The majority of these pioneers were lumbermen from Maine, farmers from the mid-Atlantic States, tradesmen and craftsmen from the cities. They were an independent lot and had grown up in an atmosphere charged with politics. At the time their numbers approached 5,000, they had begun to ask for a local government. (The list of the region's allegiances is an amazing one. Parts of this land, in some cases all, had been successively under the flags of France, England, Spain, the Colony of Virginia, the Northwest Territory, and the Territories of Louisiana, Indiana, Illinois, Michigan, Missouri, Iowa, and Wisconsin.)

◄◄◄◄◄◄◄◄◄◄◄◄◄◄◄◄◄☒►►►►►►►►►►►►►►►►►►►

Territorial Expansion

A convention called to meet at Stillwater August 26, 1848, took preliminary steps toward the organization of Minnesota Territory. To aid his Minnesota friends, John Catlin, recently secretary of the Territory of Wisconsin, set forth the "benign fiction" that he was obliged to act as Governor of that portion of the territory not included in the boundaries of the new Commonwealth. As such, he obligingly established his "capital" at Stillwater, and issued a call for an election to choose a Territorial delegate to Congress. The selection fell upon Henry H. Sibley, who also had been named by the convention. At Washington, after considerable debate, Sibley was seated, January 15, 1849, ostensibly as a delegate from the equivocal section of the Territory of Wisconsin, in reality the representative of the people of Minnesota. The adroit Stephen A. Douglas helped him to pilot the bill through Congress and on March 3, 1849, the Territory of Minnesota was formally created; its boundaries to the north, south, and east were those of today, and the western line the Missouri and White Earth Rivers. Minnesota had discarded its swaddling clothes and had begun an independent existence.

The first Territorial Legislature assembled in the dining room of a St. Paul hotel on September 3, 1849, summoned by the new Governor, Alexander Ramsey, whom President Zachary Taylor had appointed from among his eastern supporters. One of the legislature's first acts was the establishment of a system of free education.

St. Paul was incorporated as a town on November 1, 1849, having been platted two years before. A newspaper was started there on April 28, 1849, as the *Minnesota Pioneer,* the previously announced name, *Epistle of St. Paul,* having been regretfully discarded. This, and other publications that soon followed, painted glowing pictures of Minnesota's rich possibilities, and did much to increase immigration in the new Territory.

Soon it was evident that the whites could not be restricted to their comparatively small portion of the vast area included within the Territory's boundaries. Already prospective settlers were turning eager eyes toward the rich timber and prairie lands of the Indians, and were held back with increasing difficulty.

In 1851, through the treaties of Traverse des Sioux and Mendota, the Sioux were induced to relinquish their claims to much of the land in Iowa and in the present Minnesota and South Dakota, and to move to a tract reserved for them along the upper Minnesota River. The land ceded by these treaties amounted to more than 28 million acres, some of which is among the richest farm land in the world. By later negotiations, the Chippewa, at La Pointe, Wisconsin, in 1854, and at Washington in 1855, relinquished their claims to lands north of Lake Superior and in the north-central areas, tracts greatly coveted for lumbering operations.

After the proclamation February 24, 1853, of the Sioux treaties, a great tide of immigration began to flow into the southwestern part of the Territory. Steamboats on the Mississippi, the Minnesota, and the St. Croix were crowded with passengers and cargo; all the river landings bustled with colorful activity, as with every boat new arrivals disembarked and departed on stagecoaches over the newly constructed Government roads.

Many boarded the boats at Galena, Dunleith, or St. Louis. Others made the tedious journey overland in prairie schooners, driving their cattle, fording streams, and camping by the way. A few hoped to make their fortunes in commercial or professional fields, but the majority were eager for lands offered by the Government at a cost of $1.25 an acre, proof of occupancy, and cultivation.

Pioneer homes began to dot the wilderness, at first chiefly in the hardwood country nearest the watercourses. Breaking and clearing the land was a laborious task with the limited facilities at hand, and comparatively little was at first cultivated. But by the close of 1854 about 500,000 acres had been sold in Minnesota; in 1856 more than 1,000,000 acres were transferred to settlers, and in 1858 nearly 2,500,000 more.

Villages sprang up almost overnight. The clatter of grist mills was heard on a dozen streams. Merchant milling had its first substantial beginnings in the St. Anthony vicinity in 1854, and soon Mississippi River traffic began to swell with shipments of wheat and flour to eastern and southern markets.

Sawmills were overtaxed to supply required building materials. Lumbering emerged as a major industry that choked the rivers with logs. From the Red River valley there poured into St. Paul an ever increasing quantity of furs. Land offices, hotels, and livery stables were crowded with patrons. Post offices opened so rapidly that by 1856 they numbered 253. Railroads were chartered and endowed with extensive land grants. A capitol, erected from Federal funds at a cost of $32,000, was occupied in 1853.

Cultural life followed the pattern of the eastern tradition. The pioneers established churches, public schools, and academies, organized reading circles and singing classes, and maintained lyceums and lecture courses that brought to the wilderness many a distinguished visitor. A university (afterward the State university) was chartered in 1851, a building erected in St. Anthony (Minneapolis), and a preparatory department opened that fall. The Baldwin School, later to be revived as Macalester College, began its teaching in St. Paul in 1853. Hamline University was established at Red Wing in 1854 by the Methodists, and St. John's at St. Cloud in 1857 by the Benedictines.

In the meantime settlement had started at the west end of Lake Superior where a trading post and mission known as Fond du Lac had long been located. As early as 1853 a road was cut through the pines from Superior on the Wisconsin side to the lumber camps on the St. Croix. When, in 1855, a canal was built around Sault Ste. Marie Falls in Michigan, the "Head of the Lakes" was in direct water communication with the ports of Europe through the St. Lawrence River, and with New York City through the Erie Canal. Soon after the Chippewa treaties were signed in 1854–55, several villages were laid out on the Minnesota shore of Lake Superior. Among these, Duluth, of which the plat was filed in 1856, soon established its ascendency—absorbing no less than seven other villages.

By 1857 the white population in Minnesota Territory had increased to 150,037. Two-thirds of the adults had come from the eastern States; the other third was composed largely of Irish, Germans, English, and Canadians, with a sprinkling of the earliest Scandinavians. Climatic conditions, together with the anti-slavery views of the settlers, gave no encouragement to slavery in this territory. The Negro population of Minnesota, before or after the Civil War, has never been large.

With the rapid increase of settlement came the era of speculation which started in 1855 and reached its climax in 1857. Great tracts of prairie land recently obtained for $1.25 per acre were sold as "improved" by the pre-emptors for $5.00 an acre, the improvements often consisting of a mere brush hut or log lean-to and perhaps a few rods of broken sod. Town sites were platted by the hundred. Many of them were not surveyed, their locations were often uncertain, yet these "paper" lots brought high prices from buyers here and in the East. In the older settlements, a bit of land held for $500 in the morning might well sell for $1000 before nightfall. Sharpers moved in, their offices a sidewalk and their stock-in-trade a glib tongue, a roll of maps, a package of blank deeds, and alleged inside information concerning the route of a railroad. Eastern capitalists sent St. Paul bankers large sums which found ready borrowers at 3 percent a month. Every settler felt himself a prospective millionaire, and the public imagination soared high with greedy hope.

The "wild riots of financial adventure" came to an abrupt end. After the collapse of eastern business in August, the panic of 1857 cast a blight over the entire country. When the news reached Minnesota, cash and credit promptly disappeared, and with them thousands of speculators who had been caught unaware. Land agencies closed their doors. Wildcat currency was soon refused. Trade took the form of barter, but there was little enough to barter.

One effect of the financial debacle was to turn the attention of the pioneers more seriously to farming. Although the possibilities of the soil had been long known, prior to 1857 there had been comparatively little agricultural development. Many of the pioneers who had planted crops were discouraged by insect pests, drought, and prairie fires. But the collapse of their get-rich-quick schemes forced hundreds away from the towns to seek a living from the soil. By the following spring the cultivated acres of the Territory had more than doubled in number.

The growing tension between Indians and whites became more and more evident during Territorial days. Two trifling quarrels, involving the Sioux and Chippewa, led to minor outbreaks, and although promptly quelled left in their wake apprehension and unrest.

Financial straits, Indian scares, rumbling premonitions of the Civil War could not dampen the enthusiasm and self-confidence of the Territory. The population grew by leaps and bounds as European peasants continued to pour into the land. More and more desirable seemed those land grants bestowed by Congress. Representation in Congress was essential to many plans, but now especially to the success of the longed-for railroad to the Pacific. Surely the time was ripe to demand the dignity of statehood.

◄◄◄◄◄◄◄◄◄◄◄◄◄◄◄◄◄◄◄◄◄❂►►►►►►►►►►►►►►►►►►►►►►►

The New State

On May 11, 1858, Congress admitted Minnesota to the Union. From the outset, the proposal aroused violent debate in Congress. But the difficulties were at last overcome and boundaries fixed. The Enabling Act was passed in 1857. Jubilant, Minnesota chose to consider the battle won, and after an election of officers and delegates and the adoption of a constitution, the delegates ignored many legal technicalities and not only met in legislative session but passed many forward-looking bills. Henry H. Sibley was elected to the office of Governor, but it was a full seven months after the constitution had been adopted before Congress actually added the north star to the national flag. During that time all the sectional bitterness and tricky politics of pre-Civil War days seem to have been brought into play. On May 24th, 1858, the first State officers took their oaths of office and the next week the legislature reconvened. The first gubernatorial election (October 1859) following Minnesota's actual entrance into the Union, placed Alexander Ramsey in the Governor's chair and initiated a series of Republican victories that lasted many decades.

In his message in 1860 Governor Ramsey pointed out the extraordinary gains in agriculture that had taken place in the past 10 years. With a population now of 172,023, Minnesota had 22,000 farms and had produced on them during the previous year 5,400,000 bushels of wheat, nearly 4,000,-000 bushels of oats, and about 2,000,000 bushels each of corn and potatoes.

Telegraphic communication was established in 1860 between the Twin Cities and the outside world, and provision was made for the founding of three normal schools; of these Winona's opened at once and thus became the first of this kind west of the Mississippi.

Scarcely had the young State begun to recover from the panic of 1857, when the summons to war drew from it thousands of young men. The day on which the news of Fort Sumter's capture reached Washington found Governor Ramsey in the Nation's Capital. He immediately hastened to the War Department and offered 1,000 men from Minnesota, "the first tender of troops from any quarter after the fall of the Charleston fortress." One day after the publication of Lincoln's war proclamation, Ignatius Donnelly, Acting Governor, issued a call for the First Regiment. It was assembled rapidly enough to replace almost at once the regular Army units at the frontier posts and to reach the Potomac in time for the first Battle of Bull Run. The part it later played at Gettysburg is well known to all familiar with Civil War history. (Before the final muster-out, a total of 21,982 had enlisted from Minnesota.)

The first contingent of troops had hardly reached the front before the families at home were confronted with one of the most serious Indian uprisings in the country's history. Sioux problems had by no means been solved by the treaties. While various bands had moved to their reservations, it was not long before they showed an increasing tendency to roam, and so greatly did they annoy the settlers that many wished to have them completely removed from the State. The Indians on their part had many grievances: their leaders were alarmed by the weakening of tribal integrity and customs through contact with the white man's civilization; much resentment was felt against agency traders who charged them unfairly for supplies; often the Government agents were charged with distributing food unfit for consumption.

In the summer of 1862 the need for Civil War supplies superseded all other obligations, and neither money nor sufficient food was forthcoming for the Indians. Then occurred the incident that fanned the long-smoldering bitterness into flames.

In August four roving Indians killed three white men and two women after challenging them, with apparent friendliness, to a contest in target shooting. Frightened by the possible consequences of their deed, they fled to their tribesmen. After a long argument the chiefs and braves voted to stand by their fellows and to anticipate the inevitable reprisals. Could they hope for a better opportunity than this to drive out the hated invaders and to repossess their ancient hunting grounds, when so many of the soldiers had gone to the white man's war? The entire Sioux Nation of about 7,000 united in the uprising and 1,500 braves took the warpath.

From the Lower Agency near Redwood Falls on August 18th, they swept across the Minnesota River, slaughtering family after family and sparing only those women and children whom they wished to take captive. So swiftly did they move that within a few days more than 400 whites were killed, and many more taken prisoner.

A company of soldiers sent from nearby Fort Ridgely was ambushed and almost wiped out, but the heroic defense of the post, to which hundreds of refugees had fled, kept the Indians from sweeping down the valley to the more populous settlements on the north side of the river. On the south side it was the German settlement of New Ulm which barred them. Here 1,500 inhabitants, refugees, and volunteer defenders met and withstood an attack which almost annihilated the town and cost so many lives that the survivors despairingly abandoned it for weeks after the Indians had withdrawn.

Nearly 2,000 Indians and half-breeds of both sexes were either captured or voluntarily surrendered soon afterward. About 400 were given military trial, of whom 306 were condemned to death, and 18 sentenced to imprisonment. The names of 303 prisoners were telegraphed to President Lincoln who commuted the death sentence of all but 39. He maintained that while all those proved guilty of murder and rape should be executed, those accused merely of having fought in open battle merited the treatment of prisoners of war. For this leniency the general sentiment of the State turned bitterly against him, as it did against the formerly beloved Bishop H. B. Whipple, who had acted as special advocate for the condemned.

The compensation awarded to the settlers and the reimbursement to the State were paid from the Sioux trust funds, annuities were stopped, and all title to the reservation lands was wiped out.

Throughout the sixties education was a lively concern of State and county officials. The older counties were well provided with elementary ungraded schools, and in the larger centers "union schools" offered graded and high school studies. Even in the new areas most settlers were close enough to a school to give their children at least a few months' education each year. The need for trained teachers became urgent.

The second normal school was opened at Mankato in 1868 and the third, at St. Cloud, quickly followed. After a revision of tangled finances, the university reopened its preparatory department in 1867. Two years later it was fully established under a chancellor, William Watts Folwell, with a department of elementary instruction, and a college of mechanic arts. In 1863 a State school for the deaf was established at Faribault. A department for the blind was added to the school in 1866, and an asylum for the insane established at St. Peter.

Neither Civil War nor Indian uprisings could slow the development of the State. Monetary inflation, bountiful crops, soldiers' pay, plenty of work at good wages, all contributed to an increasing prosperity. Government indemnity of Indian depredations stimulated industry. Within three years after the Homestead Act of 1862 more than 1,000,000 acres had been taken over by 9,529 persons. The census showed a population of 250,099 with 18 counties not reporting. Six hundred thousand acres were now under cultivation. Railroad work had been resumed and by 1862 the first line was carrying passengers and freight between St. Paul and Minneapolis. Before the close of 1865, the railroads were operating over 210 miles on various routes.

The returning soldiers and the comrades who followed them were promptly absorbed into civilian life, and their discharge pay further augmented the circulation of money. For development of all the new State's resources more and more workers were demanded. A State board of immigration was formed and, with the railroads and other organizations, issued thousands of pamphlets in a variety of languages to broadcast the opportunities Minnesota offered. Agents appointed to attract desirable settlers and to facilitate transportation opened offices in the East and abroad. By 1870 the population had leapt to nearly a half million (439,706). Of these Europe had added 59,390 Scandinavians and 48,457 Germans. The urban population was now approximately one-third that of rural districts.

Although the cultivated area had practically trebled in five years, lumbering was still the major industry in the 1870's. Sixty percent of the farmland was planted in wheat. A new process and the middlings purifier produced a superior flour from spring wheat; they soon made Minneapolis one of the principal flouring centers of the world. Modern farm machinery was purchased in increasing quantities, and by its use the so-called "bonanza farms" harvested their thousands of acres.

During the first few years of the seventies, too, came the rapid expansion of the railroads. Until after the Civil War, the rivers were the principal highways for the shipping of both lumber and wheat. Retarded by the State's foreclosure on all railroad properties in 1860, railroad construction had been relatively slow. But once underway it developed at a lively speed. By the early seventies the Twin Cities could choose between two routes to Chicago; they were connected with Duluth and thus by the Great Lakes with the eastern markets, and with the West as far as the Red River.

With the railroads came the further extension of settlement into the open prairies. There sod houses and dugouts rather than log cabins served as pioneer habitations, but it was not long before these primitive shelters were replaced by neat frame houses supplied by the expanding sawmill industry. Villages, their sites arbitrarily selected by railroad officials, usually started with a boxcar station. This was quickly surrounded by store, church, schoolhouse, and homes. Of the older hamlets left without benefit of railway, some were moved to new locations, many others were abandoned gradually. Grain elevators and municipal water towers became characteristic features of the Minnesota landscape.

While the newcomers to the State were contentedly working their new farms and building their homes, many farmers in the older settlements were far from satisfied with what they considered a bare subsistence for their years of hard work. Bumper crops of wheat were of little value, they complained, with markets far from home, railroads discriminating against them through excessive rates, and agents grading the grain falsely. It was to adjust such farmer problems that Oliver Kelley, a Minnesota man, founded in Washington, in 1867, the Patrons of Husbandry. Popularly called the Grange, the movement spread more rapidly in Minnesota than in any other part of the country, and by the close of 1869, 40 of its 49 Granges were located in this State. Through these Granges, the farmer could not only air his grievances, but by the endorsement of Granger candidates he was able to carry his discontent to the legislature. The series of Granger Acts, all benefiting the farmer, resulted. The first of these was passed in 1871 and three years later the Grangers were in control of the legislature, where they succeeded to some extent in regulating railroads and grain dealers. A change of attitude on the part of railroads and public opinion modified these acts considerably the following year, and Granger influence waned. If the Grangers had not been able to solve the railroad problem, at least they had awakened an entire people to the fact that a problem existed, and for the first time in Minnesota history the voices of the farmer and the working people had been heard. In 1876 the Supreme Court fixed the authority of a State Legislature to regulate fares and rates.

Industrial expansion was the keynote of the 1870's, but the decade also was marked by a series of disasters. The first was a blizzard that swept over the Northwest in 1873 and took the lives of 70 persons on the prairies. The national financial panic, which in 1873 followed the collapse of the Jay Cooke interests, was felt throughout the State, but it was Duluth that bore the brunt of the disaster. That city was wholly dependent for its boom on Jay Cooke's promise to make it the lake terminus of his proposed continental railroad; it was rendered almost totally bankrupt in a few days and suffered a reduction in population from 5,000 to 1,300.

Even more grievous to the State at large was the invasion of the Rocky Mountain locust, commonly called the grasshopper. The plague affected only localized areas the first year, but in 1876 the insects invaded 29 counties, devouring every leaf and green spear, attacking even clothing and wood. Private subscriptions and legislative appropriations were needed to keep thousands of prairie settlers from starvation. The Governor appointed April 26, 1877, a day of State-wide prayer for relief. That spring the grasshoppers hatched as usual, but, when fully grown, took wing and by the middle of August had disappeared.

The decade's calendar of misfortunes was completed in 1878 with an explosion of flour dust in a Minneapolis mill. It cost 18 lives and laid waste a large part of the milling district. After this catastrophe improved safety devices were promptly introduced all over the country.

The rapid growth of the grain and railroad industries brought still another influx of immigration during the eighties. By 1885 the population had passed the million mark, and now the towns were growing five times as fast as the rural districts. The need of modernized school buildings became acute and in 1887 the State school tax was adopted. Compulsory education, textbook legislation, and State aid soon followed.

After the Rochester cyclone of 1883, Dr. William Worrall Mayo, a local health official, was offered the convent of the Sisters of St. Francis to care for 100 injured victims. Six years later this order opened St. Mary's Hospital, which they placed under the supervision of Dr. Mayo and his now famous sons, and it was here that "the Mayo boys" did the work that brought them their first national recognition.

The outstanding event for Minnesota in the eighties and nineties was the development of the ore resources through which the State was to become the richest iron-producing region in the world. In 1884 the first car-load of iron ore was shipped from the Vermilion Range via Lake Superior to eastern markets. Eight years later the first carload was shipped from the Mesabi Range. Cities sprang up in the pine forests of the Lake Superior region and grew apace with the swift progress of the industry. The panic of 1893 resulted in the transfer of most of the mining properties to the Rockefeller interest and temporarily halted the growth of the mining towns. Slavs for the first time poured into the State to work in the mines. At first the majority of the newcomers were Finns who brought a fresh knowledge and sympathy for co-operative living and trading that had a far-reaching effect. Finns, however, like little farms better than mines, and before long had surrendered their places at the mines to Czechs and Slovaks (see Tour 3).

With the growth of urban industry, labor restlessness in the cities added its voice to the agrarian protest. The Farmers' Alliance movement began to show its potential strength in Minnesota in 1881. By 1886 the alliance joined forces with the Knights of Labor and drew up a strong railroad and labor platform which it pressed the Republican Party to accept in full. By its successful backing of candidates pledged to the support of agricul-tural and labor interests, the coalition virtually controlled the legislature. In 1890 it strode out upon the political field as a definite third party. Two years later the Populist Party was born, largely through the efforts of Ignatius Donnelly, Minnesota's prophet of political experiment. This new national party absorbed many political elements, among them the Farmers' Alliance. When its candidate for Governor won second place in 1894, a third party became for the first time the dominant minority. Four years later John Lind was swept into office on a fusion of Democrats, Populists, and Silver Republicans, and the long conservative Republican regime had been broken.

During the panic of 1893 the Northern Pacific Railroad failed, and when it was reorganized James J. Hill and his associates acquired much Northern Pacific stock. Toward the end of the century, Hill, eager to con-nect with the eastern States through an independent route to Chicago, wished to purchase the Chicago, Burlington and Quincy. But Edward H. Harriman, who controlled the Union Pacific also needed this link in the transcontinental chain, for it was the only one then available. A buying duel drove Burlington stock to such heights that Harriman finally with-drew, leaving Hill in possession of nearly 97 percent, half of which he turned over to the Great Northern, the other half to the Northern Pacific. Harriman next proceeded to buy up Northern Pacific stock, hoping to gain control. The duel between the two "empire builders" was renewed with a new fury. Fortunes were made and lost and the Nation watched while stocks rose to staggering heights. When peace was finally declared Harriman was granted his connection over the Burlington, while Hill remained in control of the two northern roads, and of the Chicago, Burlington and Quincy.

In 1898, when the State was 40 years old, builders laid the cornerstone of its present capitol. This domed building, designed by Cass Gilbert, was regarded in the nineties as a model of its kind. It was Minnesota's third capitol. The first, built in 1853, was destroyed by fire in 1881, and was replaced two years later by the brick building on the same site. *(See ST. PAUL.)*

The declaration of war with Spain in 1898 found Minnesota with three regiments of militia. These units were brought to full strength by volunteers and mustered into service as the Twelfth, Thirteenth, and Fourteenth Regiments of Minnesota Volunteer Infantry; the Fifteenth was added later. The State furnished in all about 8,500 men for the Spanish-American War and the Philippine Insurrection.

<<<<<<<<<<<<<<<<<<<❂>>>>>>>>>>>>>>>>>>>

After 1900

The foundations of present-day Minnesota were well laid when the nineteenth century merged with the twentieth, and the State now faced the future with a lively optimism. The frontier had been conquered, and it was commonly believed that Minnesotans faced only the pleasant task of marching with the rest of the Nation along the unobstructed path of progress. Great business and great fortunes were now, potentially at least, within the reach of the poorest immigrant boy. Fame and success were to be the reward—if in less measure—for all who had talent for the arts or sciences. The only requisite was that everyone should work.

Miracles had been performed in converting a vast wilderness into a thriving Commonwealth in a little more than four decades. Now the pioneer Territory not only had grown up, it had caught up. If thousands of acres of rich forest lands had been laid waste, Minnesota in 1900 still ranked with the leading lumbering States. If the great flow of golden wheat had begun to slow down a little, the flow of golden butter had been steadily increasing in volume each year. Much was being learned of the advantages latent in co-operation, and co-operative groups already had begun to produce finer butter and to improve the profitable marketing of all dairy products—of livestock, eggs, and poultry. For a decade at least, more favorable railroad rates and easy credit from the rapidly multiplying local banks were to quiet the worst apprehensions of the farmer.

Minnesota's history during these years was not unlike that of her sister States. As manufacturing developed, the rural population began to drift in increasing numbers to the cities. The motorcar came and changed the customs of city dweller and farmer alike. In 1907 the legislature installed a State-wide tax for road building, and the next year the automobile license law began to yield additional highway revenue. The self-starter and short skirts for women came into common use at about the same time. Women drivers on the newly paved roads no longer seemed conspicuous, and the feminine demand for political "rights," first raised by Minnesota women in the seventies, grew more and more insistent. Movies and mounting railroad rates gradually reduced to a minimum the pleasant visits of metropolitan stars and road-shows at the Opera House, but the Art Institute and the Symphony Association stimulated a growing interest in cultural pursuits. The Mayo brothers' famous clinic already was attracting the attention of the medical world. A small boy was growing up in Little Falls who would some day become a symbol of adventure and enterprise in the air.

In 1911 still another iron-bearing region was added to the mining area of the State, when the first shipment of ore left the new Cuyuna Range. Four years later the United States Steel Corporation opened its big steel plant in the suburbs of Duluth. By the end of the second decade Minnesota was leading all the States in the value of iron ore produced and was supplying seven-tenths of the Nation's output.

In 1915 came an event long dreamed of by the entire country, but one destined to prove a setback to the State's advance. The Panama Canal was at last a reality, and Minnesota saw with dismay the great tonnage of lumber and of goods from the Orient, which had poured through her gateways, now permanently diverted into another channel. This was a severe blow not only to the railroads but to attendant industries—a loss from which the State has not yet recovered.

When the United States entered the World War in 1917, Minnesota had a seasoned militia of three regiments of infantry, and one of field artillery, all of which already had seen active service on the Mexican border. The State gave a total of 123,325 men to the service. In addition about 20,000 volunteers were enrolled in the Home Guard. They were employed later in the areas devastated by forest fires. During these years a commission of safety was created and endowed with extraordinary powers over the internal activities of the State.

From the close of the Civil War Minnesota had clung tenaciously to such national policies as were advocated by the Republican Party, although on rare occasions Democratic Governors (by reason of unusual personalities or local dissensions) had succeeded in carrying State elections. Then in 1912, Theodore Roosevelt's Progressive platform caused many a staunch voter to swing over to his support. But it was not until 1932 that the North Star State broke its lifelong precedent and voted for a Democratic President.

Toward the close of the second decade of this century the third party movement once again forced itself into State politics, and once again it was the rebellious farmer who initiated the agitation. The Nonpartisan League was organized in North Dakota in 1916 by Arthur Charles Townley, a Minnesotan. It met with a dramatic success in that State and promptly was extended to twelve others. The farmers of Minnesota, especially those in the western wheat-growing districts, had for several years been smarting under what they charged was unjust discrimination on the part of the railroads, banks, and elevators, and this new proposal to voice their discontent was welcomed with enthusiasm. Early in 1918 Townley established his headquarters in St. Paul and organized the Minnesota Nonpartisan League. An alliance with the State Federation of Labor was effected and an independent candidate for Governor endorsed. The name Farmer-Labor was adopted hastily, to comply with a ruling by the attorney general that the name of a candidate on a ticket must have a party designation. Although the Republican candidate won the contest, the election made the Farmer-Laborites the second dominant party. Thereupon a plan to make permanent the co-operation of the agricultural and labor groups was formulated. In five years the combined forces gained a full Farmer-Labor representation in the United States Senate. In the 1936 election this party secured control of all but two of the State offices. It captured the lower house, a majority of Congressional Representatives, and both seats in the Senate.

Long the main labor market of the Northwest, the Twin Cities have been the storm center of an industrial revolt that has been characterized not only by political protest but by industrial disturbances of considerable magnitude. Strikes have been frequent and bitter in Minneapolis, where organized labor has repeatedly tested its strength, and in the Range towns where the open shop has been a perennial issue. However, discontent has in a large measure relied upon the ballot in the struggle for social justice, and although many problems remain to be solved, a constantly increasing number of welfare enactments have placed the State well in the vanguard of socially-minded Commonwealths.

Minnesota suffered severely in the widespread drought of 1934. Thousands of acres of its fertile soil were converted into fine powder that day after day swirled in great clouds over towns and countryside. Farm fences were buried in sand and dirt, and farmers saw with despair their cherished topsoil lifted from their fields and piled in great mounds miles away. Rivers, ponds, and lakes went dry, and many communities were left without a water supply. Seeds shriveled and thousands of cattle starved to death for lack of forage.

In the western triangle that tapers from the Dakota lines to Minneapolis, conditions were the worst. Here the crops were a total failure and it was mainly in this region that the millions appropriated by Congress for food, feed, and seed were dispensed. In the northwestern triangle, on the other hand, there was practically no drought at all, and farmers of North and South Dakota began to drive their starving cattle into this favored area. But Minnesota needed every blade of her grass, and Governor Olson issued a decree that no cattle should cross the State borders. He followed up his order by a National Guard patrol. This mobilization was so unusual that it received national publicity as "The Cow War," although very little disorder resulted.

The drought brought to the fore the more chronic problem of soil erosion, and resulted in a series of promising agricultural experiments. Among them strip-cropping (in which plantings in contour strips are substituted for square fields) and the terracing of slopes are perhaps the most hopeful. In the succeeding years the rainfall gradually increased until in 1937 it approached normal.

‹‹‹‹‹‹‹‹‹‹‹‹‹‹‹‹‹‹‹‹✿›››››››››››››››››››››

Government

The portions of Minnesota on either side of the Mississippi fell under the jurisdiction of numerous governments and territories before their final union in the Territory of Minnesota. On January 9, 1840, St. Croix County, Wisconsin, was established, with Dakotah (later absorbed by Stillwater) for the county seat, and thus became the first local government unit in the Minnesota region.

Its early association with Wisconsin led to the adoption of that Territory's general statutes. Since Wisconsin had taken its statutes from Michigan, Minnesota's laws are indirectly based on those of Michigan.

The Organic Act creating the Minnesota Territory in 1849 contained an unusual provision for the first election, i.e., the extension of franchise and the right to hold office to every free white male resident over 21, irrespective of nationality and citizenship. The insertion of a similar franchise provision in the schedule of the State Constitution was unusual in the history of the States, and it aroused bitter opposition in Congress to Minnesota's petition for Statehood. The body of the State Constitution, adopted October 13, 1857, had a less inclusive provision (Article VII, Section 1) restricting the franchise to citizens and to mixed and pure blood Indians who had adopted the customs of white civilization.

In October 1857 after passage by Congress of the Enabling Act a legislature and a full slate of State officers were elected. Although the State was not yet in the Union, this legislature in 1858 passed bills and even amended the constitution. After admission to statehood on May 11, 1858, the officers were legally installed, and the legislature reassembled and affirmed their previous acts.

One of the acts of the first State legislature in 1858 was the submission to the electorate of the "Five Million Loan Bill," by which the State issued bonds for the financing of railroad construction. When the scheme collapsed in 1860, these bonds were repudiated by the voters, and it was not until 1881 that a settlement of fifty cents on the dollar was ratified. The demands of the powerful Patrons of Husbandry resulted in the Granger Law of 1871, regulating fares, charges, and other policies of the railroads. Stringent but ineffective, this law was followed by a second in 1874. A year later, however, a new law, much less drastic, permitted the roads to operate without severe legal restraint. A decision of the United States Supreme Court in 1876 nevertheless fully confirmed the disputed right of the legislature to regulate the railroads as "common carriers."

Woman suffrage made its first appearance on the Minnesota horizon in 1875, when a constitutional amendment gave women the right to hold office and vote in school affairs. In 1898 these provisions were extended to include public libraries.

General chaos in the administration of public funds led to the creation in 1878 of the office of public examiner, whose duties are now performed by the department of banking and the State comptroller.

Other early acts of the legislature included establishment in 1901 of the first compulsory primary election law applicable to an entire State, and regulation of campaign and election procedure, culminating in the Corrupt Practices Acts of 1895 and 1912.

Minnesota, one of the first States to discuss administrative reorganization, delayed the adoption of such a plan until 1925, when the commission of administration and finance was established. The commission is popularly known as the Big Three and controls State records, budgets, purchases, and the erection of State buildings.

From the time when a generous Congress granted Minnesota two sections of land in each township for school purposes instead of the customary one, the schools of the State have been well endowed. Minnesota has the largest public trust fund of any State in the Union with the single exception of Texas. The greatest source of this fund is the Mesabi Range where the State owns land on which 27 opened iron mines are situated. Under the constitution, the principal of the fund is inviolate, and only the interest can be used for the purpose of the original grant.

Indictment of the officers of a newly organized regional milk-distributing agency resulted in the co-operative laws of 1919, protecting co-operative organizations and regulating their operations.

The State board of health, established in 1872 (the third of its kind in the Union), and the State board of control, which in 1901 took over all charitable and correctional functions, were among Minnesota's early efforts in the field of social legislation. The Child Labor Law of 1909 was followed by a minimum wage act for women and minors in 1913; a still larger advance in child welfare legislation occurred in 1917, when the legislature enacted 37 laws for the protection of children. The first Minnesota Workmen's Compensation Law was enacted in 1913. The office of public health nurse was created in 1919; the Minnesota General Hospital was founded in 1921, and the psychopathic hospital was authorized two years later. Additional child welfare legislation regulated the employment of children in street trades, theaters, and other public amusements.

Outstanding for its long-distinguished service to the State is the Minnesota Historical Society, supported almost entirely by legislative appropriation (*see ST. PAUL*).

Government is carried on by a bicameral legislature (one of two in the Union elected on a nonpartisan basis), an executive department, and boards and commissions created by the legislature but separate from it. The executive council, composed of the Governor, Secretary of State, State auditor, treasurer, and attorney general, enjoys considerable power between legislative sessions.

One hundred and thirty-one members of the house of representatives are elected for 2-year terms, during which they receive salaries of $1,000. The senate numbers 67 members who are elected for 4-year terms and are paid $1,000 per biennial session. The Governor, elected every 2 years, receives a $7,000 yearly salary. He is commander of the State militia and possesses veto power in addition to the usual powers of the chief executive. Other State officers are Lieutenant Governor, Secretary of State, treasurer, and attorney general. All are elected for 2-year terms. Three members of the railroad and warehouse commission are elected for 6-year terms.

The judicial department is composed of the supreme court, district courts, courts of probate, justices of the peace, and such other inferior courts as may be established by the legislature. Important State boards and commissions whose officers are appointed by the Governor, with the advice and consent of the senate, include the commission of administration and finance; department of agriculture, dairy, and food; department of commerce; board of control (in charge of State institutions); department of education; department of health; department of highways; historical society; department of labor and industry; and the department of taxation.

The 87 counties are governed by local county boards of five members, one of whom is chosen chairman. Exceptions are St. Louis County which, because of its size, has seven commissioners, and Ramsey County which has six, although it is the smallest in the State. The usual county officers include an auditor, treasurer, register of deeds, sheriff, attorney, judge of probate, surveyor, coroner, clerk of court, superintendent of schools, and in many places a court commissioner.

Of the 96 municipalities now classified as cities, 24 operate under special charters or general acts and 72 under home rule charters. The State is unique in that the cities constituting the home rule group comprise approximately one-fourth of all the cities in the United States operating in this manner. Only 18 States have any home rule cities and in not one of the others does the number even approach Minnesota's.

Municipalities were given constitutional home rule by a constitutional amendment approved in 1898, which granted them the power to frame, adopt, and amend their own charters while remaining "consistent with and subject to the laws of this State." The consensus is that home rule has in no sense impaired State interests but has in fact promoted local welfare through the facility with which it provides for the enactment of special laws designed to meet local needs.

To become a home rule municipality the city must draw up a charter. This may be none other than the old charter with a few minor alterations. Then it must be adopted by four-sevenths of all voters. Several villages have advanced to the status of a city by the adoption of such charters. For a charter amendment a three-fifths vote is required. There are now 639 incorporated villages in the State.

Minneapolis, St. Paul, and Duluth, the three cities of the first class (those with more than 50,000 inhabitants), have home rule charters. The list also includes two of the second class, St. Cloud and Rochester (20,000 to 50,000 inhabitants), all seven of the third class (10,000 to 20,000), and 59 of the 82 fourth-class cities (10,000 inhabitants or less). Five cities, Anoka, Albert Lea, Columbia Heights, Morris, and White Bear Lake, operate under the city manager form of government; 16 under the commission form; and the remainder under the mayor-council form. Of the three largest cities, Minneapolis alone has mayor-council government. Two cities occupy odd positions in legal classifications: Belle Plaine enjoys the distinction of being the only borough in the State refusing to reincorporate as a city, and Hibbing, with a population of 15,000, is still known as a village—the largest in the State.

The State legislature may provide general laws relating to affairs of cities in all four population groups.

Agriculture and
Farm Life

FARMING to the Minnesota Indians was "squaw work" and was restricted largely to the harvesting of wildrice, tubers, and berries. The more spectacular fur trading, lumbering, and land speculation monopolized so much of the attention of the early immigrants that agriculture as a means of livelihood was of relatively slow growth.

The first permanent settlers to till the soil came from the Selkirk colony, in the Red River valley of Canada, who arrived at Fort Snelling as early as 1821. Although many of the immigrants from the East were farmers, it was not until about 1850 that agriculture had become the principal industry.

By 1854, the 32,000 inhabitants had bought 314,715 acres of public lands. Two years later the population, now tripled, had purchased more than 2,000,000 acres. Today the 203,000 farms embrace 32,817,911 acres and include most of the land economically adapted to agriculture—about two-thirds of the State's area. Fifty-one percent of the population of Minnesota is still rural.

In the 1850's, when agriculture was undertaken in earnest, farmers ignored the rich prairies and chose land in the wooded valleys and hills along the Mississippi, St. Croix, and Minnesota Rivers. Cutting the trees and grubbing out stumps might be a long and costly business, but they were wary of land where trees did not grow, where water was obtainable only by digging deep wells, and where cyclones and prairie fires were a periodic menace. It was not until after immigrants had followed the railroads across the State, and had proved the richness of this prairie country, that they realized their mistake.

The trend of Minnesota agriculture has been from grazing to cash crops, then to feed crops. The first stage involved only the few horses, cattle, and swine of the early settlers, and the pasturage of these animals on the wooded hills.

Wheat was shown to be an excellent crop for Minnesota soil and climate when it was raised in 1820 by the enlisted men of Fort St. Anthony (Fort Snelling). Individual farmers in the years following were soon planting most of their acreage in wheat, and when railroads spread across the State in the 1860's and 1870's, linking the southern and western prairies with a world-wide market, grain raising was almost the sole occupation of the farmers. Immigrants from Europe and settlers from the East then swarmed to the rich prairie land. For them, too, wheat was the New World's most satisfactory crop. The virgin land produced abundantly at little cost, and the grain could be converted into money the same year it was grown.

Railroads promoted the idea of large-scale wheat farming and gave rise to the bonanza farms of the Red River valley. These farms averaged 2,000 acres—several were many times as large—and by virtue of the inventions and improvements in farm machinery of 1860–70, the expense of operation was considerably lessened.

Wheat came to be measured in millions of bushels. Terminal elevators appeared at every railroad station, and the great mills of Minneapolis arose to challenge all competition. Minnesota led the Nation in flour production and was popularly known as the "bread basket" of the country.

Then economic conditions changed, farming methods improved, and recent years witnessed a shift in the agricultural scene. From 1928 to 1935 Minnesota planted yearly an average of 1,494,800 acres to wheat, of which the annual yield was 18,619,500 bushels.

Corn acreage pushed into first place at the turn of the century. While wheat from the newly broken prairies to the west and northwest was being dumped on the market, its prices sagging, the early-maturing varieties of corn were being developed and gradually introduced into the State. An influx of Iowa farmers with experience in corn raising started the swing away from cash to feed crops. Minnesota, which in 1890 produced relatively little corn, now harvests about 150,000,000 bushels each fall. Most of this crop is grown in southern Minnesota and is fed to hogs, which account for 25.2 percent of the State's farm revenue.

Flax thrived on the new prairie land. In some counties, at a time when the price of flaxseed was high, the total acreage exceeded that of wheat. About 700,000 acres are now planted annually; the average yearly production is four to six million bushels.

Oats, barley, and rye were introduced and are still grown extensively as both cash and feed crops. Minnesota leads the country in the production of barley and is second in oats and rye. The volume of oats, 150,000,000 bushels annually, is the greatest of the small grain crops. Oats are raised in all parts of the State.

Livestock raising, which before the corn era had been confined to a few animals kept on the farm for milk production or meat, has now increased to major proportions. Along with corn, much of the grain formerly raised as a cash crop is fed to livestock and sold as pork, beef, mutton, wool, poultry, and eggs. The livestock "prosperity quintuplets"—the cow, sow, hen, sheep, and steer—yield three-fourths of the State's farm income.

Diversified agriculture in Minnesota appealed to railroad promoters like James J. Hill. Foreseeing the profit returns from a heavy freight traffic over his Great Northern line, Hill campaigned strenuously to increase the farm population within his domains and to develop large-volume production there. He delivered countless speeches in the Northwest, exhorting the homesteaders to scientific farming. His railroad drew demonstration trains from settlement to settlement and conducted demonstration farms. In 1883 Hill began a spectacular ballyhoo for purebred livestock by importing costly bulls and presenting them to Minnesota farmers for free service to their herds.

Minnesota leads all the States in the production of butter. Dairying is the most important branch of its livestock industry, and contributes 27.6 percent of the total farm income. Demand for dairy products in eastern markets, the speeding up of transportation, and the improvement of refrigeration facilities aided in the rapid rise of this industry. Minnesota sweet cream is now marketed in the East; its butter and cheese are carried across the ocean. Co-operative creameries were introduced to Minnesota farmers by Professor Theophilus L. Haecker, who came to the State university dairy school in 1891. They have increased marketing facilities and the farm income.

Dairy cows are kept on the majority of farms. The most intensive dairying regions are in the southeastern part of the State, in the vicinity of the
Twin Cities, and near Duluth. Excellent natural grasses, the ease with
which forage crops can be grown, and the abundant supply of pure water
are natural advantages for the industry which has now stamped Minnesota
as "The Butter State."

In 1890 less than 15,000,000 pounds of butter were produced; the current annual production is 280,000,000 pounds. In addition, more than
9,000,000 pounds of cheese are marketed every year. This growth has
taken place in previously established dairy regions, there having been almost no increase in the number of creameries since 1910.

Poultry and egg production has increased with dairying and brings Minnesota farmers more than $20,000,000 a year.

Alfalfa is grown extensively for forage and soil enrichment. Potatoes
are the most important cultivated crop in the Red River valley, in northwestern Minnesota, and most of it is sold outside the State. Apple growing on a commercial scale is almost entirely confined to the Lake Minnetonka region, west of Minneapolis, and to the valley lands of southeastern
Minnesota. Sugar beets are a popular crop in the central part of the State.

The State is moving toward a stabilized agriculture. Since 1929 the relative acreage of wheat and corn has changed little. The earlier rapid increase in dairy cattle, swine, and egg production has slackened. But even if
crop stabilization is becoming a reality, many problems remain to be solved
before Minnesota can hope to achieve its fullest agricultural development.
The most critical of these are soil erosion, untillable or uneconomic lands
(see NATURAL SETTING), and tenant-operated farms. The last is perhaps less often recognized than others, but is nevertheless of great significance.

In Minnesota, renters make up one-third of the farm operators; in the
best farming districts they often outnumber the owners. Tenant farming
began soon after the first agricultural operations, when owners found themselves unable or unwilling to cultivate their homestead lands. As the cities
grew, many professional and business men bought land for investment,
renting it while they waited for a rise in price. In recent years the already
large number of non-resident owners has been augmented by mortgage
foreclosures. Many farms have been taken over by insurance and trust
companies and by private investors.

Soil erosion is particularly severe in the hilly, stream-cut farmlands of
the southeastern part of the State. Soil conservation experts here have illus-

trated effective methods of saving the land from gullying, and returning many acres to production (see Tour 1).

Reforestation is reclaiming thousands of acres of cut-over land in the northern half of the State. Farm families, unable to make a living on the submarginal land, are being relocated on more productive farms (see Tours 5, 6, 10, and 17).

Farm life in Minnesota has retained little of its pioneer flavor. The "farm-to-market" road building program of the Works Progress Administration began in 1935, together with other transportation improvements. It has made trips to the trading center for both meetings and shopping a common event. Newspapers, the radio, and easy transportation have done away with the earlier isolation, and the farmer of today may be as closely in touch with the world's affairs as the city man.

But despite modern advances, the era of kerosene lamps, outdoor privies, and well-house refrigeration has not wholly passed. Relatively few farm homes are modernized and equipped with labor-saving devices. Farmers of the more prosperous agricultural areas, the south-central and western parts of the State, may have many luxuries, but even the simplest comforts are too often lacking in the unproductive, cut-over regions of the northeast.

The Minnesota farmer can no longer be regarded as an isolated pioneer waging a single-handed battle with the soil. That he has learned to work together with his neighbors is shown by the leadership of Minnesota in agricultural co-operation. The Farmer-Labor Party, too, latest successor to early agrarian movements, includes a large group of the rural population. Producers' and consumers' co-operatives bring higher prices for produce and cut the cost of retail merchandise. Minnesota has more than 1,800 farmers' marketing and purchasing associations with approximately 400,-000 members. Creameries, grain elevators, and livestock- and produce-shipping associations are counted among the producer organizations.

Since Federal funds were made available by the organization in 1934 of the Rural Electrification Administration, 57 co-operative associations have been formed to bring light and power to Minnesota farms. Previously there were but six co-operatives in the field, the first of which was organized in 1914.

County agricultural agents offer and interpret to farmers the services of such agencies as the Federal, State, and University departments of agriculture, and other State departments such as the grain inspection division of the railroad and warehouse commission, the livestock board, and the State agricultural society. All of these give protection against illegal trade practices, supply technical information on farm problems, and encourage improvements in agricultural methods.

By dispensing technical information, the department of agriculture of the State university has been of incalculable value to Minnesota farmers. The department is held amply worth its cost by one achievement alone, the perfection of an early variety of corn, *Minnesota No. 13,* which has multiplied the number of corn-producing farms in the State.

Immigration
and Racial Elements

The Tides of Immigration

TO THE melting pot of Minnesota, European races made a contribution larger and more diversified than to any other of the pioneer States. Indeed the percentage here of the foreign-born to the total population has been consistently higher than in the United States as a whole. At the time of the 1930 census, although for 10 years there had been virtually no immigration, those of foreign-born parentage still made up more than 50 percent.

The first tide of settlers swept over the State with the first land sale in 1848. It was made up mostly of land-hungry and adventure-hunting easterners from New York, Pennsylvania, and New England and reached central Minnesota. In 1850, in the region now Minnesota, there were 5,354 settlers.

The population grew so amazingly that by 1858 it practically trebled, and the Territory was able to gain its statehood. Indian treaties had opened up more land and a railroad had reached the Mississippi River, making possible a long lap of the journey by train and boat. Men were wanted for lumbering, for railroad and town building, and to raise food for the settlers and their animals. The Yankee kings of industry proceeded to sell the Minnesota idea to northern Europe by methods of high-pressure salesmanship that even the predepression 1920's could not surpass. Thousands of pamphlets vaunting the region's unique opportunities were issued by the bureau of immigration created for that purpose. Agents were sent across the sea to scatter literature, and to encourage first Germans, Belgians, Scandinavians, then French and Swiss to come to Minnesota. Individual counties, through folders and newspapers, distributed stories of the soil's fertility, or of their respective manufacturing potentialities, in hotels and railroad stations throughout the land. The climate was endowed with extraordinary healing powers for tuberculosis and other pulmonary diseases. The State legislature took a hand and sponsored a prize competition for essays on the topic *Minnesota as a Home for Immigrants,* some of which they later printed and circulated. The Germans came in the greatest numbers, then the Irish, and then Canadians from beyond the border.

Ten years later the railroads had begun to spread their network over the State. Jim Hill sent his agent to Europe and Colonel Hans Mattson went over for the State Board of Emigration. Soon the Scandinavians began to pour into the land, lured by booklets whose illustrations were probably the first examples of creative art, the State produced. Immigrant houses were erected by the railroads and by Archbishop Ireland for his Irish colonists; some of these transient homes were large enough to accommodate several hundred persons at one time. By 1880 the census showed a population risen to 780,773, of which 71 percent were Europeans of the first and second generations.

All through the eighties the stream continued to flow across the Atlantic and the eastern States into Minnesota. New cheap labor crowding on the heels of earlier comers kept the labor world in a state of motion which shifted hundreds of peasants to the middle class and, in part at least, explains the rapid rise of foreign-born men in industry, and of unskilled laborers into the merchant and professional classes.

In 1890 the immigration tide reached its height. It was followed by the so-called newer immigration, that of the Finns and Slavs. Brought over to work in the mines, they came in such mounting numbers that by 1930 they constituted 53 percent of the Arrowhead region's foreign-born population (exclusive of Duluth), while each of the State's largest cities showed a marked increase in its Slavic element.

By 1900 the packing plants were in need of cheap labor. Profiting by the mine owners' experience, they sent their agents recruiting into the Balkan countries and as far north as Poland and Lithuania. Consequently, in South St. Paul today the national composition embodies Rumanians, Serbs, Slovenians, Croatians, Japanese, Jugo Slavs, Montenegrins, Mexicans, Poles, and Swedes. The Mesabi Range towns report Finns, Swedes, Norwegians, English, Irish, Germans, Poles, French, Austrians, Hungarians, Swiss, Syrians, Rumanians, Danes, Serbs, Welsh, Bulgarians, and Montenegrins. Outside of these two regions and Duluth, representatives of the Balkan countries are only occasionally found in the State.

Immigration virtually ceased in 1920, and since that date the trend has been consistently toward an ever smaller percentage of foreign-born. But there is still in Minnesota a vast group of persons only little removed from Old World influences. Nevertheless there are surprisingly few communities in the State where one can still hope to meet foreign customs or folkways. Not long ago one might still have found German the common speech on the streets of New Ulm, Czech in New Prague, Polish in a section of Winona, the three Scandinavian tongues in dozens of towns. Many churches then held their services in foreign languages. But today one finds but few children who are bilingual, and rare indeed are the communities like Embarrass, the Finnish village, where the residents still cling to Old World architecture for their barns and *saunas* (steam baths), and where their characteristic pegged, canvas-topped haystacks give a unique aspect to the countryside. On the Range one may catch an occasional glimpse of a quaint musical instrument or may chance upon a family celebration where young and old take part in a merry old country dance, but the average visitor to Minnesota may travel the length and breadth of the land and, aside from the names he glimpses on village stores and mail boxes, see few evidences of the great European immigrations.

A fondness for the foods of the homeland, however, has been retained in many quarters and at certain seasons of the year national culinary arts come strongly to the fore. The famous *smörgåsbord* suppers of the Scandinavians, served often in Lutheran churches, are experiences not to be forgotten. During the winter, *lutfisk* or *ludefisk* is featured in city and village alike. This is a species of cod which, first soaked and boiled, is served in melted butter. The tiny Swedish meat balls when properly prepared have a delicacy no Yankee counterpart can approach, and their hundreds of varieties of Christmas cakes are scarcely equaled even by the Germans. The Czechs still raise poppies in their gardens that they may have seeds for the sweet turn-over rolls, filled with citron, which they call *kolacky*, and the Poles, however Americanized, still make their special cakes and wafers for religious festivals.

◄◄◄◄◄◄◄◄◄◄◄◄◄◄◄◄◄◄◄✦►►►►►►►►►►►►►►►►►►►►►

Racial Groups

Minnesota probably owes more to Scandinavians than to any other one foreign group. They came from countries where illiteracy was extremely low. Their traditions were of thrift, respect for both intellectual and physical effort, and interest in government, and they combined to an unusual degree love of individual freedom and talent for co-operating with their neighbors. Swedes, Norwegians, and Danes have cleared Minnesota's land, built up its agriculture and dairying, laid its railroads, endowed many colleges, organized and supported its co-operatives, and contributed outstandingly to the cultural and industrial life. During the eighties their combined numbers made up half of all the foreign-born in the State. Now, when the proportion of the foreign-born has been reduced from 71 to only a little more than 15 percent, almost half of that number continues to be Scandinavian, and there is not an industry, profession, or art in which the repeated occurrence of Scandinavian names does not bespeak this people's participation. In the field of politics Governors Lind, Johnson, Nelson, Olson, Congressman Lindbergh, and many lesser-known Scandinavian figures have had a large share in Minnesota's story.

Sweden's political, social, and religious unrest were undoubtedly important factors in bringing the first Swedes to America. In 1846 Peter Cassel brought his little party of 21 to Iowa, and to him the Middle West frontier apparently was a veritable land of Canaan. His series of American Letters, published in the local newspapers of Sweden and handed on from cottage to cottage, played a large part in the immigration of individuals before the great tidal wave got under way. Not only did these letters portray a land as fabulous as Marco Polo's own, but most potent of all was the appeal made by their descriptions of the democracy that obtained in the new country. Caste lines in Sweden were severely restrictive, and here was a land where everyone was a landlord and servants sat down to table with the masters. From the first, Swedes liked Minnesota and in a few weeks felt themselves Americans.

It is said that of all the foreign groups Swedes are the most readily assimilated, an observation Minnesota's experience bears out. For they came from rural districts and went at once to the land. More than two million acres in the State are said to have been cultivated by them. Later they came from the cities, and settled in St. Paul, Minneapolis, and Duluth to make up much of the bulk of the population. They endowed three colleges, and sent thousands of their children to the State university. Although there is no county where they have not settled, their main stronghold is still where they early established it, in east-central Minnesota.

Norwegians rarely settle in areas of Swedish concentration. The Norse were great favorites in the lumbering industry, and when they had made money enough in the timber they bought their farms in the Red River valley and in some of the southeastern counties. Their admirable *a cappella* choir singing has been one of the most original of their contributions. From the faculty of their St. Olaf College at Northfield have come two of the State's most distinguished artists, F. Melius Christiansen and O. E. Rölvaag.

It is largely due to the Danes that Minnesota has achieved its enviable position as a leader in butter and other dairy products. Thousands who came into the State from Denmark after the Civil War brought with them a knowledge of dairying beyond anything the Americans had known.

They settled first in the southeastern part of the State, later in the north, and now are fairly widely distributed. In religion, as in all their convictions, they were independent spirits and were aligned to a variety of denominations—Lutherans of two types (Inner Mission and Grundtvigians), Baptists, Methodists, and Adventists. The Danes have a strong predilection for self-help, and this has led them to organize many societies, and to take a leading part in the development of the State's many cooperatives. Their folk school at Tyler is still widely used, and their home for Danish old people in Minneapolis is an eloquent witness to an understanding charity. Here both men and women are permitted to live as freely as they would in their own homes, and are even provided with weekly pocket money to assure a feeling of financial dignity.

In both 1890 and 1900 the census figures showed Germany leading all nations in the numbers it was sending to Minnesota. By 1910, however, Sweden had advanced beyond it and from 1920 on Germany has occupied the third place. Since the war, moreover, Austrians have been included in the German census listings without differentiation, so that it is impossible to make an accurate present-day generalization. The Germanic races were among the earliest of the Europeans to come to the State, and as a group have always been the best educated and most cultured of its immigrants.

As a race Germans are doubtless as adaptable to their surroundings as Swedes, but they cling to their Fatherland, its language and customs, with a sentimentality unknown to Scandinavians. Among the earliest settlers in St. Paul and New Ulm, they have left a deep imprint on the cultural and professional standards of both cities. Later they settled in farm colonies. Certain counties, Stearns and Brown for example, were almost wholly German, and in many communities for years their mother tongue was more commonly heard than English. Since the World War, however, they have become largely assimilated, and it is only among the oldsters that German is freely spoken. Their respect for organization, music, and learning is reflected in their music clubs, in their neat, precisely laid out farms, and in the efficiency with which they conduct their shops and businesses. During the rough pioneer days they managed to keep up their little orchestras and bands, and Bach, Mozart, and Beethoven were introduced by them into Minnesota even before the Paul Bunyan ditties were brought by the lumberjacks.

Owing no doubt to their recent arrival, the Finns have clung most tenaciously to Old World traditions. Deeply suspicious of all imposed government, they have bent their energies to the building up of their own co-operatives, and with the Danes are responsible for Minnesota's outstanding success in this social experiment. Strong and well built, they have provided the State with some of its finest athletes. They were drawn to the northern region by the lumbering and mining industries, but for the most part have regarded these as only the temporary means whereby they will be able to purchase a little land—the dream of all Finns. Surrounded by their own people, their *saunas,* and a few cows, they strive to bring up their children in their cherished traditions of thrift and independence. With the Scandinavians, they strongly support temperance movements and have provided leaders in this cause. If those of the older generation still sing the folksongs and recite the charms of their childhood, it is only among their contemporaries, for to their American grandchildren these have little or no meaning.

Few of the foreign groups have made as conscious an effort to retain their national heritage as have the Poles. Since the World War and the establishment of Poland as an independent nation, Polish clubs organized for the preservation of the language, dances, and folklore have sprung up in many parts of the State, scholarships are provided for Polish youths, and moving pictures are imported from their own land. Christmas and Easter are celebrated with many of the old religious practices. The Czechs, too, have become in the past few years more national-minded, and through the Sokol, the national Czech gymnastic society, have kept their youth interested in the culture of their forebears. Deeply musical, they are active in orchestras and their children share conspicuously in school music. They are also devoted to the art of the theater, and in their own clubs produce many of their native plays. Blanche Yurka, well-known actress, is the daughter of one of Minnesota's outstanding educators, Antonin Jurka, from Bohemia. Czechs have played an active part in Minnesota politics. Their rate of illiteracy is very low, and the State counts them as among its most valued citizens.

The Negro population of the State was negligible before the Civil War. In 1850 the census showed 39 Negroes, but in 1930 there were 9,445. The majority live in St. Paul and Minneapolis, where they find their principal employment in domestic and personal service. About 8 percent are postal clerks and carriers, 10 percent work in manufacturing and the mechanical trades, and a smaller group are in the professions.

Other groups include Italians, Irish, Slavs, Mexicans, and a few Asiatics. Almost every nation is represented. But with immigration practically at a standstill, and the birth rate apparently becoming stabilized, the varied national colors have already largely merged.

Despite the fact that Minnesota owes an incalculable debt to European countries, it was the first settlers—the Yankees—who set upon the region the indelible stamp it has worn ever since. Each nationality has made its contribution, but it has been quick to discard its language, its dress, its folk customs, for those of the Americans whose standards of living they have adopted. Undoubtedly color has been lost in the process, but no realistic Minnesotan questions the success of the amalgamation.

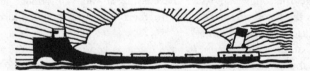

Transportation

MINNESOTA is connected with all the Nation's large centers by 10 trunk line railroads. Twenty-seven railroads crisscross the State in so close a web that scarcely a hamlet is more than 5 miles distant from one or another. Thousands of busses, trucks, and pleasure cars roll comfortably along the State's 14,000 miles of paved and improved highways. In one day they easily cover the distance which required, less than 75 years ago, all of 30 days in a Red River cart. Every few hours airplanes leave the Twin Cities for Atlantic and Pacific Coast cities; it is no unusual experience to breakfast in St. Paul and dine in New York.

Roadways of iron and cement are now commonplace; yet a hundred years ago Minnesota's means of travel were its rivers and its lakes. It was along the waterways that the region was first settled, and the first towns sprouted at landings on the Mississippi and its tributaries. Important as its rivers were destined to be in the development of Minnesota, it was by the Great Lakes that the first white men came into the region—some, like Hennepin, overland and by river routes from Lake Michigan, others (Du Luth, La Verendrye, Radisson, and Allouez) in Indian canoes on Lake Superior. These fragile shells of cedar wood and birchbark were the first craft known to travel Lake Superior's waters. They were found to be so admirably adapted to the purpose of explorers and traders that more than a century was to pass before more substantial vessels took their place, even on the Great Lakes. Designed for speed and easy portaging, they were equally able to navigate shallows and weedy sloughs, to shoot whirling rapids, or to ride through driving storms. In them trappers, explorers, traders, and missionaries paddled their way down the streams, and across the lakes from the tip of Lake Superior through the wilderness. Then up the Mississippi, following the Fox River route, came Colonel Leavenworth and his troops to establish Fort Snelling. They came in keelboats, a name given to anomalous craft that could be sailed, rowed, poled, or dragged, as occasion demanded. The American Fur Company established headquarters near the fort at Mendota and gradually the main stream of commerce shifted from the north to the Mississippi.

The first British license to trade in the upper lake region was granted in 1765 to Alexander Henry. In 1770–71 Henry built "a barge fit for navigation on the lake, and in 1772 a sloop of forty tons burden." Both were fitted with sails and are the earliest known sailing craft on Lake Superior, although a persistent but unsubstantiated legend credits a trader, La Ronde or Laland, with the operation of a sloop as early as 1731. By 1800 the Northwest Company had a vessel that made several trips each year from Grand Portage to Pine Point. That same year a resident of Grand Portage noted in his diary the arrival on July 3 of 35 great canoes, each of which carried 3 to 5 tons of goods from Mackinac. With the decline of the fur trade on the lakes, most of the furs were routed by way of Hudson Bay or the Mississippi, and there was little lake traffic. By 1840, however, there were enough prospectors, traders, and settlers in the region to make shipping again profitable, even though the boats had to be moved on sledges over the portage at Sault Ste. Marie. In 1855 the Michigan locks were finally completed and it was then possible for boats of fair size to pass into Lake Superior from the other Great Lakes.

The next 75 years brought into being a tremendous fleet of vessels of all sizes to carry eastward Minnesota's wheat and flour and her raw iron from the ranges. Duluth in that period was one of the leading freight ports of the world. In 1929, the peak year in Lake Superior's shipping history, the total volume handled at the Duluth-Superior harbor was 138,574,441 net tons, of which 50 percent was iron ore, 28 percent coal, 12 percent limestone, 7 percent grain, and the remaining 3 percent a miscellany of lumber, fish, dairy products, etc.

In 1935 the number of vessels that entered and departed from the Duluth-Superior harbor was 11,050. The average navigation season is only 8 months, and the period is governed more by local weather conditions than by the amount of business.

The advent of steamboats in 1823 inaugurated the modern era in river transportation. The first steamer to navigate the rapids at Rock Island and plow up the river to Fort Snelling was the *Virginia,* a substantial vessel, 118 feet long, 22 feet wide. It reached the levee below the fort on May 10, 1823, amid the consternation and frantic excitement of the Indians. The *Virginia's* journey was followed by the gradual establishment of a regular steamboat traffic on the upper river. For several years, however, steamer arrivals remained novel and exciting events in that sparsely settled country. The opening of the area between the Mississippi and the St. Croix in 1837 led to a sudden influx of settlers, and in order to transport them steamboat service was forced into rapid expansion. Hundreds of boats were built for this traffic, many of them of elaborate design and substantial proportions. Lumbering started on the St. Croix that same year and soon the river was crowded with barges, rafts, and steamboats. Many of the captains, wary of the turbulent waters below St. Anthony Falls, refused to go farther north and only the offer of a reward could persuade them occasionally to continue to the St. Anthony Falls levees. Eventually several steamers ran between Minneapolis and Sauk Rapids.

Steamboat traffic continued to thrive in the early days of the railroads. Each summer, wealthy planters of the South, with their families and personal slaves, traveled up to Minnesota lakes in the palatial passenger packets. Downstream the produce and lumber of the new Territory were shipped. But as early as the close of the Civil War, public attention had been captured by the prospect of railroads, and for years to come they and their builders were to hold the spotlight on the transportation stage. The riverboat traffic, which reached its peak in 1880, had by 1910 dwindled to a negligible factor in transportation.

Agitation for railroads began in the early 1850's. The first land grant was asked of Congress in 1854 but, although authorized, it was later rescinded because of the resulting controversy between the rival railroads and Territorial interests. By 1857 the Territory had granted 27 charters, but when the land grant enactment was finally obtained from Washington only 4 roads actually benefited.

By 1854 the Chicago & Rock Island Railroad had reached the Mississippi, and when a few months later a line to Galena was completed, Chicago replaced St. Louis as the metropolis of the Northwest, and the flow of traffic began to change from north and south to east and west.

The Rock Island Railroad became an active promoter of the Minnesota Territory. In June 1854 the railroad management sponsored a "grand excursion" with Minnesota as its destination. Men of national prominence—

magnates, savants, historians, editors, and politicians—were invited to make the trip over the new railroad to the Mississippi. Former President Fillmore was in the party and gave it official approval. At Rock Island the excursionists boarded five large river steamers and sailed up the Mississippi to St. Paul, there to be received with open arms. Business was suspended and western hospitality reached new heights. Indeed the excursion received so much publicity that Congress began to regard with more prejudiced eyes the aspiring Territory at the head of the Mississippi.

The land Grant Act of 1857 gave to the prospective State alternate sections of public lands six miles in width on each side of five contemplated railroad routes, with the expectation that the sale of these lands would finance construction. But before a start could be made the panic of 1857 occurred. Land could not be sold and all the ambitious plans had to be abandoned.

Minnesota became a State the following year and the new State government was importuned immediately to clear up the railroad situation. It was not until the spring of 1862, however, that the St. Paul and Pacific Railroad connected St. Paul and its sister city of St. Anthony (now part of Minneapolis) with the first section of the system which eventually became the Great Northern. On July 2, 1862, the first train puffed into St. Anthony, drawn by a wood-burning locomotive named the *William Crooks,* still preserved by the Great Northern Railway Company in its St. Paul shops. This, the first locomotive in the Northwest, was brought to St. Paul by steamboat from La Cross, Wisconsin.

By 1865 there were 22 miles of railroad in the State, and with the close of the Civil War construction began in earnest. Settlers from the eastern States and from Europe were arriving in a great tide, and new areas of Minnesota were rapidly opened to receive them.

The Minnesota Central was completed from St. Paul to Austin in 1867 and soon thereafter, by a merger with the Milwaukee, provided Minnesota with its first through route to Chicago. The Lake Superior and Mississippi in 1870 connected St. Paul with the head of the lakes. The St. Paul and Pacific reached Anoka in 1864, and extended a line in 1871 to Breckenridge, thus giving the Twin Cities their first rail connection with the Red River Valley. The Chicago and St. Paul was opened from St. Paul to Winona in 1871, and by crossing the Mississippi provided another through route to Chicago.

Another road, the St. Paul and Sioux City, completed its line in 1872. In the succeeding 10 years a number of lines in southern Minnesota, Iowa, and Nebraska territory merged into a single system under the name of the

Chicago, St. Paul, Minneapolis, and Omaha Railroad, now a part of the North Western system.

The Minneapolis and St. Louis Railroad entered the field in 1870, and the next year certain of its stockholders organized the Minneapolis and Duluth. The latter road built a line from Minneapolis to White Bear, thus giving each of the Twin Cities a direct route to Duluth. The line was later sold to the Great Northern.

In 1870 work began on the project that for years stimulated the imaginations of many people, a railroad to the Pacific Coast by way of the northwest border States. In 1883 the Northern Pacific completed its road to the Pacific, thus establishing the Twin Cities as the gateway to that Northwest which embraced all the territory from the Mississippi to the West Coast.

The Soo Line, now the Minneapolis, St. Paul & Sault Ste. Marie Railway, was encouraged by the Canadian Pacific to divert to its own lines a share of the traffic between the Twin Cities and the Atlantic seaboard. The line to Sault Ste. Marie was completed in 1887.

The Chicago, Burlington & Quincy Railroad entered the Twin Cities in the late 1880's by extending a branch up the east bank of the Mississippi from La Crosse. The Chicago and Great Western arrived in 1887, and in 1902 the Rock Island laid its own tracks from Albert Lea, where it had been connected with the Minneapolis and St. Louis.

During the early years of railroad promotion in Minnesota, a young Canadian, James J. Hill, had been employed as a shipping clerk on the St. Paul wharves. One version of his story has Hill leaving home at 18 and planning to sail for China or India. He postponed his trip to visit a friend at Fort Gary (near Winnipeg). On his arrival in St. Paul, he hoped to continue from the Twin Cities to Pembina in a Red River cart train. When he found it too late for the last trip of the year, he was forced to remain over until the following season. This incident helped to shape his career and the history of Minnesota, for as a result Hill made St. Paul his home for the remainder of his life.

On the docks Jim Hill held many jobs—warehouseman, steamer agent, shipping agent for the Canadian trappers and traders, coal dealer, railroad agent, steamer owner—and in a short time he became not only thoroughly grounded in the transportation business but enthusiastically alive to the potentialities of the country. In 1878 Hill gained control of the St. Paul and Pacific Railroad with his three partners, Norman Kittson, George Stephen, and Donald A. Smith. After Hill became president of the St. Paul and Pacific, he combined it in 1883 with various other railroad properties and formed a new road called the Great Northern. His principal extension of the Great Northern followed the route north of the Northern Pacific to Puget Sound, chosen by him for a western terminus.

Hill became the most conspicuous railroad promoter and operator of the Northwest. He died in 1916 at the height of his power and affluence.

The end of the World War saw the beginnings of a new cycle of transportation. Before the war the automobile was largely a rich man's luxury, but after 1918 the ordinary citizen could buy cars for his pleasure and his business, and inevitably he became an advocate of good roads. In 1920 a State highway system of 6,700 miles was authorized. The first modern trunk highway outside the metropolitan area was the 15-mile stretch of concrete between Northfield and Faribault, built in 1921 and still in use.

Today there are more than 11,000 miles of trunk highways. More than half are either paved or bituminous-treated, and the remainder graveled. Of the 115,000 miles of secondary roads maintained by townships, counties, or with State aid, by far the most are graveled or otherwise surfaced. Although the State maintains jurisdiction over only a small part of Minnesota's 126,000 miles of roads, it extends technical advice to all governmental units engaged in road building.

The commissioner in charge of the highway department, under whom there are eight divisional engineers, is appointed by the Governor and is responsible to him alone. Revenue for the system is derived from motor vehicle registration taxes, a gasoline tax, and Federal aid. The Minnesota vehicle registration fee is the second lowest in the country, and of the four cent State gasoline tax, part goes to the highway department and the remainder to county roads.

In 1929 the Minnesota Highway Patrol, under the jurisdiction of the highway commission, was established by legislative action. Today the patrol consists of one hundred men whose training headquarters are at Fort Ripley. The patrol covers all main-traveled roads and is designed less for arrests of traffic violators than for the convenience and protection of motorists.

Since the adoption of the State Highway Act, transportation facilities within the State have been increased by the development of bus routes. Today busses have been the cause of the railroads' reducing materially their number of local trains linking the metropolitan area with suburban and rural sections.

Hibbing was the home of the founder of the present Nation-wide bus system. In 1914 Eric Wickman, a miner, forsook his diamond drill to start a jitney-bus service between Hibbing and the mine. He found one touring car and then two inadequate to handle the growing patronage. With his associates, Wickman thereupon supervised the construction of 12-passenger, side-seat busses in a Hibbing blacksmith shop. (At that time the only other busses manufactured in the United States were built by the Fifth Avenue Coach Lines of New York for its own use.) Service was soon extended to Nashwauk, 15 miles away, and in 1916, with new capital and a larger staff, the Mesaba Transportation Company was organized. By 1918 the company was operating a fleet of 18 busses throughout northern Minnesota.

In 1922 Wickman, from his headquarters in Duluth, began buying and consolidating small bus lines, extending service from the head of the Lakes to the Twin Cities and other points. More rapid expansion followed in 1925, when the Great Northern Railroad purchased a controlling interest in Wickman's Northland Transportation Company. The company by then included both his Duluth and his original Hibbing operations. The Northland in turn became a part of the great Greyhound system.

The State railroad and warehouse commission report of 1936 lists 12 major bus companies operating as common carriers over the State highways. Transportation of livestock and package goods by truck has developed proportionately.

Two air-transport systems, both equipped for night flying, serve Minnesota and the Twin Cities with their principal terminals at the Wold-Chamberlain field, Minneapolis, and the Holman Municipal Airport, St. Paul. From the Twin Cities, air line routes radiate east to Chicago, south to Oklahoma, and west to the upper Pacific Coast.

Air mail service between the Twin Cities and Chicago dates back to Government experiments begun in 1920. Service was maintained for 9 months and then abandoned. In 1926 the late "Pop" Dickinson, octogenarian pilot, contracted to maintain an air mail service, but at the end of 3 months transferred his contract to the recently organized Northwest Airways. Northwest Airways was the corporate predecessor of Northwest Airlines. The first passenger service was offered in 1926 by the Jefferson Transportation Company, which put a Ford trimotor into operation between the Twin Cities and Rochester. Universal Airlines, a Curtiss-Wright subsidiary, inaugurated service to Chicago the same year. Soon all these pioneer services merged with Northwest Airways, and the business interests of the Twin Cities joined to maintain the consolidated system. Service eventually was extended westward along a Government-maintained and lighted route, and in 1933 reached Seattle.

Most recent of transportation developments has been a revival of river traffic, stimulated by an Interstate Commerce Commission ruling in 1922 that deprived the Twin Cities of their favorable railroad rate position. The railroad freight rate structure of the Twin Cities had been built on the potentiality of river transportation. In the controversy known as the Indiana Rate Case, however, the commission held that water transportation must be actual and not potential. Minnesota business interests thus were forced to set about making competition "actual." In co-operation with lower river interests and with the assistance of the Federal Enabling Act, the Federal Barge Lines were organized and service begun in 1927. The lines are operated by the Inland Waterways Corporation under the administration of the War Department. By 1935 they were handling a considerable tonnage in and out of the Twin Cities. A program of dam construction now under way is designed to provide a 9-foot channel and obviate past difficulties caused by low water levels.

Industrial Development

MINNESOTA'S important industries owe their variety and wealth to the State's natural resources. The climate and the vast hardwood and coniferous forests accounted respectively for the great number of richly furred animals that first brought fame to the region, and the success of its earliest industry—lumbering. The fertility of the soil and the favorable climate produced wheat crops such as the world had never seen before, and were factors, with the innumerable waterways, which permitted the attainment of new records in flour production. To the soil's fertility and lakes also goes the credit for the State's world record in butter, and for its meat packing and canning, while below the surface are deposits of iron ore and rock from which arose the great iron and quarrying industries.

Those who first appreciated these resources did not keep their discoveries to themselves. They well knew that only with the help of many thousand men could they hope to take its riches from the earth, so they recruited labor throughout the United States and Europe. The industrial and commercial history of Minnesota thus became the story of those who built up lumbering, milling, mining, and quarrying; of the rise of cities and villages around these industries; of smaller manufacturing and commerce to supply living needs; and of the bankers who held the purse strings for the whole enterprise.

Not until the twentieth century came the realization that natural resources, even so lavishly bestowed, might in time become exhausted. Wheat, lumber, and iron were still the major source of the State's wealth, but already the best forests had been reduced to great stretches of stumpland and the richest of the iron ore was being rapidly removed. Milling too began to decline, for the farmers had learned the advantages of a diversified agriculture, and the new preferential railroad rates were turning many millers from Minneapolis to Buffalo.

Pioneer days were over with the turn of the century, and the needs of a steadily increasing population demanded a shift in the industrial scene. Corn replaced wheat, and livestock and packing superseded milling, a transition which involved more intensive use of soil and water. Gradually too there developed industries not directly dependent upon natural resources or hindered by transportation problems.

Since the end of the World War period there have been many more changes in the industrial picture. Conflicts between capital and labor have caused dislocations. Labor has gained a strong political hold in the State, and has threatened repeatedly to take over the ownership of coveted utilities. Jobbing has developed in the cities at a rate far more rapid than their population growth. In 1933 Minneapolis ranked eighth as a jobbing center, while ranking fifteenth in size. Banking facilities have been extended to towns and villages, thereby providing sources of local credit and permitting more diversified buying. Chain businesses have shown a remarkable development, as have nonprofit co-operatives and co-operative associations of independent merchants who joined forces to combat their chain competitors.

Not usually regarded as an important manufacturing State, Minnesota is nevertheless the largest producer of linseed-oil products in the world, and the second largest producer of flour. Among other important manufactured products are farm machinery, patent medicines, beet sugar, and refrigerators.

<<<<<<<<<<<<<<<<<<<<<<❁>>>>>>>>>>>>>>>>>>>>>>

Lumbering

To the vast army of woodsmen who swept across the country from Maine to Oregon in their conquest of the virgin forests, Minnesota was merely a temporary encampment. For a brief period these hard-working, hard-living shantyboys furnished the most spectacular element in the life of the State. Forests by day rang with the sound of their axes and the falling of trees, their improvised songs and fantastic oaths. By night the settlers in the river towns shivered excitedly at the uproar of the loggers' drunken brawls, the shattering of the tavern's glassware, the outbursts of explosive laughter. Their physical courage and prowess in logrolling, jam breaking, and raft-piloting were the talk of the less turbulent settlers, and are still commemorated annually in community celebrations. One of these events, held at Brainerd, has won national renown, while the Paul Bunyan tales are accorded a place with those of Uncle Remus in the annals of American folklore. For a few decades the lumberjacks found Minnesota much to their liking. Wages were high, work plentiful, and even the prolonged seasons of snow and ice only made logging easier. Then, when the best of the forests had fallen, this lively crew turned their backs on Minnesota and moved westward, leaving behind them acres and acres of stumps and slash, scores of ghost towns, and several huge fortunes.

Some of the magnates of the pioneer lumbering days came from Maine and Michigan, bringing with them a knowledge of the industry. These men had learned well how to choose and acquire the richest forest property. The settlers were too occupied with the founding of their homes and villages to give much heed, and, if the methods for securing the logging rights seem more rugged than ethical today, at that time they were little questioned.

Although its operations extended over all of the southern and eastern portions of the State, lumbering before 1870 remained in a pioneer stage. The first sawmill, built at the Falls of St. Anthony in 1822, cut logs from the trees in the vicinity for the buildings of the new Fort Snelling. Only 17 years later the first commercial sawmill was erected at Marine on the St. Croix River. Before the St. Croix timber was exhausted, 133 mills were operating in that valley. Logging did not begin its second concentrated drive (in the Mississippi and Rum River Valleys) until it had been well established for 10 years on the St. Croix.

With the seventies and the coming of the railroads, the industry went forward with gigantic strides, pioneer methods were discarded, and lumbering entered the class of "Big Business." This expansion was due not only to the rapid growth of the prairie country now made accessible by the railroads, but also to the fact that the railroads themselves required vast quantities of lumber for their own building operations.

In the 1880's the industry began to move into the northern sections of the State. Larger and more efficient mills took the place of the simpler plants. Germans and Scandinavians had succeeded the original lumbermen, and with the immigration of the nineties, Russians and Finns were swept into the industry. By the end of the century 40,000 men went into the timber, and in 1901 about 552 million feet of lumber were cut in Minneapolis alone. Then, with the best forest land practically devastated, the industry quickly declined. In the next few years hundreds of mills closed down and only a very few are still operating.

Nevertheless the lumber industry is still an important factor in Minnesota's commercial life. Many companies whose mills were originally in the State, but now operate elsewhere, maintain their offices in the Twin Cities; a large amount of hardwood is distributed through wholesale yards here, and hundreds of retail outlets are handled by a few large concerns with Minneapolis or St. Paul headquarters. Millwork and paper making are also carried on extensively.

The story of lumbering in Minnesota is characterized not only by color and romance. Through it runs a sinister thread of despoliation. Practices that would seem intolerable now were accepted with scarcely a shrug. Indians were cajoled, betrayed, and robbed; legislators were coerced into complying with the demands of logging companies, while the State watched with little concern the destruction of one of its greatest resources.

Today Minnesota is planting pine, and through reforestation of national and State parks the citizens hope that this wantonly destroyed resource may be at least partially restored.

<<<<<<<<<<<<<<<<<<<<<❂>>>>>>>>>>>>>>>>>>>>>>

Milling

The first flour produced in Minnesota was milled in 1823 when Col. Snelling, hoping to reduce commissary costs, pressed the soldiers of the newly established Fort Snelling into wheat raising, and erected the first grist mill at the Falls of St. Anthony. Although their lack of enthusiasm and training for the job made Army men indifferent farmers, the attempt attracted interest to the power available at the Falls, and thus foreshadowed the rise of Minneapolis as a milling city.

During the 1850's, when each year brought thousands of new immigrants to the Territory, flour mills sprang up along nearly every river and creek. Almost from the first the high quality of Minnesota flour was acknowledged. As early as 1861 the New York market quoted it at a premium. Then came the rapid extension of the railroads, the consequent opening up of the prairies, the importation of more and more European labor for farming and town building. The invention of farm machinery made possible the "bonanza" wheat farms, the like of which the world had never seen before. One farm alone boasted 30,000 acres. By the seventies more than a million and a half Minnesota acres were bringing forth wheat.

Obviously all this grain could not be turned into flour as soon as it was harvested. A method to meet the need of storage had to be devised. The answer was the grain elevator which soon appeared along the side of every railroad station. At first ungainly red-painted buildings, they were to evolve into the masses of colossal cement pillars that distinguish Minnesota's skylines. Not until many great terminal elevators had been built was there enough storage for the streams of wheat that poured in from the prairies.

The power at St. Anthony Falls determined the choice of Minneapolis rather than St. Paul as the great milling city. By 1870 there were 12 mills operating at the falls, and with an annual production of 250,000 barrels, they gave the new city a reputation as a flour center. By 1880 the European demand was so great that one-third of the Minneapolis output was required for export. It brought the highest price hitherto ever paid for flour. But the millers were not content. Minnesota's wheat was spring wheat, and the flour made from it, while admittedly of excellent quality, was of a darker color and inclined to be speckled as compared with that of the winter wheat flour of other States. Yet spring wheat was the only variety ideally suited to Minnesota's climate.

The problem was solved when the "new process" of milling was installed in the Minneapolis mills. Edmund La Croix, a French-Canadian, perfected a middlings purifier, and this, when combined with a new system of rollers, increased the efficiency of the mills from 25 to 90 percent. With quality now enormously improved, Minnesota flour by 1885 had become the most popular in the world, and Minneapolis was definitely established as the foremost flour-producing city.

The milling industry continued to expand and develop until 1916, the peak year. Scientific methods for testing and maintaining a uniform quality were introduced. Breakfast foods, whole wheat flours, and other cereal products were added to the mills' output. The decline began in 1917 and has continued at a varying pace through the subsequent years. Several factors have contributed to this reduction of output. Among the most significant were the adverse freight rulings of the Interstate Commerce Commission and the withdrawal of storage privileges in Buffalo warehouses, with the inevitable consequence that the export trade was transferred to Buffalo, while other milling centers nearer to sources of distribution took on increasing importance. At the same time agriculture in the State turned to diversified farming and materially reduced its spring wheat crop. Nevertheless Minnesota remains a great flour-milling State, and Minneapolis still manufactures more flour than any other city in the world except Buffalo.

Today spring wheat is sown in the United States almost exclusively within the area included in the Ninth Federal Reserve District, of which Minneapolis is both the financial headquarters and the marketing seat. Grown during a short intense summer, it is harvested and moved to the market almost immediately. To insure its preservation and distribution to the mills throughout the world, an elaborate and efficient organization of many interests is required. How smoothly this operates is indicated by the fact that from the day the grain leaves the threshing machine it may be used precisely as cash.

Slightly more than half the elevators in the Northwest are farmer- or independently-owned. The remainder belong to the line companies and mills. Rural elevators are of several types; there are two groups of the so-called farmers' elevators, one is organized like a stock company, the other is owned co-operatively and its profits prorated as dividends. The independent elevators are individually owned, as the name implies, and in addition there are those held by mill owners to maintain their source of supply.

The farmer is under no compulsion to accept either the price or the grading the elevator offers. If he wishes to wait for a rise in the market, he may store his grain in the elevator and use his receipt as collateral for bank loans.

◄◄◄◄◄◄◄◄◄◄◄◄◄◄◄◄◄◄◄◄❀►►►►►►►►►►►►►►►►►►►►►►

Mining

About $100,000,000 of Minnesota's annual wealth comes from the three iron ranges which together produce annually about 40 million tons of ore. In a relatively limited area, more than 25 communities owe their existence to the mines. Fifteen thousand men are employed directly by the industry and ten thousand more on railroads and freighters for transportation of the ore.

The first French explorers thought that valuable metals might be found on Lake Superior, a belief possibly arising from the story that Champlain had been shown nuggets of copper by the Indians. This tradition was handed on, first to the English and later to the Americans. In 1826, Cass persuaded the Chippewa on Lake Superior to cede to him the mineral rights of this region. The treaty of 1854 was made with an eye to prospective mineral wealth, and from that time on the northeast triangle was the scene of geological surveys instigated by interested, if not convinced, legislatures. As early as 1865 the Eames brothers found considerable iron near Vermilion Lake, but the discovery aroused little interest since Minnesotans were convinced that gold was to be found. By December of that year the gold craze was at its height, only to collapse during the following summer when repeated assays failed to establish the promised values. It was this gold interest, however, that delayed for twenty years the appreciation of the region's richness in iron ore.

Convinced of the presence of iron ore in large quantities on the Vermilion Range, a mining group in 1883 incorporated the Minnesota Iron Company. By 1883 the Duluth Iron Range Railroads Company had engineered its charter and land grants through the State legislature and was prepared to build a road from the Vermilion mines to docks on the lakeshore. On July 30, 1884, the first load of 100 tons of iron ore was shipped in five cars from the Breitung Pit to Two Harbors.

The first ore found on the Mesabi Range was not considered of sufficiently high grade to warrant mining. But Leonidas Merritt and his six brothers, all timber cruisers, thought otherwise. In 1890 Leonidas took out 141 leases and that year one of the Merritt exploring parties struck ore in the area that later became the site of Mountain Iron Mine. Other test pits established the fact that here was another iron range. By the next year mining operations on the Mesabi were well under way and 5 years later 20 mines were producing annually nearly three million tons.

This tremendous production was due largely to the geological formation of the range. In the Vermilion district, geological upheavals had tilted the ore deposits so sharply that all mining in this region was underground and had to be done by vertical shafting. The ore in the Mesabi Range, on the other hand, lies detached in irregular horizontal masses that run lengthwise, with an ordinary depth of 200 feet. To reach these iron-laden masses it was necessary only to strip off the glacial drift. Moreover, while the Vermilion ores were hard rock, the ores of the Mesabi were soft, dusty, and friable. Their fine texture tended to clog the furnaces, and it caused Andrew Carnegie to oppose their use until, after several years, a change in furnace design eradicated the difficulty. The easy accessibility of the ore and its softness brought into being a new method of mining—the open-pit method. All costs of underground mining were thus eliminated. Now steam or electric shovels could strip, scoop out, and transfer to waiting ore cars as much as five tons at once.

The third iron range, the Cuyuna, was worked first at the Kennedy mine in 1911. Here, as in the Vermilion Range, the ore lies in vertical lenses and must be mined underground. The distinguishing characteristic of ore from this range is that it contains manganese which plays an important part in steel production.

In the early days of mining it was found that profitable shipment to distant markets required 60 to 65 percent of iron in Minnesota ore. Later the standard was lowered to 51.5 percent. But rich ores grew scarcer and it was soon necessary to improve the quality by expelling moisture, removing waste material such as silica, sintering (fusing by heat), or jigging (crushing and screening). Any process whereby the ore is improved is called in mining parlance "beneficiation." In recent years as high as 40 percent of the total annual shipments have been thus "beneficiated."

Ore railroads and lake vessels began to supply means of transportation, but in order to transfer millions of tons to the holds of ships it was necessary to invent docks of new design. These great docks, so characteristic a feature of Duluth and Two Harbors, are in reality extensions of the railroads, whose tracks reach out to deep water on trestles. Trains are backed out on these, the hopper bottoms of the red ore cars are dropped, and the ore falls into pockets on both sides of the dock from these pockets. Ten thousand tons can be emptied into a vessel's hold within six hours.

In 1937 record demands for iron-ore by railroads and munition works resulted in a boat movement of Minnesota ore amounting to 48,697,280 gross tons. This is the largest output in the history of the mines. The former peak year was 1929, when 47,478,167 tons were shipped from the State.

In the early days the ore was known by the name of the mine that produced it. It soon became necessary, however, in order to simplify shipping, not only to grade the ore according to its chemical composition, but to mix various ores for the grades desired. Today in its course from mine to furnace, the ore is repeatedly analyzed for iron, phosphorus, silica, manganese, and the degree of moisture present.

The account of the struggles for the possession of the mines is crowded with drama. Paul de Kruif in his *Seven Iron Men* presents the Merritt Story, and in the bibliography at the end of this *Guide* further references are listed which deal with the question of ownership and leases.

The taxation of mining properties has been a burning issue with many State legislatures. As a result of mining developments the population of St. Louis County leapt from 4,504 in 1880 to 206,381 in 1920. As mining towns grew with almost bewildering rapidity, they exercised their right of local taxation for schools and public improvements on valuations determined by State tax commissions, with the result that they provided themselves in rapid succession not only with waterworks, electricity, and cement pavements, but also with community houses, parks, libraries, and excellent public schools. Hibbing, for example, expended $3,800,000 for its high school and junior college. In some communities the mining companies pay over 99 percent of all taxes levied.

The question of how long the iron deposits will last is often debated. That the cream has been skimmed from the Mesabi deposits, there can be no doubt. But experiments are under way for the profitable handling of ores now considered unusable. Millions upon millions of tons of Minnesota's low grade and mixed ores have not yet been touched. Most of these experiments are conducted by the United States Bureau of Mines and at the University of Minnesota. The mining companies themselves have not yet felt acutely the threat of iron scarcity.

‹‹‹‹‹‹‹‹‹‹‹‹‹‹‹‹‹‹ ⊗ ›››››››››››››››››››››

Quarrying

The first to take advantage of Minnesota's rich building stone deposits were the officers and men of the post near Mendota who in the 1820's erected the stone buildings that remain on the site of the old encampment. Today Minnesota's many quarries produce over fifty varieties of architectural stone which are cut, shaped, finished, and shipped all over the United States. Quarrying and stone cutting constitute a mineral industry second only to that of the great iron mines. Since 1880 the State has stood twelfth among the stone-producing States and third among the States producing granite. In 1930 the value of the Minnesota industry was more than $13,000,000.

The major granite-producing area in the State, second only to Barre, Vermont, in national importance, is a small region in Stearns and Sherburne Counties. Pioneers observed and admired the stone for its beauty but regarded it as too unwieldy for practical use. In 1868, however, two partners opened a quarry in what is today a part of the State Reformatory property, and "Reformatory Pink" became a popular medium for cemetery and other monuments. Later a darker red and gray rock was found that added still further to St. Cloud's reputation. Architects began to use it extensively for many of their more important buildings, among them the Louisiana State Capitol, the Book-Cadillac Hotel in Detroit, and the Chicago Tribune Tower. The cathedral in St. Paul is perhaps the most outstanding example of its use in this State.

Near the city of St. Cloud stands the village of Rockville, on a granite outcrop said by geologists to be 5 miles thick and 30 miles deep. "Rockville Pink" is to be used for the entire exterior of New York City's new Federal courthouse. For this building with its 38-story tower, eleven hundred carloads of the Rockville stone are required.

A second but rapidly developing granite source extends along the Archean outcrops of the Minnesota River Valley from Ortonville to New Ulm. These quarries have been slower in their development than those in the St. Cloud area, although quartzite was quarried across the river from New Ulm as early as 1859. Especially prized for its beauty is the red-streaked granite from the vicinity of Morton known variously as "Rainbow," "Oriental," or "Tapestry." This decorative stone is in wide demand for facings, doorways, etc., and has been used to admirable effect in many large buildings, notably the Daily News Building in Chicago. It may be quarter-sawed and laid so that its red streaks make an effective pattern. A darker "Ruby Red" and a "Pearl White" found in this valley, together with the "black granite," a decorative foundation stone, have met with much favor.

More restricted in its use is the so-called "green granite" of the Arrowhead district, a dark stone that burnishes into a definite emerald hue. With the nearly related "black granite," it is a part of the geological formation known as Duluth gabbro.

Although Minnesota quarries no true marble, some of its limestone from Kasota and surrounding beds has been recrystallized to such a degree that it is capable of taking a high polish, and is frequently spoken of as marble. All of Minnesota's limestones are dolomitic, but some are almost a pure combination of carbonate of lime and magnesia and are specifically called dolomites. Settlers in the Minnesota River valley built their foundations with this type as early as 1868, and railroad builders before the days of concrete found it admirable for bridges, culverts, and roadbeds. When Jim Hill was ready to build his beautiful Stone Arch Bridge in Minneapolis, he sent to these quarries for the stone.

By the time concrete had replaced stone for heavier construction, quarrying and finishing tools had been vastly improved, and it was possible to use limestone much more widely in buildings. Architects became interested in variegated surface colors and textures. The cream, pink, buff, blue-and-gray mottled stones of the Kasota-Mankato quarries offered them a tempting choice for color experiment, and they rejoiced in the satiny fine texture of "old Gothic." Architects throughout the United States demanded stone from these quarries for the interiors and exteriors of some of their most important buildings. The Telephone Building in Minneapolis embodies its admirable qualities.

Some of the so-called travertine is found in the Mankato region, and in recent years "Winona Travertine" has added considerably to that city's income. A porous dolomite of the Oneota formation, the texture of this variety is very like that of the famous Italian travertine. Unlike the Italian, however, which is soft when quarried and hardens only after exposure, the Minnesota stone is hard, unaffected by climatic conditions, and extremely resistant to grease and stain.

Formerly many farmers crushed this rock and used it for a soil dressing, but architects have since discovered that it possesses not only beauty but durability. Much, however, is still broken into chips for the manufacture of "terrazzo," a flooring made up of travertine chips imbedded in a matrix and polished down to a smooth variegated surface. (The University Hospital at Iowa City, Iowa, has a quarter million square feet of this floor covering.)

A durable pinkish sandstone is found widely distributed throughout the State. It is quarried most extensively, however, in the Kettle River area. Quartz is the cementing substance between the sand grains. At first used mainly for flagging and paving, it has been chosen by later builders for many public buildings in both the Eastern and Western States. In Minneapolis it was utilized for the Union Station.

Less extensive use is made of the quartzite of the Pipestone region. This is a strong but easily worked stone which, because of irregularly spaced joints, is valuable chiefly for small decorative trimmings.

Not important economically, but of great interest to the student of American history, is the pipestone or catlinite, a dull red or flecked indurated clay of variable composition. This is found at Pipestone in a bed about a foot and a half thick with quartzite interstratifications. Indians have held this spot sacred for many centuries, and have traveled great distances for the stone from which they carved their peace pipes.

<<<<<<<<<<<<<<<<<<<✿>>>>>>>>>>>>>>>>>>>

Meat Packing

The rise of Minnesota to the front rank of livestock production has supported a thriving meat-packing industry. Almost one-third (29.8 percent) of the State's farm income in 1930 was derived from the sale of livestock. In the years from 1920 to 1934 the average value of cattle, sheep, and hogs sold annually amounted to about $120,000,000, and, while a part was shipped to Chicago and to Sioux City, Iowa, the bulk went to Minnesota packing centers.

In 1929 there were 16 packing plants in the State, with a volume of meat products valued at $201,155,942.

The meat-packing industry in Minnesota began to assume importance in the latter part of the last century, after the trend from cash-crop to feed-crop farming was well under way in the Northwest. As the demand for livestock products in the eastern metropolitan centers grew, the development of shipping facilities kept pace in a network of railroads spun from the Twin Cities, and farmers began in a small way to market their crops in the form of hogs, cattle, and sheep.

South St. Paul, the point of convergence for six railroads entering the State capital, became a watering place for livestock shipments to Chicago. In 1888 the railroads, backed by the businessmen of St. Paul, established the St. Paul Union Stock Yards. As a result, packing firms that operated on a Nation-wide scale established plants at South St. Paul. After the turn of the century, when Minnesota farmers swung earnestly into the business of livestock raising, South St. Paul was pushed into the front rank with Chicago, Kansas City, East St. Louis, and Omaha. Since 1920 the small packing houses scattered over the State have been appropriating larger portions of the packing business each year, but have not yet approached the leadership that is South St. Paul's.

Railroads were at first the chief means of transportation to packing centers, and farmers organized shipping co-operatives for more efficient marketing. The development of trucking and the direct marketing of stock has caused a decline in co-operative associations. In 1919 there were 655 associations, but the number dropped to 400 in 1932 and is lower today. The decrease in numbers has not proportionately reduced the importance of these agencies in livestock marketing, however, for the larger associations have increased their membership and volume of business.

◄◄◄◄◄◄◄◄◄◄◄◄◄◄◄◄◄◄◄◄◄◄☼►►►►►►►►►►►►►►►►►►►►►►►

Commercial Fishing

One of the little-known yet interesting and profitable industries along the southeastern edge of the Minnesota Arrowhead region is commercial fishing in the icy waters of Lake Superior. At Grand Portage, and from there north to the border, much of this industry is carried on by Indians. South of Grand Portage, most of it is handled by people of Scandinavian descent.

More than four-fifths of the many varieties caught and marketed by commercial fishermen are herring; the remainder are trout, ciscoes, suckers, and whitefish. The largest percentage are caught in gill-nets at night. Lake trout are also caught by set-lines stretched between two anchor buoys with 50 or 60 supplementary lines suspended from them, each baited with small fish called shiners. The nets are drawn up every morning, and the fish are immediately washed, cleaned, and packed in boxes between alternating layers of ice, preparatory to shipping.

Some idea of the size of this industry may be obtained from the fact that in 1935 more than 8,000,000 pounds of fish were taken by the North Shore fishermen who received about $250,000 from their sale.

Along the Canadian boundary in Namaken and Rainy Lakes and Lake of the Woods, Minnesota's commercial fishermen in 1935 caught almost 3,000,000 pounds of fish of which about one-half was pickerel. The estimated value of this catch was $139,000.

Fishing in the interstate waters such as the Mississippi River and Lake Pepin is of relatively little importance, but in 1935 there was a total catch of almost 200,000 pounds. The State is sponsoring a commercial fishing experiment, the Red Lake Fisheries Association, which enables the Indians of the Red Lake Reservation to catch and market approximately 750,000 pounds of fish each year. Pike, perch, and suckers are by far the most numerous of the several commercial varieties in the lake.

‹‹‹‹‹‹‹‹‹‹‹‹‹‹‹‹‹☼›››››››››››››››››››››

Labor and Labor Relations

In frontier days, labor in Minnesota was scarce, well paid, and independent. Employer and employee worked side by side in small shops and factories; dissatisfied employees had easy access to public lands. Even the satisfied employee, in fact, regarded his term of hire as a preliminary to the establishment of his own homestead.

Skilled labor groups made the first attempt at labor organization. The first of such groups, so far as is known, was Typographical Union No. 30, formed by St. Paul printers in 1858. Minneapolis printers followed suit a year later. These unions, which disappeared during the Civil War, were the only two known to have existed prior to 1860.

From the close of the Civil War to the depression years of 1873–77, the trade union movement experienced a slow growth, although printers, plasterers, painters, plumbers, cigar makers, and trainmen formed unions between 1867 and 1873. There was little of the spectacular about these organizations, and they exercised small influence. With the depression of 1873, trade unionism practically disappeared.

In the 1880's the trade union movement revived, only to be checked for a time by the rise of the Knights of Labor, an all-inclusive organization that dominated the labor field from 1883 to 1889. Originally a secret fraternal order, it had by this time discarded much of its ritual and become a dominant industrial union. The State-wide organization, known as District Assembly No. 79, had its inception early in 1883.

In its attempt to unite all labor in one central body, the Knights of Labor became unwieldy, and by 1890 its influence had begun to wane. The organization, however, made a number of important contributions to the labor struggle. In 1886, in conjunction with the Farmers' Alliance, it demanded the establishment by law of a State bureau of labor statistics. The bureau was created the following year, and its first two commissioners were Knights of Labor. To its credit, also, belong the celebration of Minnesota's first Labor Day on September 7, 1885, and the advocacy of such advanced reforms as the regulation of hours and conditions of child labor, arbitration of industrial disputes, and the abolition of convict labor. A master workman of the order organized what is said to have been the first retail clerks' union in America. At this period, stores were open from 7 a. m. to 10 p. m., with an extra hour on Saturdays. With the assistance of other labor groups, an earlier closing was effected, but after the victory many of the clerks dropped their membership and the union disbanded.

The theory of self-employment through co-operation, advocated by Terence V. Powderly, head of the Knights of Labor, was responsible for the beginnings of the co-operative movement in Minnesota. In the 1870's, the Minneapolis coopers formed a co-operative barrel-manufacturing company, and in the next decade co-operative stores for workmen were opened in three cities.

The organization of the Minnesota State Federation of Labor was perfected in 1890. In 1896 the federation went on record against the notorious "struck jury" law. Other federation demands of the period before 1900 included State printing of textbooks, changes in the compulsory education act to prevent child labor, health and safety regulations of shops and factories, an 8-hour day for public employees, good roads, woman suffrage, and establishment of postal savings banks. During the early years of the new century it played a vigorous part in the support of all liberal legislative measures proposed and enacted.

In 1913, labor achieved a crowning success in the passage of the Workmen's Compensation Act. Although the act was not the most favorable that could have been written, it represented the culmination of a long struggle against such laws as had heretofore permitted employers to evade responsibility through pleas of contributory negligence and other technicalities.

The outstanding figure in the annals of Minnesota's labor struggles is Le Grand Powers, whom Folwell calls the "Apostle of Labor." A Universalist minister who had become interested in labor problems, he was appointed State commissioner of labor in 1891. The list of his accomplishments on behalf of the health, safety, and general welfare of working men and women is far too long to be incorporated here. Until 1918, when he retired at the age of 71, he devoted himself tirelessly to investigating and combating social injustices and to finding means for their eradication.

Most of Minnesota's labor achievements have been won by the ballot. Relatively early, the value of affiliation with discontented farmers was recognized, and the subsequent rise of a combined third political party offered legislative opportunities which labor was quick to perceive. Nevertheless the State has been the scene of several dramatic strikes.

In the period before 1880, Minnesota experienced about 15 strikes, most of them in the Twin Cities area. The first was in 1854, when journeyman tailors of St. Paul struck for a pay increase. In the last two decades of the century there were 383 strikes, involving 1,663 establishments and about 70,000 workers; 63 percent were initiated by organized labor. The early labor contests were rarely accompanied by violence and bloodshed.

In 1889 occurred the first of the series of long and bitterly contested industrial disputes whose spectacular features were for almost fifty years to attract Nation-wide attention. That year, in Duluth, a conflict involving strikers, pickets, police, and deputized businessmen resulted in the killing of two of the citizens' army, and the wounding of fifty strikers. In the Twin Cities during a street railway strike of the same year, a mob of 10,000 tore up two miles of track and overturned cars. The company's victory on this occasion was a severe blow to labor, and one from which it took long to recover. Workers continued to carry the struggle into many fields, but their successes were few and the concessions won but minor.

By 1900 the open shop principle was so strongly intrenched in Minnesota industry that the succession of employers' victories was practically un-interrupted. This was largely due to the favorable labor market offered by the Twin Cities. Tens of thousands of migratory workers poured through the State every spring and fall. Minneapolis was for years the greatest mi-gratory labor center in the country. Usually there were plenty of workers to be had, and with the decline of the lumbering and milling industries, the supply far exceeded the demand.

In the northern part of the State, on the Iron Range, the thousands of miners in the beginning of the century's second decade began to unite on a common discontent. The famous Iron Range strike of 1916 started with a small group of miners employed by an independent company. Like a forest fire it spread until more than 6,000 strikers and all the employers were involved. Unorganized, often unable to speak any English, the miners rose up in mass protest against the contract system, low wages, the 10-hour day, monthly pay checks, and other grievances. Both sides enlisted rein-forcements. The miners welcomed the Industrial Workers of the World, and the employers deputized an army of about two thousand strikebreakers. In the end three strikers were killed and more than 200 were arrested for the killing of a deputy; six were held and, of these, three were sentenced to a maximum of 20 years imprisonment. Not one of the points for which the miners had struggled was gained, although four separate investigations served to confirm the justice of their demands. Months later, however, the mine owners, headed by the United States Steel Corporation, raised all wages 10 percent.

In Minneapolis and St. Paul the traditional open shop labor principle was militantly maintained until 1934. Then, in May of that year, Local 574 of the Teamsters' Union ordered a strike and promptly paralyzed the truck-ing industry in Minneapolis. Highlight of the strike was the battle in the market district, where between twenty and thirty thousand people watched or participated in what became known as the "Battle of Deputies Run." Pickets, police, and deputized businessmen joined the conflict in which two of the citizens' army were killed and scores of strikers wounded. Com-plaining that no settlement of the larger issues had been attained, truckers struck again in the following July. This time the killing of two pickets and the wounding of 48 brought martial law. Well organized and sup-ported by several farmers' organizations, the union finally achieved a sub-stantial advantage.

Local 544, successor to 574, presents a nominal compromise in the Nation-wide controversy over industrial as against craft unionism. Al-though recognized and chartered by the American Federation of Labor, it retains the character of Local 574 in respect to industrial organization. Among its members are skilled and unskilled workers and a section of the unemployed.

Since 1934 labor disputes have invariably resulted to the advantage of labor. The wage level during prosperity years was below the national average, but now approaches that average.

◄◄◄◄◄◄◄◄◄◄◄◄◄◄◄◄◄◄◄◄◄✿►►►►►►►►►►►►►►►►►►►►►►

Co-operatives

Co-operative ventures in Minnesota sprang mushroom-like from a soil prepared by earlier farmers', consumers', and laborers' societies, yet during the first thirty years or more few survived. The earliest organization to sponsor co-operative buying or selling was the Grange or the Patrons of Husbandry, organized in St. Paul by Oliver H. Kelley in 1868. Crusading for the elimination of the middleman and the right to market its products and manufacture its supplies, this society of farmers lived through the panic of 1873, got into politics, and was victimized by self-seekers. Then, during the later 1880's it began to lose its hold on the farm population. There were at that time no co-operative laws. Organizations were obliged to incorporate, and soon fell victim to their share-control methods.

Between these groups and today's successful associations there was little actual difference; but co-operatives had to learn that their survival depended upon certain methods of management. The fundamentals of procedure, laid down in 1844 by a group of 28 weavers in Rochdale, England, are the groundwork upon which successful co-operatives are functioning in Minnesota and the world over. The Minnesota co-operatives have accepted these principles and succeeded in codifying most of them into the State laws. These principles provide unlimited voluntary membership, democratic control, one vote for each member, no proxies, limited return on capital, selling at market price, profits returned on basis of patronage, cash purchase, federation for wholesaling or production, and allowance for education.

It is to the Iron Range and its Finns that Minnesota owes its first object lesson in modern consumer co-operative procedure. Finns and Danes came to the State already schooled in the methods of co-operatives and convinced of the necessity for united effort. From the beginning of the present century until the provisions of organization were written into State law, they kept alive the ideal of collective economic action.

In 1917 the struggles of the small, independent Finnish storekeepers in the Iron Range and Duluth area became unendurable. Delegates from 15 associations met in Superior, Wisconsin, to start their first wholesale pool. By 1934 this association, now the strongest of co-operative wholesalers, had purchased a $100,000 plant to distribute goods to member associations throughout Minnesota, Wisconsin, and Michigan.

Isolated rural associations, both producer and consumer, had in the meantime realized the necessity of unification and legal protection. Because the need for adjustment between the price of the crops they sold and the cost of the goods they bought was painfully apparent to them, the farmers were early at the front of the co-operative movement.

Once convinced of the value of a producer co-operative for the marketing of products, the adoption of the same method for obtaining supplies was but a short step. Only the mechanics of organization proved a stumbling block. Although co-operative creameries were known in New York in the late 1850's, it was not until 1889 that the first Minnesota association was organized in Biscay in McLeod County, to be followed in 1890 by a more permanent society at Clark's Grove in Freeborn County. This creamery was used as an example by Professor Haecker, university dairy expert, in his long campaign to organize Minnesota dairymen. Little opposition was encountered by these producer organizations; but in 1918 trouble arose when the farmers in the area tributary to the Twin Cities established a regional milk-distributing agency. Twin City consumers, unfamiliar with the organization, obtained an indictment against the officers. In 1919, responding to the producers' appeal for help against this action, the legislature prepared a code of laws to protect farmers' co-operatives and to prevent promoters from entering the field.

The act and its subsequent amendments assigned to the State department of agriculture the duty "to most vigorously, openly, and extensively promote, help, and encourage the co-operative movement." This department provides a free information and advisory bureau and offers help in legal matters, charter writing, and the like to any co-operative group within the State. A separate division of co-operative accounting audits the association's books on a cost basis.

The rapid growth of co-operatives in the State dates from the passage of these laws. Inexperienced organizations, ignorant of the necessity of reserve capital, are prevented by law from using all earnings as patronage returns. Nascent co-operatives over the State found themselves in an improved position and old co-operatives reorganized in accordance with the new laws. All were encouraged to widen their fields of activities and services.

Most spectacular of Minnesota consumer associations and perhaps the best known nationally is the oil-distributing society. The first oil association in the State (said to be the first in the Nation) was organized by a group of farmers at Cottonwood, Minnesota, on July 7, 1921. A year later Owatonna formed a second association and within three years 17 associations were in existence. Typical of these is the Albert Lea co-operative, organized in 1925 with $500 capital. Ten years later the capitalization had been increased by less than $12,000, but the assets totaled $125,000 and members had received $250,000 in dividends. By 1935, the 145 associations in the State had returned to members $500,000 in dividends. One of the four central wholesalers has increased its sales from about $25,000 to almost $2,500,000 in eight years. Co-operative oil sales exceed those of every commercial distributor in the State with the exception of Standard Oil's. In Kanabec County, co-operatives supplied 71 percent of the oil needs of the entire county.

Producer and consumer organizations have preceded the so-called service co-operatives. Many of these have come into existence only within the last 10 years. Fire insurance mutuals have existed in the State since its settlement. Loosely organized, these associations were little more than solicited lists of persons who pledged to share their fellows' losses and paid sums into a common pool for this purpose. Most of the truly co-operative fire insurance mutuals in the State are affiliated in the State Association of Farmers Mutual Insurance. An automobile insurance co-operative has functioned successfully at Lake Elmo for 15 years.

Public utilities co-operatives in the State date from the 1890's when telephone systems were established by farmers in rural regions and small villages. There were (1936) 1,558 rural companies in operation. Of the 80 percent of farm homes with telephone service, 90 percent are supplied by nonprofit firms. However, because of their failure to federate, these companies are at present in some danger of absorption by private interests. Electrical power has been successfully produced on a nonprofit basis at Granite Falls since 1913. Only recently has a central unit, the Federated Electric Co-operative, been incorporated; it is now in a position to plan rural electrification on a wide scale.

Credit unions are very similar to their European prototypes. Minnesota did not have a law defining their organization until 1925 when the Credit Union National Extension Bureau succeeded in arousing enough sponsors to insure the bill's passage. A union was organized that same year by the postal employees, and one year later six associations had total resources of $125,827. In 1935 the total resources were almost $2,500,000. More than 200 associations were in existence in 1936.

Co-operative trucking associations in Minnesota numbered 12 in February 1936, but many co-operatives are actively sponsoring the organization of additional groups. Burial associations have in many cases cut the cost of burials in half. Coal and fuel associations, co-operative bookstores, boarding houses, cafés, dry cleaners, meeting and recreation halls, parks, and newspapers are services which the co-operative-minded believe will lend themselves to successful nonprofit control. At least one association for each of these functions exists in Minnesota. Many of these groups are rapidly increasing their numbers. Many independent societies exist that have no relation to the larger groups, and some overlapping of function seems inevitable until unification is completed.

A 1934–5 survey of Minnesota co-operatives lists 2,866 consumer co-operatives with more than 500,000 members; 1,318 producer co-operatives with 144,000 members; and an annual volume of business for both groups of more than $125,000,000. The increase in membership and volume of business has been so rapid that even approximate totals for 1938 are unavailable.

Education and Religion

THE early priest-explorers left little mark upon the Northwest wilderness. Attracted by the fascination of discovery and the prospect of spiritual conquest, Marquette, Joliet, Hennepin, and their contemporaries made heroic expeditions into a primitive country, evangelizing along the way. The first Christian mission on Minnesota soil, established in 1727 at Fort Beauharnois by Michel Guignas and Nicolas de Gonnor, was as short-lived as the French attempts at settlement in the land of the Sioux and Chippewa. By the time immigrants began to flow into Minnesota territory, nearly all trace of French occupation had disappeared.

When settlement of the Northwest was resumed in the early nineteenth century, missionaries to the Indians and clerics of pioneer white communities often combined the offices of educator and evangelist. Among the Indians, education was a prerequisite of Christianization, since the difficulty of language had first to be overcome and primitive religious concepts replaced by a smattering of the white man's culture. Most zealous of the early missionaries in the teaching of agricultural and domestic arts were the Pond brothers, Samuel and Gideon.

Among the first settlers, the lack of public schools was an incentive for priest or pastor, the natural leader in the community—and often the only person with time for civic pursuits—to fill an educational role. As a result, most of the early schools in Minnesota were church-sponsored. This early alliance between church and school became a prime factor in developing the system of Catholic parochial schools and colleges, and the numerous colleges directed or supported by non-Catholic denominations. Ten percent of the total Minnesota school population attends these private and parochial schools.

<<<<<<<<<<<<<<<<<<<<<<✡>>>>>>>>>>>>>>>>>>>>>>>

Education

The first school in Minnesota was the post school at Fort Snelling, described by Mrs. Ellet on her visit there in 1820. Wives of the commandant and his officers taught the fort children their three R's and polite manners, and an ex-officer of Napoleon's army taught them French. The first school outside the fort was that of the Pond brothers, who, together with the Reverend Jedediah D. Stevens, opened their log school on the west bank of Lake Harriet in 1835. These lay missionaries tutored the Dakota (Sioux) Indians in farming and domestic arts as well as Christianity. Within a year they had devised the "Pond alphabet" of the Sioux language; in 1836 they published a spelling book. A 3,000-word dictionary, translations of Scripture, and a *Grammar and Dictionary of the Dakota Mission,* printed in 1852 by the Smithsonian Institution, were other fruits of their long labors with the Dakotas. The Ponds are said to have spoken the Sioux language better than any other white men.

Four years after the Ponds had begun to educate the Sioux, the first Catholic school was established among the Chippewa at Grand Portage. Not until 1847 did organized education of Minnesota's white children begin. Dr. Thomas S. Williamson, aided by the National Education Society, brought Harriet Bishop from the East that year to teach the 36 St. Paul children who were of school age. The schoolhouse was a log hovel some 10 by 12 feet, covered with bark and chinked with mud, and previously used as a blacksmith shop. Other schools soon followed—the first parochial school for white children, founded in St. Paul in 1851, and numerous missionary and denominational institutions. Poorly financed and prematurely organized, except for those under Catholic control, most of them expired during the panic of 1857.

Among these early ventures were the Baldwin School and the College of St. Paul, founded, respectively, in 1853 and 1854 by the Rev. E. D. Neill, a noted educator, historian, public official, and Presbyterian clergyman. Out of these academies grew Macalester College in St. Paul, a Presbyterian institution.

The oldest college in Minnesota, Hamline University, was founded at Red Wing in 1854 by Methodist sponsors. One of the few schools to survive the 1857 panic, Hamline continued at Red Wing until 1869 when it suspended for lack of finances; eleven years later the institution was relocated at its present site in St. Paul.

Gustavus Adolphus College, founded at Red Wing in 1862 by Erik Norelius, had for its aim "the higher Christian Education for Swedish-American Lutheran youth." In 1876 the college was moved to St. Peter, its present location.

The public school system owes its foundation to the Federal land ordinance of 1785 setting aside one section of each township for the support of the common schools; but when Minnesota became a Territory in 1849 a generous Congress granted two sections in each township for school aid. How valuable these lands were to become Congress could hardly guess, nor did it suspect that the grants in the northern part of the State were to be worth millions in timber and iron.

In 1849, only three centers, Stillwater, St. Paul, and St. Anthony, were sufficiently developed to demand schools; but two years later the second session of the Territorial Legislature took steps toward establishing a State university. In November of the same year the white two-story frame building near Richard Chute Square in St. Anthony was opened to 40 pupils by Principal Elijah W. Merrill, a Methodist minister. In 1858 the university moved to its present site on the east bank of the Mississippi River. From 1860 to 1867 no attempt was made to operate the school, and it was not until after 1868, when preparatory classes were resumed and a new charter was granted by the legislature, that the university began to play a vital role in State affairs. This was the last year that preparatory instruction was offered; in 1869 the university became a full-fledged institution of collegiate rank. The reorganization called for establishment of five or more colleges or departments, election of a new board of regents, and combination of the Congressional grants for an agricultural college and the State university.

Today the University of Minnesota, with more than 14,000 students, ranks high in attendance among the Nation's colleges and is noted for its educational research in several fields. That its board of regents honors academic freedom is attested by the reinstatement (1938) of Dr. William A. Schaper, who suffered dismissal in 1917 after unproved allegations of "pro-Germanism."

The first legislative session of the new State of Minnesota in 1858 provided for a uniform system of public schools to be supported by the sale of school lands, and for three State normal schools—just 20 years after Massachusetts had founded the first normal school in the United States. These schools for teachers were opened at Winona in 1860 (the same year that saw the opening of Minnesota's first high school), Mankato in 1868, St. Cloud in 1869. As the population increased and spread to the north and west, three more normal schools were added—at Moorhead in 1888, Duluth in 1902, and Bemidji in 1919. In 1921 the titles of these schools were changed to State teachers' colleges.

The first report of the superintendent of public schools, for the year 1851, showed only four schools and 250 students. But with the end of the Civil War schools began to open in increasing numbers. The legislatures have consistently passed measures to insure school income from land, timber, and ore royalties, and without prejudice it may be said that State administrators have handled Minnesota's school funds conscientiously and wisely. At the beginning of the fiscal year 1935 these amounted to $64,-550,076.31. It is estimated that iron ore now under lease will add at least $25,000,000, while lands yet to be sold will yield further revenue.

In Minnesota today there are 7,689 school districts. These show the widest variation in their financial resources. Some have sufficient wealth to maintain excellent schools upon a modest tax fee; others can provide only a minimum program; still others cannot maintain even a minimum program without excessive taxation. These inequalities are an outgrowth of the outmoded district school system originally set up by a Territorial act. By this provision districts were organized with no relation either to population or to taxable wealth. In its attempts to aid schools, the legislature has established four funds; an endowment fund, a current school fund, an income tax school fund, and a special State-aid fund. Despite this assistance, only one-fifth of the aid now given is based on need. The present system fails to provide equal opportunities or to equalize the burden of tax support.

It is notable that Minnesota students stay in school for a period longer than the average throughout the United States. More than one-half of the pupils in the Nation fail to complete the eighth grade; only 16 percent drop out of elementary classes in Minnesota. Including the university, teachers' and private schools, and colleges, one person in about every four residing in the State attended school in 1930—a school attendance ratio that places Minnesota fourteenth among the States.

Minnesota was the originator of the program for emergency student aid to assist students in attending college. When the Federal Government inaugurated a similar plan for both university and high school pupils, Minnesota was unique among the States in adopting a program that supplemented Federal assistance by giving additional aid to needy children under the age of sixteen.

The junior college movement has progressed slowly in Minnesota, probably because the State does not subsidize these schools. With nine junior colleges, and an additional two which are church schools, Minnesota ranks sixteenth among the States in the number of such institutions. Those maintained by the public are supported through appropriations from local school funds and by tuition fees, the maximum fee being $100 per year.

In its program for handicapped children, Minnesota has made unusual advances. As early as 1863 the State school for the deaf, dumb, and blind was opened. Today nearly 2 percent of the common-school population is enrolled in special classes for the defective in speech, the mentally subnormal, the blind, the deaf, and the crippled. With the entire administration of the program under State aid and supervision, 8,677 were enrolled in special classes during the school year 1935–36. However, since each of the laws concerning aid for the handicapped, mentally and physically, was separately written, the various types of handicapped children are not equally well cared for. Rural schools do not have enough students to justify classes with special teachers and equipment.

Crippled children are comparatively well cared for, the State providing transportation for each child or living expenses near schools to the extent of seventy cents per day.

The State schools for the blind, the deaf, and the feeble-minded are situated in Faribault and are governed by the State board of control. Schools for crippled children, such as Michael Dowling in Minneapolis, and Lindsay in St. Paul, while not under State direction, are subsidized by the State department of education.

The department of education administers the Federal program of vocational rehabilitation. Thus the schoolboy or girl who is physically handicapped can be prepared specifically for the 2-year Federal training period restricted to those over sixteen. The rehabilitation division of the State department of education aims also to place all physically handicapped persons in remunerative positions.

Music and art are taught in most schools in the State. In high schools, four courses in music and one in art are commonly offered. In the larger high schools, universities, and colleges, facilities for advanced study are available to talented students. According to a recent survey, however, the offering of music in Minnesota schools is smaller than in many other States. The larger schools, paradoxically, tend to have less musical activity than the smaller, perhaps because of heavier extra-curricular programs.

The development of opportunity for education has not been an orderly process in Minnesota. The early 1900's found a complete and unified system of schools in the thickly populated sections, but too often merely a one-room log school in the sparsely settled northern portion.

In 1937 there were 23 school districts in Lake of the Woods County (the most northerly part of the United States); only 16 of these qualified for State aid. In the same year the school at Penasse was held in a 14- by 16-foot log building, whose plastered interior alone made it distinguishable from the St. Paul smithy where Miss Bishop taught in 1847.

At present one Indian boarding school for institutional cases, with an enrollment of 300, is maintained at Pipestone by the Bureau of Indian Affairs. All other Indian pupils attend the public and reservation schools; funds for their education, which in 1936–37 amounted to $82,900, are derived from tribal funds and State equalization funds.

The State has two folk schools, both Danish, one at Askov and the other at Tyler.

◄◄◄◄◄◄◄◄◄◄◄◄◄◄◄◄◄◄◄✹►►►►►►►►►►►►►►►►►►►

Religion

The efforts of early missionaries to proselyte Minnesota Indians were largely unproductive. They were hampered by the difficulty of language, the Indians' primitive religious concepts, the uninspiring example of white traders, and a general mismanagement of Indian affairs by the Government.

The Protestant missionary felt obliged to give the Indian a book religion; consequently he had to begin by studying their speech and creating a written language, or, more rarely, by acquainting his prospective converts with English. Boutwell and Ayer, the first Protestant missionaries to the Chippewa, collaborated on a Chippewa grammar and on translations of the Bible, but Ayer's mission, like many others that followed, was soon abandoned. Another Presbyterian, Dr. Thomas S. Williamson, established a Sioux mission at Lac qui Parle in 1835, the same year that a Catholic mission was opened among the Chippewa of the Lake Superior region. Mission societies began to send their emissaries to Minnesota in 1836. Grand Portage acquired a Catholic mission and Fort Snelling an Episcopal chaplain in 1838. In 1841 Father Galtier built the first permanent Catholic church in the territory, the Chapel of St. Paul, from which the city takes its name. Father Augustine Ravoux, who succeeded Galtier late in 1841, built churches in Mendota and St. Anthony. Between 1845 and 1848 Episcopal missions were established in St. Paul, Stillwater, and Red Wing, and, about 1850, Episcopal activities were extended to the Chippewa.

A slave, James Thompson, purchased and freed by the Rev. Alfred Brunson, a Methodist minister, helped erect the first Methodist Church in St. Paul, which was also the first Protestant church in the State. The ex-slave became one of the church's first members.

The first immigrants in the great influx of the fifties were largely Irish and German Catholics, and by 1851 the Catholic population had so increased that St. Paul was made the seat of a bishopric. The Right Reverend Joseph Cretin was appointed first bishop of Minnesota and a rapid expansion of Catholic activities followed. Schools were opened in St. Paul and St. Anthony in 1851 by the Sisters of St. Joseph. The first hospital in the State, St. Joseph's, was opened in St. Paul in 1854; the foundation for St. John's University, near St. Cloud, was laid by the Benedictine order in 1857.

When the Upper Sioux were removed to their reservations on the Minnesota River after 1851, all their mission stations—Red Wing, Kaposia, Oak Grove, and Prairieville—were abandoned, and with the exception of Dr. Williamson, who was transferred to a new station among the Wahpeton near the Yellow Medicine Agency, the clerical missionaries remained as pastors of local white congregations.

Organized evangelism by the Methodist Episcopal Church and by Swedish Lutherans began in the early 1850's. The story of their early religious activities is one of haphazard meeting places and lay preachers, of persistent but usually unsuccessful attempts to obtain ordained ministers, and of intense competition among the various sects—often within a single church. This competitive spirit, at first a stimulus to the pastors, resulted ultimately in the over-building of church structures and the division of members into small congregations.

First on the scene, the Methodists made a determined but only partially successful attempt to enroll the Scandinavians, who began to settle in Minnesota in the early 1850's. The circuit riders and their camp meetings and revivals offered welcome interludes in pioneer life. Perhaps the most famous of these riders was John Dyer, who was appointed to the Caledonia Circuit Mission in 1857 and later was transferred to the Austin Circuit. "Brother" Dyer, according to an early account, "had hard going in a godless, drunken region," though for the most part people were not then surfeited with sermons.

Among the oldest Swedish settlements in Minnesota is Vasa, still a Swedish stronghold. Erik Norelius organized Lutheran congregations at Vasa and at nearby Red Wing in 1855. Followed by a few constituents from Indiana, he took personal charge of them in 1856, supplanting the lay leader, Col. Hans Mattson. Norelius became both a religious and a political power. Among other accomplishments, he started the *Minnesota Posten,* the State's first Swedish paper, founded an orphanage, started a private school which was the nucleus of Gustavus Adolphus College, and rose to leadership in the Minnesota Conference and the Augustana Synod.

Originally directed from Illinois, Swedish Lutherans gained a measure of independence by the formation of the Minnesota Conference in 1858 at Chisago City. In 1860 the Swedish Lutherans of Minnesota and other States established their own church authority, the Scandinavian Evangelical Lutheran Augustana Synod of North America. Between 1854 and 1884 there was little co-operation among them, and their churches multiplied alarmingly in poverty-stricken frontier settlements.

The Swedish settlers began to establish parochial schools in the 1860's, but it fell to the Methodists to found Minnesota's first college, Hamline, which opened its doors at Red Wing in 1854. The Protestants' effort to establish a permanent parochial school system, however, was relatively unsuccessful.

The Protestant Episcopal Church was headed by Henry Benjamin Whipple, who became the first Minnesota bishop in 1859. Whipple lived at Faribault, where Episcopal schools were established during the next decade. After the Sioux uprising in 1862, Whipple was said to be the only man in public life who dared oppose wholesale executions of the Sioux captives. His representations to Abraham Lincoln, in which he laid much of the responsibility for the outbreak on mistaken Government policy, are said to have influenced the President to investigate and finally commute the sentences of all but 39.

The Rev. Lars J. Hauge, a Baptist, led a group of Danes to Freeborn

County in 1862. Hauge, a dairying enthusiast, had a hand in the organization of the first permanent co-operative creamery in Minnesota, started at Clark's Grove in 1890.

Both Swedes and Norwegians, accustomed to a state church, were slow and haphazard in organizing church bodies in the New World. Later, especially among the Norwegians, many synods were formed, and not until 1917 did Minnesota Norsemen merge three synods to form the Norwegian-Lutheran Church of America, now second to the Roman Catholic in church membership in Minnesota.

Religious instruction was a characteristic activity among pioneer Norwegian congregations. At first the weekday and vacation schools were conducted in various private homes. Weekday schools were held during the winter when no public schools existed; summer vacation schools generally extended over a two-month period. Sunday schools in nearly all congregations, and parochial schools in several, were a later addition.

In the early Norwegian communities, life revolved about the church and the pastor. His word was law in spiritual matters and hardly less authoritative in civil affairs. An early reminiscence states, "We were Lutherans, so there were no parties. Going to church was our only amusement."

At the time Minnesota Territory was established in 1849, English and French were the common languages, and both religious services and civil business were carried on in those tongues. The new immigrants, however, included Irish, Germans, Bohemians, Poles, Italians, Hungarians, Belgians, Rumanians, Scandinavians, Czechoslovakians, Icelanders, Greeks, Russians, and lastly Finns and Mexicans; and soon after their arrival churches were organized to conduct services in their respective languages. But with Americanization of these groups and the cessation of immigration the practice of holding services in a foreign language has steadily declined.

At the beginning of 1850 there were few churches in Minnesota. In 1870 there were 877 organized churches and 582 church edifices. By 1900 the number of churches had increased to 4,000, but, owing to improved transportation facilities, economic factors, and the shifting of residential districts in the cities, some consolidation of parishes has occurred. The result has been, that with a noticeable increase in population since 1900, the number of churches remains about the same.

An amendment to the State constitution in 1877, prohibiting religious instruction in the public schools, served to increase the number of parish schools in the State and caused many a taxpayer to groan under the double burden. Faribault Catholics exploded an educational bombshell by announcing, just before the beginning of the school year 1891, that the

Faribault parochial school would not reopen. Lacking facilities for the 150 parochial pupils, public school officials, much as the Catholics had expected, accepted the suggestion that the parochial school be rented to the school board for one dollar per year. Three nuns remained as teachers, but the city superintendent had full jurisdiction and no religious instruction was allowed during regular school hours. Modeled after experiments in other cities, notably Poughkeepsie, the plan had the support of the highest Catholic authorities. Wide publicity given the experiment stimulated a similar effort at Stillwater, where the opening of the school year had been delayed by an epidemic, but after concerted opposition by Protestant ministers, particularly in Minneapolis, the plan was discontinued by common consent. The Faribault alliance was disapproved by the annual Faribault school meeting in 1892, and the system was abandoned in 1893 when Catholics objected to the replacement of two nuns by public school teachers.

In 1923 an amendment to the compulsory education law permitted children to be excused from public schools for not more than 3 hours a week to attend church-maintained religious schools.

Since 1925 Minnesota has been a center of the Liturgical Movement in the Catholic Church, owing to the efforts of the Benedictines of St. John's Abbey at Collegeville and of priests at St. Thomas College and St. Paul Seminary. The movement aims to revive the communal spirit of the early Roman Church, substituting for a formalized choir a communal rendition of hymns and responses. It has been extensively publicized and promoted by periodicals, books, and pamphlets published by priests and laymen in these localities.

The anti-evolution controversy of the 1920's, which attained its height in Tennessee's Scopes case, also had its legislative counterpart in Minnesota. W. B. Riley, a Baptist pastor who had engaged in a long controversy with university officials and had denounced evolutionary teachings, particularly at the university and at Carleton College, headed a group of Fundamentalists who sponsored an anti-evolution measure in the legislature in February 1927. The introduction of the bill was the signal for concerted agitation, pro and con, by ministers, educators, students, and laymen. University students, whose casual reaction to a series of lectures by the Rev. W. B. Riley had been that the speaker was "a very nice looking man," turned out five thousand strong at a mass meeting and affixed five thousand names to a protest petition. After a preliminary hearing, the Minnesota Senate laid the "Monkey Bill" effectively to rest by a vote of 55 to 7.

Press and Radio

CLOSE on the heels of western settlement came the printers. From the often crowded and highly competitive centers of the East they followed the opening of new lands, tempted by the opportunities offered in the printing of official documents and the tracts and translations the missionaries demanded. Some hoped to establish a medium of expression for their political convictions. Still others were brought by land companies to help boom their chosen sites.

No sooner did it appear that Minnesota was to achieve territorial status than two firms in Ohio and a publisher in Wisconsin almost simultaneously decided to seize upon the first fruits of the new Territory's office printing, and to establish its first newspaper. The earliest to arrive, bringing his press by boat, was James M. Goodhue, publisher of the *Grant County Herald* at Lancaster, Wisconsin, who landed in St. Paul four weeks before Congress welcomed Minnesota as a Territory. Undaunted by his lack of subscribers, pledges, or political acquaintances, he issued the first copy of the *Minnesota Pioneer* on April 28, 1849. His slogan exhorted readers to "put our trust in the people, not in princes." A graduate of Amherst College, where he seems to have been a conspicuous leader in undergraduate fights and pranks, Goodhue was successively schoolteacher, lawyer, and farmer. In Lancaster he took up law for the second time, but soon decided to renounce its practice and to buy the local newspaper. In St. Paul he set up his primitive press in a building of which he said, "Open as a corn rick . . . not that we would find fault with the pigs for it is all owing to their bringing up; but really our equanimity is somewhat ruffled if our chair is not jostled by the movements of their hard backs under our loose floor." But Goodhue was compelled to overcome greater handicaps than a drafty office. His hand press was capable of only 225 impressions an hour, the closest type foundry was at Chicago, paper and ink were even farther distant, and all mechanical equipment had to be hauled in summer, since overland freight in the winter months was both uncertain and prohibitive in price. He delivered his papers himself, noting on his route each new development in the growing town, and recording it in the next issue. He lived only three years after his arrival—not long enough to see the *Minnesota Pioneer* become the Territory's first daily newspaper—but in that short period he saw his little weekly gain steadily in influence, while his caustic editorials and trenchant comments on local and national politics won for him a fame that still endures.

His Ohio rivals refused to grant him the credit of publishing the Territory's first newspaper although they had to acknowledge him its first resident editor. The *Minnesota Register*, published in Cincinnati, was rushed to St. Paul and, when unwrapped, copies were found to be dated both as of April 7, and of April 27, 1849—both earlier than the *Pioneer's* first issue on April 28—but there is some doubt about their having actually appeared on the dates claimed. Nevertheless they carried the proud boast: "We have to congratulate ourselves on being the first to undertake the establishment of a paper in the new territory of Minnesota." Not until July 14 did the *Minnesota Register* actually print copies in Minnesota, and before then another Ohioan had reached St. Paul, issuing the *Minnesota Chronicle* on May 31. The following August these Ohio papers, both Whig in their affiliations, combined as the *Minnesota Chronicle and Register*.

The next printing concern to enter the region was motivated by an impulse far removed from the economic one. Its press arrived in 1849 at Cass Lake, and was paid for by students of Oberlin College and Ohio Sunday schools, who sent it to the Reverend Alonzo Barnes for his Chippewa Indian mission. The religious material it turned out was printed in both Ojibway and English. The *Dakota Friend,* edited by the Indian missionary Gideon Pond, was issued in St. Paul in 1850, and performed a similar service for the Christian Sioux.

Two years after the birth of the first newspaper, the *St. Anthony Express* appeared at St. Anthony Falls piloted by Elmer Tyler, a tailor, and Isaac

Atwater, an attorney, both ardent Whig partisans. To oppose the *Express* came the *Northwestern Democrat,* founded in 1853, which moved the next year to the west side of the river, and, under J. B. Bassett's direction, espoused the then new and radical cause of Republicanism. Later it merged with the *State Atlas* of William S. King, the Congressman, State fair manager, cattle-fancier, and publisher, who is said to have put Minneapolis journalism on a permanent, paying basis. Out of the *Atlas* evolved the present Minneapolis *Tribune.*

The first decade in the history of Minnesota's newspapers brought them great hardships. Not only were there mechanical difficulties to be overcome, but news from the outside world was scanty, the post uncertain, and the returns were small. Nevertheless during these 10 years, 90 papers were founded, and although most of these were short-lived, 12 pioneer papers have survived to the present day. (They are The St. Paul *Pioneer Press,* 1849; the *Minnehaha,* 1855; the Winona *Republican Herald,* 1855; the Chatfield *News,* 1856; the Hastings *Gazette,* 1856; the Hokah *Chief,* 1856; the Stillwater *Post-Messenger,* 1856; the Mantorville *Express,* 1857; the Monticello *Times,* 1857; the Red Wing *Republican,* 1857; the St. Cloud *Daily Times and Daily Journal-Press,* 1857; and the *Wabasha County Herald-Standard,* 1857.)

The opening of land in the early fifties brought thousands of settlers, and a new town was scarcely platted before it could boast its own news sheet. Many served as advertising prospectuses for attracting settlers, and thousands of copies were mailed to the eastern States and to Europe. In the years 1854–56 papers were founded in settlements as widely scattered as Winona, Stillwater on the St. Croix, Shakopee and St. Peter on the Minnesota, Sauk Rapids on the upper Mississippi, and on the lower river, Red Wing, Wabasha, and Brownsville.

It was also during the fifties that a number of Minnesota's most renowned editors came to the Northwest. Earle S. Goodrich, often called "the gentleman journalist of Minnesota," arrived in 1854 to edit the Goodhue paper, that year grown to a daily. Sam K. Whiting, an arctic explorer and adventurer, came in the same year to edit the Winona *Argus* and later to establish the Winona *Republican.* In 1856 Ignatius Donnelly left Pennsylvania to plat his city of Nininger and founded the *Emigrant Aid Journal* to help him in building and promotion. The following year Jane Grey Swisshelm, Minnesota's most famous newspaper woman and one of its most colorful personalities, left her *Saturday Visiter* in Pittsburgh to start a paper by the same name in St. Cloud. In that decade, too, came

Joseph Wheelock, later of the *Pioneer Press,* who for fifty years was to be the acknowledged dean of Minnesota journalists.

The weeklies of the fifties and sixties were pretty nearly the only contact between settlers and the outside world. True he did not depend wholly on his local papers. In 1856 the new State was sending almost three thousand subscriptions to the New York *Tribune*—more than any local paper could boast. But it was to the local papers that he looked for legal and government information, local business news, and the doggerel verse that passed as poetry. Occasionally these papers carried really good literature. Local news might be meager enough but political and other national news appeared, rewritten from eastern papers and freely commented upon by the editor. There was little competition from periodicals, and the large amount of space given over to magazine material furnished reading matter for the entire family.

Even the early Territorial days had a few foreign-language papers, and their number increased steadily with the great tides of immigration. First of these were the German, led by the *Minnesota Deutsche Zeitung* of St. Paul. The Norwegian *Folkets Röst* and the Swedish *Minnesota Posten* followed in 1857, the latter under the well-known church leader, Erik Norelius *(see EDUCATION AND RELIGION).* Col. Hans Mattson's *Minnesota Stats Tidning* of 1877 exerted a powerful influence on Swedish culture in Minnesota. Like many other foreign-language publications, the *Stats Tidning* was devoted to matters of church interest and to the causes of reform and temperance. Still larger in scope was the *Svenska Amerikanska Posten,* established on a permanent basis in 1885, and which boasted, under its editor, Swan J. Turnblad, the largest paid circulation of any Swedish periodical in the United States. Prominent among Norwegian publications was the Minneapolis *Tidende,* successor to *Emigranten,* and the first Norwegian newspaper in the United States to attain any degree of permanence. Minnesota's only French newspaper was *L'Echo de l'Ouest.* From its birth in 1883 to its demise some 45 years later *L'Echo* played a major part in preserving the French language and French traditions in the Northwest. Today there are 24 foreign-language papers in the State: 10 German, 4 Finnish, 4 Norwegian, 3 Swedish, 2 Danish, and 1 Polish.

Negro newspapers, dating back at least as far as 1885, have always played a vital part in shaping public opinion within the group. At present there are three Negro weeklies in the State, the Minneapolis *Spokesman,* Twin City *Herald,* and St. Paul *Recorder.*

In the seventies it began to be obvious that a marked change in the character of many country papers was taking place. Ready-print and boiler-plate had appeared, and by 1880 all papers were using non-shopset material for their foreign, national, and State news. The growth of the metropolitan dailies served further to lessen the significance of local editorial comment, and more and more the country editor curtailed his contributions on large issues and confined himself to local happenings. With the passing of the ready-made columns, after the turn of the century, news of a foreign nature was given still less importance, until by 1929 it occupied less than 5 percent of the news space. At the same time magazine material (which in the last half of the past century had filled 40 percent of the weekly) was in its turn steadily displaced as libraries, periodicals, and metropolitan dailies extended their circulations and supplied more and more successfully the people's reading requirements. Despite these changes in the country newspaper, many characteristics have remained surprisingly constant. All of them still attempt urban daily make-up, and divide their space about equally between advertising and news, a general practice since 1860.

From the land exploitation and violent political partisanship of pioneer days, Minnesota papers turned to merchandising and other services to emerge at last in their present form. However naïve and quaint seem the news sheets of the past when compared with the urban dailies today, it is necessary to consider the wide influence and varied interests of the pioneer newsmen. Among the State's early editors were Erik Norelius, father of Gustavus Adolphus College; Isaac Atwater, judge of Minnesota's supreme court; and Russell Conwell, who left his paper, after having been instrumental in organizing the Minnesota Editors' Association, to found Temple University in Philadelphia and later to help 3,000 young men through school.

Since 1900 the story has differed little from that in other States, but the Northwest witnessed in that time one large-scale venture in journalism. In 1918 A. C. Townley established the Northwest Service Bureau in the interests of the Non-Partisan League, and for a time operated the 36 papers to which it supplied machinery, personnel, and selected news. The central news bureau gradually dissolved, however, and most of its papers were absorbed or discontinued. Largest of these organs was the *Minnesota Daily Star,* founded in 1920, and, as the Minneapolis *Star,* taken over by a conservative management in 1935.

In 1937 the newspapers in Minnesota numbered about 500, of which 8 were metropolitan dailies, 26 smaller dailies, the remainder weekly and monthly sheets. Of the metropolitan papers, six are in the Twin Cities: the

Minneapolis *Tribune, Star,* and *Journal;* and the St. Paul *Pioneer Press, Dispatch,* and *News.* In Duluth the *Herald* and the *News-Tribune* share the field. Of the five hundred, more than 125 have passed the half-century mark, and 12 have celebrated their diamond jubilee—a remarkable record in view of Minnesota's youth, and of the fact that in the entire country only about 160 had passed the century mark at the time of the study.

Most significant of all recent journalistic events occurred on July 1, 1931. The United States Supreme Court ruled that the Minnesota newspaper suppression law was unconstitutional. The court held that libel laws gave sufficient protection to persons attacked, and hence it was unnecessary to suppress the publication in which the attack was printed.

In the last two decades radio has become an important supplement to newspapers as a medium for disseminating information and entertainment. In 1936 there were 15 broadcasting stations in the State, 13 commercial (1 with television equipment) and 2 educational stations.

Although it is not the first radio station in the State, WCAL, St. Olaf College, is the oldest still operating under its original call letters. Established in Northfield in 1921, WCAL since its inception has broadcast a variety of educational, religious, and musical programs. The other institutional station is the University of Minnesota's WLB, which broadcasts courses by professors and others in cultural subjects such as music appreciation (in which it was a pioneer) and foreign languages, in addition to agricultural programs by experts of the university's farm school.

In November 1922, two Minneapolis newspapers rushed on the air in a furor of competition; the *Tribune* with station WAAL, the *Journal* by arrangement with a local experimental station. The St. Paul *Pioneer Press* entered the commercial field about the same time, but a surplus of expenses over income impelled the three dailies to retire in favor of the 500-watt Western Electric transmitter WLAG. The latter was succeeded after two years by WCCO, present outlet for the Columbia Broadcasting System. Among other early Twin City stations were WDGY, a small commercial unit, and KSTP, member of the National Broadcasting Company's Red Network.

It is interesting to note that today, some 14 or 15 years after their original venture, the newspapers are back on the air, the *Tribune* and *Pioneer Press* with their own station WTCN (an outlet for NBC's Blue Network), the *Journal,* in alliance with KSTP, and the *Star* affiliated with WCCO.

Six of Minnesota's radio stations are now in the Twin Cities, leaving nine distributed in Duluth, Virginia, Moorhead, Rochester, and other of the larger towns.

Sports and Recreation

LONG before the turn of the century, Minnesota had achieved a reputation as a summer haven. Before the Civil War, southern planters with their slaves came up the Mississippi to vacation at St. Paul or St. Anthony. By 1880 they were going to fashionable Lake Minnetonka (*see Tour 10*), to Lake Elmo, Prior Lake, the Dalles of the St. Croix, St. Croix Lake, or Frontenac. In 1886 citizens of St. Paul braved frigid temperatures to see its first Ice Palace and Winter Carnival. The climate was advertised during the eighties as a cure for tuberculosis.

The land of sky-colored waters has been celebrated in many a song and story, from Longfellow's *Hiawatha* to the fabulous tales of Paul Bunyan. Surprisingly, its title, "The Land of Ten Thousand Lakes," is no exaggeration, for more than eleven thousand lakes and as many rivers and streams comprise one-fourteenth of the total area of the State—an expanse of 3,607,680 acres. These waters drain into three great watersheds; north to the Red River and Hudson Bay, east to Lake Superior and the Atlantic Ocean, and south to the Gulf of Mexico via the Mississippi River. The remains of a vast primeval forest still blanket a large area; in the southeastern section a belt of hardwood—oak, maple, elm, and birch—and in the northern half, the conifers—mostly second-growth, with here and there a stand of virgin pine. The Nation's largest wilderness park lies within the

Superior National Forest; some of the State's most interesting historical sites are within the boundaries of the Chippewa National Forest.

From its southeastern tip to the famous Arrowhead District, the State affords recreation of almost every kind. Approximately twelve hundred lakeside resorts—many of them in the heart of the wilderness—and innumerable cabins, tourist camps, and camp sites are provided for the traveler. More than two million tourists come to Minnesota each year to fish, hunt, swim, or sail in the summertime, or for skating and skiing in the winter.

Minnesota's lakes and streams are well stocked with fresh-water fish. Brook trout are plentiful in the cold streams that tumble into Lake Superior on the North Shore; in the numerous creeks farther west that surround Itasca Park *(see Tour 2)*, Walker, Park Rapids, and Detroit Lakes; in central Minnesota near Alexandria, Osakis, and Long Prairie; near the Wisconsin boundary in the streams that feed the St. Croix; and to the south in Whitewater State Park. The St. Croix is famous for its small-mouth bass; Lake of the Woods (especially the Canadian side) and the Mantrap chain near Park Rapids claim the rarer muskellunge. Wall-eyes abound in the central and northern regions, and large-mouth bass, northern pike or pickerel, and panfish may be taken almost anywhere. The much-prized lake trout inhabit the deep, cold waters of Lake Superior and the lakes along the Canadian border. Fourteen State fish hatcheries, seven in year-round operation, produce fish fry and fingerlings that run annually into hundreds of millions.

The Arrowhead region offers many inducements to the recreation-seeking tourist, not the least of which is fishing. In numerous lakes—to mention only Vermilion *(see Tour 8)*, Burntside, and Basswood—bass, pike, trout, and landlocked salmon are plentiful. Lakes along the international boundary, although difficult of access, reward the visitor with catches, the tales of which his friends find scarcely credible.

The hardy canoeist can traverse the entire length of Minnesota waters from south to north and rarely have to portage his craft. Setting out at the southeastern tip, the modern *voyageur* follows the eastern boundary on the Mississippi and passes Winona and its famous Sugar Loaf Mountain. At Hastings, after a widening of the river called Lake Pepin, he can either head up the St. Croix and by short portages reach Lake Superior, or swing northwest to the Twin Cities. The canoeist can follow the Minnesota River south, then northwest through Lac qui Parle and Big Stone Lake to the Red River; from the Red River the adventurer can paddle through many wilderness miles to Hudson Bay (as two Minneapolis youths once did). Due north from the Twin Cities the Mississippi winds upward to Brainerd, the adopted land of the mythical Paul Bunyan. Beyond lie many lakes—among them Gull, Winnibigoshish, and Cass. From the tip of Lake Bemidji, the Mississippi (here but a small and winding stream) bends southward to Itasca State Park within whose lake-spotted boundaries the Father of Waters has its source. Despite the insistence of scientists, popular legend maintains that the real source was none other than Babe, Paul Bunyan's Blue Ox, who inadvertently capsized a water tank and started the long flow of waters to the Gulf.

To the north and east, in the Superior National Forest and the adjoining Canadian territory, the Quetico Reserve is the continent's most concentrated canoe area. Shaped by glacial invasions, which gouged long, narrow depressions in its surface and then melted into them, the Arrowhead is a wonderland of water and virgin forest, a labyrinth of lakes and streams. Especially in the area north of Lake Superior, between Rainy Lake on the west, and Grand Portage on the east, the lakes and streams open one into another except for occasional short portages that are welcome variations in the paddler's day. In the countries of this region are 2,272 meandered lakes, many thousands still unsurveyed; of Superior National Forest's 1,713,610 acres, one-fifth are covered by water *(see SUPERIOR NATIONAL FOREST and CANOE TRIPS).*

The Chippewa National Forest *(see Tour 7)*, which covers much of Itasca County and juts on the northeast into Beltrami and on the south into Cass, is another protected playground of lakes and woods.

Less rugged than the national forests, though scarcely less inviting, are the regions in the vicinity of such towns as Detroit Lakes, Park Rapids, Alexandria, Brainerd, Bemidji, and many others. Itasca State Park, third largest in the country, contains the most extensive area of virgin Norway pine left standing in the United States and is Minnesota's most frequented State park.

The lakes to which Minnesota owes its recreational renown range in size from tiny unnamed ponds to Red Lake, which covers 274,994 acres and is the largest fresh-water body within a single State. Although Lake of the Woods, part of which lies within Canada, has more than 200 square miles of surface, its fourteen thousand islands assure an almost constant sight of land from every point. Mille Lacs *(see Tour 3)*, only 100 miles north of the Twin Cities, is the third largest lake in Minnesota; duckhunters as well as fishermen frequent its numerous cabins and resorts. Other lakes that have an area of more than 10,000 acres are Leech, Winnibigoshish, Vermilion, Kabetogama, Cass, Gull, two of the Pelicans, Lake Pepin and Rainy Lake.

A glance at the names of Minnesota's meandered lakes reveals a disappointing lack of originality. For every Minnetonka there are 99 Longs; for each Elkhorn, 91 Muds, and 76 Rices. The poetic settlers who christened Albion, Sylvan, Elysian, and Alpine were greatly outnumbered by the realists who named Little Dead Horse, Full of Fish, Dirty Nose, Big Spunk, Pug-Hole, Split Hand, and Skunk. Inexplicable indeed is the whim which started the series that goes One, Two, Three, and up, and then began another list with First, Second, Third, Fourth, Fifth . . . More than a hundred names are repeated five times or more, and over a thousand meandered lakes have no official names at all. Scandinavian names such as Big Ole, Peterson, Nelson, Olson, Kolstad, Swede, and Knutson one expects to find, but they are not much more frequent than are the Irish names —O'Leary, O'Brien, Murphy, Kelly, and Ryan. Indicative of the State's diverse racial character are—Moses, Cameron, Davis, Gould, Wagner, Doerfler, Selinsky, Knaus, and Heikkila. Many couples appear, like John and Isabella, and Jacob and Annie, while close to Terry are Anna, Mary, Emily, and Ruth. The anatomist would be interested in Bladder, Foot, Elbow, and Hand; but Coffin, Grave, and Devil strike a more ominous note. A single county has all these: Kettle, Spider, Spoon, Cup, Knife, Pickle, Plum, Rabbit, Deer, Duck, Rice, Partridge, Pike, Pickerel, Bass, Fire, Fry, and, happily, a Cook; Spring, Turtle, Goose, and Silver are pleasant, but too oft repeated; Rum, Whiskey, and Bootleg suggest a thirst quite out of line with the waters to which they are applied. Difficult indeed for the inexperienced are No-To-She-Bun, Kabetogama, Winnibigoshish, Kabetona, and Ogish-Ke-Muncie, but once conquered they charm the visitor who delights in originality.

Minnesota was once a mecca for eastern magnates and sportsmen, who came in luxurious special trains to slaughter partridge and prairie chicken. Then, with the retreat of the forest, the amount and variety of wild game inevitably diminished. The white-tailed deer, however, are still plentiful in the north country and may be shot every other year; the hardy ring-necked pheasant, introduced to replace the partridge and prairie chicken, ranges over all but the most northern areas and withstands a formidable annual cannonading. Migratory game are subject to many protective restrictions. Squirrels and rabbits, though numerous, are not particularly popular with Minnesota hunters. (See GENERAL INFORMATION.)

Facilities for other sports besides hunting, fishing, and canoeing are also available everywhere in the State. There are more than 260 golf courses scattered over Minnesota. Golf, it is said, takes on added zest when the fairways wind along the shores of a northern lake and clusters of virgin pine form a backdrop for the greens. Minnesota resorts stage numerous summer tournaments. If experts are welcome, so is the duffer; many of the meets encourage a huge entry list and offer generous prizes.

Those interested in riding and in horse shows concentrate their activities chiefly near the Twin Cities—at Fort Snelling (horse-show and polo center), at the State Fair, and at private clubs—although several scattered resorts have horses for hire and maintain bridle paths and trails.

For a region with so many lakes and rivers it is surprising to find that only in the vicinity of the Twin Cities are yacht races popular, but outboard motorists find ample facilities throughout the State.

Archery clubs have been established in several cities and their number is growing rapidly. Not only do they stage local and State tournaments, but many archers hunt deer, rabbits, and other game with bow and arrow.

When Lewis Rober, a member of the Minneapolis Fire Department, introduced the "Kitten League Game" to fellow firemen in 1893, no one imagined it might become the recreational park's most popular sport for people of all ages. Yet today diamondball, or softball, as it is often called, is played throughout the State and other States as well; many cities and clubs stage tournaments, and in several places the players enjoy floodlighted enclosed fields.

Minnesota utilizes several months of freezing temperatures each year, to make its hills and lakes a winter sports center. As early as 1886, St. Paul celebrated the first of several winter carnivals by building a mammoth ice palace 106 feet high. For several years this annual fete was repeated, nationally advertised, and well attended. But interest flagged and it was not until the winter of 1937 that the carnival was revived as an annual event.

The Scandinavians, who swept into Minnesota on the tide of westward immigration, soon introduced the winter sports of their homeland. On home-made skis they flew over snow-packed hills, scudded over the deep drifts of midwinter, or planed behind their horses in their popular *skikjöring*. Early in the 1880's the country's first ski-jumping clubs were organized in Minneapolis and Red Wing, and soon others were established in nearby towns. Eight of them in 1893 formed the Skiing Association of the Northwest, an organization that perished only when two capricious winters passed without abundant snowfall. Today Minnesota is one of the ski capitals of the United States. Ski jumps and cross country races are held throughout the State, and slides of championship size have been erected at Bush Lake *(see Tour 14)* and in Red Wing.

Even more popular is ice skating. Lakes and artificial rinks are crowded from December to February. Since the days of the fabulous John S. Johnson, speed-skating champion during the 1890's (and world's champion bicycle racer as well), the Twin Cities have developed a long list of champion skaters. A well-known figure-skating center, the Twin Cities are hosts to annual exhibitions and competitive meets and contribute many skilled performers to the figure-skating troupes that barnstorm the country. Numerous hockey rinks, many of them lighted for night play, are used by hundreds of teams. An annual State hockey tournament is held in Minneapolis.

The winter sports season has its climax in ice carnivals and officially declared "Winter Sports Weeks," in which thousands participate and compete in skiing, skating, ice hockey, ice boating, log rolling, curling, tobogganing, snow modeling, dog derbies, costume parades, and bobsled and sleighing parties.

The Arts

WHEN the white man first came to Minnesota, sophisticated criticism had not yet discovered primitive art. The pictographs of the Indians, the weird rhythms of their music and dancing, the sculptural modeling of their pottery, the poetry of their folklore—all these the explorers and traders regarded merely as "curiosities," of value chiefly as color for their travelers' tales. For the best examples of this native art one must visit the museums. Contact with the white man has been disastrous to the culture as well as to the physical well-being of Minnesota's Indians. At Pipestone the tourist will look in vain for the beautiful carving with which they used to ornament their famous pipes; no longer are rocky caves being decorated with their drawings. In music alone the Chippewa still preserve and express their racial spirit.

The settlers in Minnesota, like other pioneers the world over, had neither leisure nor impulse for a conscious art. But even in a menacing wilderness the universal urge to express in written words the day's experiences or to sing with one's neighbor impelled many to record their adventures by fire or candlelight, and to travel many trackless miles to sing the familiar tunes or to listen to the nostalgic notes of an old fiddle. Thus Minnesota's first literature was largely in the form of diaries and autobiographies, its first music that of "singing schools" and village fiddlers.

Despite the general impression that the Midwest has until recently been almost a barren desert in the world of culture, the truth is that no section of the country has had a more earnest desire for cultural facilities, or shown a more rapid development in the appreciation and expression of art. The artistic taste of those early Minnesotans may be questioned, but their abiding faith in the necessity for mental and spiritual food was obvious from the first. Credit for this faith must be given largely to New England, where the importance of culture was early recognized as second only to that of church-going.

At the time of the first migration of easterners into the Northwest, the "golden age" of New England culture was just beginning. Minnesota's settlers as a whole could have taken little part in this renaissance or they would never have come so far away from the springs of enlightenment. Henry Thoreau hurled blasts of scorn on covered-wagon New Englanders who turned their backs on their intellectual opportunities "to escape more than rocks." Nevertheless they brought with them the culture-respecting traditions with which they had been surrounded and these have colored the State ever since. No sooner was settlement well under way than schools began to spring up in every community. With the first post offices came subscriptions to the literary magazines of Boston, and the "singing schools" became not only the opportunity for music but also for the exchange of last month's *North American Review,* or the latest installment of a Dickens novel.

A little later the music-loving peoples of Europe began to pour into the Territory, and soon Bach, Beethoven, and Mozart became familiar household names. Germans in Winona and Czechs in New Prague had their orchestras and bands, the Scandinavians brought with them their ritual-loving pastors, who saw to it that each church had its trained choir, while America created its own folksongs, as from river and forest rose the ballads of the logging industry's shantyboys.

As early as 1862, four German musicians in St. Paul formed a string quartet. Soon other music lovers gathered around them and a year later the St. Paul Musical Society had been organized and boasted 200 members. In 1870 an orchestra, whose members were local musicians, under the director, George Seibert, was giving concerts not only in the Twin Cities but in Stillwater, Duluth, and other communities.

By the 1880's, St. Paul and Minneapolis had become not only thriving trade centers, but the educational and cultural hub of the Northwest. Study clubs and lyceum courses were immensely popular. Many a world-renowned lecturer came up the Mississippi, partly to satisfy his curiosity, but also in response to the call of culture-hungry citizens. Emerson, Mark Twain, Oscar Wilde, and Fredrika Bremer lectured in those early days. Each left behind a quickened intellectual appetite, to be fed by a humbler lecturing group that, under the distinguished leadership of William Folwell, was gathering at the new university. Noteworthy among these local teachers was Maria L. Sanford, who came to the university in 1880. In her forty years of teaching and public addresses she probably did more to advance the love of literature in Minnesota than any other person.

A grand opera house soon succeeded the "upstairs" amusement hall from whose balconies brass bands had summoned the passers-by. To the cities came the famous Adelina Patti, Jenny Lind, Ole Bull, and many itinerant opera companies, as well as Edwin Booth, Lawrence Barrett, Joseph Jefferson, Modjeska, Duse, and Bernhardt. Provincial and crude as the Twin Cities doubtless were in the eighties and nineties, it was nevertheless in those decades that they had their only first-hand experience of supremely good acting. With the new century was to come the gradual decline of the road show, the rise to popularity of the moving picture, and the almost complete inanition of the legitimate theater in Minnesota.

In the graphic and plastic arts, the new State was less fortunate. Probably the first original Minnesota painting was that done for the lurid lithographs and posters scattered by the thousands throughout the eastern States and Europe to incite immigration. A few farmers still retain these fantastically exaggerated picturizations of Minnesota's largess, but of the dozens of daubers who perpetrated them the names of only a few have been preserved. That of Edwin Whitefield is worthy of special note. This artist came to Minnesota in 1856 for the Whitefield Exploration Association whose purpose was to develop and explore the Kandiyohi Lake region. He left many water color sketches that in recent years have won for him a significant place in the Nation's pioneer art. To the average town dweller of the 1880's, art was mainly represented by the traveling panoramas on whose thousands of feet of canvas were depicted in great detail historic scenes such as the battle of the *Monitor* and the *Merrimac*. These attracted large audiences and were thought to offer valuable educational advantages.

Nevertheless art was taken seriously in the cities. As early as 1870, Minneapolis had founded an Athenaeum Society and provided funds for the purchase of art books. In 1883 the Minneapolis Society of Fine Arts was established, soon to be followed by the Minnesota State Society of Arts. Paintings were produced, many of which were excellent in the traditional academic sense and need no apology today. At this time also, interest arose in the acquisition of collections, private and public. This in turn led to the establishment of museums.

The Minneapolis Society of Fine Arts had its own art school and galleries by 1915. In 1933 the University of Minnesota opened a gallery in Northrop Auditorium to which come many of the most interesting foreign and American exhibits. The gallery has started its own permanent collection with notable modern American paintings. St. Paul's frequent exhibits as well as its permanent collection were shown for years at the St. Paul Institute. Today most exhibits are shown at the library, or in the galleries at the St. Paul School of Art founded in 1927. Various civic organizations bring exhibits of both paintings and prints to the smaller cities, notably Winona, Rochester, Owatonna, and others, and to all those in which colleges are located.

One indication of the growth of an art consciousness in Minnesota is the fact that requests for murals for schools and other civic buildings are more numerous than can be met by the Federal Art Project.

The State's more specific contributions to American art require more detailed treatment.

◄◄◄◄◄◄◄◄◄◄◄◄◄◄◄◄◄◄◄◄◄☿►►►►►►►►►►►►►►►►►►►►►►►

Architecture

The history of architecture in Minnesota goes back no more than a hundred years, yet it embraces an unusual variety of structures and designs, and the names of several architects whose ingenuity and creative ability brought notice to the State and fame to themselves.

The first buildings in Minnesota of which there is record were the impermanent gabled dwellings the Sioux built at their "capital" on Mille Lacs prior to the Chippewa invasion from the region of Lake Superior early in the eighteenth century.

Military penetration preceded settlement, and a log fort was built in 1820 on the bluff overlooking the junction of the Minnesota and the Mississippi Rivers. The log structure was first occupied in 1822, and about two years later a diamond-shaped enclosure around it was defined by a

10-foot stone wall, with corners accented for defense by round towers. At first called Fort St. Anthony, the name of the military post was changed in 1825 to Fort Snelling. Of this early work, only traces of the stone wall and two of the towers remain.

The earliest domestic structures were limited in plan to the barest essentials and constructed of materials readily at hand. In wooded regions the earliest houses were built of logs; on the prairies, they were of sod. Cabins in the forest regions were made of peeled logs, either round or roughly squared, fitted together by notching the ends. Chinked with moss or clay, they afforded protection against the severe cold. The floors were generally of hardened earth. The sod houses of the prairie regions were made by cutting pieces of turf and placing them on top of each other like stones. The roof was made of poles covered with sod.

After 1840 settlers from New England built frame structures strongly reminiscent of Colonial types in the East. Characteristic details were remembered—clapboards, shutters, simple gabled roofs, small-paned windows—while plain but vigorous classic moldings and cornices served further to recall this earlier architecture. The wooden Colonial phase lasted for about four decades. Details which might be traced to specific eastern localities were lost; and only the most typical characteristics of the styles were retained. But it is possible to pick out, here and there in many parts of the State, old houses that remind one of the single-story cottages of Cape Cod, or of the rectangular, symmetrical two-story houses of New England. Of such a New England type is the Indian Agency house at St. Claire, a short distance from Mankato. It was built in 1855 by the United States Government for the Winnebago Indian Agency. This superior structure, a central hall type of two stories and attic, has brick gable ends rising above the roof to form what, in Portsmouth, New Hampshire, would be called a "Captain's walk."

The symmetrical façade is executed in variegated red local sand-mold brick, with solid wood lintels over the windows and doors, and solid wood sills. The doorway, in place of the southwest window, is so designed as to preserve the effect of balance in the openings of the façade. The main doorway has side and top lights, framed by very simple trim, with almost no moldings. Where moldings do occur, they follow pure Georgian Colonial precedents. The effect of an exterior cornice is achieved by a sawtooth arrangement of bricks, set at an angle to the face of the wall, and resting on two rows of corbeled brick courses.

Unusual also, because of their infrequent use in other Minnesota houses of this date, are the fireplaces in the diningroom, the office, and two bedrooms. Severely plain in design, they were utilitarian rather than ornamental. The general plan of this house is obviously studied, and it seems probable that it was prepared in the East for the Government, and executed in the Territory of Minnesota from drawings. Certainly the general plan elements were too well articulated to have been designed at that early date in Minnesota.

At Mendota, below the bluffs of Fort Snelling, Henry Hastings Sibley in 1835 built a house of native stone, with white wood cornice and trim. It is curiously like many of the stone houses of Pennsylvania. The laths were of interwoven willow sticks which were readily obtainable along the river bottoms. The house with its several outbuildings is now the property of the Daughters of the American Revolution, who have attempted to recreate the atmosphere of the original house with furniture of the period.

On the whole, the architecture of this period followed current trends in the East. In the fifties the octagonal house had a certain vogue, and two interesting examples of this quaint experiment are the Dr. William Thorne house at Hastings and one at Afton on the Saint Croix.

Of unusual interest was the marked influence of the "Greek Revival" just prior to the Civil War. Houses with temple fronts—that is, with two-story, colonnaded, and pedimented porches, and one-story wings projecting symmetrically from the main mass of the house—were very popular. There are at least a half dozen good examples still extant in the old Irvine Park section of St. Paul. Numerous survivals of the style are still to be found in villages and on farms in the eastern part of the State. These houses were particularly fine in detail. The purity of the original Greek stone architecture has been ably adapted to wood. The Doric columns, the finely molded cornice in correct classic proportion, and the balanced masses of the style are embodied in a four-columned house, built in the 1850's, on Sherman Street just north of West Seventh in St. Paul.

The period from the end of the Civil War to about the year 1893 may be considered the Victorian era, architecturally. Insofar as Minnesota is concerned, the period is one of eclecticism. National influences obscured local tendencies, except for those interesting minor notes introduced by immigrants, which are found at random, frequently in churches. One can readily detect the application of Byzantine detail on the otherwise ordinary churches of the Syrians; and the ornate, pinnacled, Gothic motifs of churches used by those of German extraction. The German congregation of the Assumption Catholic Church in St. Paul had the plans of its church made in Munich in 1871 by Edward Riedel.

The Romanesque influence of H. H. Richardson was widely apparent in a variety of buildings; and interesting survivals of the style are the Minneapolis City Hall and Pillsbury Hall at the University of Minnesota. Simultaneously, the French influence of the Ecole des Beaux Arts was evident in innumerable mansard-roofed dwellings and mansions of the château type. The older sections of Summit Avenue in St. Paul and Park Avenue in Minneapolis testify to the variety of architectural styles.

Materials used at this time were largely those obtainable within the State: Kettle River sandstone, dull red in color; Mankato limestone; St. Cloud granite; and, of course, lumber, for lumber played a very important part in the economic history of the State. Easily obtainable lumber was frequently used to imitate a variety of other materials and by means of the jigsaw was cut into innumerable tortured forms and applied indiscriminately from cellar to ridge pole. Then, as if the applied ornament were not adequate, structural forms such as porte-cocheres, towers, balconies, dormers, and elaborate turrets were added to the buildings.

The most notable contribution to architecture in this period was made by Leroy S. Buffington of Minneapolis. In the early 1880's, when he worked in Chicago, he is known to have discussed with various architectural associates his idea of building a steel frame as a structural support for the fabric of stone or brick which clothed the building. At that time, for every floor of increased height above three or four stories, the stone walls of the foundations and lower floors had to be made thicker, and the space in the lower floors was thus increasingly sacrificed. Moreover, stone or brick subjected to the weight of many stories imposed definite restrictions upon the height of buildings owing to limitations in compressive strength. Buffington's idea was to erect a steel frame to which thin veneers of brick or other material of relatively light weight could be attached, and the frame itself was to carry the mass, rather than the masonry walls. In 1887, after many years of work on his idea, he applied in Washington for a patent on a 28-story steel frame building. On May 22, 1888, the patent on "Iron Building Construction" was issued to him, whereupon he became the object of widespread derision by short-sighted critics. In 1889 the architects of the Tacoma Building in Chicago made use of the idea for a thirteen-story building. A precedent was set for the use of a cage or "skeleton" construction; and the principle, once demonstrated, was thereafter more and more frequently used. Buffington fought against what he considered patent infringements, both in the law courts and by writing, but without success until 1929, when Rufus Rand of Minneapolis voluntarily paid a royalty for the use of the skeleton construction adopted for the Rand Tower in Minneapolis. Buffington's claim to priority has caused widespread discussion and heated controversy. In its issue of June 1929, the *American Architect* concludes with finality that he must be given credit for the method of steel construction now so commonly in use.

Buffington's work as a practicing architect has generally been overlooked because of the more sensational aspects of his architectural theories. Nevertheless, he designed numerous buildings that, as examples of the period, and considering the influences then at work on architecture as a whole, are creditable. Among his designs were Pillsbury Hall and the Old Library Building at the University of Minnesota. Pillsbury Hall is Romanesque in the best Richardson manner; the library is Greek in style with a portico copied from the Parthenon in Athens. He also designed numerous residences for a rising class of wealthy people and planned commercial buildings, factories, and warehouses for their businesses. His work was restrained and almost invariably in good taste.

The Columbian Exposition at Chicago in 1893 gave impetus to the various tendencies of the classic and Renaissance styles, and during this epoch such well-known examples of neoclassicism as the new State Capitol were brought into existence. Minnesota also nurtured numerous architects who later rose to national prominence. Among these were E. L. Masqueray, a Frenchman from the Ecole des Beaux Arts in Paris; A. H. Stem, one of the architects of the Grand Central Terminal in New York and designer of many charming houses; and James Knox Taylor, who later became supervising architect for the United States Treasury Department at Washington. Though not natives of the State, these men while residing here produced some of their best work, most of it in the classic tradition.

Masqueray's French training was very evident in his designs, and whether he was designing the cathedral in Saint Paul, the Basilica of Saint Mary in Minneapolis, or the buildings for the St. Louis Exposition, he invariably displayed a taste for the baroque and the dramatic.

In 1893 the State of Minnesota announced a Nation-wide competition for a design for a new State Capitol, and from the projects submitted by architects of national prominence, Cass Gilbert's plan was selected. He was then a young man with his first large commission, which in time brought him an increasing number of opportunities for designing buildings of importance. So successful did this young Minnesotan become that he moved his offices to New York, where he supervised plans for such widely known structures as the Woolworth Building in New York, the West Virginia State Capitol, and the Supreme Court Building in Washington.

The Capitol Building for the State of Minnesota is an impressive structure of white marble, expressed in a Renaissance vernacular. It served as model for most of the State capitols built in the ensuing twenty-five years, and it was not until the spell was broken by Bertram Grosvenor Goodhue in his design for the Nebraska State Capitol that any notable deviation from the academic, domed statehouse was attempted.

One other monumental scheme of State-wide interest, also Cass Gilbert's, was the rearrangement of the University of Minnesota campus. This plan also was chosen by competition, and since its adoption the buildings have been cast in rigidly conceived and symmetrically fenestrated structures of brick trimmed with stone. Individually and collectively the buildings are planned to be monumental (an effect which they have achieved) but the diverse elements of a large university are housed not too happily in structures that bear no relation to their functional requirements.

To this period, although advanced in style, belongs what is to architects probably the most interesting building in Minnesota: namely, the National Farmers' Bank in Owatonna, begun in 1907. Its board of directors must be given credit for casting aside the prevailing Greek and Roman modes in bank buildings, and searching for an architect who could design a utilitarian structure to meet special requirements. They asked Louis Sullivan to design the building, and so admirably was it done that it is still one of the best examples of modern architecture in the State.

Minnesota is now entering the period called "modern," or "functional," which is too international in spirit to be affected by specific movements within the State. All major commercial work is now being done in the modern manner, and the latest civic structures bear the stamp of modernism.

The new city hall and courthouse in St. Paul was one of the first important structures of its kind to accommodate various civic functions in a skyscraper type of building. An interesting feature on the ground floor is the Memorial Hall, three stories high, finished in black glass. It is the dramatic setting for a *Peace Memorial* created by Carl Milles.

As a domestic style, the modern has made relatively little progress. However, within the State are two examples by Frank Lloyd Wright, one of the greatest living exponents of modernism, and a pupil of Louis Sullivan. The house owned by Mr. Philip Little, Jr., at Lake Minnetonka represents the earlier phase, and the M. M. Willey house in Prospect Park in Minneapolis is characteristic of Wright's current work. The Willey house has the long low lines and the widespread eaves of Wright's "prairie" style, and is still the most satisfying of domestic designs in any contemporary style within the State.

Indigenous to Minnesota, and almost completely ignored by its people, are the stark, unornamented, functional clusters of concrete—Minnesota's grain elevators. These may be said to express unconsciously all the principles of modernism, being built for use only, with little regard for the tenets of esthetic design. Everyone has seen the rhythmic repetition of these cylindrical forms accented by the shadows made by the hot summer sun, and the whole dignified mass set against the sky; yet it remained for European visitors to discover that while Minnesota sought for artistic expression in other directions, it had achieved in its grain elevators a signal triumph of functional design.

‹‹‹‹‹‹‹‹‹‹‹‹‹‹‹‹‹‹✕›››››››››››››››››››››

Literature

During its pioneer stage Minnesota produced a considerable literature which today is valued chiefly for its historical significance. Most of these writings were of the nature of travel books, and served not only to acquaint the world with a new country where "they till the land but own the land they till," but also to inspire distant writers. Among these latter were the great German poet, Friedrich Schiller, and New England's Henry Wadsworth Longfellow, at that time regarded as equally talented. (Carver's Cave was immortalized by Schiller, who received his inspiration from *Carver's Travels,* published in 1792 and later translated into German. Longfellow was led to write *Hiawatha* after reading Mrs. Mary H. Eastman's *Dahcotah; or Life and Legends of the Sioux around Fort Snelling,* published in 1849, and "the various and valuable writings of Mr. Schoolcraft." For his descriptions of Minnehaha Falls, which he never saw, he used a photograph by Alexander Hesler, a Chicago photographer.) A less-famed writer who found in Minnesota a fund of local color was the Indianan, Edward Eggleston (1837–1902), who spent several years in the State preaching, making soap, and collecting material for his *Mystery of Metropolisville.* He is thought to have written *Hoosier Schoolmaster* here. Eggleston was St. Paul's first librarian.

Of all the writers of pioneer days, the fiery Ignatius Donnelly (1831–1901), "Sage of Nininger," was the most picturesque. For forty years he threw himself into the turbulent whirlpool of pioneer politics, and, when defeated, withdrew to make a living and to salve his sores by writing controversial books of which his thousands of admirers demanded repeated and enormous editions. It is claimed that 700,000 copies of his novel *Caesar's Column* were sold here and abroad, while *Atlantis* went into 21 editions and was published in both England and France. Donnelly is said to have quoted Epictetus (in the original Greek) on the floor of the United States Senate and to have surprised erudite Europeans by the extent of his learning. His best known book, *The Great Cryptogram,* was devoted, as were many of his lectures, to his alleged proof that Bacon wrote the Shakespearean plays.

Early "western" writing was nearly all highly romanticized. To Hamlin Garland belongs the credit of being the first writer to cast aside the romantic tradition and to picture pioneer living in an honest realistic fashion. Garland used Minnesota, which he repeatedly visited, as a source of much local color, and he must be regarded as the direct forerunner of the State's two outstanding realists, Sinclair Lewis and Ole Edvart Rölvaag.

The first generation of the twentieth century not only popularized Minnesota writers but brought several to the attention of that smaller audience whose prime interest is in scholarship and style. To the latter group the State university has made a notable contribution. Among these are Oscar Firkins (1864–1932), whom William Archer declared to be America's outstanding critic; William Watts Folwell (1833–1929), Minnesota's beloved teacher and historian (author of the four-volume *History of Minnesota*); William Stearns Davis (1877–1930), whose historical novels (including *A Friend to Caesar*), written as relaxation between periods of research, are among the best novels of that genre America has produced; and Joseph Warren Beach, critic and poet.

From the university, too, came Minnesota's outstanding lyric poet, the young Arthur Upson, who was drowned in 1908 at the age of thirty-one when contemporary critics, both American and British, were predicting for him the glory of a poet of the first rank. Many of his poems appeared first in the *Bellman,* the little literary magazine published in the early 1900's by William C. Edgar, editor and publisher of the technical journal, *Northwestern Miller.* Upson's lyrics are for the most part concerned with the sensitive and wistful response of a poet to the gentler phase of beauty, but it is their almost Greeklike purity of form that won him his reputation among contemporary critics. Poets still make pilgrimages to the Arthur Upson Room in the University Library, endowed by Ruth Phelps, another University writer. Before Miss Phelps's marriage to the French author,

Paul Morand, she taught Italian literature, the subject of her critical essays. Elmer E. Stoll, held by many to be the greatest contemporary Shakespearean student, and Martin Ruud, an authority on medieval culture, have gained international recognition.

Better known to America at large are F. Scott Fitzgerald, who first revealed with bitter and brilliant incisiveness the cynical desperation of early post-war adolescents; Charles Flandrau, whose *Viva Mexico* is one of the most delightful accounts of that exciting Republic; his sister-in-law, Grace Flandrau, writer of novels about St. Paul and short stories of Africa; Martha Ostenso, author of *Wild Geese,* a prize-winning novel concerned with life in northern Minnesota.

Others are James Gray, literary commentator and novelist *(Wake and Remember);* William McNally, playwright and novelist *(The House of Vanished Splendour);* Darragh Aldrich *(Earth Never Tires);* Maud and Delos Lovelace *(Gentlemen from England);* Lorna Beers *(A Humble Lear);* Dagmar Doneghy *(The Border);* Charles A. Eastman, the distinguished Sioux *(Indian Boyhood);* and Margaret Culkin Banning, prolific magazine contributor and novelist, who has not only established herself as an acute observer of Minnesota's social scene, but also has given of her time and counsel to many State and civic enterprises.

Three writers overshadow the Minnesota literary field: Thorstein Veblen, economist and social philosopher, Ole Edvart Rölvaag, novelist, and Sinclair Lewis, first American winner of the Nobel Prize for literature and member of the American Academy of Arts and Letters.

Thorstein Veblen (1857–1929) lived in Minnesota from his eighth year, when his family moved from Wisconsin to a farm near Northfield, until his early twenties and graduation from Carleton College. He knew the State also as a refuge during his scholastic career. His people were Norwegians who migrated from their first homes to escape poverty and oppression.

At Carleton he read intensively in the social philosophers from Hume and Kant to Spencer, absorbed the current equalitarian ideas in politics, and evidently found his direction as a critical analyst of modern industrial civilization. His direction does not lend itself to easy classification. While he definitely discarded the classical in economics, he did not adopt Marxism as such although his approach was distinctly social and opposed to capitalism on moral and practical grounds.

In subsequent years of study, teaching in universities, and writing, Veblen evolved his theoretical system. He saw history as a succession of conflicts between the predatory and the industrious. Few men of his time could relate Veblen's thinking with the problems he attacked, and a highly complex manner of expression diminished his circle even more. But our contemporary scientific economists acknowledge an immense debt to him, while lecturers and writers make common coin of many of his characteristic epithets and phrases.

Of the 10 works he published, *The Engineers and the Price System* (1921) has become widely known among students of social and economic organization. His first book, *The Theory of the Leisure Class* (1899), is a popular reprint and best-seller among works of this nature.

Ole Edvart Rölvaag (1876–1931) left a fishing career in Norway to come to America when he was twenty years old. Almost penniless when he arrived in the Northwest, it was only after many tribulations that he finally was given a professorship at St. Olaf College, at Northfield, where he taught until his death. In *Giants in the Earth,* he presented the physical and spiritual experiences of pioneering with such truthfulness and sympathetic beauty that the novel's permanence in American literature seems assured. Published originally in Norway, where it was widely praised, when rendered into English it met with almost phenomenal success, and was acclaimed immediately by some critics as the "most powerful novel that has ever been written about pioneer life in America." Although Rölvaag's succeeding novels never achieved the simple but profound greatness of this first work, they demonstrated again his integrity and craftsmanship.

Sinclair Lewis, native son of Minnesota, has been regarded with mixed emotions by many of his fellow Minnesotans. Indeed it was not until the Swedish Academy had awarded him the Nobel Prize in 1930 that their full approval was bestowed upon him. Local pride was outraged by the ruthless manner with which in *Main Street* he stripped Minnesota small-town life of any suggestion of charm and romance. But in 1920, young Americans, suffering from the disillusionment and frustration of the war and sick of pretty phrase-making, found in *Main Street* a satisfying and exciting expression of many of their feelings.

Its incisive, almost reportorial realism struck a new note in American literature. Stephen Crane, Ambrose Bierce, and Theodore Dreiser, it is true, already had awakened an appreciation of realistic writing, but they were enjoyed only by the discerning. Lewis' success was due not only to the fearless expression of his penetrating insight, but to his seemingly artless power of arousing, in critical and uncritical alike, immediate recognition of his portaits and their backgrounds. His influence was soon reflected in the books of dozens of young writers and continued to expand with each new novel he issued until about 1930. He lists among his accomplishments 16 novels, 6 of them best-sellers. Translated into foreign languages they brought him international fame. If in common with other prophets Lewis has had to wait for full appreciation from his own townsmen, few will be found now who will deny to the red-headed young rebel Sauk Center once knew as "Doodle," the credit of having become, with Dreiser, the primary liberating force of the writers of his day.

❮❮❮❮❮❮❮❮❮❮❮❮❮❮❮❮❮❮❮❮ ❁ ❯❯❯❯❯❯❯❯❯❯❯❯❯❯❯❯❯❯❯❯❯

Music

Minnesota has made at least three outstanding contributions to America's music and has nurtured several concert artists and composers of distinction. Among the concert artists are Eunice Norton, distinguished pianist born in Minneapolis, and the two Metropolitan Opera singers, Florence Macbeth born in Mankato, and Olive Fremstad brought from Sweden at the age of six to Minnesota where she made her first public appearances. Of its composers three warrant special mention: Dr. John J. Becker, whose modern compositions have been played and approved both in New York and Europe; Donald N. Ferguson, the classicist; and Stanley Avery, who, between his distinguished organ recitals, has composed scores played by several leading orchestras.

The brilliant and comprehensive study of Indian music (Chippewa and Sioux) made by Frances Densmore for the Smithsonian Institution; the interpretive work of the Minneapolis Symphony Orchestra; and the revival and adaptation of medieval church music by F. Melius Christiansen, leader and inspirer of the famed choir at the College of St. Olaf, Northfield, are the State's major contributions to American music.

Miss Densmore, who was born and still resides in Red Wing, Minnesota, spent many months on Indian reservations analyzing and recording the music which is still, as it has always been, one of the greatest pleasures of the Chippewa tribe, and their only art that retains, unchanged, its primitive form. According to Miss Densmore's observations, rhythm—the dominant element in every Chippewa song—is unaltered by the singer, although he may and frequently does vary the words as he sees fit. The instruments used are the drum, the rattle, and the flute, the latter reserved wholly for love songs. Drum and voice are given independent expression, seldom sounded simultaneously, and it is the accent of the former that determines the nature of the rhythm. Songs are usually of accomplishment rather than of yearning or self-expression, and are sung over and over for several hours. The singer does not move the lips, but creates the tone by the contraction of throat muscles. Minute gradations smaller than a semitone are commonly used. The descending interval of the minor third occurs with special prominence and frequency.

The inception of the Minneapolis Symphony Orchestra dates back to the nineties, when Emil Oberhoffer, a talented music-loving German, organized the Philharmonic Club from a local chorus of mixed voices and a small string orchestra. The club's concerts grew steadily in popularity, but as more ambitious programs were undertaken, Oberhoffer felt increasingly the need of skilled and professional players other than the community could provide. He interested a group of businessmen, who, in 1903, formed the Minneapolis Orchestral Association and guaranteed financial support of a 40-piece orchestra for five years. E. L. Carpenter was chosen president and has not only continued in this office but remains its outstanding patron. Oberhoffer conducted the orchestra until 1922, when he resigned to go to California, where he repeated his Minneapolis successes. By that year the orchestra had grown to 80 players, many internationally known, and in its previous season had given 115 concerts. Henri Verbrugghen (1873–1934), who followed Oberhoffer as conductor, was a scholarly and talented Belgian violinist, widely known in Europe, Australia, and America. Under his direction the orchestra won for itself a place among the country's best orchestras and visited more than 300 cities.

During Verbrugghen's regime the Orchestral Association and the University of Minnesota completed an unusual arrangement whereby the latter accepted sponsorship and offered its auditorium, with a seating capacity of 5,000, for the permanent housing of the orchestra. This affiliation has been of mutual benefit. The university remains entirely free from financial obligation, receives reduced rates for students and staff, and has at its disposal the association's valuable music library, while the orchestra has the advantages of close co-operation with the university's musical department and an appreciable reduction in its overhead expenses. Since 1930 all symphony concerts have been held on the campus.

When Verbrugghen's health failed after seven years of conducting, he was succeeded (in the fall of 1931) by the young Hungarian, Eugene Ormandy, whose personality and greatly diversified programs aroused new enthusiasm and interest. In 1936 he resigned to conduct the Philadelphia Symphony Orchestra, and his place was taken by Dimitri Mitropoulos, a Greek conductor, whom the critic Olin Downes and the distinguished Boston conductor Koussevitsky have declared to be one of the world's outstanding conductors.

The Minneapolis Symphony Orchestra has grown from a group of 40 amateur musicians to one composed of 100 trained artists. Its contribution to the enjoyment and cultural development of this midwestern State has been made possible through the talent of foreign-born artists and the financial support of American businessmen.

It is not surprising that Minnesota with its predominance of Lutheran churches should be the home of some of the finest *a capella* choirs in the country, since Lutherans from the sixteenth century have regarded choir singing as essential to their ritual. One of the most distinguished of these choirs is at Glenwood *(see Tour 9),* and its Bach recitals have become well known throughout the Midwest. The Bach choir at the State university is also worthy of special note. The *a capella* choir at the College of St. Olaf, at Northfield, is the only one of its type in America. It owes its renown to the genius of its conductor, F. Melius Christiansen, who was born in Norway in 1871, came to America at the age of 17, and joined the St. Olaf faculty in 1903. From approximately 300 students—most of them children of Scandinavian farmers—Christiansen chooses 60 boys and girls, of whom about one-third are lost each year by graduation. By means of rigid discipline and his own fervor, he trains them to sing, in perfect pitch and tone, the most difficult and austere church music, unaided by either notes or accompaniment. The choir has made two concert tours to northern Europe where it was received with the same enthusiastic praise it has invariably met in American cities.

Dr. Christiansen had achieved world recognition for his adaptations of sixteenth and seventeenth century church music, and today there are few sacred choral programs that do not include one or more of his compositions.

As Lutheran music is based largely on Bach, so is that of the Roman Catholic Church on Palestrina. Opportunity to hear this early Catholic music is offered at intervals at St. John's Abbey, at Collegeville *(see Tour 9),* which, through the efforts of the Benedictine fathers, has become a recognized center of the liturgical movement.

◄◄◄◄◄◄◄◄◄◄◄◄◄◄◄◄◄◄◄◄ ☿ ►►►►►►►►►►►►►►►►►►►►

Painting

Until recent years Minnesota's canvases bore few marks to distinguish them from those produced in other sections of the country. At the turn of the century such men as Simmons, La Farge, and French did the murals and sculpture of its more noteworthy public buildings. Nevertheless the State had painters who were trained in New York and abroad and whose works, exhibited in the various art centers, were purchased by outstanding museums. Foremost among them was Homer Dodge Martin (1836–1897). Born in New York and usually associated with the Hudson River group, Martin identified himself in his later years with St. Paul. Others were Cadwallader Washburn, etcher and painter; Nicholas Brewer, portrait painter; and S. Chatwood Burton. That the politicians were proud of their State's art is shown by the fact that Minnesota women in 1903 succeeded, surprisingly enough, in persuading the legislature to pass an appropriation for the State Society of Art.

Minnesota had become accustomed to the conventional and formal styles of painting, and thus early in the present century few were prepared to appreciate a group of young men and women who painted with new vigor and independence. Like the writers, these artists were through with mere prettiness. Shocked comment and sharp criticism did not deter them. True, they made few sales, but they were used to that, and they were thoroughly enjoying themselves as they plunged into a succession of lively experiments. The lithographs of the witty Adolph Dehn derided Main Street as ruthlessly as did the works of Sinclair Lewis. Wanda Gag added a sprightly note of fantasy in her woodcuts. Both artists have been unsparing with their social comments. Many others found subject matter for brilliant realistic compositions in Minnesota villages, grain elevators, silos, mining towns, and stretches of concrete road. Theodore Haupt, Elizabeth Olds, Clement Haupers, Dewey Albinson, Erle Loran, Cameron Booth, Frances Greenman, and others became familiar names to New York dealers, and the interest of those who follow art trends turned to the Northwest. The *American Magazine of Art,* reviewing the State's contribution, in 1934, remarked: "We are led to suspect that perhaps Minnesota, despite all the troubles of the day, is finding herself the possessor of a genuine tradition."

A comparison of Minnesota painting today with that of older groups leaves the feeling that here is a quality of breeziness and a solid rejection of outworn conventions that promises much for the future. Many signs point to a correspondingly active interest in the world of art on the part of Minnesotans generally. The annual exhibitions by Twin Cities artists in the Minneapolis Institute of Art are viewed by thousands; State Fair galleries in which annually hundreds of local canvases are shown, together with traveling collections of famous paintings by European and American artists, attract the largest crowds at the fair. Private and public galleries are visited by increasing numbers, and the art work of the Federal agencies has been supported enthusiastically.

◄◄◄◄◄◄◄◄◄◄◄◄◄◄◄◄◄◄◄◄◄✿►►►►►►►►►►►►►►►►►►►►►►

Sculpture

Minnesota's early sculpture, architectural or detached, was for the most part commissioned, and unfortunately offers little to excite the imagination. Like the State's earlier painters, its sculptors almost invariably have been craftsmen of sound technique. Their work, with the possible exception of Paul Manship's, belongs to the academic school. The most prolific was Jacob Fjelde, who designed several bronze portrait figures which have been placed in Twin City parks and public buildings.

Fjelde emigrated from Norway to Minnesota in the late nineteenth century. He had studied in both Italy and his own homeland. His bust of Henrik Ibsen at Como Park, St. Paul, was modeled from life, and its replica has been placed in Bergen, Norway. Other works include the somewhat idealized bronze of Ole Bull, the violinist, and the *Reading Woman* figure at the Minneapolis Library entrance. Fjelde's romantically treated *Hiawatha and Minnehaha* group, placed on a stony island a short way above Minnehaha Falls, is enjoyed by the many lovers of the Longfellow idyl. His commissions included many portrait busts, and the 24 spandrel figures representing the arts and sciences on the old library building of the State university. His son, Paul Fjelde, also a sculptor, is at work in the State on commissions for busts and memorial plaques.

Paul Manship, formerly of St. Paul, is Minnesota's best-known sculptor.

Many consider him a distinguished exponent of an archaic but highly stylized art; other critics hold that he is really an adroit emulator of the later Hellenic and Italian Renaissance artists. The cleverness with which he echoes the graces of Olympia and Pompeii is beautifully illustrated in *Playfulness,* the figure of a woman and child in the Minneapolis Institute of Arts. *Spring Awakening,* in the St. Paul Institute of Science Museum, is delicate and charming. His bronze fountain group, *Indian Hunter,* at Summit and Western Aves., is another embodiment of the decorative conventions he loves. Manship's free archaistic style has gained for him enormous prestige with architects, and may influence American sculpture in this generation as definitely as French's realism did in the last.

The most important sculpture that Minnesota can boast is the 37-foot Indian figure at the end of the concourse of the Ramsey County Courthouse *(see ST. PAUL).* The creator of this mammoth statue is Carl Milles, a native of Stockholm, Sweden, and today an instructor at the Cranbrook School, near Detroit, Michigan. Milles emphasizes the functional relation between sculpture and architecture. Free from conventional flourishes and meaningless ornamentation, his St. Paul group (which he regards as his most successful expression in stone) becomes an integral part of the building.

Most eminent in the realm of academic sculpture is the work of Daniel Chester French (1850–1931), New Hampshire artist, whose figures in the attic and dome of the State Capitol are marked by dignity and simplicity of line. French is remembered as a facile craftsman, who tended to sentimentalize the human figure.

A Minnesota sculptor whose work is not represented in the State is James Earle Fraser, of Winona. His fame rests chiefly on his well-known equestrian statue, *The End of the Trail* (purchased by San Francisco), memorials and figures for Government buildings in Washington, and the Indian head chosen for the buffalo nickel.

Today Minnesota is experiencing a more spontaneous and widespread desire for art expression and appreciation than ever before. Its pioneer crudities are outgrown, and its New England heritage has been enriched by later European ideas.

PART II
Cities and Towns

The Tale of Two Cities

NUCLEUS of the Northwest, in the hub of an area where 900,000 people live, the Twin Cities, Minneapolis and St. Paul, are at the head of navigation on the Mississippi River—1,596 miles from where it pours into the Gulf of Mexico—and near the geographical center of North America. Following the river, Minneapolis lies 15 miles upstream from St. Paul, but a crow flying from city hall to city hall would find them only 10 miles apart. Together they form one metropolitan trade center, which ranks eighth in the United States.

To a stranger they seem already to have merged. Connected by a common zone, each has grown up on both sides of the river, their residences intermingled; to the north only a surveyor's line divides them, farther south the mythical "center" of the river marks the boundary. But their citizens know that although born at almost the same time, their culture shared wholeheartedly, each maintains, as it has from the beginning, a personality differing sharply from that of its twin.

Even the casual visitor (when he overcomes his bewilderment and determines into which city he has wandered), cannot fail to note certain obvious differences. The St. Paul skyline is all of a piece, Minneapolis sprawls; St. Paul is hilly, Minneapolis level; St. Paul's bridges leap down from the high shore to the loop; in Minneapolis they snake across the river with no regard for distance; St. Paul's loop streets are narrow and concentrated, while in its twin city the center of activity extends many blocks along the broad shopping avenues. Minneapolis marks its streets and ornaments its lakes, but leaves its river shore ragged and unkempt below the cream-colored elevators. St. Paul makes much of its river shore but illumines no street sign for a nervous driver. St. Paul has already attained a degree of mellowness and seems to be clinging to its Victorian dignity, while in Minneapolis dignity is less prized than modern spruceness. The visitor from the East will perhaps feel more at home in St. Paul; if from the West he is likely to prefer Minneapolis.

Less obvious, but quite as distinctive, are the cities' social differences. While Minneapolis has outstripped its neighbor in wealth and population, St. Paul has clung more tenaciously to its cherished New England traditions and to the tenets of family aristocracy. St. Paul's largest foreign immigrations were German and Irish. Minneapolis, on the other hand, was built largely through the help of Scandinavians, most of whom were of peasant stock whose descendants today hold important positions in banks, industry, politics, and the professions, as they also make up in large measure the thrifty middle class of small business folk. This difference in racial element is again suggested by the great cathedral dome that dominates St. Paul's hill and proclaims the city the seat of a Roman Catholic archbishopric, even as the spires and towers of scores of Lutheran churches proclaim Minneapolis the Lutheran center of the same area.

The contest for leadership that repeatedly in the days of their growth broke out in bitter, vituperative, schoolboyish quarrels, has always been conspicuously lacking in their cultural activities. Music particularly has been communally enjoyed. From the first when string quartets played in the wooden hotels, when chorals preserved the conglomerate temper of immigrant races and ranged from the intricacies of Gregorian chants brought over by the French Catholics to simple *lyrics* of the Indians, or Paul Bunyan songs of the lumberjacks and "whistle-punks," down to recent times when together they support a symphony orchestra, the Twin Cities have been the united music center of the Northwest. In all other fields of art the story has been likewise one of a common pride and enjoyment in the achievements of both. Art galleries, painters, writers, composers are invariably claimed by the Twin Cities as a unit, rather than by the one or the other, and the trend toward a regional art expression is watched with undivided interest. In this unifying process the University of Minnesota has figured largely. Between its main campus and the agricultural college campus, one in Minneapolis, the other in St. Paul, a special trolley carries back and forth hundreds of students who daily attend classes on both. Its open concerts, athletics, forums, and speakers attract large Twin City audiences, while the Golden Gophers' football contests annually cement the two towns into one almost rabid fraternity. Research workers of both cities take equal advantage of the university library in Minneapolis, the James J. Hill Reference Library, or the fine collection at the Minnesota Historical Society, both of which are in St. Paul. Enjoyed by both cities are the famous Botanical Gardens, the many miles of park boulevards and highways that skirt the Mississippi, famous Minnehaha Falls, and the lakes. Sports too have had their integrating effect, and the sports fans of the two cities have little regard for city boundaries as they dash to St. Paul's ice palaces and colorful parades, or to the national skiing and skating exhibitions Minneapolis stages; to St. Paul's municipal auditorium to watch ice hockey contests, or to the Golden Gloves Tournament at the Minneapolis auditorium. Twin City professional hockey and baseball, to be sure, arouse considerable rivalry, but it is the rivalry of good sportsmanship and has nothing to do with the jealousy of older days.

Nevertheless it cannot be gainsaid that there still survives a remnant of the old distrust that marked their industrial struggle in that long period when, suspiciously on guard against the threat of absorption, they watched with jealous eyes as their territories each year drew more nearly together. Some newspapers, with very little intercity circulation, still enliven their editorials with barbed thrusts at their neighbors' pretensions, and rarely encourage combined activities. Until 1936, when the Twin City sewage project was finally agreed upon, two bridges represented the sum of their joint public undertakings. The visitor who mildly suggests that a merger might offer advantages, may well be surprised by the heat with which his idea is rejected.

Nowhere else in this country have two cities in such close proximity, born at almost the same time, grown to a status so nearly equal. To understand how this happened and why, it is necessary to go back to the days of settlement and to trace briefly their development.

First a steamboat landing and then a waterfall determined the locations and likewise the economic growth of the Twins' progenitors, Pig's Eye and St. Anthony, which in the 1830's squatted on the banks of the upper Mississippi. Already there were two other little settlements in the area, but these existed only by sufferance of the U. S. Military Reservation that stretched for 10 miles up and down the river and blocked all other newcomers. Mendota, at the confluence of the Minnesota River and the Mississippi, was then the focal point of the Red River fur trade and the live-

liest and busiest community of the Northwest. It seems more than probable
that had legal ownership been granted the village before the fur trade
shifted to St. Paul, Mendota might have become the capital city of a vast
region and have swallowed up both of the neighboring villages before
they had taken on any true significance. But governments moved slowly
in those days, and by the time its residents could claim the right to own
and improve the land they lived on, Mendota was already fading into the
drowsy site of memories it is today.

The other settlement that preceded the embryo cities had a far less colorful, and an even briefer duration, but nevertheless has a greater bearing
on the story, for it was this forlorn group of squatters who were the real
founders of St. Paul. French-speaking Swiss refugees who had wandered
down from the Selkirk colony on the Red River, were allowed to locate on
the west bank of the Mississippi within the reservation's boundaries. In
1838 they were ordered to vacate, and a few families moved across the river
under the mistaken impression that they were now well outside the military limits. There they found Pierre Parrant, a French Canadian, who a
few weeks before had put up a shack where he lived and sold whisky to
the soldiers. Parrant was thus the first actual settler within the present
limits of St. Paul.

The nature of his business gave rise to the popular quip that "while
Minneapolis was conceived in water power, St. Paul was born in whisky."
(Mark Twain, visiting St. Paul in 1882, expanded this idea in one of his
classic perorations. "How solemn and beautiful is the thought that the
earliest pioneer of civilization, the van leader, is never the steamboat, never
the railroad, never the newspaper, never the Sabbath School, but always
whisky! The missionary comes after the whisky—I mean he arrives after
the whisky has arrived; next the trader, next the miscellaneous rush; next
the gambler, the desperado, the highwayman, and all their kindred of sin
of both sexes, and next the smart chap who has bought up an old grant
that covers all the land, this brings the lawyer tribe, the vigilante commit-
tees, and this brings the undertaker. All these interests bring the newspaper; the newspaper starts up politics and a railroad; all hands turn to
and build a church and a jail and behold! Civilization is established forever in the land. Westward the jug of Empire takes its way!")

All settlers on both sides of the river were forcibly expelled from reservation lands in 1840, and then it was that some of these French-Swiss
wanderers moved a few miles eastward and became the real founders of
St. Paul. Parrant built another cabin at the river landing there, and resumed his business. Nicknamed Pig's Eye by soldiers and traders, this

sinister-looking scoundrel seemed destined at one time to become immortalized in the name of the future city. The little settlement that grew up about him was long and widely known as Pig's Eye, a euphonious title that survives on the bottoms farther down the river where he later moved. But the church proved stronger than whisky. Father Lucian Galtier erected a little log chapel at the landing in October 1841 which he consecrated, November first, to St. Paul, and the community gratefully took over the name of the apostle.

The refugees from the reservation were agriculturists and it was mere chance that led them into possession of the head of Mississippi navigation. They gave no thought at all to the opportunities the river landing offered, and little guessed that their happening upon this site was to determine St. Paul's rapid rise to wealth and leadership. Henry Jackson, later the first justice of the peace, who opened the first store among them in 1842, was probably the first to dream of commercial possibilities. Three years later, however, only about 30 families made up the settlement, most of them farmers.

While the fathers and mothers of St. Paul were still being shifted about, Henry Sibley, later the first Governor, then a prosperous fur trader and a famous host, was living at the trading post, Mendota. He had seen the commercial possibilities of the region and induced his future brother-in-law, Franklin Steele, to act as sutler at the fort whose reservation at that time embraced most of what is now Minneapolis. Steele watched with considerable interest the two mills Colonel Snelling had built (1821–23) on the west side of St. Anthony's Falls, one to cut lumber for his buildings, the other to grind flour from the wheat his men half-heartedly raised. In 1838 Steele erected a cabin on the east side of the falls and paid a man to live there. Six years later, Bottineau, a half-breed guide who had drifted down to St. Paul from the Red River country, took out an adjoining claim. (Bottineau is one of the State's most colorful legendary characters. Handsome and reckless, he has been called the Kit Carson of the Northwest. In 1936 an old-timer recalled vividly being one of an admiring group of youngsters for whose edification he was wont to "skip" silver dollars across the surface of the Mississippi.) In 1847 Steele's workmen started building a sawmill and dam on the east side of the falls. Steele and Bottineau now emerged as sole owners of the land along this east bank. French colonists, mostly part Indian, followed Bottineau to the new settlement, and St. Anthony, later the East Side of Minneapolis, was born, with American workmen busy at the falls and half-breeds scattered about on nearby claims.

That same year the town of St. Paul was platted, a school was opened, and steamboats made the settlement their official terminus with regular scheduled visits. What with the establishment of the American Fur Company's headquarters in the new town, ever-increasing cartloads of pelts from the Red River country coming here to unload, and the Hudson's Bay Company's trade, St. Paul quickly became the most significant trading post in the Northwest.

When the Territory of Minnesota was created in 1849, St. Paul had a population of 840, while 10 miles away St. Anthony had about 250. St. Paul boasted a chapel, school, hotel, post office, warehouses, and stores, a total, including residences, of 142 buildings. St. Anthony had its mill, a store, a post office, and a school, with not nearly so many dwellings. The name Minneapolis had not yet been conceived, but St. Anthony was platted that year on Steele's land. Bottineau at once followed suit and platted the addition that still bears his name.

Between St. Anthony and St. Paul stretched the military reservation, largely on the west side of the river. It required a special Government permit for Col. John H. Stevens, Mexican War hero, to build a residence on the west bank of the falls in 1849. But the incoming Yankee settlers cared little for Government paper. Despite the opposition of the soldiers at the camp, who repeatedly tore down their cabins, they persisted in their determination to occupy the land surrounding Stevens' home. Then in 1855 Washington curtailed the boundaries of the reservation and gave these obstinate squatters their legal patents. By that time a village had grown up on Stevens' claim, now the Minneapolis loop district. Someone proposed a name for the new hamlet derived from "Minne," Sioux word for water, and the Greek suffix "polis." The editor of the first St. Anthony *Express* added an "a" for euphony's sake and Minneapolis it became.

Attempts to incorporate the city of St. Paul were first made in 1849, but it was not until 1854 that city government was a reality. The next year St. Anthony became an acknowledged city. Both it and Minneapolis were booming. In 1858 St. Anthony had a population of 3,500 and Minneapolis on the other side of the falls, 1,500; most of the former were French-Canadians, and the latter principally Yankees, British, and later Scandinavians. (Minneapolis was not incorporated as a city until 1867, and it was not until 1872 that the two united as one city.)

In the fifties, following the Indian treaties, all three towns expanded at a rate almost incredible even to their own optimistic founders *(see IMMIGRATION AND RACIAL ELEMENTS)*. With the first great tide of immigration, St. Paul, the landing port of the thousands who came up the river, became the center for immigrant supplies and laid the foundations for its extensive wholesaling and jobbing interests. By 1853 it had established the first bank in the Northwest (Borup & Oakes). St. Anthony, on the other hand, was ideally situated with its abundant water power to manufacture the lumber the newcomers required for their homes, to turn into flour the wheat they soon began to raise. The boom brought a train of land speculators to all three of the new towns, and by 1856 lots were selling for as much as $2,500. St. Paul was still far in the lead in wealth and population, but the lumber and milling industries that later made Minneapolis famous the country over, already had a healthy start.

Then came the panic of 1857 with its attendant collapse of grandiose dreams. One of the byproducts was its indirect effect on the future expansion of the Twin Cities. Some time before, having decided to abandon the fort, the Government sold the reservation to Franklin Steele, who made a preliminary payment, and on the site of the fort platted a beautifully designed metropolis which he named Minnesota City. The proposed town, still on paper, was seriously advocated as the capital of the State whose admission to the Union was now assured. But the panic so depreciated Steele's resources that he was unable to complete his payments, and the Government took back the fort to reopen it at the beginning of the Civil War. The area once laid out in broad streets and avenues is today occupied by administration buildings, barracks, and parade grounds.

By the end of the decade the division of function that distinguishes so sharply the early development of the Twin Cities was already well established. St. Paul's river advantage for years gave it leadership in trade and commerce, and the city paid far less attention to manufacturing. Its two steam lumbermills produced only enough for local consumption. For a brief period, St. Anthony, refusing to submit to St. Paul's boast that it headed Mississippi navigation, persuaded steamboat captains to risk the hazards of the falls by the promise of rich bonuses. In 1857, 52 steamboats loaded down with goods and passengers, docked at St. Anthony, and took lumber and grain on their return trip. But the next year low water defeated hopes of grand-scale river navigation, and the two sister villages at the falls resigned themselves to their dependence on St. Paul for needed goods. On its commercial facilities they leaned more and more heavily as they built up national markets for lumber and flour. These differences in function—St. Paul, the trade and commercial center; Minneapolis, the industrial—arising directly from their respective locations, are today largely eliminated, but for years they were the leading factor in the almost parallel growth of the Twin Cities.

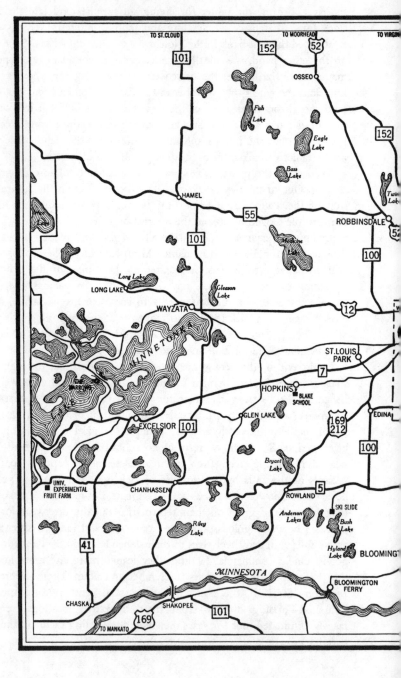

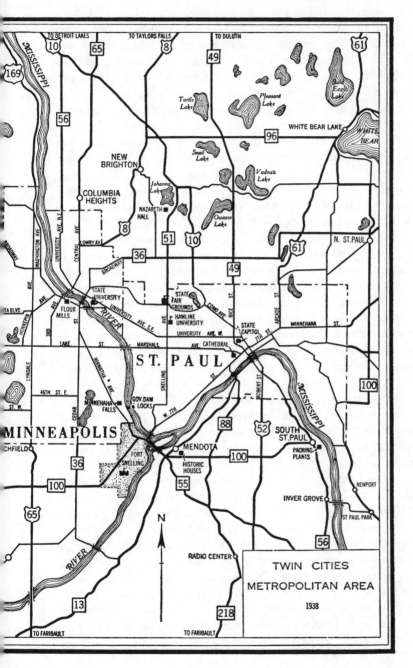

TWIN CITIES
METROPOLITAN AREA
1938

With the development of steamboat traffic above the falls, the fur trade shifted to St. Cloud, but by this time St. Paul had a well-established whole- sale business, and the loss was not too disastrous. Merchants in the new prairie villages followed the established custom and stocked from its wholesale houses. The rapid extension of the railroads in the early seven- ties meant not only more towns and new markets, but advanced still fur- ther the city's trade ascendancy, for while Minneapolis had equal railroad facilities, St. Paul was the official terminus of the roads running to Duluth and to the East. St. Paul's present and future alike at that time could well have been painted in glowing colors, but the picture had one dark blot. There was no escape from the fact that Minneapolis was rapidly catching up. Already it was called "the sawdust city," and its fame for the flour it milled from the State's expanding wheat supply had extended its market even into European countries (see INDUSTRIAL DEVELOPMENT).

It was during the period when Minneapolis was perfecting the "new process" milling methods, which carried the quantity and quality of its flour output to new records, that the city was suddenly threatened with a loss of all its water power. In 1869 it was discovered that the two tunnels under construction beneath the falls, one for waste and the other for a traffic route, had hastened erosion to a point where the falls themselves might be completely swept away. But the Government quickly came to the rescue, and, aided by private contribution, built a cut-off wall and saved the 120,000 horsepower by a project started in 1870 and completed in 1879.

By 1880 Minneapolis began to boast that it had passed St. Paul in the race for supremacy. This was the decade in which the Twins, totally un- mindful of their mutual dependence, slashed at each other with a vindic- tiveness that today seems incredible. A book published in 1885 and en- dorsed by the mayor of Minneapolis, refers to the *Dual City Blue Book* (St. Paul) as follows: "According to the above authority, Minneapolis is shown to be much the stronger society; that is, there are more spike-tail coats, high collars, more silks, satins, diamonds, jewelry, and gim-cracks generally; more *ton*. We have always contended this was true, but we did not expect to demonstrate it so clearly by cold statistics." Rival sparring was kept up more or less continuously and mainly by the newspapers. Al- though it was largely "literary" in character, it must have fanned the jealous flames, for over the 1890 census the feud attained such scandalous proportions that the Government was forced to take a hand. St. Paul con- tended that in the previous decade the two cities had maintained a popu- lation substantially equal—Minneapolis scorned equality. Charges and countercharges were hurled back and forth. Census takers were kidnapped, evidence seized, arrests were frequent. At last the Government ordered a recount of both cities. The results showed that in guilt at least they were equal. Both had increased their figures by fictitious children and boarders, by counting workers at home and shop, by inventing residences, by the registration of transients. When the smoke cleared away, the lead granted to Minneapolis was 10,000 less than its own figures showed, while St. Paul had basely boosted its figures only a little less. The count officially declared, amity was soon re-established. Joint subscription paid the fines of two convicted enumerators, and charges against 31 others were good-naturedly dismissed. Thus ended the worst and the last rowdy quarrel between the Twins.

Although by 1880 Minneapolis was thoroughly established as an industrial city, St. Paul as the Northwest's commercial stronghold, the demarcation between the business activities of the two cities was by no means as clean-cut as this might seem to imply. St. Paul had a few local sawmills and a number of industries of which boot and shoe manufacturing was most profitable, while Minneapolis was by no means devoid of commercial interests. St. Paul's jobbing at the time far exceeded that of Minneapolis, yet Minneapolis merchants, wholesale and retail, handled the supplies required by the army of transients who seasonably passed through the city on their way to the north woods.

Gradually St. Paul's river trade died, and Minneapolis' twin industries, lumber and flour, declined. Their sharply defined differences, so important historically, began to fade and lose significance.

That the Twin Cities should have developed as two separate metropolitan centers is readily explained by their respective functions, but the reason they did not merge after these functions no longer operated is found in the railroad situation. The Mississippi-Minnesota River valley involves a belt 1 to 5 miles wide of river and marsh bordered by steep bluffs 120 feet high, and while this gives easy access to railroads from the south it has formed a barrier to lines that must cross it. St. Paul is at the exact northern limit of this valley, and has the advantage of breaks in the bluffs that occur in its immediate vicinity. Minneapolis on the other hand was nearer the grain fields of the West, and had in Nicollet Island the most convenient river crossing for routes passing north around the valley. Thus each city had reason to have a railroad center of its own. But to obtain the business they needed, rival railroads from whatever direction were forced to secure entry into both cities. Had the distance between them been less, one railroad center might conceivably have handled the traffic of both, but before the days of automobiles, the 10 miles separating them barred such a possibility. Today, although the cities' borders almost overlap, their commercial centers are almost as far apart as in the beginning. To change this situation would require so tremendous a loss in invested capital that it seems hardly possible that it will ever be undertaken.

With their industrial and commercial differences largely eliminated, the Twins welded their economic life and their establishment as one metropolitan trade center that serves a vast area and includes roughly the northwest quarter of Wisconsin, all of Minnesota, North and South Dakota, Montana, and portions of Iowa and Wyoming; a more recent tendency is toward a closer relationship also with the northern peninsula of Michigan. Since the establishment of a Federal Reserve Bank in Minneapolis in 1914, the Twin Cities have become likewise the financial headquarters of the Northwest.

Minneapolis has continued to maintain a considerable lead over St. Paul in both population and business wealth since 1880. (Between 1920 and 1930 the population increase of Minneapolis was 22 percent; of St. Paul 15.7 percent. The percentage of foreign-born at the same time dropped from 20.5 percent to 19.4 percent in Minneapolis; in St. Paul, however, the decline was far greater, i.e., from 22 percent to 16.2 percent. These figures are interesting when compared with those of the United States as a whole, which showed 13.2 percent of foreign-born in 1920, and 11.6 percent ten years later.) Manufacturing establishments in Minneapolis number 923, in St. Paul, 639. Jobbing, in which St. Paul once surpassed its Twin, has forged ahead in Minneapolis until that city claims a "billion-dollar market." But, while jealous irritation still occasionally bubbles up to the surface in quarrels little more serious than shadow boxing, the question of supremacy is no longer an issue. Psychological antagonism may still exist, but in the economic field both cities have come to a realization of the wisdom of Jim Hill's dream in which he saw not one but both together constituting the industrial heart and arteries of the great body of the Northwest.

Symbolic of this conception is the Midway district sandwiched between the two cities and within the boundaries of each. When the four railroads to the Pacific coast were completed, all freight from the West was routed through what was called the Minnesota Transfer in the Midway district. Around this transfer developed an industrial and commercial center and blocks of residences for the workers. Through it were carried the goods of the Orient, the lumber and fruit from the Pacific States. The double centers became a unit, and promised to become the nucleus of a railroad empire. Before 1915 this Midway was the scene of extraordinary railroad and shipping activity. Then the Panama Canal was opened and the activities languished. But today the Midway is a flourishing industrial and business center and has practically wiped out the cities' official dividing line.

Minneapolis

Railroad Stations: Great Northern Depot, foot of Hennepin and Nicollet Aves., for Burlington, Northwestern, Omaha, Great Northern, Northern Pacific, Great Western, and Minneapolis & St. Louis; Milwaukee Station, 3rd Ave. S. and Washington Ave., for Milwaukee, Soo Line, and Rock Island; Minneapolis Northfield & Southern R.R. Station, 710 3rd Ave. N., also for Anoka Line.

Bus Stations: Union Bus Depot, 29 N. 7th St., for Greyhound, Jefferson Transportation Co., and Twin City Bus Lines; Sioux Limited Bus Depot, 706–1st Ave. N., for Sioux Limited Lines, Grey Goose, and Great Western Stages.

Airport: Wold Chamberlain Field, 60th-66th Sts., and 34th Ave. S., 10.8 m. from loop; for Northwest Airlines Inc., and Hanford Airlines, taxi fare 75¢, time 30 minutes.

Taxis: 25¢ first ½ m., 10¢ each additional ½ m.; no passenger limit.

Streetcars: Fare 10¢ or 6 tokens 45¢; 5-15 minute service before midnight, hourly service 1-5 a.m.; transfers on all carlines and cross-town busses.

Street Busses: Hennepin Ave. 10¢, no transfers; Minneapolis-St. Paul busses, University Ave. (10 min. service before midnight), Lake St.-Marshall Ave. (20 min. service until 7 p.m.), 2 tokens 25¢, 1 fare for each city, no transfers.

Traffic Regulations: Regulation traffic lights in business district; 5 min. to 1 hour loop parking 8 a.m.-6 p.m.; no all-night parking; no U-turn at traffic lights, whether in operation or not; L. turn prohibited where posted; chief one-way streets, Emerson Ave. S. (N. to S.) between Hennepin and 36th; Dupont Ave. S. (S. to N.) from 36th St. to Hennepin Ave.

Accommodations: More than 100 hotels. Rates higher in winter and spring. Tourist homes on highways entering the city. Tourist camp, Minnehaha Park and the Mississippi River, open May 20th-Oct. 15th.

Information Service: Gateway Tourist Information Bureau of the Minneapolis Civic & Commerce Association, Washington between Hennepin and Nicollet Aves.; A.A.A. Tourist Information Bureau, 13th at LaSalle.

Radio Stations: KSTP (1,460 kc); WCCO (810 kc); WDGY (1,180 kc); WLB (760 kc); WMIN (1,370 kc); WTCN 1,250 kc).

Theaters and Motion Picture Houses: Lyceum, 85 S. 11th St., theater and concert hall; Gayety, Washington and 1st Ave. N., burlesque; University Little Theater, Music Bldg., University of Minnesota Campus; 9 first-run motion picture houses.

Athletic Fields: 143 parks with 11 lakes provide complete recreational facilities.

Swimming: Camden Baths, Washington near Colfax Ave. N.; Lake Calhoun, N. Calhoun Blvd. (W. Lake St.) and Dean Blvd.; Lake Nokomis, Cedar Ave. and E. 50th St.; Glenwood Lake, east side of lake and Western Ave.

Golf: Municipal Courses: (All have 18 holes with grass greens, and charge rates that vary (30-75¢) according to quality of the course and time of play.) Armour, St. Anthony Blvd. and 22nd Ave. NE.; Columbia, Central and 33rd Aves. NE.; Glenwood, Plymouth Ave. N. and Glenwood Pkwy.; Hiawatha, 46th and Cedar; Meadowbrook, 4.5 m. Excelsior Blvd.

Baseball: Nicollet Park, 31st and Nicollet, American Association.

Tennis: The Parade, Kenwood Pkwy. and Dupont Ave. S., clay courts; Nicollet Field, Nicollet and 42nd, cement courts; and nearly 200 courts (123 cement) in city parks.

Boating: Lake Harriet, canoes 30¢ per hr., rowboats for fishing $1 per day, launch trip around lake 10¢, canoe docks, reasonable fee; Lake Calhoun, same facilities,

launch trips cover Lake Calhoun, Lake of the Isles and Cedar Lake 25¢, 1½ hrs.
Sailboat dockage, Lake St. and E. Calhoun, $5 (includes use of tender). Lake of the
Isles, canoe docks.
Polo: Fort Snelling, Hiawatha Ave., State 55.
Archery: (Summer) William Berry Park, south shore of Lake Calhoun; (Winter)
Armory, 500 S. 6th, Nov.-Apr., Sun., 8:30 a.m.-12:30 p.m. (Twin City Archery
Club, see J. A. Dashiell, Sporting Goods Dept., The Dayton Co.).
Sailboating: Lake Minnetonka, 12 m. State 7.
Riding: Joe Lacy Riding Academy, 2816 Dupont Ave. S.; Eddie Merfeld Riding
Stables, 2815 Emerson Ave. S.; and the Pastime Riding Club, 5626 W. Lake St.
(St. Louis Park) supply horses; 11 miles of bridle paths around Lakes Cedar, Cal-
houn, Harriet, and the Isles.
General Recreational Information: Minneapolis Park Board, City Hall, for informa-
tion about 134 diamondball fields, 38 football gridirons, 36 baseball diamonds, 153
horseshoe courts, more than 50 skating and hockey rinks, and other facilities.

Annual Events: Winter Sports Play Week, Jan. (10,000 Lakes Speed Skating, Snow-
modeling Contest [Loring Park] John S. Johnson Memorial Skating Meet); N. W.
Golden Gloves Amateur Boxing Contest, Jan.; N. W. Ski Meet, Bush Lake, 5 m.
SW. of city *(see Tour 14),* Jan.; Winter Ice Carnival, March; Figure Skating,
March; State Amateur Hockey Tournament, March; Bach Society Concert (U. of M.),
April; Lilacs in Bloom (Lyndale Park), 1st wk. May; Swedish Art Exhibit,
May, n.f.d.; *Syttende Mai,* Norwegian national holiday, May 17, Loring Park; Peo-
nies in Bloom, 2nd wk. June; Minn. Trapshooting Championship, June; Park Con-
certs, June, July; Twin City Archery Meet, William Berry Park, or Highland Park
(St. Paul), June; Roses in Bloom, beginning 1st wk. July; Playground Pageant, 4th
wk. July; Park Board City Tennis Tournament, July; A.A.U. Swimming Meet,
Aug.; State Rifle Championship (Ft. Snelling), Sept.; Chrysanthemum Show, Park
Board Greenhouse, 38th and Bryant Ave. S., Nov.; Twin City Art Exhibit, Minneapolis Institute of Arts, autumn, n.f.d.

MINNEAPOLIS (812 alt., 464,356 pop.) is the largest city in Minnesota
in both area and population, and ranks fifteenth among American cities.
The visitor who comes in the summer by plane and circles above its residential districts looks down upon what seems to be a forest dotted with
houses, threaded with the blue of lakes that loop the town from the Mississippi to the Minnesota River like a chain of beads each in a green velvet
setting, and crossed by dozens of straight white lines which lead with
scarcely a curve or an angle into the city's business heart. The narrow Mississippi winds through the downtown section, spanned by bridges and
bordered by its new levees, the State university, great flour mills and their
towering elevators, while diverging east and west as far as the eye can follow, extends a network of railroad trackage.

If the traveler comes by train to the Union Station, after winding over
Jim Hill's beautiful stone-arched bridge, he will catch a glimpse of the
buildings of the city's major industry—flour milling—rising above swirling water, and of a ragged skyline that refuses to compose. When he steps
out on the street his first impression is of broad radiating avenues. To be
sure, flophouses, employment agencies, beer parlors, little shops whose
overcoats and pants are padlocked to the street racks, flank those wide
streets somewhat disconcertingly for two or three blocks—reminders not
only of pioneer days, but of the grim law that growth and decay in cities
as elsewhere exist side by side. But the tourist, accustomed to shabby settings for his country's railroad terminals, is likely to hurry on to his hotel,

stopping only to note approvingly the spaciousness and the beginnings of a city's planning suggested by the new post office at the left, the Gateway Building and the Nicollet Hotel at the convergence down the street of the city's proudest shopping avenues, Nicollet and Hennepin.

If, however, the traveler be of those who like to sense a city's personality, he will do well to pause for a moment and look around him. For this is Bridge Square, and here, and in the immediate vicinity more than in any other part of the town, are gathered those forces that have shaped Minneapolis in the past, and may well determine its temper for a long time to come. Here, at the foot of the square, Minneapolis was born beside the river whose falls Father Hennepin admired, blessed, and named in 1680, and which 150 years later attracted the first settlers. The bridge to the left is the successor of the bridge they built, the first, although they did not know it, to cross the main current of the Mississippi in all its long course from northern Minnesota to the Gulf. The bridge ended at the island (Nicollet Island) that shunts the river's force to the west, now the site of straggling warehouses and decrepit dwellings, but then covered with maples and oaks, and there the west-bank settlers boarded a ferry that carried them across to St. Anthony for their supplies, or for the festivities held at the seat of Northwest hospitality, the Winslow House.

An observer will have to give his fancy free rein, for not a visible remnant of those early days remains to guide it. Even the falls of which the priest wrote so glowingly have been tamed and harnessed, and suggest not a trace of their former wild beauty. Yet only by recalling the wilderness of a century ago will he be able to comprehend the city that rose in its place; for the spirit of the founders has, throughout the century, dominated the social and commercial life of Minneapolis. True, the big industry builders came for the most part in the seventies and eighties, but they were brother Yankees of the same stock and tradition. As the settlers exploited the Indians, so they exploited the forests and other natural resources, and both groups shared the powers of ruthlessness and vision that characterize all conquerors, making it possible for them to build a great city in a phenomenally short time; a city that carried two infant industries to world records in a little more than a single generation. Scarcely more than a stone's throw from the square are the great flour mills and elevators which brought wealth to the city as well as to their owners, wealth that has built art galleries and schools, and financed a fine civic orchestra; around the river's bend on its opposite side, high on the bluffs, is the State university they founded that educated many of their sons; down by the river's borders the new levees proclaim the grandsons' plans for a resurrected river traffic whereby they hope to emerge from the economic shadow cast by the Panama Canal and the Interstate Commerce rulings on freight rates of the railroads whose thousands of miles merge here.

But courage and vision and water, mighty as they were, could not alone build a State or a city. For that, manpower was needed. Men came from northern Europe, thousands upon thousands of them, and for thirty years poured into this square to sit shoulder to shoulder on the curbs all day, by night to sleep shoulder to shoulder in the dreary flophouses that topped the employment offices, while they waited to be sent to the timber, to the wheat fields, to the railroad camps, or to the mines. The square became the greatest labor center in the Northwest. Most of the jobs offered were seasonal, and back again came "whistlepunks," "shovel stiffs," and harvest hands by the hundreds to spend their pay in ways often highly disturbing to the more respectable citizenry. Bridge Square was a sore spot then, as it is now, but much of the time it could be ignored by a proud city growing steadily away from it, and after all, those high-booted, checked-shirted lumberjacks, and those solid, blond Norse harvest hands brought good money to the merchant's coffers. In those hey-days of expansion there was a job for every man, and Bridge Square, while admittedly ugly and perhaps not very fragrant, was generally regarded as an inevitable symptom of the city's youth and vigor.

Those days are gone as irrevocably as the pristine wildness of St. Anthony Falls. Today, listlessness rather than vigor stamps most of the homeless men, who, between jobs or long since despairing of any, mill about the beer parlors and the shabby movie houses. To Minneapolitans, Bridge Square symbolizes not alone struggles with an enemy-infested wilderness, but the even more dramatic present-day struggle for power between the grandsons of the early builders and the grandsons of the men they summoned from Europe and distant States to help them, a combat in which both sides still fight with ruthlessness and vision. The pioneer spirit has been diluted by new race mixtures, its confidence shaken by new social trends, still it survives as the motivating force behind much of the city's optimism and ferment.

The sordidness of the city's gateway was condemned in 1917 by the new planning board, which replaced it—on paper—with public buildings designed to convert the area into an impressive transportation center. The World War and the decline in industry during the 1920's checked the building program, and the site has remained practically unchanged except for the recent addition of a new post office. Meanwhile the square is far from indicative of what the city has to offer, and is soon traversed. When the Minneapolis visitor departs, the impression he carries with him is usually of space, trees, boulevards, and homes, and more likely than not he is willing to concede that Minneapolis comes justly by its reputation—one of the Nation's most beautiful cities.

The founding fathers from the first envisaged an orderly town. The Mississippi determined the direction of the first streets they platted, and they ran them from northwest to southeast, parallel and at right angles to the river, as they still are in the downtown district. As the city stretched outwards, however, they straightened out the wide roads on which they built their residences, and platted the avenues due north and south and the cross streets east and west, in a regular geometric pattern. The streets were numbered as they are today, but the avenues, originally named, were mostly changed to numbers soon after the city was incorporated, and, true to their New England memories, they planted the streets with double rows of elms. They had a great unpeopled prairie on which to build their city, with only the St. Paul line to the east checking their advance. With no reason for building in brick or brownstone rows, each house, whether mansion or cabin, could have not only a personality of its own, but a barn, lawn, and a vegetable garden.

The liking for independent dwellings has persisted through the years. Minneapolis has its apartment houses and its many two-family duplexes, but apartment living never has been as popular here as in many cities, while each duplex has its green setting and almost invariably puts up a brave front of appearing, at least, to be a one-family house. Today, when barns have been displaced by garages, vegetables and chickens by flowers and shrubs, it is claimed that approximately 50 percent of its citizens own their homes—homes large and small, attractive and ugly, but nearly all with tree-shaded lawns and flowery shrubs, scattered over the city's 58 square miles of gently rolling land. This means an average of only 12 persons to an acre.

Ask a Minneapolitan to show you the "best" residence street, and he will be hard-put to make a choice, for in Minneapolis people of wealth have shown little inclination to congregate in one district. In the nineties they tried it when the aldermen, exasperated by the fame that came to St. Paul's Summit Avenue, elected to make Park Avenue its rival. Today a long line of Victorian houses gradually being taken over by business testifies to their mistaken judgment. Minneapolitans who could build houses in keeping with the traditions of wealth selected sites in a dozen districts: on the hill surrounding Loring Park, about Lake of the Isles, in Lynnhurst that includes and stretches back from the east side of Lake Harriet, about the Art Institute, or along the River Road. Surrounding these widely separated islands of the financially elect, are the thousands of stucco, brick, and frame residences of the professional and upper business group. Architecturally many no doubt warrant criticism, but see them in summer, miles upon miles of them, standing to their knees in flowering shrubs, their only fences glowing borders of blossoming perennials, and one is likely to forget any architectural shortcomings.

The workingman's family is no less likely to have a garden where he and his wife raise flowers, tomatoes, onions, and lettuce. And he too has a dozen or more districts from which to choose his residence. Minneapolis has its shabby neighborhoods, of course, and there are dingy stretches, particularly in the older sections, but of congestion there is almost none. In the sense usually implied by the word, Minneapolis has no slums, even though it admits to neighborhoods where substandard housing conditions prevail. One such was razed in 1936 by a Federal housing project whose plans include 65 buildings with 613 family living units on an area of 26 acres. Another such district has been replaced by the municipal public market.

As one looks over downtown Minneapolis today, it is amusing to recall the description of the city that the St. Anthony *Republican* printed in its issue of May 7, 1857: "Business:—Never before have the streets of this dual city seen such business activity. Steamboat whistles sound at both ends of the city. An unending number of goods-laden wagons and carriages. . . . Crowds of strangers. . . . Spring goods are landed and unpacked everywhere. . . . All the ladies are out to get first choice. . . . Continual rattle of machines. . . . New buildings shooting up to right and left. . . . Everyone in a hurry. Such is the life just now in St. Anthony and Minneapolis." This was ten years after R. P. Russell opened the first store in St. Anthony, and four years after Thomas Chambers invited the settlers on the west bank to make their purchases at his Pioneer Store on their own side of the river. The boom that skyrocketed land prices up 500 percent was at its height, its collapse obviously unsuspected by the exuberant editor.

Today, only 80 years later, near the site of the Pioneer Store, acres of elevators and flour mills proclaim Minneapolis a bread basket and grain bin for the Nation. South from the river loom massed office and commercial buildings; head and shoulders above them rise the obelisk-like Foshay Tower, the streamlined Rand and Telephone Buildings, and embedded in the heart of the city is the Federal Reserve Bank that has made Minneapolis the financial capital of the Northwest. Piercing this granite-made district, the city's smartest retail street, Nicollet Avenue, extends southward, its long array of plate-glass-fronted shops a far cry, indeed, from Chambers' Pioneer Store.

Often called the Fifth Avenue of Minneapolis, Nicollet resembles it at least in having no carline to mar its broad expanse, while none can deny that the models displayed behind its windows have their originals in New York and Paris. But despite elegant motorcars, well-dressed matrons, smartly turned-out Junior Leaguers and working girls, the people hurrying along the streets or staring into windows in general look quite different from those in New York. There is here a predominance of fair hair and high cheekbones to remind one of the great Scandinavian immigrations that during its first 25 years made up more than 45 percent of the city's population, frequently farmers in overalls and mud-coated thick-soled boots, or in wide-checked mackinaws, proclaim again how close to the soil is Minneapolis, for all its boasted cosmopolitanism.

All Minneapolitans may and largely do share in the outdoor sports provided by its lakes and parks. The town was very young and sprawling when Charles M. Loring—the "Father of Minneapolis Parks"—realized the potentialities for beauty and recreation offered by the lakes within its borders, and persuaded the State legislature to create a park board. Fortunately, despite opposition on the grounds of expense, its members from the first kept firmly to their determination to establish one of the most beautiful and widely used park and boulevard systems in the United States. But it is to Theodore Wirth, park superintendent from 1906 to 1935, that credit is due for most of the major park improvements. Today Minneapolis has 144 parks embracing 5,253 acres, or one park acre for every 92 of its people.

The social life of people of wealth in Minneapolis furnishes ample wordage for the society page. Descendants of the early Yankee builders are leaders of this group, and this perhaps explains the hospitable tradition and the indifference to rigid formality in their entertaining. Although bankers and professional men of Scandinavian origin are occasionally found within this upper group, the social life of the Swedish and Norwegian families of substance, as well as that of the middle classes, is largely confined to members of their own race. The guest at one of their dinners or New Year's parties may feel that, aside from the language spoken, he might easily be in Europe, and he will long remember the good talk, the snowbirds, the aqua vitae, and the Swedish punch his host imported from his homeland specially for the occasion.

Minneapolitans as a whole do little of their entertaining outside their homes. For this reason cafes and restaurants have less glamour than they offer on either the eastern or western coast. Everyone goes to the movies (since there is practically no theater), after which a host is more likely to take his guest home for a late supper than to a nightclub. The most colorful restaurants are those that cater to Swedish patronage, and here is often a jolly crowd made up mostly of workingmen with their wives or girls, with here and there a professor from the university, all sharing with gusto the beer, the *lutefisk,* and the occasional outburst of song.

Well provided with churches, 290 of which are Protestant, 27 Roman Catholic, and 10 Jewish, every creed is represented in the city—even the Orthodox Greek. By far the largest number of churchgoers have Lutheran affiliations. In the social life of middle-class Scandinavians, their church plays a large part. The *smörgasbord* and *lutefisk* suppers prepared by the women's organizations, not only provide needed funds, but are occasions also for music and general sociability. Lutheran pastors have today, perhaps, less weight than in pioneer days, when their authority was almost absolute, but they are still active forces in the community, especially in behalf of temperance movements and in the sporadic attacks on the city's underworld conditions.

In a rapidly growing city, amalgamation of foreign groups tends to take place very quickly, and the evaluation of the contribution of each grows increasingly difficult. If to the Scandinavians and Finns can safely be ascribed much of the success of the co-operatives, of the city's smaller national groups, the French, German, Polish, Ukranian, Greek, Negro, and others, it can be said with assurance that all have shared in the making of Minneapolis, and that all have made cultural contributions. The names of several of the city's streets—Hennepin, La Salle, Marquette, Nicollet—commemorate seventeenth century French explorers and missionaries. Almost two centuries later the French-Canadians formed the settlement at St. Anthony. Many of these were half-breeds, but some were descendants of French families from Brittany and Normandy. Others, exiled from Acadia, after wandering about for years, established homes beside the falls. Until 1900 the French continued to come to Minneapolis, most often by way of Canada, and for years they struggled to conserve their language and traditions, but it was a losing fight in the face of the hordes of Scandinavians who were all but taking possession of the city. Today their only stronghold is their church, Our Lady of Lourdes (Notre Dame de Lourdes), where sermons in French are still preached every Sunday and in whose parochial school at least a part of the teaching is carried on in the language of their ancestors.

The first known Swede to come to Minneapolis territory was Nils Nyberg, a shoemaker, who settled in St. Anthony in 1851, and was always referred to as the "foreigner." Until Civil War times a Swede was regarded with lively curiosity and interest. The story is told that one day in the later 1850's a yellow-haired blue-eyed giant wandered into the settlement, his only luggage what he could carry in a red plaid cotton handkerchief. Weary and ragged, he sat himself down on the street where Hennepin Avenue crosses Washington. Yankee John Wilson came out of his blacksmithy and when he could make nothing of the stranger's replies to his questions, sent for Mousseau the Frenchman. But to Mousseau's "parlezvous" the traveler merely stared dumbly. A German was sent for, but soon retired abashed. A crowd gathered to chatter and stare at this strange being who was unable to understand even one of the three languages common to respectable Minnesota communities. John Broderick, the Irishman, was pushed forward and bashfully offered his Gaelic. At last someone remembered the "foreigner," Nyberg, and ran to fetch him. At the first Swedish words, the stranger leapt to his feet, and amid general rejoicing the problem was solved.

After the Civil War Scandinavians swept into Minneapolis in ever increasing numbers. They opened the city's first boarding houses, they became storekeepers, tailors, milk dealers, lawyers, doctors, and bankers. By the seventies there was not a business, trade, or profession in which Scandinavian names did not occur. Washington Avenue became their main business street. At first the Scandinavian population was almost equally divided between Swedes and Norse, with far fewer Danes. But by 1880 Swedes began to outnumber the Norse, and after that date the discrepancy grew greater. With the practical cessation of immigration, and the frequent marrying into other racial groups, the proportion of Scandinavians in the population has been steadily growing smaller. Today foreign-born Scandinavians make up less than 10 percent of the city's population. Their language and customs are rapidly disappearing as with each oncoming year they grow more and more truly American (*see IMMIGRATION AND RACIAL ELEMENTS*).

Minneapolis is not yet 90 years old, a youthful city, but during these brief years its population has been multiplied many times; its two industries have increased to more than one hundred; it has built up a school system that compares favorably with any in the Nation, and it has kept the percentage of illiteracy to the lowest point achieved by cities in its class; it has its orchestra, its art museums, and is the seat of a univeristy third in total registration in the United States. It has had, and still must solve, its problems arising from railroad rates, from the diminished purchasing power of farmers, from labor unrest; and it knows that its future may well depend on how these are met. It has been obliged to resign some of its dreams of an empire capital, but its optimism is no less vigorous because it is more realistic.

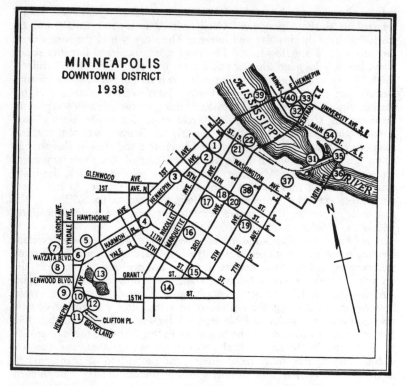

POINTS OF INTEREST

(The Heart of Minneapolis)

1. The GATEWAY BUILDING, Washington Ave. between Nicollet and Hennepin Aves., houses the Tourist Information Bureau. The building and park are on what was once known as "Center Block," site of the Old City Hall. In the waitingroom are MURALS painted by David Granahan, graduate of the Minneapolis School of Fine Arts, depicting incidents in Minnesota's history.

2. The SITE OF THE OLD NICOLLET HOUSE, Washington Ave. between Hennepin and Nicollet Aves., is occupied by the modern Nicollet Hotel. The old frontier inn, built in 1857 of local stone, was popular in the "Mill Town" whirl when Minnesota was still a Territory and Minneapolis not yet a chartered city. The hotel was named, as is its present successor and the avenue on which it stands, in honor of Joseph N. Nicollet, a French exile, who was commissioned by the United States Government to make scientific observations in the Minnesota Territory in 1836–38. The present red brick structure was begun in 1923.

3. The WEST HOTEL, Hennepin Ave. and 5th St., designed by Leroy Buffington (1847–1931), is typical of the eclectic architecture of the period, incorporating in its design both Gothic and Renaissance detail. Its construction rather than its design entitles it to architectural notice, for upon this building Buffington bases his claim to priority in the invention of the braced skeleton. In his memoirs he describes the framework and adds, "So, here, in the West Hotel, was first constructed in 1882, the embryo state of the column and the supporting shelf of the skeleton of steel construction." Inasmuch as Buffington did not apply for his patent on the "skyscraper" until 1887, after the erection of the modern Home Insurance Building in Chicago by Jenney, the local architect's claim rests upon the incorporation of this principle in the West Hotel. Today it is generally conceded that, although the plan was an advance in lobby construction, the new idea was applied here only in partial form because the West Hotel was constructed while Buffington was evolving his "skyscraper" design.

The hotel was the center for most of the social and political life of the 1880's and 1890's.

4. The MINNEAPOLIS PUBLIC LIBRARY (*open weekdays, 9-9; newspaper and technical room, Sun. 2-9*), 1001 Hennepin Ave., was established by legislative act in 1885 and opened December 16, 1889. The bronze statute, *The Goddess of Wisdom* by Jacob Fjelde, is above the entrance on Hennepin Avenue. The building itself, of red granite and bearing the unmistakable stamp of the 1880's, is architecturally undistinguished. Besides its regular collection, it houses the Minneapolis Athenaeum Library. The Athenaeum, organized in 1859 to lend books to shareholders and subscribers, has grown to its present status largely through the bequest of Dr. Kirby Spencer, a pioneer Minneapolis dentist, described as an "eccentric man of unique methods and scientific tastes." When Dr. Spencer.died in 1870, he bequeathed to the organization his personal fortune of $20,000 and the entire income from his Washington Avenue and Third Street property, a gift which has added nearly 100,000 volumes to the library collection. Largely through the efforts of Herbert Putman (now of the Library of Congress), who came to the Minneapolis post in 1884, the Public Library entered into a 99-year contract with the Athenaeum by which the latter's books were made available for free public use.

The collection in the main library numbers 590,000 volumes. The library includes special collections of business, art, social problems, and Scandinaviana, the latter containing more than 8,000 volumes in Swedish, Norwegian, Danish, and Icelandic. The nucleus of the notable collection of the Art Library on the third floor was the rare books bought in 1892 in France, Germany, and Belgium.

Outstanding of persons associated with the library is Gracia Countryman, who retired in 1936 after 45 years of service, 30 of which she spent as chief librarian.

5. The BASILICA OF ST. MARY (Roman Catholic), Hennepin Ave. and 16th St., surmounts the rise of ground at the sweeping curve of the Avenue. It is a striking version of Renaissance architecture, typical of the 19th century. The architect was Eugene L. Masqueray. The familiar char-

acteristics of the basilican plan are discernible in the broad nave with side aisles ending in semicircular chapels, in the dome on four great piers set apart from the main body of the church by a great arch, and in the arched apse for the organ and choir.

The central portion of the façade contains the rose window and is surmounted by a broken pediment with a sculptured group representing the Assumption. Tower-motifs enframe the central composition, and a pillared portico completes the façade. The architectural composition of the plan is further expressed on the exterior—in the long nave with its rhythmically spaced windows, as well as in the square massive sanctuary, defined by a pedimented gable. From this base the square drum of the dome is lifted and, in the superstructure, becomes octagonal.

The walls of the vestibule are lined with honed pink stone from Mankato. The vaulted ceiling is colored, and above the doors are stone panels bearing religious symbols. The baptistry contains a well-designed font of Siena marble and bronze, and at the sanctuary ends of the outer aisles are chapels dedicated to St. Anne and to St. Anthony of Padua with altars and walls of marble.

The nave, lined with Mankato gray stone, is arranged with alternating piers and small columns that support an impressive ceiling that springs from a stone cornice 43 feet above the floor and rises to a height of 75 feet at the crown of the vault. It is suspended from six steel girders that support the concrete roof.

The sanctuary, together with its appended aisles and chapels, occupies one-third of the area of the church and is spacious enough for the most elaborate liturgical functions. It is separated from the ambulatories by twelve monolithic columns of Swiss cipolin marble. In the spaces between the columns are hand-forged iron grilles with symbolic decoration. The columns supporting the entablature form the pedestals for the 6-foot marble statues of the Apostles, only existing copies of the 12 figures in the Basilica of St. John Lateran, Rome.

The altar is of white Italian statuary marble, and over it is an imposing marble baldachino whose ceiling is of brilliant gold and azure mosaic. The distinctive colors—white, blue, gold, and red, associated with the Virgin Mary, to whom the church is dedicated—are used throughout. The stained glass in the edifice is of Renaissance design.

Although the building was begun in 1907, formal dedication did not take place until August 15, 1915, when only the exterior was completed. The sanctuary and altar were finished in 1924, and the nave and other parts in 1926. In 1926 the building was formally designated as a "basilica" affiliated with St. Mary Major and St. John Lateran, both in Rome.

6. The STATUE OF FATHER LOUIS HENNEPIN stands in front of the basilica in a small triangle. It was designed by Fred A. Slifer of St. Paul, and placed there in 1930 by the Knights of Columbus to commemorate the 250th anniversary of the Franciscan monk's discovery of the Falls of St. Anthony.

7. DUNWOODY INSTITUTE, 816 Wayzata Blvd., is on a tract of ground equal to six city blocks. It was founded in 1914 with a $5,000,-

ooo endowment by William Dunwoody, to furnish instruction in the industrial and mechanical arts to the youth of Minneapolis and Minnesota; tuition fees are very low. The school is said to be the country's largest endowed trade school. During the World War the institute trained more than 2,000 men for trades pertaining to military activities, primarily radio and telegraphy. The present enrollment of 4,000 is divided into two general classes; the regular day school for boys beyond the eighth grade, and an evening school for men already experienced in a trade who can register for "shop courses" of varying length to meet their individual needs.

8. The PARADE, Wayzata Blvd., Erie Ave., Lyndale Ave., and Kenwood Pkwy., is the hub of the Park Board's summer recreational activities. On this tract of 65.56 acres are 26 diamondball fields, a number of baseball diamonds and football gridirons, and 13 clay-surfaced tennis courts. At the floodlighted diamond at the corner of Lyndale Avenue and Wayzata Boulevard, seats are available for about four thousand spectators and standing room for several thousand more. Most popular of Park Board competitive sports is diamondball, which had its inception in Minneapolis in 1895, the invention of Lewis Rober, a local fireman.

9. The WALKER ART GALLERIES *(open Tues.-Sat., 10-5; Sun. 12:30-5; adm. 10¢)*, 1710 Lyndale Ave., housed in a one-story ornate terra cotta structure of Byzantine design, contain the paintings, jade, and early ceramics collected by the millionaire lumberman, T. B. Walker. The collection of jade and ceramics is noteworthy both for its size and quality. The building also is headquarters for the Minnesota Archeological Society.

10. ST. MARKS EPISCOPAL CHURCH, 15th St. and Hennepin Ave., erected in 1910–11, has a parklike setting similar to many English parish churches. The building was designed by Hewitt and Brown of Minneapolis. The general architectural style, although somewhat modified, is Perpendicular Gothic. The typical English plan of a long nave with side aisles, a deep choir space, shallow chancel, and square apse is reproduced in this structure. There are, however, no transepts. The exterior, of Indiana limestone, is very simple, with a square crenellated tower; the plainness of the walls is relieved only by the perpendicular tracery of the windows and the occasional use of ornament.

The plain walls of the interior provide a suitable foil for the decorative color and woodwork. Octagonal piers support Gothic arches along the nave and above them are the stained-glass clerestory windows, which thus far are without their proper glass. The ceiling vaults are groined, with a continuous rib parallel to the nave along the crown of the vaults. The vaults themselves are formed of tile laid in herringbone pattern and supported by heavy cross ribs.

The windows over the entrance and the one in the apse, of Renaissance design, by Charles Connick, are hardly suitable to the Gothic interior. In better relationship to the interior are the lower aisle windows. A small chapel at the right of the sanctuary is charming in detail and furnishing. Noteworthy are the font, the pulpit, the lectern, and the choir stalls and

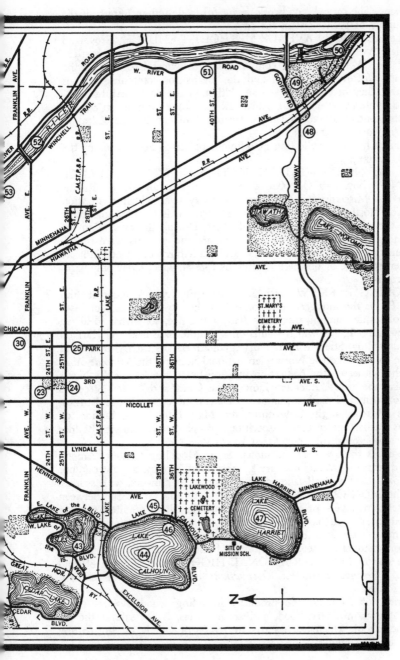

choir screens. The carved woodwork, beautiful in design and finish, is the finest example of such work in the city.

11. The HENNEPIN AVENUE METHODIST CHURCH, Groveland and Lyndale Aves., designed by Tolz, King and Day, is the city's best example of the "Akron" plan of church structures whose basic idea is the radial seating of the auditorium and the means for combining various units so that they may be used as one. Although the non-ritualistic treatment of the interior is undistinguished, the limestone exterior, an adaptation of the central octagonal lantern treatment of the Ely Cathedral in England, is worthy of note.

The church houses a collection of religious paintings bequeathed by the late T. B. Walker.

12. In the NORTHWESTERN NATIONAL LIFE INSURANCE BUILDING lobby, 430 Oak Grove St., are MURALS by H. W. Rubins depicting the Mississippi as the water highway over which civilization came to the Northwest. The simplicity and restraint is in admirable keeping with the earnest purpose of the pioneers. During the excavation for this building many fossils of preglacial plants and animals were found. The remains of white spruce, tamarack, and white birch unearthed indicate the former existence of northern coniferous forests where today only hardwoods grow.

13. LORING PARK, W. 15th St., Hennepin Ave., Willow St. and Harmon Pl., is the most centrally located of the city parks. It contains a number of statues, among them *Ole Bull*, a life-size, somewhat idealized bronze by Jacob Fjelde which stands on a granite base near the Harmon Place and Willow Street corner. Norwegian-Americans each year meet at the statue to celebrate the Norwegian national holiday, the *Syttende Mai*. Those who witnessed the dedication in 1897 heard the son of the Norse fiddler play one of his father's melodies. Near Grant and Willow Streets is a group of memorial markers; among persons honored are Maria Sanford, for years a teacher at the State university; Mary Burr Lewis, founder of the Lewis Parliamentary Law Association; Joseph Smith Johnson, builder of the first house on this tract (1856).

The park is the scene of an annual Snow Modeling Contest. Among the varied recreational facilities are a lighted roque court, a giant outdoor checkerboard, and a small lake which, in winter, is crowded with skaters.

14. The MUNICIPAL AUDITORIUM, 14th and Grant Sts. between Stevens and 3rd Aves., of Bedford stone with St. Cloud granite base, was completed in 1927. It has a seating capacity of 15,000. Most elaborate of its equipment is the $120,000 organ, which has a five-manual concert console, a four-manual theater console, and a built-in grand piano.

15. In the MILLER VOCATIONAL HIGH SCHOOL, 11th St. and 3rd Ave., is a mural decoration, *Occupations,* by Lucia Wiley of the Federal Art Project.

A variety of student-made products, including wooden ware, metal work, clothing, millinery, food, and art novelties, is for sale at the art shop. The school, which teaches arts and crafts of widely varying nature, is closed in the summer.

16. The FOSHAY TOWER *(observation balcony at the 32nd floor open daily; adm. 25¢)*, 821 Marquette Ave., conspicuous in the Minneapolis skyline, is unique both in design and in history. This strange building was the headquarters of a far-flung public utility empire, which, in 1929, soon after dedication ceremonies, collapsed into a receivership with prosecution of the promoters. The luxurious apartment designed for the would-be utilities king has never been used, except—so the story goes—by a plumber who once bathed in the regal bathtub.

The design of the building was a result of Foshay's admiration for the Washington Monument. Foshay commissioned the architects to design the office building to simulate the form of the monument. The sloping walls reduce the floor area as the building rises, and also serve, with the necessary cross bracing, as a natural windbracing. The framework is of steel and reinforced concrete, with horizontal bracing extending into the foundation. The building is faced with slabs of Indiana limestone, which, owing to the gradually receding walls, are not interchangeable and had to be cut and delivered in sequence.

The shaft is centered in a city square and is set back about 60 feet from the street. A two-story building surrounds three sides of the tower, which is reached by a block-long arcade. The tower is 81 by 87 feet at the base, narrowing to 59 by 65 feet at the top, each side sloping 11 feet from grade to top. Atop the 447-foot tower are two aviation beacons, one fixed and the other revolving.

The building has an original Houdon bust of Washington, together with two bronze copies. The original stands in the center of the tower lobby, directly in front of the elevators. The interior of the lobby is designed in the modern manner, decorated with wrought iron, marble, and bronze.

The lavish dedication ceremonies on Aug. 30, 31, and Sept. 1, 1929, were widely publicized. More than one hundred thousand dollars is said to have been spent for dinners, special trains, and for visiting celebrities among whom were Sousa and his band.

17. The RAND TOWER *(open)*, 6th St. and Marquette Ave., is a 27-story structure designed by Holabird and Root of Chicago and constructed in 1928–29. It was awarded a prize in 1930 by the American Institute of Architects. From an 82-foot square base the building rises in a series of setbacks, some of them very shallow and used only to emphasize the terminal treatment of the tower.

The lobby and hallways are decorated in marble, glass, nickel, and vividly colored enamel. The lobbies on the Marquette Avenue side are faced with Tosa grey Nelle marble set in large slabs with panels of matching grain. The marble is accented by inserts of hand-carved glass in modern patterns. A small bronze-plated statue by Oskar Hansen stands on a black marble base in the lobby. Indirect lighting and panels of glass etched to simulate clouds add to its effectiveness as a symbol of aviation. The circular stairway from the main lobby is composed of various marbles, with balustrades and handrails of nickel.

18. The NORTHWESTERN BELL TELEPHONE BUILDING

(guides available for tours), 224 S. 5th St., begun in 1930 and completed in 1932, was designed by a Minneapolis architect, Rhodes Robertson, of the firm of Hewitt & Brown. All of the materials, with the exception of a small amount of marble, came from Minnesota; the steel, from Mesabi Range ore, was fabricated in Minneapolis; the cement came from Duluth; Minnesota firms supplied all equipment used.

The design is the characteristic American perpendicular skyscraper style, with horizontal lines subdued and the vertical lines emphasized. This effect is amplified by the dull-finish aluminum covering the spandrels between the tops and bottoms of all windows. The effect from a short distance is one of light and dark vertical stripes which give an upward movement to the design.

Details symbolic of communication are incorporated into the decorations. The metal work of the 755 windows is of steel and cast aluminum. The doors are of bronze. The walls on the ground floor are finished with marble. Its 26 stories, each unusually high to accommodate special equipment, rise 346 feet above the street level; below, the three basement floors extend 42 feet resting on the solid rock stratum that underlies the Mississippi riverbed above St. Anthony Falls.

19. The ARMORY, 500 S. 6th St., headquarters for Minneapolis units of the National Guard, is a modern cream-colored brick building with granite base and limestone trim, completed in 1935 and used for public gatherings and recreational activities. In the trophy room *(open daily 10-5; Mon., Tues., and Wed. 8-10 p.m.)* are TWO MURALS in true fresco technique done by local artists under the Federal Art Project. One of these, symbolizing Minnesota resources and early history, is by Elsa Jemne, and the other, representing the history of Minnesota National Guard, is by Lucia Wiley.

20. The CITY HALL AND HENNEPIN COUNTY COURTHOUSE, 4th St. between 3rd and 4th Aves., contains city and county offices and jails, and the Minneapolis police headquarters.

The five-story, red granite structure, 300 feet square and covering the entire block, is an interesting survival of the Romanesque influence of H. H. Richardson. The surmounting tower rises 400 feet above the street. In the Fourth Street rotunda is the colossal statue, *Father of Waters,* the work of Larking Goldsmith Mead, an expatriate American sculptor. It was carved in Florence, Italy, of stone from the famed Carrara quarries, for a citizen of New Orleans. When he failed to buy it, the city of Minneapolis brought the huge statue to the headwaters of the Mississippi. The symbolic figure resembles ancient personifications of the Nile and Tiber.

The LAW LIBRARY *(open only to members of the bar)* on the fourth floor, has complete State and Federal statutes and reporter systems of all English-speaking countries. The $250,000 collection, which was started in 1883, is maintained by municipal court bail forfeitures.

21. PIONEER SQUARE, Marquette Ave. between 1st and 2nd Sts., immediately in front of the new post office, contains a sculptured monument, *Pioneers,* honoring the city's first settlers. The statue was carved from a single block of St. Cloud granite by a local sculptor, John K. Daniels.

MINNEAPOLIS

22. The MINNEAPOLIS POST OFFICE, 1st St. between Marquette and 3rd Ave., is a four-story building with a base of black granite and superstructure of Shakopee dolomite. The modern structure, designed by Leon Arnal of the local firm of Magney & Tusler, stands on the site of the earliest Minneapolis post office. The cornerstone was laid in July 1933; in February 1935, the building was ready for occupancy.

The main building is in the approximate center of a three-block area; its four stories reach a height of 100 feet. The design—dignified and impressive—is based on utility rather than artistic embellishment. In addition to mail-handling facilities, there are a cafeteria, an assembly room, meeting rooms, a gymnasium, and rifle range. Mail is gathered and distributed by electrically operated conveyors; one of these, with a capacity of 50,000 pounds of mail per minute, extends through an enclosed bridge connecting the second floor of the main building with the Great Northern Express office.

(Beyond the Loop)

23. The INSTITUTE OF ARTS (open daily 10-5, except Sun. and Mon., 1-5; adm. 25¢; Wed., Sat., and Sun. free), 201 E. 24th St., is an impressive structure of Greek design, notable for its beauty of proportion and simplicity of detail. Of the seven units planned, only two have been built; completion cost of the entire structure is estimated at three million dollars. The building was designed in 1912 by McKim, Mead, and White, leaders of the American neo-classic movement. The well-proportioned façade of white Vermont marble has a rusticated basement story surmounted by a story of large windows set between pilasters, which support a cornice and solid attic parapet. The flanking wings are designed in the manner of the Florentine Renaissance. The design of the principal façade belies the existence of another story behind the cornice and parapet, which contains a series of skylighted galleries. The severed relationship of the façade is justified, perhaps, by the necessity of wall spaces for hanging pictures. On the central axis of the plan are the rotunda, secondary lobby, and lecture hall. To the right and left, symmetrically disposed, are the various galleries. Administrative offices in the basement are lighted by windows in the rusticated base of the façade.

The institute is the home of the Minneapolis Society of Fine Arts, organized in 1885 to "take art off its pedestal" and bring it into everyday life. Pursuing that goal, the institute sponsors extensive radio and lecture programs and gallery tours, and each November displays the works of Twin City artists.

Furthering no special school of art, the institute seeks to make the museum a compendium of the evolution and history of art as a whole. Its permanent collections are almost all originals, with emphasis on paintings, period rooms, decorative arts, prints, and early material from the cultures of the American Southwest.

Clifton Morrison in 1910 donated the site, Dorilus Morrison Park, opposite Washburn Fair Oaks Park, and civic-minded patrons raised $500,-000 toward financing the building. The society's funds were augmented in

1914 by a million dollar bequest from Mr. Dunwoody, used to establish a permanent art collection. Gifts and bequests to the society total five million dollars.

Although the exhibits are rearranged from time to time, choice pieces of 18th-century jade are usually on display in the rotunda. On the right of the auditorium is the French period room, and on the left are classical casts. The east corridor of the main floor is devoted to Egyptian, Greek, and Roman collections. Several specially designed chambers—all unusually fine examples of their times—are the American Georgian Colonial rooms and front entrance of the Stuart House from Charleston, South Carolina, in the east wing, and the Elizabethan room, the Queen Anne room, and the English Georgian pine room in the west wing.

The period from the Gothic to the Renaissance is represented in the west wing. *The Miraculous Field of Wheat,* painted in 1500 by Patiner and Matsys, is one of the earliest landscape paintings; the *Nativity* by Perugino has significance in the history of perspective. A *Dante,* a *Virgin Tapestry* from the period of 1450–1750, and three Gothic tapestries, the *Millefleur,* the *Esther,* and the *Burgundian Falcon Hunt* are notable.

The second floor is given over to later paintings, prints, sculpture, and the decorative arts. Titian's *Temptation of Christ* hangs in the center gallery with other examples of the classic masters, Rembrandt, Rubens, Tiepolo, and El Greco. English, French, and American schools from the 19th century to the present are near the center gallery, while the earlier paintings are in the west wing. The print gallery contains etchings and the prints of Holbein, Dürer, Rembrandt, Hogarth, and others. *Playfulness,* the sculptured figure of a woman and child, is by Paul Manship of St. Paul.

24. The MINNEAPOLIS SCHOOL OF FINE ARTS *(open Sept. to Feb. 9-4; June, July 8:45-3:30),* 200 E. 25th St., occupies a modern, well-equipped building. Here, under the patronage of the Society of Fine Arts,

KEY TO MINNEAPOLIS ART INSTITUTE

B-1. Foyer
B-2. Rotunda—Jade Collection
B-3. East Corridor—Early American Furniture
B-4. Egyptian Room
B-5. Classical Room
B-6. Connecticut Room
B-7. Providence Room
B-8, 9. Charleston Room
B-10. Gothic Gallery
B-11. First Renaissance
B-12. Second Renaissance
B-13. Tudor Room
B-14. Queen Anne Room
B-15. Georgian Room
B-16. West Corridor— Tapestries
B-17. South Hall—Fountain Room and Tapestries
B-18. French Gothic Gallery
B-19. French Study Room —Regency

B-20. Library—Louis XV
B-21. Louis XVI Bed Alcove
B-22. Antechamber to Louis XVI Room
B-23. Louis XVI Salon
B-24. Sculpture Gallery
B-25. Sculpture Gallery
B-26. Sculpture Gallery
B-27. Sculpture Gallery
C-1. Print Gallery
C-2. American Painting, New Vanderlip Collection
C-3. American Painting, New Vanderlip Collection
C-4. American Painting, New Vanderlip Collection
C-5. Old Masters
C-6. French Paintings
C-7. French Paintings

C-8. American and English Paintings
C-9. Loans—Special Exhibits
C-10. East Corridor—Loan Exhibits
C-11. West Corridor
C-12. Medallions, Objet d'Arts
C-13. Chinese Collection
C-14. Chinese Collection
C-15. Lace and Costumes
C-16. Temporary Collection, Near East
C-17. Temporary Collection, Near East
C-18. Textiles
C-19. Japanese Collection
C-20. Searle Collection— Jades, Snuff Bottles
C-21. Ceramics
C-22. DeLaittre Room— Collection of Drawings

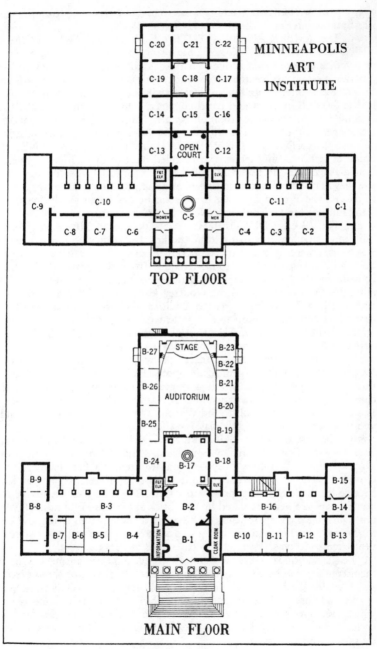

TOP FLOOR

MAIN FLOOR

a group of well-known teaching artists conducts classes in painting and illustration, interior decoration, and industrial art.

25. The AMERICAN INSTITUTE OF SWEDISH ARTS, LITERA-TURE AND SCIENCES *(open Thurs. 2-4;)*, 2600 Park Ave., a center of Swedish culture in the United States, has exhibits of inventions and industries, peasant art, textiles, glassware, porcelain, and antique furniture. Of particular interest are the original drawings of the war vessel, *Monitor,* by the Swedish inventor and naval engineer, John Ericsson. The collection is housed in the former mansion of Swan J. Turnblad, a Swedish-American newspaper editor and philanthropist who founded the institute in 1929.

26. ST. ANTHONY OF PADUA, Main St. and 9th Ave. NE., the oldest church in Minneapolis, was founded in 1849 by a group of French-Canadians under the leadership of a pioneer priest, Father Ravoux. The site was donated by Pierre Bottineau, and the present structure was erected in 1861. The French members were soon outnumbered by the incoming Irish and left the parish to join Notre Dame de Lourdes.

27. The ALEX COULTIER HOUSE, 915 2nd St. NE., a single-story building, is believed by many to be the first frame dwelling in the city. It was built, according to family records, in August 1848 by Alex Coultier, a French-Canadian who came to St. Anthony from Montreal with 60 others to work for the Hudson's Bay Co. If this date is correct, the Coultier house antedates by several months the Godfrey House, usually accredited as the first dwelling. In this home Harriet Coultier was born in August 1848, the first white child to be born in the settlement of St. Anthony.

28. ST. MARY'S CHURCH (Russian Orthodox), 1625 5th St. NE., is a part of the orthodox bishopric of Alaska and the Aleutian Islands and is the social and religious center for a colony of more than two thousand Carpatho-Russians residing in Minneapolis. Formerly the home of the denomination's seminary and still a center of orthodoxy in America, the church is notable for its a cappella choir, its beautiful altar screen, and its liturgy conducted in English and Slavonic. Of interest are the midnight and morning services at Christmas and the liturgical Easter service.

29. The first unit of the SUMNER FIELD HOUSING PROJECT, 11th Ave. between Dupont and Emerson Aves., stands on the site of the birth place of Floyd B. Olson (1896–1936), Minnesota's first Farmer-Labor Governor. The area was once a middle-class residence section, but later became the city's nearest approach to a slum. The tumble-down shacks and dump heaps are being replaced by neat brick apartment buildings. The first unit consists of 12 apartments, each having a combination living and dining room, a kitchen with ice box and gas stove, a bathroom, and two well-ventilated bedrooms. There are no basements or garages.

The 50 additional units vary slightly in size and arrangement. One of them contains the heating plant. The estimated total cost of the project, a PWA undertaking, is three and one-half million dollars. Only those renters are admitted whose incomes fall within certain fixed limits—limits which are, however, higher than the average of the people who formerly lived in the area. Rental is determined by total cost of the project and the estimated running expenses.

30. The LYMANHURST CLINICS BUILDING *(open by permission)*, Chicago Ave. and 18th St. S., a long two-story light-colored brick structure, houses the Lymanhurst Health Center. Here a children's heart study clinic, and venereal disease and tuberculosis control clinics, are conducted as WPA projects directed by the Minneapolis Commissioner of Health. The land was donated in 1915 by George E. and Ella R. Lyman.

The clinic contains X-ray, fluoroscope, and electrocardiograph equipment; special diets and medication are provided. In the two 20-bed wards of the heart clinic more than two hundred needy children have been cared for since the study of incipient heart conditions was begun in 1935. Four persons direct the classroom studies, as well as bedside teaching for patients who must have complete rest.

In the tuberculosis clinic in the south wing adults from families of infected children are given Mantoux tests, and X-ray and pneumothorax treatments. Transients referred by the health commissioner and other persons unable to pay for treatment are cared for in the venereal disease control clinic. Once each week there are skin and orthopedic clinics for the city school children.

In the Lymanhurst Hospital playroom is a MURAL, *Mother Goose,* painted in 1937 by Miriam Ibling of the Federal Art Project.

TOUR 1—2.3 m. *(On foot only)*

To Flour Mills and Grain Exchange

SE. from the Gateway Building on Washington Ave. S.; L. on 3rd Ave.; S. across Mississippi River.

31. The GREAT NORTHERN STONE ARCH BRIDGE, downstream below the 3rd Ave. bridge, curves across the river just below St. Anthony Falls. This, the second railroad bridge to span the Mississippi, suggests a Roman viaduct. Its twenty-three arches of limestone and granite, each locked with a keystone, support a double-track roadbed over which transcontinental trains rumble daily into the Great Northern Station a few hundred yards upstream. "Hill's Folly" many called it, when he planned and supervised the bridge's erection in 1881, but it is now known simply as the Stone Arch Bridge.

3rd Ave. S. becomes Central Ave. SE.

32. The SITE OF THE OLD WINSLOW HOUSE, corner Central Ave. and Ortman St. SE., is occupied by the Exposition Building built in 1886. The pioneer hotel was built in 1857 and overlooked the Falls of St. Anthony. Much prized by the old hotel owner was a bronze archangel, 8 feet tall, which had been made in Lyons, France, for that country's exhibit in the New York Exposition of 1853. After repeated disappearances this gilded form finally was placed atop the Exposition Building, which is now empty and awaits the wrecking crew.

33. The GODFREY HOUSE *(open Mon.-Fri. 9-4)*, Central Ave. between University Ave. and Ortman St. SE., is the older of two pioneer structures preserved in the city parks, and one of the first frame dwellings on

the east side of the Mississippi in the settlement called St. Anthony. It was built in 1848 of lumber from the village's first sawmill. Ard Godfrey, an experienced Maine millwright, and Franklin Steele's foreman, built the doors and windows and made the floors and outer walls of three thicknesses of board. Originally on Main and Pine (now Second) Streets, the house, when presented to the city in 1909 by a local pioneer association, was moved to the Square. At this time the one-story kitchen wing was removed, and the dwelling was converted into a museum. The story-and-a-half frame structure is simple in proportion and design, with New England details of cornices, divided window sashes, pilasters, and moldings. The post-Colonial doorway is paneled with sidelights and framed by pilasters supporting a cornice heading. The interior is finished in lime plaster and pine woodwork.

Among the pioneer relics displayed are the cradles of Harriet Godfrey, one of the first white children born in the village, and of Mary Stevens, the first white child born on the west side of the river; the Godfrey piano; the village's first flag; the first city directory, printed in 1859; early surveyor's instruments; Pierre Bottineau's snowshoes; and furniture used by the early inhabitants.

Retrace Central Ave. SE.; L. on 2nd St. SE.; R. on 3rd Ave. SE.

34. The PILLSBURY "A" MILL *(tours weekdays 9-12; 1-3)*, 3rd Ave. and Main St. SE., is the world's largest flour producer. Its capacity is 14,000 barrels per day.

In 1880, when Minneapolis was becoming prominent as a center of flour milling, the Pillsbury Company built its "A" mill, incorporating parts of earlier buildings, and unifying the whole by a new façade. The building is six stories high, of local limestone, laid in rough-coursed ashlar with walls about three feet thick at the base. The Victorian exterior has narrow windows with segmental heads, and a heavy cornice. The interior is framed by wooden timbers in "mill" construction manner. An interesting feature is a circular stairway of cast iron, ornamented with the classic acanthus leaf motif.

On the first floor of the original "A" mill visitors are supplied with coats for protection from flour dust. Here the air is heavy with the smell of grain being crushed in the world's largest aggregate of wheat grinding machines, whose total weight is 675 tons. Each machine is equipped with breaker rolls that reduce the wheat kernels to middlings. The wheat is crushed between horizontal, corrugated steel rolls, revolving in opposite directions at different speeds. The product varies from coarser grindings to the finished cereal.

In the motor room is a leather belt (150 feet long and 4 feet wide) which has been in operation since 1883. The hides of 250 cattle were used in making it. Continuous wear has reduced its original thickness of three-quarters of an inch to five-eighths.

On the sixth floor the grain enters the mill from adjacent storage bins, having previously been blended to meet the requirements of each specific flour. The wheat is cleaned and scrubbed and the fine hairs, detrimental to color and quality, removed. After an electro-magnet has removed all metal particles, the wheat passes to a tempering machine where heat and moisture overcome the brittleness of the bran that would otherwise be pulverized and darken the flour. After its descent to the grinding machines, the product reaches the sifters that shimmy from side to side with almost incredible velocity, dropping the breakstock through flexible canvas spouts to machines on the floors below. When the bran has been removed by the middlings purifiers, the flour is sent to steel rolls for further grinding and finally to the reels that sift it through close-mesh silk. Approximately 70 percent of the wheat kernel becomes flour, the remaining 30 percent bran or shorts. In the process the product is ground 17 times and undergoes 180 separations.

L. from 3rd Ave. SE. on Main St.

35. LUCY WILDER MORRIS PARK, Main St. and 6th Ave. SE., has in it a bronze marker indicating the spot where in 1680 the first white man, Father Louis Hennepin, looked upon the raging cataract of St. Anthony Falls.

A short distance upstream and about halfway down the riverbank were the Chalybete Springs. Early residents of St. Anthony Village, impressed by the reputed healing properties of the waters, built paths and steps to their outlet. But the spring lost its reputation, its steps, and its platform, when an analysis, urged by skeptics, showed that it drained a neighboring swamp which was responsible for the bitter odor and taste.

R. on 6th Ave. SE. across river, 6th Ave. SE. becomes 10th Ave. S.

36. The TENTH AVENUE BRIDGE *(open only to foot traffic)*, an old steel span adjacent to the park, is one of the finest vantage points in the city. Some distance above the bridge, the upper dam diverts water to the mills whose windowless walls tower above the riverbanks—a massive stone front that dwarfs the river-drop, where the once raging cataract is now an ordered flow of harnessed waters over man-made spillways. On the left bank, looking upstream, are the huge Washburn Crosby mills and elevators, grouped with the King Midas, Russell-Miller, Northwestern, and older structures. On the right is Pillsbury's long row of interconnected silos—a magnificent architectural mass. Upstream is the graceful curve of old Stone Arch Bridge, and beyond are the Third Avenue and Hennepin Avenue bridges. In the distance the new Minneapolis Post Office intercepts a view of the Great Northern station, successor to a sawmill that in turn succeeded a Swede, his pigs, and an open prairie.

R. from 10th Ave. S. on Washington Ave. S.; R. on 6th Ave. S.

37. The WASHBURN CROSBY "C" MILL, 6th Ave. S. at 1st and Canal Sts. *(hourly tours Tues.-Fri. 9-11, 1-3; Sat. 9-11;)*, largest of the Washburn mills, stands on the site of the Washburn "A" Mill destroyed in 1878 by a fire that followed a terrific explosion of flour dust. A tablet on the east wall of the plant, to the left of the visitor's entrance, commemorates the fourteen employees who lost their lives in the city's worst industrial disaster.

Retrace 6th Ave.; R. on Washington Ave. S.; L. on 4th Ave. S.

38. The CHAMBER OF COMMERCE GRAIN EXCHANGE *(open*

Mon.-Fri. 9:30-12), 4th Ave. S. at 3rd St., is the country's largest wheat, barley, rye, and flax market and is second among the twenty-one grain exchanges in the country. The gallery for visitors is on the fifth floor. In the trading room, 180 feet long and 80 feet wide, about half of the space is given over to cash grain tables upon which sellers display their samples. (Minneapolis is preeminently a sample market.) In the center of the room is a space devoted to the telegraph terminals; nearby are the batteries of local and long distance telephones; the pits devoted to the trading in futures are at the end of the room. During trading hours these pits seem a bedlam to the eyes and ears of the uninitiated as bids and offers are shouted back and forth by bellows-lunged traders. In the "pulpit" a recorder keeps official account of the prices established by the transactions. On either side of him are operators who file the prices over the wires to the other exchanges and to the ticker service. A record of local and out-of-town transactions is kept on a blackboard. Centrally located in the room are the press tables from which information is dispatched to local newspapers, press associations, and the radio.

TOUR 2 (Parks and Boulevards)—23.7 *m.*

NE. from Gateway Building on Hennepin Ave.

39. The HENNEPIN AVENUE BRIDGE marks the site of the first bridge to span the main channel of the Mississippi River (1855). The old bridge was replaced in 1878 by a second one, and it was replaced in turn in 1890 by the present structure.

Hennepin Ave. crosses Nicollet Island, once a St. Anthony village park. Attempts in the 1870's to buy it for a civic center were unsuccessful.

Hennepin Ave. becomes E. Hennepin; R. from E. Hennepin Ave. on Prince St.

40. NOTRE DAME DE LOURDES (Roman Catholic, French), at end of Prince St., built in 1857, now consists of the original church and two additions. The exterior with its rugged limestone walls resembles that of a small Gothic church. The broad-ribbed surface of the vaulted ceiling of the transept exemplifies the plainsman's taste for ecclesiastical ornament. Closely connected with the French parish was *L'Echo de l'Ouest,* the only French newspaper in Minnesota. Founded in 1883 by Zephirin Demoules, a French-Canadian member of the parish, this four-page sheet recorded the history of French activities in the Northwest. It was discontinued in 1928. The church maintains a convent and the only French Catholic school in the city.

Retrace on Prince St.; R. on E. Hennepin Ave.; L. on Johnson St. NE.; L. on St. Anthony Blvd.

41. DEMING HEIGHTS, St. Anthony Blvd. at Fillmore St. NE. *(parking space),* highest point in the city's park system, is 963 feet above sea level and affords an excellent view of the north residential and industrial sections. The Boulevard crosses Camden Bridge at the junction of 36th and 37th Avenues, then becomes Webber Parkway as it crosses the intersection of Washington and Lyndale Avenues. Webber Parkway skirts Cam-

den Park and the John D. Webber Baths, passes Camden Pond into which Shingle Creek, an old millstream, flowed, and becomes Victory Memorial Drive. This Boulevard was dedicated in 1918 by the Minneapolis Park Board to the memory of the Hennepin County World War dead. Of its 860 trees, 568 are marked and dedicated to fallen service men. The entire Drive, although easily followed, is variously marked. THE ABRAHAM LINCOLN STATUE is at the left as the Drive curves past the G.A.R. circle of ten trees. A few miles beyond is Sunset Hill (parking space) with an excellent view of the park and residential area of northwestern Minneapolis.

The 45th Parallel of Latitude is marked by a boulder at Glenwood Parkway (the southern part of Victory Memorial Drive) and 19th Avenue. Here the drive leaves the newer section with its young trees and enters an older and more naturally wooded area.

42. GLENWOOD PARK, adjoining Victory Memorial Drive bet. 21st Ave. N. and Wayzata Blvd., is the largest playground in the city (681.16 acres). When established, in 1908, it was known as Saratoga Springs for the large stream that once arose in its center. In the northern part of the park near the road (R) is the ski jump and the first tee of the 5,539-yard golf course. Beyond 6th Avenue N. the parkway passes through a heavy grove of evergreens, among which are representatives of all temperate zone conifers.

GLENWOOD LAKE, shoreline 1.51 m., is to the left.

Beyond the Loring cascade, an artificial waterfall, the parkway divides; the right fork leads around Birch Pond; the left fork passes a plainly marked footpath (L) leading to the ELOISE BUTLER NATIVE FLANT RESERVE *(open weekdays 9-12, 1-5; Sun. 10-2)*. Here are most of the native wild flowers and plants of the State, the city's oldest white oak (700 years), as well as an unusual variety of native birds. The botanical garden was informally begun in April 1907 through the efforts of teachers of botany who found it difficult to find native plants near the city. In 1911 the Minneapolis Women's Club and the Park Board agreed to maintain the park jointly, and Eloise Butler, a former botany teacher, was appointed curator. After her death, in 1933, the reserve was dedicated to her memory.

The left fork follows the slope overlooking the reserve and tree-bordered Birch Pond and merges with the right fork at the base of the hill.

Victory Memorial Drive crosses Wayzata Blvd. and becomes Cedar Lake Road. L. from Cedar Lake Blvd. on Benton Blvd.; L. on Dean Blvd.; R. on W. Lake of the Isles Blvd.

43. LAKE OF THE ISLES (shoreline 3.86 m.), before improvements were begun in 1886, was an unsightly swamp and dump grounds. Now beautifully landscaped, its swamp drained, the long narrow lake with its wooded islands is a favorite of tourists, riders, and hikers. Along its boulevard are many of the city's most attractive residences.

R. at E. Lake Calhoun Blvd.

44. LAKE CALHOUN was named for John C. Calhoun, under whose direction as Secretary of War Fort Snelling was established and the map

of this area drawn. It is the largest lake within the city limits, although its shoreline is only three and five-tenths miles. Sailboat races are popular in summer, and ice boating in winter. At Lake Street and East Calhoun Boulevard, near the boathouse, is a group of Naval Memorials.

45. The SITE OF THE POND BROTHERS' LOG HUT, E. Calhoun Blvd., is marked by a tablet at 35th St. Samuel and Gideon Pond, missionaries to the Sioux, built the cabin in 1837. It was torn down in 1839 and its logs used in a fort to protect the whites from hostile Indians.

46. The SITE OF AN INDIAN VILLAGE is marked by a bronze tablet at E. Calhoun Blvd. and 36th St. The land between Lake Calhoun (once called Medoza or Lake of the Loons) and Lake Harriet was for many years inhabited by Indians who were known as the Island Sioux or "water people." Their "village of roofed cabins," derided by less provident Indian neighbors, was long presided over by chief Cloudman or Man-in-the-Sky, to whom Fort Snelling sent Philander Prescott (1801–1862), one of the first agricultural teachers in Minnesota. The Island Sioux lost their home in 1851 when, by the Treaty of Mendota, the encroaching settlers bought the land for twelve and a half cents per acre.

L. at 38th St. on the Interlake Blvd.; R. on W. Lake Harriet Blvd.

47. LAKE HARRIET (shoreline 2.8 *m.*) was named for Harriet Leavenworth, wife of the first commandant of the military post at Fort Snelling. Near the Boulevard at 42nd Street is a marker indicating the SITE OF THE LAKE HARRIET MISSION SCHOOL, the first school within the limits of the present city. It was built by Jedediah D. Stevens and Gideon H. Pond in 1835, and was taught by Lucy Stevens, the missionary's niece.

R. from Lake Harriet Blvd. on Minnehaha Parkway.

Minnehaha Parkway, the longest single unit in the park system, skirts Minnehaha Creek across the southern part of the city, and crosses the new park areas of Lake Nokomis and Lake Hiawatha with their playgrounds and golf course.

48. The LONGFELLOW BRANCH LIBRARY, Minnehaha Pkway. at Hiawatha Ave., occupies the house built by the proprietor of the old Longfellow Gardens. The admirer of the poet built this copy of the Longfellow residence, from which it differs only in minor details. Federal funds enabled the city to restore the residence as a branch library in 1937. Early American decorative features as well as several Longfellow relics are preserved here.

49. Historic MINNEHAHA PARK, Minnehaha Blvd. at Minnehaha Ave., includes 142.04 acres of rugged woodland, purchased at a cost of $1,372,004.

The park is bordered on the east by the Mississippi River which flows past steep 100-foot sandstone and limestone cliffs. A deep ravine divides the park from north to south. This area was at one time a channel of the Mississippi River; the land on which the tourist camp and the Soldiers Home are located was then an island. The ravine joins another deep glen, the bed of Minnehaha Creek, which cuts the park from the south to the northwest. In this glen is the FALLS OF MINNEHAHA, known to every school child through Longfellow's *Hiawatha*. The waters of Minnehaha

Creek fall 93 feet over a limestone ledge in their course to the Mississippi, more than a half mile distant.

When, in 1855, Longfellow published his *Song of Hiawatha* he started a still unsettled controversy as to the origin of the material. The poet's notes state:

This Indian Edda—if I may so call it—is founded on a tradition prevalent among North American Indians, of a personage of miraculous birth, who was sent among them to clear their rivers, forest, and fishing grounds, and to teach them the arts of peace. Into this old tradition, I have woven other curious Indian legends, drawn chiefly from the various and valuable writings of Mr. Schoolcraft, to whom the literary world is greatly indebted for his indefatigable zeal in rescuing from oblivion so much of the legendary lore of the Indians.

The poet later quotes the following description by Mary E. Eastman:

The scenery about Fort Snelling is rich in beauty. The Falls of St. Anthony are familiar to travelers, and to readers of Indian sketches. Between the fort and these falls are the "Little Falls" forty feet in height, on a stream that empties into the Mississippi. The Indians call them Mine-hah-hah, or "laughing waters."

In the manuscript collection of the Minnesota Historical Society is a letter written by an early daguerreotype artist, Alex Hesler of Chicago, to Russell Blakely of St. Paul, which throws further light on the source of the poet's inspiration. Hesler visited Minnehaha Falls in 1852 and made several daguerreotypes, one of which, on his return to Galena, he gave to George Sumner of Cambridge. In January 1856 much to his surprise he received a copy of *Hiawatha* on the fly leaf of which was written

Mr. A. Hesler
with compliments
of the Author
Jany. 1856

In the letter Mr. Hesler said:

I remarked that the author must have seen the falls to be able to describe it so perfectly. Mr. Sumner laughed and said "Longfellow never was there and never saw the falls. Do you remember that daguerreotype you gave me at Galena?' I said: 'Yes, perfectly.' 'Well when I got home, being neighbors, I showed him the pictures you gave me and he selected *Minnehaha,* took it out in the woods with him and from it conceived the thought and poem of Hiawatha. And this is why he sent you the book—one of his first copies."

Dr. Warren Upham has pointed out that the name *Minnehaha* was coined by white men from Indian roots, and that its use by Longfellow was probably its first appearance in print. It is agreed that while the theme of the poem was of Iroquois origin, the courtship of Minnehaha was wholly imaginative. No record exists of an Indian maiden, beautiful or otherwise, at Minnehaha Falls. But however inspired, it was a happy choice that directed Longfellow's fancy to the "land of the Dahcotahs,"

Where the falls of Minnehaha
Flash and gleam among the oak trees
Laugh and leap into the valley.

While many Minnesotans deplore the present state of the falls, insisting that in the early days a mighty cataract thundered into the ravine, historical records do not support their contention. Colonel Snelling, looking for water power for a sawmill, undertook to build a dam across the ravine, but abandoned the site in 1820 because of low water and chose St. Anthony Falls instead. In 1854 Ard Godfrey used the site for a gristmill, and remnants of both dam and mill can still be seen. In 1893 Mr. Charles Steiner of Switzerland urged upon the Engineers Club the utilization of the falls, estimating that the flow would produce 1,600 horsepower. The engineers maintained, however, that his figure was based on a very wet season and that "for several years the entire amount of flowage in Minnehaha Creek could be taken care of in a box 12 x 24 inches and not more than half full."

The conversion of the area into a park had been long advocated, but it was not until 1885 that a bill for appointment of an appraisal commission was introduced into the legislature. Dissatisfied landowners stopped action until 1889, at which time the legislature had no funds. The city of Minneapolis then provided the money, secured title to the land, and now maintains the tract under the name of Minnehaha State Park.

When special visitors arrive, the falls are augmented by water from a large artesian well, for only in the spring is the natural flow sufficient to satisfy local pride. A stone arch bridge near the foot of the falls affords a splendid view of the drop and ravine. A few yards above the falls on an island is a romantically treated bronze group, *Minnehaha* and *Hiawatha* by Jacob Fjelde, purchased by pennies contributed by Minnesota's school children in 1893.

R. from Minnehaha Pkwy. on Minnehaha Ave.; L. on a paved rd. beyond 50th St.

50. The STEVENS HOUSE, on a paved rd. at Minnehaha Creek, was the first frame dwelling on the west shore at Minneapolis. John H. Stevens received a special permit to build it in 1849 and in return agreed to ferry troops and supplies across the stream to St. Anthony. He built his single story-and-a-half frame structure, reminiscent of New England Colonial houses, near the site of the present Great Northern Depot. Only the simplest rooms compose the rectangular plan. All interior walls are finished with lime plaster, in most cases flush with the pine trim, painted white; the pine floors were unpainted. The undecorated exterior cornice is of planed wood; at the corners are vertical boards like slender unembellished pilasters.

In the parlor of this house Hennepin County was organized and its first officers elected; the county's first courts, agricultural society, school district, singing school, and literary society were all founded here. Here, too, religious services were held. The name "Minneapolis" was proposed within its walls, and here on April 30, 1851, was born the West Side's first white child—Mary Stevens. In 1896 the house was acquired by the Minneapolis Board of Park Commissioners. Mounted on wheels it was pulled by relays of Minneapolis school children to Minnehaha Park, to be preserved there as a historical monument. Nearby is a Roman bronze statue of Colonel Stevens done by Jacob Fjelde.

Retrace Minnehaha Ave. to Minnehaha Blvd.; R. on Minnehaha Blvd.

which becomes Godfrey Rd. passing under Ford Intercity bridge viaduct.
Godfrey Rd. becomes River Rd. W.
  51. MICHAEL DOWLING SCHOOL FOR CRIPPLED CHILDREN
(open by permission), 3900 W. River Rd., is housed in a red brick building on the wooded shore of the Mississippi River. The school, under the
direction of the Minneapolis Public School System, provides academic
courses as well as special corrective training. In physical equipment the
school ranks second in the Nation among institutions of its kind. Many
remarkable improvements in muscular coordination are attributed to the
special musical training. So successful are these treatments that special
funds have been raised to increase the musical equipment. The State cooperates with the city by reimbursing the local board with a stipulated
amount for each child enrolled in special classes.

The school is a memorial to Michael Dowling who, as a 14-year-old
boy, came to Minnesota from Massachusetts in 1880. He bought a pony
and herded cows, but during his second winter was caught in a blizzard
and so badly frozen that both legs, one arm, and several fingers had to be
amputated. Despite his handicaps he led an active life, becoming in turn
a schoolteacher, school superintendent, real estate agent, country editor,
and banker. Following his death in 1921 the Minnesota Associations of
Bankers and Editors donated $50,000 to the city school board to help in
the erection of the school. The land was donated by William H. Eustis.

52. The CAPPELIN MEMORIAL BRIDGE, bet. River Rd. E. and
River Rd. W. at Franklin Ave., forms an important connecting link between the south and southeast sections of the city. The bridge, with its
simple detail and fine structural proportions, harmonizes well with its park
and residential surroundings. There is a minimum span length of 300 feet
for the major arch and a minimum clearance of 52 feet. The center span
is balanced on either side by 200-foot arches, which in turn transmit their
loads to the walls of the river gorge through smaller 50-foot arches. The
balustrade consists of a plain, pierced railing of concrete.

River Rd. W. becomes Franklin Terrace.
53. RIVERSIDE PARK, Franklin Terrace between Franklin and 26th
Aves., is a 42.28 acre plot of land formerly known as Murphy's Woods. It
contains the most rugged stretch of riverbank in the city and provides the
recreational and community gathering place for the preponderantly Scandinavian population in its vicinity. The old rock quarry that supplied limestone for many of the old Minneapolis mansions has been transformed
into a large baseball and football field and is used as a skating rink in the
winter.

TOUR 3 (University Campus)—3.3 *m.*

NE. from the Gateway on Hennepin Ave. which crosses the river and
becomes E. Hennepin Ave.; R. on University Ave. SE.
The University of Minnesota, with approximately fourteen thousand
students, ranks second in full-time student enrollment among State universities and third among all universities and colleges in the Nation.

In 1936 the physical plant of the main campus included approximately 130 acres with 46 major and 15 minor buildings valued at $15,508,805, lying roughly within a triangle bounded by the Great Northern tracks, Oak Street, and the Mississippi River. The old campus centered about the knoll on University Avenue between 14th and 15th Avenues. Its buildings house only a small part of the university, having been largely replaced by the newer buildings to the east and south.

Previous to 1910 there had been no coordinated building program; thus examples of the worst and the best of the period's architecture will be found in the older structures near University Avenue and 15th Street SE. In 1908 the regents offered $1,000 for the best design for the rapidly expanding campus. A young St. Paul architect, Cass Gilbert, won the contest and was commissioned in 1909 to amplify the plan and complete detailed designs. More than half of his $10,000 fee was obtained in gifts. Since 1910 all buildings have conformed to the submitted design, invariably referred to as the Cass Gilbert Plan. Its central motif is a wide mall more than 1,000 feet long and 275 feet wide, at whose head is Northrop Auditorium (one of the largest university auditoriums in the country), and at whose foot will stand the Union Building, center of student activities. Grouped around this mall are the technical and professional schools and dormitories.

The general exteriors of all the new buildings are of the same classical design with dignified stone colonnades against a background of red brick in Georgian architecture. There are no outward indications of the widely varied functions of the different buildings, and, although the general effect is considered by some to be a little monotonous, the campus has achieved a pleasing unity.

Although it was established in 1851 as a Territorial University, by 1868 the University of Minnesota had accomplished little more than the erection of two buildings in which sporadic preparatory classes were held. Its early history is largely that of the struggle to realize the educational aims of its first president, William Watts Folwell, who was only 36 years old when he came to Minnesota to direct its university in 1869. Many of his educational experiments of half a century ago are regarded even today as "modern." Of these, his junior college was short-lived, but his efforts to obtain State aid for high schools, a State geological and natural history survey, and his farmers' short course met with surprising success.

On his arrival he found 154 students and a faculty of eight men. The presence of 57 women students did not disturb him. "Experience," he wrote, "has proven that men and women students can associate freely without danger." Folwell's Irish humor served him well through years of conflict with a board of regents whose conceptions of education lagged far behind those of the young president. They seem to have felt for him a grudging respect, and he often succeeded in gaining an advantage even from their blunders.

The lack of harmony between Folwell and the board caused him to retire from the presidency in 1884 and to accept a professorship in political economy. Until his death in 1929 he was a familiar and beloved figure on the campus in his black-caped overcoat and black broad-brimmed hat, his finely modeled features framed by snow-white hair and beard. His later years he devoted almost wholly to his history of Minnesota and to his autobiography.

The administration of the second president of the university, Cyrus Northrop (1884 to 1910), was a period of rapid growth. His first three years, however, were difficult ones; the university was considered by many a godless institution; farmers were opposed to it because it then offered no agricultural training; and the legislature had no comprehension of its financial needs. Nevertheless, by 1887 Northrop had won confidence. Three divisions, Agriculture, the Experiment Station, and Engineering and Mines had been added. Law and Medicine followed in 1888; then came the College of Dentistry. Other departments followed, and by 1910, forty structures stood on the campus. The Graduate School, which granted the first Ph.D. degree in 1888, has (1937) graduated 954 persons with this degree.

The governing body of the university, the board of regents, consists of 12 members; they serve terms of six years, appoint the president and his assistants, and direct the activities of the university.

Minnesota was the first State to recognize the value of school aid in helping to meet the emergency of a large number of unemployed youths. The student-aid program operating with Federal aid, was established during 1933–34. In 1936 more than one thousand of its students received funds from the Federal grant of $138,105. The State provides additional aid (which in 1937–38 totaled $50,000) for needy students. From these two sources more than 10 percent of the students receive assistance. The competence of the group so employed is attested by the survey of staff members who rated 88 percent of the Federal- and State-aid students as "superior workers" or "better than average."

Although it follows, in most of its activities, the conventional plan of State universities throughout the country, the University of Minnesota achieves distinction in several fields. Among the more recent experiments is that of the University College, established in 1930, by which an advanced student may register in diverse colleges for his major sequence. The student is thus freed from limitations imposed by registration in any one college and permitted to work in two or more specialized fields. Noteworthy additions have been made to the curricula of several schools. A two-year graduate course in public administration, first offered in 1936, trains men and women for public office and requires a year's internship in a Government post. A five-year course prepares social workers for public and private institutions. This department was one of the few in the Nation utilized by the Emergency Relief Administration in its social work training plan.

University Avenue passes the first of the campus buildings, Sanford Hall, the women's dormitory, at 12th Avenue SE.

R. from University Ave. SE. at 14th Ave. SE. through Campus Gates curving left around the Knoll.

Most of the streets on the campus are unnamed and can be identified only by their proximity to buildings. The Campus Knoll, center of the original campus, is the scene of traditional school activities such as band concerts and the engineers' annual festival.

54. The INSTITUTE OF CHILD WELFARE on the Knoll drive, a two-story red stone building, was established in 1925 when only two other such institutes existed in the United States; today it is one of the leading child welfare departments in the country. Besides maintaining a campus nursery school and kindergarten for child observation and for demonstration of teaching methods, the institute performs three major services: it

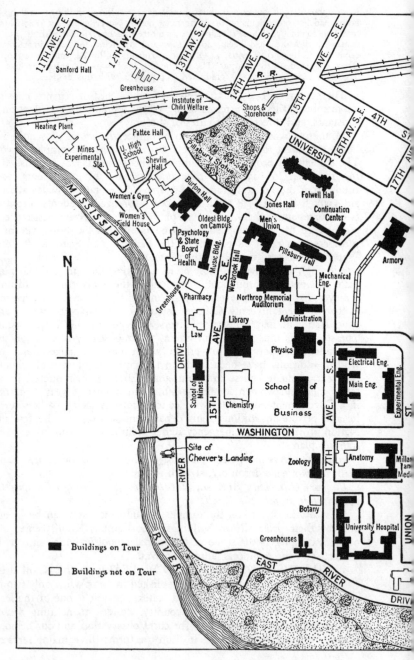

N

Buildings on Tour

Buildings not on Tour

UNIVERSITY OF
MINNESOTA
MAIN CAMPUS

studies child development, trains future workers in the field of child welfare, and provides programs and bulletins for parent education.

55. In the gray stone BURTON HALL, the "Old Library" on the Knoll drive, are the offices and classes of the Social Science and Geography Departments and the offices of the College of Education. The principal façade of this two-story building has 24 spandrel figures representing the branches of science and the arts, executed by Jacob Fjelde, a Minnesota sculptor of Norwegian birth. The building was designed by Buffington in classic Greek style with a portico copied from the Parthenon in Athens.

56. The life-size bronze STATUE OF JOHN S. PILLSBURY, facing Burton Hall, is the work of Daniel Chester French; it was unveiled in 1900. John S. Pillsbury is called the "father of the University." His connections with the institution began in 1863, when he became a member of the board of regents, a position he held continuously until 1895 when he was named a life member of the board. He and his family have been responsible for numerous benefactions.

57. The OLDEST BUILDING ON THE CAMPUS, at the corner of the Knoll drive and intersecting rd., is a red brick structure erected in 1886. Until replaced by the new Business School Building, Vincent Hall, it housed the offices and classrooms of the School of Business.

R. from the Knoll drive on the first rd.

58. The MUSIC BUILDING (R), like all the newer structures, is of red brick. It is occupied by the Music and Dramatic Departments and the University Little Theater. The regular staff of the music department is assisted by members of the Minneapolis Symphony Orchestra and other Twin City musicians.

A faculty of four trains students for the stage, Little Theater production, and for teaching dramatics. Five major productions and various experimental performances by student groups are staged annually. The Little Theater appeals to a wide audience aside from that on the campus, for it offers almost the only legitimate theater fare in the Twin Cities, presenting Broadway successes and revivals and the première of at least one play each year.

59. WESBROOK HALL (L), the old Dentistry Building, constructed of cream-colored brick, was named for an early dean of the medical faculty. Here are the offices of the General College, the University Press, the Art Education Laboratory, and the Anthropology Department. In the GENERAL COLLEGE students, through a widely diversified course, may obtain orientation for later vocations. Minnesota was the first of the large universities to make its General College a separate division and to grant a certificate to students who complete its two-year course. The Visual Education program includes a technical course in the use of motion pictures, the preparation and collection of slides and films for other departments.

The ANTHROPOLOGY MUSEUM *(open weekdays 8:30-12, 1-4:30)* has exhibits of cultural development up to and including the Neolithic Age. Outstanding is the Mimbres collection of prehistoric pottery, consisting of 1,000 bowls found in New Mexico, and the skeleton of the 20,000-year-old "Minnesota Man" *(see FIRST AMERICANS)*. There are 6,000 implements from the culture of the African Caucasoid man.

60. NORTHROP MEMORIAL AUDITORIUM (L), erected in 1928, is fronted by 10 Ionic columns. It dominates the "new" campus and is approached by wide flights of stone steps. From these steps the wide landscaped mall extends to Washington Avenue, beyond which are the tennis courts (to be displaced by a new Union) and the river. To the left and right are the symmetrically disposed buildings of several colleges.

The auditorium, with a seating capacity of 4,840, is equipped for stage productions, concerts, and lectures. The offices of several special services are in Northrop Auditorium. The UNIVERSITY TESTING BUREAU, first university bureau of its kind, keeps elaborate records which enable the personnel division to aid maladjusted students and to determine for what fields of study a student's abilities fit him. Several hundred thousand test records of high school students, as well as enormous numbers of special test results enable the staff to give careful attention to more than three thousand students each year; each case requires an average expenditure of twelve hours' time by staff members.

The regular series of classical concerts by the Minneapolis Symphony Orchestra, supplemented by Sunday afternoon popular concerts, have been presented in Northrop Auditorium since 1930. Members of the orchestra have made the teaching of all symphonic instruments available to students on a fee basis.

The LITTLE GALLERY, top floor of Northrop Auditorium *(open daily 12:30-5:30 except Sat. & Sun.; and during Symphony concerts)*, is a feature rarely found in a university. It brings to the Twin Cities exhibitions of contemporary artists, sponsors the work of local artists, and loans prints to students. Although opened only in 1933, the foundation of an excellent permanent collection has already been acquired. Included are paintings by John Marin, Georgia O'Keeffe, J. B. O. Nordfeldt, and Catherine Kleinhart, besides many prints and reproductions, and a collection from the Federal Art Project.

On the third floor of the building is a FINE ARTS ROOM. The furnishings form a unit of modern design, arranged by cooperation with the Modernage Group in New York. Opposite the Fine Arts Room is the PRINT ROOM with student exhibits, prints, and art literature. Four oil panels, by Gerome Kamrowski of the Federal Art Project, on the plaster walls of the third and fourth floor corridors represent *Music, Plastic Arts, Science,* and *Invention.*

61. The UNIVERSITY OF MINNESOTA LIBRARY *(open; regular session, weekdays 8-10, Sat. 8-6; vacations, 8-5, Sat. 8-12; summer; first session, 8-8:30, Sat. 8-12; second session, 8-6, Sat. 8-12)*, flanking Northrop Auditorium on the right is one of the finest of the new buildings. It was completed in 1923. The interior is finished in Mankato limestone, the stairways and foyers are spacious with well-arranged card files and circulation desks. One of the reading rooms is 200 feet long. The library contains more than 800,000 volumes. Notable collections include that of the biological sciences; 17th-century English history; and a Scandinavian li-

brary of 100,000 volumes with the Nation's only complete record of parliamentary proceedings of the three Scandinavian countries.

In addition to the general reference, periodical, biological, medical, reserve, and seminar reading rooms, the library building contains the ARTHUR UPSON ROOM *(open regular session, 2-6, 7-10 p.m.)* of Italian Renaissance design, a memorial to a Minnesota poet. Its 4,800 classic and contemporary books provide students with a variety of literary subject matter. In this room no studying is allowed, no book may be borrowed, and no notes taken; the collection is intended as a literary retreat and not a study room.

The League of Minnesota Municipalities and the Municipal Reference Bureau cooperate with the university in collecting and circulating information for the member cities. The league, among the earliest in the country, was organized in 1913 and today has 371 members varying in size from small villages to the Twin Cities. Questions of varied nature—health, recreation, charter problems, taxation, and the like—are answered by the staff or referred to specialists in governmental research. Publications include the Yearbook, a bi-monthly magazine, and special bulletins.

62. The SCHOOL OF MINES (R), became a part of the newly established Institute of Technology in 1935. The School of Mines and Metallurgy was established in 1888; it was designated as a separate college in 1897. Its consolidation with the College of Engineering and Architecture, and the School of Chemistry in the new technical school permits students to move freely from one course to another in the separate colleges. The unification prevents duplication of courses and makes the facilities and staffs of the various departments available to a much larger number of students.

The school cooperates with the United States Bureau of Mines, with whom it shares its laboratory, and with the mining companies of the Iron Range in whose factories and mines the students watch actual operations. Among its interesting studies are investigations to determine the possibility of using the low-grade ores that occur in almost unlimited amounts in the State.

R. on Washington Ave.; L. on the E. River Rd. When River Road is closed follow Washington Ave. to Church St.; R. on Church St.; L. on Delaware.

63. The SITE OF CHEEVER'S LANDING is marked by the Old Portage Trail Tablet, a bronze marker on a boulder. Here Indians, traders, and explorers, among them Hennepin and Carver, portaged around the Falls of St. Anthony. William A. Cheever, a pioneer of 1847, originally claimed the area now included in the campus. On this land, known as Cheevertown, he built a 90-foot tower which he labeled "Pay a dime and climb." Cheever was instrumental in effecting the first commercial development of water power at the Falls of St. Anthony.

64. The GREENHOUSES of the Botany Department, at the foot of the curving E. River Rd., contain an unusually wide variety of plants for study and class demonstration. The first greenhouse, an old structure farther upstream on the riverbank, was in existence before 1873. The present structure, replacing a second greenhouse, was built in 1925 in an abandoned

quarry. Among its unusual plants are rare cycads, orchids, and date and fig trees. Some seeds left over from experimental work on the embryology of the ginkgo, undertaken in 1904, were planted and grew well despite the severity of the Minnesota climate. Two of these so-called Maidenhair trees, stand on the south side of the greenhouse. There are others in protected spots on the campus. The tree, a native of the Orient, is the only plant genus to survive from prehistoric times.

L. from E. River Rd. on Harvard St. SE.

The tour passes Pioneer Hall, southernmost building of the campus. The red brick block-square building is the men's dormitory.

L. from Harvard St. SE. on Delaware St. SE.

65. The MEDICAL SCIENCE BUILDING (1930) and MILLARD HALL (1912), Delaware St. SE. at Union St., house the offices and classrooms of the Schools of Medicine and Dentistry.

Since its first courses were taught in 1883, the College of Dentistry has graduated more than 3,000 students. Pioneering for higher standards in this branch of medical science it has achieved wide recognition; its graduates staff many well-known institutions.

66. The MINNESOTA GENERAL HOSPITAL QUADRANGLE encircles three sides of the block. In 1883 the Department of Medicine of the university was established with a faculty of five whose duties included the licensing of medical practitioners. When a State Board of Examiners was appointed in 1887, the department was empowered by the legislature to begin courses in medicine, but it remained in a building at Ninth Avenue South and Sixth Street until 1893 when, despite objections of certain persons who feared that medical students would disturb the quiet college atmosphere, it became a part of the main campus. The six-year academic and medical course was adopted in 1904. The hospital, which began as a single teaching unit in 1911, admits any needy legal resident of the State recommended by an authorized physician. The Todd unit was added in 1924 and is devoted to the care of the eye, ear, nose, and throat. The Cancer Institute (1925) was the first in the United States to be developed and operated by a medical school. The Pediatrics Department was aided materially by a million dollar bequest from William H. Eustis, himself a cripple, providing for a hospital for crippled children. It forms part of the west wing of the quadrangle and contains a series of murals by the Federal Art Project. One, on the porch of the children's ward, is entitled *Fairy Tales,* and was painted by Daphne Haig, who also painted the animal and bird murals designed by Florence Budge, which decorate four other rooms.

The Student Health Service, providing dental and medical care for all students, was established in 1928 and has been used as a pattern for many such departments. The five-year course for medical technicians was a pioneer course. The most recent addition to the medical plant is the Psychopathic Unit built in 1936 on the top floor of the Todd wing. This division is unusual in that it combines teaching, research, and treatment. Its furnishings are exceptionally pleasing; many of the devices to insure the safety of both patients and staff are unique.

L. from Delaware St. SE. on Church St.

67. The ZOOLOGY BUILDING, cor. Church St. and Washington
Ave. SE., erected in 1917, contains the MUSEUM OF NATURAL HISTORY
(open weekdays 9-5; and from Jan. to March, Sun. 2-5). An aquarium
and several mounted groups of birds and animals set in reproductions of
their natural habitat are supplemented by displays of lower animal forms
and colored plates of plants and animals. During the Sunday openings,
there are tours conducted by the museum staff as well as free lectures and
motion pictures.

Church St. continues across Washington Ave.

68. VINCENT HALL, the new school of business building, named in
honor of the university's third president, George E. Vincent, replaces
(1938) the old building on the Knoll drive. Statistical research is a
notable feature of the work done by this school. In 1935 it completed its
most ambitious project, an exhaustive economic and business survey of the
Northwest, conducted in conjunction with the Psychology Department. As
an outgrowth of this study the school publishes a monthly financial and
investment review.

69. The three ENGINEERING BUILDINGS (Main, Electrical and
Experimental) are in a group (R). The first courses in civil and mechanical
engineering were taught in 1871; electrical engineering was added in 1887
and architecture in 1912. The courses in agricultural engineering were begun in 1925, those in aeronautical engineering in 1928. All technical
courses in the college are taught by men who have had practical field experience as well as professional training. The college is now a part of the
Institute of Technology. The Engineering and Architecture Libraries are in
the Main Building; here also is a MURAL by Hollis Arnold, painted while
he was a student in the college. In the Electrical Engineering Building is
the university radio station, WLB, which broadcasts weekly convocations,
special lectures, farm and home discussions, and music and foreign language courses. A valuable addition to the engineering facilities is the
hydraulic laboratory built in 1937 on Hennepin Island in the Mississippi
River about a mile upstream from the campus.

70. The PHYSICS BUILDING (L) includes in its unusual equipment a machine popularly called the ATOM SMASHER, sealed in the 35-
foot steel cylinder back of the building and adjoining the road. The tank
which houses the generator is arc-welded and will withstand 100 pounds
pressure per square inch. The machine is used for manufacturing artificial
chemical elements, such as radio-active phosphorus, sodium, and potassium
for medical and research purposes. The mechanism is controlled from the
Physics Building where operators are separated by a six-foot wall of earth
and concrete from the destructive rays emanating from the tank during the
operations.

71. The ADMINISTRATION BUILDING (L) faces the mall and
houses the president's office as well as a number of administrative bureaus;
the office of information is on the main floor.

72. PILLSBURY HALL (L), a much photographed, red sandstone
structure, was designed by Leroy Buffington in Richardson Romanesque
style. Although one of the oldest, it is still one of the best designed of all

campus buildings, with rough stone walls, massive arched openings, and tiled roof. On the lower floors are the offices of the student publications and the Department of Journalism. The Geology Department and Museum occupy the upper floors. The MUSEUM *(open weekdays 9-5, free)* has a varied collection of specimens including meteorites, fossil remains of prehistoric animals, and rocks found during geological surveys of the State. *L. on rd. in front of Pillsbury Hall.*

73. The CENTER FOR CONTINUATION STUDY, opposite Pillsbury Hall, was opened in the fall of 1936 to enable special groups of adults to extend or supplement their previous training. The intensive short courses are designed for doctors, lawyers, ministers, engineers, and a number of other groups. Half of the students are more than 40 years of age. The building includes living quarters, an auditorium, classrooms, a chapel and organ, a 200-car garage, and a library. The design of the Center departs somewhat from that of the newer buildings that it may better harmonize with Folwell Hall. The brick is golden brown, to approximate the appearance of the Folwell brick, now no longer manufactured.

74. The MEN'S UNION (L), a double-winged massive building of light brown brick with red stone trim, was erected in 1890. It is a clubhouse and recreation center for the entire university. *R. on rd. at Caleb Dorr Fountain.*

75. FOLWELL HALL, 15th and University Aves., an ornate old brick structure of Jacobean design erected in 1907, is the largest of the old campus buildings. It contains many of the divisions of the School of Science, Literature and the Arts, i.e., the Departments of English, Mathematics, Philosophy, Speech, and Languages. *R. on University Ave.*

76. The OLD ARMORY, University and 17th Aves. SE. (R), built in 1896, was once the scene of cultural as well as athletic activities. Most of these functions have been taken over by newer buildings, but the Armory remains—a solid fort-like landmark of weathered brick in the growing maze of newer units. Its architect, Charles R. Aldrich, designed it to resemble a Norman castle.

77. MEMORIAL STADIUM, University Ave. and Oak St. SE., of red brick has a pleasing simplicity. It was constructed in 1924 and seats 50,400 persons. Its facilities include handball and squash courts and gymnasiums. At its open end is the modern Athletics Building, completed in 1934.

78. The FIELD HOUSE, opposite the Stadium on Oak St. and University Aves. SE., was built in 1928. It is a huge shell with windowed ends and arched roof and is connected with the stadium by an underground tunnel. The structure which seats 13,000, enables students to participate in athletic activity throughout the winter. It is the scene of basketball and other indoor athletic competitions.

POINTS OF INTEREST IN ENVIRONS

Sibley and Faribault Houses at Mendota, *8 m.;* Fort Snelling, historic military post, *6 m. (see Tour 9).* Lake Minnetonka, recreation and historic points, *11.8 m., (see Tour 11).*

St. Paul

Railroad Stations: Union Station, 4th and Sibley Sts., for Northwestern, Northern Pacific, Great Northern, Burlington, Great Western, Milwaukee, Rock Island, Omaha, Soo Line, and Minneapolis & St. Louis.
Bus Stations: Union Bus Depot, 397 St. Peter St. for Greyhound, Jefferson Transportation Co., and the Twin City Bus Lines; Sioux Limited Bus Depot, 391 St. Peter St., for Sioux Limited, Grey Goose, and Great Western Stages.
Airport: Holman Municipal Airport, 2 m. from loop on south bank of the Mississippi River, for Northwest Airlines Inc. and Hanford Airlines; taxi fare 55¢, time 7 minutes.
Taxis: 25¢ first ½ mile, 10¢ each additional ½ mile; no passenger limit.
Street Cars: Fare 10¢, or 6 tokens for 45¢; 5-15 min. service before midnight, hourly service 1-5 a.m.; transfer privileges on carlines, and cross-town busses.
Street Busses: Minneapolis-St. Paul busses, University Ave. (10 min. service before midnight), Lake St.-Marshall Ave. (20 min. service until 7 p.m.), 2 tokens 25¢, 1 fare for each city, no transfers.

Traffic Regulations: Regulation traffic lights in business district; 30 min. to 2 hrs. loop parking, 8 a.m.-6 p.m.; no all-night parking; no U turns at traffic lights, whether in operation or not; L. turn prohibited where posted.

Accommodations: Adequate hotel facilities. Rates higher in the winter and spring. Tourist homes on highways entering city. Tourist camp at Lake Phalen, reasonable rates.

Information Service: A.A.A. Tourist Information Bureau, 85 E. Kellogg Blvd.; State Tourist Bureau, 9 State Capitol Bldg.; St. Paul Assn. of Commerce, Athletic Club Bldg.

Radio Stations: KSTP (1,460 kc); WCCO (810 kc); WDGY (1,180 kc); WMIN (1,370 kc); WTCN (1,250 kc).
Theaters and Motion Picture Houses: St. Paul Auditorium, 145 W. 4th St., opera and stage plays; five first-run picture houses.
Athletic Fields: Dunning Athletic Field, Dunlap St. at Marshall Ave.; Highland Park, S. Snelling Ave., at Highland Parkway; 91 parks and 2 lakes.
Swimming: Municipal pool adjoining Highland Park, at Lexington Parkway, S. Montreal Ave. and Edgecumbe Rd.; Lake Phalen.
Golf: Municipal Courses: (All have 18 holes, grass greens, and charge rates that vary [25-60¢] according to quality of course, and time.) Highland Park Course, at Highland Park; Phalen Park Course, at Phalen Park; Como Park Course, at Como Park.
Baseball: Lexington Park, University Ave. at Dunlap St., American Association.
Tennis: Dunning Field, Marshall Ave. and Dunlap St.; and 118 courts in city parks, all crushed rock.
Polo: Fort Snelling, W. 7th St. *(see Tour 9).*
Archery: May-Oct., Highland Park; Nov.-Apr., Minneapolis Armory.
Sailboating: Bald Eagle and White Bear Lakes, 10 m., US 61 *(see Tour 1).*
General Recreational Information: Department of Parks and Playgrounds, City Hall.

Annual Events: Winter Carnival, 9 days, including last Sat., Jan.; North American Indoor Skating Championship, Feb.; State Gallery Rifle Matches at Como Range, April; Twin City Archery Meet, Highland Park, or Wm. Berry Park (Minneapolis),

June; Minnesota State Fair (1st Saturday before Labor Day, 1 wk.), Aug.; State
Skeet Championship, Aug.; Chrysanthemum Show (approximately 2 wks.), Nov.;
Junior Livestock Show, South St. Paul, 4 m., State 56 *(see Tour 9)*, Nov.; Twin
City Art Exhibit, Minneapolis Institute of Arts, autumn, n.f.d.

ST. PAUL (703 alt.; 271,606 pop.), capital city of Minnesota, is terraced
on the north bank of the Mississippi River on a great bend whose southwest end is the point of confluence of the wide, forest-lined Minnesota
Valley with that of the narrower Mississippi. Here at the merging of these
valleys, following Zebulon Pike's negotiations, the Government erected
the fort from whose reservation St. Paul's first citizens came *(see HIS-
TORICAL SURVEY)*. On its way to this point the Mississippi wanders
diagonally through the business section of Minneapolis, before the bluffs
at Mendota force it to flow north again into the heart of St. Paul, after which
it turns abruptly southward once more. St. Paul, like Minneapolis, has thus
grown up on both sides of the river, a fact often surprising to visitors who
expect to find the river a dividing line between the Twins, much as the
Missouri separates the two Kansas Cities. At St. Paul the right or south bank
rises steeply from 100 to 200 feet above alluvial flatlands. The left or north
bank, about half as high, takes the form of a stone terrace backed by a series of plateaus surrounded by morainic hills. It was on this river terrace
that the city's business section started. At the foot of Robert Street was the
claim Pierre Parrant sold for $10, now worth millions. Business spread
back from the landing to the plateaus, fortunes were made, and the hills
provided scenic sites for the residences of the families of wealth who succeeded the Selkirk farmers and the French-Canadians.

As in Minneapolis, the city's founders loved trees, and elms and maples
border most of the streets. Like Minneapolis too, this is a city of home
lovers, and half of the residences are occupied by owners. There is less
spaciousness, perhaps, and the air of suburban spruceness characteristic of
nearly all of Minneapolis's residence districts is less obvious. In contrast to
its twin, the city seems to have been here a long while and to have changed
but little since the turn of the century.

The hilly conformation made it impossible for St. Paul's founders to
plat their city in the regular squares and rectangles of its twin. Many of
the present streets that seem sometimes to zigzag at unreasonable angles
were once old trails leading back from the river to the hills, and to not a
few St. Paulites their narrowness and irregularity are endearing mementos
they would be reluctant to change. Nevertheless considerable widening has
been accomplished in recent years. Historic Third Street, for many years
the city's main business thoroughfare, has been paved, broadened, and
landscaped into Kellogg Boulevard, a transformation that has solved one
of St. Paul's most acute traffic problems, and has provided the city with a
boulevard that offers a superb outlook over the lower city, the river valley,
and the mounting bluffs on the opposite side. The widening of West Seventh and Eighth Streets, and University Avenue are additional accomplishments of the city-wide improvements projected in 1922 by the planning commission.

The narrow streets and the compactness of the downtown district are largely responsible for St. Paul's seeming, even to the casual observer, more like an eastern than a midwestern city. This impression extends beyond mere appearance, for in more ways than one this city has escaped much of the insularity commonly associated with the Middle West. As far back as the days when the settlement was the Northwest's most important fur-trading center, it was in contact with merchants in New York and Albany, and a close commercial relationship with the eastern seaboard was an essential element in the city's growth. While Minneapolis was concentrating its attention on logs and wheat, St. Paul was going regularly to New York and to Europe for capital for its banks, to Washington for grants for its railroads.

Of St. Paul's earliest days there remains little to be seen. Nevertheless ample records survive to enable reconstruction, with fair confidence, of its strenuous and dramatic evolution from a little settlement into a thriving city whose rapid growth was the wonder of the West. Its river location made the village comparatively easy of access, and as the head of Mississippi navigation it attracted a long line of more or less distinguished visitors eager to see the new Northwest. Many recorded their impressions for posterity, as did a large number of resident chroniclers, and when are added to their accounts the lively paragraphs of James Goodhue's *Minnesota Pioneer,* established in 1849, there emerges a vivid picture of frontier living. At first the population, whose shacks, log cabins, and tepees collected about the boat landing, was made up of French-Canadians, dispossessed Selkirk colonists, Yankees, and Indians. French was then, and for several years afterward, the common language. Of St. Paul in 1843 one observer writes: "It had but three or four log houses, with a population not to exceed twelve white people, and was a mixture of forests, hills, running brooks, ravines, bog mires, lakes, whisky, mosquitoes, snakes, and Indians." Three years later the Reverend Thomas Williamson reported four stores. By June 1849 the population had grown to 840, the buildings to 642, an increase of more than 600 from the previous April when Goodhue first arrived.

American frontier towns were much alike the West over, and St. Paul's records imply that it was no exception. It is the story of rough and fearless men given to a prodigious amount of whisky drinking, spitting, and brawling, who staked claims and put up cabins, first of logs hewn flat with a broadax, and later, when the new mills provided lumber, houses of clapboards, for wives who struggled persistently to preserve in this raw life such civilization as they might for their children. The habit of idealizing the pioneer man was easily acquired by their grateful descendants, but the student of contemporary records is unable to accept too seriously the generally accredited picture. Of the pioneer woman, however, the more we learn the greater grows our admiration and wonder. Even more amazing than her resourcefulness and courage in facing physical hardships, is the gaiety of her spirit. Twin City records are filled with stories of dances, of sleigh-ride parties on the river, of weddings and bridal finery, of dinners cooked with primitive utensils and with extemporized substitutes, but offering a variety of delicacies almost incredible. She organized the Ladies Sewing Society that earned the first payment on the lumber for St. Paul's first schoolhouse, a reading circle to procure books and magazines from the East; she helped the preacher with his church, and was the mainstay of Harriet Bishop's day and Sunday schools; by scolding and feeding she kept the Indians in order. Her unceasing attacks on whisky were both amusing and pathetic. In 1852 the State at last consented to vote on the adoption of the Maine Law, and then her efforts seemed destined to be rewarded. This is the way Harriet Bishop describes that momentous election: "The first day of April . . . was bright and glorious. Every voter was at the polls. A day of more general commotion had never been known in St. Paul; the ladies were at the 'Sons Hall' (Sons of Temperance) where a free sumptuous entertainment was prepared for all who would come and partake. Each guest was required to leave his autograph and over three hundred names were entered. With what emotions both friends and foes of temperance await the counting of the 'Yes' and 'No.' The sun has set, courier after courier arrives at the capital, and hark! the bells are ringing! Six bells are announcing VICTORY! VICTORY! VICTORY!" But the triumph was shortlived. In the next legislative session the law was repealed.

In 1849 St. Paul became the capital of the new Territory, and in 1858 under the leadership of Henry Sibley the fight for statehood was won. The first tide of immigration was at its height, and almost every day large, wood-burning, side-wheeler boats drew up at the landing to disembark 500 or 600 passengers, and plowed back again down the river laden with furs, moccasins, and dried buffalo tongues brought regularly by the caravans of Red River oxcarts from the far north to the offices of the American Fur Company.

The railroads' influence began to be felt in the late sixties, and by the seventies they had materially reduced river traffic. But by that time St. Paul, with 62 jobbing firms and a wholesale grocery larger than any in Chicago, was absorbed in its dream of becoming the great railroad center of freight transfer and distribution for all of northwest America, and had every confidence in Jim Hill's plans to make it the capital of an empire.

James J. Hill came to St. Paul in 1856 and at once was imbued with a dynamic faith in the possibilities of the Northwest. His first opportunity came in the panic of 1873 and five years later when with Canadian capital he gained control of the bankrupt St. Paul and Pacific Railroad. His contribution to Minnesota's development extended beyond his home city and his railroads. His story is one of the most dramatic—as it is often one of the most appalling—of America's success stories, and embodies much that was great and much that was ruthless in the world's Clives, Cecil Rhodeses, and Rockefellers. His wife was a Catholic, and for this reason and because he was convinced the Church was "the only authority they (the workers) fear and respect," he gave the diocese many gifts, including $50,000 for the St. Paul Cathedral. He collected famous paintings, and gave the city its reference library. It was said that "in thirty years Hill and his partners took from the Great Northern 407 million dollars exclusive of dividends and other emoluments."

An equal genius at organization was Archbishop Ireland. James J. Hill and John Ireland together had perhaps a greater influence in the development of the city and State than any other one or two men. Divergent as was their philosophy of life and the methods they used to express it in action, there is nevertheless an interesting parallelism in their lives. Both were born in poverty and came to St. Paul in the same decade, as unknown and unremarked as thousands of other young men who crowded into the city; both were imbued with an almost fanatical faith in their adopted country; indefatigable workers, neither spared himself nor his associates; in the colonization of the newly opened land both saw a long step toward a richer nation; each achieved fame and lived to see a great part of his dream become a reality. Each helped the other.

John Ireland was born in Burnchurch, Ireland, at a time (1838) when famine and poverty were causing thousands of his countrymen to emigrate to America. John Ireland's father, having come to Vermont in the late forties, moved his family first to Chicago and then to St. Paul where they arrived in May 1852. The boy, educated first at Bishop Cretin's school in St. Paul, was sent to France to complete his preparation for the priesthood. In 1869 he started his work for temperance instigated by three drunken men who came to his home with a paper signed by a saloonkeeper and his patrons on which was written "For God's sake organize a temperance society."

In 1876 he settled 800 destitute Irish families in Swift County upon 117,000 acres of railroad land he obtained for the purpose. By purchase and grant he acquired thousands of additional acres in southern Minnesota on which dozens of colonies were established. He built up one of the country's great Catholic dioceses—a work that culminated in the erection of the cathedral. Catholics and Protestants alike recognized his magnetism and force, his patriotism, and his devotion to humanity. Jim Hill also colonized, but to him the immigrant was but a cog in the machinery by which he strove to build and rule an empire. Archbishop Ireland's empire was his church and his country, to whose glories he felt that every immigrant was a legitimate heir.

The real builders of present-day St. Paul came to the settlement early in its history and a considerable number arrived soon after the Civil War from New England, New York, and not a few "younger sons" from old England. Most were men of education and business experience and their stamp on the village gave it a degree of culture that early eliminated many frontier crudities, and won for the growing city the title of the Boston of the West. They not only ruled the banks, railroads, and industries, but with the families they established in stone mansions on Summit Avenue they became the arbiters of the city's social life. Summit Avenue was long the seat of this dynastic rule, and its Victorian houses with their towers and porte-cochères still wear an air of dignified, carefully attended aloofness like that of arrogant dowagers who have retired in disdain from the haste and confusion of modern living. As the city grew, Summit Avenue stretched westward, landscaping its center as it went. But by the new century Colonial and English-type houses began to line its twin traffic lanes and to bear witness to a new taste and smaller fortunes. Many of the younger generation then chose sites on Crocus Hill, along the River Road, or in the section once a part of Fort Snelling's reservation and long known as "Old Reserve Town." Yet Summit Avenue epitomizes St. Paul's golden days, and remains the most attractive residence street in this section of the country.

Like other cities, St. Paul broadened its conception of parks when the automobile made them so much more accessible for recreational centers and emphasized the pleasures derived from scenic boulevards. In many instances these boulevards merge imperceptibly with those of the Minneapolis system and together these chains offer to the motorist hundreds of miles of beautifully parked highways all within the limits of the two cities. With fewer lakes than has its twin, St. Paul has made more of its river front, and has never allowed industry to monopolize and mar its banks to the extent long ago permitted by Minneapolis.

The five accredited colleges within the city's boundaries testify to the respect for education that has been one of its distinguishing traits ever since Harriet Bishop came from Vermont in 1847 to establish Minnesota's first common school. Among the colleges is Hamline, the first institution of higher learning founded in the State.

When immigrants by the thousands and tens of thousands poured into Minnesota, it was the Germans and Irish who stayed in St. Paul to make up the main body of the population. To them is due much of the credit for the city's culture, its love of music, its fondness for politics, and for the dominant position of the Roman Catholic religion. Among the Germans were physicians trained in what were then the best scientific schools in the world, and they contributed largely to the city's high standards of medical practice. Germans too were responsible for the early establishment of music clubs and have played a generous part in the city's widespread interest in every phase of that art as evidenced by its enthusiastic support of the Minneapolis Symphony Orchestra and its own Civic Opera Association. To Germans, again, St. Paul owes its breweries. The professional men among the Irish here as elsewhere turned largely to the law and politics. The Scandinavians came to St. Paul later, and in fewer numbers than to Minneapolis, and thus played a relatively small part in determining the permanent color of the city. As in Minneapolis, numerous small foreign groups recall their national customs in occasional festivals, and here the International Institute sponsored by the Y.W.C.A. has done much to promote civic interest in its foreign-born and to preserve Old World cultural traditions for the younger generation.

Although St. Paul is pre-eminently a Catholic city, its 248 churches represent 28 denominations with 19 additional classed as undenominational. Several of the Catholic churches hold services in English and in German, French, Bohemian, Italian, and Polish. The Rumanians, Russians, and Syrians have their own buildings in which the service is that of the Greek Orthodox Church.

Most persons who know the Northwest regard St. Paul as a definitely conservative city, and it cannot be denied that it occasionally displays a complacency doubtless engendered by railroading and banking—both conservative businesses—and by its distinction as the seat of government. Yet it has shown a far greater disposition toward experiment than most Midwestern cities. It was the first city of its class to adopt successfully the commission form of government; in its courthouse and Women's City Club it solved difficult architectural problems and produced examples of modern architecture that won national recognition; it has produced a surprising number of men who have helped to make American history in politics and in the arts. Labor has long played an important part in the city's politics, but, while 10 miles away Minneapolis has been the scene of a succession of violent labor struggles, St. Paul has had relatively few serious strikes.

If Minneapolis is indeed, as a recent writer puts it, "a man in the late thirties not quite sure of himself," then St. Paul is a gracious hostess of 45, who, secure in her mature attractiveness, observes the upward struggles of her neighbors with detached indulgence.

POINTS OF INTEREST

(The Heart of St. Paul)

1. The CITY HALL AND RAMSEY COUNTY COURTHOUSE, 15 W. Kellogg Blvd., erected in 1931–32, is an excellent example of modern municipal architecture. The building is composed of a 19-story (265-foot) tower that faces south on Kellogg Boulevard, and the Memorial Concourse, entered from 4th Street, that makes up the northern section. The tower rises boldly from a one- and two-story base set-back in the form of a plain shaft with slab-like masses attached to each face and crowned by two smaller set-backs. The imposing effect of its lofty silhouette is almost lost except when the building is viewed from a distance.

Throughout, the architects have planned the disposition of materials to bring out their intrinsic and essential values as decorations. Careful arrangement of offices has resulted in a freedom from congestion on all floors. Municipal units open directly into the north and south corridors. By careful allocation a far greater percentage of the floor area than is usual has been utilized. The cost of the completed building with its furnishings was four million dollars.

The carvings around the entrance on Kellogg Boulevard and over the Fourth Street doorways are by Lee Lawrie of New York, a pupil of Augustus Saint-Gaudens. These panels, although less pretentious than his noted work at the Nebraska State Capitol, are typical of the artist's technique and spirit. The panels on the elevator doors are by Albert Stewart of New York and depict the history of St. Paul.

The tower houses the courtrooms, council chamber, and the numerous offices necessary to the business of the city and county. In the council chamber are murals by John Norton of Chicago. In the courtooms are several innovations; one of these is the location of the judge's bench to the left of the room rather than in the middle where precedent places it.

The most striking unit of the City Hall is the War Memorial Concourse, known to many as the Fourth Street lobby. It is 85 feet long, 24 feet wide, and 41 feet high. Here the structural columns were replaced by a series of buttresses projecting into the central space. The lobby, illuminated by concealed lights in the buttresses, has a light marble floor, walls and piers of blue Belgian marble (almost black in appearance), and a gold mirror ceiling. On the face of each buttress and extending from about eight feet above the floor to the ceiling are vertical bronze fins behind which the lighting grows gradually dimmer toward the ceiling, where the mirrors give the impression of indeterminate height.

At the end of the concourse is the famous onyx PEACE MEMORIAL STATUE by the Swedish sculptor, Carl Milles. This memorial, the largest carved onyx figure in the world, was designed in plaster in the artist's Stockholm studios and reproduced in a St. Paul workshop by Giovanni Garatti and 19 craftsmen. The completed statue, weighing 55 tons, was cut in 98 blocks and joined into 38 sections, In order to show the details on the back of the figure, it was placed upon a turntable base that slowly oscillates, completing a 90-degree arc every hour.

The memorial is of Prapada Mexican onyx that resembles white marble, with veining shading from ivory to deep bronze. It harmonizes in color and texture with the marble buttresses, the bronze figures, and gilded mirrors. Its base, about eight feet high, is composed of five crouching Indians smoking their pipes of peace. In a thin veil of smoke rising from behind the base is the majestic figure of the Indian God, the dominant feature of the massive composition. One hand holds a peace pipe, and the other is raised in a gesture of friendliness. On the back is a fantasy of tiny figures, hunting, camping, fishing, and finally falling, as the legend goes, at the feet of the gods. The entire design is representative of the dream of peace. Based on curves symbolic of the southern Indian, the work is at once monumental, serene, and graceful.

It is still the most widely discussed element of the whole Courthouse Project. The expenditure of $75,000 in the midst of the depression caused dissension in the city council, while its design aroused equal dissension in artistic circles, the whole affair furnishing news items of national interest. Nevertheless the onyx Indian is judged by many artists, as well as by the sculptor himself, to be Milles' finest work. A miniature of the statue will be placed in the permanent collection of the Metropolitan Museum of Art. Dedication of the memorial took place May 30, 1936.

2. The WOMEN'S CITY CLUB BUILDING *(open by permission)*, 305 St. Peter St., in modern style, was designed by Magnus Jemne of St. Paul. The architecture of the structure, restricted by the limitations of the site and the peculiar requirements of the project, is an achievement in functional planning.

The exterior is faced with yellow Mankato travertine above a black granite base. The modern elements are most conspicuous on the interior. In the auditorium, to the left of the foyer, a series of projecting wings defines the proscenium; the color scheme is a monotone of bronze silver, accented by copper lights of charming design. Above the fireplace in the small foyer is a mural by Elsa Jemne. The terrazzo floor of the foyer is inlaid with diagonal metal strips. The lounge on the second floor is ultra-

modern, with clusters of boxes for lighting fixtures and a sculptured brass by Brancusi. The expanse of glass forming one end of the diningroom permits an exceptional view of the Mississippi Valley, a vista which seems to be an integral part of the decorative scheme of the room itself.

The building stands on the site of the city's First Presbyterian Church, built in 1850 by the Reverend Edward D. Neill.

3. The WEST PUBLISHING CO. PLANT *(open; business hours)*, 5 W. Kellogg Blvd., occupies a modern eight-story building. The company, which employs 600 persons, was founded in 1876 and is the world's largest publisher of law books. Its publications include the 10 weekly law journals that constitute the *National Reporter* System originated by J. B. West of St. Paul.

4. The ST. PAUL PUBLIC LIBRARY and THE HILL REFERENCE LIBRARY, 80-90 W. 4th St., although separate institutions, are housed in one building.

This structure was designed by Electus D. Litchfield and erected in 1916. Its design is based upon the Italian Renaissance style of architecture. Details include a rather flat ornament, delicate arabesque, a relatively subdued cornice, and third story windows incorporated into the design of the frieze in the manner of the Roman palazzi. The exterior is finished in pink Tennessee marble, and the principal rooms are of Mankato gray stone. The woodwork is gray of stained maple—an excellent background for the polychrome decorations. The open side of this U-shaped building faces Kellogg Boulevard and overlooks the river in conformation with Cass Gilbert's city plan. The detail of this side of the building is attractively planned.

The St. Paul Public Library *(open Mon.-Fri. 9-9; Sat. 9-6; Sun. 2-6)*, is entered by the right of the two symmetrically placed openings. To the left is the reading room; to the right are the circulation desk and open shelves. Notable are the successive increases in depth of the west windows. The walls are of honed sandstone and ceilings are beamed and decorated. The Children's Library occupies the basement. On the second floor is the Greenleaf Clark Reference Room. The *Arundel* prints of famous paintings are along the passage to the third floor where frequent exhibits of both local and foreign artists are shown. Of special interest is the collection of 51 cuneiform tablets dating back to 2500 B.C. and two volumes, *Investigations* and *Studies in Jade,* valued at $1,500 each.

The first St. Paul Library was begun in 1857 with 300 books; now the collection numbers almost 450,000 volumes.

The Hill Reference Library *(open weekdays 9-10, Sun. 2-6)*, left entrance, was established through a million dollar endowment fund donated by James J. Hill and is maintained by gifts of the Hill family. It was opened in 1921. The interior is an impressive two-story hall surrounded by Roman Ionic columns and faced with Kettle River sandstone. Its collection of 40,000 volumes includes authoritative works of technical, classical, and cultural nature. As a reference library, it is unusually valuable for its comprehensive works in history, philosophy, economics, science, and religion.

5. The MUNICIPAL AUDITORIUM, 145 W. 4th St., was built in 1907 and remodeled in 1932, when an addition of light-colored brick was built. The building was designed by Charles Bassford, then city architect, assisted by Ellerbe and Co. of St. Paul. Of modern brick and steel construction, the exterior has little aesthetic distinction and offers nothing of special architectural interest. Its interior arrangement, however, is unusually well adapted to all the varied functions of a municipal recreational and meeting center. The older section has been converted into a theater whose seating capacity is 2,801. The recent addition has an arena capable of seating 15,000 persons and, when cleared, it is used for industrial exhibitions and national and local events. The floor space totals 101,506 square feet; the building cost was $1,386,385.

6. The OLD POST OFFICE AND FEDERAL COURTS BUILDING, 106 W. 6th St., was completed in 1900. The structure, of early French Renaissance design, is marked by numerous battlements, Gothic towers, embrasures, pillars, and pinnacles, and has both pointed and square-topped windows. In addition to the uptown station post office, the building now houses the Federal Courts and other Government offices.

7. The RAMSEY COUNTY MEDICAL SOCIETY LIBRARY *(open*

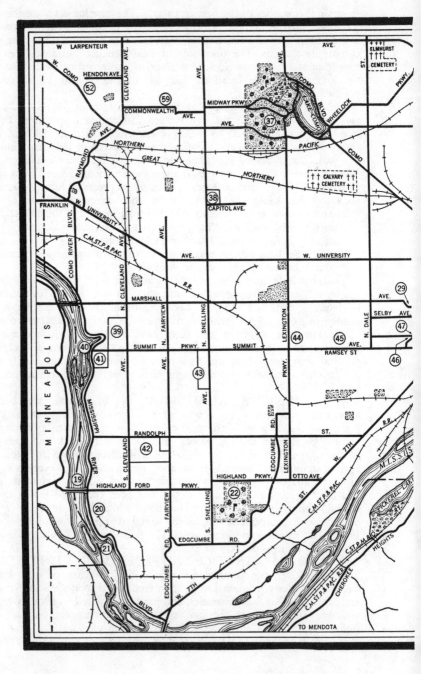

ST. PAUL
1938

Mon.-Fri. 9-5, Sat. 9-12), is in the Lowry Medical Arts Building, 350 St. Peter St. The library, which was founded in 1897, contains, in addition to current medical literature, a notable collection of medical Americana, obsolete medical and surgical instruments, and documents relating to the history and development of the science in Minnesota. Publications include a complete file of early Minnesota medical journals and many of the earliest medical periodicals published in the United States.

8. The OLD CUSTOMS HOUSE, 5 W. 5th St., the most pretentious of St. Paul's early buildings of its type, was begun in September 1867. After the erection of a new Federal building it became known as the Old Customs House. A rectangular building with modified Romanesque detail, its design is less vigorous than the later Richardsonian type popular in St. Paul during the eighties. The oak beams and trim, and the many finely proportioned details give it considerable charm. Its preservation has been recommended by an architectural committee.

9. The MINNESOTA STATE CAPITOL, 700 Wabasha St. *(tours Mon.-Fri. 9-10-11-1:30-2:30-3:30; Sat. 9-10-11),* is a wide, porticoed, marble-domed building approached on all sides by wide terraces and topped with a cupola, visible at night for miles. (Minnesota's first capitol was erected in 1853 on a plot of ground on 10th and Cedar Streets, donated by Charles Bazille, and was in use during the last of Minnesota's Territorial days and the first period of its statehood.) In 1893 a commission was appointed to select a site and an architect for a third and more commodious capitol to replace the second that was built in 1883 on Wabasha and 10th Streets. Cass Gilbert, a young St. Paul architect, was awarded the contract; a 10-year tax levy provided funds, and ground was broken for the present building May 6, 1896. The cornerstone was laid July 27, 1898, and the building, completed late in 1904, was first occupied by the legislature January 3, 1905.

As part of the project to provide an adequate setting, a public meeting was called December 12, 1903, at which the architect presented tentative plans. The distinctive elements of the design were the symmetrical plaza in front of the capitol, with central approaches from Seven Corners, the Cedar Street Mall, and from Summit Avenue. The layout of the eastern half of the capitol grounds and the treatment of the entourage around the State Historical Society building give some indication of the original scheme. The further development of the plan, closely bound with St. Paul's City Plan, depends upon the still moot question as to the proper division between the State and the city of the cost of the project.

For the capitol's design, Gilbert drew his inspiration from the Italian High Renaissance, incorporating such characteristic elements as a high peripteral dome, an arcaded loggia, rusticated masonry, and an ordinance of Corinthian columns. A general Board of Design consisting of Gilbert, La Farge, French, Garnsey, Blashfield, and Simmons, was appointed to coordinate all decorative elements, and together they achieved a harmony of detail rarely found in public buildings.

The approach consists of broad terraces that are broken by secondary flights of steps. The main entrance is through three large arched openings in the rusticated base of the central pavilion. Above the entrances at the second and third stories is an arcaded loggia, adorned with coupled Corinthian columns. The design is strengthened by two slightly projecting corner piers and by a high attic parapet. Two end pavilions repeat the dominant motif of the central pavilion and, with their flat copper domes, terminate the long symmetrical lines of the façade. The large central dome is a copy of Michelangelo's for St. Peter's in Rome, from which it varies only in minor details.

Above the central loggia are six heroic marble statues by Daniel Chester French. These highly idealized figures, with their long straight lines of drapery and conventional arrangement of hair, are executed with an impressionistic absence of detail. They represent the six virtues essential to an evolved State—from left to right *Wisdom, Courage, Bounty, Truth, Integrity,* and *Prudence.* Above the parapet at the base of the dome is a quadriga of gilded copper, by French and Edward Potter. The figure represents *Prosperity,* whose triumphal car is drawn by four horses.

The length of the building, east to west, is 433 feet; the average width is 120 feet. The central portion, which includes the north wing, is 228 feet from north to south. The outer walls are 69 feet high, while the dome reaches a height of 220 feet.

The entrance portal leads into a large vestibule with corridors extending the length and width of the building and meeting at the central rotunda. The floor of the latter is marble with a large glass star in the center that serves both as a decoration and as a means of lighting the rotunda basement. Around the walls are alcoves whose display cases contain historic flags. Above is a circling balustrade of Hauteville and Skyros marble from France and Greece. The rotunda is octagonal, its walls extending upward to form the piers and pendentives that support the dome.

The murals in the four pendentives of the dome, by Edward Simmons, are notable. They are mostly in deep blues and gold, and represent the *Civilization of the Northwest.* Originally painted on a seamless canvas in the artist's studio in Paris, they were afterwards fastened to the curved surfaces of the wall by a thick coat of white lead, thus making their removal impossible.

Large stairways on either side of the rotunda give access to the Senate Chamber and to the Supreme Court Room. On the second floor surrounding the stair well are highly polished columns of Breche Violette marble. A rosette representing the State flower, the pink ladyslipper, has been introduced into the design of the capitals of the Corinthian columns on the second floor.

The Governor's ornate Reception Room off the west corridor of the main floor provides a background for a series of historical paintings. Best known are Frank J. Millet's *Treaty of Traverse des Sioux* and Douglas Volk's *Father Hennepin Discovers the Falls of St. Anthony.*

The Supreme Court Room in the east end of the second floor is furnished in dignified but simple style and contains four La Farge murals, one in each of the recessed lunette panels. The Justices' Consultation Room is a copy of the Supreme Court Room in Independence Hall in Philadelphia. In the north wing are the House of Representatives and Retiring Rooms. The Speaker's desk is backed by an Ionic colonnade, while above are tiers of spectators' seats. The Retiring Room, designed in the elaborate style of Francis I, has a beamed ceiling adorned with carved brackets and soffits.

10. The STATE OFFICE BUILDING *(open daily 9-4:30)*, 425 Park Ave., faces the Capitol Terrace, and contains the offices of a large number of divisions, among them the departments of conservation, criminal investigation, insurance, and agriculture, and the boards of parole, health, and education.

The Minnesota Traveling Library, also housed here, extends its service to every part of the State where library facilities are lacking. Its collection of 41,000 books and 25,000 pictures is available to clubs, rural schools, small town libraries, isolated farmhouses, and CCC and transient camps.

11. The MINNESOTA HISTORICAL SOCIETY BUILDING *(open weekdays 9-5)*, 651 Cedar St., of St. Cloud granite, is designed in the neo-classic style with Ionic two-story columns and was completed in 1917. It houses the oldest cultural institution in the State, the Minnesota Historical Society, established in 1849 by the first Territorial legislature. From its inception the society has collected museum articles, books, newspapers, and manuscripts until its library contains, besides its extensive genealogical material, the most complete collection of Minnesota memorabilia in existence. Its collections also include those of the Minnesota Diocese of the Protestant Episcopal Church and of the Swedish-American Historical Society.

The aim of the society is to acquire all available Minnesota material, and toward this end it already possesses a comprehensive series of maps, 18,000 volumes of State newspapers—many of them complete photostats of privately held material, files of the Minnesota War Records Commission, State archives, archeological and historical objects.

The HISTORICAL SOCIETY MUSEUM, on the third floor *(hours, same as bldg.)*, contains implements, furniture, and other relics of pioneers, historic documents, Indian relics, and miniature reproductions of pioneer villages, characters, and events.

12. The ST. PAUL INSTITUTE *(open weekdays 9-5:30; Sun. 2-5)*, 51 University Ave., to the rear of the State Capitol, has exhibits in anthropology, biology, other sciences, and applied arts. In 1927 the association acquired this red sandstone mansion that was built in the 1880's for John L. Merriam, pioneer St. Paul banker whose son, William R. Merriam, became Governor of Minnesota.

Spring Awakening, a small nude figure in the fine arts section, is the work of Paul Manship, formerly of St. Paul. Although this bronze displays a marked freshness of feeling, it nevertheless conforms to his usual mode of realistic portraiture of the quattrocento.

13. The UNION DEPOT, 214 E. 4th St., of gray sandstone with a classic façade of Doric columns, was completed in 1920 at a cost of $16,000,000. The salient feature of this modern railway station is a wait-

ing room longer than a city block. All passenger trains entering St. Paul use this depot.

14. The SITE OF THE SETTLERS LANDING is at the Steamboat Wharf, on the Mississippi River at the river end of Jackson St. James J. Hill's warehouses and yards once stood at this point on the river flat that today is used as an excursion boat dock.

15. The SITE OF THE CHAPEL OF SAINT PAUL, between Minnesota and Cedar Sts., is marked by nails, almost imperceptible now, driven into the macadam roadway. At this spot, in 1841, Father Lucian Galtier established the town's first church, the Chapel of St. Paul. Most of the communicants were Canadians of French and Irish extraction who quickly seized upon the name of the church as a more suitable one for the pioneer village than the earlier name *Pig's Eye.*

16. The ROBERT STREET BRIDGE, Kellogg Blvd. and Robert St., built in 1926, is the newest and most impressive of the St. Paul bridges. Of chief interest is the center span over the main channel of the river— two arcs of reinforced concrete from which the platform of the bridge is suspended. They rise boldly and sharply above the roadway. The remainder of the bridge is carried on the crowns of a series of arches across the river flats, to make a total length of 1,920 feet. The piers and abutments, of modern design, are characterized by a simplicity made necessary by the cast concrete construction.

The bridge and street were named for Captain Louis Robert (1811–1874), a fur trader who came to St. Paul in 1843, and became active in its business and political life.

17. The WABASHA STREET BRIDGE, together with the Robert Street bridge, carries the city's major south-bound traffic. The original structure, completed in 1858 at a cost of $161,956, was one of the first bridges across the Mississippi River. Its construction was undertaken by a company of local businessmen, but when they were unable to finance it the city was obliged to issue bonds, and used the tolls to help pay for the cost. In 1867 the city took over the bridge and the tolls were abolished in 1874. An Englishman, Sir James Caird, who visited the city in 1858, noted "the curious bridge which connects the low level bank with the high chalky bluff on which the city stands—a most distressingly untraditional bridge, all on the oblique and very awkward, like a great clumsy fire-escape propped up against a high wall." The piers of the old bridge were retained for the present structure.

(Beyond the Loop)

18. ST. MICHAEL'S APOSTOLIC GROTTO *(open)*, Rose and Arkwright Sts., is little more than a church in miniature—only 18 feet long and 12 feet wide. Gabriel Pizzuti, whose studies for the Catholic priesthood were terminated by his marriage, built it in 1934 in memory of his little daughter. He molded the cement and cut the stone by hand, and salvaged the wood for the three pews from the wreckage of the old courthouse. The altar—an Easter gift to his little daughter—he brought from

his home next door. Each weekday morning at six and each Sunday at nine, Mr. Pizzuti and his son conduct services, assisted by a daughter who plays the organ. A picturesque rock garden surrounds the tiny chapel; nearby is a drinking fountain with a shrine to St. Anthony and a stone shrine to St. Mary. A new chapel that will accommodate a larger number is being fashioned by hand near the stone grotto.

19. HIGHLAND-FORD PARKWAY BRIDGE (intercity bridge) Highland-Ford Parkway and the Mississippi River Blvd., was plannned by a Twin Cities commission and was completed in 1927 at a cost of $1,600,-000. The 1,521-foot bridge leads to Minnehaha Park and the Minneapolis municipal tourist camp.

20. The FORD MOTOR PLANT *(open daily 10-2)*, 966 Mississippi River Blvd., is one of the city's largest industrial units, employing as many as 1,800 men. The main assembly plant of ivory-colored brick covers 19.7 acres of floor space and faces the river on a beautifully situated 219-acre tract. At one time glass was manufactured from the sand under the plant where two and one-half miles of electric railway were laid in the tunnels in the deep sand formation. Power is supplied by U. S. Government Dam No. 1, also known as the High Dam or the Ford Dam, which, in 1923, was leased to the Ford Company for a 50-year period. Only five percent of the maximum daily power of 318,000 kw. is used in the plant, the remainder being sold for commercial distribution.

21. HIDDEN FALLS PARK, adjoining Mississippi Blvd. 0.8 *m.*, below the Ford plant, a wooded ravine with a 20-foot waterfall in its upper end, has long been a favorite spot for picnics. The park has been recently improved through Federal aid; the sharp footpath has been replaced by massive stone steps, and a wide automobile road leads to the river level. A stone-walled lookout on the crest of the bluff overlooks the park and the river valley.

22. HIGHLAND PARK, Edgecumbe Rd. between Snelling and Hamline Aves. *(golf course)*, surrounds a hill that reaches an altitude of 1,023 feet. An athletic stadium seats more than 10,000; a modern clubhouse, an outdoor swimming pool, an archery range, and tennis courts add to the recreational features. Highland Park water tower at the northwest corner of the park, built in 1928, affords an extensive view of both St. Paul and Minneapolis.

23. The HIGH BRIDGE spans the river from the low north bank to the high bluffs on the opposite shore of the river at a height of 200 feet. It was built in 1888–89. The steel superstructure, more than a half mile long and 40 feet wide, has 28 supports.

24. CHEROKEE HEIGHTS PARK AND LOOKOUT, Cherokee Blvd., overlooks the river valley; on clear days Minneapolis as well as St. Paul is visible. The night view is unexcelled. A ravine on the north shore of the river leading from Fountain Cave is visible directly over the south end of the railroad bridge. It was at this place that Pierre "Pig's Eye" Parrant, St. Paul's first settler, erected a hovel in June 1838, and sold whisky to Indians and to Fort Snelling soldiers. The cave was an excellent cache, and indignant military officials found it impossible to curb Parrant's illegal

sales. Within a week of his arrival this pioneer bootlegger was joined by the Abraham Perry family, Swiss immigrants from the Selkirk colony. The new settlers chose a claim directly east of Parrant's and built a log house near where Ancker Hospital now stands. Parrant remained only a year, moving to his second claim at what is now the north end of the Robert Street Bridge, and finally to the island far downstream which still is called Pig's Eye.

Along the river bank beneath the bluffs in this so-called West Side area are numerous caves used for growing mushrooms and, recently, for the ripening of a domestic Roquefort-type cheese. The humidity and temperature of these caves are similar to those in France, and the cheese, although of the mild cow's milk variety, is considered excellent and is being developed for commercial production. The experiments are being conducted by the division of dairy husbandry of the University of Minnesota.

25. HUMBOLDT HIGH SCHOOL, 640 Humboldt Ave., a light-colored brick building, is the smallest of the city high schools. In the auditorium at the right of the stage is a MEMORIAL to a former teacher, Mary G. Fanning. The work is plaster of Paris, and represents two high school boys examining a lizard they have found while working in a garden. One figure is half-nude and has a shovel, symbolizing physical education. It is the work of Samuel Sabean, of the Federal Art Project, and a former student at the school. Miss Fanning, a native of Texas, graduated from the University of Minnesota, and began teaching at Humboldt High in 1899, a position she held until her death in 1935.

26. RASPBERRY AND HARRIET ISLANDS, below the Wabasha Street Bridge, are reached by stairway and ramp. On Raspberry Island are the clubhouses and docks of the Eleventh Naval Reserve Battalion and the Minnesota Boat Club. The club sponsors an occasional rowing regatta at this point on the Mississippi.

Harriet Island, named for Harriet Bishop, St. Paul's first school teacher, has picnic grounds and playfields.

27. BATTLE CREEK PARK, on the Point Douglas Rd. near the SE city limit, is marked by a sign. It has grown from its original 25 acres until it comprises 60 acres of natural woodland. The park is well lighted, but the entire area and its surrounding cave-marked cliffs are kept in their natural condition. A stream in the center of the park is crossed by a log-covered steel bridge. There are cooking stoves, fireplaces, and benches for picnickers.

TWO MARKERS at the entrance to the park commemorate the battle of Kaposia or Pine Coulee, fought in June 1842 by the Mille Lacs Chippewa and the Kaposia Sioux. The battle was the result of the murder of two Sioux squaws by a band of Chippewa warriors who had passed unobserved from the head of Lake St. Croix to a point opposite Little Crow's village at Kaposia on the west bank of the Mississippi River. The invaders were repulsed after fighting several hours.

Across the river and visible from the Point Douglas Road are the packing plants of South St. Paul (see Tour 9).

28. The ST. PAUL SCHOOL OF ART (open Mon.-Fri., 9-4; Sat.,

9-12), 343 Selby Ave., established in 1927, occupies a two-story frame building. Of its more than 100 students, many are scholarship holders. Special classes admit children, and adults not specializing in art. Exhibits are displayed at the school gallery; occasional lectures on art are open to the public.

29. ST. JOSEPH'S ACADEMY, Marshall and Western Aves., between Carroll St. and Virginia Ave., a Catholic preparatory school, is the city's oldest school for girls. The buildings, Gothic in design, form a pleasant cloistered group surrounding a court and enclosed by an iron fence.

In 1851 four sisters of St. Joseph arrived in the wilderness village to establish a school for girls and, in the vestry of Father Galtier's church, opened classes in the fall of that year. The little school expanded rapidly and after numerous changes in location began instruction in 1863 in a building on the present site. Students at one time reached the school by cable cars over Cathedral Hill. St. Joseph's may be said to have mothered St. Catherine's College, for its boarding students were transferred to that institution in 1905.

30. The CHURCH OF THE ASSUMPTION, 9th and Franklin Sts., designed by Edward Riedel of Munich, Germany, and built in 1871, is the oldest Catholic church in St. Paul and was the first in which the German language was used. Its original cornerstone was laid in 1855. The church is constructed of local gray stone, roughly dressed and laid regular coursed, but with quoins and corners of smoothly dressed stone. The interior is of plaster. The church was designed in the manner of a German Romanesque basilica with round arches and decorations. The plaster was originally painted to imitate marble, but recently has been redecorated. Two towers flank the façade, and, although extremely severe, compose well in mass.

On the west corner of the church property at the West Exchange St. junction is the Assumption School, built during 1861–1864 of quarter-cut limestone. It stands today with nearly every detail of its pioneer construction intact.

TOUR 1 (Churches, Schools, and Parks)—25.2 *m.*

NE. from the Courthouse on E. Kellogg Blvd.

31. The KELLOGG VIADUCT, E. Kellogg Blvd. between John St. and Hastings Ave., is named for the Minnesotan, Frank B. Kellogg of peace-pact fame. It is one-half mile long, its length composed of 41 spans, the longest of which is 100 feet. Forming part of Kellogg Boulevard, the main traffic artery between the city and Wisconsin, the viaduct is part of an ambitious civic improvement plan initiated at the beginning of the depression.

R. from E. Kellogg Blvd. on Hastings Ave.; R. on Mounds Blvd.

32. INDIAN MOUNDS PARK, Mounds Blvd. between Clermont St. and Johnson Parkway, comprises 77 acres on a high bluff overlooking the Mississippi River. Its ledges rise abruptly from the river and offer the best eastern vantage point for viewing the broad valley lowlands, the loop

and industrial sections of the city, and the surrounding hills of Dakota County. Directly below the park, on the opposite shore of the river, is the Holman Municipal Airport.

Preserved within the park along the margin of the bluff are several aboriginal mounds that undoubtedly contain human bones. Jonathan Carver reported watching the burial procedure here on his visit to the Sioux in this locality in 1767. When thoroughfares in this locality were graded, many traces of aboriginal habitation, such as bones and fireplace stones, were uncovered. CARVERS CAVE *(inaccessible)* is below the bluff in the limestone ledges.

R. from Mounds Blvd. on Burns Ave.

33. The MUNICIPAL FOREST RESERVE, Burns Ave. between Johnson Parkway and Birmingham St., in the wooded valley at the eastern edge of Mounds Park, covers approximately 26 acres.

R. from Burns Ave. on Pt. Douglas Rd.; R. on first surfaced rd.

34. A STATE FISH HATCHERY *(open daily 8-5)*, below Mounds Park, is the distributing point and general headquarters for the Lanesboro and St. Peter hatcheries, and for several smaller rearing ponds. The station is headquarters for the State's fleet of distributing and fish-rescue trucks. A yearly total of thirty million fish are hatched at the station; of these almost twenty-five million are wall-eyed pike, for southern Minnesota lakes; 275 thousand trout are hatched. Fish of all stages from the minute newly hatched stock to the fingerlings ready for planting, and a few mature broodstock can be seen in the rearing ponds.

Retrace surfaced rd., Pt. Douglas Rd. and Burns Ave.; R. from Burns Ave. on Johnson Pkwy.; L. at entrance to Phalen Park on Ivy St.

35. The GILLETTE STATE HOSPITAL FOR CRIPPLED CHILDREN, Ivy St. between Forest and Earl Sts., was opened in 1911 to provide a separate hospital for children who had been cared for in the City and County hospital in St. Paul. Minnesota undertook the treatment of indigent and crippled children in 1897, and was the first State to attempt this project at public expense. Specialists from the Twin Cities direct the medical work; the residence staff is composed of medical students from the State University. Children under treatment are given educational training. In the diningroom are MURALS representing occupations and activities of the modern world, painted by Edwin Holm of the Federal Art Project.

Retrace on Ivy St.; L. on Phalen Parkway.

36. PHALEN PARK AND LAKE, Phalen Parkway between Maryland St. and north city limit, named for St. Paul's third settler, Edward Phalen, is the largest park in the city. The road skirts the lake with its beaches and docks. A footpath from the bathing beach leads by flagstone steps to the hilltop that overlooks the entire park.

The road curves left from the lake drive beyond the bathing beach to the southwest entrance.

R. from Phalen Parkway across Arcade St. on Wheelock Parkway; L. on Como Lake Drive.

37. COMO PARK, E. Como Blvd. and Hamline Ave. bet. Union St. and Hoyt Ave. W., in the early 1880's marked the north city limit. It is

a municipal center of both scenic and recreational interest, with golf course, play fields, concert pavilion, zoo and conservatory.

Lake Como during the winter is one of the city's largest outdoor skating rinks. The band pavilion on the west shore is the scene of summer concerts. At the indoor rifle range beneath the pavilion the State Gallery Rifle Matches are held each April.

Retrace along lake shore 0.1 m.; R. on winding rd.

A bronze BUST OF HENRIK IBSEN modeled from life, in Norway, by Jacob Fjelde was erected in 1907. A replica is in Bergen. Near the Ibsen bust is a bronze STATUE OF JOHANN FRIEDRICH SCHILLER, the German poet, by an unidentified sculptor, placed there in 1907 by the German people of St. Paul.

The BOTANICAL CONSERVATORY can best be located by watching for its glass dome on the summit of a hill about one-quarter mile west of the pavilion and immediately south of the golf course. Among its unusual displays are a number of plants indigenous to the tropics. Its flower shows are widely known.

Immediately back of the conservatory is the COMO PARK ZOO, with a collection of nearly 100 varieties of birds and animals. The $60,000 limestone zoo building of modern design was constructed as a WPA project in 1936. The stone was taken from piers set in the Mississippi River for a bridge that was never completed. A favorite attraction is the outdoor "Monkey Island," where the animals are kept during the summer. A STATUE ST. FRANCIS OF ASSISI, patron of the animals, by a local sculptor, Donald Shepard, stands near the zoo and the conservatory.

Adjoining the conservatory is Flower Hill with its numerous flagstone walks and its succession of blossoms. It is covered with peony, iris, and rose gardens; there are several lily ponds.

W. from the conservatory on an unnamed rd. across Hamline Ave. The rd. becomes Midway Parkway; L. on N. Snelling Ave.

38. HAMLINE UNIVERSITY, Snelling Ave. N. between Hewitt and Capitol Aves., is an outgrowth of the school founded in Red Wing, Minnesota, in 1854. It was named in honor of Bishop Leonidas L. Hamline of the Methodist Episcopal Conference. The first classes were held above a store. Soon after its founding a number of businessmen of the river community, then embracing only three hundred people, donated a block of land in the center of the town. A three-story red brick structure was built and occupied in the winter following. Beginning with 33 preparatory students under Jabez Brooks, it established its college course—the first to be offered in the State—during the panic of 1857. By 1869, however, contributions had so decreased that it was heavily in debt and unable to continue.

When reopening of the school was contemplated, the Midway district between the Twin Cities was chosen for the location of the new college which opened September 22, 1880.

The college, whose 11 buildings are grouped on a 25-acre campus, has an enrollment of more than 600 students. Its most recent addition is the Norton Field House, whose gymnasium seats 3,000. The building, designed by F. A. Slifer, is a one-story modern structure of red brick. The Gothic-styled brown brick library, erected in 1907, was enlarged in 1936, and contains 40,000 volumes. Behind the library is modified Romanesque University Hall, the college's oldest building, which houses the administration offices and classrooms. In general the buildings have little architectural distinction.

R. from N. Snelling Ave. on Summit Ave.

39. ST. THOMAS COLLEGE, Summit Ave. between N. Cleveland and N. Cretin Aves., was founded in 1885 by the Reverend John Ireland. Until 1894 it served both as an academy for lay students and as a seminary for training priests. Since that time the college has concentrated its efforts in giving a Catholic education to young men in the secondary and collegiate grades. In 1915 the secondary department was separated from the college proper and is now known as ST. THOMAS MILITARY ACADEMY. As such it is one of the two schools in the United States designated by the U. S. War Department as "Essentially Military." The college chapel is an adaption of a Byzantine basilica of northern Italy and was designed by E. L. Masqueray. It is of red brick trimmed with Bedford stone and accommodates 800. The college and miltary school together occupy eight buildings. Included in the library of 20,000 volumes are good collections of French and Celtic literature. Almost a third of the 600 students are from other States or foreign countries.

40. SHADOW FALLS, Summit Ave. at the Mississippi River, contains a concrete memorial shaft erected in 1922 in memory of service men of the World War. It was designed by the late Thomas J. Holyoke and donated by the Daughters of the American Revolution.

L. from Summit Ave. on Mississippi River Blvd.

41. The ST. PAUL SEMINARY, Mississippi River Blvd. between Summit and Goodrich Aves., occupies three large buildings, two of red brick and one of stone. It was endowed in 1892 by James J. Hill, as a training school for Catholic clergy. The seminary is also the headquarters of the Catholic Historical Society of St. Paul, founded in 1905 by Archbishop Ireland. Included in its collection are books, manuscripts, and furniture of early priests and missionaries, as well as complete publications of the Wisconsin and Minnesota Historical Societies. The organization publishes the yearly Journal *Acta et Dicta,* which, with the exception of two intervals, has appeared regularly since 1907.

L. from Mississippi River Blvd. on Randolph St.

42. The COLLEGE OF ST. CATHERINE, Randolph St. between S. Cleveland and S. Fairview Aves., was founded in 1911 by Archbishop Ireland and his associates. It is the city's only women's college. Its campus of 100 acres (with 10 buildings) overlooks the valleys of the Mississippi and Minnesota Rivers and occupies a part of the Reserve Township organized in 1858. This area, known as "old Reserve Town," was originally within the Fort Snelling Reservation. A colony of squatters, Selkirk colonists, and others who had settled here were driven off in 1840; ten years later, the land was thrown open for settlement. In 1880 the principal occupation of the 490 residents was still farming, and not until 1915 did

the area begin to assume its present appearance of a city residential district.

In St. Paul's early days the site of the College of St. Catherine was an unbroken stretch of red and white oaks, traversed by a Government road along which Indians, traders, and settlers traveled between the fort and the tiny settlement which was to become St. Paul. A surviving remnant of this once broad trail is a narrow footpath which cuts diagonally across the campus.

George Nason was the landscape architect; his plans, calling for two quadrangles about which the college buildings should be grouped, are not yet fully developed. The campus is used by more than 600 students.

The beautiful limestone chapel, Our Lady of Victory, overlooks a landscaped terrace. It was designed by H. A. Sullwold in early Romanesque style and is modeled after the Cathedral of St. Trophime at Arles, France. It is constructed of Bedford travertine inlaid with brick. The interior, with Byzantine features, is faced with polychrome tile. Housed in the chapel building, which was dedicated in 1924, is a library of 30,000 volumes.

L. from Randolph St. on Snelling Ave. S.

43. MACALESTER COLLEGE (Presbyterian), Snelling Ave. S. between St. Clair St. and Grand Ave., is an outgrowth of the Reverend Edward D. Neill's many educational ventures, earliest of which was the coeducational Baldwin School, founded in 1853 and reestablished in 1872. Out of this grew Macalester College, the name having been changed in 1874. The present school was founded in 1885.

An old bell is housed in a special tower on the campus. After arriving by steamer in 1850, it was hoisted to the belfry of the new Presbyterian Church. Its first tones are said to have caused "consternation among the Indians."

The college has 10 buildings of which the oldest is Old Main, erected in 1885 and housing the administration offices. Many of the buildings follow the Georgian Colonial style of architecture. The enrollment is approximately 600.

R. from Snelling Ave. S. on Summit Ave.

44. ST. LUKE'S CHURCH, Summit Ave. at Lexington Ave., of Italian Romanesque design, is considered the finest work of the architect, John T. Comes. It is faced with New Bedford stone and has a Spanish tile roof.

The body of the church is cruciform in plan with very shallow transepts. A vaulted ceiling, ribbed and coffered, spans the nave; the transverse ribs rest upon monolithic Romanesque columns. The interior walls, banded in light and dark gray stone, are reminiscent of the ecclesiastical architecture found in Sienna, Italy. The whole effect of the church, though the structure is incomplete in many details, is one of fine proportion.

Noteworthy is the crypt, built in 1919, with its flat vaulted ceiling, its fine coloring, and the altar triptychs. The severity of the façade is relieved by three beautiful portals, a rose window, and a row of small surface arches. The octagonal baptistry, instead of being placed in the narthex of the church or in a separate wing, is incorporated into the west transept. The detail of the interior is Byzantine in feeling. Through a traceried stone screen at either end of the narthex two deeply colored rondel windows glow in an otherwise unlighted space. The carving in the column caps is particularly fine. A carved stone reredos fills the center arch back of the main altar.

The shrine of the Blessed Virgin, rich in color and exquisite in detail, is in a secluded chapel. The series of symbolic rondel, stained-glass windows in the Baptistry are noteworthy as are the triptychs over the several minor altars, the canonical colorings, and ecclesiastical legend.

45. HOUSE OF HOPE CHURCH, Summit Ave. at Avon St., with its buildings grouped in the traditional English manner, is dominated by a tower housing a Belgian carillon of 28 bells. The architects were Ralph Adams Cram, and Goodhue and Ferguson of Boston.

The plan is characerically English Gothic with a long nave, short square transepts, chancel and square apse, and a Lady Chapel beyond on the axis. The tower is over the west transept and is joined by arcades to the parish offices and Sunday school building. The interior is comparatively simple, with pointed aisle arches.

The collar-braced roof trusses rest upon corbels bearing carved scenes from the life of St. Paul. A pleasant decorative touch in an otherwise plain interior is a line of pierced ornament at the junction of the wall and roof. The windows, both in aisle and apse, are designed with English Gothic curvilinear tracery filled with colored glass. A rich band of carved interlaced decoration defines the chancel arch which frames the embryonic oak reredos.

46. A STATUE OF NATHAN HALE, Summit Ave. at intersection of Portland and Western Aves., commemorates the Revolutionary War hero and martyr. The sculptor was William Ordway Partridge of Massachusetts.

47. A BRONZE FOUNTAIN GROUP, Summit Ave. at intersection of Portland and Western Aves., directly opposite the Nathan Hale statue is done in formalized manner. The group, entitled *Indian Hunter,* is by Paul Manship, a native of St. Paul, and was donated by Thomas Cochran of New York.

48. The JAMES J. HILL HOUSE, 240 Summit Ave., a large red stone residence, was the show place of the city when erected in 1887 at a cost of $200,000. James J. Hill was remembered by his associates as the bright but penniless youth whose climb to fame rivaled the most incredible of the Alger stories. The ornate sandstone buildings standing near that of the "Empire Builder" were the nucleus of the long double row of solemn but elaborate houses of the less famous "City Builders." The three-story Hill home originally had 32 rooms but was remodeled for its present occupants. The building houses the St. Paul Diocesan Teachers College.

49. The CATHEDRAL OF ST. PAUL, Summit Ave. between Selby and Dayton Aves., designed by E. L. Masqueray, begun in 1906 and still incomplete, was dedicated in April 1915.

The general mass resembles that of St. Peter's in Rome as laid out by Bramante and Michelangelo. The dome, 175 feet high and 96 feet in diameter, is raised on pendentives supported by immense piers and by four barrel vaults over the short arms of the Greek cross. The main entrance is under a monumental arch that frames the central rose window. The interior, finished in buff and gray Mankato limestone and lighted by 24 large windows at the base of the dome, is the work of Maginnis & Walsh of Boston. The polychrome decorations on the wall of the sanctuary and chapels are noteworthy additions to the decorations of vari-colored marbles and bronze. The nave, 60 feet wide and 84 feet high, is flanked by two large chapels, one consecrated to the Blessed Virgin and the other to St. Joseph. The former is of blue and white Italian marble; the latter is finished in American marble. The short transepts on either side, lighted by large rose windows, contain the two great chapels of St. Peter (L) and St. Paul (R).

The sanctuary is surrounded by marble columns and arches filled with magnificent bronze grilles. Beyond it are the ambulatory and six chapels, dedicated to the apostles of the several countries that sent colonists to the city and State. The sanctuary contains an exceedingly fine altar and baldachino designed by Whitney Warren of New York. The altar itself is a simple rectangle of white marble. The Italian baldachino has six monolithic black-and-gold Portora marble columns which, with the red Verona marble above and the florid canopy, complete a graceful composition. The decorations of the sanctuary ceiling represent the Seven Gifts of the Holy Ghost; the seven windows symbolize the seven sacraments. The theme of the colored decorations with the large painting over the altar is that of the coming of God's grace. Between the piers surrounding the sanctuary are the Te Deum and Magnificat grilles. Special recognition is given to St. Paul in the top panels which, from left to right, portray episodes in his life, from his conversion to his martyrdom.

Behind the central axis and the organ pipes is the separate small-domed sacristy; under the towers are the crypt entrances.

TOUR 2 (The Farm Campus and Fair Grounds)—9.5 m.

NW. from Courthouse on Wabasha St.; R. on Rice St.; L. on Como Blvd.; R. around Lake Como; R. on N. Lexington Ave.; L. on Larpenteur Ave.

The Farm Campus of the University, Larpenteur and Como Aves., includes 28 major buildings, most of which are of red brick of varied architectural types bearing little regard to either use, or beauty of design. The total value of the buildings including 58 minor structures is approximately $2,200,000. The campus of 465 acres, midway between the Twin Cities and adjoining the State Fair Grounds, is beautifully wooded and rolling.

Experimental work in agriculture was an early project of several groups of Minnesotans. The old Territorial Agricultural Society was first organized to push the ideal of an experimental farm and a school of agriculture. In 1858 a Minnetonka farmer introduced a bill for the location of a State agricultural farm in McLeod County. By 1862 funds were set aside for the purchase of some land between the university and Prospect Park, adjoining the main campus. Experimental attempts soon proved this land too poor for farming, and it was sold. In 1862 the Bass Farm of 155 acres (nucleus of the present school grounds) was purchased. Impetus to the school's development was given by the Hatch Act of 1887, which provided $15,000 for agricultural experiments.

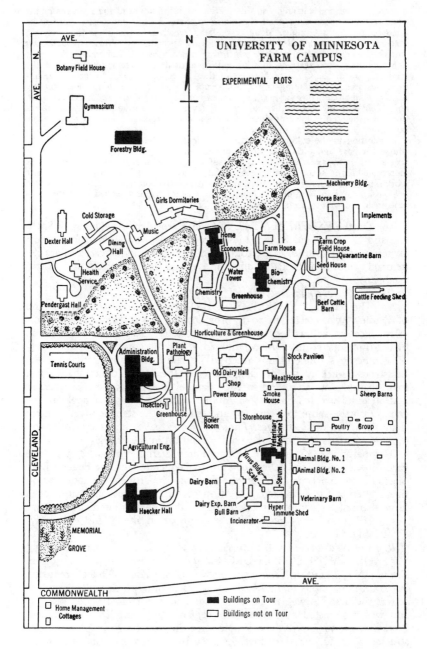

UNIVERSITY OF MINNESOTA
FARM CAMPUS

EXPERIMENTAL PLOTS

Botany Field House

Gymnasium

Forestry Bldg.

Machinery Bldg.

Horse Barn

Implements

Girls Dormitories

Cold Storage

Music

Dexter Hall

Dining Hall

Home Economics

Farm House

Farm Crop Field House

Quarantine Barn

Seed House

Health Service

Water Tower

Chemistry

Bio-chemistry

Cattle Feeding Shed

Pendergast Hall

Greenhouse

Beef Cattle Barn

Horticulture & Greenhouse

Plant Pathology

Stock Pavilion

Tennis Courts

Administration Bldg.

Old Dairy Hall

Shop

Meat House

Sheep Barns

Insectory

Greenhouse

Power House

Smoke House

Boiler Room

Storehouse

Poultry Group

Agricultural Eng.

Veterinary Medicine Lab.

Animal Bldg. No. 1

Animal Bldg. No. 2

Dairy Barn

Virus Bldg. Scale

Serum

Veterinary Barn

Haecker Hall

Dairy Exp. Barn

Bull Barn

Hyper Immune Shed

Incinerator

MEMORIAL GROVE

AVE.

COMMONWEALTH

Home Management Cottages

Buildings on Tour

Buildings not on Tour

Experimentation, teaching, and distribution of information to the residents of the State, are the prime concern of the divisions, both Federal and State, that are located on the Farm Campus. Many of the staff members divide their time between teaching and research, and a number of students, specializing in various courses, are employed in experimental work in which they can receive practical training.

Minnesota's investigations in the field of agricultural economics antedated the establishment of the Office of Markets of the United States Department of Agriculture. Research in marketing at the Minnesota station resulted in the first comprehensive textbook on this subject. Experiments on drainage tile, farm structures, farm equipment and power are other noteworthy contributions. In the field of plant breeding alone the studies have produced disease- and cold-resistant varieties whose value far outweighs the cost of the experiments.

In addition to the collegiate courses in agriculture, the school offers a three year course for boys and girls who have completed the 8th grade and have had at least six-months farm experience. This unusual course includes a winter term of six months, which is spent studying general farming and special practices, and summer work on the farm itself. The Minnesota extension division annually conducts a free one-week course in farming and home management, that is attended by three thousand men and women from all parts of the State.

50. On the EXPERIMENTAL PLOTS, Larpenteur Ave. between Snelling and N. Cleveland Aves., studies are made by various divisions of the Experiment Station. Disease-, cold-, and drought-resistant varieties are developed, culture methods studied, and production and planting records established.

L. on N. Cleveland Ave.

51. The red brick FORESTRY BUILDING, N. Cleveland Ave. at end of Dudley Ave., erected in 1938, provides quarters for Experimental Forestry offices as well as for the School of Forestry. Despite the organization of a Minnesota Forestry Association in 1876, the conservation and study of Minnesota's timber lands received little consideration until after the disastrous Hinckley fire of 1894. Already President Folwell had urged investigations, however, and in 1898 Samuel B. Green of the Experiment Station published his *Forestry in Minnesota,* one of the first books in the country on the subject of forestry, and for years the standard text in more than 14 agricultural colleges. *Prairie Forestry* gave the first information on hardy varieties of trees for woodlot planting in the prairies.

The major research is at the Cloquet Forest Station 3,000-acre farm. The Experiment Station and School of Forestry cooperate with the Federal Lake States Forest Experiment Station and the State Department of Conservation in an attempt to rehabilitate the Minnesota forests that once supplied a large share of the country's timber. Despite their concentrated efforts, Minnesota still imports 85 percent of its supply at an annual cost of twenty-eight million dollars.

R. from N. Cleveland Ave. on Hendon Ave.; L. on Branston St.

52. OLD MUSKEGO CHURCH *(open by permission, Prof. O. E. Brandt, No. 3, Luther Seminary Campus, Como Ave.),* end of Branston St., is on the campus of Luther Theological Seminary (United Lutheran). It was the first Norwegian Luthern Church in the United States (1843), and was constructed by pioneer Norwegian immigrants from Drammen, Lier, Skien, and Larvik. The simple structure, cruciform in plan, is constructed of great hewn-oak logs. In 1869 the church was moved from its

original location in Racine, Wis., once called Muskego, to the Jackson farm at the foot of the hill, where for nearly forty years it was used as a barn. In 1904, largely through the efforts of Hjalmar R. Holand, it was moved to its present site. The renovated exterior has lost much of its original rugged charm, but the interior has been restored as a memorial to its builders.

Retrace Branston St. and Hendon Ave.; R. on N. Cleveland Ave.

53. MEMORIAL GROVE, N. Cleveland Ave. at Carter Ave., dedicated to the school's war dead, is marked by a bronze tablet on a boulder.

L. on Campus Main Drive, a continuation of Carter Ave.

54. HAECKER HALL, on Main Drive, was named for Theophilus Haecker, who, although popularly known as the "father of Minnesota's dairy cooperatives," is best known among professional men for his early research on feeding standards for dairy cows. Mr. Haecker's early schooling was interrupted by the Civil War, in which he served, and was resumed at the University of Wisconsin, where, after several interruptions, he was employed as dairy specialist. He came to the University of Minnesota as an instructor in 1891 and was placed in charge of the Dairy School two years later. He authored a saying, oft repeated among dairymen, "Treat the cow kindly, boys; remember she's a lady—and a mother." A plaque in Haecker Hall notes his contributions to the dairy industry during his service at the university from 1891 to 1918.

55. The ADMINISTRATION BUILDING *(open Mon.-Fri. 8 a.m.-10 p.m., Sat. 8-5 during sessions),* on Main Drive, facing tennis courts, contains executive offices, the AGRICULTURAL LIBRARY, and the research laboratories and classrooms of the Division of Entomology. There are numerous entomological exhibits on the top floor. The Division of Publications, in the basement, supplies the numerous requests for technical bulletins and other information.

R. from Administration Bldg.; L. on first rd.

56. The HOME ECONOMICS BUILDING, at top of hill, of white brick with darker brick trim, contains one of the important divisions of the Agricultural College. Training for specialized technical work as well as for homemaking is featured in the school. Here are displays of primitive handicrafts as well as of modern industrial products.

Retrace to dirt rd. branching L.; L. on dirt rd.

57. The BIOCHEMISTRY BUILDING, at intersection of rd. and intercampus carline, is of golden brown brick and has numerous displays of chemical processes of both agricultural and industrial nature. Of special interest are two old French burr millstones from the Spring Lake mills, and a display of modern milling processes. The division is widely known for its early work on the chemistry of wheat products; its more recent work in colloid chemistry has brought international recognition. A practical result of the research in wood utilization is the probable use of aspen for the production of cellulose.

R. at rd. paralleling intercampus carline, continuing beyond carline loop on east campus rd.

58. In the VETERINARY MEDICINE LABORATORY, on the east

campus rd., a research staff studies many of the diseases of domesticated animals. The division of veterinary medicine was established in 1888. Largely through its efforts Minnesota is officially recognized as an accredited tuberculosis-free area; all Minnesota cattle are tuberculin-tested. From 1910 to 1918, during the drive to stamp out hog cholera, the division distributed more than one hundred thousand doses of serum and virus. In 1934 studies were begun on Bang's disease of cattle; by April 1935, more than a third of a million agglutination tests for the disease had been made. Among the numerous other valuable studies are those on grass poisoning and diseases of wild game.

L. from campus on graveled rd.

59. The MINNESOTA STATE FAIR GROUNDS, bounded by N. Snelling, W. Como, and Larpenteur Aves., and the University Agricultural Campus, were visited in 1936 by more than 636,000 people who came to view the 10,000 exhibits at the 77th State Fair. The first fair, sponsored by the Hennepin County Agricultural Society in 1854 at Bridge Square in Minneapolis, was opened with impressive ceremonies. This fair boasted more than 50 exhibitors and several hundred dollars in cash prizes.

Since this first effort, the fair has grown to such value that its resources, including land and buildings, total $3,750,000. The grounds include 260 acres. One of the few self-supporting activities of its kind, it has operated since 1911 at an average yearly profit of $35,000. The highlight of sports history of the fair was a run on September 8, 1906, by *Dan Patch,* who paced the mile track in 1.55 flat, a record that stood for 31 years. On the track, north of the grandstand, automobile races have almost displaced the horse races, but riding enthusiasts rent horses at the stables and try the track, or canter to Como Park along the bridle path.

Near the south entrance to the grounds on Como Ave. is the HIPPO-DROME, a large amphitheater used for livestock judging and the State Fair Horse Show. In winter the building is used as a natural-ice skating rink, where on the quarter-mile track the North American Indoor Skating Championship is held each February.

Among recent additions are the poultry building and horse barn erected in 1937 with Federal aid. DECORATIVE PANELS of concrete representing prize-winning exhibits flank the main entrances of both buildings. Above each entrance is a conventionalized medallion involving the State Seal. The panels were designed and cast by Samuel Sabean of the Federal Art Project.

POINTS OF INTEREST IN ENVIRONS

Sibley and Faribault Houses at Mendota, *14 m.;* Fort Snelling, historic miltary post, *12 m.;* packing plants and site of Kaposia at South St. Paul, *5 m. (see Tour 9).* White Bear Lake recreation, *17.9 m. (see Tour 1).*

Duluth

Railroad Stations: Omaha Station, 200 S. 5th Ave. W., for Canadian National, and Omaha; Union Station, 605 W. Michigan St., for Great Northern, Northern Pacific, Duluth & Iron Range, and Duluth, Missabe & Northern; Soo Line Station, 6th Ave. W. & Superior St., for Soo Line, and Duluth South Shore & Atlantic.

Bus Station: 507 W. Superior St., for Northland Greyhound Lines.

Airport: Williamson-Johnson, Municipal, 5.5 m. N. on Stebner Rd.; taxi fare, $1.75, time 30 minutes (auxiliary seaplane base, Duluth Boat Club, no scheduled service).

Passenger Docks: N. P. Docks 1 & 2, Bayfront slip, Northern Navigation Co. (Canadian); City Dock, 5th Ave. W. and St. Louis Bay, Clow and Nicholson Transp. Co. dock, foot of 5th Ave. W.; Duluth Boat Club Dock, 1000 Minnesota Ave.

Boat Excursions: Montauk steamer to Fond du Lac, and harbor, morning, afternoon, and evening excursions (refreshments, dancing), fares 25¢ to 75¢; Clow and Nicholson dock, scenic trips, regular and charter, 50¢ and $1.00; City Dock, and Duluth Boat Club.

Taxis: 25¢ first ¾ mile, 10¢ each additional ½ mile regardless of number of passengers.

Street Cars: Fare 10¢, tokens, 6 for 45¢.

Toll Bridges: Arrowhead Toll Bridge, Lesure St.; Interstate Toll Bridge, Garfield Ave.; (autos 10¢, passengers 5¢ each; on busses, two tokens, or 20¢).

Traffic Regulations: Regulation traffic lights in business district; no all-night parking; restricted parking in business district; turns in either direction at all intersections; no U-turns on any street.

Accommodations: Six hotels. Tourist camps: Brighton Beach, on US 61 at 62nd Ave. E.; and Indian Point, 68th Ave. W. and Pulaski St.

Information Service: Chamber of Commerce, Medical Arts Building, 324 W. Superior St.; Minnesota Arrowhead Association, Hotel Duluth, 3rd Ave. E. and Superior St.; Duluth Automobile Club (A.A.A.), 602 W. Superior St.

Radio Stations: KDAL (1,500 kc); WEBC (1,290 kc).

Theaters and Motion Picture Houses: Little Theater, 6 S. 12th Ave. E.; Orpheum, 207 E. Superior St., occasional road shows; 11 motion picture houses.

Athletic Fields: Athletic Park, 34th Ave. W. and Superior St.; Public Schools Stadium, 44th Ave. W. and 3rd St.; Chester Park Bowl, under end of Chester Park (15th Ave. E.); Wheeler Field, 3415 Grand Ave.; Ordean Field, 40th Ave. E. and Superior St.

Swimming: Beaches with lifeguards at 10th and 43rd Sts., Minnesota Point; Oatka Beach, 3900 Minnesota Ave.; 63rd Ave. W. on St. Louis River; Riverside and New Duluth suburbs on St. Louis River.

Golf: Municipal Courses: (18 holes, 50¢) Enger Park Course, Skyline Blvd.; Lester Park Course, US 61 and E. Lester Blvd.

Riding: Lester Park Paddock, 5916 E. Superior St.; Fond du Lac Riding Academy, Fond du Lac.

Hunting and Fishing: Seasonal angling in streams emptying into lake within and near city; lake fishing from boat and shore. Deer and game birds in season outside of city game reserve.

Annual Events: Winters Sports' Week, Jan. 16th; Northwestern Annual Curling

Bonspiel, Jan.; Annual Ski Tournament, Feb. 15th; Finnish and Scandinavian Midsummer Day, June 24th; Peony Show, July.

DULUTH (602 alt. at lake level; 101,463 pop.), third of Minnesota's cities in size and importance, is like a Lilliputian village in a mammoth rock garden. From the western tip of Lake Superior the city rises on rock bluffs 600 to 800 feet above the lake level, houses and business buildings alike dwarfed by the rugged volcanic juttings and the vast expanse of cold blue water.

From northeast to southwest it extends for 24 miles along the edges of Lake Superior, the Duluth-Superior Harbor, and the lower reaches of the St. Louis River, with a width sometimes less than a mile and never exceeding four. Occasionally the hills slope gently to the water line, but more often the highlands rise into abrupt cliffs and crenelated ledges.

Astride these promontories are many of the residential sections, and even some of the business areas have mounted part-way. Many of the avenues rise at a breathless angle and demand good brakes and steady nerves. On more than one occasion trucks have stripped their gears, and, running wild downhill, have hurtled into walls—once into a bedroom.

The visitor approaching Duluth either by steamer, railroad, or automobile cannot fail to be charmed by the city's setting, and will also sense in the scene an exciting difference from most Middle Western cities. For the first view of the city and its environs he can do no better than to come by US 61 and stop at Rest Point. If it be a typical day in June or July, the air will have the clear, clean, winy quality characteristic of the North, and the hills will be a glinting gold from millions of buttercups. Far below, the lake sparkles and glistens, a great patch of vivid blue, rimmed by the narrow city extending for miles along its shore that vanishes at last among the curving gray bluffs.

To the east, spanning the ship canal, the Aerial Lift Bridge is patterned against the sky, and Minnesota Point, a slim crescent of land, curves out into the bay toward Wisconsin to separate the lake from the river. To the west and south the parallel smokestacks of the steel mills and cement plants rise black and sharply defined, and beyond, the shining blue arms of the St. Louis River, on their way to the lake, wind between the many densely wooded islands. Skirting the opposite shore is the city of Superior, Wisconsin.

Down in the business section the city presents to the casual visitor a face not unlike that of many another young industrial city. But the observer will now and again catch glimpses of a frontier past lurking behind the modern make-up. A buckskin-trousered, woolen-clad lumberjack, or a dark-skinned Indian is not a too uncommon sight on the streets and recalls the days when "river-hogs" by hundreds came down with the spring drives to celebrate in wild orgies their release from winter camps, and when Chippewa bartered pelts trapped at Duluth's back door. Automobiles bearing canoes pass through the town on their way to the watery pathways of the *voyageurs*, and, in season, carcasses of deer killed just beyond the city's limit can be seen on many a running board. Not too infrequently deer, porcupines, and great horned owls are seen within the city. In 1933 a huge black bear broke into the restaurant of Duluth's largest hotel, while in 1936 a man shot one on his doorstep; on another evening a citizen came home to find a cub playing with his children in his front yard.

To the layman scarcely less than to the scientist, the geology of Duluth has unusual fascination. The line of hills on which the city is built is formed from an ancient lava flow called Duluth gabbro, one of the oldest rock formations on the continent. The entire lake shore is the edge of a geologic fault, its steepness only a little modified by glacial action. Striae, or shallow grooves on exposed rock—footprints of the Pleistocene glacier —can be seen on the Point of Rocks and at many other places where there are bedrock outcrops.

Lake Superior, its basin the collapsed shell of a dead volcano, is the remnant of glacial Lake Duluth, whose successive shores are clearly marked along the Duluth escarpment (see GEOLOGY). Dammed by the ice cap to the north, this prehistoric reservoir drained westward and south to pour in a mighty flood into the Mississippi River. Of this torrent all that remains is a little runnel, Otter Creek, now flowing in the opposite direction into the gorge of the St. Louis River. Lake Superior, though but a remnant of its glacial predecessor, is still the largest body of fresh water in the world—383 miles long, 160 miles wide, and 1,290 feet deep—and has a tide which at maximum is about three inches.

This great inland sea has a profound effect on Duluth's climate. Its waters vary in temperature only a few degrees throughout the year. In those occasional winters when the lake remains open, lake winds tend to temper the cold, but more frequently there is ice for 20 or more miles from the shore. Despite Duluthians' claim that their city is the healthiest on earth and that their thermometers go no lower than the Minnesota average, they cannot deny their joy when the end of the long winter is heralded by the breaking up of the lake's ice. On that day all downtown seems atingle with a new excitement. The common salutation "Have you seen? The ice is going out!" is heard again and again. All who can, get into cars and drive along the North Shore to see for themselves the crumbling and shifting of the great gray sheets before the determined advance of blue water.

The opening of navigation meant even more to the Duluth pioneers of 1869, as shown in the following excerpt taken from Duluth church records of 1870:

It was Sunday; the congregation had assembled and the [Episcopal] service had proceeded with due order, until nearly the close of the morning prayer when the steamer *Keweenaw*, the first boat of the year, blew her whistle. Almost instantly the church was emptied of all but Mr. Gallagher [the pastor]; whether he completed the service is not recorded; at all events, that evening after service, he made the following announcement:

"Service next Sunday morning at half past ten, Providence permitting, and if the whistle of the *Keweenaw* doesn't blow."

Long after the ice has gone from the lake the fantastic ice architecture created by the spray and waves on the rocky shores remains in glittering beauty, and compensates, in part at least, for the delayed spring whose flowers and trees come into bloom almost a month later than those of the Twin Cities. Even ardent Duluthians have been known to complain at this season that the city has "nine months of winter and three months of poor sledding." But only in the bitterness of the moment, for summers in this city usually have an average temperature range of from 68 to 82 degrees. The autumns, too, are delightful with their riot of color in the mountain-ash berries, the staghorn sumacs, native hard maples, and golden birches. The modifying influence of the lake postpones the killing frost several weeks beyond its arrival in the surrounding territory, and the air, warm in the sun, cold in the sharply defined shadows, has a tang that makes mere breathing a conscious pleasure.

Hay fever sufferers have long been a source of tourist trade, and since the turn of the century the Hay Fever Club of America has chosen this city for its headquarters.

Because of the city's narrowness, the countryside seems always, in Duluth, to be crowding down to its very back doors. Indigenous pines and birches cluster in its landscaped gardens, wild trillium springs up by the steps of many of its most pretentious houses. Rocks, pine-covered woods, wild flowers, wild strawberries, spring-fed creeks plunging through gorges to the lake, or pausing to form swimming-pools, coasting and skiing slides, skating ponds—all within the city itself, accessible to everyone—are woven indelibly into the pattern of its youth. On warm Sundays it seems as if at least a tenth of the entire population pack picnic baskets and go out to the shores of the lake to loaf and play, and to stop on the way home to buy fat lake-trout from the fishermen drying their nets beside their little cabins. Today, as in the past, it is the lake, more than any other factor, that dominates the life of the city.

Little is known of the Duluth territory previous to the coming of the white man other than that there was an Ojibway village at Fond du Lac in 1630. Some historians hold that Etienne Brulé visited the foot of Lake Superior in 1622, but Radisson and Groseillier are generally given credit as the first white men to explore the southern lake shore (1654–60). Ten years later Father Allouez is known to have been at the mouth of the St. Louis River. Daniel Greysolon, Sieur Du Luth, for whom the city is named, made his first visit in 1679, when he tried to make peace between the Ojibway and the Sioux so that the country around the head of Lake Superior might be safe for trapping and trading.

From the period of the 17th century explorations until settlement, the story of the Lake Superior region is concerned mainly with fur-trading. The words Fond du Lac were used at first to embrace the entire area of the western end of Lake Superior. The name occurs for the first time in 1750 and the Mackinac Register of 1753 shows a baptism record of Marie Josephs Tellier, legitimate daughter of Jean Baptiste Tellier of Fond du Lac. In 1792 Cadotte was located at the Northwest Company's trading-post there, and we are told that he had not only a large garden but several head of cattle. Although Fond du Lac was a minor post, it was the gateway to an extensive fur-bearing region and from there a canoe route led to Sandy Lake, where in 1794 the Northwest Company built what became the most important post in their territory. It was in Fond du Lac in 1826 that Gen. Lewis Cass, Governor of the Territory of Michigan for whom a Minnesota lake and county were named, negotiated the Treaty of Fond du Lac with the Ojibway, and here six years later Schoolcraft paused on the expedition in which he discovered the main source of the Mississippi. Accompanying him was the Reverend W. T. Boutwell, preacher of the first English sermon in the region, who recorded his surprise at finding "400 souls, half-breeds and whites" at the post.

The fur trade departed from Lake Superior in 1847. It had been operated by a succession of companies while a little settlement grew up about the stockade at Fond du Lac although it as yet gave no suggestion of permanence. Permanent settlement did not actually begin for Duluth until 1852, the year that George P. Stuntz first came to the region under orders from Surveyor-General George B. Sargent whose Federal Headquarters were at Davenport, Iowa. On this first visit Stuntz became so excited by the possibilities of this wilderness country, that he returned the following year to remain. It is Stuntz, a man not only of courage but with creative imagination, who is usually credited with being Duluth's first settler.

The years 1854 and 1855 marked a boom in the unnamed town. Rumors of immense copper deposits along the North Shore, and of iron ore at Lake Vermilion had long been prevalent; in 1854 the Treaty of La Pointe was signed at Fond du Lac, by which the Grand Portage and Fond du Lac Indians relinquished their rights to mineral tracts in the region. But before it was ratified by the Senate, miners and settlers, convinced of a new El Dorado, rushed into the territory and built their cabins, hoping to be able to establish their claims by pre-emption. Prospectors came in from northern Michigan and St. Paul, and land speculators from the Central States, believing land values would skyrocket, scrambled for sites. Wildcat speculation followed. In 1856 the village, consisting of 14 buildings, was named and made the seat of St. Louis County; the following year the towns of Duluth, Fond du Lac, Portland, Belville, and Oneota—all later to be absorbed within the limits of Duluth—were incorporated as separate villages.

In 1855 Robert E. Jefferson built the community's first frame structure about 500 feet north of the present Duluth ship canal, on what is now Lake Avenue.

The national panic of 1857 brought disaster to the region. Eastern creditors demanded money, and debtors paid as long as a dollar remained. Towns were left wholly without funds and hundreds of families abandoned their homes. For ten years not a store was open on the Minnesota shore of Lake Superior. Close on the panic followed the devastating scarlet fever epidemic of 1859. By 1865 only two houses in Duluth were occupied.

A year later, however, thousands of men poured into the area. They came because in the summer of 1865 geologists had reported finding iron ore and gold-bearing quartz at Lake Vermilion, and a stampede for the supposed gold bonanza ensued; and because Jay Cooke, eastern financier, decided to make Duluth the northern terminus of the Lake Superior and Mississippi Railroad, which was to replace the old Military Road from St.

Paul. By 1869, with an added influx of the lumbermen from Maine who built mills throughout the Lake Superior district, the population of Duluth reached 3,500. In March 1870 Duluth was granted its first charter and at its first election the following April Col. J. B. Culver was elected mayor. In August of that year the Lake Superior and Mississippi Railroad was opened for traffic. (This road later became the St. Paul and Duluth, and is now a part of the Northern Pacific System.)

It was in 1871 that Duluth sprang into national notoriety through the famous speech made in Congress by the Kentucky Representative, J. Proctor Knott. Congress was soon to adjourn and the contesting supporters of two railroad land-grant bills knew that only one could be passed in the allotted time. As it happened Mr. Knott's constituents had the right of way. But this lively Kentuckian—to whom Minnesota was doubtless as remote as darkest Africa—had somehow confused the railroads and, with the political zeal wealthy constituents inspired in the 1870's, arose to prevent a vote on the opponents' bill. Fantastically exaggerating the pretensions of poor little Duluth he was so wittily satirical that the House rocked with laughter. Amid cheers and shouts he continued to elaborate his theme until the time for the bill had been all consumed. It was only then he learned that the bill he had killed was the one he should have supported. The joke was on Mr. Knott, even though his speech was recognized as a classic of ironic oratory; as for Duluth, it could well afford to laugh, for now its fame was spread to thousands. Not only did the city get its railroad grants, but in less than 20 years most of the predictions made in flamboyant mockery by the Congressman were literally fulfilled. Knott himself graciously admitted this at a banquet in 1890, adding, "Possibly the mention of the name 'Duluth' may bring my own to the recollection of millions long after I shall have mouldered into dust, and everything else pertaining to my existence faded from the memory of man."

Soon after the completion of the first railroad, the Northern Pacific made Duluth its terminus on Lake Superior. In 1870 this road built the Immigrant House, at what is now 5th Ave. W. and Michigan Street, to house immigrant settlers en route from Montreal to the Dakotas. As many as 700 are known to have been accommodated there at one time.

By 1870 Duluth was booming and proudly regarded itself as a "City of Destiny." To the impersonal observer the town might appear for the most part a heterogeneous settlement of cheap frame buildings, log cabins, and tar paper shacks, manifesting all the rowdiness and vitality of the usual frontier town. Organized gangs vied for power and wealth and their fights often enough ended in bloodshed and murder. But at the Clark House (between First and Second Aves. W., on Superior St.) where the eastern settlers gathered at banquets, parties, and balls, no hopes of Duluth's future were too extravagant for either expression or belief. The city, they believed, was soon to be "one of the largest if not the largest on the continent." Had not Jay Cooke, one of the world's greatest financiers, tacitly implied as much? For three years optimism was boundless. Then in 1873 came Jay Cooke's failure and for Duluth "it was as though the very heavens had fallen." Banks failed, real estate slumped, there was no work to be had, and the population dwindled from about 5,000 to 1,300. The city government found itself so heavily in debt that it could not continue. On March 12, 1877, it held its last council meeting after which it burned up its bonds and lapsed once again into a "village" status. For ten years the more settled parts were known as Duluth village, the surrounding fringes, the "district."

Already by 1878, however, Duluth's prospects had begun to brighten again. Lumbering got under way, grain from the prairies began to pour into the port; the village boundaries had to be enlarged and hope was again in the ascendant. The first street railway franchise was granted in 1881, and that same year was installed the first telephone exchange with 30 subscribers. By 1886 the population had leaped to 26,000 and in 1887 the legislature once again gave Duluth permission to call itself a city.

By the end of the century the six communities, originally platted along the lake shore and incorporated in the early days of settlement, had been gradually absorbed into Greater Duluth. On December 3, 1912, the present charter providing for a commission form of government was adopted.

The development of the railroads, elevators, docks, and sawmills was accompanied by a continued rise in the city's population, and by 1890, with the beginning of ore shipments, it had increased to 33,115. At the turn of the century it was 52,969; by 1910 it was 78,466, and the 1930 census revealed a city of 101,463 persons.

The economic history of Duluth is the history of its harbor. This famous harbor is cut off from the open lake by two narrow sandbars—Minnesota Point, which extends almost six and a half miles from the north shore, and Wisconsin Point, reaching two and a half miles out from the south shore. Together they form a perfect landlocked basin and between them is the channel by which the waters of the St. Louis and Menadji Rivers reach the lake. This outlet, 500 feet wide, is the Superior Ship Canal, and, improved by the Federal Government with bulkheads, concrete piers, and a breakwater, it admits the largest ships on the Great Lakes.

In 1871 Duluth decided to dig an artificial entry to the lake through Minnesota Point so that its fishing boats could get out directly and thereby eliminate the seven-mile stretch to the only natural entry near the Wisconsin shore. Work was started with one steam shovel, but the City of Superior, across the bay, appealed to Washington to halt operations.

On a Friday in April word came that an Army engineer was on his way with the injunction. That night all Duluth shoveled and spaded. Saturday and Sunday they worked without pause. On Monday morning the injunction arrived, but the canal had been dug, and the little tug, *Fero,* was steaming through in triumph, its tied-down whistle shrieking defiance. In 1873 the United States Government assumed control of both canal and harbor, and in 1893 named it the Duluth-Superior Harbor.

An idea of the present commercial importance of the harbor may be gained from the fact that in the United States it is second in total net tonnage only to New York, and this with but an average eight-months navigation season. The average yearly tonnage is 48,000,000 net, although during the peak year of 1929 there was a total net tonnage of 60,385,767. Of this, 50 percent was iron ore; the balance coal, limestone, grain, and miscellaneous products. The value of the shipments exceeded 485 million dollars. In 1935 the average cargo received and shipped per day was 124,190 tons, and 11,050 vessels passed in and out of the harbor.

Ninety percent of the docks are modern, and some are among the largest in the world. One modern cement elevator has a storage capacity of 114,000 barrels, and an unloading capacity of 1,000 barrels an hour. The largest grain elevator has a capacity of 12,800,000 bushels, and one of the elevators unloads 20,000 bushels an hour. Seven iron ore docks (nearly three miles long) have a storage capacity of 819,000 tons.

Thirty-eight steamship companies, two of which are passenger lines, operate out of Duluth. But although its 19 square miles of harbor and 49 miles of water frontage offer ample port facilities, Duluth is still far from content. Long before it became a city, its settlers dreamed of an inland waterway that would connect the head of the Great Lakes with the Atlantic. Of recent years this ambition has grown so insistent that its opponents say derisively that Duluth is the "old-maid city, looking under her bed every night for an ocean." With the seaway a reality, enthusiasts retort, Duluth and Superior, forgetting jealousies, would unite to form a great inland metropolis rivaling New York or Chicago.

After the harbor, Duluth is perhaps proudest of the chain of boulevards, called the Skyline Parkway, that make up the 29 miles of scenic drives above the city; of its educational facilities that include its State Teachers' College, 37 grade schools, six junior high schools, three senior high schools and one junior college, together with a Roman Catholic parochial system of 12 elementary, four high schools, and one college; and of its Civic Symphony Orchestra, an organization showing great promise.

Shipping facilities and the diversity of raw materials in the region have attracted to the city jobbers and manufacturers, who provide a livelihood for the foreign-born workers, a large number of whom came during the height of each of the region's rapidly changing industrial phases. In 1930 the foreign-born population totaled 24,929. More than half of this number came from the Scandinavian countries and Finland, and settled largely in what is known as the West End. Many Scandinavians, once woods lumbermen, are employed now in lumber's related industries. The Finns were first attracted by the forests and the mines, but are now usually employed as longshoremen and stevedores, although they are happiest at farming— the city workers dreaming of the few acres and stock they will own when they are financially independent. Their zeal for co-operative undertakings brought from their homeland has accounted for much of the success of co-operatives throughout the State. Finland-Swedes (Swedes who have lived for centuries in Finland, but who have only rarely intermarried with Finns and have retained their Swedish speech), of whom there are a few hundred, also have settled in West Duluth. They are now mainly interested in carpentering and fishing. When the United States Steel Corporation built its model town, Morgan Park, for its employees, about 700 of the Yugoslavs who had been imported to work in the plants were segregated there, although many are in Gary and New Duluth. French Canadians came with the railroads; Italians came first to the mines, but those who have stayed in Duluth are for the most part unskilled laborers. The Poles came first in 1868 as a result of Prussian oppression, and their numbers were increased in 1880 by a group from Galicia driven from their country by a similar situation. The Germans are scattered throughout the city and are represented in almost every trade and activity. Before the depressio. of 1929 there were many Negroes in the city, but their number has since diminished to a few hundred.

The topography of Duluth has facilitated the sectional segregation of these nationalities, yet few are the traces of Old World customs that survive today. A few years ago all foreign groups had their respective churches in which services were held in their native languages. Today, the Serbian Orthodox Church, St. Elizabeth's for Croats and Slovenians, St. Peter's for Italians, St. Josephat for Poles, and St. Jean Baptiste for French Canadians, alone conduct regular services in foreign tongues. The predominating Lutheran churches, once conducted almost universally in Swedish, Norwegian, or Danish, now hold only occasional meetings in these languages, and are agreed that with the passing of the present generation even these will be discontinued.

The children and grandchildren of the foreign-born, however, are beginning to take a conscious pride in the literature, drama, dancing, and handiwork of their forebears, and numerous small groups, notably among the Scandinavians and Poles, have been formed to revive and keep alive Old Country customs and traditions. Of all foreign groups the Finns cling most tenaciously to their native mode of living.

The Duluth *Skandinav* is a Norwegian weekly newspaper. One of its pages is printed in English for the benefit of the younger generation. In the city are published also the monthly *Ledstjarnan* (Swedish) and three Finnish sheets, two of which are dailies, the third a weekly.

Whether it be due to the stimulating atmosphere, the rugged setting, or to the adventurous spirit inherited from its settlers, there can be no doubt that the Duluth temperament is to an unusual degree, even for Minnesota, buoyant, optimistic, expansive. A passive attitude toward anything is inconceivable to a true Duluthian—whether the subject be of national or local interest. He is vitally interested in politics and in all suggestions for social betterment, and he believes with all his might in the glamorous potentialities of his city. He is a strong party man and he enthusiastically supports his local symphony, his little theater, his Community Chest, and his service clubs. His intense individualism is equaled only by his faith in organization, a characteristic which is as widespread among the workers as among the financiers. The businessmen's service clubs have their counterparts in the Labor Forward Movement sponsored by the Duluth Federated Trades Assembly, and in the Labor Advancement Association made up of unorganized workers.

Because of this city's unique topography the great majority of tourists come into Duluth from the northeast and southwest over US 61. For this reason the Points of Interest have been grouped as far as possible in the order in which they are met by the motorist approaching the heart of the city.

POINTS OF INTEREST

(Approaching the Loop from the northeast)

1. KITCHI GAMMI PARK, London Rd. between Lakewood Rd. (81st Ave. E.) on the shore of Lake Superior and E. Lester Blvd. (61st Ave. E.), includes 154 acres of woodland. In addition to its groves of native trees there are several from foreign countries. There are excellent picnic sites along the lake shore.

2. THE UNITED STATES FISH HATCHERY *(open daily, 8-5)*, 6008 London Rd., the largest hatchery in the State, is the only one under Federal control on Lake Superior. The Federal Government cooperates with the State department of conservation in all phases of its work. Excess supplies of eggs from the State hatcheries together with those collected from the lakes or purchased from other States are reared to fingerling stage. Although no brood stock is kept here, most of the species common to the small lakes and streams as well as the Great Lakes are reared for distribution throughout the State. The young trout can be seen in the outdoor troughs, but the pike and whitefish must be reared indoors.

3. EAST JUNIOR HIGH SCHOOL, cor. Hawthorne Rd. and 4th St., in a beautiful setting overlooking the lake, is of red brick, designed much like an English manor. It was completed in 1927.

4. The CHILDREN'S MUSEUM *(open weekdays 9-5, except Wed. and Sat. 9-12; free)*, 1832 E. 2nd St., was opened in 1930. In 1935 it was moved to the present building donated by Mrs. Archibald Chisholm. To further its plan of visual education, exhibits are so arranged as to supplement the work of the public schools. The collections cover a wide range, including natural history, industry, and commerce. Many dolls in native costume, weapons, utensils, miniature houses and vehicles, and examples of foreign handicraft are displayed. Other exhibits depict early American, Indian, and Eskimo culture. A glass used by George Washington and a paint brush of Rosa Bonheur are novel possessions. Children are assisted in making notes, drawing pictures, and studying displays.

5. The CHILDREN'S THEATER, 114 N. 15th Ave. E., occupies a rebuilt barn with a seating capacity of 200. The Theater Association was organized in 1932 by Frances Hoffman and Mrs. D. K. Harris, and is one of the few such organizations in the country. It began as a branch of the Little Theater, giving its initial performance, *The Wizard of Oz*, in 1928. Its first presentation, as a separate organization with its own building, was *Aladdin and His Lamp*. The players—boys and girls from the colleges as well as from the elementary and high schools—are chosen by tryouts and trained by a volunteer staff. Four plays are presented during the season.

6. The DULUTH CURLING AND SKATING CLUB BUILDING, 1328 London Rd. *(open, nonmembers, daily 2-5, adm. 25¢; daily 8-10:30 p.m. except Wed. and Fri. 8-10 p.m., adm. 35¢)*, a two-story red brick structure of reinforced concrete and steel is 279 feet long. Its curling and

skating rink, and amphitheater, place it among the best-equipped curling clubs in the country.

7. The DULUTH ARMORY, 1305 London Rd., of red brick and rein-forced concrete, was built in 1916 and has a seating capacity of 3,500. The city's outstanding musical organization, the Duluth Civic Symphony Orchestra, with a membership of 65, presents its concerts here. The or-ganization was established in 1925 when a group of citizens raised fifteen thousand dollars, interested volunteer musicians, and hired some profes-sionals. The early concerts overflowed the Orpheum Hall and later perform-ances were given in the Central High School Auditorium. But the funds lasted only until 1928 at which time activities were discontinued. A new association was formed in 1933, and by 1934 the orchestra had progressed so rapidly that it undertook the performance of several radio broadcasts. Its personnel still consists of volunteer as well as paid musicians. Many of its concerts are presented in conjunction with the Civic Symphony Choral Society of 250 people, which was first assembled in 1935.

8. In the 15-acre LEIF ERICCSON PARK, London Rd. between 8th and 14th Aves. E., is the LEIF ERIKSON OF BERGEN, a little craft patterned after Leif Ericcson's dragon ship. The gunwales are hung with replicas of the traditional Norse shields bearing the devices of the Vikings. Captain Gerhard Folgero of Sannesjoen, and his crew, sailed it from Bergen, Nor-way, on May 23, 1926, and arrived in Duluth on June 23, 1927, after stopping at the Sesqui-Centennial Exposition at Philadelphia; later it was taken to Chicago for the dedication of Leif Ericcson Drive.

9. The LITTLE THEATER, 6 S. 12th Ave. E., one of the country's earliest, was established in 1914. The association owns its hall, trains its players, and has sponsored summer courses in all phases of play produc-tion, for which it hired guest instructors. Seven plays are presented during the winter season. Several of its plays have later been produced on Broad-way or in the movies. An annual Beaux Arts Ball augments the funds re-ceived from ticket sales.

10. The JAY COOKE STATUE, London Rd. and 8th Ave. E., is the work of Henry M. Schrady. Jay Cooke (1821–1905), a Philadelphia finan-cier, planned to make Duluth the terminus of his transcontinental railroad. The line had already been completed across the State to the Red River val-ley when the crash of 1873 reduced his fortunes and halted the project.

11. The SITE OF THE OLD VERMILION TRAIL, Washington Ave. and 1st St., is marked by a bronze plaque. Washington Ave. follows this historic route between Lake Superior and Vermilion Lake The Indian trail was used by explorers and finally surveyed by George R. Stuntz.

12. The MILLER MEMORIAL HOSPITAL, 502-510 E. 2nd St., of cream-colored face brick, and limestone from Kasota, Minnesota, is five stories high and modern in design. It was established in 1932 through a trust fund created by Andreas M. Miller, in memory of his son, and is open to any needy patient.

13. ST. PAUL'S EVANGELICAL CHURCH *(belfry open weekdays, except Sat., 10-12),* 932 E. 3rd St., contains a nine-hundred-pound bell cast from a cannon used in the Franco-Prussian war. The bell was presented to

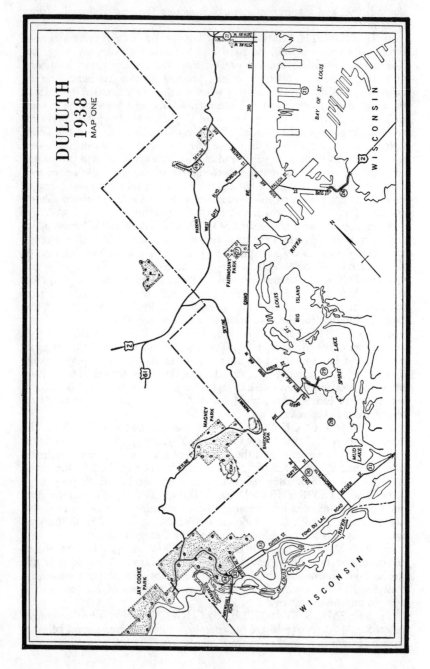

DULUTH
1938
MAP ONE

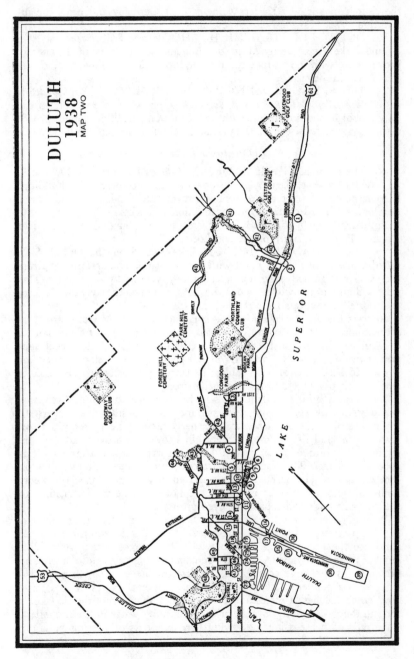

DULUTH
1938
MAP TWO

the church in 1874 by Kaiser Wilhelm I, of Germany and bears the inscription "Aus Franzoesischem Geschuetz."

14. DULUTH CENTRAL HIGH SCHOOL, 2nd St. between 1st Ave. E. and Lake Ave., designed in the Romanesque style is of Minnesota brownstone, with a 230-foot rectangular tower. Its enrollment, 2,700, is the largest in the city.

15. The red brick WASHINGTON JR. HIGH SCHOOL (broadcasting station open 8:15-8:30 a.m. schooldays), 305 Lake Ave. N., is the only school in the Northwest with a student-built, double-program broadcasting system, consisting of a radio and public address microphones.

(Downtown Duluth)

16. The U. S. ENGINEERS' OFFICE (open Mon.-Fri. 9-4:30; Sat. 8-12), 600 Lake Ave. S., in a grey stone and cream-colored brick building, has charge of all river and harbor improvements, navigation and power development, flood control, and construction of docks, bridges, etc., in the Duluth district, which extends east from the Lake Superior watershed to Iroquois Point just north of the Soo Locks.

17. The AERIAL LIFT BRIDGE, Lake Ave. S. at the Duluth Ship Canal, connects Minnesota Point with the mainland. The first bridge across the canal was a footbridge four feet wide suspended by wire ropes. This was used only in the winter; when the canal was open to navigation a ferry transported the settlers from the Point to the mainland.

In 1905 the first aerial bridge was constructed by the Modern Structural Steel Company of Wabasha, Wisconsin, from the design of C. P. Turner of Minneapolis. It consisted of an overhead span of riveted steel supported by high towers, and a rigidly suspended, electrically-operated car which ran back and forth on cables; its carrying capacity was six vehicles and enough passengers to fill two large streetcars.

The present bridge, built in 1930 by the Kansas City Bridge Company, was designed by Harrington, Howard and Ash, consulting engineers. In the new structure, the basket that formerly carried the passengers is replaced by a solid lift, although the original towers and overhead span are retained. The bridge has an over-all length of 510 feet and a vertical clearance of 138 feet. The 900-pound lift is counterbalanced by two 450-ton concrete blocks, and is electrically operated at an annual cost of twenty thousand dollars. This lift is one of the fastest in the world, rising 120 feet in 55 seconds and capable of even greater speed.

Invariably tourists will be found parked here both day and night during shipping seasons watching the boats go by. Three deep throaty blasts announce the approaching ship to which the bridge replies with a like number of shrill signals. A warning bell sounds, the gates close down, and presently, as the huge counterweights descend the entire span rises skyward with a ponderous clanking of chains. The boat glides by to a rattle of opening hatches, a screeching of winches, a shout from the deck, or a song in the galley, until only the rush of churning water in the propeller's wake tells her passing. Following her, hundreds of herring gulls dip and dart or glide slowly with the wind.

18. The CIVIC CENTER, 1st St. between 4th and 6th Aves. W., designed by Daniel H. Burnham of Chicago, consists of the central COURT-HOUSE, built in 1910, with the FEDERAL BUILDING on the left, and the CITY HALL on the right. The ST. LOUIS HISTORICAL SOCIETY MUSEUM and LIBRARY occupy two rooms on the 4th floor of the courthouse *(open Mon.-Fri. 8:30-5; Sat. 8:30-4)*. In addition to a collection of books, charts, maps and war records, there is an exibit of paintings and sketches of Indian types by Eastman Johnson. The City Hall was finished in 1927; the Federal Building, completed in 1930, contains the post office and other governmental units. All three structures are of granite and are neo-classic in design.

19. The SOLDIERS AND SAILORS MONUMENT, 5th Ave. W. and 1st St., in the open square at the Civic Center was designed by Cass Gilbert; it is entitled *Patriotism Guarding the Flag*.

20. The INCLINE RAILWAY, 7th Ave. W. and Superior St. *(fare 10¢)*, built in 1891, has two electrically-operated cars counter-balanced on an endless cable controlled from a station at the top of the hill. The cars make the 3,000-foot ascent on a 15-25 percent grade, to a height of more than 600 feet above the lake level. The view from the summit is excellent; on clear days during the summer months, ships 60 miles distant have been sighted through the powerful telescope mounted on a platform at the top of the hill.

A spectacular fire in 1901 provided onlookers with a thrill. An amusement pavilion at the top of the incline burned, and the fire rapidly spread to the station, severing the cable and releasing the flaming, heavily constructed car. The fiery mass, speeding comet-like down the hill, hit the retaining wall hurling the iron roof of the car across Superior Street. Much smaller passenger cars have replaced the massive structures that carried a couple of teams and drays in addition to a number of passengers.

(Approaching the Loop from the Southwest)

21. The IRON ORE DOCKS, an extension of the Duluth, Missabe and Iron Range Ry. trestle, which crosses 3rd St. and 33rd Ave. W. *(open by permission from offices in the Wolin Bldg.)*, are of steel and concrete. The most modern is 2,304 feet long and has 384 loading pockets, each of 400-ton capacity. A record loading from these docks was made in 1926 when 225,258 gross tons were transferred to 26 vessels in 24 hours.

22. LINCOLN PARK, 3rd St. between 25th and 26th Aves. W., is notable for its unspoiled natural beauty. The 38-acre park borders a small swift stream, Miller's Creek, between high, wooded hills. Fireplaces, tables, benches, and shelters for picnickers have been built throughout the park. Each June the Scandinavian Midsummer Festival, featuring folk songs and dances in native costume, is held here.

23. The POINT OF ROCKS, adjoining Superior St. between 8th and 14th Aves. W., is a massive outcrop of Duluth gabbro. Atop can be seen striations made by glaciers.

24. An INDIAN VILLAGE once stood where Mesaba Ave. intersects Superior St.

25. The HEADQUARTERS OF THE NORTHERN BIBLE SOCI-
ETY *(open weekdays, 9-5; free)*, 715 W. Superior St., is a modern cream-
colored brick building with lancet windows in the upper story. Here is
the Rev. Henry Ramseyer's private collection of Bibles and testaments,
representing 550 languages and 60 alphabets, and phonetic scripts. Among
these are a first edition *King James Bible,* 1611; an *Archbishop Cran-
mer's Bible,* 1541; a 17th century Hebrew scroll (from Aden, Palestine),
handwritten on 52 sheepskins; and a *Luther's Bible,* 1560, in Gothic type.

(In Old Duluth)

26. The ARROWHEAD TOLL BRIDGE, Lesure St. and St. Louis
Bay *(cars, 10¢; passengers, 5¢)*, leads to Superior, Wisconsin. It was built
in 1926, and was designed by the Scherzer Rolling Lift Bridge Company
of Chicago. It is an unusually long jacknife type of bridge, measuring
2,200 feet.

27. The DULUTH ZOO, in Fairmont Park (56.21 acres), 72nd Ave.
W., has a fine natural setting. The buildings, constructed by Federal aid
in 1936, are of blue stone. There is a Big House, circular in shape, for
large animals, and a crescent-shaped Little House. In addition to the native animals such as bear and deer, there are several imported specimens
including a hippopotamus, an elephant, a rhinoceros, and a giraffe.

28. The AMERICAN STEEL AND WIRE CO. PLANT *(open by permission at gatehouse or office, guides; free)*, 1434 88th Ave. W., is one of
the largest industrial units in the State.

The plant, opened in 1916, was the first in the State to manufacture
steel wire. Visitors may watch many of the processes by which steel is manufactured from the crude ore brought from the adjacent iron ranges. For
these processes the plant imports coking coal from the East, limestone
from Michigan, and manganese from Brazil and elsewhere.

At a temperature of 3,000° F. the oxides are removed; the melted ore
is drawn off from the bottom of the furnace. After further purification in
open-hearth furnaces, it is cooled in molds to form six-ton ingots. These
ingots, again heated, are fabricated by pressure into long thick sections
called blooms, then further thinned and lengthened in the billet mill. The
product begins to assume final shape in the merchant mill which produces
round, square, or flat bars, small angles, fence posts, T-bars, and reinforc-
ing bars; or in the rod mill which produces steel wire. After baths of sul-
phuric acid, other solutions, and water, and tempering in ovens, the wire
passes through dies on a drawing block. It emerges as nails in more than
nine hundred sizes; and in more than one hundred varieties of barbed and
woven wire.

By-products from the coking process include ammonia, tar, benzol, and
other substances; from the blast furnace comes the slag utilized in the
nearby cement plant.

29. SPIRIT ISLAND is in Spirit Lake (a widening of the St. Louis
River), east of Morgan Park. Here a battle between the Chippewa and
Sioux is supposed to have been fought before the coming of the white
man. According to an old Indian legend, the son of a Sioux chieftain fell

in love with a princess of the enemy Chippewa. They fled to this island during the night, but when morning came, the pursuing parties, who had surrounded the island, could find no trace of the lovers. Various theories were advanced concerning their disappearance—suicide, drowning, the will of the gods. Since that time the island has been called Spirit Island.

30. In ST. GEORGE'S SERBIAN ORTHODOX CHURCH, 1218 104th Ave. W., a red brick building of Byzantine design, the liturgies are spoken in old Slavonic, the sermons in Serbian. The church was founded in 1923 and serves a parish of 250 families.

31. The DULUTH-OLIVER BRIDGE, McCuen St. and St. Louis River, built in 1910, leads to South Superior via Oliver. It is the only double-decked bridge at the Head of the Lakes.

32. The SITE OF FOND DU LAC includes an area adjoining the St. Louis River near the Wrenshall Rd. (State 23) bridge. Today a well-kept suburb has grown around this little settlement, one of the most historic spots in the State. Originally an Indian village, it later became a fur-trading post; in 1834 a school and mission were established here by the Reverend Edmund F. Ely, whose wife, in 1835, gave birth to the settlement's first white child.

33. The SITE OF A CHIPPEWA VILLAGE at the foot of 133rd Ave. W., is marked by a bronze plaque just above the approach to the excursion dock. Here in 1826 the first Minnesota Chippewa treaty was signed. Du Luth stopped here in 1679, and an Astor Trading Post was established at this site in 1817.

34. A REPRODUCTION OF A TYPICAL ASTOR TRADING POST, in Chambers Grove, Wrenshall Rd. (State 23) at the St. Louis River, is a composite of the features found in several Minnesota posts. The log stockade is of the type used at the Leech Lake Post where the Indians and whites were not on friendly terms; the bastions and turrets are reproductions of those at Sandy Lake. Some of the old logs bearing the Astor stamp are rebuilt into the structure.

TOUR 1 (Minnesota Point)—3.3 m.

S. from intersection of Superior St. and Lake Ave. on Lake Ave. S. across lift bridge.

Minnesota Point, a narrow strip of land, is basically nothing more than a sand bar. In places scarcely a block wide, but extending nearly six miles from the Duluth Canal to the Superior entry, it is one of Duluth's most distinctive features. Before the days of the automobile, the more prosperous of the city's residents established a summer colony here where they had a boat and yachting club and a swimming beach. But modern transportation put an end to the seclusion and the Point began to decline in popularity. Recently it has become popular again, for hay fever sufferers have found that its air is almost always free from irritating pollen. For about half of its length it is well built-up with homes, stores, a modern school, and fire department—a village apart. A bus line connects it with the Duluth street railway system. The back yard of a Point resident is a sand beach; if he lives on the bay side of the avenue, often scant; but if on the lake side, wide, white and gently sloping. Often the sand forms small dunes, constantly moving about, burying vegetation; most yards have high board fences or snow fences to keep it back. After a big blow from the lake, a stroll along the Point may prove a pure adventure of discovery. Anything is likely to turn up: logs, trees, boxes, dead gulls, perhaps a beaver or a porcupine, wreckage from ships, light bulbs, and always an assortment of flasks.

R. from Lake Ave. S. on 10th St.

35. The DULUTH BOAT CLUB, 10th St. and Minnesota Ave., has docking and storage facilities for crafts up to 50 feet in length. The building, once an exclusive clubhouse of early 18th Century Italian Rococo design, has been reconstructed as a public clubhouse and dock.

Retrace on 10th St.; R. on Lake Ave. S.

36. The U. S. COAST GUARD STATION AND WATCHTOWER *(open)*, 1225 Lake Ave. S., has both lake and bay frontage.

Retrace on Lake Ave. S.; R. on 12th St.

37. At the U. S. NAVAL BASE, 12th St. and Minnesota Ave., is the *U. S. S. Paducah* training ship *(open while in harbor)*. It makes week-end cruises early in the spring and fall. The regular two-weeks' cruises begin in early July and last until early September.

L. on Minnesota Ave.

38. MINNESOTA POINT DEVELOPMENT PROJECT, Minnesota Ave. and 43rd St., is a 200-acre summer playground. The park proper, though sandy, is landscaped with Black Hills spruce, Scotch pine, and birch, in a background of 400 varieties of vegetation. Duluth's most popular beach, once located north of this point, is being replaced by a new swimming beach in the park. The uninitiated will generally choose a fine, warm day to go swimming in the lake, very probably when a hot southwest breeze is blowing. Native sons know better than this. During, or soon after, a brisk northeaster is the time to go swimming in Lake Superior. Then the wind blows in enough of the warm surface water to make swimming a delight. The atmosphere will be chillier, but the water is marvelously refreshing. For one who can swim well there is little danger from the undertow.

39. The REMAINS OF THE FIRST LIGHTHOUSE at the Head of the Lakes, a brick structure reminiscent of early harbor life, are near the tip of Minnesota Point. The lighthouse stood by the only natural channel into the harbor. Its first keeper, R. H. Barrett, in foggy weather, used a warning horn which he blew with his mouth. The ruins have almost disappeared but the site still is used as "Zero" for marine surveys.

TOUR 2 (The Skyline Parkway)—21.7 *m.*

N. from London Road (US 61) on 60th Ave.; R. on Superior St.; L. on Occidental Blvd.; R. on Snively Blvd.

40. LESTER PARK (46.81 acres), Snively Blvd., between London Rd.

and Graves St., with its pines, footpaths, and its swift, tumbling trout stream is the starting point for the Skyline Parkway.

41. AMITY PARK adjoins the road. Here the city began a reforestation project in 1926 by planting more than twelve thousand pines. Five thousand spruce were added in 1932. The road circles a 200-foot cliff, and overlooks the wooded heights of Moose Mt. and Lester Park, Lake Superior, and the extensive residential section.

L. from Skyline Parkway on Woodland Ave.; L. on 5th St.

42. The DULUTH STATE TEACHERS COLLEGE, 2205 E. 5th St., occupies four buildings of classic and Romanesque design set high above the lake in spacious grounds cleft by a stream and a ravine wooded with birch and pine. The school, the fifth of the State's normal schools, was established in 1902. A two-year course for elementary teachers, and a four-year course leading to a Bachelor of Education degree, are supplemented by special courses for school supervisors. A practice training school occupies one building. Enrollment at the college averages 400.

43. CHESTER PARK, between Chester Park Drive and Chester Parkway (108 acres), like other Duluth parks, owes its beauty to its natural setting. In the upper end is Chester Park Bowl, where are toboggan slides, skating rink, tennis courts, athletic field, clubhouse, and a 125-foot artificial ski slide.

R. from Skyline Parkway on Kenwood Ave.

44. The VILLA SANCTA SCHOLASTICA, corner Kenwood and College Aves., is a girls' school conducted by the Sisters of St. Benedict. Its impressive buildings of native blue-trap granite in English Gothic design, were constructed in 1909. The school, set high on a bluff in an isolated spot, overlooks the lake and wooded ravines. The enrollment is 300. The school offers a four-year college course and awards bachelors' degrees in Arts, Science, Home Economics, and Nursing Science.

45. The U. S. WEATHER BUREAU STATION *(open weekdays 9-4)*, Skyline Parkway and 7th Ave. W., forecasts weather conditions for Lake Superior and the surrounding territory, and sends out storm warnings by radio, signal flags, and lights.

L. from Skyline Parkway on 8th Ave. W.

46. ST. PETER'S ITALIAN CHURCH (Roman Catholic), 8th Ave. W. and 3rd St., of blue, yellow, and grey native granite, was hand-built by its congregation. It was completed in 1927 and is of transitional Romanesque-Gothic design.

R. from 8th Ave. W. on 3rd St.

47. DARLING OBSERVATORY *(open by appointment)*, 910 W. 3rd St., was built by Prof. John H. Darling, a former Government engineer stationed at the Head of the Lakes. After retiring in 1913, Mr. Darling devoted himself to the study of astronomy which long had been his hobby. Through the aid of the Extension Division of the University of Minnesota, and an endowment fund for operating the observatory, he has insured its continued use by the public. The building, of red brick and stucco, has plain walls and a mansard roof. The dome is 19 feet in diameter.

R. from 3rd St. on 10th Ave. W.; L. on Skyline Parkway.

48. ENGER PARK (329.89 acres), adjoining the Parkway bet. 13th and 24th Aves. W., is a popular recreation center. Twin Lakes are among its many natural scenic features.

R. on a branch which encircles the bluff; L. on a steep rd.

ENGER PEAK with its 40-foot octagonal observation tower *(open at all times, free)*, of native blue granite with retaining wall, grilled windows, and balconies, affords a fine panoramic view of the lake and forests. Here also are picnic grounds and a shelter house.

49. In ONEOTA CEMETERY, Skyline Parkway between 65th and 68th Aves. W., one of the oldest in Duluth, are buried the "Seven Iron Men" as De Kruif named the Merritt brothers—discoverers of the Mesabi iron range; George R. Stuntz (1820–1902), explorer, surveyor, and discoverer of the Vermilion range; and many others notable in early Arrowhead history.

(From its intersection with US 61 the Skyline Parkway continues along the bluff as part of State Tour 1.)

POINTS OF INTEREST IN ENVIRONS

North Shore Scenic Drive; Jay Cooke State Park, *8.7 m.*, Cloquet, paper mills and Forest Experiment Station, *21.5 m. (see Tour 1, Section b.).*

St. Cloud

Railroad Stations: Great Northern Station, 16th & Breckenridge Aves. N., for Great Northern Ry. and Northern Pacific Ry.
Bus Station: 5th Ave. & St. Germain St. for Northland Greyhound Lines.
Airport: A. G. Whitney Memorial Airport, on the northwestern boundary of city. No scheduled service.
Taxis: 25¢ minimum.

Traffic Regulations: Parallel parking (90 min.) in the business section; 45-degree angle parking in other areas.

Accommodations: Five hotels; rates constant year-round.

Information Service: Junior Chamber of Commerce, second floor of the Recreation Hotel, 6th Ave. N. at St. Germain St.; St. Cloud Auto Club, Breen Hotel, 905 St. Germain St.

Radio Station: KFAM (1420 kc.)
Theaters and Motion Picture Houses: Four motion picture houses.
Athletics: Teacher's College and the Technical High School athletic fields.
Golf: Hillside Golf Course, on Washington Memorial Drive near Calvary Cemetery, 9 holes, greens fee 50¢, or $1 per day per person.
Baseball: St. Cloud Ball Club, between 27th and 29th Aves. N. on 1st St.
Riding: Cater Stables, 1527 8th Ave. S.

Annual Events: War Memorial Service on Mississippi River, May 30; Benton County Fair, Aug. 21-23; Winter Carnival, either Jan. or Feb.

ST. CLOUD (alt. 1,032; pop. 21,000), on the Mississippi River, which forms the eastern boundary of Stearns County, is the county seat and trade center for a large agricultural area that extends in all directions and, to the east, includes a major portion of Benton and Sherburne Counties. In other parts of the country St. Cloud's importance rests on its numerous quarries, the stones of which have been used since the 1870's by builders and architects throughout the United States for many of their most noteworthy structures. The city, however, has none of the usual aspects of an industrial community. Its quarries lie beyond the city limits, and the picture the town presents to the visitor is one of wide clean streets, modern shops, and business blocks, tree-lined avenues of attractive houses interspersed with schools and churches—a prosperous, thriving little city whose residents obviously harbor a strong civic pride.

St. Cloud was settled largely by men and women from eastern States who brought with them the educational and other traditions of Yankee forbears, and it was they who fixed the cultural pattern that dominates the contemporary scene.

The city's architecture reflects both its early history and its principal industry. The Colonial architecture of many homes suggests the eastern background of the pioneers, and the prevalence of granite construction witnesses the growth of quarrying.

The second and third generations of Germans, Scandinavians, Scotch, Irish, and Poles, who later were attracted to St. Cloud by Government gifts of land, are fused in a staunch Americanism, even while they still, on gala occasions, love to revive the customs of their ancestral homelands. Those of Polish descent, who predominate in the western part of the city, delight in colorful church festivals at which they feast on the *bouja* (meat and vegetable stew) of their ancestors. The *lutefisk* (boiled, cured cod) suppers served by those of Scandinavian descent are characterized by all the abundance for which their north European forbears have long been famed.

Before its settlement the immediate vicinity was first Sioux territory, but the Chippewa who drove out the Sioux centered their activities around Mille Lacs, to the north. In the forties, one of the fur trails from the Red River country met the Mississippi at St. Cloud, and here the teamsters, happy at reaching this important milestone on their long haul to Mendota, forded the stream, rested their tired oxen, and built their campfires under the shelter of the bluffs, to appease their hunger with pemmican and their spirits with roistering songs and robust stories.

The first stage line was operated through the region in 1851, and in 1859 the route was extended a considerable distance up the Mississippi, and later to the north and westward through the Sauk Valley to the Red River country. The stages brought the mails upon which the people depended almost entirely for their communication with the outside world. Stage officials and drivers were big-hearted, fun-loving men, kindly and accommodating, prime favorites of all with whom they came in contact, and vital figures in the pioneer life of the community. With the coming of the railroad from Minneapolis in 1866, the stage extensions assumed additional importance but were gradually discontinued after 1871 when the railroad reached the western boundary of the State.

With an eye to the beauty of the location far above the bed of the river, Ole Bergeson, a Norwegian, squatted in what is now the business section of St. Cloud early in 1853. In the summer of that year, John L. Wilson, a native of Maine, paid Bergeson $250 for his rights, and the following year platted a town that he named for the French city which, in his repeated readings of Napoleon's biography, had taken a deep hold on his imagination.

The geographical position of St. Cloud, near what was then the head of upper Mississippi River traffic, brought it into prominence in the fifties and sixties as an outfitting post for the fur trade. A vast tonnage of furs from the territory west and north was loaded upon steamboats here, after they had discharged cargoes mainly of supplies for the wilderness forts and for the distant Canadian posts of the Hudson's Bay Company. The goods were carried inland by trains of one hundred or more ox and pony carts that came and went in a steady flow, week after week. The last regular steamboat trip was made up the river in 1874. By that time the railroads had absorbed the traffic.

Early settlers who located in central and western Minnesota found St. Cloud a convenient center. To the United States land office, moved here from up the river at Sauk Rapids in 1858 and operated until 1906, came immigrants from northern Europe to look over the maps and pick out the quarter section of 160 acres which was their gift from the Government. After the Homestead Act was passed in the early sixties, a quarter section was available to any actual or would-be citizen who occupied the land for five years and made reasonable improvements. This time could be commuted on payment of the usual $1.25 an acre. Still wearing the costumes of their native countries, speaking the various languages of their homelands, the immigrants swarmed into the office, placed their fingers on the chosen tracts, and went their way to establish homes and rear families of American citizens.

Although most towns erected log stockades to protect their inhabitants from Indian attack in 1862 at the time of the Sioux outbreak, the citizens of St. Cloud built a novel fort of parallel log walls filled with earth, floored the inside of the structure with timber and sod, and topped it with 12 lookouts with firing holes.

With the addition of "Upper Town" and "Lower Town," adjoining the original plat, the village was ready to receive the newcomers. Among them came exponents of both the political parties whose differences were destined soon to plunge the Nation into civil war.

Gen. Sylvanus B. Lowry, one of the town proprietors, was a typical southerner, dignified and courteous, strongly imbued with the southern view of slavery, a recognized leader of the Democratic party.

Opposed to General Lowry was Jane Gray Swisshelm, who came in 1857 and assumed the revival and editorship of the newspaper, the *Minnesota Advertizer*. This sheet was discarded and her new paper, the *Visiter*, established some months later. Already known as an author and lecturer on feminine and political subjects, the vitriol of her editorial attacks and the vigor of her denunciations soon made her a storm center in the little community. Annoyed by her attacks on some of his southern visitors who brought their household slaves to St. Cloud, and incensed by what he construed to be editorial aspersions cast upon the wife of a Democrat friend, General Lowry and a group of sympathizers broke into the Swisshelm office one midnight in 1858 and threw parts of the press and most of the type into the Mississippi. An indignation meeting of the editor's friends was promptly held and steps taken to purchase a new outfit. (This meeting, which Mrs. Swisshelm attended under protection of an armed volunteer bodyguard, was presided over by Theodore N. Barrett who, several years later, as brigadier general at the head of his Negro troops, fought the last land engagement of the Civil War at Palmetto Ranch, near Brownsville, Texas, on May 13, 1865.) After repeated public denunciations Mrs. Swisshelm agreed never to mention the affair again in the columns of the *Visiter,* keeping the letter of the agreement by changing the name of the newspaper, and the following day resuming her attack.

In 1864 a detachment of Hatch's battalion of cavalry camped in St. Cloud with 400 Indian captives who had fled toward the Canadian border after the Sioux outbreak. From its first trip to Pembina and Fort Abercrombie in 1864 until its muster out in 1866, detachments of the battalion had their rendezvous here, the soldiers mingling with the other pioneer characters and adding much to the town's activity and color.

Soon after the town was platted, parents of the village children started a free public school by private subscription and named it for Edward Everett, of Massachusetts. Informed of the honor accorded him, Everett presented the school with a set of books that was the nucleus of the present public library.

The city was incorporated in 1868. Its first mayor was Judge Edward O. Hamlin who won wide notice as a member of the platform committee at the Democratic National Convention in 1864, where he vigorously opposed the adoption of a plank that declared the conduct of the Civil War by the Lincoln administration to have been a complete failure.

In 1912 St. Cloud adopted a home rule charter, with a joint commission and council form of government. The officers include a mayor, a finance commissioner, a street commissioner, and five councilmen. So close has been the cooperation of the people with the officials that for five successive years, 1929 to 1934, St. Cloud received the Minnesota award as the cleanest city in the State.

An interesting situation in newspaper control is shown in the editorship and management of the St. Cloud *Times*. Through a consolidation Republican Alvah Eastman became editor of the sheet, and Democrat Fred Schilplin its publisher. The paper is an independent daily that ranks high among the newspapers of the State.

Among the distinguished people who have made their homes in St. Cloud are Jacob Vardenberg Brower, archeologist and author; William Bell Mitchell, editor and historian; Stephen Miller, brigadier general and Governor; Myron D. Taylor, scholarly jurist; and Christopher C. Andrew, major general, author, lawyer, and diplomat.

The first quarry, opened as a private local enterprise in the fall of 1868, was rapidly followed by others. There are 50 privately owned establishments in and around the city that employ about 600 St. Cloud residents and account for nearly 20 percent of the city's industrial payroll. Production of monuments vies in importance with the cutting and dressing of building stone. One company has the reputation of being the largest monument-manufacturing plant in the world, and the city is one of the leading monument-producing centers in the country.

Ninety percent of the granite workers in the area are native-born. Forty percent of these are of German descent, and the remaining 60 percent are Poles, Scandinavians, Irish, and Scotch, in about equal proportions. Among them are artisans of the highest technical skill and several sculptors of talent, for in the early days the industry attracted young Germans ambitious to become sculptors. Their artistic talents are evident in statues among the widely scattered cemeteries and public parks.

The fine-grained stone of the region ranges in color from almost coal black through red and pink of varying shades to a clear white. It is widely used in public and office buildings, churches, bridges, and memorials. In

Minnesota it is used in many buildings, including the massive foundation and broad granite steps of the capitol at St. Paul, in the cathedral in that city, and in the courthouse in Minneapolis. Notable buildings in Washington, Philadelphia, Chicago, and Detroit—to mention but a few among the many throughout the country—owe their beauty and stability to the rock taken from the quarries of St. Cloud *(see INDUSTRIAL DEVELOPMENT: QUARRYING).*

POINTS OF INTEREST

1. The ST. CLOUD STATE TEACHERS' COLLEGE, in the southern part of the city, covers seven acres of oak-shaded land on the west bank of the Mississippi. The location of the institution was determined by a public donation of the old Stearns house and a tract of land. The doors were opened in the remodeled building in September 1869. Today the college, which cooperates with the extensive city, parochial, and rural school system, has approximately 800 students.

2. ST. MARY'S CATHOLIC CHURCH, 9th Ave. S. and 1st St., is Romanesque in style and has a simple, austere interior, with tall granite pillars flanking the nave. The largest Catholic church in the city, St. Mary's is a tribute to the diligence of the early Benedictines, who came here in the spring of 1856. Coming from the Abbey of St. Vincent, near Latrobe, Pa., and headed by Rev. Demetrius De Maragona, the Brothers, determined to found an educational center, established themselves on a farm on the banks of the Mississippi, a short distance below the present St. Cloud Orphanage, and started conducting services in the surrounding settlements. True to the custom of their order, the Benedictines, after securing a seminary charter from the Territorial Legislature in 1857, opened the second institution of higher learning in the State. Five students, housed, fed, and tutored in a rude farm building which was the home of the Brothers, constituted the first class of what is now St. John's University at Collegeville. The Benedictines moved their seminary from St. Cloud in 1864, but their early efforts resulted in an extensive system of Catholic institutions, and eventually in the designation of the city as the seat of the diocese which bears its name.

3. The ST. CLOUD HOSPITAL *(open 2-5)*, 1406-6th Ave. N., is under the direction of the Sisters of the Order of St. Benedict. It was completed in 1928 at a cost of $1,500,000, and has 375 beds. The modern, exceptionally well-equipped hospital buildings present an imposing picture, towering above the groves of oak and pine.

4. ST. CLOUD ORPHANAGE, 9th Ave. S. and 17th St. E., was erected and equipped at an original cost of $350,000. The Sisters of St. Francis are in charge. Twenty infants between the ages of 3 months and 3 years, and 110 children between 3 and 14 years can be cared for at one time. The extensive landscaped grounds are 1.5 miles from the business center and overlook the river.

5. The STEARNS COUNTY COURTHOUSE, 7th Ave. near St. Germain St., was built in 1921 of local granite in Italian Renaissance style, the

architects being Toltz, King & Day of St. Paul. The classic façade with its broad steps, its massive columns, and the dome above give quiet grandeur to the building. The exterior walls are of brick, but into the construction has gone with fine harmony a considerable amount of Stearns County granite and terra cotta. At the head of the main stairway is a mural by Elsa Laubach Jemne of St. Paul, depicting life in pre-Territorial days.

6. The PUBLIC LIBRARY *(open 9-9, weekdays)*, 5th Ave. S. and St. Germain St., made possible by a gift of $25,000 from Andrew Carnegie, was opened in 1902. A casket of earth from St. Cloud, France, and a collection of pictures of the famous palaces and gardens sent by the ancient aristocratic city to its lusty young namesake are on view in the library building.

7. In RIVERSIDE PARK is a PINE LOG CABIN, one of the oldest in the region. It was built about 1855 by Balthasarr Rosenberger, and has been variously used as a home, a hotel, a fort, and a jail. It is preserved as a memorial to the early days of St. Cloud.

8. A MONUMENT FACTORY *(open by permission)*, is at St. Germain St. and Cooper Ave. Visitors can go through the plant and see rough granite trimmed down by hand and air drills, polished and lettered by the sandblast method.

9. The ST. CLOUD PRESBYTERIAN CHURCH, 4th Ave. and 3rd St. S., a granite structure, was founded in 1856 by the Rev. David Lowry, pioneer Indian school teacher, a fearless man of large frame and great physical strength. It is said that on several occasions when too much liquor made the Indians troublesome he dashed in among them with a club and, laying to on right and left, quickly brought them to order.

10. The NEW POST OFFICE, 720 St. Germain St., is of modern Gothic design, constructed of stone from local quarries. In the main room hangs a mural painted in oil on canvas by David Granahan, a Minneapolis artist. The mural was sponsored by the Treasury Dept. Art Project. On the 9-foot panel are depicted three scenes in the stone quarrying industry.

POINTS OF INTEREST IN ENVIRONS

Minnesota State Reformatory, *3 m. (see Tour 16)*; St. Benedict's Convent, *8 m. (see Tour 9)* and St. John's University, *11 m. (see Tour 9)*; Rockville, granite quarrying and finishing center, *10 m. (see Tour 9)*.

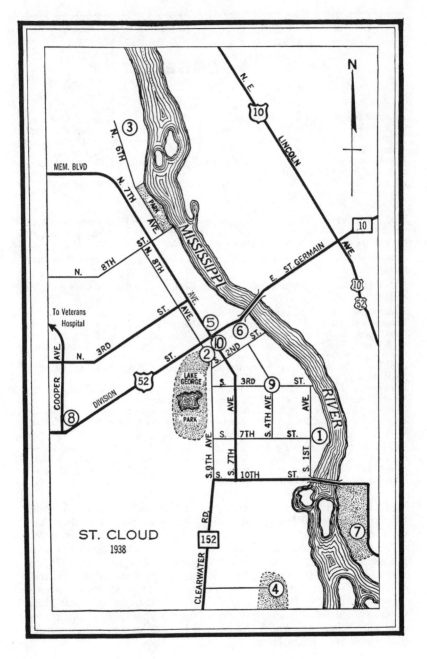

ST. CLOUD
1938

Winona

Railroad Stations: Milwaukee Station, 11th & Center Sts., for Chicago, Milwaukee & St. Paul R.R.; North Western Station, 2nd and Bluff Sts., for Chicago and North Western Ry.; Burlington Station, 102 E. 2nd St., for Burlington, Green Bay & Western R.R.
Bus Station: Arcade Restaurant, 116 Main St., for Northland Greyhound Lines, Merrillan Line and Stewart Line.
Airport: Conrad Airport, 4 m. W. of city on US 61. No scheduled service.
Taxis: 25¢ flat rate within city.
Street Cars: Fare 10¢, 4 tokens 25¢.

Traffic Regulations: Turns in any direction at all intersections except 3rd and 4th Sts. between Washington and Market Sts. inclusive; no U turns on Main and 4th Sts.; no traffic officers or traffic light signals.

Accommodations: Hotels, boarding houses, and inns (uniform rates throughout year).

Information Service: Winona Association of Commerce, Arlington Club Bldg., 57 E. 4th St.

Radio Station: KWNO (1200 kc.)
Theaters and Motion Picture Houses: Anvil Theatre, 57-61 E. 4th St., local productions; Community Playhouse, High School auditorium, W. 5th St. entrance, local productions; Teachers' College auditorium, Sanborn & Johnson Sts. lecture courses; five motion picture houses.
Athletics: Athletic Park, 5th & Minnesota Sts.; Maxwell Field, Sarnia St., numerous fields throughout city for diamondball.
Swimming: Lake Park, south side of city on Main St.; Latsch Public Bathing Beach across Mississippi River; cross High Bridge at north end of Main St.
Golf: Municipal course, 9 holes, reasonable fees, west end of city; street car service.
Riding: Saddle and Bridle Club, admission by invitation, near Winona Country Club.

Annual Events: Winona County Fair, last week in August; Merchandise Fair in autumn; golf and diamondball tournaments in late summer; poultry and grain shows in spring; Winter Carnival; Old Settlers' Day, Feb. 22nd, Red Men's Club, 4th & Franklin Sts.; annual horse show in autumn.

WINONA (alt. 664; pop. 20,850), the seat of Winona County, is on the Mississippi River. When the Mississippi leaves Lake Pepin to flow down to Winona, it spreads out over the broad valley making countless bayous of marshland, surrounding innumerable islands, while above its banks granite bluffs and hills with rounded, pointed, or squared contours, rise against the sky to form an idyllic back drop for the long narrow city lying at its level. The once teeming levee is now a formal garden that runs 1,500 feet along the river front. Across the bottoms where in ages past glacial waters poured down from the north, a long S-shaped bridge joins Minnesota with Wisconsin, whose tree-covered hills make a graceful unbroken line against the eastern horizon.

In 1851 the site of Winona was a barren, low-lying plain often partially submerged by the Mississippi, of interest only to an occasional fur trader and to the dwindling band of Indians who pitched their tepees on its treeless sands. Since then a city has been born. It has survived a childhood whose every day was crowded with frontier excitement and adventure; an adolescence in which six great industries brought fortunes to their eastern builders who erected massive Victorian houses, founded banks and established colleges; a maturity when, its major industries gone or obviously declining, it has settled down to the leisurely and cultural life it enjoys today, content that its first fifty years of drama shall fade into history, pleased that with every advancing year it assumes more and more an air of conservative sophistication.

The city's dominant population element is of New England stock. Among the earlier settlers were Germans who came as early as 1856 in sufficient numbers to establish their own church, and to introduce Beethoven and Mozart to the prairie. Yankees and Germans together planted trees and built up fortunes in lumber, wheat, steamboating, and railroading, which at one time gave Winona the reputation of having more millionaires than any city of its size in the country. The names on the signs of its leading law offices, factories, newspapers, land agencies are still largely those of pioneer days. In surprising numbers young Winonans, sent East to college, have come back to intermarry and carry on the family business and professional traditions. With more sophistication than their building fathers possessed, they have used much of their leisure in the cultivation of the arts, and, aided by the facilities and student bodies of the three colleges, they have given to their city an atmosphere of culture and dignity often lacking in young midwestern communities. Among the foreign groups arriving since the middle of the nineteenth century, Poles predominated. They number (1938) about 3,500, live mostly in the east end of the city, and all are Americans of the second and third generation. Other nationalities have but minor representation. A large number of transient channel and dam workers and ice cutters drift through the city and are its only unassimilated element.

In spite of its two modern banks and its skyscraper tower, Winona's business streets, like most of its residences, are more suggestive of the nineteenth than of the twentieth century. The old red hotel, with its spacious lobby, elaborate decorations of colored glass, carved pillars, balcony, and lofty diningroom, seems haunted with ladies in Merry Widow hats, and with bewhiskered and Prince-Alberted men who entertained and banqueted many of the Nation's notables here.

The visitor who comes in the summer will find it difficult to believe that this city could ever have been without trees, for its many steeples and towers rise above a sea of green. All of its broad residence streets are lined with double rows of elms and maples; the grounds of its colleges and religious institutions are landscaped; trees crowd to the foot of the granite bluffs and up the ravines to the prairies.

The earliest explorers of the upper Mississippi, French, English, and American, all make mention in their records of *Prairie aux Ailes,* or Prairie with Wings, and many landed here. Fur traders settled in the neighborhood of the Indian bands before the Black Hawk War of 1831–1832.

Aside from scrubby growths along the river's banks, the entire prairie had but a single tree. Despite this, Winona owes its beginning and its greatest prosperity to wood. The founder of the village was Capt. Orren Smith of the steamboat *Nominee* that plied between Galena and St. Paul. The ship's boilers were great consumers of cordwood, and the captain conceived the idea of locating a townsite whose prospective settlers might be induced to supply his fuel. The two landing places on Wabasha's Prairie impressed him favorably, and, deciding to secure both, he left his ship's carpenter, Erwin H. Johnson, and two others on shore with instructions to hold the landings and to cut wood from the opposite (Wisconsin) bank. Thus it was that Winona was born to the clanging of a bell, the hiss of escaping steam, and the splash of paddle wheels, at exactly 10 o'clock on the night of October 15, 1851.

The same year Chief Wabasha's band moved to an island under the Wisconsin bluffs. For the entire prairie they received from the white men only six barrels of flour; in 1852, when the treaties of 1851 were ratified, the last Indian claim to the region was obliterated.

In 1852 came settlers, among them a group from the East that had originally set out for the ill-fated co-operative colony at Minnesota City *(see Tour 1)*. The river town was platted and named Montezuma for the Aztec Emperor, but the proprietors reconsidered and gave their village the less pretentious name, Winona, a modification of the Sioux name Wenona invariably given to every Sioux girl who was the first-born child in the family.

The boom years of the new village began in 1855, when the local land office was established. Winona entered this, its fourth, year with some 50 unplastered shanties scattered along its river front. When the year ended, it had put up an average of two buildings a day, was supporting a newspaper, a steam mill, wagon factory, mail routes, saloons, hotels, loan sharks, jewelers, milliners, and had begun to survey for a railroad. Although not incorporated until two years later, the town published its first business directory in 1856 and listed 82 industries.

In 1855 the first lumberyard and the first sawmill were started on the prairie. Stock had first to be purchased from mills on Wisconsin streams and brought down on rafts with sweep and pole. There was easy access to the timber supplies of the upper Mississippi and the St. Croix, hordes of new settlers to the west were clamoring for building material, and before long Winona had 10 sawmills, 2,000 loggers, 1,500 mill hands, and its harbor was jammed with rafts. In a little more than fifty years, however, every mill was abandoned and the last lumber raft to pass down the Mississippi floated by Winona in the fall of 1915, behind the *Ottumwa Belle*. Yet the city's industrial life is founded on those early lumbering days, just as its present buildings rest upon thousands of tons of sawdust used to reinforce the sand.

In the early fifties settlers began to plant wheat. Soon bumper crops

poured into Winona from the southern triangle. A flour mill was established in 1856 and by 1868 Winona, too barren to grow even a spear of
grain, had become the fourth primary grain market in the United States.
Warehouses lined the levees; paddle-wheeled steamboats, barges, flatboats,
backed into the landings. In one year no less than 8,585 boats rounded the
bend at Winona. For the competing railroads the scorn of the rivermen
was boundless, and for years they expressed it by spitting a vociferous
curse on every track they came upon. Day and night hip-booted rivermen
challenged swaggering lumberjacks to contests of drinking, cursing, singing, or fighting. Farmers, 200 miles back in the country, packed up wives,
children, shotguns, and milk cows, came with wheat-laden oxcarts to the
city, and purchased their winter's supplies.

The Winona and St. Peter Railroad, with its river terminus at Winona,
replaced the oxcart from the West. The first load of wheat was shipped
over the new road in 1862, and by 1873 the line had tapped the fields of
South Dakota. The grain business reached its peak in 1877. In 1878 a
prolonged hot and dry period ruined the wheat crop. Grainmen and farmers alike learned the hazards of the one-crop idea. Winona lost the wheat
trade, but the farmers learned diversification.

Lumbering and wheat shipping were closely identified with steamboat
traffic, but as early as 1823 the Winona bluffs echoed to the shrill whistle
of the *Virginia,* and before the village was founded steamboat lines were
in regular operation. From its beginnings river traffic was vital to the existence of Winona, and when it was threatened in 1857 drastic action was
inevitable. That was the year when the unruly Mississippi tried to plow a
new main channel through what is now the bathing beach slough north
of Latsch Island. Steamboats, with officers none too friendly to the growing settlement their rival captain had founded, began to follow the new
course of the river, ignoring Winona's landings. But the village grimly
met the emergency. The county officials, in a carefully concocted scheme,
voted to erect an elaborate stone courthouse. They awarded the contract
to one of their own number, who started to get out the required stone
from the Wisconsin bluffs. The first load was piled on a huge barge and
started down the river. But at the debouchure of the new channel it met
with an "unfortunate accident." The barge was wrecked, its load of stone
permanently blocked the new course of the river, and again steamboats
were forced to swing into the Winona landings. From that time until the
end of the century the river was Winona's great highway. Then steamboating declined and with it ended one of the most vivid chapters of Winona's
history.

While its builders were bringing in from other regions the timber for
thousands of pioneer homes, an extensive supply of a more substantial
building material was at hand in the town's own crags and bluffs. Early
settlers had used stones they found in the vicinity for foundations. Later
the lime-burning industry grew up, and the bluffs were still further serrated
with quarries from which miniature railroads carried tons of rock to the
flaming kilns on the shore. Winona's limestone came into relatively late

recognition by architects, but today it is regarded as comparable to much of Italy's finest travertine *(see INDUSTRIAL DEVELOPMENT: QUARRYING)*.

Side by side with the stone industry has grown the making of brick. The first brickyard was opened in 1870, and in 1920 the yearly output of the leading plant was 3,000,000 bricks.

Winona's octogenarian newspaper, the *Daily Republican* (later the *Republican Herald*) claimed to be the first daily published after Minnesota's admission into the Union. The Leicht Press, now known as the National Weeklies, Inc., established by an early German settler, is one of the largest foreign language periodical syndicates in America; it publishes English, German, and Polish newspapers, weeklies and monthlies, including the *Lincoln Freie Presse,* the *American Farmer,* and others.

Every subsiding wave of industry left an aftermath of riches. When the decline of grain, lumber, and steamboating threatened its continued development, the results of the new agriculture began to fill its coffers once again. Soon it was an important dairy and meat-packing center; then with the cabbages brought in by the farmers it made itself the largest sauerkraut producer west of Chicago; still later the second largest hay and clover seed market in the country, and with the farmers' straw it made insulating sheets. Today with many profitable industries Winona claims to be the wealthiest city of its size in the Nation, and much of its $3,000,000 annual payroll still comes directly or indirectly from the farmers in the back country.

For miles on either side of the city the wilderness of the Mississippi bottoms, the ancient hunting grounds of the Sioux, is a natural terrain for fishermen and hunters. Trout, small-mouth bass, sunfish, pike and other game fish are more abundant here than ever, since the river's artificially dammed chain of lakes has increased their breeding grounds. These flatlands are on the natural flight route of northern ducks, and are the protected habitat of quail, partridge, and ring-necked pheasant. Countless sloughs and inland pockets, navigable to boats of light draft, are perfect ambushes for bird hunters.

POINTS OF INTEREST

1. SUGAR LOAF, a truncated monolith of limestone, tops a bluff that rises 500 feet above the city along its southwestern margin. It is 1¾ miles from the center of the city, and it can be reached only by a foot trail that starts from Lake Boulevard and US 61 and State 43. For countless generations before white men came up the river, the Mdewakanton Sioux, whose hereditary overlords were the successive chiefs named Wabasha, ranged the upper Mississippi, and each year their chiefs and medicine men gathered at the foot of this peak to celebrate with barbaric splendor the ceremonies of Ke-ox-ah, the *Homestead.* On the bluff top, called by the Indians Wabasha's Cap, signal fires were kept burning, while a brave kept constant watch for approaching friends or raiding Chippewa. White settlers found many acres of graves and burial scaffolds along the riverbank.

2. The BAY STATE MILLING PLANT *(open by permission),* Front

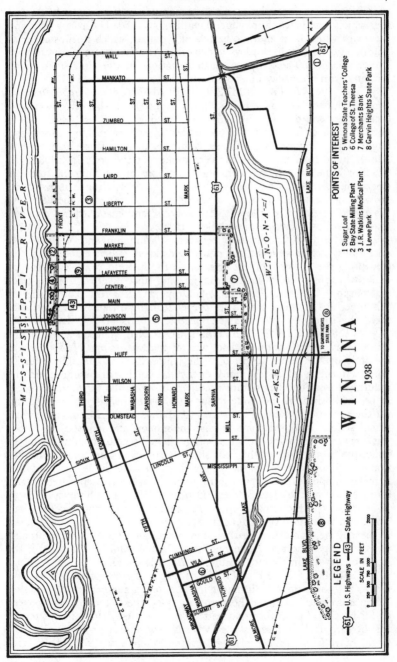

WINONA

1938

POINTS OF INTEREST

1 Sugar Loaf
2 Bay State Milling Plant
3 J.R. Watkins Medical Plant
4 Levee Park

5 Winona State Teachers' College
6 College of St. Theresa
7 Merchants Bank
8 Garvin Heights State Park

LEGEND

61 — U.S. Highways   43 — State Highway

SCALE IN FEET
0   250 500 750 1000   2000

and Franklin Sts., occupies an eight-story building of concrete, brick, and tile, which dominates the skyline. The plant has a daily capacity of 4,500 barrels of wheat flour and 500 barrels of rye flour, which it ships as far as Europe and Africa. It employs 200 workers. Its two grain elevators hold 750,000 bushels. The company began operations in 1874 in a small frame building with a capacity of 250 barrels of flour a day.

3. The J. R. WATKINS MEDICAL PLANT *(open by appointment)*, 150-178 Liberty St., is topped with a stone-faced 10-story tower and occupies an entire block. Its liniment, "good for man or beast," was a popular product in a town that specialized in harness making. Horse and buggy days are gone, but liniment continues to flow from Winona at a rate of more than three bottles every minute of the year. In 1868 J. R. Watkins came to Winona with high ambitions and a liniment formula. Concocting his product on his kitchen stove and peddling it in a basket, he was soon compelled to hire a salesman. Today (1938) the company has 9,000 salesmen, employs 1,520 workers, and manufactures 150 varieties of spices, medicines, and toilet articles.

4. LEVEE PARK, Riverside between Washington and Walnut Sts., once a busy steamboat levee, is a quiet, landscaped garden, extending 1,500 feet along the Mississippi. At one end is the historic WATERTOWER. Its galleried cap is open to visitors, though long since diverted from its original purpose. The tower encases a standpipe 210 x 4 feet. The raising of this pipe, all in one piece, to its perpendicular position was a feat that taxed the ingenuity of several engineering experts of that day (1862).

5. WINONA STATE TEACHERS' COLLEGE, Johnson and Sanborn Streets, was the first normal school west of the Mississippi. No sooner was the State of Minnesota admitted to the Union in 1858 than Dr. John D. Ford, a member of the Winona district school board, wrung from the indifferent first State Legislature a meager appropriation for normal schools to be established in the three towns that made the largest contribution for the purpose. Dr. Ford, known as the father of the Minnesota normal school system, hastened home to raise the money, and in 1860 the school was opened. When the principal resigned to become an army major in 1860, the greater part of the male students followed him, and the institution was closed for the two succeeding years. In 1876 the legislature failed to make an appropriation, but contributions from the resident director, and tuitions paid by the State Soldiers' Orphans' Home for the instruction of its wards kept the school open. Its annual enrollment exceeds 600. The PAUL WATKINS ART COLLECTION *(open during school hours)*, housed at the college, comprises nearly 4,000 pictures—originals, and reproductions, etchings, engravings, and portraits. In the exhibit of statuary is the figure of Sappho in Carrara marble, by Antonia Garella.

6. COLLEGE OF ST. TERESA *(open)*, corner of Wabasha and Gould Sts., owes its establishment in Winona to another town's disaster. When a cyclone devastated Rochester in 1883, the Sisters of the Convent of St. Frances, by converting a part of their academy there into a refuge for the care of the injured, started what is now St. Mary's Hospital, a unit of the Mayo Clinic *(see Rochester)*. Forced to find a new site for the acad-

emy, they fixed upon a building in the western part of Winona that at one time housed a Franciscan boarding school for girls. Here in 1893 they established the Winona Seminary, which developed into the College of St. Teresa, a girls' college with an annual enrollment of 600. It offers the B. A. degree.

7. The MERCHANTS' BANK, 102-4 E. Third St., designed by Purcell, Feick, and Elmslie of Chicago, was built about 1910. The structure is of brick, with terra cotta ornament. An immense glass window comprises most of the façade, with an enriched doorway as a note of accent. The coloring is dark but rich, and the ornament crisply modeled and recognizable at once as typically Sullivanesque. At the time of its construction this building was a noteworthy step in the progress of modern design in Minnesota— a good example of the "prairie style" of the Chicago school of Sullivan and Wright. It is an early attempt at functional and organic design, as a departure from the traditional "temple" fronts that had come to symbolize the "Bank." Two large murals by Oskar Gross representing dairying and harvesting occupy the semi-circular spaces opposite the windows. The decorative panels over the doors, and the lighting fixtures are noteworthy; the shades are miniatures of the whole building. The furniture was especially designed and is of quarter-sawed white oak.

8. GARVIN HEIGHTS STATE PARK (reached by a steep road from Lake Boulevard near Huff St.), a 117-acre tract on the western bluffs of the city, was the gift of H. C. Garvin of Winona. Roadway and footpaths ascend through birch and oak woods to the tip of Inspiration Point, 500 feet above Lake Winona. From this spot on the high-bluffed river valley, Lake Pepin, 40 miles distant, and the Trempealeau Wisconsin hills can be seen on a clear day. The park has picnic and camp grounds, and a natural amphitheater.

POINTS OF INTEREST IN ENVIRONS

Old mill at Pickwick, *14 m. (see Tour 1, Section c.);* St. Mary's College, *1.6 m. (see Tour 12);* Whitewater State Park, *29.9 m. (see Tour 12);* John Latsch State Park, *10 m. (see Tour 1, Section c.).*

Rochester

Railroad Stations: North Western Station, 4th St. NW. and 1st Ave. NW. for Chicago and North Western Ry.; Great Western Station, 19 2nd St. SE. for Chicago Great Western R. R.

Bus Station: Union Bus Depot, 15 W. Center St. for Northland Greyhound, Jefferson Transportation Co., and Stewart Line. (City is classified as all-year tourist point with reduced rates on all railroads and busses.)

Airport: Rochester Airport Service, 1½ m. SE. of city on 3rd Ave. SE. for Northwest Airline, taxi fare 75¢, time 10 minutes; bus service within 3 blocks of field.

Taxis: Minimum fare 25¢; no passenger limit.

Intracity Bus Service: Fare 5¢.

Traffic Regulations: Turns in either direction at intersections of all streets except on Broadway and 1st Aves. No U turns on above streets nor on 2nd Ave. from 1st St. to 3rd St. inclusive. Watch street signs for parking limitations.

Accommodations: Hotels, boarding houses, restaurants, and inns have adequate facilities; rates are uniform throughout year.

Tourist Information Service: Chamber of Commerce and Rochester Automobile Club, Chamber of Commerce Bldg., 212 1st Ave. SE.

Radio Station: KROC (1310 kc.)

Theaters and Motion Picture Houses: Chateau Theater, occasional road shows; four motion picture houses.

Recreational Facilities: Soldiers' Memorial Field, end of 2nd Ave. SW.; Mayo Park, center of city.

Swimming: Soldiers' Field Municipal pool, end of 2nd Ave.; Lake Zumbro, 15 m. from city on Oronoco Rd.; Silver Lake, in North Rochester.

Golf: Soldiers' Memorial Field Municipal Course, end of 2nd Ave. SW., 18 holes, grass greens, moderate fees.

Tennis: Numerous courts throughout city.

Riding: Rochester Riding Academy, Olmsted County Fair Grounds.

List of Annual Events: Southeast Minnesota Peony Show, June; concerts and recitals in season sponsored by the Civic Music Assn.; tri-weekly band concerts during summer in Mayo Park; Mayo Clinic Tower carillon recitals, Sunday, Wednesday, and Friday; special lectures (year round), Mayo Clinic.

ROCHESTER (988 alt., 20,621 pop.), seat of Olmsted County, began in 1854 as a crossroads campground for the immigrant wagon trains then pouring into Minnesota's southern triangle, and was founded by George Head of Rochester, N. Y. In 1858 the settlement's population had reached 1,500 and it was incorporated as a city.

Had a certain young Englishman been content to remain in the chemist's shop where he was employed, Rochester would have undoubtedly developed into a pleasant little trade and railroad center for the farmers whose rich claims surrounded it, and been no better known to the world at large than countless other thriving Middle Western towns. But the year the town was born the English chemist became an American doctor and began a career destined to make this crossroads settlement the world's most renowned privately owned medical center.

Rochester's census returns are misleading for they tell only half the story. A constant transient population more than doubles the official figures. Forty hotels, 84 apartment buildings, 200 rooming houses, 20 restaurants, and a 20-acre municipal tourist camp shelter annually 20,000 travelers, each year provide bed and board for more than 150,000 health seekers, their relatives, and friends.

The large majority of these transient sojourners are still, as they have been ever since "Dr. Mayo and the boys" first hung out their shingle, farmers, small tradespeople, typical middle-class Americans, but the number of foreigners on the streets and in the hotel lobbies gives the town a cosmopolitan air wholly unexpected in a southern Minnesota city. South Americans from the Argentine and Brazil, wealthy Indians from the oil fields of Oklahoma, East Indians in turbans, their shy wives in graceful floating veils and scarves, Mexicans, Filipinos, a trio of Japanese research workers sent by their government to pick up the latest "methods"—one or all of these, as well as French, Italian and Russian doctors, are encountered any day on Rochester's broad streets and are no longer of more than passing interest to its merchants and citizens. In the cheaper boarding houses, and especially in the crowded tourist camp, can be heard dozens of tales—enough to fill a volume—of humbler folk who have traveled thousands of miles, with much the same hope of salvation that takes Mohammedans to Mecca; of a woman who in order to get here crossed all of Alaska in a dogsled, of a crippled child sent along from farthest Canada with a simple address tag around his neck, of a girl with a mortal disease hitch-hiking from Texas. Too often these form the tragedies of Rochester, for hundreds come for whom there is nothing to do but send them home again. During the summer it is no uncommon sight to see an ancient motorcar laden with an entire family and all its household goods, rattling down the street toward the clinic with a huddled figure that tells the reason for the journey. Practically penniless, their license plates bearing the name of a distant State, they have yet met few difficulties, since local officials, told of their destination, have gladly supplied gasoline and food to carry them from town to town, fearful that otherwise they may become permanent charges. It is because so many who come to Rochester require help other than medical that social service has become an important adjunct of the city's as well as of the clinic's activities.

Social life in Rochester is maintained by two distinct groups although some individuals occupy places in both. The town group amuses itself in ways that differ little from those of other Minnesota cities. Social life for the clinic group, however, resembles that of a university or even more of an Army post. At the head stand the two Mayos and their families, affectionately dubbed by their assistants "the Royal Family." Next in the scale are the heads of the various departments and their wives; then the hundreds of young student Fellows, many of whom are married, and at the bottom the army of nurses and technicians. Not that these lines are sharply or snobbishly drawn, but they exist, are generally recognized, and are rarely crossed except on large ceremonial occasions. The constant incoming and outgoing stream of distinguished visitors provides a reason for much entertaining by the upper group; and since among these guests are outstanding artists as well as scientists, social life here has a far more sophisticated flavor than that of some cities many times its size. Wives of the busy doctors bring lecturers, concert singers, and art exhibits to the community, and the 95-mile trip to the Twin Cities is regarded as a mild jaunt, gladly undertaken for a symphony concert in Minneapolis, or the opera in St. Paul.

Rochester lacks none of the essentials of a completely modern community. Excellent schools, many attractive churches, perfectly kept parks, playgrounds, golf, tennis, a zoo—all provided by a city intensely aware of its importance, and alive to its responsibilities. Along its elm-lined residence streets and perched on its surrounding hills are many attractive houses built by members of the clinical staff, and surrounding it is a countryside the beauty of which is surpassed by few areas in Minnesota. Yet to sightseeing tourists Rochester remains a town of hospitals, which are often, surprisingly enough, a part of the hotels in which they find themselves registered.

This unusual combination of hotel and hospital grew up naturally with the rapid growth in the demand for both types of accommodations, concomitant with the clinic's swift rise to fame. Until 1907 St. Mary's Hospital with constantly added stories and wings could meet the need for beds and operating rooms. But by that time it was recognized that new buildings must be erected, and a company with one of the hotel managers as its head was organized for the purpose. A new hospital was built, to which later was added, as a convenient and economic feature, a number of hotel rooms. This arrangement was repeated in several instances, and when the larger hotel-hospitals were connected by underground passages with the clinic building, it seemed ideally suited for ambulatory patients who were obliged to go to the clinic for their treatments. It must be conceded, however, that the combination is sometimes a little disconcerting to the healthy and casual visitor, even as he may find the many bandaged and afflicted who roam the downtown streets and linger in the lobbies somewhat inhibiting to a festive holiday spirit.

Rochester's industrial chart is unique among cities of its size, and here, too, the influence of the clinic is manifest. The influx of sick keeps more than a hundred agents writing life insurance. The yearly florist bill amounts to about $200,000. Manufacturers of remedies and health foods, discerning profit in the Rochester postmark, have chosen the city as headquarters for their small laboratories. Purveyors of luxuries, gifts, and books, with an eye to the enforced leisure of convalescents and accompanying friends, import their stocks from Europe and New York and find a ready market for goods of a quality rarely sold in small cities. The fact that the proportion of women workers is higher here than in any other city of the Northwest is again due to the hospitals and hotels.

But the clinic is by no means the sole source of Rochester's wealth. When railroad scouts arrived in the sixties with orders to route lines through the richest inland spots, they sent back reports of an almost unbelievable volume of crops flowing into this village from the fertile soil of southeastern Minnesota.

One of Minnesota's first dairy farms was started at Rochester in 1865. Dairy herds multiplied in the surrounding area until the city came to be regarded as the hub of this industry in the State.

The lush soil, warmth, rainfall, and a rolling loamy prairie nearly 1,000 feet above sea level were soon found by farmers to be ideally adapted to market gardening. They began raising the crops of peas and sweet corn that finally brought into Rochester one of the largest pea canneries in the world.

Fancy foodstuffs, as well as hundreds of gallons of milk in special cars daily leave the city for eastern markets. Flour, baby chicks, and phonographs boost the annual export figure to four million dollars.

POINTS OF INTEREST

1. MAYO CLINIC BUILDING, 102-110 2nd Ave. SW. *(tours: weekdays, 5:30; Sat., 10:30 a.m., 3:30 p.m.; Sun., 3:30)*, dominates the entire city. This huge modern building opened in 1929 owes much of its functional efficiency to Dr. Henry S. Plummer, a member of the clinic staff who for years was at work planning a structure that would combine under one roof every facility for diagnoses, dressings, laboratories, meeting rooms, and library. The architects were Ellerbe & Co. of St. Paul. The building has 22 stories, the first two of limestone, the others brick with terra cotta trim.

Minnesota has no more dramatic success story than that of the rise to international fame of the two Mayo brothers and their medical center.

The story begins in 1845 when William Worrall Mayo, a youthful English chemist, joined the army of emigrants to New York, and nine years later obtained his medical degree in Indiana. The following year, unable to resist the lure of the rapidly developing Northwest, he moved to Minnesota. Here in Le Sueur, his oldest son, William James Mayo, was born in 1861. After serving as a surgeon in the Civil War, Dr. Mayo moved to the little village of Rochester in 1863, where two years later was born Charles Horace Mayo.

From their earliest days the brothers were conditioned to the profession of medicine. Their father was renowned throughout the southern portion of the State for his skill in surgery and medicine. He taught his sons a knowledge of human bones with the aid of the skeleton of an old Sioux, and familiarized them with the uses of a microscope while they attended the Rochester public schools. They accompanied him on his rounds at an age when most boys are busy with baseball, and when they entered their respective medical schools at Michigan and Chicago they were not only grounded in many of the medical sciences as then taught, but were completely at home in the routine of a busy practitioner's life.

Following a cyclone in 1883, the Sisters of the Convent of St. Francis, who had established a convent here in 1877, offered to build and operate a Rochester hospital if Dr. Mayo and his sons would consent to direct it.

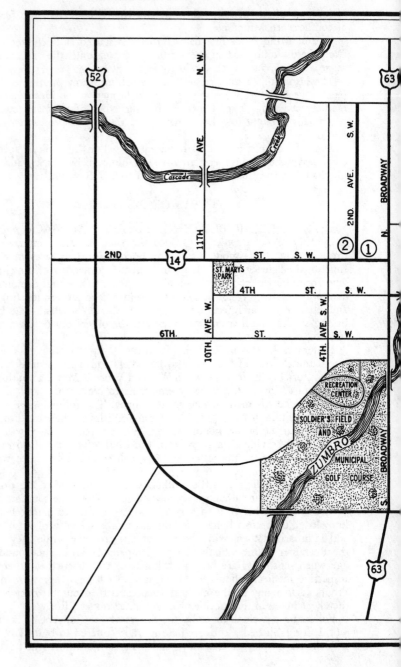

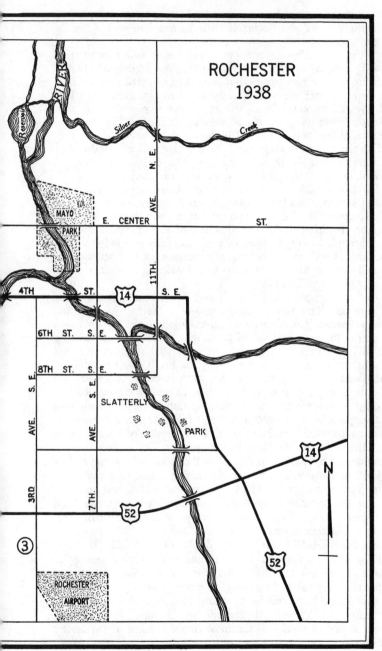

ROCHESTER
1938

Thus in 1889 with 40 beds the now famed St. Mary's, built by the Sisterhood, became the nucleus of a Rochester chain of hospitals with a bed capacity of 1,400.

Until 1892 the three Mayos were able themselves to take care of their rapidly growing surgical practice, but during that year it became obvious that they had to increase their staff. Gradually they gathered around them more and more assistants; at first only surgeons, then physicians, then laboratory and research workers. Again and again they were obliged to seek larger quarters to meet the demands of their increasing practice. In 1929 the new clinic building was opened. This building has no counterpart in the world. Designed to meet every need for the diagnosis of hundreds of patients, it operates with all the efficiency of a great department store, yet manages to maintain an atmosphere of reassuring friendliness.

In 1915 the Doctors Mayo affiliated with the University of Minnesota and established a foundation they endowed with $1,000,000 to which they later added $500,000. The income from the Mayo Foundation is used for medical graduate teaching under the direction of the university medical department. Through its aid, Fellows who are carefully selected from the graduates of schools with the highest standing may work in Rochester for three years and become masters of science, and after two or three additional years, doctors of philosophy.

The story of man's fight against death and disease contains names of many great surgeons. The Mayo brothers would be the first to deny that their skill has surpassed that of many operators whose names are unknown to the layman. But their genius was unique in that it combined outstanding professional ability with a vision and capacity for organization that had heretofore been effected only in industry—by the Fords, the Rockefellers, the Marshall Fields of the world. It is due to their executive genius and to their indefatigable devotion quite as much as to their distinguished surgical talents, that Rochester has grown from a country village to a thriving city, to which come daily hundreds of sufferers from the world over, many with the almost superstitious awe and faith of the cripples of Lourdes, who hope to leave their crutches on the cathedral walls.

From the tower of the Mayo Clinic a 23-bell carillon tolls at the end of the day and fills outlying valleys and nearby market streets with the sound of Gregorian chimes and hymns. The bells were cast in England and consecrated by the late archbishop of Canterbury, the Most Reverend Lord Randall Davidson. They can be played either by the carillonneur or automatically from the electric keyboard on the 19th floor.

2. The MAYO FOUNDATION MUSEUM OF HYGIENE AND MEDICINE, housed in a reconditioned building in the park opposite the Clinic entrance *(visiting hours: 10-12, 2-4, daily; 10-12, Sat.; 2-5, Sun.)*, includes exhibits of normal and pathological tissues and organs of the human body, and modern treatments of many injuries and diseases. The museum collection was greatly enlarged for the Chicago Exposition and has since been added to until it is the most comprehensive of the State's medical displays.

3. REID-MURDOCK VEGETABLE CANNING PLANT, 3rd Ave. and SE. 12th St. *(visiting hours 10-10 weekdays from June 15 to July 15, and from August 15 to September 15)*, is one of the largest pea canneries in the world. Its output in 1930 was valued at 2 million dollars.

POINTS OF INTEREST IN ENVIRONS

A-1-A Airport, *0.5 m. (see Tour 9)*; municipally owned Hydroelectric Plant, *20 m. (see Tour 18)*; Niagara Cave, *45 m. (see Tour 9)*.

PART III

Tours

Tour 1

(Port Arthur, Ontario)—Duluth—Pine City—St. Paul—Red Wing—
Winona—La Crescent—(La Crosse, Wis.); Ontario 61 and US 61.
Canadian Border to Wisconsin Line, 486.9 m.

The Duluth, Missabe & Northern Ry. parallels highway between Two Harbors and
Duluth; the Great Northern Ry. and the Northern Pacific Ry. between Duluth and
Twin Cities; the Chicago, Milwaukee, St. Paul & Pacific R.R. between Twin Cities
and Wisconsin Line.
Graveled and bituminous-treated roadbeds to Two Harbors; paved to Wisconsin
line; open all year.
Tourist accommodations north of Duluth restricted to summer season.

This route begins in the Canadian Twin Cities, Port Arthur and Fort
William, which annually attract a large number of visitors, and proceeds
in a southwesterly direction across the ridges and promontories of the ancient Pigeon River valley, a region of great historic interest, to the International Border.

South of the border, at Pigeon River, the highway runs through former
Indian and fur-trading country near Grand Portage and follows what is
perhaps the most beautiful drive in Minnesota, past high, rocky points
that line the northern shore of Lake Superior.

US 61 skirts the lumbering region around Cloquet. An alternate route
from Duluth to Carlton leads through beautiful Jay Cooke State Park, at
the mouth of the St. Louis River. From Carlton to St. Paul the transition
from the evergreen forests to farming country is apparent.

South of St. Paul the route parallels the Mississippi River. This southern portion of the State is excellent farm land. US 61 overlooks elongated

Lake Pepin between Red Wing and Wabasha and continues along the broad river valley until it crosses the Wisconsin Line.

Sec. a. PORT ARTHUR *to* DULUTH, *199 m. Ont. 61 and US 61.*

PORT ARTHUR, 0 *m.* (602 alt., 19,818 pop.), and Fort William are the Canadian Twin Cities. Port Arthur is a modern community with golf courses, motor drives, parks, and tourist camps. There are fine hotels in the town, and stores where visitors from the United States can indulge in Canadian shopping.

FORT WILLIAM, 4 *m.* (608 alt., 20,551 pop.), is at the end of the Lake Superior-International Highway. The city *(good accommodations)* is probably best known for its woolens, particularly Hudson Bay blankets, and its linen and china shops. There are golf courses and riding trails within a short distance of the town.

From Port Arthur and Fort William regular daily sailing schedules are maintained in summer to Isle Royale in Lake Superior about 35 miles away. The island is also on the route of occasional boats from the Upper Michigan Peninsula and launches from Grand Portage and Grand Marais, Minn.

ISLE ROYALE, largest island in the world's largest body of fresh water, is 160 miles northeast of Duluth and 55 miles northwest of the Keewanaw Peninsula, Mich. This island, 45 miles long and 7 miles wide, is surrounded by hundreds of small reefs. Long before the arrival of the white man, it was known to the Indians for its wealth of copper. On Isle Royale's copper range, still called by its original Chippewa name, Minong, many vestiges of this primitive industry have been found. An exploring party in 1872 and investigators sent in more recent years by the Milwaukee Public Museum, discovered remains of mining pits and 30-foot excavations, some with 60-foot timber-covered drains where ungrooved cobbles, once used as hammers, were collected by the cartload. Charcoal and half-burned sticks nearby suggested that primitive workers had crumbled the rock by alternately applying fire and cold water, after which the slivers of metal were hammered out. Today the island has resumed its natural state. Deep spruce woods, narrow fjordlike channels winding back for miles between timbered ridges, and 32 scattered lakes make it an ideal wildlife refuge. Many of its plants are rarely found in Minnesota. The saskatoon, which resembles the juneberry, is found here; the crowberry grows in rocky places on the island.

In 1664 Pierre Boucher made the first known record of a "mine of copper on an island in Lake Superior," which he describes according to the report of the band of traders who went to the lake in 1660 and returned in 1663. By 1670 French Jesuits had written in their Relation of 1669-70, "As the savages have told many people, the metal exists here in abundance. . . . Pieces of copper, mingled with stones, are found at the water's edge almost all around the island—along the inlet— under the strata of the steep clay—in the copper formed islets that surround it." Although Jesuit maps thereafter called Minong "Isle Royale" in honor of the French Monarchy, history made little mention of the copper island for almost 200 years. When the Northwest was opened up in the middle of the 19th century, and Chippewa treaties ceded Isle Royale to the United States, explorers, prospectors, and surveyors swarmed to its wilderness. But by 1855 the great stampede into the Mississippi Valley had begun, and Isle Royale's adventurers had moved on to the new frontier.

Twice again during the next 50 years surveys and half-hearted booms seemed about to restore its forgotten industry, but the attempts at development proved unprofitable.

The 146,000-acre island, now maintained by the Federal Government as a national park, is visited by many tourists. It is best known to mariners for the lighthouses of its deep harbors; the shacks of commercial lake-trout fishermen line its shore. Radio and lake boats provide communication with the mainland.

A short distance south of Fort William Ont. 61 (the International Highway) swings close to the base of MOUNT MC KAY, a rock formation nearly 1,000 feet high, and then follows the Pigeon River valley southwestward. On both sides of this route great ridges, promontories, and high palisades rim the valley.

At 41 *m.* is the junction with a country road.

Left on this road to HIGH FALLS, 2 *m.*, a 120-foot cataract about 2 miles above the mouth of the Pigeon River. Along the northern side of the river is a flume down which logs are slid during the spring logging drives.

Below the falls and on the U. S. side near the river's mouth is the SITE OF PARKERSVILLE, once an important trading post and village. All that remain are mounds and cellar cavities outlining the position of former log structures.

At 44 *m.* the MIDDLE FALLS are visible from the highway *(parking spaces and picnic grounds near falls).*

At the INTERNATIONAL BORDER, 48 *m.* (900 alt.), the highway crosses the Pigeon River on the steel INTERNATIONAL BRIDGE. This border region is of striking beauty. The bridge spans a canyon through which plunge the churning rapids of the river far below, named, tradition holds, for the large flocks of passenger pigeons that formerly frequented the vicinity. Canadian and U. S. customs and immigration officials have quarters on opposite sides of the river.

Crossing the Pigeon River, the route traverses Minnesota's famous Arrowhead recreational region. This vast area of 16,000 square miles extends from the extreme northeastern corner of the State to International Falls, almost touches Bemidji on the west, borders Lake Mille Lacs on the south, and includes the city of Duluth. The name was chosen in a Nation-wide contest and is descriptive of the shape of the area.

Southwest of the Canadian Border the route traverses a rocky area covered with evergreens and follows the shore of Lake Superior to Duluth.

At 49.4 *m.* is GRAND PORTAGE TRAIL CROSSING. A swath through the woods, crossing the highway, marks the famed overland passage from Lake Superior to Pigeon River. This 9-mile portage was used by voyageurs and fur-traders to avoid falls and rapids in the Pigeon River. The first white man to record its existence was La Vérendrye, who passed over it in 1731; but it probably had been used by Indians for centuries before that. Eventually the portage fell into disuse and became overgrown with brush, but it is now cleared and hikers can follow its entire length.

Right on the Grand Portage Trail to the SITE OF FORT CHARLOTTE, 5 *m.*, an 18th-century trading post. Accessible overland only by portage, it is marked by mounds indicating the position of buildings, and a few timbers of the old dock that extended into the Pigeon River.

Glaciers have marked and grooved many of the rock formations of the area. In earlier geological periods these were gigantic ranges; today only a few precipitous slopes remain. The soil in the irregular valleys is rich but rocky; boulders are scattered over much of the area. Farms, replacing the richer forests, are productive only of crops that are adaptable to the short growing season of this region. The high precipitation and the moderating influence of the lake upon the climate make for an abundant vegetation.

MINERAL CENTER, 54.5 *m.*, is a small village.

Left from Mineral Center on a country road to GRAND PORTAGE, 5.8 *m.*, whose population is almost entirely Indian. Chief Mike Flat rules this remnant of a once influential band of Chippewa.

The Northwest Company, long a loose partnership of independent merchants and traders, came into existence during the period of the American Revolution, and by 1792 it had posts all over the Northwest, with its central depot at Grand Portage, the "metropolis" of Lake Superior. The story of Grand Portage and of the trail that ran 9 miles northwest from the lake to the Pigeon River, is one of the most romantic in all frontier history. Even before the Declaration of Independence was signed, more than 1,000 miles away in the heart of this Northwest wilderness, there was already established a busy settlement with flourishing trade, said to have included shops, French fashions, drinking places, and even police. In 1793 the post consisted of a high stockade surrounding 16 log buildings; these provided lodgings for officers and clerks, a huge mess hall, storage for furs and supplies, and goods for barter. Beyond the enclosure were the camps of the "pork-eaters," as the tenderfoot canoemen were called, the wigwams of the Indians, and a canoe yard that accommodated 150 canoes; about 70 new canoes were added each year. Here foregathered hundreds of Indians, imperturbable and watchful; here was the goal of the dashing *voyageurs,* naively vain and dramatically colorful with jauntily perched plumed caps of red wool, blue capotes and gaudy sashes, bare thighs, deerskin leggins and moccasins, and their ubiquitous pipes.

These *voyageurs,* mostly French, were an extraordinary group of men; the majority came from Canada in the region of the St. Lawrence River. Short of stature, they were nevertheless exceedingly strong; unmoral and boastful, it was their faithfulness and loyalty to their contracts that made the vast fur trade possible; taking great pride in their manners, their dancing and singing, they were yet voluntary exiles, their ambition being to become "les gens libres" or free traders.

By 1790 these fearless, skilled boatmen had reached the Pacific Coast and in the years following repeatedly crossed and recrossed the western upper half of the continent from the Pacific's Columbia River to Lake Superior's Grand Portage in regular trips. Arrived at Grand Portage and their cargoes unloaded, the *voyageurs* swaggered about the post, chaffing in their own patois, soon riotously drunk.

Trading negotiations were usually completed in July, after which there always followed a celebration to which factors, *voyageurs,* and Indians—all who could possibly get there—came from miles around. The opening banquet was followed by a dance in the mess hall whose puncheon floor was 60 feet long. Gallons of rum were drunk, and to the music of bagpipe, violin, and flute, they danced the night through with their Indian girl partners. The fiesta over, the *voyageurs* set off once again in their canoes, loaded now with trade goods and camp supplies, and cheered by their own songs, paddled and portaged back through the wilderness to face long months of hardship and loneliness. In the shipping of furs on Lake Superior the average canoe carried more than 5 tons of furs and supplies, and was manned by 8 *voyageurs.* (Boats used on the interior lakes and rivers carried 1 or 2 tons and were manned by 6.)

Grand Portage now consists of a few houses, some cabins, a general store and post office, and an old cabin used as a HISTORICAL MUSEUM housing relics and Indian handiwork. At the northern edge of the village stands a wooden structure on the SITE OF THE FIRST CATHOLIC MISSION SCHOOL established in the state (1838).

Under the direction of the State and local historical societies the old landmarks, including the stockade, are being restored. Various Indian articles of birchbark and beadwork can be purchased here.

This region is the most rugged in Minnesota. The rough topography is the result of complicated geological processes; a huge fault (slipping of rock masses) left the depression now filled by Lake Superior. Many plants not found elsewhere in Minnesota are hardy along the north shore and in the adjacent forests. Stands of leatherleaf cover acres of muskeg; Labrador tea is abundant; billberry grows only in this upper tip of the state. Swamp laurel, bog- and autumn-willow, and black currant are only a few of the plants characteristic of this region. Trailing-arbutus is found in the sandy forests, and aromatic wintergreen covers the forest bed in much of the drier area. Pine, fir, and spruce are interspersed with groves of birch.

RESERVATION RIVER, 61.3 *m.*, is the northernmost of a series of trout streams crossed by the highway. While the entire North Shore area affords excellent trout fishing, the best will probably be found in the cool, swift streams of Cook County; but even here the fisherman will usually find his maximum catch some distance upstream from the highway.

HOVLAND, 67.2 *m.* (50 pop.).

Right from Hovland on an improved country road to a SUMMER RESORT, 16 *m.*, near McFARLAND and PINE LAKES, where trout fishing is good.

At 72.3 *m.* the highway crosses the ARROWHEAD RIVER (formerly the Brule) on which is a large summer resort. A species of juneberry *(Amelanchier stolonifera)* common farther east, has been collected in Minnesota only at the mouth of this river, where it blooms in late June.

KADUNCE *(diarrhea)* CREEK, 77.5 *m.*, is a good trout stream despite the water's mineral content, which suggested its name.

At the point where the highway crosses KIMBALL CREEK, 78.4 *m.*, the stream is choked with trees and is suitable only for bait fishing.

DEVIL'S TRACK RIVER, 83.1 *m.*, originating in Devil's Track Lake, flows from behind a rock escarpment near the lake shore.

At 84.9 *m.* is the junction with a country road.

Right on this road to the second terrace of an ANCIENT LAKE BED, 0.8 *m.*, where fine agates and occasionally an amethyst crystal are found. The matrix is so hard, however, that it is difficult to remove the stones.

CHIPPEWA CITY, 86.3 *m.* (702 alt.), adjoining Grand Marais, is inhabited by Indians and a few whites who have married into the tribe. Most of the cabins composing the town are concealed from view by the woods on both sides of the road.

GRAND MARAIS, 87.9 *m.* (602 alt., 618 pop.) *(see SUPERIOR NATIONAL FOREST: Canoe Trips)*, seat of Cook County, is the center of a large summer-tourist traffic. This village has an excellent natural harbor, often filled with acres of floating logs to be converted into wood pulp; commercial fishing is the predominant industry. On an arrow-shaped point of sharp, columnar, rose-colored rocks is the FOREST LOOKOUT TOWER *(visitors permitted)*. Here, too, is the NORTH SUPERIOR COAST GUARD STATION, which operates 25 boats. The village still has a fur-trading post; it also has a newly constructed airport.

Right from Grand Marais the Gunflint Trail, an improved road *(trail usually in good condition but inquire in Grand Marais before driving over it)*, swings northwest through the eastern section of the SUPERIOR NATIONAL FOREST *(see SUPERIOR NATIONAL FOREST: Canoe Trips)*, a region of many lakes and of towering, overhanging pines. Moose, bear, deer, porcupine, and other wild animals are numerous in this region.

Campgrounds and picnic grounds, identified by signs, are maintained by the U. S. Forest Service. Canoe routes interlace the maze of lakes in this northeastern triangle of Minnesota. The canoeist can start at Lake Superior and paddle to the western border of the state.

The campgrounds here listed all have tables, benches, fireplaces, tent and trailer sites and water, unless otherwise noted.

The SOUTH BRULE RIVER CAMPGROUNDS, 14.4 *m.* (R).

The NORTH BRULE RIVER CAMPGROUND, 18.8 *m.* (R).

The SWAMPER LAKE CAMPGROUND, 25.1 *m.* (L).

At 26.8 *m.* is the junction (R) with a dirt road.

Right 3 *m.* on this road to the EAST BEARSKIN LAKE CAMP AND PICNIC GROUNDS *(swimming beach)*.

At 29.2 *m.* is the junction (R) with a dirt road.

Right 2.5 *m.* on this road to the FLOUR LAKE CAMPGROUND.

At 30.4 *m.* is the junction (R) with a dirt road.

Right on this road 1.5 *m.* to the WEST BEARSKIN LAKE CAMP AND PICNIC GROUNDS *(swimming beach)*.

The first IRON LAKE CAMPGROUND, 34.5 *m.*, is (L) on the east end of Iron Lake.

The second IRON LAKE CAMPGROUND, 38.3 *m.*, is (L) on the west end of Iron Lake.

At 39 *m.* is the junction (R) with a dirt road.

Right on this road 1 *m.* to the CRAB LAKE CAMPGROUND.

The LOON LAKE CAMPGROUNDS, 41.3 *m.* (R).

At 46.7 *m.* is the junction with a graveled road.

Right on this road 1.5 *m.* to GUNFLINT, a village at the western end of GUNFLINT LAKE, to the south of which lies the GUNFLINT IRON RANGE, where Minnesota ore was first discovered. In 1850 J. G. Norwood, assistant geologist with the D. D. Owens Survey, took samples from this range and sent them to the Smithsonian Institution; some were exhibited at the International Exposition in Paris. The range was never opened because the ore contained too much titanium, and could not be mined profitably.

At 48.6 *m.* is the junction (R) with MAGNETIC ROCK TRAIL.

Right on this trail 1.9 *m.* to MAGNETIC ROCK, an ancient Indian landmark 42 feet high, whose location was unknown for many years and only recently rediscovered. The rock is highly magnetic and causes compasses in the vicinity to function inaccurately.

SEA GULL LAKE CAMP AND PICNIC GROUNDS *(swimming beach)*, 56.4 *m.*, are (L).

BIG SAGANAGA LAKE *(resorts, swimming, fishing, canoes)*, 59.5 *m.*, is at the end of the trail.

CASCADE RIVER, 97.5 *m.*, is in the center of CASCADE STATE PARK, which covers 2,300 acres. An ideal camping spot has been created by extensive clearing, trail construction, and the erection of fireplaces, tables, and benches. The Cascade River is a fine trout stream, and its upper waters can be reached by roads branching R. from the main highway. Fishing shacks dot the rocky lake shore. Fishermen, mostly Scandinavians, combine primitive methods with modern. The nets that hang gossamer-like in the lofts, drying after use or preservative baths, are purchased ready-made but mended by hand. Motorboats are replacing rowboats, but the essentials of the work are little changed.

At LUTSEN, 107 *m.* (700 alt., 50 pop.), the route crosses the Poplar River, which flows between vertical cliffs. From the resort lodge a path leads to the bottom of the gorge, where there are a number of pot holes. The fishing is only fair in the lower river but improves nearer the headwaters. The hills are well-forested, having escaped disastrous fires; the trees along the road are mostly birch, aspen, and other deciduous types.

ONION RIVER, 110.4 *m.*, derives its name from the Paul Bunyan legend that wild onions grew in such abundance in the vicinity that Minnesota's legendary logger was faced with the necessity of checking the tears of his crew as they cut timber.

TOFTE, 114.7 *m.* (695 alt.), is a small settlement *(lodge accommodations and a public camp site).*

CARLTON PEAK (1,529 alt.), a barren, rounded knoll, rises back of the town. It affords an excellent view of the lake and forest, but can be reached only on foot.

At 116.2 *m.* is CAULDRON TRAIL and HIDDEN FALLS, near the mouth of the TEMPERANCE RIVER *(public campground).* Like most North Shore streams, this river abounds with shady trout pools and spectacular waterfalls; it gained its name from the fact that it is the only north-shore stream with no bar at its mouth.

At 117.3 *m.* (L) is a marker commemorating FATHER BARAGA'S CROSS, erected by the priest in thanksgiving for his safe crossing of Lake Superior in a canoe during a severe storm in 1846. The name Cross River was suggested by this incident. The original wooden cross has been replaced by a granite one that stands on the lake shore at the end of a footpath.

SCHROEDER, 118.2 *m.* (690 alt.), is a small resort and fishing settlement. A bridge spans Cross River close to a beautiful WATERFALL.

Right from Schroeder the old highway leads into the back country, roughly paralleling US 61.

CRAMER, 10 *m.,* an old lumbering village, is now practically deserted.

Left from Cramer the road parallels the lake shore beyond the rock escarpment. It continues southwestward, crossing various trout streams.

At FINLAND, 22 *m.* *(see Tour 8),* the road intersects the Ely-Finland Trail *(see Tour 8)* and in several places crosses the old logging-road grades. At one of these points is the DESERTED VILLAGE OF LONDON, 44 *m.,* where the roads divided during the days of extensive logging operation.

At 57 *m.* the old road returns to US 61.

Southwest of Schroeder on US 61 is TWO ISLAND RIVER, 120.2 *m.,* so named because of the two islands in the lake directly opposite the river's mouth. In this area lake trout can be caught by trolling *(boats for rent).* Agates and thomsonites are frequently found on the beach. Many gulls nest on the ledges of the high basaltic cliffs of the islands.

At 126.8 *m.* the highway crosses CARIBOU RIVER, another famous trout stream; its upper reaches literally teem with small trout. About a mile above the highway the river shoots over the cliffs in a dazzling waterfall, and above the falls it runs through a burnt-over area where gaunt, dry stumps stick up among the rocks like gray ghosts. In this desolate rocky stretch of underbrush the river flows through a precipitous chasm. An anglers' foot trail leads upstream from the highway, slightly above, or north of, the crossing. Often at night the plaintive calls of the whippoor-will echo through these lonely valleys.

The highway reaches MANITOU RIVER at 129.1 *m.;* a road (L) leads to the lower river ravine and the falls. Most trout fishermen use ropes to climb down to the mouth where fine rainbow and speckled trout usually lurk beneath the protective rocks. Sometimes a sand bar, 10 to 15 feet in width, closes the mouth and forms a shallow lagoon into which the waterfall plunges, but this bar has a transient existence, coming and going according to,the action of waves and current. On the cold, wet rocks near the mouth of the Manitou grows a typically northern flower, the little white rock-saxifrage, which in this locale blooms nearly a month later than on the hills farther south. Also growing among the damp, decaying leaves on the steep slopes facing the lake is the dainty little blue birdseye or wild primrose.

At 129.6 *m.* US 61 crosses Two Island River and follows a birch- and aspen-lined road across the backs of the jutting points.

LITTLE MARAIS, 133.9 *m.* (642 alt., 25 pop.), was the site of the old Crystal Bay corundum mine and plant that operated in 1903. Corundum, an exceedingly hard crystalline mineral, was once in great demand as an abrasive, but it has been almost completely displaced by synthetic abrasives, such as carborundum. The crushed corundum from this mine was carried to Duluth by boat, but poor harbor facilities caused abandonment of the enterprise. During its short existence the industry sustained the village, which consisted of a school and several homes and office buildings. Only the foundations of the crushing plant, remnants of machinery, and an old scaffold remain to mark the mine. Today the village is a resort center with a hotel and tourist camp.

Here the road crosses the Little Marais River.

At 138.3 *m.* is the junction with State 1, still called the Ely-Finland Trail *(see Tour 8).*

At 139.4 *m.* US 61 crosses the deep ravine of Baptism River.

At 140.9 *m.* is the junction with a dirt road.

Left on this road to PALISADE HEAD *(picnic grounds),* 0.5 *m.,* an 80-acre headland of volcanic rock whose highest point is 314 feet above lake level. The lookout point is on the edge of a sheer vertical wall of rose-colored rock splotched with sea-green lichen. Far below, the ring-billed gulls loop above the deep blue of the lake. Distinguishable in the far-off haze are the Apostle Islands and the Wisconsin shore. At West Lookout is the best view of the Minnesota shore line—a serrated rocky margin of bays and points across which the shining highway follows a more even course.

BEAVER BAY, 146.2 *m.* (620 alt., 500 pop.), at the mouth of Beaver River, is one of the oldest settlements on the North Shore. The community existed long before it was platted in 1856, but exact records of its founding are lost; it was the only lake settlement between Duluth and Grand Portage to survive the panic of 1857.

SPLIT ROCK LIGHTHOUSE, 150.9 *m. (open to visitors),* is perched (L) on the crown of a high cliff overlooking dangerous reefs. The warning light (370,000 candlepower) is of great value to mariners, for the magnetic attraction of the metallic rock formations in the area diverts compass needles by several degrees. During fogs the throaty blast of the siren is heard at 16-second intervals, and at night the beam of the beacon warns the mariner of the jagged reefs. The modern houses of the lighthouse employees are grouped at its base. An iron stairway leads from the top of the rock down to the lake shore.

At 153.9 *m.* the road crosses SPLIT ROCK RIVER, a slow little stream in a shallow grassy meadow.

At 155.8 *m.* is a PUBLIC CAMPGROUND *(running water).*

At 158.1 *m.* the road crosses a bridge spanning the rocky ravine of Gooseberry River in GOOSEBERRY STATE PARK *(campground, picnicking, refectory, playgrounds).* The river meanders through the park to reach the lake a half mile below the highway; the upper and lower falls are clearly visible from the bridge.

CASTLE DANGER, 159.7 *m.,* was so named because a boat, the *Castle,* was wrecked on the reefs offshore near here.

At ENCAMPMENT RIVER, 164.7 *m.,* a dry rocky bed except after heavy storms, the highway cuts through a fine stand of virgin timber, saved by the owners of neighboring summer homes who refused to allow it to be logged.

The road partly ascends the precipice of SILVER CREEK CLIFF, 166.3 *m.,* and winds around its sheer wall of red and gray rock, with Lake Superior directly below. A marker (L) at a parking space commemorates Gitche Gumee, the lake made famous by Longfellow's *Hiawatha.*

The Stewart River is crossed at 169 *m.* Here is the junction with an old logging road *(see above side tour from Schroeder).*

At 170.3 *m.* (R) is the LAKEVIEW GOLF COURSE *(9 holes, reasonable fee),* owned by the city of Two Harbors. To the L., at 170.9 *m.,* are LAKEVIEW PARK and a PUBLIC CAMPGROUND *(running water).*

TWO HARBORS, 172 *m.* (635 alt., 4,425 pop.), is the seat of Lake County. Chippewa Indians gave the settlement its first name, Wass-wewining *(spear by moonlight).* Subsequently Agate Bay became the white man's name for the village because of the adjacent bay of that name. On the shore of Agate Bay's twin harbor, Burlington Bay, the town site of Burlington was platted in 1857, but its founders did not realize their ambitions, for the hard times of those years caused Burlington's prospects to fade.

Completion of the railroad and the ore docks in 1884 at Agate Bay gave birth to a new city, Two Harbors, named for the two bays. Incorporated as a village March 9, 1888, it became a city on February 26, 1907.

Two Harbors is the ore-shipping terminal of the Duluth Iron Range Ry., later merged with the Duluth, Missabe & Northern. The first locomotive, *Three Spot,* brought in on a scow in 1882, stands on the west side of the passenger depot. The first load of ore from the Minnesota mines was shipped from here in 1884. At one time the No. 1 iron-ore dock, 1,388 feet long and 59½ feet high, was one of the largest in the world, with a loading capacity of 12,500 tons in 16 minutes. Pulpwood and lumber, as well as ore, are shipped from this port. The U. S. Coast Guard maintains a base here.

Two Harbors High School has a junior and a senior division, an enrollment of 624 students, and a staff of 30 instructors. Students from outlying districts travel by bus, sometimes as far as 35 miles, to the school, or receive $15 each month for board in the town. The two grade schools have 880 pupils, served by a staff of 33 teachers.

At KNIFE RIVER, 179.6 *m.*, a few families live near the rocky stream that drains the adjacent forest. This was once a thriving lumber town— the terminal of a logging railroad whose branches spread through thousands of square miles of virgin timber.

At 182.8 *m.* is a marker (R) indicating the SITE OF BUCHANAN, where in 1856 the first Federal land office at the head of the Lakes was established.

At 183.5 *m.* the road crosses the Sucker River, which flows in a green valley whose hillsides in late June and early July are a mass of yellow buttercups.

At FRENCH RIVER, 186.3 *m.*, is a STATE FISH HATCHERY (R).

Out on the lake the ore boats ply their way; in the distance each loaded boat looks like two, so deeply submerged is its shallow center.

The vegetation at this point is typical of the North Shore. Blooming in early spring is the trailing-arbutus with its fragrant pink blossoms. The aromatic sarsaparilla, a bristly shrub, bears its white flowers in June; its tiny, black fruit ripens in August. Another common shrub is a variety of dogwood closely resembling that found on the Pacific Coast; its white flowers appear in late June and are followed by the white fruit.

At 191.8 *m.*, just after the Lester River is crossed, is the junction with 60th Ave., E. This is the point from which the northern section of the Skyline Parkway starts *(see DULUTH: City Tour 2)*. Straight ahead to Superior St. and Piedmont Ave.

DULUTH, 199 *m.* (626 alt., 101,463 pop.) *(see DULUTH)*.

Points of Interest: Aerial Lift Bridge, ore docks, Skyline Parkway, Incline Railway, Minnesota Point.

At Duluth are the junctions with US 53 *(see Tour 5)* and US 2 *(see Tour 7)*.

Sec. b. DULUTH to ST. PAUL, 154.2 m. US 61.

US 61 crosses the city of Duluth on Superior St. to Carlton St.; R. on Carlton St. to Grand Ave.; L. on Grand Ave. to Cody St.; R. on Cody St.

At 5.6 *m.* US 61 crosses the tracks of the Duluth, Missabe & Northern Ry. This road brings all the iron ore to the Duluth docks, and long trains can be seen chugging down the incline at almost any hour of the day or night.

Just a few feet past the bridge over the tracks is the junction with the Skyline Parkway *(see DULUTH; City Tour 2)*, an alternate and more attractive route between this point and Carlton.

Left on the Skyline Parkway, an exceptionally beautiful graveled road that passes through many miles of scenic parks. For several miles the Skyline cuts back into an area within the Duluth city limits.

At 1.8 *m.* is SNIVELY PARK, a 50-acre woodland tract, and at 3.8 *m.* is BARDON'S PEAK (R).

MAGNEY PARK, 4 *m.*, is a rugged natural woodland of rocks and mixed trees, one of the most beautiful parks along the route. Balsam and second-growth pine are not uncommon, but maple and linden predominate. In the early spring, before the countryside is green, the white-flowered bloodroot pushes up among the dry leaves. The maples are usually vividly colored after the first frost. Among the trees are picnic grounds equipped with benches, tables, and fireplaces.

At about 4.5 *m.* and 4.7 *m.* foot trails lead L. through the park.

ELY'S PEAK (L), 6 *m.*, is one of the highest points at the head of the Lakes and overlooks a striking panorama of the surrounding country, including the St. Louis River Bay and the Wisconsin shore. Directly below the peak the Canadian National Ry. tracks run through a tunnel in the rocks.

At 5.7 *m.* is the junction with Becks Rd., a paved highway. The route turns R. on Becks Rd., about 500 feet, and then continues L. on the graveled parkway, winding among successive hills through a rocky clay terrain. Within a half mile it crosses five stone bridges spanning a little stream that empties into the St. Louis River at Fond du Lac.

Many of the terraced hills are densely wooded with pine, birch, aspen, and balm-of-Gilead. Occasionally a tall old virgin pine or spruce has been spared by fire and woodcutter.

Formerly along this entire western extension of the boulevard masses of trillium bloomed in the spring. The large, showy *Trillium grandiflorum*, the most common, still sprinkles the hillside with its snowy blossoms, but it is not so abundant as formerly; thoughtless picnickers have gathered huge armfuls, including the root stalks.

At 7.4 *m.* is a fork in the road. The left fork (Mission Creek Parkway) leads to Fond du Lac. On the right fork at 8.1 *m.* is the junction with the Oldenbury Parkway.

The route continues R. and at 8.7 *m.* crosses the northeast boundary of JAY COOKE STATE PARK, which comprises 3,375 acres—an area of rugged woodland, jagged rocks, evergreens, and rushing water. Directly through it, bordering the road, the St. Louis River cuts a picturesque gorge, dropping 395 feet within a few miles. The original land, 2,000 acres, was given to Minnesota in 1915–16 by the administrators of the estate of Jay Cooke (1821–1905), eastern financier, who took a great interest in the development of the Northwest. Since then the park has been greatly enlarged and improved.

At 9.4 *m.* is LOOKOUT POINT, about 500 feet above the rocky river bed. This is one of the most beautiful views along the route. Far below, the river winds from the distant valleys and densely wooded hills into the delicately shaded waters of the bay. The wooded or craggy terraces left by the receding waters of old Lake Duluth are plainly marked.

Early *voyageurs* who came to the head of the Lakes entered the dalles and rapids a short distance up the St. Louis River, in what is now Jay Cooke Park. Thence they carried their canoes across country to other streams. Two of these old trails still traverse the park.

Behind Lookout Point is a MEMORIAL PLAQUE and a TOURIST CAMP SITE *(overnight camping in tent or trailer; firewood, tables, and benches provided)*.

From this point the parkway continues downhill and at 11.8 *m.* forks into two one-way roads parallel for about 3 miles. When the water is high, the river gorge is filled with a swirling torrent of green-white water. At low water the rocks project in jagged fashion, and many smoothly rounded pot holes are uncovered; dried-out pools are filled with pebbles and crayfish claws. When the river is at its lowest, it is possible to cross in places by stepping from rock to rock.

On the lower road, crossing the river, is the SWINGING BRIDGE, a suspension of steel cables with stone towers and a wooden walkway. The deep pools directly below are sometimes used for swimming. Across the bridge a network of foot trails spreads over the hillside. Above the road near the bridge is a fine picnic shelter.

Right on the upper route, which runs between rock walls and seems to enter a tunnel overhung with evergreens, to THOMSON, 14.6 *m.*, a little village on the western edge of Jay Cooke State Park.

Above the bridge, 14.9 *m.*, is (L) the THOMSON DAM, which furnishes power for Duluth. At high water the current roars over the huge spillway, but when the water subsides there is excellent fishing below the dam—big trout and pike from the river and Lake Superior. Rock formations near the bridge show splotches of white stone, much like snowbanks against the background of gray rock. Cedar, spruce, pine, and balsam find a precarious foothold on the shaggy cliffs.

At 16.1 *m.* is CARLTON (1,084 alt., 687 pop.) *(see below)* and the junction with US 61.

ESKO, 14.9 *m.*, is a small Finnish dairy community with a co-operative creamery.

The Finns are a clannish people who cling to their Old World manners and customs, and to a stranger may sometimes seem unfriendly. At one time a suspicious farmer accused them of practicing magic and of worshipping pagan deities. Entire families, he claimed, wrapped themselves in white sheets and retreated to a small square building set apart from the dwellings and worshipped their gods, calling upon them to bring rain and good harvests to Finns, and wrath upon their neighbors. On investigation, however, it was discovered that although they did wrap themselves in sheets and visit these "shrines" almost daily, it was not in the zeal of religion but for the purpose of taking baths. The Finns here are almost fanatical advocates of cleanliness, and each has his own "sauna" or steam bathhouse *(see IMMIGRATION AND RACIAL ELEMENTS)*.

At 16.4 *m.* the highway crosses the St. Louis River, which seethes over a confusion of rocks. At this point the bed and banks of the river are of solid rock, and the water is subject to sudden rise after even a slight rainfall.

At 18 *m.* is the old lumbering town of SCANLON (435 pop.).

Right from Scanlon on State 45 to CLOQUET, 2 *m.* (1,209 alt., 6,782 pop.). Cloquet's chief industry is still the manufacture of wood products, despite the fact that the coniferous forests that once covered northern Minnesota have been greatly reduced. Here is the WOOD CONVERSION COMPANY PLANT *(open 10:30-3 daily)*, with modern manufacturing operations and an imposing array of machinery. Here also is a PLANT OF THE NORTHWEST PAPER COMPANY *(guides provided, 9:30-2:30 daily)*, one of the largest and most progressive of its kind. More than 1,000 people are employed here in manufacturing paper.

One of the largest co-operative retail associations in North America is in Cloquet; it has a membership of 2,104, and its sales amount to almost a million dollars yearly.

The present Cloquet is built upon the ashes of an earlier town. One of the State's most devastating forest fires swept over northeastern Minnesota during the afternoon and night of October 12, 1918. Fifty to seventy-five separate fires merged and were fanned to huge proportions by a 70-mile wind. The flames advanced over a vast area with incredible speed. More than 8,000 square miles were in the path of the flames and approximately 2,000 square miles, mainly within a radius of 50 to 100 miles of Duluth, were completely burned over. Nearly 400 persons lost their lives, 2,000 suffered burns, and about 13,000 were left homeless. Property loss, including standing timber, was approximately 25 million dollars.

Cloquet suffered the heaviest loss, its residential and business sections being almost entirely destroyed. Quick action on the part of railroad officials and citizens saved the lives of all but five. Residents who fled from the fire returned and built a new city. Most of the buildings are constructed of brick, giving Cloquet a thoroughly modern appearance.

PINEHURST PARK, comprising about 20 acres, is well improved and attractively landscaped. It has a pavilion, grandstand, bandstand, playground equipment, and artificial ponds. Beautiful flower beds and winding driveways are outstanding features.

The highest part of Carlton County is near the town of Cloquet. The hills, well timbered with conifers, are interspersed with maple and birch.

Left from Cloquet on State 33 1.2 *m.* to an INDIAN HOSPITAL on the FOND DU LAC INDIAN RESERVATION, a 25,000-acre area with about 725 residents. There is no agency on the grounds since the reservation is under the direction of the Consolidated Chippewa Agency at Duluth.

At 4 *m.* on State 33 is the CLOQUET FOREST EXPERIMENT STATION. This sub-station of the State Agricultural Experiment Station is under the direction of the State university. It is the research agency for the solution of land-use and forestry prob-lems, as well as a training station for students in game management and forestry. The 3,000-acre farm, established in the early 1900's, is one of the three most intensively managed timber areas in the country. Complete records of harvests, plantings, and operation costs enable forest specialists to direct the conservation procedures through-out the state on both private and public lands. On the tract are approximately 4 million feet of saw timber, 2 million cubic feet of pulp and bolt wood, and a large stand of immature timber. Within recent years game management records and ex-periments have increased the usefulness of the farm.

CARLTON, 19.5 *m.* (1,084 alt., 687 pop.), seat of Carlton County, has two large gravel pits in which many fine agates have been found. When the building of Northern Pacific Ry. was begun, the first spike was driven here.

The town, almost surrounded by wooded hills and prosperous dairy farms, lies in the bed of an ancient glacial river. The St. Louis River has cut through a great terminal moraine, and the polished tops of the rocky knobs indicate the great glacial burden. Here the hemlock, common in the States farther east, finds its only favorable Minnesota habitat.

The JAY COOKE TOURIST CAMP, within Carlton's village limits, at the entrance to Jay Cooke Park, is about 1,000 feet from the St. Louis River. The camp has 15 cabins, all with modern conveniences, and is near two streams, Otter and Crystal Creeks, in which speckled trout are plentiful.

Here is the junction with the Skyline Parkway, an alternate of US 61 between this part of the town and Duluth (*see above*).

A short distance south of Carlton is the divide between the drainage basin of Lake Superior and that of the Mississippi River. Usually the temperature difference between the two sides of this divide is great.

At 22.5 *m.* is the junction with US 210 (*see Tour 15*).

The route passes through ATKINSON, 27.6 *m.* and MAHTOWA, 31.7 *m.,* small agricultural communities.

BARNUM, 37.9 *m.* (1,122 alt., 271 pop.), and the surrounding terri-tory have earned state-wide fame for fine Guernsey cattle and white Leg-horn chickens. The soil is excellent, especially for potatoes and red clover. Barnum was originally a lumber town and proud of it; but when the for-ests were razed the reason for a community was gone and the lumberjacks drifted away to other camps. One went as far as Louisiana where he be-came so despairingly homesick he decided that, come what might, he must return to Barnum. Then chance placed a poultry magazine in his hands and he learned of the easy money chicken-raising offered. Back to Barnum he hurried to invest all his earnings in a farm that he stocked with 2,000 chickens, despite the neighbors' conviction that no chicks could withstand the northern cold. The next spring only 500 had survived but Jack persisted and eventually his faith was rewarded. Today Barnum is one of the largest egg-producing centers in the State and the majority of its people makes its living by poultry raising.

The town has a large school and library, a creamery, a poultry hatchery, a farmers' co-operative society, and a weekly newspaper, the Barnum *Herald*. Moose Horn River flows through the town; on the southern limits are the FAIRGROUNDS (L).

MOOSE LAKE, 42.6 *m.* (1,085 alt., 742 pop.), came into existence in the early 1860's as an overnight stop on the stage route between Superior and St. Paul. It consisted then of a hotel, barns, a few dwellings, and several Indian tepees.

The Lake Superior-Mississippi River R.R. was constructed in the early 1870's; most of the work of building grades, bridges, and track was done by hand. As its roadbed was about 3 miles west of the old stage line, the people of the original hamlet moved to a site near the railroad, now Moose Lake. The depot was built about 1873. The early engines, vastly different from modern locomotives, were wood-burning and hence were forced to pick up a fresh supply of fuel every 5 or 6 miles; a full-size train was made up of 10 to 18 freight cars.

The only work of the early settlers was logging. The country was covered with a virgin stand of white pine, which was cut, hauled to the edge of the lake, and floated to the sawmill. The scattered settlers came to town for supplies twice a year, in the spring and fall. The trips were made by sled while frost and snow covered the ground, for the mud and the lack of bridges made travel almost impossible during the summer months.

Like Cloquet, Moose Lake was wiped out by the forest fire of 1918; a marker (R) commemorates the hundred victims.

At 62.8 *m.* is the junction with State 66.

Left on State 66 to ASKOV, 4 *m.* (1,157 alt., 298 pop.). Through the efforts of the Danish People's Society, founded in 1887, 20,000 acres of cut-over and burned-over land in Pine County were purchased in 1905. Ten years later the town of Askov had about a thousand inhabitants and was surrounded by clean, well-tilled farms. Soon it had its folk school, and its fame was rapidly spreading in Europe and at home as one of the most truly co-operative communities in the United States. Askov is now known as the rutabaga center of the country. It is estimated that about one-third of the Nation's rutabagas are produced in this district. A feature of the village is its remarkable record for lawfulness; it has never had or needed a jail.

Characteristic of the villages in this district are the aluminum-painted water towers—the first indications of the approaching towns. The roadsides are lined with flax, sumac, hazel, and milkweed. Between Moose Lake and Sandstone the hardwood groves become more numerous, the evergreens more sparse.

SANDSTONE, 66.3 *m.* (1,086 alt., 1,083 pop.), was settled in 1885 when quarries were opened in the sandstone outcrop along the Kettle River. The stone, which varies from pink to dark red, has been used in building throughout the Middle West. A forest fire in September 1894 destroyed the village; today its chief industries are agriculture and dairying. Summer colonies are numerous on the nearby lakes.

HINCKLEY, 76.7 m. (1,030 alt., 682 pop.), was the center of the raging forest fire of 1894, in which more than 400 persons lost their lives.
The hero of the disaster was Northern Pacific's engineer, Jim Root, who
backed his train through a wall of flames and on over the burning Grind-
stone Creek bridge all the way to Duluth. He saved 350 lives, but his
hands were burned fast to the throttle.

Left from Hinckley on State 48 to a MONUMENT TO THE FIRE VICTIMS, 0.1 m.
The scenic ST. CROIX RECREATIONAL AREA, 20 m., belongs to the Federal
Government and consists of approximately 21,000 acres in Pine County, along
the west bank of the St. Croix River. The road at this point leads south to a
PUBLIC CAMP, a GIRLS' CAMP, and a CCC CAMP. All but the latter are of log or
rustic construction and will be operated by social service agencies.
At 28 m. is the ST. CROIX RIVER. The canoeing enthusiast can easily float and
paddle down the St. Croix in one day to the toll bridge (about 30 miles), across
which State 70 leads from Wisconsin back to US 61 at Rock Creek; or he can continue about 40 miles farther downstream to Taylors Falls.
The river is a small-mouth bass stream; the only rapids are at Kettle River and
offer no difficulty. Many of the St. Croix's small tributary streams have good trout
fishing; springs supply drinking water (food and lodging obtainable along the way,
but camping equipment is recommended).

At 80.2 m. is the junction with State 23. A Chippewa mission was established near this spot in 1838 and destroyed by the Sioux in 1841. Here
the lakes and thickets become more numerous; wild plum and raspberries
make a background for the mass of blossoms—lupine, thistle, and goldenrod—which color an otherwise barren stretch of road. The power-line
poles are oddly placed along this stretch and seem to lean upon each other
for support.

Right on State 23 to BROOK PARK, 6 m., where a monument stands in memory
of those who lost their lives in the forest fire of 1894.
MORA, 18 m. (1,001 alt., 1,014 pop.), was platted in 1881 and named for Mora,
Sweden. A boom town of lumbering days, it is now dependent upon its co-operative
creamery, its gristmill, and a machine shop which manufactures buttermilk driers.
In Mora the Minnesota Izaak Walton League has its largest per capita membership and the league's only women's auxiliary. The IZAAK WALTON LEAGUE MU-
SEUM (permission to visit museum obtainable at bakery next to post office), housed
in a log building erected in 1930, contains more than 3,000 exhibits, including a
complete set of tools and equipment of early lumber days, a large archeological
collection (mostly copper implements from local mounds), more than 300 Nordic
copper cooking utensils, a collection of old pueblo pottery, and some rare books,
among them Church Fathers in Latin. The museum also contains the silver cup
presented to the local chapter of the league for its work in constructing dams at
Knife and Fish Lakes, and in establishing the Ann Lake Game Refuge of 2,000
acres.
Right from Mora 7 m. on State 65 to KNIFE LAKE, which is identified by
some historians as the rendezvous of Radisson, Groseilliers, and small bands of
Chippewa, Huron, and Ottawa Indians, following the Frenchmen's wintering along
Lake Superior. A great feast was held, which many Sioux attended; the lake is said
to have been so named because Radisson gave them the first steel knives many had
ever seen.

The region about PINE CITY, 89.9 m. (955 alt., 1,343 pop.), once the
site of an Indian village, consists of undulating hills with a sandy clay
soil. Pine City is a translation of the Indian word "Chengwatana," now
the name of the outlet of Cross Lake into Snake River, which runs through

the town. Along the river, from its lake source to the St. Croix, are basaltic lava flows; several old shafts made by copper prospectors remain along the north bank.

South of Pine City the pointed tops of the spruce and the feathery contours of tamarack become less frequent in the swamps. Oak, elm, maple, and basswood replace the softer deciduous trees, and patches of corn, wheat, and potatoes are interspersed among the deep meadows.

RUSH CITY, 100.1 *m.* (922 alt., 908 pop.). The highway here is within 5 miles of the St. Croix River (L). At this point the transition from wooded and burnt-over area to fenced fields is especially noticeable.

HARRIS, 107.1 *m.* (924 alt., 584 pop.).

Left from Harris on an unsurfaced road to SUNRISE, 10 *m.,* a boom town in the lumbering era, but now a small dairy community. It lies in the valley of a once mighty river, which drained the melting glaciers.

At 11 *m.* is the junction with State 95; L. on State 95 to ALMELUND (Swed., *elm valley*), 15 *m.* Gold is being washed from the moraine here, about one dollar's worth to the ton.

NORTH BRANCH, 112.1 *m.* (921 alt., 691 pop.), is on the edge of the wide sand plain. To the L. are occasional glimpses of the wide St. Croix Valley and the Wisconsin hills.

The most southerly transition forest of any extent along this route lies between North Branch and Wyoming. Here tamarack and birch are intermixed with oak and other hardwood, and the shrubs include both northern and southern types.

WYOMING, 124.8 (905 alt., 214 pop.), is at the junction with US 8 *(see Tour 19).* South of Wyoming US 8 and US 61 are united for 5.3 miles.

FOREST LAKE, 128.6 *m.* (937 alt., 916 pop.), is the center of a popular summer and fishing resort area. The town adjoins a lake of the same name. To the west is the wide sand plain with its scattered dunes; eastward the country becomes more roughly rolling until it reaches the heavily wooded St. Croix Valley.

At 130.1 *m.* is a junction (R) with US 8 *(see Tour 19),* known as the Forest Lake Cut-off, a direct road to Minneapolis.

BALD EAGLE, 139.8 *m.,* was named for the lake (R) where bald eagles once nested on an island. The fine lakes in the district have made this a popular suburban territory.

WHITE BEAR LAKE, 142.9 *m.* (941 alt., 2,600 pop.), is a resort town favored by St. Paulites. Indians believed that the lake, whose shores are lined with summer homes, was haunted by the spirit of a white bear, slain by a brave as it was about to attack his beloved.

An annual 3-mile swimming meet is held here in July.

Left from White Bear Lake on State 96 to a private entrance, 0.3 *m.,* over a bridge to MANITOU ISLAND, called Spirit Island by Indians who visited it annually to obtain sap for maple sugar. Today this 54-acre isle is an exclusive residential district.

Right from State 96 on a road skirting the lake to the WHITE BEAR YACHT CLUB, 2.3 *m.,* where an annual regatta is held in August.

For the next 3 miles the road passes through a group of interconnected towns:

DELLWOOD, 3.1 *m.*, where is the WHITE BEAR COUNTRY CLUB; MAHTOMEDI (Ind., *gray polar bear lake*), 4 *m.*; EAST SHORE PARK, 4.9 *m.*; and WILDWOOD AMUSEMENT PARK, 5.8 *m.*, with picnic grounds.

US 61 follows Arcade St., in St. Paul, to 7th St.; R. on 7th St. to the junction with Hastings Ave.; L. on Hastings Ave. to the junction with Kellogg Blvd.

ST. PAUL, 154.2 *m.* (703 alt., 271,606 pop.) *(see ST. PAUL).*

Points of Interest: Capitol Square, City Hall, Cathedral of St. Paul, Government dam and locks.

In St. Paul are the junctions with US 12 *(see Tour 10)*, US 10 *(see Tour 16)*, US 52, *(see Tour 9)*, and US 212 *(see Tour 11).*

Sec. c. ST. PAUL *to* WISCONSIN LINE *133.7 m. US 61.*

In St. Paul US 61 and US 10, which are united at the junction of Hastings Ave. and Kellogg Blvd., 0 *m.*, follow Hastings Ave. to the junction with Point Douglas Rd.; R. on Point Douglas Rd.

RED ROCK, 5 *m.*, is a small settlement.

Right from Red Rock across the railroad tracks to RED ROCK PARK (L.), 0.1 *m.*, early Methodist mission site and an annual camp-meeting ground since 1869. The mission was founded in 1837 on the west side of the Mississippi River just below Kaposia. It was moved in 1840 to the east side where several buildings were erected. The main building was of hewn logs, 18 feet square, 1½ stories high, with a shed addition 14 by 18 feet. Here the Rev. Benjamin Kavanaugh sought to convert the Indians. In 1905 it was moved to its present site. One of the oldest buildings in Minnesota, it became a nucleus around which a group of buildings has been built, housing activities of camp-meeting followers. The HOTEL was built about 1870, and the open PAVILION, which seats 1,800 persons, in 1880. At the turn of the century these camp meetings drew as many as 30,000 on a single Sunday, when famous evangelists occupied the pulpit. The park was named for a red granite rock, an unusual sight in a limestone area. It was venerated by the Indians and annually painted in various designs.

At 15.2 *m.* is the junction (L) with US 10 *(see Tour 16).*

At 15.4 *m.* US 61 crosses the Mississippi on an unusual SPIRAL BRIDGE. Its shape was planned to bring the end of the bridge to the main street of Hastings, but the width of its curve, although adequate when travel was slower, scarcely accommodates modern motor traffic. A short distance downstream the Mississippi is joined by the wide St. Croix, giving the first really impressive indication of the huge stream the Mississippi becomes as it flows on to the Gulf. There is a Government DAM on the Mississippi about 1 mile north of Hastings.

HASTINGS, 16 *m.* (706 alt., 5,086 pop.), seat of Dakota County, was originally known as Oliver's Grove, because in 1819 Lt. William G. Oliver and his troops camped here. Among the group was Joseph R. Brown (1805–1870), who became Hasting's first settler when he established a trading post here in 1833.

Hastings manufactures flour-milling implements, paper and clay products, and skis. It is the trading center of a diversified farming district to the south and west. At the Vermilion River is a large FLOUR MILL, and nearby the remains of an OLD MILL erected by Governor Alexander Ramsey (1815–1903).

HASTINGS STATE ASYLUM for mental cases is in the southeastern part of the town near the Vermilion River.

Less than a mile south of the business district US 61 passes (L) the limestone MANSION OF GEN. WILLIAM GATES LE DUC (1823–1917), which is almost completely hidden by trees and now houses an antique shop *(open by appointment during summer)* marked by a roadway sign.

The house, first in the State to be built in the Victorian Gothic style, was copied exactly from Robert Downing's book of architectural designs. The New England and Greek Revival styles had prevailed until 1860, when the house was begun. During its construction the Civil War started and General Le Duc was called to the service. Work was continued, however, and he came from the South on a furlough to supervise its completion.

Architecturally the house is a graceful structure, built simply when simplicity was not considered a virtue; for this reason it is considerably less outmoded in style now than its contemporaries. Its 15 rooms, designed for entertaining and luxurious living, were arranged about a center hall. All were planned with good taste and without the numerous and superfluous nooks and alcoves so frequent in that period of architectural history. Many of the interior details, not shown in the book from which the design was taken, were constructed from General Le Duc's own sketches.

Originally the livingroom had a dark maroon wallpaper with an all-over gold tracery design. The bronze chandeliers, said to have been made in England, were brought from an old Episcopal church in Batavia, N. Y. The original furnishings were Victorian, and included a square rosewood piano and a sideboard copied from an Eastlake design shown at the Philadelphia Exposition in 1876.

The exterior walls are of a cream-colored limestone quarried in the vicinity, laid with larger blocks in regular-coursed mason-work of squared stones in the front and side walls, but with smaller pieces laid in random ashlar at the rear. The trim, inside and out, is pine. There is an absence of elaboration, except for a jigsawed, running Gothic ornament under the gable ends. The effect, architecturally, is one of general good proportion and pleasing disposition of the openings. The front door opening is a Gothic arch, a form which is repeated at intervals in the house. Here, as in so many houses of the period, the high and narrow motif prevails in doors, windows, porches, and tower.

The house is in fairly good repair. Except for the recent addition of dormers in the attic, it is practically the same as at the time of its construction.

At Hastings is the junction with State 55.

Right on this road 3.1 *m.* to the junction with a marked road; R. here to NININGER, 5.2 *m.*, the home of Ignatius Donnelly (1831–1901), "Sage of Nininger," "Apostle of Protest," politician, and author of the *Great Cryptogram,* which attempted to prove that Lord Bacon was the author of Shakespeare's plays *(see THE ARTS).*

Nininger was boomed as the coming metropolis of the Northwest by a group of Philadelphia lawyers and businessmen, including Donnelly. Donnelly was the town's greatest "booster" and continued his residence there after the disastrous bank failures of the late 1850's. The rest of the population, once numbering more than 500, moved to Hastings and St. Paul. Donnelly's first house was moved to Hastings, but was soon replaced by the present dwelling which is visited annually by scores of his admirers, whose names fill a guest book on his desk.

Nininger was a center for gay parties and the seat of long political discussions from its founding in 1857 until its decline in the 1860's. Lyceum courses were given in the winter and church services were held in private homes, two features of the village life that distinguished it from the cruder life of the towns nearby. Large sawmills, a flour mill, dance pavilion, hotel, and homes of ambitious pioneers were built in a short time and then abandoned. Only Donnelly remained.

It was just below Hastings that the steamboat *Chippewa Falls* grounded on a bar in the low water of 1864. She drew only 12 inches and the pilot ever after insisted that he floated her free by a quick starboard-to-port shift of his "chaw" of tobacco.

To the south the route leaves the river and crosses excellent farm lands.

At RED WING, 42.7 *m.* (712 alt., 9,629 pop.), the highway enters the greatly widened Mississippi Valley. Here, indeed, the panorama justifies the superlatives used by Mark Twain (1835–1910) in the record of his journey along the upper Mississippi. "There it was," he said, "this amazing region, bristling with great towns projected day before yesterday, so to speak, and built next morning. The majestic bluffs that overlook the river, along through this region, charm one with the grace and variety of their forms, and the soft beauty of their adornment. The steep, verdant slope, whose base is at the water's edge, is topped by a lofty rampart of broken, turreted rocks, which are exquisitely rich and mellow in color— mainly dark browns and dull greens, but splashed with other tints. And then you have the shining river, winding here and there and yonder, its sweep interrupted at intervals by clusters of wooded islands threaded by silver channels; and you have glimpses of distant villages, asleep upon capes; and of stealthy rafts slipping along in the shade of the forest walls; and of white steamers vanishing around remote points. And it is all as tranquil and reposeful as dreamland, and has nothing this-worldly about it—nothing to hang a fret or a worry upon."

The white steamers are rare now, but the river towns are quiet—a reminiscent quietness that gives them time to take a backward glance at a glamour which, though fleeting, left its indelible mark.

When Zebulon Pike came in 1805 he found a village of the Dakota Indians, for whose chief, Whoo-pa-doo-to *(wing of scarlet)*, the city was named; his descendant, Hazen Wakute, now (1938) lives here.

In 1836 a Swiss Protestant missionary society sent three missionaries to establish posts among the Sioux. One was erected at Red Wing. Here, on a low plateau above Lake Pepin, an Alpine chalet of hewn logs was constructed by the missionaries. It stood in the midst of a large garden enclosed by a wooden fence. It was abandoned in 1840, and though it was re-established temporarily, the post was given up by the society in the middle forties and taken over by the American Board of Commissioners for Foreign Missions in 1846.

Red Wing has the country's second MUNICIPALLY OPERATED THEATER, which is housed in the T. B. Sheldon Memorial Auditorium. The recreational center of the community is COLVILL PARK. The 100-acre SOLDIERS' MEMORIAL PARK on the broad plateau and wooded hillside is accessible to cars and hikers and overlooks the surrounding hills and river valley. A. P. PIERCE PARK, on the banks of the river, commonly known as Levee Park, is a beautiful spot with shady elms and garden paths.

From the foot of Main St. a concrete stairway ascends MOUNT LA GRANGE, formerly known as Barn Bluff, the translated form of the original name that has since been restored. From a distance the bluff resembles a huge barn. Cambrian trilobites (crustaceans) and other fossils have been found in its strata.

The city's chief industry is the manufacture of pottery and clay pipe. Other Red Wing products include marine motors, used by the Federal Government and many foreign countries, shoes, plate glass, linseed oil, and dairy, tannery, and foundry products. Most plants offer personally conducted tours.

The annual ski meets held in January are the second largest in the State.

At the eastern city limits is (R) the MINNESOTA TRAINING SCHOOL FOR BOYS, a reformatory.

At Red Wing is the junction (L) with US 63 *(see Tour 18)*, and from this point to Lake City US 63 and US 61 are united.

At 47.8 *m.* is WACOUTA STATION.

Left from Wacouta Station on a graveled road to the pioneer river community of WACOUTA, 0.5 *m.* This little village at the head of LAKE PEPIN teemed with lumberjacks and rivermen during the late 1850's. Millions of logs from the Mississippi and St. Croix Rivers were assembled into rafts and floated to mills downstream. At one time the town was forced to move inland a short distance, after a change in the river channel.

At this point the Mississippi broadens out to form Lake Pepin. This bluff-walled lake, 34 miles long, is formed by the entrance of the swift-flowing Chippewa into the Mississippi. Five hundred feet wide at its mouth, the Chippewa has a strong descending current from the high tablelands of western Wisconsin. Pebbles and silt are carried along this fast stream and deposited in the bed of the sluggish Mississippi, which, unable to carry the load, backs up and spreads out to the high bluffs. In addition to Lake Pepin, only Lac qui Parle and St. Croix of Minnesota's 10,000 lakes were formed in this way.

Called by the Indians Pem-vee-cha-mday *(Lake of the Mountain)*, Lake Pepin was first seen by a white man when Father Hennepin and two companions were taken along its channel by their captors, the Sioux. The Franciscan renamed it Lac des Pleurs *(Lake of the Tears)* because the Indians, while camping on its banks, wept until daylight in the hope of gaining their leader's permission to kill one of their white prisoners. The present name is derived from the Pepin family of Three Rivers on the lower St. Lawrence in Canada, two of whose members accompanied Sieur du Luth to the upper Mississippi in 1679.

FRONTENAC STATION, 53.2 *m.*, is the post office and railroad station of another early river settlement.

Left from Frontenac Station on a country road to FRONTENAC, 1.2 *m.* The town is named for Louis de Buade, Comte de Frontenac (1622–1698), a French Colonial Governor of Canada. At 1.5 *m.* (R) is the LITTLE GREY EPISCOPAL CHURCH, of "box" type design with vertical siding battened together with narrower strips. It was built in 1867 through the efforts of Henry Benjamin Whipple (1822–1901), first Episcopal bishop of Minnesota.

At 1.9 *m.* is the junction with a dirt road; R. to ST. HUBERT'S LODGE *(not open)*, 2 *m.*, built by Gen. Israel Garrard (1825–1901), a Kentuckian, after the style of the pre-Civil War houses, with whitewashed vertical battens on a wood frame, with an upper veranda or gallery. The shuttered windows, two-story porch, and general details all show southern influence. The structure provided accommodations for many southern and eastern vacationers. The coat-of-arms of the house, a stag's head with a cross between the antlers, the insignia of St. Hubert, patron saint of hunters, is in the lodge. Some of the furnishings and interior woodwork were brought by steamboat from Cincinnati. Many of the original furnishings remain, and the interiors have been little changed since the death of the owner.

Grant La Farge and George L. Heins spent part of the winter of 1883–84 at St. Hubert's Lodge, visited the quarries, and admired the rich creamy color of the limestone. Later Heins and La Farge, architects of the Cathedral of St. John the Divine in New York City, selected the Frontenac stone for the interior of the sanctuary and apse of the cathedral.

William McNally in his novel *House of Vanished Splendor* tells of the gay 1870's and 1880's, when Gen. Charles King, John La Farge, Joseph Jefferson—who excelled in painting as well as acting—Henry Ward Beecher, and others came here to write and paint.

General Garrard donated land for a railroad station 2 miles inland, to prevent encroachment on his domain, which he ruled in a baronial manner. This gift isolated Frontenac, and its streets today are grass-grown. Only one house has been built in the little town during the past 40 years.

In Meyer's pasture the general raced thoroughbreds from his 22-horse stable. He brought in 200 Tyrolese workmen to remake and beautify his purchased village, which he called Westervelt. The Westervelt home is a short distance beyond the lodge. It, too, is an old house of white frame construction, surrounded by a fine hedge. Evert V. Westervelt had purchased an early trading post on the site several years before Garrard's arrival.

At 3.5 *m.* south on the lake shore road, which branches L. from St. Hubert's Lodge, is VILLA MARIA, a severe gray-shingled building whose red spire is all that can be seen of the town from the main highway. It stands on a wooded knoll overlooking the lake and the bluffs to the north and south. The school was first established at Lake City in 1856 by nuns from St. Louis. They chose this site from the several that General Garrard offered them. Roman Catholics for two centuries have been attracted to this vicinity.

East and south of Villa Maria is SAND POINT, a wave-built spit of sand and gravel jutting into Lake Pepin. It is believed to be the site of Fort Beauharnois, built in 1727 and rebuilt in 1732 after abandonment in 1728. The new site may have been in the immediate vicinity. Wells Creek, which flows into the Mississippi here, was called Sand Point River on Nicollet's map in 1843. The site apparently was a favorite with traders, for James Wells had a post here as late as 1850. Perriere, De Gonnor, Guignas, St. Pierre, Carver—all are names associated with its early history.

Return along the lake shore and down a curving road to FRONTENAC INN, 5.4 *m.*, a spacious, white frame structure with the green shutters characteristic of the old village's houses. At one time it was an important hostelry for tourists who visited the upper Mississippi by steamboat. Its registers begin in 1871 and contain well-known names. Now the inn caters to the leisurely tourist and an occasional group of professional and amateur ornithologists, who find Frontenac one of the best spots in North America for the study of bird migrations. The entire upper valley of the river is notable for the number of species to be seen in migrations, but in the portion of the state contiguous to the stretch of river south of Red Wing, nesting species can be seen that do not ordinarily fly so far north. Among these are the blue-gray gnatcatcher, the tufted titmouse, the prothonotary warbler, and others.

To the north are the bluffs of POINT-NO-POINT, from whose summit the whole of Lake Pepin is visible. It was named by boatmen who found that each point, when approached, seemed to be replaced by another farther on.

LAKE CITY, 59.7 *m.* (713 alt., 3,210 pop.), lies along the stretch of Lake Pepin most dreaded by steamboat skippers because of the sudden, violent winds that sweep the narrow channel. Although several boats have been lost here, the worst disaster was the wreck of the *Seawing,* which turned over in a storm just above Lake City on July 13, 1890, with a loss of 98 lives. An early resort town, Lake City was also a trading center with sawmills and flour mills. The nursery business has been an important one since it was established shortly after the Civil War. Several popular varieties of crab-apples originated here.

The Lake Pepin clamming industry, once of major importance to river towns, centered at Lake City. A quarter of a century ago, between 500 and 600 river clammers operated their picturesque outfits on the surface of the lake, and the button factories on the shores did a flourishing business. With the increasing use of synthetic products for the manufacture of buttons, the industry declined and the factories closed. But here and there along the lake shore, clam-gatherers, sometimes living in transient communities, eke out a precarious existence by this seasonal industry.

READ'S LANDING, 69.8 *m.* (683 alt., 475 pop.), was once one of the busiest sites on the Mississippi. During the American Revolution a trader in the British service was sent here for the purpose of preventing the Sioux from aiding the Americans farther down the Mississippi. The man was the father of Augustin Rocque, later a trader at Wabasha. It was not until 1840 that the post then established made Read's Landing famous to fur-traders. It was during lumbering and steamboat days, however, that this river town came into its own. Lumberjacks and raftsmen gathered here for their Saturday night's roistering, and the 20 or more saloons did a thriving business. Seventeen hotels and boarding houses were required to take care of the passengers who stopped over here in the 1850's on their way to the upper Mississippi settlements. Fifteen hundred travelers are said to have been put up at the Landing at one time. In the spring 32 steamboats lay waiting for the ice in Lake Pepin to melt and permit their passage, while during the winter captains and pilots gathered about the stores and hotels to swap river stories and boast of their crafts. When wheat turned the eyes of the world to Minnesota, Read's Landing became one of the greatest wheat-shipping ports in all the country, and settlers drove miles from the west to bargain on the levee for the sale of their grain.

Today only a row of buildings and the old posts to which the steamboats were tied remain of that colorful river traffic. Even "Landing" has been dropped from the village name and its inhabitants know it as Reads.

WABASHA, 72.6 *m.* (708 alt., 2,212 pop.), once a trading post, is on the flood plain with bluffs shutting out the tableland west of the river. In the days of river traffic it was one of the largest primary wheat markets in this area. Although later renamed in honor of the family of Sioux chiefs, the town was once called Cratte's Landing, for an Englishman, Oliver Cratte, who built a blacksmith shop on the levee in 1838. The spot was a favorite of fur traders from a period shortly after the American Revolution, when Augustin Rocque had posts in the vicinity. Later, after 1834, Alexis Bailly operated a post on the site; Joseph La Bathe was established here in 1840.

Wabasha is on the edge of the WINNESHIEK BOTTOMS, a network wilderness of sloughs and bayous extending 300 miles southward along the Mississippi Valley to Rock Island, Ill. Approximately 175,000 acres of land and 100,000 acres of water-surface comprise this great area, which is now a national game preserve—the first refuge to include fur-bearing animals, fish, and plant life. The quiet waters of expanded lakes resulting from spring floods make this reputedly one of the greatest breeding grounds for small-mouth bass, a natural hatchery closely guarded by the Government.

Through this section the route winds along the river valley following the base of limestone bluffs. In summer the bottom lands are covered with feathery light-green willows and a variety of swamp and river plants. Farther up the hillside the white bluffs are almost hidden by the heavy dark hardwoods. Eastern adventurers found much in this lovely stretch to remind them of the far-away Hudson River Valley.

Left from Wabasha is a toll bridge crossing the Mississippi into Wisconsin.

MINNEISKA (Ind., *white water*), 89.7 *m.* (670 alt., 192 pop.), was first settled in 1851, and gradually became an export center, shipping in 1870 a total of 330,000 bushels of wheat. Subsequently it was added to the list of river ports that declined with the coming of the railroads. Here, as elsewhere in river towns, the true riverman made a practice of spitting a curse upon each railroad track he crossed.

Picturesque dwellers of the tents and shantyboats here dig clams during the summer season and sell the shells to button factories. Sometimes river dwellers tend Government navigation lights, sound the channel, or engage in commercial fishing.

At 94.8 *m.* is the JOHN LATSCH STATE PARK, extending along the Minnesota side of the river for 2 miles and covering an area of approximately 350 acres. FIVE PEAKS offer a wide view of the river valley. Back of the ridge are sheltered, well-wooded, spring-fed valleys. Near the areas reserved for CAMP SITES are good fishing grounds and sand beaches.

It was here that Jonathan Carver (1732–1780), ascending the Mississippi in a canoe with two companions, came ashore one April evening in 1766 to cook his supper on the grassy terraces near the mouth of the Whitewater River. Carver was the first white man to find the strange-looking REMAINS OF THE INDIAN TURF HOUSES in this valley. This extensive system of artificial mounds on the marshy ledges below the river road is almost obliterated.

At 99.4 *m.* is the junction with an improved road.

Right on this road to ROLLINGSTONE, 3 *m.* (289 pop.). Along the Rollingstone River near the town are more than 50 MOUNDS, many 100 feet long, from which pots, beads, and blankets have been removed.

Most of Rollingstone's citizens are descendants of German colonists who came here before the Civil War. They have clung to their land, language, and native culture for more than 75 years.

MINNESOTA CITY, 99.7 *m.* (673 alt., 151 pop.), is a small village that grew up on the site of a prospective Utopia, the communal dream of a group of New York mechanics known as the Western Farm and Village Association. The story of the Rollingstone colony is one of the most tragic in Minnesota history.

In the spring of 1852, steamboat captains plying the upper Mississippi were astonished when approached at Galena by groups of eastern immigrants bound, they declared, for Rollingstone City. When told no such place existed, the hopeful travelers refused to accept the rivermen's word, and produced as evidence an illustrated map of the metropolis. The steamboat officers, men who knew every inch of the upper river, were amazed. The map plainly indicated that on their river route was a beautifully planned city with a glass-enclosed winter house, surrounded with radiating shaded streets, bordered by fireproof public buildings and comfortable homes.

The explanation that finally came to light led back to New York City, where some mechanics and others, a year before, had formed an association whose aim was to obtain free Government lands on which they planned to settle. A committee went West to select a site and brought back a rough plat of an area on the Mississippi; but before this was shown, it was transformed into a complete town and lithographed. Each member was to draw by lot a village home and a farm up the valley.

The steamboat captains finally identified the site as one a few miles above the scattered huts on Wabasha Prairie, later to become Winona. There they unloaded the colonists and their goods, and left them to reach their prospective homes as best they could.

From the start the venture was doomed. The advance committee had mistaken a shallow, unnavigable slough for the main channel of the river, actually several miles away, and the settlers found that all their goods and cattle had to be transported over a long rough trail and across dangerous fords. But it was too late to check the flow of land-seekers from the East. By the end of May the community numbered 400.

Ignorant, for the most part, of even the rudiments of farming and wholly unsuited for pioneer life, the city dwellers suffered intensely. Women and children were crowded into a community tent, while the men slept in "gopher tents" whose sloping log sides were covered with grass. Many died and the mortality among the children mounted daily. It was not until after the middle of June that word of the situation reached New York and the exodus was checked. Some of the survivors found their way back to New York. Many settled at Winona and other neighboring communities. A few moved on to their farms where their descendants still live.

Nameless graves, a decaying warehouse never used, a mill, and a few farmhouses were all that remained of the Utopian city Rollingstone. On the heights farther up the valley another village was later to take over the name, but this second Rollingstone *(see above)* has no other connection with the paper city of the New York promoters.

WINONA, 104.6 *m.* (666 alt., 20,850 pop.) *(see WINONA).*

Points of Interest. Sugar Loaf Mountain, Garvin Heights State Park, Lake Winona, College of St. Teresa.

At Winona is the junction with US 14 *(see Tour 12)*.

Beginning at Winona's south city limits and lying entirely within the Gilmore Creek watershed, 5,600 acres of land have been included in a Federal soil conservation project by co-operation of farmers with the Federal Government. The work, begun in 1935, consists of dam-building, terracing, reversion to timber in certain areas, crop control, and the like. *(Inquire for guides at local office in Winona Federal Bldg.)*

Between Winona and La Crescent US 61 and US 14 are one route. The highway follows the eroded river gorge, which varies in width from 3 to 6 miles. The present cities of the valley stand on alluvial terraces built up by glacial floods. The many streams that join the river flow in deep-cut rocky coulees, fed by springs that issue from the strata near the foot of the bluffs. Numerous footpaths leave the highway for the uplands. The well-forested woodlands extend for some distance to the west of the river bluffs. Even a casual observer will note the great dissimilarity between this region and the rest of the State. Many of the trees and shrubs common throughout the woods to the north are scattered through these ravines and bluffs. Here are the most varied forests in the entire State; they include black oak, shellbark, hickory, and black walnut, as well as more common northern varieties. In the lowlands the usual swampland growth is varied by the black maple and Kentucky coffee tree. The confusion of hills typical of glacial regions to the north is lacking, and the tableland has an almost imperceptible roll; the ravines, deeply cut by small streams, are weathered and worn. It is old terrain, unchanged for centuries except by the slow weathering of the seasons.

Many of the villages that once thrived along this narrow bench have disappeared, to be replaced by the numerous country homes of the prosperous neighboring villages. The landscaped, terraced grounds harmonize with the luxuriant natural foliage to make the entire highway seem a stretch of pleasant park.

At HOMER, 111.8 *m.* (662 alt., 50 pop.), François du Chouquette, a half-breed blacksmith, built a shack in 1830, seeking to establish trade with the Wabasha tribe then ruling this area. Frequent raids upon the Sioux by the Sac and Fox Indians caused him to move, first to what became known as Blacksmith's Island and finally to Prairie du Chien. His forge and anvil on the island are the only remaining evidence of this first attempt at white civilization in the region.

A GOVERNMENT FISH HATCHERY is at Homer.

Through the deep layers of limestone the Mississippi and its immediate tributaries in this vicinity have cut their valleys. The ledges in places are extremely sharp; others have been almost obscured by an unusually heavy growth of vegetation. Along the river bottoms grow slender red birches, rare or absent elsewhere in the state. They are typical of many species of trees and flowers found in Minnesota only at this unglaciated southeastern tip. Shagbark hickory and red mulberry are frequent in the deep woods; the rare Soulard crab grows in the thickets with several species of highbush blackberry and, in more rocky places, the Appalachian cherry and the shrubby chinquapin oak. The upland soils are a good quality loam, resting upon a yellowish clayey subsoil loess, or wind-deposited rockflour, mixed with rotted limestone and sandstone, which is exceedingly fertile.

At RICHMOND, 120.3 *m.* (660 alt., 603 pop.), about 1835, George Catlin (1796–1872), painter of North American Indians, daubed his name in red on the rocks. The spot was afterwards known as Catlin's Rocks.

An INDIAN MOUND in the shape of a bird is near the town.

DAKOTA, 125 *m.* (658 alt., 250 pop.), another trading post, was the headquarters of Jeremiah Tibbitts, who came to this region at the age of 17 with a band of Indians and carried on trade up and down the river until 1853.

At DRESBACH, 126.7 *m.* (675 alt., 175 pop.), the widely used limestone called Winona travertine is quarried.

In MINERAL BLUFF, rising 405 feet at the northern end of the village and split from top to bottom on its river side, lead, silver, and coal have been found—none, however, in commercial quantities. Excavators also unearthed a skeleton into whose skull was sunk a copper hatchet and a dart 9 inches long. The hills in the vicinity are frequently bordered with prostrate juniper and creeping savin and occasionally topped with white pine—all three characteristic of northern coniferous forests.

QUEEN'S BLUFF, or Gwinn's Bluff, like the surrounding area, is unglaciated and contains some of North America's most interesting plant relics, descendants of botanical species that were forced into this region by the advancing glacial ice. Uncommon mountain flora and mosses, whose natural range is usually above 5,000 feet, thrive on this spot at an altitude of 900 feet. Most interesting of these expatriate species is a variety of the springbeauty *(Claytonia virginica),* usually found only in the Rockies and in Alaska. On the summit is a clump of stunted white cedar trees, natives of the wet lands of northern Minnesota. At the northern base of the bluff the witchhazel reaches its northernmost habitat; the blue or winter grape, a native of eastern states, grows along the eastern side.

At the mouth of Burns Valley on Burns Creek is an ancient pottery kiln, and farther up the creek are the remains of what may have been an arrowmaker's dwelling.

LA CRESCENT, 131.8 *m.* (647 alt., 520 pop.) *(see Tour 12),* is at the junction with US 14 *(see Tour 12)* and US 16 *(see Tour 13).*

At 133.7 *m.* US 61 crosses the Mississippi (the Wisconsin Line), 2 miles south of La Crosse, Wis. *(see Wisconsin, Tour 11).*

Tour 2

Junction with State 11—Bemidji—Wadena—Sauk Center—Willmar—
Redwood Falls—Windom—Jackson—(Spencer, Iowa); US 71.
Junction with State 11 to Iowa Line, 421 m.

Route is paralleled by Minnesota & International Ry. between Littlefork and Be-
midji, and by Great Northern Ry. between Park Rapids and Sauk Center.
Improved roadbed between junction with State 11 and Northome, paved between
Northome and Sauk Center, improved between Sauk Center and New London,
paved between Windom and Jackson, and improved between Jackson and Iowa
Line. Open all year.
Tourist accommodations at short intervals, except between International Falls and
Northome.

This route, which crosses the central western portion of the State from
north to south, begins just below the Canadian Border, passes through the
northwestern section of the Arrowhead region, penetrates the leading resort
and lake areas of the Paul Bunyan playground, and crosses the diversified
dairying and agricultural belt of southwestern Minnesota. Canoe trips can
be made from points on the route.

At 0 m. US 71 branches south from State 11 *(see Tour 6)* with which
it has been united for 11.1 miles from International Falls *(see Tour 5)*
and the bridge across Rainy River, the Canadian boundary.

LITTLEFORK, 8.4 m. (1,153 alt., 475 pop.), in a horseshoe bend of
the river of the same name, is in the center of a rich agricultural area. It
is the largest village in Koochiching County and is growing steadily.

When first settled, about 1905, the Littlefork area was covered with a
heavy growth of fine timber, including spruce, balsam, cedar, tamarack,
white pine and some hardwood. Much has been removed, but a considerable amount of timber remains and furnishes a substantial revenue to
the district. During the winter 60 trucks haul timber products from this
vicinity to the big paper mills at International Falls.

The future of Littlefork, however, and that of the country it serves as
a trading center—lower Little Fork and Big Fork Valleys—depend upon
the development of agriculture. Thousands of acres have been added to
the cultivated area, the greatest development having taken place during the
depression years, beginning with 1929. There were no crop failures during these years and, except for generally low prices, the farmers did not
suffer the losses or hardships that overtook the more highly developed
agricultural areas to the south. Clover seed, which yields from 6 to 10
bushels on the cut-over lands, with cash returns of $100 to $150 per acre,
has for several years been the chief money crop of the country. The Littlefork area, known as the place "where clover makes the seed," is recognized

by national authorities as being one of the country's most favorable regions for the production of clover and alfalfa seed.

The Little Fork River offers good fishing, and the deer hunting here is excellent. The floor of the river valley is heavily wooded, mostly with large elms, which are among the finest in northern Minnesota. Back from the banks of the stream rise hills that enclose the valley for the greater part of its course. These hills, bold, rugged, and abrupt, were formerly covered with a heavy growth of coniferous timber, but at the present time many are so denuded that bare rocks and the effects of soil erosion are plainly visible. On the slopes of others young trees of various kinds have already attained a height of 6 to 12 feet.

At 25.7 *m.* the highway crosses the BIG FORK RIVER *(good fishing and deer hunting).*

South of BIG FALLS, 27.7 *m.* (1,240 alt., 450 pop.), the highway runs along the watershed that diverts the waters of this area toward Hudson Bay on the north and the Gulf of Mexico on the south. In this region US 71 passes through grazing grounds with thousands of acres of bluejoint and redtop hay meadows.

In NORTHOME, 58.8 *m.* (1,451 alt., 250 pop.), one of Koochiching County's two annual fairs is held in early autumn.

At BLACKDUCK, 75.4 *m.* (1,404 alt., 704 pop.), is the oldest co-operative creamery in Beltrami County, producing more than 410,000 pounds of butter a year, an indication of the extensive dairying in this region.

At 75.5 *m.* is the junction with a graveled road.

Right on this road to BLACKDUCK LAKE, 0.5 *m.* *(cabins, tourist camps, fishing).* Blackduck is the largest lake in this locality and has a prehistoric VILLAGE SITE and INDIAN BATTLEFIELD on its southern shore.

HINES, 81 *m.* (1,424 alt., 210 pop.), is on the divide. For years it was predicted that Hines, like other northern towns, would be abandoned when the stands of excellent pine and cedar had been cut. In 1915, however, the Augustana Synod of the Lutheran Church decided to establish a colony here. The Lutherans who settled in the territory held religious services in schoolhouses and homes until their church was completed in 1920.

During the years 1915 to 1920 a musical group of 32 members was organized to sing on festal occasions and give concerts in nearby towns. Music has continued to be one of the major social activities. The village has a keen interest in social welfare and maintains that among its citizens are more nurses, teachers, college students, and musicians than in most communities twice its size. Community sunrise services, held annually on Easter at 6 a.m., were inaugurated locally some years ago and are now held in country churches in many districts throughout the territory.

Indicative of its agricultural pioneering are its crib silos, the first in Minnesota. The largest local unit of the Minnesota Farm Bureau has its headquarters in Hines. A commodious TOWN HALL, where athletic clubs and other organizations hold meetings, was built in 1921.

Fourteen good fishing lakes *(pike, bass, crappie, bluegill)* are within a 5-mile radius.

At 91.7 *m.* is the junction with a dirt road.

Left on this road to LAKE BEMIDJI STATE PARK, 1.5 *m.* *(camping, picnicking, recreational facilities),* 265 acres of exceptional stands of Norway pine. The park is on three separate tracts, each of which fronts LAKE BEMIDJI.

BEMIDJI, 102.3 *m.* (1,362 alt., 7,202 pop.) *(see Tour 7),* is at the junction with US 2 *(see Tour 7).*

This extreme southern portion of Beltrami County lies in the Mississippi Valley and slopes to the south and east. It is drained by the Mississippi and Turtle Rivers and their tributaries.

Drought and depression forced many farmers throughout this area into tenancy; their land was taken over by the State-operated Rural Credit Bureau from which they had obtained loans. The bureau, attempting to liquidate its investment, experimented with a new seed potato developed by the University of Minnesota. Although the cut-over land and drained muskeg would produce no corn or hay, the new seed potato with the trade name "Shelterbelt" grew to maturity 10 days earlier than the old Cobbler and, with careful handling, had a disease frequency of only 1/5 of 1 per cent (the Government allows a 4 per cent margin). By 1937 more than 100 farmers were raising the seed crop of which 170,000 bushels went into storage. More than 1,000 acres were sown, one farm producing 400 bushels on an acre of land. The potato, already receiving a premium in the market, may again make Minnesota a favorable seed-producing State and enable a good number of the tenant farmers to repossess their farms.

At 130 *m.* US 71 reaches the eastern gateway to ITASCA STATE PARK AND FOREST *(information about picnic grounds, tourist accommodations, bathhouse, hiking and bridle trails, recreational features, and a detailed map of the park may be obtained at Douglas Lodge, about 1.5 m. from US 71 entrance).*

Itasca State Park has within its boundaries LAKES ITASCA, ELK, and HERNANDO DE SOTO, each bordered by magnificent virgin pines. Established in 1891, it has since been enlarged to nearly 32,000 acres. Its attractions include (on the second floor of the bathhouse) a MUSEUM of Itasca Park's flora and fauna. Among the trails are the LIND SADDLE TRAIL, beginning at DOUGLAS LODGE, circling through the trees for 13 miles and passing within sight of 28 lakes and ponds before returning to the starting point; DEER PARK TRAIL, connecting Douglas Lodge with De Soto Lake—equally suitable for hiker or equestrian; EAGLE TRAIL, built by Boy Scout troops and leading through attractive woodland from the southwest patrol cabins to De Soto Lake; and BOHALL FOOTPATH, built for fire patrolling, which begins at the west arm of Lake Itasca and runs 2 miles through virgin timber to Bohall Lake and Park Drive. The Park Drive is open to motorists and affords an excellent one-way route through this section.

MANTRAP LOOKOUT STATION is just beyond the southeast corner of the park. The ANCHOR HILL STATION at the northwest corner has a 100-foot steel tower *(visitors admitted to both stations).*

INDIAN MOUNDS are scattered throughout the park. Stone implements and shards of pottery have been taken from a number and are now preserved by the State Historical Society in St. Paul.

While it is possible that Lake Itasca was discovered by William Morrison (1785–1866) in 1803, credit for being the first white man to visit the source of the Mississippi *(see HISTORICAL SURVEY)* is generally given to Henry Schoolcraft (1793–1864). Guided by the Indian, Yellow Head, Schoolcraft reached this lake in 1832. According to the best evidence Schoolcraft formed the name by combining the last two syllables of the Latin "veritas" *(truth)* with the first of "caput" *(head* or *source).* Despite the ingenuity of this etymological contention, the origin of the name is still disputed. Some maintain that it is from a Chippewa legend, according to which the beautiful daughter of Hiawatha, named Itasca or I-tesk-ka, was borne away to the region of darkness by Chebiabo, ruler of the netherworld. Tears shed by the maiden mourning her fate united with springs and rivulets to form the source of the Mississippi.

The outstanding surface features in this district are the central ridge, a rugged morainic belt crossing the country from east to west, beyond which the rolling till-plain extends to the north, the smooth outwash plain to the south. The central ridge, now sharply rolling, now hilly, rises with precipitous slopes, in places 100 feet above the deep depressions. South of the ridge the land gradually slopes from gentle hills to level plains, and most of the lakes lie in this belt of hills. Extensive peat bogs are numerous both to the north and the south.

At 146.5 *m.* is the junction with County Rd. 32.

Right on this road to WEIGELWOOD RESORT on TWO INLETS LAKE, 8 *m.* From this point a canoe trip can be made requiring one and a half days and covering approximately 27 miles. The route traverses Island, Eagle, Potato, and Fish Hook Lakes, noted for their wall-eyed and great-northern pike, bass, crappie, and bluegill.

Northwest from Weigelwood on Two Inlets Lake is HAY CREEK, 0.8 *m.* About 100 yards down this stream, which flows slowly, is a portage over a road bridge; another such portage is at 2.3 *m.* There may be one or two beaver dams that will require portages. At 8.3 *m.* is ISLAND LAKE; at 9.5 *m.* is PINE PARK CAMP; and at 9.8 *m.* is an excellent place for lunch. A brief run of fairly rapid water leads southeast to EAGLE LAKE, at 10.8 *m.* Another short outlet of fast water leads into the west arm of POTATO LAKE, 11.8 *m.* POTATO RIVER, 17.8 *m.,* is a good place to camp for the night. Down Potato River is a DAM, 18.2 *m.,* which must be portaged; this river is fairly swift, and there are some hazards in the form of rapids and rocks; it will take about 2 hours to reach FISH HOOK LAKE, 24.2 *m.* The outlet, FISH HOOK RIVER, is at 25.7 *m.* PARK RAPIDS, 27.2 *m.,* should be reached about noon of the second day.

PARK RAPIDS, 153.5 *m.* (1,426 alt., 2,081 pop.), was founded in 1880. Its leading industries are lumbering and lath-making. Good roads lead to 300 lakes in the vicinity, which offer excellent canoeing and fishing. Parklike groves are visible beside the dammed rapids of the Fish Hook River.

When this region was first settled, wheat was the staple crop, and until the 1880's it was practically the only money crop. The prairies produced heavily, and during the loading season long wagon trains of wheat were sent to the elevators in towns to the south. Every railroad station had its grain trader. The very low price of wheat in the 1890's forced farmers to diversify, and now the country has become one of the best dairying regions in the State.

A TOURIST PARK *(free camping, running water, swimming)* is at the eastern edge of town.

MENAHGA (Chippewa, *blueberries*), 165.3 *m.* (486 pop.), was originally a lumber town, later becoming a trading center and shipping point for wheat, and finally a general agricultural and dairying district. Industrious Finns have developed much of the surrounding territory. An annual

2-day fete during summer *(variable date)* is held to promote neighborliness among the farmers and villagers.

SEBEKA, 174.1 *m.* (1,398 alt., 548 pop.), is a modification of "Se-be-kaun" (Chippewa, *by the made ditch* or *channel*). The early settlers probably tried to choose a term meaning *by the river*. The first stock of merchandise was hauled here by team in 1890, and the village was platted in 1891. Lumbering was the early industry, and what is open farming land today was still so wooded in 1894 that fire destroyed nearly the entire village. Some fine farms have been developed in this territory which also has a large Finnish population.

In the HIGH SCHOOL *(open during school hours)* is a MURAL that demonstrates a new process in which casein paint is used in fresco-painting. It is the work of Richard Haines of the Federal Art Project, who has used events of local history for his subject.

LEAF RIVER, 181.8 *m.,* once a settlement of some consquence, has almost disappeared. A copper knife, evidently a relic of prehistoric times, was found in Leaf River in 1903.

WADENA, 188 *m.* (1,337 alt., 2,512 pop.) *(see Tour 16),* is at the junction with US 10 *(see Tour 16).*

South of Wadena on US 71 is an area in which the bedrock is in places still unobscured by glacial drift, although it has at three periods been covered with ice.

BROWERVILLE, 215.2 *m.* (1,284 alt., 700 pop.), was named for Abraham D. Brower, a Todd County pioneer, who settled in Round Prairie Township in 1860 and became chairman of the first board of county commissioners in 1867.

ST. JOSEPH'S ROMAN CATHOLIC CHURCH (R) in the center of Browerville is designed in the early Romanesque style; it has a clock tower with chimes and a $10,000 pipe organ. The SCULPTURES in the church, particularly *Our Lady of Lourdes* and the *Gethsemane Group,* are considered among the finest in the Northwest. They were carved by Joseph Kieselewski, who was born at Browerville in 1901, studied art in the Twin Cities and in New York, and won a European scholarship in 1925. Later he was awarded the Prix de Rome; he was one of the youngest artists ever to be so honored.

In 1874 John Bassett built a large boat and began floating wheat from his farm one-half mile east of Browerville down the Long Prairie River to Motley. His success led the firm of Chandler, Fisher & Wait to build a steamboat for transporting freight on this river. Wait, the district's representative in the legislature, secured an appropriation of $2,500 a year for the purpose of clearing the river channel. The boat operated until 1877, when the water dropped so low that the river was no longer navigable.

LONG PRAIRIE, 223.1 *m.* (1,298 alt., 1,854 pop.), seat of Todd County, was incorporated in 1883. In 1848 the Government established an Indian agency here to which a tribe of troublesome Winnebago Indians was moved from Iowa to act as a buffer between the Chippewa and the Sioux. A large number of Government employees and traders soon gathered in the new settlement. About 150 buildings were erected and 1,000 acres of land were broken for planting. In 1851 a mission school for the Winnebagos was established in Long Prairie by Francis Vivaldi, an Italian nobleman who, because of political activities, was forced to leave Italy. He became a priest, later married, but deserted his wife, and after years of penance was readmitted to the priesthood. President Lincoln appointed him consul at Rio de Janeiro and also in Argentina. There were 160 white residents in Long Prairie before Minneapolis existed and when St. Anthony Falls was only a village. By 1855, the arrangement with the Winnebagos having proved unsatisfactory, the Government moved them to a smaller area southeast of Mankato, and abandoned the Long Prairie Agency.

Andrew Northrup bought all the Government land and buildings and sold them to the Long Prairie Land Company, an organization with headquarters in Cincinnati, Ohio. Settlers were reluctant to buy the land, however, and in 1859 only three families were living in the settlement. At a Fourth of July celebration in 1860 a pole was erected on the site of the present courthouse, and for many years the place was known as Liberty Pole, instead of Long Prairie.

Long Prairie has a tourist park *(cabins, reasonable rental)* in the northern end of town.

SAUK CENTER, 241.3 *m.* (1,248 alt., 2,716 pop.) *(see Tour 9)*, is at the junction with US 52 *(see Tour 9)*.

US 71 crosses the Kandiyohi County line at 268.1 *m.* "Kandiyohi" is the Sioux name of the habitat of the buffalo fish, which spawn in the nearby rivers during May and June.

At 272.3 *m.* is the junction with State 23.

Right on State 23 to SIBLEY STATE PARK, 1.2 *m. (hiking, camping, picnics, water recreation)*, 365 acres of virgin red cedar and hardwood on the shores of LAKE ANDREW. In the early days this was a favorite feeding ground for elk, and here General Sibley, first Governor of Minnesota, for whom the park is named, spent much time hunting.

A noticeable feature of the landscape is MOUNT TOM (alt. 1,372), a morainic hill. The park, which is included in the Mongolia game refuge, where grouse, pheasants, and prairie chickens abound, has three lakes within its boundaries.

NEW LONDON, 276.8 *m.* (1,281 alt., 483 pop.), a charming little village, is built around the mill ponds formed by the MILL DAM that was started before the Indian outbreak of 1862 and finished in 1865. These ponds, with their many islands, peninsulas, and needle points, lie half-hidden among the hills in this wooded, semi-wild country. The area is part of a great glacial moraine extending for 40 miles.

Between New London and Willmar US 71 crosses scenic lake country.

The clear greenish-tinged water and the heavily timbered shore line of GREEN LAKE, 278.9 *m.*, were admired by the early explorers of the region. They were accustomed to the beauties of nature, but this expanse of water and the rare loveliness of its setting led them to linger and share in the early settlement of the area. Green Lake is now a popular summer resort; the native beauty of its shores remains unspoiled.

At 289.9 *m.* is the WILLMAR STATE HOSPITAL for mental cases

(L), a secluded colony of 1,394 patients. It has red-roofed, vine-covered stucco buildings, attractive gardens, broad and well-lighted private streets, a private auditorium, a bakery, and its own water and lighting systems.

WILLMAR, 291.9 *m.* (1,131 alt., 6,173 pop.) *(see Tour 10)*, is at the junction with US 12 *(see Tour 10)*.

Through Renville County the highway traverses an expanse of broad, undulating prairie land.

OLIVIA, 317.3 *m.* (1,076 alt., 1,475 pop.), seat of Renville County, named by a railroad official for one of his friends, is at the junction with US 212 *(see Tour 11)*. Here (L) is a TOURIST PARK *(free camping, running water, pavilion)*.

At 327.7 *m.* is a junction with a county road.

Left on this road to BIRCH COULEE STATE PARK, 2 *m.* *(camping, picnicking)*, established in 1895, and containing 80 acres. The drive along the winding hill by the brooklet is usually delightfully cool. The park commemorates the battle fought with the Sioux during the uprising of 1862, when about 160 United States troopers were attacked, and more than a third of that number killed or wounded. Several markers indicate the sites of battles *(see below: LOWER AGENCY)*.

At 328.3 *m.* on US 71 is the junction with State 19.

Left on State 19 to MORTON, 0.5 *m.* (845 alt., 756 pop.). At the quarry of the Cold Springs Granite Company, the largest in Renville County, is a boom derrick with a 120-foot mast and a boom swing of 200 feet, whose hoist will lift 100 tons of stone. It is the largest derrick of its kind in Minnesota. Beautiful banded granite-gneiss is quarried here.

At 1.5 *m.*, high on a bluff, are two tall MONUMENTS erected in memory of the Indians who remained friendly to the whites during the outbreak.

At 3 *m.*, on the north bank of the Minnesota River, a marker points to the SITE OF AN AMBUSH where Capt. John Marsh, an interpreter, and 46 men were attacked by the Sioux *(see below: LOWER AGENCY)*.

At 333.4 *m.* US 71 crosses the MINNESOTA RIVER into Redwood County. The bluffs along the river are from 175 to 200 feet high, and the river valley is about 2 miles wide. In the late glacial period the River Warren, draining ancient Lake Agassiz, eroded the covering and exposed the granite for a distance of 16 miles along the Minnesota, northwest of where the highway crosses it. To the southeast the exposures are smooth and rounded, and the upper surfaces show grooves and pot holes caused by the rushing water of this mighty stream, which no doubt filled the entire valley.

At 333.6 *m.* is the junction with a dirt road, marked by a sign pointing to the Bishop Whipple Mission.

Left on this road to an active INDIAN AGENCY, 0.5 *m.*, of about 1,000 acres. Twenty-five or thirty families of Mdewakanton Sioux live here; their children attend a regular district school with white children, and most of them continue in high school at Pipestone or Flandrau.

At 3 *m.* are the remains of a building of the old LOWER AGENCY (L). The stone in this well-preserved building, which now serves as a farmhouse, is 2½ feet thick. On this site occurred the first attack in the Sioux uprising of 1862.

The smouldering resentment of the Minnesota Sioux flamed into actual insurrection at the Lower Agency on the morning of August 18, 1862, and within a few weeks nearly 500 whites had been killed.

When the settlers began pouring into the Minnesota Valley the treaties ratified in 1852 proved not entirely satisfactory either to settlers or to Indians. The settlers wanted Minnesota for a white man's country. The Indians, on the other hand, wanted to continue their old manner of living. They had signed the treaties, but with little understanding of terms, and with no conception at all of . the private ownership of land.

Most of them had moved unresistingly to the lands reserved for them by the Government along the upper Minnesota, where the Upper and Lower Agencies had been established at the mouth of the Yellow Medicine River and near Redwood Falls. The Government's intention was to make farmers of the Sioux. Although there was plenty of good farming land within these reserves, most of the Sioux were not ready for agriculture and with the loss of so much of their good hunting grounds it was extremely difficult for them to find food. The natural result was that more and more they tended to roam beyond bounds. The settlers, on the whole, rarely felt active antagonism toward their red visitors although the constant begging and occasional thefts were sources of considerable annoyance. Some whites, however, never lost their apprehension, and their fears had been greatly augmented by the Inkpaduta Massacre. This had happened in 1857, when a small band of renegade Sioux had murdered more than 30 persons across the Iowa Line, and in their retreat to South Dakota had killed several Minnesota settlers near Spirit Lake in Jackson County. Although this band had been outlawed by their own kinsmen, the memory and horror lingered in white minds, while the fact that the leader, Inkpaduta, escaped unpunished led the Sioux to discount the military power of the Great White Father.

By 1862 the dissatisfaction of the Indians was widespread. Forced to depend on the treaty agreements and farming for their subsistence, they asserted that these agreements were being violated by the whites. Especially did they resent the manner in which their money was handled. Agency traders, who repeatedly issued supplies on credit, were paid by Indian agents from the Government allotments even when the Indians protested that the bills were inaccurate. Food distributed by Government contractors was often short in weight and unfit to eat. Medicine men were particularly hostile; with growing alarm, they observed that tribesmen were adopting the religion of the white man. All this was aggravated by the failure of the Indian corn crop in 1861.

Early in the summer of 1862 the Upper Agency Indians assembled to receive their annual payments. Although supplies were in the warehouse, the agent, following a precedent, refused to issue them until the gold payment was received. But the gold was delayed owing to the exigencies of financing the Civil War. A threatened demonstration was quickly quelled by soldiers, and the Indians were appeased for the time being by a small issue of food. Protests continued. Then occurred an incident that transformed a smouldering resentment into a desperate attempt at reprisal and vengeance.

On Sunday, August 17, four "blanket" Indians, members of a small band of malcontents then roving about in Acton Township (Meeker County), became involved in a truculent discussion of cowardice; the question had arisen from a proposed theft of a few eggs. Before the argument was settled, to prove their courage, they killed three white men and two women.

Fearful of the settlers' retaliation, they hurried to the reservation and told their story. An all-night tribal conference resulted in a decision to take the warpath before the whites could inflict the inevitable punishment. They argued that the white men were themselves at war and had left many communities practically defenseless; that these whites could not be very strong for they had recruited a company of half-breeds to help them; that now at last they could drive out the white invaders and resume their ancient mode of life.

Fifteen hundred men made ready for the warpath under the leadership of Little Crow. Traders, clerks, and helpers at the Lower Agency were the first victims. A heroic ferryman carried surviving refugees across the river until he himself was killed.

Bands of Sioux dispatched to Renville County swept through the peaceful German settlements wiping out entire families. Only a few women and children were spared and these were taken captive.

Terrified refugees, escaping through swamp and thicket, brought word of the disaster to Fort Ridgely. Volunteer Capt. John S. Marsh at once set out for the agency with 46 men and an interpreter. Ignorant of Indian warfare, Captain Marsh led his men in close formation to the Redwood Ferry landing. There they were met with a withering fire from ambushed Indians. In an attempt to lead the trapped survivors to shelter across the river, the captain was drowned. Only half of the command lived to make their way back to the fort.

Other bands struck with deadly swiftness at settlements farther away from the agency. In Brown County a group of unarmed Germans started their Monday work with no suspicion of danger. Before nightfall 50 were dead and the survivors were fleeing to New Ulm.

Tuesday was another day of horror. Murders, mostly of fleeing refugees, continued in Renville and Brown counties. In a concerted attack against New Ulm, the Indians did not spare even long-acknowledged white friends. For the next few days the area of slaughter was extended far up the Red River Valley and south almost to the Iowa border. The inhabitants of 23 counties fled to older settlements, some never to return. Folwell states that a region 200 miles long and averaging 50 miles wide was devastated or depopulated.

The crushing of the Sioux outbreak was accomplished in the main by troops from Fort Snelling in training for the Civil War. These were supplemented by volunteers who responded to Governor Ramsey's summons. In charge of the volunteer forces was Henry H. Sibley, who had been asked by the Governor to take command because of his long experience with Indians. Sibley marched his troops up the valley to relieve Fort Ridgely and then used the post as a base of operations. Scouting parties and small detachments were sent out to patrol the countryside and to act as garrisons for the stockades throughout southwest Minnesota. Following the successful defense of Fort Ridgely (August 20-22) and the two battles of New Ulm (August 19-23) came the battle of Birch Cooley (September 2). Although the last encounter had proved more disastrous to the whites than to the Indians, the reinforcement by Sibley's forces the following day caused the Indians to retire up the valley of the Yellow Medicine to a point between the Upper Agency and Wood Lake, 2.5 miles south, from which isolated bands continued their forays, and where, on September 23, the final battle of the Sioux uprising was fought. Many of the hostile chiefs then set off for North Dakota with their adherents, a goodly number of whom escaped General Sibley's insufficient punitive force. In a few days nearly 2,000 Indians, the majority women and children, were under guard. Two hundred and sixty-nine white captives were turned over to Sibley at Camp Release. Arrests of the Indians continued, and by November 5 a military commission of 5 officers had tried nearly 500 prisoners, of whom 321 were found guilty; 303 were condemned to death. That only 38 were hanged was owing to President Lincoln's commutation of the sentences of all but those proved guilty of murder and rape (see Tour 12: MANKATO). This leniency was largely the result of the efforts of Bishop Henry Benjamin Whipple, who Folwell states was the "one public man in Minnesota not subjugated by the passion of the hour."

When Congress assembled in December 1862, steps were taken for the drastic punishment of Minnesota's Sioux. All treaties were abrogated, land grants and annuities annulled, their reservations sold and the money used to pay the damages. In May 1863 all but 25 families, known to be "friendlies," were transported from the State. A number of the descendants of these families still live here.

At 3.3 m. is the SITE OF THE OLD INDIAN MISSION (L), in the middle of a pasture near the road. A box-elder tree has grown in the center of the ruins.

At 336.3 m. is the SITE OF LITTLE CROW'S VILLAGE (marked). Little Crow was the leader of the agitation that led to the serious Sioux outbreak of 1862.

REDWOOD FALLS, 339.7 m. (865 alt., 2,552 pop.), seat of Redwood County, is on a high bank of the Redwood River, now a shipping center for granite quarried in the vicinity and extensively used for building throughout the United States. The town is near the site of the old steamboat landing, where boats came up the mouth of the Redwood River and unloaded supplies that were carried by ox team to Williston, N. Dak. Parks, rivers, gorges, and bluffs surround this beautiful place. The river drops 140 feet in 3 miles, in a series of falls and rapids, between gently rolling hills of clay till, a glacial moraine deposit.

At the northwestern edge of Redwood Falls lies the ALEXANDER RAMSEY STATE PARK, often called a miniature Yellowstone. Its 200 acres embrace winding streams, deep gorges, picturesque rock cliffs, groves, attractive drives, and a zoo. Beautiful RAMSEY FALLS is within the park. The cliffs contain substances such as kaolin, which investigators have studied with a view to commercial use. Several attempts to manufacture paint from the clay have met with fair success.

The Indian name for the Redwood River is "Tschan-chiyapi" *(river by the tree that is painted red)*. The following legend explains its origin: A party of Sioux, while camping near Redwood almost 300 years ago, discovered that a band of strange Indians had come down the river. They feared that these Indians might occupy a strategic point on the Minnesota and Redwood Rivers and cut off travel on those waterways. The Sioux marked the trail to the camp of the strangers by putting red paint on the trees, and subsequently they attacked and defeated the intruders. After the battle they painted a tree at the spot, and for several years continued to repaint it in commemoration of the successful battle.

At 363.3 *m.* is the junction with US 14 *(see Tour 12)*.

SANBORN, 365.3 *m.* (1,099 alt., 525 pop.), is in the diversified, rich farming and dairying belt. The country has many rolling hills of glacial origin, where bare rocks are frequently exposed. A TOURIST CAMP *(camping, running water)* is in the southern section of town on the bank of the Cottonwood River.

At 389.2 *m.* is the junction with State 60.

Left on State 60 to MOUNTAIN LAKE, 10.4 *m.* (1,350 alt., 1,388 pop.), the home of a Mennonite colony that migrated to this country from Russia, where it had gone from Germany. Of the 254 families living here, 191 are Mennonites, conspicuous for the simplicity of their life and of their dress. Their confession of faith, adopted in a conference at Holland in 1632, enjoins the practice of footwashing, intermarriage only with members of the same faith, and nonresistance to violence. They do not believe in infant baptism, refuse to take oaths, accept no public offices except those connected with school, and strictly observe all church holidays, which are celebrated as family days. The Mennonites have five churches, and the combined congregations have built a HOSPITAL, NURSES' HOME, and HOME FOR THE AGED. During the spring they hold a music festival in which all the choirs unite. They serve *borscht,* a well-spiced Russian beet soup. *Porzelchen,* raised cakes fried in deep fat, are a special New Year's dish.

WINDOM, 390 *m.* (1,359 alt., 2,133 pop.), seat of Cottonwood County, was named for William Windom (1829–1894), distinguished statesman and member of the Cabinets of Presidents Garfield and Harrison. Just before the bridge over the Des Moines River is the fine ISLAND PARK MUNICIPAL TOURIST CAMP *(cabins, $1.00).*

Right from Windom on State 60 to HERON LAKE, 12 *m.*, the largest lake in southwestern Minnesota—11 miles long and 2.5 miles wide. To its marshy shores come numbers of wild geese, ducks, other water-fowl, and sportsmen. Chinese ring-necked pheasants, prairie chickens, and several other game birds are numerous in this region. During recent years efforts have been made by various organizations to conserve the game by protecting their eggs and supplying food for the birds in winter. There is an abundance of small animals in the vicinity, including mink, muskrat, weasel, badger, fox, coyote, skunk, wildcat, and gopher.

At 13 *m.* is HERON LAKE (1,423 alt., 786 pop.), whose inhabitants are mostly German and Irish farmers, with an intermixture of Slavs and Scandinavians. Only a few settlers had homes near the lake before 1870, but, when it was rumored that a railroad was to be laid out, a town named Sibley was planned near the present town of Heron Lake, and a store was built but later abandoned.

In 1871 John T. Smith and C. H. Carroll built a general store, and a well was dug in the middle of the main street; the town grew and one year later it had a population of 50. Since it was the only railroad town for many miles around, its retail trade came from great distances, and the settlers visioned its growth into a city.

Then, on June 14, 1873, swarms of grasshoppers appeared, the beginning of the grasshopper scourge. A light harvest was gathered that fall, but conditions grew steadily worse until 1877, when not a green leaf was left in the area. The grass-hoppers came in clouds so thick that they hid the sun and flew down to the earth at night with a sound like roaring wind. They were piled up to a depth of 1 or 2 feet; horses could hardly be driven through them, and railroad trains were block-aded. Immigration ceased and many people left, never to return. Some lacked even the railroad fare with which to leave and could not sell their land, as it was value-less. A few tried to make a living by trapping, and many sought employment in other counties. In 1877 the grasshoppers providentially disappeared, and the region has not been troubled by them since.

Between this point and Jackson, US 71 crosses a high plateau of gently rolling surface with a cover of glacial drift, so deep that no underlying rocks protrude—an area well suited to agricultural production. The soil is extremely fertile, and its ability to resist drought is remarkable. In very dry weather a thin crust forms on the surface but does not pack firmly enough to interfere with plant growth. As soon as the frost leaves the ground in the spring, the loam is free from water and ready for cultivation.

At 410.8 *m.* is the junction with US 16 *(see Tour 13)*. Between this point and Jackson, US 16 and US 71 are united.

JACKSON, 440.5 *m.* (1,485 alt., 2,206 pop.) *(see Tour 13)*, is at the junction with US 16 *(see Tour 13)*.

At 421 *m.* US 71 crosses the Iowa Line, 41 miles north of Spencer, Iowa *(see Iowa, Tour 7)*.

<<<<<<<<<<<<<<<<<<<☼>>>>>>>>>>>>>>>>>>>

Tour 3

Junction with US 53—Hibbing—Grand Rapids—Minneapolis—Mankato
—Blue Earth—Elmore (Fort Dodge, Iowa); US 169.
Junction with US 53 to Iowa Line, 367.9 m.

This route is paralleled by Great Northern Ry. between Virginia and Grand Rapids
and between Milaca and Minneapolis; and by Chicago, St. Paul, Minneapolis and
Omaha Ry. between Minneapolis and Iowa Line.
Paved roadbed between junction with US 53 and Grand Rapids, bituminous-treated
between Grand Rapids and Onamia, paved between Onamia and Iowa Line. Open
all year.
Accommodations adequate.

This route, between the western region of the Arrowhead and the
eastern part of the Paul Bunyan resort region, includes the iron mines of
the Mesabi Range with the towns their wealth created; it traverses the
scenic country of northern Minnesota's lake district, industrial Minneapolis, and the agricultural belt of southern Minnesota.

Along the highway are the iron mines of the Mesabi Range and the
towns where live the miners, mine officials, professional men, and tradesmen. Since all of these towns owe their origin to a common industry, they
have few distinguishing differences other than their size. Yet together they
offer a definitely characteristic type of village and small city, in a setting
that is not found anywhere else in the country.

The open-pit mines at the edges of these communities are of spectacular
interest. The red and purple sides of these great craters in the earth descend
for hundreds of feet in uneven terraces. Winding up from the depths in a
spiral path over a network of steel trackage, one after another come the
long chains of hopper-bottomed ore cars, hauled from terrace to terrace
by puffing locomotives. At the base of the crater, huge power shovels, like
rhythmically moving monsters, scoop out the red earth 5 tons to a bite,
and load it on waiting empties. Masses of strippings and ore stock piled
above the terraces intensify still further the feeling of vastness and depth.
From the observation platform, through the rising, red dust clouds, the
men, cars, and shovels seem like marionette performers in the first scenes
of the drama of steel-making.

Local taxation of mining properties has enabled all of the range towns
to carry out great civic improvements. Almost unprecedented public spend-
ing has provided waterworks; electric, gas, and heating plants; cement
pavements, community houses, hospitals, municipal golf courses, libraries,
public conservatories, indoor swimming pools, ice-skating rinks, auditoriums, parks, and the "most lavish school system in the world," almost
simultaneously or in rapid succession. Not only are the school buildings
and their equipment the envy of all schoolmen, but teachers are paid high

salaries, instruct only small classes, and have every facility placed at their command.

Minnesota's range-town officials, with money enough for any civic project, have never had to face meetings of thrifty taxpayers. These communities have never felt any urge to economy since they well know that a half dozen or so mine owners are obliged by law to bear over 90 per cent of the local tax burden. As might be expected, it has not been with either enthusiasm or complaisance that the mining companies have relinquished the millions thus devoted to public projects. Mine taxation has been repeatedly a hard-fought issue in State politics and has long been contested on the floors of the State legislature.

During the busy years in which Minnesota as a whole was developing from a wilderness, there was nothing to indicate that the present sites of these mining towns were ever to be anything more than stretches of pine, destined like so many others to be cut over and left in stumps and slashings. Then in 1890 came the discovery of iron ore on the Mesabi Range (see INDUSTRIAL DEVELOPMENT: MINING).

When test pits revealed the presence of the ore throughout the district, a railroad was completed to the head of the Great Lakes (the first shipment was made in 1892), and the Mesabi boom was on. Villages were necessary to supply the needs of miners and railroad workers. Both Hibbing and Virginia were literally chopped out of the forest. Trees were cut down to make room for the buildings and sidewalks into which they were converted. At the very outset of their history came the economic disasters of 1893. Many financial leaders lost their fortunes; investors were compelled to relinquish holdings which they knew to be worth potential millions; workers who had helped to construct the railroad received their pay in warrants which were worthless until many months later. But neither financial panics nor fires could retard permanently the development of the mines.

Although bitter feuds between lumberjacks and miners were common in the early nineties, a tacit understanding existed between roisterers and police authorities. One officer during the most turbulent years went unarmed into even the roughest frays. Jail was accepted cheerfully as a sobering institution, the natural accompaniment of the pay-day's sport. The killing of a bartender by a "husky" was regarded merely as an incident.

Into this rip-roaring melting pot, labor agencies dumped Slavs, Finns, Germans, Scandinavians, Latins, Greeks, English, and Celts. Praying, swearing, and love-making were carried on in 20 different languages and dialects. During this period the schools were confronted with a most difficult situation. The parents of most of the children had never learned to read or write, many pupils had never heard a word of English in their homes, and some knew no accepted language, and used only the polyglot patois of a Balkan borderland. The very multiplicity of languages, however, proved to be a flux in the melting pot. With so many mother tongues, English was agreed upon as a common medium of communication. Today the Slavic type is seen everywhere on the range, but it is only among the older people that traces of the Old World culture persist.

Homes in the range towns are of three or four distinct types. The spacious mansions of the mine executives are readily distinguishable from the comfortable residences of the higher salaried mine employees and the business and professional men; more humble are the neat houses and gardens of the domestically established laborers; and scattered everywhere, but chiefly on the outskirts, are the swarming neighborhoods of typical mining-town shacks. But even the smallest cottage, however dreary its exterior, is equipped with electricity, water, plumbing, gas, and, it may be, with municipal heat; and from it the family steps into its own community center where games, dances, lectures, and music are provided for the amusement and participation of both old and young.

Today, as the range towns approach maturity, they are developing yet another asset. Already many show indications of becoming centers of an important dairying business.

Sec. a. JUNCTION with US 53 to MINNEAPOLIS, 237.2 m. US 169.

At the junction of US 169 and US 53 is VIRGINIA, 0 m. (1,537 alt., 11,963 pop.), the second largest municipality of the three Minnesota iron ranges. Platted in 1892 by the Virginia Improvement Company, when the Mesabi boom was at its height, the town was named for the home State of the company's president.

Eager buyers, many of whom had not seen the region, paid from $300 to $400 for small business sites at the public sale held in Duluth in 1892.

Pine was slashed out along Chestnut St., rough buildings were put up, and lumbermen, investors, lumberjacks, and cruisers flocked in. The erection of a small portable mill on the east side of the lake marked the beginning of industry.

The village was burned to the ground in 1893 but was rebuilt immediately. A second fire in 1900 burned everything but two hotels. Incorporated as a full-fledged city in 1894, by 1895 it had a population of 3,647, and reached its peak of 14,022 in 1920. It was one of the first cities in the State to adopt a commission form of government.

The extension of the railroad into pine lands far to the north made the city one of the leading sawmill towns of northern Minnesota. Although lumbering here has long since lost its industrial importance, a single company has a daily output of 35,000 feet of pine. More than 20 iron mines, both underground and open-pit, have made Virginia primarily a mining city. The MISSABE MOUNTAIN MINE, at the end of Chestnut St., is one of the largest open-pit mines in the world and ships about 7,000 tons of ore a day.

Finns form a large portion of the mining population. A group of them early formed a Finnish Temperance Society. The Finnish and Scandinavian interest in co-operative effort is evident in Virginia's five co-operatives.

A trade center for 50,000 persons, Virginia has 264 retail establishments, a number of small manufactories, 2 privately owned creameries, 2 foundries, and 2 machine shops.

The ROOSEVELT HIGH SCHOOL, 5th Ave. S. and 2nd St., completed in 1929, is designed in the Gothic style. The JUNIOR HIGH SCHOOL, 5th Ave. S. and 3rd St., has an auditorium with a seating capacity of 1,500 and is equipped with sound-movie apparatus. Both have swimming pools.

The school system—financed, like all the range towns' municipal undertakings, by a heavy tax on mining properties—employs a full-time dentist, part-time doctor, and full-time nurse, and provides special classes for the deaf, the undernourished, and exceptional pupils. The music department offers free instruction in all phases of music and free use of many types of musical instruments.

The MEMORIAL BUILDING, 3rd Ave. S. and 1st St., commemorates local men who died in the World War. This $500,000 building contains 50,000 feet of floor space. The main floor is used for dancing during the summer; in winter it is flooded for skating and hockey. The basement contains a 7-lane curling rink, a 450-guest dining room with kitchens, and a women's clubroom.

The community has four musical organizations—a municipal band, municipal symphony orchestra, high school band, and high school orchestra. Weekly winter concerts are held in the Technical School Building; in summer, concerts are given on Wednesdays in South Side Park and on Sundays in Olcott Park.

OLCOTT PARK, at N. 9th St. and 9th Ave., contains approximately 40 landscaped acres and a Zoo.

US 169 branches west from US 53 *(see Tour 5)* at the northern edge of Virginia.

At 3.2 *m.* is the junction with a county road.

Left on this road to the junction with another road 0.2 *m.;* L. on this road to the WACOOTA MINE, 0.3 *m.,* an active open-pit.

In MOUNTAIN IRON, 3.8 *m.* (1,510 alt., 1,349 pop.), the school buildings are among the finest in the State.

LUCKNOW, 10.8 *m.,* is a small village.

Right from Lucknow on a county road to KINNEY, 1.5 *m.* (737 pop.), where an active OPEN-PIT MINE has yielded over 6 million tons of ore.

BUHL, 11.7 *m.* (1,500 alt., 1,634 pop.), primarily a mining community, has eight mines, the majority open-pit, operating in the vicinity. The WABIGON, now inactive, holds the record for cheap mining, for, after the overburden was removed by electric machinery, a crew averaging five men a day took out 500,000 tons of ore in two seasons. This was the first open-pit mine on the Mesabi to be completely electrified; it used a power shovel with a dipper capacity of 14 tons. The school district was the first on the Mesabi to build an elaborate high school, an imposing building easily seen when approchiang Buhl from any direction.

At 16.7 *m.* is the junction with a county road.

Right on this road to the SHENANGO MINE, 0.5 *m.,* both open pit and underground; the lowest level is about 300 feet.

CHISHOLM, 17.4 *m.* (1,492 alt., 8,308 pop.), on the shore of LONG-

YEAR LAKE *(bathing beach, tourist camp, zoo)*, has five active mines. Since the Mesabi Range was first opened, 45 mines have shipped ore from the Chisholm district.

Chisholm holds the distinction of having the largest school enrollment in proportion to its population of any community in the State. Its educational system ranks with those of the leading range towns.

Finns, attracted to the range by mining operations, are the largest group in the foreign population. It is estimated that in this district there are 60,000 Finns, principally in St. Louis, Itasca, Carlton, and Wadena counties.

HIBBING, 25.3 *m.* (1,527 alt., 15,666 pop.), although the largest municipality on the Mesabi, Vermilion, and Cuyuna Iron Ranges, prefers, for technical reasons, to retain its original village form of government.

The town was platted in 1893 by a lumber company on a part of the township called "North 40," now the rapidly vanishing North Hibbing, and was incorporated 4 months later. A portable sawmill was hauled through the forest and set up; amid the stumps, stores and houses arose.

Progress at first was slow; supplies had to be hauled over roads and streets that were a morass of mud and slush, or piled high with drifted snow; preference was given to fodder for the horses and oxen used in railroading, mining, and logging, so deficiencies in the family larders were made up by the addition of wild game; the nearest available drinking water, except for a limited supply at one of the test pits, was at Carson Lake, over 3 miles away. Typhoid was common.

A burst of municipal pride in 1895 resulted in the purchase of the light and water systems installed the previous year by Capt. Frank Hibbing, for whom the village was named. To achieve this purchase 1,100 votes were cast by a recorded population of 1,085, with an enfranchised citizenry of less than 300. Perhaps similar conditions prevailed 4 years later when the furor that followed the installation of a sewer system culminated in the hurried departure of the mayor who had fathered the plan.

Miners and lumberjacks, men from nearly every country in Europe, swarmed to the town. Saloons outnumbered the stores. In the "snake rooms" adjoining the bars, many of the patrons slept off their drunkenness on the floors, pillowed on their baggage. Foremen looked over the huskies crowded in these rooms to pick their crews, and then herded them into camps and mines. One saintly Lutheran clergyman, failing in his search for a friendly home to shelter him on his first visit, was taken in by a bartender who furnished him a sleeping place on the floor of his already crowded saloon.

A school was started in a store in 1893 but was housed in a building of its own the following year. Here the pupils received what was to most of them their first taste of American culture.

Between 1898 and 1900 the substantial sawmill of the Swan River Lumber Company replaced the original portable. A mile east of the town 1,500 men were sheltered in a single camp. Logs were transported to Hibbing by rail or by steam-haulers and lumber was shipped out by rail to Swan

Lake, the first leg of the journey that would send it floating down the Mississippi.

By 1900 the town was so prosperous that, seeking to dispose of a substantial sum raised for charity, a committee could find only three or four individuals in the entire village who needed help, and they were widows.

An event of 1900 was the inauguration of the Hibbing Fair, now the annual St. Louis County Fair.

When valuable ore was found under Hibbing's streets, an iron company bought the land and in 1919 moved the village to its present location, a mile farther south. Towed by log-haulers, churches were slowly moved down the street—spires, pews, and decorations all intact. Buildings were sometimes cut into sections. Christ Memorial Church was moved stone by stone and rebuilt after Cass Gilbert's original plan. Graves were "reverently scooped up with steam shovels," and the occupants given a new resting place.

This moving of the village, a slack season in the mines, and the failure of a would-be automobile agent to sell a single car, resulted in the establishment of the Northland-Greyhound lines, a nucleus of the Greyhound Lines Inc. Carl Eric Wickman, failing as a salesman, started a small livery service between old and new Hibbing, and into the range district. Soon he and Andrew G. Anderson had established the first motorbus route outside of New York City.

The HIBBING HIGH SCHOOL building, Mesaba St. between 7th and 9th Sts., was completed in 1921. This $4,000,000 structure is E-shaped, with a frontage of 596 feet. The main corridor section, or north wing, contains classrooms, laboratories, and offices; the south wing has a study hall, library, auditorium, two gymnasiums, an indoor running-track, and a swimming pool. Equipment for industrial work includes an electrical laboratory, machine shop, automotive and aeronautics shops, forge and foundry shops, home economics and sewing rooms, a greenhouse, and an industrial-art room. The auditorium has a seating capacity of 1,805, a $25,000 pipe organ, and a stage 40 by 60 feet with electrically controlled settings and unusual lighting effects. The interior of the building is decorated with murals of history and industry.

The PARK SCHOOL, between North and South Hibbing, known as the "Glass School" because of its large wall areas of structural glass, is a four-room building designed by J. C. Taylor. An electric eye controls the lighting and the venetian blinds. The desks are movable so that they can be grouped informally.

The WAR SERVICE MEMORIAL BUILDING, Josephine St. between 4th and 6th Sts. *(open daily 8 a.m. to 5 p.m.)*, covers an entire block. Within are the Memorial Hall, the arena with bowling alleys, and curling club quarters that have a seven-lane rink and a spectators' gallery, and the Labor Temple. The arena has a terrazzo floor that can be converted into a hockey rink with space for 2,400 spectators, or into a basketball court accommodating 5,000.

A radio station, WMFG, Androy Hotel, 5th Ave. and Howard St., owned and operated by the Head of the Lakes Broadcasting Company, is in Hibbing. The ore deposits interfere to some extent with radio reception and broadcasting.

Hibbing's MAIN LIBRARY, 703 3rd Ave. N., built in 1916 of Kettle River pink sandstone, is decorated with murals and paintings and has a bookmobile that carries books to all the outlying districts of Stuntz Township.

The VILLAGE HALL, 4th Ave., South Hibbing *(open daily 8 a.m. to 5 p.m.)*, of red finishing brick, is modeled after Faneuil Hall in Boston and houses all the departments of municipal administration. There are four murals of the history of Minnesota and of the mining industry; two others symbolize Law and Justice.

Hibbing maintains six municipal parks. Of these the 47-acre BENNETT PARK, 3rd Ave. and Park St., is completely developed. In the eastern section is the administration building of the park department; adjacent are the municipal greenhouses; two are showhouses, and three supply the plants and flowers used to beautify all public parks and buildings as well as to furnish decorations free of charge for public events, or for church holidays. In the greenhouses are held annual Easter exhibits, a chrysanthemum show in November, and an exhibition of roses, poinsettias, and cyclamen at Christmas. Also in the eastern section of the park is a Zoo. A Winter Sports Frolic is held in Bennett Park every February.

At 33.6 *m.* US 169 crosses the Itasca County line. At the present time (1937) this county has more than 2,000 miles of improved highways. Yet only a few years ago, when removal of pine timber was the main industry, there were almost no roads other than rude tote trails built and maintained by the logging interests, over which supplies were hauled to the camps. Communication in the summer was mainly by lakes and streams. During the winter season the tote roads followed direct routes, crossing swamps, lakes, and rivers on the ice.

At KEEWATIN, 34.3 *m.* (1,505 alt., 2,134 pop.), large ore reserves were discovered about 1904, but the village developed quite slowly until 1909, when its mining became more active. Keewatin's early operations were at the St. Paul and Mississippi mines. Later came the Bray, the Bennet, the Sargent, and, within more recent years, the Mesabi Chief. Mines at Keewatin during the recent depression years have been maintained better than many others in Minnesota by reason of their diversity of ownership and their type of operation.

At 34.8 *m.* is the junction with a county road.

Right on this road to the MESABI CHIEF MINE, 0.5 *m.*

US 169 passes under a bridge, and at 34.9 *m.* is a junction with a country road.

Left on this road to the MESABI CHIEF WASHING PLANT, 0.3 *m. (open by permission);* here sand and other foreign material are washed out of the native ore.

NASHWAUK, 38.9 *m.* (1,500 alt., 2,555 pop.). In 1902, where the village of Nashwauk now stands, was a large logging camp. Then iron ore was discovered and Nashwauk was founded. At first comprising only a few straggling houses and stores, it developed with astounding rapidity. Nashwauk's first mining wealth came from the early operations of three properties, the Hawkins, Crosby, and Larue mines. Later others were developed, and Nashwauk became one of the important mining communities on the Mesabi Range.

COOLEY, 40.9 *m.* (368 pop.), has a MAGNETIC SEPARATING PLANT *(open to visitors)* to free the ore from foreign material.

CALUMET, 45.8 *m.* (1,400 alt., 805 pop.), newest of the Mesabi communities, is centered around the operations of the Hill Annex Mine *(see below)*.

Calumet's main thoroughfare is Gary St.

1. Right from Calumet on Gary St. to the junction with a dirt road, 0.2 *m.;* R. on this road to the junction with another dirt road, 0.5 *m.;* L. on this road to the HILL ANNEX MINE, 1.3 *m.*, a large electrified open-pit, which has electric shovels with a capacity of 10 cubic yards. The entire mine is visible from the road.

2. Left from Calumet on Gary St. to the junction with a dirt road, 0.3 *m.;* L. on this road to the HILL-TRUMBULL WASHING PLANT, about 1 *m.*

At 47.7 *m.* on US 169 is the junction with a country road at the outskirts of Marble.

Right on this road to the junction with a dirt road, 0.3 *m.;* L. on this road to the ARCTURUS MINE, 2 *m.*, an active open-pit.

At 0.5 *m.* on the country road is the HILL-TRUMBULL MINE, an active open-pit.

The village of MARBLE, 47.8 *m.* (738 pop.), was laid out by the Oliver Iron Mining Company for its employees at the Hill Mine. In 1908 the present site of Marble was a dense forest. A year later a modern village with many public improvements had been constructed.

Near TACONITE, 50.6 *m.* (485 pop.), was some of the earliest mining on the Mesabi Range. Experiments at the Diamond mine were carried on in the late 1860's near the present village; the first experimental ore-washing plant on the western Mesabi was erected here.

BOVEY, 52.8 *m.* (1,354 alt., 1,248 pop.), on the northeast corner of TROUT LAKE, is another mining community settled by merchants and others from Nashwauk and Grand Rapids. When it was incorporated, in 1904, it had hardly enough persons to meet the legal requirements of a village government. Within 3 years it had a population of 1,200, and every home and room were occupied by workers engaged in the development of the mines.

The Farmers' Festival held here in summer *(date varies)* is interesting and elaborate.

Here is the junction with a country road.

Left on this road to the TROUT LAKE WASHING PLANT, 2.3 *m.* *(guides available)*, the largest ore-washing plant in the world.

COLERAINE, 53.5 *m.* (1,343 alt., 1,243 pop.), a "model village" on the shores of beautiful Trout Lake between undulating hills, was built by the Oliver Mining Company for its employees. Its public buildings are artistically grouped on wide and well-laid-out streets amid a profusion of flowers and trees. The company financed public improvements and built most of the residences, all different in design and some quite elaborate. The town has a modern hospital, a grade and high school, and a junior college.

Coleraine is a trading center for the nearby agricultural sections where further development may offer a partial solution to the problem of seasonal mining employment.

South of Coleraine US 169 enters the eastern part of the Paul Bunyan region, a forest, lake, and resort area, rising in low rolling hills that gradually flatten toward the west. There are numerous lakes with sandy bottoms and beaches, and sandy loam soil predominates. Most of the timber is second-growth, but a few protected virgin forests still exist.

The divide of watersheds, passing east-west through this region, creates three drainage basins, carrying the waters respectively to Hudson Bay, to the St. Lawrence River, and to the Gulf of Mexico via the Mississippi River.

GRAND RAPIDS, 60.7 *m.* (1,290 alt., 3,206 pop.) *(see Tour 7)*, is at the junction with US 2 *(see Tour 7)*.

Right on 3rd Ave. E. from its intersection with US 169 to the junction with 11th St., 0.7 *m.;* R. on 11th St. to the junction with 12th St., 0.9 *m.;* R. on 12th St. to the junction with a dirt road, 1.2 *m.;* L. on this road to the GREENWAY MINE, 3 *m.,* at the end of the road, an active open-pit.

This region marks the western limit of the Mesabi Range.

In HILL CITY, 78.9 *m.* (1,312 alt., 515 pop.), pails and other wood products are manufactured.

At 84.5 *m.* is the junction with a county road.

Right on this road to the LAND O' LAKES STATE FOREST, 9 *m.,* covering 138,241 acres (gross) and including numerous lakes. The area shows practically no agricultural development but is favorable for timber-growing and recreation.

At 105.4 *m.* is the junction (L) with US 210 *(see Tour 15)*, which for 7.9 miles unites with US 169.

Around AITKIN, 113.3 *m.* (1,205 alt., 1,545 pop.) *(see Tour 15)*, much of the fertile soil has resulted from prehistoric Lake Aitkin, which covered a large area to the north and whose shallow waters were drained by the deep channel of the Mississippi. Bogs and swamps are numerous in the old lake bed. This section of Minnesota rarely suffers from drought; the average rainfall is about 30 inches.

At 127.5 *m.* is the junction with State 18.

Left on State 18, which runs along the lake shore, to a natural high pike formed in centuries past by the waters of MILLE LACS *(tourist camps, cottages, bathing beaches, resorts, fishing, hunting, golf, tennis, horseback riding, and water sports)*. This ridge is in some places 25 feet high and from 16 to 20 feet wide.

Mille Lacs Lake is one of the largest and most beautiful in Minnesota. It has approximately 150 miles of shore line. The region surrounding it is of unusual scenic beauty and contains about one thousand INDIAN MOUNDS.

This is a sportsman's paradise. Wall-eyed and northern pike abound in the lake, as do perch, whitefish, bass, and crappie. Deer, a few bear, quail, grouse, pheasants, and squirrels frequent the wooded regions.

Mille Lacs connects with many smaller lakes and with numerous streams, including the beautiful Rum River, once an important logging waterway. Many ruins and relics of the old logging camps are still visible along its banks. Panfish are abundant in Rum River.

Father Hennepin, a member of La Salle's western expedition, was captured by Sioux Indians during the first exploration of the upper Mississippi Valley, and held prisoner at the Indian village near the southwestern shore of this lake *(see HISTORICAL SURVEY)*. Many legends, both gruesome and romantic, center about Mille Lacs. The lake is said to be inhabited by ghosts, whose white, vague forms are often seen among the trees, and whose low, sighing moans are heard at night. The Indians and many settlers in the vicinity believe that these moaning forms are the souls of Indian warriors who died in battle.

MALMO, 13.1 *m.* (50 pop.), is at the junction with State 56; R. on State 56 to the junction with State 27, 22.1 *m.;* R. on State 27, which continues around Mille Lacs, providing excellent views of the lake.

South of GARRISON, 132.7 *m.* (25 pop.), a summer resort, US 169 follows the western shore of Mille Lacs for almost 19 miles. Handiwork can be purchased from the Indians who display their wares along the road. The baskets and souvenirs are hung on lines running between trees and are most colorful against the background of foliage.

At VINELAND, 142.1 *m.,* is an INDIAN TRADING POST *(visitors welcome)* with an interesting collection of Indian weapons, buckskin work, basketry, and beadwork; many of these are for sale, as are furs, wildrice, and maple sugar. More than 300 Chippewa make this post their headquarters.

During the summer, squaws bend over charcoal fires and small Indian children play with primitive toys beside their low willow huts, to which they move for the tourist trade. Sometimes these shelters are covered with birchbark, but as often they are little more than willow frames with branches laid across the top.

The Indians hold a Rice Dance here every September before the harvesting of wildrice begins *(see Tour 5: NETT LAKE).*

ONAMIA, 153.6 *m.* (1,260 alt., 514 pop.), touches the shore of Onamia Lake. At the northern outskirts of this village (R) is CROSIER COLLEGE, a monument to the industry of the Crosier Fathers, who came to Onamia in 1913. The preparatory school and college have 65 students; 7 brothers and 9 community priests occupy the monastery. The order was founded in Belgium in 1211, and the present mother house is at Agatha, Holland. The seminary has been moved to Hastings, Neb. Hastings and Onamia have the only English-speaking branches of this order in existence.

MILACA, 175.2 *m.* (1,072 alt., 1,318 pop.), the seat of Mille Lacs County, is on the shore of the Rum River that flows from Mille Lacs to the Mississippi. The name is a corruption of Mille Lacs.

Left from the highway, at the center of town, is the TOWN HALL, an attractive structure of rustic architecture, constructed by the WPA of salvaged granite stones; above the doorway is a bas-relief whose subject is historical matter of the region. It was executed by Samuel Sabean. In the council room are eight MURAL PANELS by Andre Boratko, depicting phases of the lumbering industry. The murals are enhanced by an unusual wainscoting of knotty pine. Both sculpture and painting were made possible by the Federal Art Project.

The town was started by a lumber company, owned by James J. Hill, which built houses on the site and rented them to its workers. Lumbering has long since been superseded by dairying, now the principal industry.

A TOURIST PARK is in the western part of town. Milaca also has a 9-hole GOLF COURSE *(reasonable fee)*.

PRINCETON, 188.1 *m.* (970 alt., 1,636 pop.), is a shipping center for the agricultural area surrounding it. Its creamery association ships a half-million pounds of butter annually.

In 1862, during the Sioux Indian outbreak, a stockade was erected at Princeton, then the seat of Mille Lacs County.

A TOURIST PARK *(free camping, running water)* is in the center of town on the Rum River.

ELK RIVER, 207.2 *m.* (924 alt., 1,026 pop.) *(see Tour 16)*, is at the junction with US 10 *(see Tour 16)* and US 52 *(see Tour 9)*. Between this point and Anoka, US 169, US 10, and US 52 are united.

ANOKA, 218.7 *m.* (904 alt., 4,851 pop.) *(see Tour 16)*, is at the junction (L) with US 10 *(see Tour 16)*.

MINNEAPOLIS, 237.2 *m.* (812 alt., 464,356 pop.) *(see MINNE-APOLIS)*.

Points of Interest: Minnehaha Falls, University of Minnesota, Chain of Lakes, flour mills at St. Anthony Falls.

Minneapolis is at the junction with US 52 *(see Tour 9)*, US 12 *(see Tour 10)*, US 212 *(see Tour 11)*, US 65 *(see Tour 14)*, and US 8 *(see Tour 19)*.

Sec. b. MINNEAPOLIS *to the* IOWA LINE, *130.7 m. US 169.*

West on Lake St. in Minneapolis from its junction with Lyndale Ave., around the north shore of Lake Calhoun to Excelsior Blvd.; L. on Excelsior Blvd., which US 169 follows. From Lake St. US 169 and US 212 *(see Tour 11)* are united for 17 miles.

At 3.7 *m.* is France Ave., the west city line.

At 19.2 *m.* US 169 branches L. from US 212 *(see Tour 11)*, and at 19.9 *m.* crosses the Minnesota River along whose shores layers of limestone called the Shakopee formation are visible.

SHAKOPEE, 20.1 *m.* (750 alt., 2,023 pop.), seat of Scott County, was named for Chief Shakpa *(Little Six)* of the Dakota Indian band, beside whose village the town was founded in 1851. In 1858, 300 braves fought the "Battle of Shakopee," the last skirmish between Chippewa and Dakota Indians.

At the eastern end of 1st St. is the TAMARACK LOG CABIN built by Oliver Faribault (1819–1851) in 1844. It is still used as a dwelling and stands as originally built except that the logs are covered with unpainted siding. *(Visitors can inspect grounds and view house from outside.)*

Carl Schurz, German writer and statesman who visited Shakopee in 1859, said that this part of the Minnesota River, with its gently sloping banks, was as beautiful as the Rhine. This favorable comparison is thought to have encouraged the heavy German immigration to this territory. The town is built on one of the terraces of the receding glacial river. Several levels are distinguishable along the broad river valley.

Shakopee, the retail center for a diversified farming district, manufactures stoves, bricks, lime, and ironware. It also has a marble works, a bottling plant, and a distillery. The STATE REFORMATORY FOR WOMEN was established here in 1915.

Between Shakopee and Mankato US 169 follows the Minnesota River Valley, a scenic area of tree-bordered river and rolling farm land.

MUDBADEN, 29.6 m., a sulphur- and mud-bath sanitarium, is on the R. of the highway. The sloping hillside bogs result from the heavy growth of moss, sedge, or other vegetation which clogs the seeping water of the springs. The finely pulverized mud used in the treatment is bentonite, an ash believed to have come from a prehistoric volcano.

JORDAN, 31.6 m. (755 alt., 1,119 pop.), was named for the Biblical river. Most of the inhabitants are of German descent. The profits derived from a municipal saloon are sufficient to make local real-estate taxes unnecessary. A canning factory here employs a large number of people.

1. Left from Jordan on the street leading toward the river and the railway station and across the tracks to the SITE OF ST. LAWRENCE, 2.9 m. In anticipation of a real-estate boom that never materialized, Samuel Burton Strait in 1857 built here a sturdy buff limestone HOTEL (L) at a cost of $5,000 in gold coin. The foundation rests on solid limestone, and the three-story structure is a rectangular, hipped-roof affair, laid up in regular-coursed ashlar with a rough-tooled surface. There was a dance hall on the top floor, and the well-fabricated construction made possible very slender interior supports. The important doorways in the hotel were of black walnut, made in Pennsylvania and brought to Minnesota by steamboat. The stone walls taper from 3 feet thick at the bottom to 2 feet at the top, and because of their solidity the old hotel is now used as a barn by the present farmer-owner. At present only the shell remains. Interior woodwork and trim have been removed, and now hay, feed, and harness clutter the space where hotel rooms used to be.

2. Left from Jordan on State 21 to NEW PRAGUE, 9 m. (1,543 pop.), whose main street is the dividing line between Scott and Le Sueur counties. The town was founded by a group of Bohemians seeking a site for settlement. They had been directed by Bishop Cretin at St. Paul to follow the Mississippi River, but followed the Minnesota instead, and settled at what is now New Prague. Dairy farming is the principal industry in the surrounding territory, and the town itself has a flour mill, creamery, foundry, publishing plant, and small stockyard. The annual Southern Minnesota Livestock Show is held here during November.

At 18 m. on State 21 is MONTGOMERY (1,570 pop.), where the Kolacky Day celebration is held annually on September 27. This affair centers around the serving of kolacky, a Bohemian bun made with dried fruit and spice fillings, at a festival that includes sports and other events. Thousands of kolacky buns are served to visitors. Montgomery has a large flour mill and is a canning center.

At 23 m. is the junction with State 99; R. on State 99 to LE CENTER, 29 m. (769 alt., 948 pop.). Originally called Le Sueur Center, it became the county seat after a lengthy dispute with the village of Le Sueur. Ginseng, a valuable herb abundant in this vicinity in pioneer days, was a source of revenue to the settlers when their cultivated crops failed.

On the Le Sueur County Fairgrounds in Le Center is PIONEER HOUSE, a log cabin built in pioneer fashion, and housing a collection of frontier relics (open during day, see caretaker for key to cabin). During the county fair, usually held in August, the cabin is a meeting place for old settlers. At 45 m. State 99 unites with US 169 at St. Peter (see below).

BELLE PLAINE, 39.6 *m.* (728 alt., 1,236 pop.), is named for the beauty of the valley at this point.

On April 9, 1861, a Government agent chartered the *Fanny Harris* to bring troops to St. Paul from Fort Ridgely. Spring floods had converted all the waterways into raging torrents, uprooted houses and fences, and inundated the countryside. At Belle Plaine the boat's officers decided to leave the tortuous channel of the Minnesota River and to pilot the *Fanny Harris* straight across the flooded fields. The boat was nosed toward a place where the bank could be hurdled without serious interference by trees.

The passengers hung on frantically, the throttle was thrown open, the boat flew across the river and cracked into the trees on the shore. No serious damage was done, however, and in a short time she was sailing blithely across the plain. After a 10-mile overland journey, the *Fanny Harris* cut back toward the wooded bank, glided safely through the trees, and steamed on down the channel.

The 300 miles by river from St. Paul to Fort Ridgley were covered in 4 days, a record never since equalled.

LE SUEUR, 54.9 *m.* (757 alt., 1,897 pop.), is named for Pierre Charles Le Sueur, who at the end of the 17th century explored the valley of the Minnesota River *(see HISTORICAL SURVEY)*. On the main street (L), marked by a tablet, is the MAYO HOME, from 1858 to 1863 the residence of Dr. W. W. Mayo (1819–1911), father of Drs. William J. and Charles Mayo of Rochester; William was born in this house in 1861.

The founder of the Mayo Clinic built this story-and-a-half frame house in 1858, while he was still a country doctor. Around the doorway are Greek Revival decorative features. The entrance projects slightly to define the doorway and has a classic entablature with flat pilasters and sidelights. Directly over the entrance is a gable that is actually only an oversized dormer. In other respects the house is very plain, with one projecting bay and only slightly emphasized window heads.

Le Sueur has a large cannery, concrete-block, ice-cream, sugar, and cigar factories, and a creamery.

The MEXICAN VILLAGE in Le Sueur is a collection of tiny, pastel-colored adobe houses built around a court. The Mexicans are mostly single men who migrate from Texas and are willing to work for small wages. In early summer they thin and weed beets; in midsummer they go to the cornfields and snap sweet corn for the canneries. In the fall they return to work in the beet fields before going home for the winter.

At Le Sueur US 169 crosses the Minnesota River.

At 62.8 *m.* (R) is the 5-acre TRAVERSE DES SIOUX STATE PARK *(picnic grounds)* named for the ford where Indians and pioneers crossed the Minnesota River. Near the ford the Treaty of Traverse des Sioux was signed in 1851. By the terms of this treaty with the Upper Bands, and that of Mendota with the Lower Bands, the Indians ceded to the Federal Government a tract estimated at nearly 24 million acres; 19 million were in Minnesota. The amount to be paid the Indians in annuities extending over a period of 50 years has been computed at 12½ cents an acre. Dissatisfaction by the Indians with the manner in which the provisions of the treaties were executed by the Government was one cause of the Sioux war of 1862; after that conflict the annuities were canceled. At the time of the treaty there was a trading post and mission here.

ST. PETER, 64.8 m. (812 alt., 4,811 pop.), was founded in 1853 by Capt. W. B. Dodd (1811–1862), who built the first section of a military road into Minnesota; he was killed at the battle of New Ulm. The city was named for the Minnesota River, formerly called the St. Peter River.

In 1857 the territorial legislature attempted to remove the capital from St. Paul to St. Peter; although the maneuver failed, the building, asserted by many to be the original CAPITOL, prematurely erected by the citizens of St. Peter, stands at 3rd and Walnut Sts. and is marked by a tablet. The bill, passed by both chambers of the legislature, was being held in a council committee for enrollment and for the Governor's signature when Joseph Rolette, chairman of the committee, disappeared, taking the bill with him. Until the assembly was adjourned by constitutional time limitation, he remained in hiding in a hotel room. The Governor thereupon signed a copy of the bill and it was printed with the laws of 1857. But the territorial supreme court nullified the act with the decision that there was no evidence that the bill signed was that passed by the legislature.

The ST. PETER STATE HOSPITAL FOR MENTAL CASES, established here in 1868, is the largest (2,000 patients) of its kind in the State. It was among the first of these hospitals to employ occupational therapy in the treatment of mental diseases. Exquisite needlework done by the patients can be purchased at the office.

In St. Peter is the GUSTAVUS ADOLPHUS COLLEGE. Its 25 acres on the west bank of the Minnesota include the highest land in the town. Established in 1876, this coeducational institution is maintained by the Minnesota Conference of the Augustana Synod of North America. The campus, containing 13 buildings, is landscaped with trees and shrubs and has ample space for tennis courts and ball fields.

Old Main, now a science hall, is built of Kasota stone. It was erected in 1876, and for 8 years was the college's only building. It houses classrooms and a cafeteria.

The auditorium, a brick structure built in 1904–5, has an assembly hall seating 1,000 and contains administrative offices and recreation rooms. The gymnasium, which will seat 2,000, is a handsome edifice of Menominee colonial sand-mold brick, trimmed with marble. The outside dimensions are 112 by 72 feet. It has room for two full-size basketball courts, a cork 20-lap-to-the-mile track, a swimming pool and gallery, dressing rooms, and offices for athletic instructors. The stadium, erected in 1929, seats 3,000, and the gridiron is lighted for night games.

Johnson Hall is a modern fireproof dormitory housing 70 girls. The men's dormitory, a three-story fireproof brick building designed on the Harvard unit plan, has a main hall 174 by 57 feet.

St. Peter was the home of five of Minnesota's Governors: H. A. Swift, Horace Austin, A. R. McGill, A. O. Eberhart, and John A. Johnson; a STATUE OF JOHN A. JOHNSON is on the courthouse grounds.

The city has a woolen mill, an overall factory, and two creameries, and is a livestock-shipping center.

South of St. Peter US 169 again crosses the Minnesota River and at 67.2 *m.* is the junction with a State-aid road.

Right on this road to KASOTA, 0.8 *m.* (811 alt., 593 pop.), where is quarried the Kasota limestone used extensively for building purposes throughout the country (*see INDUSTRIAL DEVELOPMENT: Quarrying*).

MANKATO, 76.4 *m.* (781 alt., 14,038 pop.) (*see Tour 12*), is at the junction with US 14 (*see Tour 12*).

South of Mankato this route closely parallels the Blue Earth River to the Iowa Line, through one of Minnesota's finest agricultural and dairying sections.

At 80.4 *m.* is the 120-acre MINNEOPA (Ind., *two falls*) STATE PARK. Near the highway the TWO WATERFALLS drop 50 feet into a gorge surrounded by high hills. Included in the park is an old stone windmill, designed and erected by Louis Seppman, a stonemason from Westphalia. He started this building in 1862 with funds earned by erecting another mill at Mankato, but because of the Sioux outbreak the construction was not completed until 1864.

The mill, 32 feet high, is of native stone carried by hand and in wheelbarrows up an inclined roadway built to the top from the northwest side. The fourth of the original five stories contained the smut mill, operated from the main driveshaft by a belt and pulley. Two large beveled cogwheels and the millstone were brought from St. Louis, Mo., at a cost of $6,000; the rest of the machinery was home-made.

Although struck several times by lighting, the mill continued to grind flour until 1880 and was used as a feed mill until 1890, when it was severely damaged by a storm.

The Blue Earth Historical Society became interested in its preservation, and in the summer of 1930 the Seppman heirs donated the mill to that organization. The society repaired the most obvious damage and gave the mill and its site to Minneopa State Park in 1931.

GARDEN CITY, 91.4 *m.* (969 alt., 275 pop.), a cluster of 75 frame houses, at the point where US 169 crosses the Watonwan River, is not incorporated. It was chartered as a village until 1905, when the bridge washed out; after this catastrophe the council dissolved, throwing on the county the expense and responsibility of building a new bridge. Through the will of Sir Henry Wellcome, London millionaire who died in July 1936, the hamlet will inherit $400,000. It is provided that $250,000 be used to build a combined library and auditorium and an athletic field. The remaining $150,000 is for maintenance.

The citizens want the athletic field, but have decided that sidewalks, a sewage system, a water system, and an electric light plant would be more useful than the combination library and auditorium.

Wellcome came to Garden City in 1865 with his father, a roving missionary and apothecary, and spent his boyhood here. As a young man he went first to Rochester, Minn., where he became a drug clerk. From

Rochester he moved to Chicago, to Philadelphia, and finally to London, where he established a pharmaceutical supply house and amassed a fortune of 10 million dollars. Research in ethnological and chemical fields took him to South America and later to Africa, where he aided in Stanley's search for Livingstone. He was knighted in 1932, and, in the words of a Garden City oil-station operator, "King George patted him on the head and said he was O.K."

Sir Henry Wellcome always visited Garden City when he was in the United States and, as his will indicates, was extraordinarily attached to the little village. His last visit was in May 1936, two months before his death.

AMBOY, 102.7 m. (1,046 alt., 593 pop.).

Left from Amboy on State 30 to the junction with State 22, 15 m.; R. on State 22 to the OLD HAUNTED MILL, 22 m. (open), a relic that attracts tourists from all parts of the State. Despite the penciled and carved signatures of a thousand visitors, the mill is well preserved.

Coming from Holland in the early 1860's, Gottlieb Shastag settled in this section and took up farming. Needing a mill to grind corn, he undertook to construct one patterned after those in the old country. In the district which is now Mankato, Shastag set to work carving parts for his mill out of trees. He was forced to use the crudest of home-made tools, so the work was slow and laborious. His brother was his only assistant. The pieces of the mill were hauled by ox teams over the open prairie; en route the brothers were threatened by Indians but reached their home in safety; here a "raising bee" was attended by farmers from miles around.

The gears and wheels, some of them 10 feet in diameter, are of hardwood and are fastened together with wooden dowels. The main drive shaft is an oak log 16 inches in diameter. There are 4 fan blades 25 feet long, so built that they can be set by hand to catch the wind. The entire top of the mill can be turned and anchored to hold the blades against the wind. The exterior is a truncated pyramid with horizontal wood siding, strengthened by vertical corner-boards.

For 10 years Shastag served as miller for the entire neighborhood. The mill performed perfectly, but the Indians, frightened by the gyrations and the squeaking of the fan, made several attempts to destroy it.

When his mill showed signs of wear, and competition had taken most of his business, Shastag began to brood, and became obsessed with the idea that a devil, in the form of a black rabbit, had taken up its abode in the mill. To drive out the unwelcome inhabitant, he stood guard, day and night, for two weeks. Local historians say he was successful; to prevent the black rabbit's return, Shastag boarded up three of the doors leading into the building and literally covered the outside walls with signs, warning against entrance upon pain of death. On a fence built around the mill he reiterated his warning against anyone attempting entrance, including his own family. While attempting repairs, he was struck on the head by a revolving fan blade and died a short time later.

WINNEBAGO, 110.9 m. (1,098 alt., 1,701 pop.), a business center for this agricultural region has a corn- and pea-canning factory, a poultry company, two hatcheries, and a co-operative creamery.

Scottish settlers here are said to have introduced the game of curling to Minnesota in the 1850's; they used their wives' flatirons.

In Winnebago was Parker College, a Baptist institution that later belonged to the Methodists. When it was returned recently to the Baptists, they closed the school, but transformed its new dormitory into the BAPTIST HOME FOR THE AGED, a completely modern, comfortable home accommodating about 30; the grounds are neat and attractive.

Across from the Baptist Home, in a well-shaded spot, the Commercial

Club of Winnebago maintains a PUBLIC TOURIST CAMP *(water, light, kitchen, firewood)*.

At 115.4 *m.* is the RIVERSIDE TOWN AND COUNTRY CLUB *(9 holes, reasonable fee)*, halfway between Winnebago and Blue Earth and shared by the two communities.

BLUE EARTH, 120.1 *m.* (1,086 alt., 2,884 pop.) *(see Tour 12)*, is at the junction with US 16 *(see Tour 13)*.

ELMORE, 130.2 *m.* (1,130 alt., 744 pop.). In August 1855 Crawford W. Wilson came from Iowa. He was the first settler in this township and was interested primarily in farming land. He was followed by others who moved into the surrounding country because of its agricultural possibilities.

In 1858 the town was named Dobson, in honor of James Dobson. In 1862 an act of the legislature changed the name to Elmore for Andrew E. Elmore of Wisconsin, a friend of several early settlers.

Here is a small CITY PARK and a TOURIST CAMP *(running water)*.

Elmore has a school building that houses eight grades and a high school, with a library that serves the entire community. Its population is descended chiefly from Norwegians and Germans, but shows few racial or Old World traits.

In season there is excellent wild-fowl and pheasant shooting here.

At 130.7 *m.* US 169 crosses the Iowa Line, 90 miles north of Fort Dodge, Iowa *(see Iowa, Tour 6)*.

◄◄◄◄◄◄◄◄◄◄◄◄◄◄◄◄◄◄❀►►►►►►►►►►►►►►►►►►►

Tour 4

(Winnipeg, Manitoba)—Noyes—Crookston—Moorhead—Breckenridge—Ortonville—Pipestone—Luverne—(Sioux City, Iowa); US 75.
Canadian Border to Iowa Line, 434.1 m.

The Great Northern Ry. parallels the route between Canadian Border and Breckenridge; and Chicago, Milwaukee, St. Paul & Pacific R. R. between Moorhead and Breckenridge; the Chicago, Milwaukee, St. Paul & Pacific R. R. between Breckenridge and Ortonville; and the Chicago, Rock Island & Pacific Ry. between Pipestone and Iowa Line.
Roadbed bituminous-treated or graveled throughout; good condition all seasons.
Tourist accommodations at short intervals.

This route along the western edge of Minnesota crosses the entire State, following, in the north, the fertile Red River Valley and bordering the Detroit Lakes resort area; midway it approaches Lake Traverse and Big Stone Lake; and in the south it passes the Indians' sacred quarries of pipestone in a prosperous farming country.

Sec. a. CANADIAN BORDER (NOYES) *to* MOORHEAD,
173.6 m. US 75.

At 0 *m.* US 75 crosses the Canadian Border, 67 miles south of Winnipeg.

NOYES, 0.1 *m.* (792 alt., 64 pop.), is a small village and a United States port of entry, with an almost cosmopolitan air of bustle and excitement emanating from the U. S. CUSTOMS AND IMMIGRATION OFFICES. The American and Canadian flags flying not far apart, the trim uniforms of the officials, and the constant commotion usual to international boundaries contrast with the quiet of this remote north-woods country. A large force of railroad officials is necessary to take care of incoming and outgoing passengers and freight on both the Soo Line and the Great Northern Ry. passing through Noyes.

At 7.2 *m.* is the junction (L) with US 59.

HUMBOLDT, 8.2 *m.* (793 alt., 139 pop.), originated as a "Jim Hill town." James J. Hill, the railroad builder, owned the town site and platted it. The present name, honoring the great German naturalist, Baron Alexander von Humboldt, was a tribute from Hill to the German people, many of whom had invested in railway bonds.

The land in this vicinity is typical Red River prairie, an open expanse of gently rolling fields, broken only by farmstead windbreaks. The soil is clay and sandy loam, adapted to diversified agriculture, and so fertile that descriptions of the farms sound like Paul Bunyan legends. Records show the yield has been as high as 45 bushels of wheat or 500 bushels of potatoes to the acre, and farmers here have plowed furrows straight ahead for 7 or 8 miles without a twist or turn.

NORTHCOTE, 15.4 *m.*, although considered a village, is administered as part of Hampden Township. The village, named for Sir Henry Stafford Northcote, English statesman and financier, was settled chiefly by Irish and Scottish Canadians.

The FLORENCE FARM at Northcote *(open to visitors)*, once owned by James J. Hill, consists of about 25,000 acres (15,000 under cultivation in 1937) and is one of the largest successfully operated grain farms in the United States. The farm residence alone, built by Walter Hill in 1912, cost $49,000. Among the other structures are a powerhouse large enough for a city of 1,500, two immense silos, and two grain elevators with capacities of 55,000 bushels and 25,000 bushels respectively. Of the 15 tractors in use, 9 are equipped with Diesel engines and 6 with 10-horsepower gasoline engines. In a recent year the planted acreage of this completely mechanized farm was 3,600 acres of wheat, 4,000 acres of flax, 500 acres of rye, 2,000 acres of barley, and approximately 1,500 acres of oats.

The country along the highway between Northcote and Hallock, more rolling than that along the northernmost portion of the route, is broken by the curving branches of Two Rivers, whose banks are lined by graceful elm and ash trees.

HALLOCK, 20.4 *m.* (820 alt., 869 pop.), seat of Kittson County and in an area abounding with game, was named for the journalist and editor,

Charles W. Hallock (1834–1917), founder of *Forest and Stream* magazine. In 1880 Hallock, who was a great sportsman, erected in the newly founded town a $10,000 hotel with water on every floor, bathrooms, speaking tubes, a barber shop, kennel rooms, gun rooms, and other facilities unusual in the far Northwest at that time.

The HALLOCK COMMUNITY RINK cost $19,000. Hockey is the major sport in the village, curling is also popular, and there is a community SWIMMING POOL.

Honey from more than 3,000 colonies of bees is extracted centrifugally and shipped in carload lots, some of it to European markets. Pollen carried by the bees fertilizes the sweetclover seed, an important source of revenue to the local farmers.

The highway through this area follows the old Pembina Trail, now unmarked, used for generations by pioneers and in earlier times by the Indians. Some scholars believe that this route was used as early as 1362 by a Norse-Gothic party, which reputedly penetrated deep into the territory that later became Minnesota, as evidenced by the Kensington Runestone *(see Tour 9)* and the Norse anchor stones *(see Tour 16)*.

Along this same ancient trail creaking oxcarts once carried valuable loads of furs to the distant settlements. These carts at first had solid wooden wheels, about 3 feet in diameter, sawed from the ends of logs; later spokes were formed by removing V-shaped pieces from the solid discs of wood, and finally rim wheels with 10 or 12 spokes were constructed. The carts were also made entirely of wood, usually oak, held together by wooden pins. The wooden hubs turning on the axles made a harsh, screeching sound, nerve-racking when large trains were in motion. In some instances rawhide tires were used, but the carts remained little changed until the advent of railroads ended their usefulness.

Norman Kittson (1814–1888), for whom Kittson County was named, first made use of the oxcart on a profitable scale. While stationed at Pembina as agent for the American Fur Company he sent his first oxcart train of furs to Mendota in the 1840's. It was only after two years of valuable experience, however, during which he lost about $1,000, that he succeeded in making his oxcart transportation business profitable. He learned that carts, in order to operate safely and successfully, must move in large trains. Three men were in charge of each brigade, and a leader was in charge of the whole train; his post was considered very responsible and desirable. Loaded carts generally weighed about 800 pounds; the plodding oxen seldom covered more than 15 miles a day.

Kittson's first train of six carts carried $2,000 worth of furs. In 1850 the carts transported furs valued at $15,000 and returned with $10,000 worth of supplies. In the following year 102 carts reached St. Paul, and by 1857 there were 500 carts in service. The chief exports were beaver, otter, mink, fisher, marten, muskrat, and fox pelts, and buffalo hides.

At 30.1 *m.* is KENNEDY (827 alt., 279 pop.), named for John Stewart Kennedy, who was connected with the James J. Hill interests. The immense farms formerly operated in this vicinity have been broken up into smaller tracts.

Left from Kennedy on a country road to a spring-fed gravel-pit pool, 4 *m.*, an excellent SWIMMING HOLE, 200 by 450 feet *(picnic facilities)*.

At 35.2 *m.* is the junction with State 11 *(see Tour 6)* and DONALD-SON (825 alt., 133 pop.), in an area of bonanza farms. The enormous 65,000-acre property of the Donaldson-Ryan interests was managed in early days by Capt. Hugh Donaldson, a former Civil War officer. When bonanza farming was "the colossus that bestrid" the Red River Valley, such a position as Donaldson's carried with it considerable importance; if a man wanted a job or wished to buy a farm he was told to "See the captain." The phrase was used constantly in the vicinty and even marriage-bent swains were so admonished.

STEPHEN, 43.9 *m.* (833 alt., 474 pop.), adopted the name of a farm owned here in early days by Lord Ramsey; it was called Stephen Farm in honor of Lord Mount Stephen, an official of the Canadian Ry. As the southern terminus of the stage line, Stephen became an important trade center when the railroad was built to this point in 1897.

Farming in the vicinity is diversified. This small village has the county's largest creamery (privately owned), and ships a large volume of livestock. Today feed crops are of greater importance than wheat, the former main-stay of the Red River Valley farmer. Stephen also has tourist cabin camps, one with a swimming pool and baseball diamond.

ARGYLE, 52 *m.* (850 alt., 700 pop.), formerly called both Louisa and Middle River, was given its present name after Scottish immigrants out-numbered the other settlers. There is a tourist camp here.

WARREN, 62.3 *m.* (858 alt., 1,472 pop.), seat of Marshall County, almost lost that distinction when in 1881 the county commissioners from Argyle and Stephen, constituting a majority, resolved that "the county seat of Marshall County is hereby located in the townsite of Argyle." They moved and seconded that the county safe and its content of legal papers be placed in the sheriff's charge and conveyed to Argyle. Then for almost 10 years it became, to quote the Argyle *Sheaf,* a game of "Who's got the safe?" Loyal citizens of each town delighted in gathering together and with sleigh or wagon removing the safe and all other office equipment from one town to the other. County government of a sort would be temporarily set up in the town having possession of the safe until the citizens of the rival town could gather sufficient strength to repossess it. At times only the counsel of a few calm heads averted the swinging of fists or the brandishing of firearms. After the battle had been carried on in private arguments and heated newspaper editorials over a period of years, it was decided to take the issue to the voters, and the matter was finally settled on election day, when in a violent snowstorm almost every voter turned out. Warren received a majority of 303 votes.

NORTH STAR COLLEGE *(closed)* was established here by the Swedish Lutheran Synod. This synod also controls the WARREN HOSPITAL, which has made the town a medical center of the area for 30 years.

With the exception of the Snake River there are no lakes or streams near the highway in this vicinity. As far as the eye can see is flat land covered with waving fields of grain and alfalfa, broken only by giant silos and modern farm buildings. Because wells in this area are not adequate to water the stock, the farmers have dug large open-pits 6 to 15 feet deep, 20 to 60 feet wide, and 50 to 100 feet long; the clay subsoil in these "dig-outs" holds the rainwater and keeps it comparatively clear. These ponds are easily mistaken for the natural pot holes that occur in southern Minnesota.

At 85.5 *m.* is the junction with a country road.

Left on this road to DOROTHY, 10 *m.* (902 alt., 25 pop.), a little hamlet distinguished by a beautiful CHURCH with stained-glass windows.

Right from Dorothy to the OLD CROSSING MEMORIAL PARK (L), which borders the Red Lake River at HUOT, 16 *m.,* a small village. Close to the road is the MEMORIAL IN COMMEMORATION OF THE OLD CROSSING TREATY, signed on October 2, 1863, by the chiefs of the Pembina and Red Lake tribes and by Alexander Ramsey, representative of the Federal Government. This treaty gave to the United States nearly 10 million acres, the greater portion of the Red River Valley.

Behind the monument is a foot trail; R. on this trail circling through the park at 0.5 *m.* from the main road to a small granite monument marking the OXCART TRAIL. Close to the monument stands a giant cottonwood tree, probably the one used by old settlers as a post office, where letters were placed in a box to be picked up by the drivers of the oxcart trains. The Pembina Trail crosses the Red Lake River at a point about 50 feet above the monument.

At 24 *m.* is the little village of GENTILLY (946 alt., 172 pop.). Most of the inhabitants are of French-Canadian origin. Their parish priest for many years was Father Eli Theilon, born near the town of Limoges in France. He urged his parishioners to organize a co-operative plant and make Limoges cheese from the recipe he had obtained from his old monastery in France. Within a year of its founding in 1895, the Gentilly Dairy Association produced 15,000 pounds of Limoges cheese; by 1927 its output was 150,000 pounds, most of which went to eastern markets. Prosperity came to farmers and town alike. Father Theilon served as president of the association and manager of its factory until his death. He refused any personal reward, but his grateful parishioners built for him the impressive CATHEDRAL that stands on the outskirts of the village.

Right from Gentilly; at 32 *m.* is the junction with US 75.

At 90.8 *m.* is a junction (R) with US 2 *(see Tour 7)*. Between this point and CROOKSTON, 92.1 *m.* (872 alt., 6,321 pop.) *(see Tour 7),* US 75 and US 2 are one route *(see Tour 7).*

ADA, 128.6 *m.* (906 alt., 1,285 pop.), seat of Norman County, was named for the daughter of a railway official. Although this town owes its genesis to the lumber industry, it stands now in the midst of a vast prairie. In 1897 a large sawmill began operations. From forests about 75 miles to the east logs were floated down the Wild Rice River; lumbering activities continued until 1924.

Ada is now the leading shipping center for Norman County; its prosperity depends upon dairying and potato-raising. This town has a CIGAR FACTORY utilizing tobacco imported from other States, although a small quantity of tobacco is experimentally raised here.

In Ada US 75 turns R. until it almost reaches the Red River. In this section a vast expanse of prairie spreads out to an almost unbroken horizon. During summer mirages are not uncommon and the reflections of far-off towns are occasionally seen hanging inverted at the edge of the sky. Near the scattered farmsteads, trees, windmills, and wind-propelled

generators are grouped to break or use the force of the strong gales that
sweep down from the north.

At 143 *m.* US 75 turns L. and parallels the Red River, which lies 1 mile
to the west. Along its course, tall prairie grass provides shelter for numbers of prairie chickens, pheasants, white-breasted grouse, and rabbits.

Between HENDRUM, 144.7 *m.* (877 alt., 326 pop.), and Georgetown,
US 75—still following the Pembina Trail—is bordered on the west by
the Red River and on the east by fertile plains where 75 or 80 years ago
vast bison herds were hunted by the Sioux and Chippewa.

Near GEORGETOWN, 158.1 *m.* (886 alt., 183 pop.), the *Anson
Northup,* first steamboat on the Red River, was launched in the winter of
1859. The boilers and heavy parts of the machinery were loaded on sleds
at Brainerd and drawn over ice and snow through hostile Indian country
by a crew of 60 men and 34 oxteams.

At 158.5 *m.* (L) is the marked BOUNDARY BETWEEN THE SIOUX AND
CHIPPEWA COUNTRY as defined by the Treaty of Prairie du Chien of 1825.

MOORHEAD, 173.6 *m.* (929 alt., 7,651 pop.) *(see Tour 16),* across
the river from Fargo, N. Dak., is at the junction with US 10 *(see Tour
16)* and US 52 *(see Tour 9).*

Sec. b. MOORHEAD to ORTONVILLE, 114.9 m. US 75.

Between Moorhead and Breckenridge US 75 runs in an almost straight
line and is bordered on the R. by the meandering Red River. This part
of the State is comparatively high and is excellent, rolling farm country.

At 25.8 *m.* (R) a marker indicates a point on the west bank of the Red
River, about one mile (R) from here, where is the SITE OF FORT ABER-
CROMBIE, begun by United States troops in August 1857, to protect the
northwestern frontier against attacks by the Indians. The post withstood
several Sioux attacks during the outbreak of 1862 and was garrisoned
until its abandonment in 1877.

At 40.6 *m.* are (R) the FEMCO FARMS *(open to visitors),* a 6,000-acre
demonstration farm of the Minneapolis *Tribune,* devoted to the development of choice breeds of Shropshire sheep, Holstein cattle, and Percheron
horses. Its Holstein herd is one of the finest in the United States; Femco
Alma, a registered Holstein cow of royal breeding, in 1937 produced
1,002 pounds of butter-fat (the equivalent of 1,252.5 pounds of butter),
thereby completing a new world record for junior 2-year-old cows of all
breeds.

BRECKENRIDGE, 45 *m.* (1,000 alt., 2,264 pop.), seat of Wilkin
County, is at the confluence of the Otter Tail and the Bois de Sioux Rivers
(the Red River is called by the latter name south of this point). The town
was established in 1857 and named for Vice President John C. Breckinridge.
Its progress was retarded by Civil War enlistment in 1862, when it was
all but abandoned. Only three men remained behind in the hotel and on
August 23, 1862, they were killed by the Indians. The same day a mail
stage was attacked near the town and its driver killed. It was not until
the advent of the Great Northern Ry. in 1871 that the town began to

develop. The railroad made the rich prairie land of the Red River Valley profitable for agriculture, and the region grew into a great wheat-raising area. Later, farming became more diversified, and today, although wheat is still the principal crop, other grains and potatoes are raised, and dairying and stock-raising have become important industries. Breckenridge with its many rail facilities is the trade and shipping center of the region.

Wilkin County thrice named itself and twice repudiated its choice. When organized in 1858, the settlers chose the name of the Senator from Georgia, Robert Toombs; but when he deserted the Union for the Confederacy the honor was promptly transferred to Andrew Johnson and Toombs County became Johnson County. Johnson's politics also displeased the residents, however, so they renamed the county for Col. Alexander Wilkin (1820–1864) of Minnesota.

The country near WHEATON, 78.5 m. (1,019 alt., 1,279 pop.), is famous for water-fowl and pheasant shooting; many sport clubs lease land in the vicinity. The CITY TOURIST PARK (free camping, running water) is at the southern end of town.

Right from Wheaton on State 27, which skirts the eastern shore of LAKE TRAVERSE, to SAM BROWN STATE PARK, 26 m. Joseph R. Brown (1805–1870), who came to Minnesota as a drummer boy with Colonel Leavenworth in 1819, lived here in the early 1860's. His two-story LOG HOUSE is preserved in the park named for his son, Samuel Jerome, head of an Indian scout patrol at Fort Wadsworth, Dakota Territory, in 1866. During one of the many Sioux threats Sam Brown rode 120 miles on horseback, during the night of April 19, 1866, through a storm to warn the settlers. This hero of western Minnesota is often compared with Paul Revere.

On State 27, between Lakes Traverse and BIG STONE, is BROWNS VALLEY, 27 m. (981 pop.); here the prehistoric "Browns Valley Man" was discovered in a gravel pit at the southeastern end of the village (see FIRST AMERICANS: Archeology). The waters of Lake Traverse drain northward to Hudson Bay; those of Big Stone southward to the Gulf of Mexico through the Minnesota River.

Left from Browns Valley on State 28 is the junction with US 75 at 48 m.

GRACEVILLE, 95.9 m. (1,100 alt., 969 pop.), is in the midst of a prosperous farming and dairying region. Here is the junction with State 28 (see above side tour).

TOQUA LAKES STATE PARK, 97.5 m. (camping facilities, 9-hole golf course), has 40 acres. Long-continued drought and constant drainage and cultivation have dried the lakes in this ancient glacial area.

ORTONVILLE, 114.9 m. (985 alt., 2,017 pop.) (see Tour 10), is at the junction with US 12 (see Tour 10).

Sec. c. ORTONVILLE to IOWA LINE, 145.6 m. US 75.

Southeast of Ortonville US 75 follows the Minnesota River east for about 7 miles from its source in Big Stone Lake, then crosses the river and turns south. Here is one of the major water-conservation attempts in Minnesota—a flood-control project using Big Stone Lake as a reservoir for the waters that each spring inundate the Minnesota River Valley.

MADISON, 28.2 m. (1,100 alt., 1,916 pop.), is the seat of Lac qui Parle County. The village was founded by Jacob F. Jacobson, who led

Iowa settlers to the site. He was a gubernatorial candidate in 1908 but was defeated by John A. Johnson.

Madison has a LUTHERAN NORMAL SCHOOL *(not open)*, a CO-OPERATIVE CREAMERY, a livestock-shipping association, a FLOUR MILL that produces 24,000 barrels a year and ships 75 per cent of its output, several GRAIN ELEVATORS, and a municipally owned ELECTRIC POWER PLANT. An excellent GREENHOUSE AND NURSERY with a large display of evergreens and other plants has a country-wide trade and does considerable exporting. Near the nursery, set in a delightful flower-filled landscape, is a LOG HUT *(open to visitors)* with a sod roof, a reproduction of the nursery owner's boyhood home in Norway. The fireplace and furniture are relics from Norway. Madison also has a tourist park.

Lac qui Parle County is named for the lake formed by the widening of the Minnesota River in the northeastern part of the county. It is a French translation of the Indian name meaning *lake that speaks*.

At 33.8 *m.* is the junction with US 212 *(see Tour 11)*.

At 52 *m.* is the CANBY TOURIST PARK *(free camping, running water)*.

CANBY, 52.8 *m.* (1,243 alt., 1,738 pop.), is the seat of Yellow Medicine County. The county was named for the roots of the yellow moonseed used by the Indians for medicinal purposes. Canby has a large electric power distributing plant and co-operative livestock, wool-shipping, and creamery associations.

IVANHOE, 71.6 *m.* (1,655 alt., 556 pop.), seat of Lincoln County, some parts of which contain the highest land in southwestern Minnesota, was named for the hero of Sir Walter Scott's novel; the streets bear the names of leading characters in the book. There is a tourist park here.

Nestled among the hills, LAKE BENTON, 87.2 *m.* (1,755 alt., 903 pop.) *(see Tour 12)*, at the junction with US 14 *(see Tour 12)*, lies on the southwestern shore of the lake for which it was named.

At 87.3 *m.* is a 4-mile gap running southwest between picturesque bluffs that rise 150 to 200 feet. The Indians called this place, which was the channel of an ancient river, Hole in the Mountain. Here the elongated hills are part of the Altamont moraine, the terminus of the Keewatin glacier. The moraine follows the crest of the Coteau des Prairies, a large stretch of elevated prairie country crossing the southwestern corner of the State from South Dakota to Iowa. The crest, more than 1,500 feet above sea level, is reached by a slope so gradual as to be almost imperceptible.

At 105.7 *m.* is a gate (R) leading to the PIPESTONE INDIAN TRAINING SCHOOL *(open)*.

Right, through the gate, to the 33 modern school buildings, 0.5 *m.*, most of which are built of native rock quarried on the reservation. The institution was founded in 1893 and students co-operate in performing the manual labor. *Hiawatha* is given as a pageant each year by the eighth-grade graduating class.

Left from the Indian Training School, on Hiawatha Ave. N., to the PIPESTONE QUARRIES (L), 1.5 *m.*, famous in Indian legends and historic documents as the source of the unusual reddish-colored stone used for many centuries by the Indians to make pipes. For generations bitter warfare was waged for the possession of these quarries. A legend common to both Omaha and Yankton Indians relates that Wahegela, an Omaha wife of a Yankton Sioux, discovered the pipestone while trailing a white bison whose hoofs uncovered the red stone. The Omaha based their claims of ownership on Wahegela's blood relationship to them, while the Sioux maintained that since she had lived and died among them tribal law made them heir to all her discoveries. Ultimately an agreement was reached whereby the territory became sacred and neutral ground, shared in common by all Indians. In 1937 Congress approved an act setting aside 115 acres in which the quarries are situated, to be called the Pipestone National Monument.

Indians believe this is the spot where the Great Spirit created man and that the dark red quartzite was the flesh of their ancestors, hardened by the waters of the great flood. None but Indians are allowed to quarry or carve the pipestone. In years past the Indian carvers were skilled craftsmen, but today examples of distinguished workmanship are rare.

HIEROGLYPHICS carved on the quarry wall symbolically depict the early life of the tribes. From a SHEER PILLAR OF ROCK, separated from the main wall by several feet and known in Indian legends as "Leaping Rock," the ubiquitous maiden is said to have jumped to her death. Nearby are THE THREE MAIDENS, a group of gigantic rocks believed to have been formerly a solid piece. The Indians relate that their present race sprang from three maidens who fled here for refuge, when all the rest of their tribe were killed in battle.

Longfellow referred to this spot in *Hiawatha* and many travelers and explorers who followed George Catlin visited the locality. In 1836 Catlin (1796–1872), artist and explorer, described and sent back samples of the rock, the substance of which has since been known to mineralogists as catlinite. He was followed 2 years later by Joseph Nicollet (1786–1843) and his party, whose names, carved on the rocks, are still decipherable at Winnewissa Falls. In Nicollet's party was John C. Frémont, who was to be the Republican candidate for President in 1856. In addition to the quarries and rock formations, the district has numerous Indian shrines, waterfalls, and creeks.

PIPESTONE, 106.8 *m.* (1,725 alt., 3,489 pop.), seat of Pipestone County, is on the western slope of the Coteau des Prairies. Pipestone has two large creameries and a produce plant. In its RECREATION FIELD are tennis courts, playground equipment, and a $12,000 swimming pool. Many of the buildings in Pipestone, notably the LIBRARY, the imposing COURTHOUSE, and the adjacent JAIL, are constructed, in part at least, of the beautiful red granite quarried here. In the courthouse are many INDIAN RELICS including petroglyphs, or carvings on rock believed to have been made by prehistoric mound builders. Additional Indian relics are displayed in the window of a local store (123 Hiawatha Ave. S.), and various articles carved by the Indians from pipestone can be purchased at several shops.

In the newly established MOUND SPRINGS STATE PARK, 129.9 *m.*, is BLUE MOUND, visible a mile or so to the L. of the highway, a massive bluff of quartzite about 3 miles long. This is the rock for which Rock County is named; stories relate that Indians used to drive herds of buffalo over it to their death below.

It was in the hills of this wild country that the notorious James and Younger brothers hid after their raid on the bank at Northfield in 1876.

LUVERNE, 134.8 *m.* (1,450 alt. 2,644 pop.) *(see Tour 13),* is at the junction with US 16 *(see Tour 13).*

At 145.6 *m.* the route crosses the Iowa Line, 87 miles north of Sioux City, Iowa *(see Iowa, Tour 9).*

◄◄◄◄◄◄◄◄◄◄◄◄◄◄◄◄◄◄◄◄◄ ✿ ►►►►►►►►►►►►►►►►►►►►►

Tour 5

(Ft. Frances, Ontario)—International Falls—Cook—Virginia—Eveleth—
Duluth—(Superior, Wis.); US 53.
Canadian Border to Wisconsin Line, 158 m.

The Duluth, Winnipeg & Pacific Ry. parallels the route.
Bituminous-treated roadbed between International Falls and Virginia; paved be-
tween Virginia and Duluth. Open all year.
Tourist camps and hotels.

The northern end of the route at the Canadian Line crosses a lonely
deforested area that was once the scene of extensive logging operations;
the route passes through Virginia, important iron-mining town of the
Mesabi Range, and its south end is in commercial Duluth.

INTERNATIONAL FALLS, 0 *m.* (1,124 alt., 5,036 pop.), is on the
southern bank of the RAINY RIVER, the boundary between the United States
and Canada from Lake of the Woods to Rainy Lake. Jacques de Noyon
(about 1690) was probably the first white man to visit this site; in 1731
a post called St. Pierre was built in the vicinity by a son and nephew of
La Vérendrye.

International Falls is the headquarters of the Border Patrol. The three
branches of this service can be identified by their uniforms: the Immigration Border Patrol wears forest green, the Customs Border Patrol dark
gray, and the Customs Inspectors dark blue. Immigration and customs regulations *(see GENERAL INFORMATION)* are designed to make passage across the border as unrestricted as possible, a factor that has resulted
in an ever-increasing volume of traffic. Because of "border jumpers,"
motorists are warned not to pick up hitch-hikers.

It was not until 1904 that International Falls became industrially important. At that time a paper company, attracted by the hydro-electric possibilities of KOOCHICHING FALLS, brought about a settlement of Canadian
and United States riparian rights and contracted for the development of
water power. The establishment of various manufacturing industries followed. The falls, known to early French as the Cauldron, had a natural
drop of 24 feet. Today they supply 25,000 horsepower from a 27-foot
head and have made the town an industrial center. The MINNESOTA &
ONTARIO PAPER COMPANY'S MILL *(guides)* is one of the largest in the
country. The company also operates an insulite mill, a sawmill, and a planing mill.

In the paper mill the pulpwood is first sent through "slashers," which
cut the 8-foot pieces into shorter lengths; then through huge "barking
drums" where all bark is removed from the blocks; and next to "chip"
machines in which each "stick" is cut into thousands of small pieces. The

chips are conveyed to the sulphite house, dumped into large cookers, and steamed in an acid that disintegrates the wood. Huge stones reduce the wood to a fine fiber. This pulp is mixed with an equal amount of sulphite pulp, which then undergoes a series of treatments until it is spread out in a semiliquid state on a fine wire screen to drain; then pressed through a series of heavy rollers. The web of damp paper travels over and under a series of great steam-heated drying rolls and emerges completely dry, to be wound on spindles. The pulp, which is 90 per cent water when it leaves the headbox, emerges as dry paper in less than a minute. The factory works night and day and produces 1,100 feet of paper a minute.

In the INSULITE MILL, opened in 1913, waste from the paper plant becomes wallboard, decorative tile, roofing, or other insulating material. Today 750,000 board feet of insulite are made at this mill every 24 hours.

The SAWMILL, with a capacity of 300,000 feet every 10 hours, is the largest in the State. Adjoining is the PLANING MILL which finishes the rough lumber; it has a capacity of 400,000 feet every 10 hours.

At 434 Third St. is a CURIO COLLECTION *(open 9 a.m.-midnight)* of mounted animals and birds and old firearms gathered by O. J. Masters. Dozens of exhibits line the walls in lifelike poses or are perched on convenient shelves.

A TOURISTS' BUREAU *(open 9-6 except Sun.)* is in the *Daily Journal* office, 3d. St.

International Falls' entertainment in the summer includes: log-rolling contests; the July Fourth Lumber Festival and Paul Bunyan Parade; exhibits for the Better Homes and Gardens Week in May; and the annual Flower Show. During the winter there are hockey games, tobogganing, and, in January or early February, a carnival featuring the Dog Derby.

Southeast of International Falls US 53 runs through a sparsely settled country which has acres of wild blueberries and raspberries. Originally extremely rugged, the terrain has been rendered even more stark by deforestation and consequent erosion. At some points on each side of the road are great heights of rock—its gray relieved only by the green of second-growth balsam firs. During the winter and early spring this section of the road is bordered by great piles of pulpwood, ties, and sawed lumber. Villages are infrequent; small, fragile buildings seem to lean upon each other for support; tarpaper shacks are common. Bleached piles of sawdust and rusted hulks of old steam engines add to a general appearance of desolation and abandonment.

CUSSON, 49.8 *m.*, during logging days was the headquarters of the Virginia & Rainy Lake Logging Company. Today the homes of one or two settlers and a CCC camp are its only signs of civilization.

In the spring the Indians in this section erect temporary shelters resembling wigwams, in which they live while making maple sugar. When the sap begins to run, they drill holes in the trunks and allow the liquid to collect in birchbark vessels called *nak-gan*. The filled containers are emptied into pails by carriers who take the sap into camps, where it is strained and boiled down in great kettles. While still a thick, heavy syrup, some is poured into variously shaped molds to harden; the Indians call the molded sugar "cake sugars"; the "gum sugar" is put into other containers. The remainder is cooled and pulverized with ladles in "sugar boats," wooden vessels 5 or 6 feet long.

ORR, 52.9 *m.* (100 pop.), is on the east shore of PELICAN LAKE, a large body of water whose outlet was blocked by the moraine on its southern shore.

Left from Orr on an unpaved road to the junction with a second unpaved road, 19 *m.,* at the crossing of the Vermilion River; L. on this road to BUYCK, 23 *m.,* whose few scattered inhabitants engage in farming. Here is the junction (R) with the ECHO TRAIL *(see Tour 8).*

At 35 *m.* on the second unpaved road is HARDING, a small village on CRANE LAKE *(canoe trips).* The lake, although not large, offers entry to the chain of wilderness lakes that forms the Canada-Minnesota boundary. From Crane Lake are accessible some of the greatest inland canoeing waters on the continent. This chain of border lakes, now so sparsely settled, was once the scene of great historic conflicts. It was on these lakes that the Sioux fought losing battles in their retreat before the ruthless, savage Chippewa, who had determined to secure for themselves the rewards of the fur trade. This wilderness playground is a land of sharp hills, gaunt masses of lichen-covered granite, dark forests heavy with undergrowth, and vast black spruce and tamarack swamps (called muskegs). Here the winters are long and cold, but the short summers and long autumn days are ideal for adventurers. The lakes abound with game fish—wall-eyed pike, northern pike, called by the natives "fighting jack," and crappie. In its forests deer, bear, and moose are still common. Although much of this country is still unexplored, the Crane Lake resorts offer comfortable accommodations and can equip tourists for water journeys *(see SUPERIOR NATIONAL FOREST: Canoe Trips).*

Several of the Indian pictographs in this region have been chipped by chemists in search of the formula for their durable paint. It is probable that the pigment used is red ochre reduced to ashes and mixed with animal fat or root oils. Border lake pictographs include a variety of figures: moose, men, handprints, footprints, sundials, totems, otters, wolves, foxes, turtles, and snakes.

Old village sites and dwelling places have been traced near the shore lines of many northern lakes; some have been found in an area normally under water. Household debris, broken pieces of pottery, ashes, stone implements, and cobblestones have been found mixed with surface soil or buried several feet deep. Ruins of underground houses or dugouts, 15 to 30 feet in diameter, with central fireplaces, have been discovered 4 to 6 feet below the surface level.

At some points are boulder dams, apparently built by an early race to eliminate rapids by raising the water level, thus making navigation easier. Some of the dams are constructed of huge rounded boulders, several tons in weight, and are situated where such boulders are naturally scarce. Though most of this region is extremely rocky, areas of improved, cleared land suggest early cultivation by human beings. If ancient inhabitants worked the soil at all, they did so in a crude manner. Some writers believe, however, that they made excavations in solid jasper, one of the hardest of known rocks. Recent discoveries indicate that cannibalism was practiced, perhaps for ceremonial sacrifice. Whatever the nature of these aborigines they apparently lived in the border-lake region of Minnesota many centuries before it was visited by white men.

At 54.8 *m.* is GLENDALE (1,299 alt.), a small settlement.

Right from Glendale a graded road bordered by tall maples, birches, and oaks skirts PELICAN LAKE *(excellent duck hunting)* for 9.5 *m.;* at 16 *m.* is NETT LAKE in the BOIS FORT INDIAN RESERVATION *(accommodations for visitors),* one of a group of five Indian reservations under the jurisdiction of the Consolidated Chippewa Reservation at Cass Lake.

The village is a group of old log cabins and tarpaper shacks. The fine virgin timber that once blanketed the area has all been cut and second-growth trees have taken its place. Here is the INDIAN EMERGENCY CONSERVATION CAMP, where more than 200 men are regularly employed. The employees engage in a comprehensive athletic program; contests with CCC camps nearby are a part of the recreation schedule.

In the surrounding area are some of the State's most extensive blueberry marshes. Indians from miles around gather here during the berry season; they pick the fruit and sell it to buyers who follow their camps.

Wildrice grows profusely in Nett Lake. To gather it Indians paddle into the swamp, two men in each canoe; while one rows the other threshes the rice heads into the boat with two sticks. On shore the rice is heated in large kettles over open fires to loosen the hulls and enhance the flavor. Then it is poured into wide, bark baskets and is tossed and shaken until hulls, stalks, and foreign substances have blown away. The rice is then placed in a cement or wooden vat, and a man or boy with moccasins on his feet "jigs" it, with a peculiar tramping step, to loosen all shells from the grain. Again the rice is tossed, then bagged and marketed.

During the rice-gathering season occur many of the ceremonial dances. Early in the evening natives carrying packs and bundles begin to file into the "coliseum" to the roll of the tom-tom. An occasional jingle of bells and the moving crowd direct visitors to the building in front of which serious-faced men are skillfully drying and stretching the drums over the fire. Within the dimly lighted octagonal dance hall, the drummers on a raised center platform begin a measured beat, and the chorus of voices swells into a musical story of wars, victories, love, and hate. Out of the darkness colorfully dressed girls dance into the circle, using a halt step to the rhythm of the tom-toms. Bending the right knee at each inflected beat, they shuffle to the left and continue the circling, swaying motion. Suddenly youths, dressed in brilliant, bead-trimmed suits with feather and fur ornaments, rush into the room keeping time with the rhythmic sounds. Each youth wears a headdress· which partially covers his face. He steps lightly on his toes but thumps his heels on the floor twice with each beat of the music. His body twists and turns, almost touching the floor, and the dance is concluded with extraordinary skill and agility *(see THE ARTS: Music).*

SPIRIT ISLAND, a short distance from shore in Nett Lake, has figures in a smoky, reddish brown film seemingly embedded in the gray rock. Legend maintains that these pictures were on the island when the first Indians visited the lake. Sometimes they heard sounds as of children playing on the island, but knowing it to be uninhabited they dared not venture near it, for they attributed both the noise and the pictures to spirits.

COOK, 70.3 *m.* on US 53 (1,452 alt., 272 pop.) *(see Tour 8),* is at the junction with State 1 *(see Tour 8).*

At approximately 92.4 *m.* the road crosses the divide from which rivers flow north to Hudson Bay and south to Lake Superior. At about this point the area of light, sandy soil, marked by scrubby sparse growth, merges into the regions of iron mines.

VIRGINIA, 90.1 *m.* (1,574 alt., 11,963 pop.) *(see Tour 3)* is at the junction with US 169 *(see Tour 3).*

At 93.6 *m.* is an OUTCROPPING OF TACONITE (iron-bearing rock). In many places gaping holes and huge piles of strippings indicate mining operations.

EVELETH, 99.1 *m.* (1,574 alt., 7,484 pop.), "The Hill Top City," is an important range town. Named for Edwin Eveleth, a Michigan lumberman, the village was platted in 1893, but its growth was slow until 1900 when extensive mining operations were begun. Between 1900 and 1910 the population increased from 2,752 to 7,036. Mining is the principal industry and 50 per cent of Minnesota's iron ore now comes from mines lying within a 50-mile radius of the city. Agriculture and dairying supplement the local income. The rapid development of the public school system is a source of pride to the citizens; school buildings are of modern design. Fishing and canoeing bring many tourists on their way to the Superior National Forest, a few miles north, while an equable summer climate and a generous rainfall make its local golf courses *(reasonable fees)* unusually attractive. Eveleth's hockey team has trained many well-known professional and amateur players. An annual Winter Sports Frolic is held here in March. Eveleth has three beautiful parks that serve adequately every outdoor recreational need of the community.

Left from Eveleth on State 37 to the junction with State 35, 4.1 *m.;* R. on State 35 to BIWABIK, 11.4 *m.* (1,472 alt., 1,383 pop.), on the historic Vermilion Trail; the name is derived from the Chippewa word for iron.

Right from Biwabik on an improved road to the junction with another improved road, 4.7 *m.;* R. on this road to the St. Louis County 4-H Club LOG CLUBHOUSE *(open to visitors),* 5.1 *m.,* which was won by the organization for outstanding work. The clubhouse stands on beautiful ESQUAGAMA LAKE *(golf course, swimming, fishing, camping, picknicking),* whose shores are heavily wooded with birch and pine.

At 16.6 *m.* on State 35 is AURORA (1,478 alt., 1,463 pop.), which has five open-pit mines and is at the eastern edge of the Mesabi Range; Aurora has the fine school buildings characteristic of the range towns.

At 26.6 *m.* is the junction with the Embarrass Rd.; R. on this graveled road to EMBARRASS, 27.7 *m.,* a small Finnish settlement where Old World culture and customs are preserved. The village name is derived from the French "embarras," meaning *obstacle,* and refers to the nearby river, which at the time of the fur-traders was so littered with driftwood that canoeing was very difficult.

Numerous little farmhouses in this valley have pole-anchored birchbark or shake-shingle roofs, rounded or "gumdrop" canvas-covered haystacks, "toothpicked" to the ground with pegs like a circus tent, and outside bathhouses where hot stones are dropped into a pool to create steam for baths indulged in by the Finns even in subzero weather *(see IMMIGRATION AND RACIAL ELEMENTS).* The Dummola Shake Shingle Mill is operated like mills in Finland. Shake shingles of any thickness, not only of cedar as is usual, but also of jack and Norway pine, are cut by a one-man circular ripsaw.

With deft hands the women card their wool on hand-made carders of curved pine boards studded closely with half-inch steel teeth. They feed the wool to imported wheels and knit it into a variety of woolen products; black and white are mixed to form the familiar gray. They also make felt moccasin-boots 10 inches high, by pasting and pressing wool into shape by hand. The men wear these felt boots inside rubber overshoes.

At 99.6 *m.* on US 53 is the junction with the paved Fayal Rd.

Right on this road to the junction with the paved Mine Rd., 0.3 *m.;* L. on the Mine Rd. 1 *m.* to the LEONIDAS MINE. Named for Leonidas Merritt, the discoverer in 1890 of the first ore on the Mesabi *(see INDUSTRIAL DEVELOPMENT: Mining),* this is one of the most active mines and has shipped a total of over 16 million tons of ore. An open-pit is operated in connection with the underground workings.

The EVELETH MUNICIPAL TOURIST CAMP *(shelters, ovens, firewood)* is at 101.1 *m.*

A STATE RANGERS' STATION with an observation tower is at COTTON, 119.4 *m.,* a small village on the west bank of the Whiteface River.

Mixed with the black spruce and tamarack of the peat bogs and swamps grow Labrador tea, cranberry, pitcherplant, and Indianpipe. Often the low ground is lush with sphagnum, or peat-moss, which during the World War was used as a substitute for cotton in surgical dressings.

At 149.4 *m.* is the DULUTH HOMESTEADS PROJECT (R), built by WPA labor. Adjoining US 53, this project, the only one in St. Louis County, includes 1,220 acres of rolling land well suited to agricultural purposes. On July 1, 1937, 40 houses had been completed and 44 more were in the process of construction; they vary in size, are of 4 styles, and stand on lots of from 3½ to 10 acres. The homesteaders on this project may work at any occupation that gives steady employment, and these low-cost houses, with easy access to good roads and schools, are equipped with electric power and telephone service.

At 153.9 *m.* US 53 descends over the rock escarpment, affording a fine panorama of Duluth's East End, Lake Superior, and the Duluth-Superior Harbor.

DULUTH, 158 *m.* (626 alt., 101,463 pop.) *(see DULUTH).*

Points of Interest. The Aerial Lift Span across the ship canal, the ore docks, the Skyline Parkway, the Incline, Minnesota Point.

At Duluth are the junctions with US 61 *(see Tour 1)* and US 2 *(see Tour 7).*

Southeast of Duluth US 53 crosses the INTERSTATE BRIDGE, 159.6 *m.,* into Superior, Wis. *(see Wisconsin, Tour 10).*

<<<<<<<<<<<<<<<<<<<<<<<<✿>>>>>>>>>>>>>>>>>>>>>>>>

Tour 6

(Ft. Frances, Ontario)—International Falls—Baudette—Warroad—Roseau—Greenbush—Donaldson—(Drayton, N. Dak.) ; State 11.
Canadian Border to North Dakota Line, 200.9 *m.*

Minnesota, Dakota & Western Ry. parallels highway between International Falls and Loman; Canadian National Rys. between Baudette and Warroad; and Great Northern Ry. between Warroad and Greenbush.
Graveled and bituminous-treated roadbed; rough in early spring. Open all year.
Accommodations limited west of Baudette.

This route is the only east-west highway traversing the extreme northern part of Minnesota. It parallels the United States-Canada boundary between International Falls and Baudette on the southwestern tip of Lake of the Woods, an area with abundant fish and game, and proceeds in a southwesterly course through peat lands that were drained at great cost and are now being farmed with fair success.

INTERNATIONAL FALLS, 0 *m.* (1,124 alt., 5,038 pop.) *(see Tour 5)*, is at the junction with US 53 *(see Tour 5)*.

East of International Falls State 11 follows the beautiful southern shore of RAINY LAKE, called "Lac de la Pluie" by the French explorer La Vérendrye (1685–1749), who crossed its waters in 1732.

In a rugged area of rock escarpments as rich in color as in minerals, its primeval beauty has won for Rainy the title, "Queen of the Lakes." It is about 50 miles long and from 3 to 15 miles wide, with numerous long arms and bays, giving it a total area of about 325 square miles. The most westerly of the border chain of lakes, it drains a watershed of almost 15,000 square miles. All the water from this vast area must pass through Rainy Lake on its way to Lake of the Woods, Lake Winnipeg, Hudson Bay, and the open sea.

Rainy Lake's 1,600 islands vary in size from mere upthrusts of stone to areas of several square miles. Most of them are heavily wooded and all have beautiful rocky shore lines interspersed with occasional sand beaches; many are occupied by summer homes.

At 3.1 *m.* on State 11, where the Duluth, Winnipeg, & Pacific Ry. crosses the border, is RANIER (202 pop.), the only United States village on Rainy Lake and an important port of entry. Its officials collect more than $500,000 in duties on foreign goods annually. In addition they supervise the operation of about 200 boats plying Rainy River and Rainy Lake and inspect all passenger trains *(see GENERAL INFORMATION)*.

At the STATE FISH HATCHERY in Ranier, the largest in Minnesota and one of the largest in the country, about 1,000,000 wall-eyed pike are hatched in a season. The spawn hatches in from 18 to 26 days, in water taken directly from Rainy Lake by a powerful electric pump that distributes it through glass jars containing the eggs, and then returns it to the lake. This circulation of water continues night and day during the hatching season. The percentage of fish hatched by this artificial method of propagation is much larger than if the fish were left in the rivers and bays, where the spawn is often eaten by other fish.

On AMERICAN ISLAND *(accessible by boat from Ranier)* are GOLD WORKINGS *(open to visitors)*, opened in 1935. Gold was discovered on this island in 1893–94 and was intensively mined for some time, but the amount obtained did not justify the expense and labor. Recent prospectors with modern equipment and advanced knowledge of mining hope to extract gold in commercial quantities.

From Ranier another extension of State 11 penetrates the district eastward along the foot of Rainy Lake to BLACK BAY, 12.7 *m.* *(excellent pike fishing)*.

This route climbs through the highland country, which affords a magnificent panorama of Rainy Lake. In natural beauty the Black Bay district is rarely excelled. Within a radius of 2 miles are dozens of well-wooded islands, in the vicinity of which wall-eyed and northern pike are numerous.

West of International Falls, State 11 is bordered (L) by forest and swamp and (R) by meadows and fields that roll gently toward Rainy River. During the winter considerable timber-cutting is done in the region by farmers, who supply a large amount of pulp, logs, and cedar posts to the mill at International Falls. Trapping of fur-bearing animals—chiefly wolves, mink, ermine, and muskrat—is also a source of income. The development of agriculture here, as in other parts of Koochiching County, has been slow because of the expense of clearing the timber land and the difficulty of draining the area.

At 11.1 *m.* is the junction (L) with US 71 *(see Tour 2)*.

LAUREL, 17.9 *m.,* is a very small settlement. On the PICNIC GROUNDS of the Fred Smith farm is a group of five INDIAN MOUNDS, including the GRAND MOUND, largest in the State, 325 feet in circumference and 45 feet high. In another mound, known as LAUREL MOUND NO. 4, a group of scientists from the State university made careful explorations in 1933. The mound, 50 feet in diameter and 4½ feet high, contained 5 succeeding levels of Siouan bundle burials. On three levels whole bodies had been buried, and with them many artifacts. Complete, though broken, pots were found, some, of Algonkian type, with tapering or conoidal bottoms. This mound, only a couple of rods from the Rainy River, is believed to be at least 500 years old.

Rainy River (R) was at one time used for commerce; a fleet of large boats made regular trips between Kenora, Baudette, and International Falls. The "bones" of the old *Itasca,* one of the early steamboats, now lie on the south bank of the river on the Fred Smith farm. The railroads built along the north bank and the highways on both sides of the stream supplanted river travel.

At 35 *m.* (R) is the MANITOU RAPIDS CAMP *(cabins, firewood, picnic grounds, ovens).* MANITOU RAPIDS, roaring through a short rocky gorge, is visible from the highway and is reached by a foot trail. Here is one of the two places where nature has bridled the waters of the Rainy River. Elsewhere resembling a narrow lake, the river drifts placidly from Rainy Lake to Lake of the Woods.

At CLEMENTSON, 63.7 *m.,* a small village, the highway crosses rock-bound Rapid River, a favorite spot for anglers and campers.

SPOONER, 69.5 *m.* (225 pop.), is on the south bank of the Rainy River. At the peak of lumbering activities Spooner and Baudette, its twin village, had a combined population of approximately 2,200. The Spooner mill cut over 60 million feet of lumber a year and the Engler mill in Baudette, 70 million. In the fall of 1910, after an extremely dry summer, the sporadic peat fires that had been menacing the countryside for months blazed up along the Canadian National Rys. tracks and completely destroyed Spooner and Baudette; 34 lives were lost.

At 71.5 *m.* is BAUDETTE (1,083 alt., 822 pop.). At the western edge of the village is the MUNICIPAL TOURIST CAMP (L).

Baudette is the headquarters of a Farm Security Administration project, involving 745,000 acres in parts of Beltrami, Lake of the Woods, and Roseau Counties which have been purchased by the Federal Government as a forest and game reserve. Families are being moved from this unproductive area to more fertile lands toward the west, north, and northwest. Each tenant selects his own farm from available tracts, and plans for its development, buildings, and equipment are worked out jointly by him and by the local Farm Security authorities. Long-time loans are granted by the Government as well as every possible assistance by which the client can acquire a reasonably profitable farm. Already more than 300 families have been moved from this area (October 1937), and the resettlement of perhaps a hundred more will be completed in 1938.

Right from Baudette on State 72 to WHEELER'S POINT, 12 *m.,* on FOUR MILE BAY.

The first settlers on the United States side of the river were William Zippel, who crossed over from Rat Portage in 1887 and built a home at the mouth of a creek that has since borne his name, and Alonzo Wheeler, who in the same year settled at the mouth of the Rainy River at what is now Wheeler's Point. Here is the ROWELL BURBOT OIL EXTRACTING PLANT *(open to visitors)*. From liver of the burbot, a fresh-water member of the cod family, is extracted an oil with an anti-rachitic potency reputedly higher than cod-liver oil. It is put up in capsules and is used also in the compounding of a burbot-liver oil ointment.

At 77.9 *m.* the road passes over a high gravel ridge at the hamlet of PITT, where a large pit was dug to supply ballast material for the Canadian National Rys. tracks. The ridge marks an old shore line of the Lake of the Woods where tons of gravel were deposited.

At WILLIAMS, 88.9 *m.* (262 pop.), are FLOWING WELLS (R), some of which have been continuously active for 25 years without any appreciable diminution.

Left from Williams on an improved road to BELTRAMI ISLAND STATE FOREST, 6 *m.,* 445,440 acres of pine hills and peat swamps; it harbors one of the large HERDS OF CARIBOU in the United States.

This region abounds with big game. It is also well known for its abundance of blueberries.

SWIFT, 102.3 *m.,* possibly named to described its mushroom growth, was formerly a lumber town; today it has only one small mill.

WARROAD, 107.9 *m.* (1,068 alt., 1,184 pop.), on the bank of the Warroad River where it flows into Muskeg Bay, is the only United States port on the Lake of the Woods *(boats to American Point, Oak and Flag Islands, and Kenora, Ont.).*

When La Vérendrye came to this region, it was common ground for Sioux and Chippewa, and the old Indian "War Road" that passes this point was a familiar trail traversed by war parties. Many bloody encounters occurred on the Kabeckanung *(dark and bloody ground)*. Visible from Warroad is Gull Rock, a small, bare island in the bay; it is regarded with such awe by the Indians that not one will set foot upon it, as is explained in the following legend:

At one time the Cree, Chippewa, and Assiniboine made war upon each other until their bravest men were dead, and they had no strength to resist the advance of the Dakota. In a beautiful land of plenty there was only bloodshed, and the enemy was about to drive the people from the land of their fathers. Then the Great Spirit descended and spoke to his children. One midsummer day a terrible heat gripped the land. The morning had dawned sultry and oppressive, and as the day wore on the heat became more and more intense. People from the islands and from the land flocked to the shores. Mothers carried crying children into the lake to dip them into the cooling waters, and even wild animals, driven from the forests by the oppressive heat, ran to the water's edge unheeding the presence of man. The people sat together in groups, like hares cowering before a storm, their hearts filled with dark foreboding. Suddenly there was a blinding flash of light, and a great voice, which seemed to fill every corner of the earth, spoke to them.

"I am the Great Spirit. I have come to tell you to be friendly with one another. The land in which you dwell is your own. Far to the west and south is a big nation whose eyes are turned in this direction, and unless you who live upon this lake become brothers the enemies from the plains will fall upon you and drive you hence. You must no longer quarrel with one another. The same sun pours its beneficent light over you all and the watchful eyes of the Great Spirit are never turned away from his children."

The last syllables of the great voice rolled away like the reverberation of distant thunder, and a silence fell. The heat lifted, and cool breezes began to come in from the lake. The Indians, who had fallen prostrate with their faces to the ground, slowly arose and some lifted their eyes in time to see the Great Spirit ascending as a mist into the heavens; and those nearest saw that the mist arose from the Rock of the Gods. This island, but a few moments before covered with trees and grass, was now stripped of every sign of life, and the startled natives beheld only a naked rock. Obeying the command of the Great Spirit, the local tribes united and were able to repel the invading Dakota.

In the VILLAGE PARK on the lake shore are a plate and a stone marking the approximate SITE OF THE AMERICAN FUR COMPANY POST, established about 1820.

The town's important industry is its FISHERIES, which ship 2 million pounds of fish annually. Here also is a MILL FOR GRINDING FELDSPAR. The pulverized mineral is so fine that it will float in air. Feldspar, chiefly used in making enamelware and porcelain, serves as a flux to bind together the flint and clay. It is also a prime ingredient in the glaze for chinaware and tiles, and plays a less important part in soap-making, the manufacture of polishes, and dentistry. Warroad's co-operative FISH MEAL FACTORY converts tullibees, or whitefish, and burbots (see above) into chicken feed and fertilizer.

LAKE OF THE WOODS (for boats, see above). When the treaty that gave the United States independence was signed in Paris in 1783, the Mississippi River was believed to be west of the Lake of the Woods. This geographical misconception was the primary factor in the agreement that gave the United States not only the southern shore of the lake, but also many islands and the NORTHWEST ANGLE.

The Angle is entirely isolated from the mainland and is the northernmost portion of land in the United States; there are no roads to this area. During the summer it is reached by boat from Warroad, the nearest settlement, and by dog team, plane, or wind sled in the winter. From the village of Penasse in the northwest corner of the Angle it is 40 miles across water or ice to Warroad, and it is approximately 75 miles to Baudette, the county seat. For several weeks during the fall and spring, when the ice is forming or breaking up, the people on the Angle and the islands are entirely isolated from the mainland except for shortwave radio communication.

At the northern peak of the Angle, leading northwest from Harrison Creek, runs the old DAWSON ROAD; this historic overland route to Winnipeg and the Northwest carried the traffic of the eastern seaboard from the terminus of the water route. The old turnpike is well defined for almost 9 miles. Before the railroad was built it was the only thoroughfare into the Canadian Northwest and was traversed by several hundred Red River ox carts.

Two miles across open water from the Point on the Angle mainland is the FELDSPAR MINE, operated until 1934, when a low-water stage hindered barge movements and forced its abandonment. The Angle feldspar dike is one of the largest in North America, with an estimated possible volume of 16,000 to 18,000 tons. In bright sunlight the feldspar, strewn with fragments of dynamited rock, glows like fire.

Of historical interest, in addition to the SITE OF FORT ST. CHARLES (marked), on the southern shore of the Northwest Angle Inlet about 2 miles west of American Point *(see HISTORICAL SURVEY)*, and the Dawson Road, is MASSACRE ISLAND, in Canadian waters, where, in 1736, 21 Frenchmen—among them Jean-Baptiste, eldest son of the Sieur de la Vérendrye, and Father Aulneau—perished at the hands of the Sioux. Their bodies were brought to Fort St. Charles and buried under the chapel.

The lake abounds with small- and large-mouth bass, crappie, pickerel, salmon, trout—some weighing up to 40 pounds—muskellunge (one weighed 59½ pounds, the largest ever caught), perch, sauger, sucker, sunfish, and whitefish. At one time sturgeon—some of which weighed 285 pounds—were here in almost incredible numbers. In 1895 the catch in the lake's U. S. waters alone amounted to 1,300,000 pounds with roe totaling 97,500 pounds; sturgeon are now very scarce. The hunting in this region is excellent; deer are numerous, and ducks, attracted by the abundant wildrice, are plentiful.

All of the U. S. islands in the Lake of the Woods are north of the 49th parallel. Despite their rocky composition they are beautifully forested with pine and spruce. The gray, worn rock is cracked and broken; the ground is covered ankle-deep with carpet moss and ground-clinging underbrush. A gray-green lichen marks the rocks in strange designs. Saxifrage, one of the earliest flowering plants, and rough *Erigeron* or fleabane grow on the ledges; both are rare in Minnesota. Although the temperature drops to 40° below zero each winter, and the summer season is very short, the little cactus known as prickly pear survives on several of the small barren islands.

Between Warroad and Roseau, State 11 follows the old Sandridge Trail, used successively by Indians, fur-traders, and early settlers.

A tall NORWAY PINE, at 112 *m.*, was an early landmark.

At 114.6 *m.* is a portion of the ALGOMA SWAMP, which only a few decades ago was a trackless and dangerous quagmire. Drainage projects financed by the State as well as destructive forest fires have helped to change much of this former muskeg into workable land, and today some cultivated crops grow in the burnt-over region that formerly had only sedge and aquatic plants.

SALOL, 120.3 *m.*, a short time ago was a thriving timber town; today only a few bleached and settling piles of sawdust remain from its lumbering days. According to tradition three Swedes were delegated to ask help of Roseau's leading citizens in choosing a name for the new town; but when they reached the county seat, the delegation fell in with gay company, and so hospitable was their welcome that the Swedes lost all track of time. With sunrise the painful prospect of greeting their still unnamed town bestirred their groggy minds. Inspired, at last, they strode into the local drugstore, grasped a drawer marked "Labels," and drew forth "Salol," and Salol it remains to this day.

Right from Salol on a country road to LOST CREEK, 5 *m.*, which, at times 15 feet wide with a noticeable current, often merges with the quagmire and then disappears entirely.

The name of ROSEAU, 129.4 *m.*, (1,047 alt., 1,028 pop.), is derived from "Riviere aux Roseaux" (Fr., *river of the rushes*). Roseau is the seat of Roseau County and the dominant trading center and shipping point of the surrounding area; there is also a creamery here.

Two artifacts of apparent antiquity have been discovered near Roseau—a ROUND STONE displaying incised figures within a circle, believed by some authorities to be prehistoric writing, and an IVORY FISH SPEAR. The ROSEAU COUNTY HISTORICAL MUSEUM is on the second floor of the MUNICIPAL AUDITORIUM.

Left from Roseau on State 89 to the junction with an improved road at 4.8 *m.*; L. on this road to MALUNG, 8 *m.*, a small community settled by immigrants from Dalarne, Sweden.

At 132.7 *m.* the highway ascends a high gravel ridge. This is CAMPBELL BEACH of the glacial Lake Agassiz *(see NATURAL SETTING)*, once the historic Sandridge Trail on the route of the old War Road. State 11 follows the ancient shore line for approximately 35 miles.

The post office of FOX, 135.9 *m.*, was named by the community's first citizen, T. S. Nomeland, who, it is reported, selected the name of an animal because the ridge already contained a Badger Village and a Skunk Creek. Platted in 1909 by Nels K. White, Fox never attained a population large enough to admit its incorporation as a village, although in 1917 and 1918 there were four stores, an elevator, and a lumberyard.

Right from Fox on County Rd. B to ROSS, 5 *m.*, a small community settled largely by immigrants from the Halling Valley region in Norway.

Right from Ross on a country road to the JESSE NELSON FARM, 1 *m.*, on the site of an old Indian village. The legend of the Windego, Ghost of Roseau Lake, centers about this place. This ghost terrified the inhabitants for generations, not so much because of its spectral appearance as by the fact that its coming presaged death. The Nelsons saw the ghost on several occasions; a vivid description is included in the *Nelson History:* "I was in the yard at the Mickinock house about mid-afternoon, looking south I saw that apparition rise by the side of the muskeg and start walking westward; it stumbled and nearly fell; then it started to run and several times stumbled, but each time it recovered and ran on for about a quarter of a mile. Finally it went out of sight behind the east end of the grove on the small ridge on Bertilrud's homestead. The apparition was about fifteen feet tall, dressed in some material that looked like white lace. Whatever it may have been it was not a hallucination of superstitious fears in the dark, for I saw it in broad daylight. Mrs. Mickinock died the following morning."

At PINECREEK, 11.5 *m.* on County Rd. B., a port of entry, stands the FIRST CHURCH in Roseau County; the building was constructed of logs cut in 1891 and intended for a fort.

BADGER, 143.8 *m.* (325 pop.), in the days of early settlement was on the route followed by home-seekers north to the Roseau River.

GREENBUSH, 153 *m.* (1,071 alt., 387 pop.), sprang up in 1904 when the Great Northern Ry. was built to the sand ridge; it was incorporated a year later. The town site was purchased from Ole O. Hereim for whom the township is named. The name Greenbush was applied first to the old town to the east, where a heavy coppice of evergreens became a landmark and stopping place for settlers traveling the Sandridge Trail.

In the early days the flat lands were mostly covered with water. Next to the ridge lay a floating bog—almost impossible to cross. Today the territory has been drained and is built up into farmsteads; even some of the erstwhile bog is under cultivation. Much of this soil is adapted to growing sweetclover; dairying and seed-raising are the principal types of agriculture. Greenbush has a modern, farmers' co-operative creamery, producing approximately 375,000 pounds of butter annually.

The village has a CITY HALL and THEATER and a fine water system with a tower and power-house.

At 160.9 *m.* State 11 cuts through one of three INDIAN MOUNDS about whose origin early settlers heard an explanation by the Indian, Mickinock. The tale concerns the time when Campbell Beach and the Cypress Hills of Manitoba were islands in a great lake. One autumn a boat was beached by a storm and 14 strange people of fair skin and light hair escaped from the wreck. The little marooned band built three sod wigwams (the three mounds). Famine and illness took their toll, and in the spring only one man and five children were left alive. The Indians on the Cypress Mountains saw the smoke of the white man's fire and came to help. The children intermarried and Mickinock maintained that his auburn-haired wife was a descendant of these white men. The mounds have never been investigated.

PELAN, 163.4 *m.*, a ghost town where the South Fork of Two Rivers cuts the ridge, was named for Charles Pelan, an Englishman who squandered a considerable patrimony in the saloons between Winnipeg and Crookston. He arrived here about 1880 and started a cattle ranch "for pleasure and for sport." Neither Pelan nor Long, another settler, remained, but by 1890 a steady stream of pioneers was arriving to take up homesteads on this northern frontier. A rumored Indian uprising in 1891 checked the growth and many frightened families left the Roseau Valley, traveling by ox team through Pelan. The uprising, however, was averted.

One of the earliest establishments in the village was the Pelan Hotel or Halfway House, on the stage route between Stephen and Roseau. Once each week broncos pulled the stages into the town, usually at a speed of 6 miles an hour—sometimes as fast as 10 miles an hour.

An early advertisement in the Pelan *Advocate* read: "Girls, here's your chance! A handsome young man with a good income offers a good home to the right party. Address all communications to Box 76, Pelan, Minnesota." Women here, as in many frontier towns, were scarce.

Only the weed-grown foundations and bits of high rickety boardwalks remain in this once boisterous village.

KARLSTAD, 172.5 *m.* (1,048 alt., 364 pop.), on the Sandridge Trail, was settled in 1883 by August Carlson and his family, who were its only inhabitants for a decade. In 1904, Soo Line officials platted a town and built their railroad; the village grew rapidly, drawing its population from nearby towns farther removed from transportation lines.

Karlstad has a number of business establishments, including a co-operative creamery. There is a theater, a hotel, and a 9-hole public golf course.

Karlstad is at the junction (L) with US 59 *(see Tour 17)*, which unites with State 11 for 4 miles.

DONALDSON, 187.8 *m. (see Tour 4)*, is at the junction with US 75 *(see Tour 4)*.

At 200.9 *m.* State 11 crosses the Red River (the North Dakota Line), 57 miles east of Langdon, N. Dak.

◄◄◄◄◄◄◄◄◄◄◄◄◄◄◄◄◄◄ ✿ ►►►►►►►►►►►►►►►►►►

Tour 7

(Superior, Wis.)—Duluth—Grand Rapids—Bemidji—Crookston—East
Grand Forks—(Grand Forks, N. Dak.) ; US 2.
Wisconsin Line to North Dakota Line, 269.2 m.

Route is paralleled by Great Northern Ry. between Duluth and North Dakota Line;
Northern Pacific Ry. between Crookston and East Grand Forks.
Bituminous-treated roadbed between Duluth and Grand Rapids, paved between
Grand Rapids and Deer River, bituminous-treated between Deer River and Bemidji,
and paved between Bemidji and the North Dakota Line. Open all year.
Accommodations available at the larger towns.

This route winds westward and slightly northward from commercial
Duluth across upper Minnesota, through the Arrowhead region and the
Chippewa National Forest, where it runs between Leech and Winnibigosh-
ish Lakes, and enters the Paul Bunyan resort area; it traverses the fine
farm land of the Red River Valley to the Red River, the boundary between
Minnesota and North Dakota.

Section a. WISCONSIN LINE (DULUTH) *to* BEMIDJI. *156.2 m. US 2.*

US 2 crosses the Wisconsin Line in Duluth *(see Wisconsin, Tour 14).*
DULUTH, 0 *m.* (626 alt., 101,463 pop.) *(see DULUTH).*

Points of Interest. Aerial Lift Span across the ship canal, ore docks, Skyline Parkway, Incline, Minnesota Point.

Duluth is at the junction with US 61 *(see Tour 1)* and US 53 *(see
Tour 5).*

US 2 crosses the ST. LOUIS RIVER, 28.3 *m.*, at this point a turbulent,
rushing stream churning along a rocky bottom on its way to Lake Superior.
The river was probably named by the Sieur de la Vérendrye, who began
explorations in this region in 1731.

FLOODWOOD, 47.3 *m.* (1,257 alt., 343 pop.), was named for the
natural rafts of driftwood that obstructed the nearby stream. North of this
point the St. Louis River meanders through a broad, marshy valley once
covered by glacial Lake Upham. The silt deposits of this ancient lake are
visible here, but in much of the area they are covered with peat bogs and
swamps.

At one time the region around ISLAND, 53 *m.* (1,274 alt.), a small
village, was dry farm land surrounded by densely wooded spruce swamps.

Entering Itasca County at 57.9 *m.*, US 2 follows a northwesterly course
through rugged, hilly country.

SWAN RIVER, 64.5 *m.* (1,279 alt.).

Right from Swan River on State 65 to GOODLAND, 5.7 *m.*, a small community,
where the co-operative is the only method of merchandising in use.

At 76.2 *m.* (L) the MISSISSIPPI RIVER is only a short distance from the highway. Between this point and 88.8 *m.* US 2 parallels the river.

At 82.7 *m.* is the ghost town of LA PRAIRIE. Poor judgment was exercised in platting this hamlet on a site below the head of navigation, now commanded by Grand Rapids. Although all the buildings have been moved away, the outlines of the old street are still visible.

GRAND RAPIDS, 83.7 *m.* (1,290 alt., 3,206 pop.), the seat of Itasca County, is a gateway to the Arrowhead fishing region. Four beautiful lakes lie within its limits, and more than 100 resorts are within short driving distance. An artistic BRIDGE in the heart of Grand Rapids spans the Mississippi, and a few hundred feet north of it is the Blandin PAPER FACTORY *(guides available during the summer),* with a DAM to supply water power. This ultra-modern plant is built without windows, which not only gives more space but insures precise control of air-conditioning and lighting facilities—important factors in paper-making. The mill, largest in the Northwest, has operated profitably all through the depression. It employs 225 people at prevailing wages for 6-hour days, and in the last 20 years has increased its daily output from 25 to 150 tons; it also creates a convenient market for the products of loggers and farmers within a radius of 60 miles.

The ITASCA COUNTY FAIRGROUNDS, 45 acres, on the northern outskirts of Grand Rapids, are among the most beautiful in the State. They lie in a natural theater, oval in shape, on the shore of CRYSTAL LAKE, entirely surrounded by virgin pine.

Grand Rapids is at the junction with US 169 *(see Tour 3).*

Right from Grand Rapids on State 38 to BIGFORK, 32.9 *m.* (1,292 alt., 295 pop.), a logging center; many million feet of timber are moved out of the area by truck each year. The old logging road parallels State 38 and offers glimpses of logging activity.

The Paul Bunyan tales depicting the lumberjacks as profane and boastful do an injustice to these woodsmen, whose energy is the basis of prosperity in the timber belt. In recent years there has been a decided change in the nationality of the woodsmen. From 1875 to the turn of the century, natives of Sweden outnumbered all other immigrants in the big timber operations that began just above the Twin Cities and gradually moved northward as the timber line receded. Today the Finns are the most numerous among European-born jacks, but native-born Americans are in the majority.

Right from Big Fork on a graveled road to SCENIC STATE PARK *(camping, fishing, boats, tackle),* 39.9 *m.* One of Minnesota's most interesting natural parks (1,632 acres), it was set aside by the State to preserve an original stand of virgin pine and includes within its borders four beautiful lakes, COON, SANDWICK, LAKE OF THE ISLES, and CEDAR. Bass, bluegill, crappie, and great-northern and wall-eyed pike abound in these lakes.

The natural beauty of the park has been emphasized and its recreational facilities increased by the work of the CCC. New trails have been made through the timber, and there is an excellent TOURIST CAMPGROUND *(electric lights, hot and cold water, free kitchen facilities, ice house, and a fish house; recreational buildings, log cabins, free; staple groceries and supplies).*

COHASSET (Ind., *place of pines*), 88.8 *m.* (1,287 alt., 299 pop.).

US 2 now runs in an almost straight line among numerous lakes with sandy beaches. Sandy loam soil predominates in the area, and most of the timber is second growth. A divide crosses this part of the State distributing the water to three watersheds; the Hudson Bay, the Gulf of Mexico, and the St. Lawrence.

At DEER RIVER, 98.9 *m.* (1,294 alt., 832 pop.), the highway enters the CONSOLIDATED CHIPPEWA INDIAN RESERVATION. In this town is the STATE FORESTRY STATION'S HEADQUARTERS. Deer River is also the base of supplies for a large number of summer resorts and fishing camps on the shores of the surrounding lakes.

The country is not naturally adapted to farming, but farms have been literally carved from the stump lands adjacent to Deer River. The businessmen of the village, realizing the value of agriculture in the vicinity, gave every possible assistance to the farmers; markets were established for the purchase of their products and a creamery was built.

In addition to a huge amount of pulpwood that passes through Deer River, the town supplies about 8,000 cords of wood annually for the production of matches. A packing company maintains a box factory here.

The centralized grade and high school is one of the few public schools in the United States having dormitories; here about 100 boys and girls are accommodated.

At 100.9 *m.* is the junction with State 46.

Right on State 46, through the superb scenery of the Cut Foot Sioux district of the Chippewa National Forest, to the TURTLE AND SNAKE INDIAN MOUND, 16.5 *m.,* along the shore of CUT FOOT SIOUX LAKE. This mound is in the shape of a turtle, about 25 feet wide by 30 feet long, with the head pointing north. Around the turtle is built a snake of proportionate size with the head and tail meeting and pointing south.

The mound's origin and interpretation are interesting. This region originally belonged to the Sioux but was coveted for its rich resources by the Chippewa. In 1748 a major battle, ending in the complete rout of the Chippewa, was fought on the spot where the mound now stands. The Sioux, jubilant and eager to commemorate the victory, built the turtle part of the mound with the head pointing north to signify that the enemy had been driven in that direction.

The defeat suffered by the Chippewa only increased their determination; they returned in the summer of 1748. In the ensuing battle, the Chippewa surrounded and massacred the Sioux to the last man and built the snake around the turtle, to signify that the Sioux had been surrounded and annihilated. The head of the snake was pointed south as a warning to other Sioux tribes and as an indication of the future path of Chippewa conquest.

The morning after the battle, while the Chippewa were still dividing the spoils, some of their squaws found on the lake shore an unconscious Sioux warrior whose foot was almost severed. The squaws dispatched the warrior with alacrity, and the Chippewa thereafter referred to this lake as the "Lake of the Cut Foot Sioux."

The CUT FOOT SIOUX RANGER STATION *(information about the forest)* is at 17 *m.* The original ranger station, built in 1904 on the site of an old camping ground at the head of the portage, was vacated about 1918 but is still in good condition.

At 18 *m.* (R) is the Inger Rd. (marked), which closely follows an old portage, approximately 4 miles long. This portage between Little Cut Foot Sioux Lake and the Bowstring River crossed the divide and was used by the Chippewa and Sioux for generations.

Right on the Inger Rd. to INGER, 21.3 *m.,* and an INDIAN VILLAGE.

At 22 *m.* is a STATE FISH HATCHERY *(open to visitors).* More than 75,000,-000 fry are hatched here annually and planted in the various lakes of the district.

At 24 *m.* is the CUT FOOT SIOUX CCC CAMP, and at 32 *m.* a roadside sign marks the spot where the highway crosses the divide.

In the deep forest of Norway pine covering this area, pine-thinning experiments are being carried on by the Minnesota Department of Conservation. The entire Cut Foot Sioux region is nationally known for its water-fowl shooting and for its excellent "duck passes," strips of land between two lakes with blinds from which hunters shoot. Ducks of every variety are found on the many lakes, where wildrice beds supply their favorite food. The region abounds also with partridge, prairie chicken, and pheasant. Various resorts remain open for the fall hunting season. On the lake shores are free public campgrounds under the supervision of the Forest Service.

West of Deer River US 2 traverses the hilly, wooded country of the CHIPPEWA NATIONAL FOREST, whose original gross area of 312,-659 acres, approximately 60 per cent Government-owned, was established as a national forest in 1902. The boundaries now enclose 325,000 acres, and 1,105,000 acres are in the process of acquisition. Lake-shore summer homesites of one acre can be leased for $15 a year.

During the early logging operations near here, millions of feet of lumber were cut; large areas once considered inexhaustible are now waste lands. A half-million dollars has been spent buying back large tracts of exhausted lands for reforestation and conservation, but there has been no mass re-settlement movement; small tracts capable of supporting communities will remain in private hands. With the decline of lumbering many of the towns that once flourished have disappeared or become mere hamlets.

Although fire and logging have in the past been almost equally destructive, the former is today the greater hazard in the fight to reclaim the land; 90 per cent of the fires in the Chippewa Forest are caused by man. The Forest Service posts warnings at all camps and distributes fire-prevention literature; practical demonstrations and motion-picture exhibits are constantly employed. Twelve Federal lookout towers and nine State towers help to guard the forest. One hundred and eight miles of telephone lines, well-kept roads and trails, water tanks, tools, fire pumps, and trucks are all maintained primarily for the fight waged by rangers and farmers against fires that average thirty-two a year. The one at Crooked Lake in 1933 covered 4,165 acres of an area that was mostly meadowland. The source of every fire is investigated, and persons found guilty of fire-law infractions are vigorously prosecuted.

There are 200 million board feet of merchantable timber in the Chippewa Forest today. Replanting, begun in 1911, has added 15,000 acres, mostly of Norway pine, to the forest area; yearly planting of 15,000 acres is anticipated by 1940.

At BALL CLUB, 105.9 *m.* (50 pop.), is an Indian village named for nearby Ball Club Lake whose form suggested a lacrosse racket to the Indians.

At BENA, 118.7 *m.* (1,311 alt., 145 pop.), is a CCC CAMP and a RANGER STATION.

Bena is at the foot of LAKE WINNIBIGOSHISH (Ind., *miserable, wretched, dirty water*), a mudbottom lake so shallow (probably not more than 20 or 25 feet) that the water becomes roiled during storms. Adjacent LEECH LAKE, on the south, is the site of the last Indian uprising in the

State; today the United States Indian Service maintains tribal headquarters here. In the 1880's the largest undertaking in this territory, with the exception of timber-cutting and railroad-building, was the construction of headwater dams at Leech and Winnibigoshish Lakes, two of the Government's great series designed to control the flow of water on the lower Mississippi. To this end engineers surveyed the Minnesota, the Wisconsin, and all other important rivers of the North. Several hundred men were employed; sawmills were erected; oxen, boats, and horses were kept busy bringing in materials and supplies. The problem of transporting materials into the new country was a difficult one. There were no roads, and during the winter materials had to be brought from Brainerd to the southern end of Leech Lake on sleighs drawn by horses or oxen; from this point they were taken across the ice to the dams.

The Leech and Winnibigoshish dams were built in 1882–83 of white pine mostly 12 by 12 inches, but they lasted only 15 years. The one at Leech Lake could not sustain the heavy head of water and started to go down. Winnibigoshish dam also proved inadequate. In 1898 the dams were rebuilt of steel and concrete.

An annual Pow-Wow is held at Bena on July Fourth.

SCHLEY, 126.1 *m.*, a small hamlet named for Rear Admiral Winfield Scott Schley of Spanish-American War fame, was established in 1898–99.

At 133.8 *m.* is (L) a PUBLIC CAMPGROUND *(free camping, swimming, tables, fireplaces).*

CASS LAKE, 137.8 *m.* (1,321 alt., 1,409 pop.) *(see Tour 20)*, is at the junction with US 371 *(see Tour 20).*

BEMIDJI, 156.2 *m.* (1,351 alt., 7,202 pop.), seat of Beltrami County, was named for Chief Bemidji (Ind., *Cross Lake*), a Chippewa whose band of about 50 made their home at the site of the present city on the southern end of LAKE BEMIDJI. The town is equidistant from three Indian reservations, Red Lake Reservation to the north, White Earth to the west, and Leech Lake to the east.

This was one of the last areas opened to settlement along the Mississippi between Lake Itasca and the Gulf. In 1894 homesteaders found some quartzite pebbles on the lake shore and, thinking them diamonds, purchased many acres in the vicinity. The little boom that followed soon collapsed and in 1895 tamaracks still grew in its streets. Then came the lumber barons and within 20 years all the timber thereabouts had disappeared. In these two decades sawmills sprang up as by magic until there were 14 that among them cut a million feet of lumber every day. Railroads connected the village with the outside world and the town became one of the most lawless lumber centers in the Northwest.

Of all these sawmills that once ran day and night, today there remains only one. The lake shore, once buffeted by rafts of logs and trampled by calked boots of swampers, is now serene with parks and gardens. But the names of Bemidji's streets still suggest the stream of woodsmen who once poured into the town—Chippewa and French Canadians, Scottish and Irish, Polish and Scandinavian, German, Finnish, and Icelandic.

Bemidji is now a trade center for the surrounding district. The sawmills have been replaced by smaller woodworking plants, and dairying has become an important industry. Four creameries are within the city. The Interstate Hydro-electric Plant supplies light and power to the surrounding area. Bemidji, however, is best known as the hub of a large recreational area that abounds with lakes and virgin timber, fish and game.

The BEMIDJI CIVIC AND COMMERCE ASSOCIATION BUREAU, 3d St. and Bemidji Ave., will furnish information concerning the town and surrounding area. On the shore of beautiful Lake Bemidji, at a point where all Federal and State highways passing through the city converge, this tourist bureau is one of the best in the State. Constructed as a Government project, its building shows excellent workmanship; even the shingles and doors are hand-made. The immense fireplace, known as the FIREPLACE OF STATES, contains stones from every State, from almost every province in Canada, and from several foreign countries. The PAUL BUNYAN FIGURE, on the lake shore to the R. of the building, is 18 feet high and built of steel and concrete.

In LIBRARY PARK, on Bemidji Ave. between 3d and 6th Sts., is a STATUE OF CHIEF BEMIDJI carved from a log. One story of its origin says that it was made by a lumberjack for a man who had aided him, and another that it was done by a man to show his gratitude to the chief, who had saved his life during a massacre.

An annual Winter Carnival is held here in February.

At Bemidji is the junction with US 71 *(see Tour 2)*.

Section b. BEMIDJI *to* NORTH DAKOTA LINE, *113 m.* US 2.

West of Bemidji US 2 crosses lumbering country where a considerable amount of cutting is still being done. The pine forests in this territory furnish excellent cover for game. Ranger station towers rise above the dense forest every 15 miles.

At 8.1 *m.* is the junction with State 89.

Right on State 89 to the junction with State 1, 26.3 *m.;* R. on State 1 to RED LAKE VILLAGE, 27.3 *m.,* on Lower Red Lake; here are the INDIAN SCHOOL *(open to visitors)* and ADMINISTRATION BUILDINGS OF THE RED LAKE INDIAN RESERVATION. The land for this reservation was originally set aside by the treaty negotiated by Governor Ramsey with the Chippewa at the old crossing of the Red Lake River in 1863.

Indians on the reservation augment the small Government annuity they receive by hunting and gathering wildrice and berries. Blueberries are plentiful, and besides the supply they gather for their own use the Indians sell a large quantity to tourists; they also sell hand-made trinkets. During the winter many of them trap fur-bearing animals whose pelts they dispose of at points along the Canadian Border.

The forest in this region is primitive, and tourists will find an interesting cross-section of early backwoods American life. The Indians still travel almost entirely by canoe or on foot, as there are very few horses and no roads through the forest— only narrow, deeply grooved trails. Their houses are mostly of logs.

The combined UPPER AND LOWER RED LAKE, which contains no islands and is very shallow in proportion to its size, is about 30 miles in diameter and is divided into two sections by long peninsulas projecting from its eastern and western shores, forming a strait about 2.5 miles wide.

At REDBY, 33.3 *m.,* is a CO-OPERATIVE FISHERY, organized by Indians of the

Red Lake Reservation, which provides a market for the entire reservation; in addition there is a community-owned mill *(see FIRST AMERICANS)*.

At 37.5 *m.* is the junction with a newly constructed all-weather road, that circles the eastern end of Lower Red Lake.

Left on this road to the village of PONEMAH, 60 *m.*, inhabited by Indians who cling to their ancient religion and still observe most of the customs of their forefathers. They have an unusual burial ritual and are often referred to as pagan Indians because of their reluctance to use Christian graveyards. They bury their dead in little houses near the road and place food on a shelf for the spirit of the dead relative. In the summer these Indians move out-of-doors; nearly every house has a tepee of some kind near it. These are not conical but are built with rounded tops that give them a blunt streamline admirably adapted to resist windstorms.

At 66 *m.* is an INDIAN VILLAGE at RED LAKE NARROWS, where Upper and Lower Red Lakes join. On this narrow spit of high land stands one of the finest forests of virgin pine in the State—an isolated remnant overlooked by the lumber interests.

At 25.3 *m.,* near Clearwater River, US 2 passes through a stretch of muskeg in which beautiful wild flowers bloom in the summer.

In BAGLEY, 26.3 *m.* (1,446 alt., 885 pop.), seat of Clearwater County, is a FOREST RANGER SUBSTATION *(information about surrounding country).*

The last heavy forest of pine and spruce is at 36.6 *m.* The forest's floor is a thick carpet of pine needles, and in places the foliage is so dense that no sunlight can enter.

FOSSTON, 43.7 *m.* (1,298 alt., 978 pop.), has developed since 1884 from two shed-roofed frame buildings to a bustling modern village. Potatoes are raised extensively near Fosston, and some flax is grown on drained marsh land, but the drainage was so expensive that flax-raising is not very profitable. Moreover the drainage project, planned to affect only marsh lands, has changed many formerly clear and beautiful lakes in the vicinity to weed-grown lake beds, surrounded by arid sand beaches. The restoration of these lakes is being undertaken by the State conservation department, which is buying land from the farmers in hopes of reviving the natural beauty of the region and its former splendid fishing and wild-fowl shooting.

A TOURIST PARK *(camping, running water)* is at the southeastern edge of town.

Westward from the forest region, agriculture becomes more intensive. Light corn and grain crops are varied by an occasional field of sweet clover, a potato patch, or lowland pasture. Heavy crops are rare except where US 2 penetrates Red River Valley.

In tamarack swamps of the area are pink and white moccasin flowers, also called ladyslippers or Indian shoes; this, the State flower, is now almost extinct because of ruthless picking.

At 57 *m.* is (R) the WIN-E-MAC GOLF CLUB *(9 holes, reasonable fee),* owned jointly by the neighboring villages of Winger, Erskine, and McIntosh, from whose first syllables its name is derived.

ERSKINE, 57.8 *m.* (1,201 alt., 511 pop.), on the Minneapolis, St. Paul & Sault Ste. Marie Ry. and the Great Northern Ry., is at the southern edge of LAKE BADGER. It is the principal marketing and shipping point for the surrounding territory.

Erskine is at the junction with US 59 *(see Tour 17)*.

At 71.7 *m.* is the junction with State 32.

Right on State 32 to RED LAKE FALLS, 9 *m.* (1,210 alt., 1,386 pop.), seat of Red Lake County. In 1798 a Northwest Company trading post was established at Red Lake Falls under Jean Baptiste Cadotte. Lured by the wealth of furs and skins that brought fortunes in European markets, French settlers swarmed into the territory; today this dairying community is still predominantly French.

At 76.3 *m.* US 2 descends 159 feet in 12 miles from a ridge that runs north and south, one of the beaches of ancient Lake Agassiz, and enters the Red River Valley. Near the highway are occasional bunches of bittersweet, tangles of juniper, and brakes of balsam and cedar. On the low hills are apple thickets, hazel brush, sumac, dogwood, and wild currant.

At 86 *m.* is the junction (L) with US 75 *(see Tour 4)*.

CROOKSTON, 88.2 *m.* (863 alt., 6,321 pop.), seat of Polk County, was named for Col. William Crooks (1832–1907), chief engineer of the first railroad to reach this vicinity. The surrounding region's outstanding topographical features are a broad level valley once filled by glacial Lake Agassiz and a series of ridges or beaches marking the recessional stages of the lake.

Composed of the fine-grained lacustrine sediment of this ancient lake, the fertile topsoil has been long famous for its production of hard spring wheat. Annually Polk County averages more than 2 million bushels of wheat, double that of any other Minnesota county. It is also a great producer of barley, flax, and potatoes. Agricultural diversification is increasing yearly, however, and the income from small grains, potatoes, and sugar beets is being nearly matched by dairying and livestock-raising. Turkeys and wool, too, are important sources of income.

First settled in 1872 and incorporated 1879 as a city, Crookston today is a major trade center in northern Minnesota with over 35 wholesale and 300 retail establishments. Among these are a flour mill, flax fibre factory, honey refinery, and two creameries.

Hundreds of farm youths from the valley come to the NORTHWEST SCHOOL AND EXPERIMENT STATION at Crookston, a branch of the University of Minnesota, designed to further agricultural knowledge throughout the Northwest. Under its auspices are held the annual Red River Valley Agricultural Expositions, with displays of grain, potatoes, livestock, and poultry. Thousands attend these exhibits to learn of advances in all phases of farming.

MOUNT ST. BENEDICT, a Roman Catholic school for girls, is in the southern part of the city. The city has 18 churches, 2 hospitals, and a tuberculosis sanatorium; the latter is on the banks of the Red Lake River.

CENTRAL PARK *(tourist camp, swimming, tennis court, playgrounds)* is one of the city's three large landscaped parks.

At 90.4 *m.* is (R) the junction with US 75 *(see Tour 4)*.

FISHER, 99 *m.* (836 alt., 297 pop.). After the panic of 1873, the

Minnesota & Pacific Ry. tracks to Warren were torn up and relaid to Fisher, then called Fisher's Landing. Since it was at the head of navigation on the Red River, Fisher at once became an important frontier center, and soon outstripped Crookston in population. Steamboat navigation on the Red River declined, however, and the railroad was rebuilt through Warren to Winnipeg. After these changes, Fisher became an abandoned village.

In this community is the large plant of the American Crystal Sugar Company, supplied by the sugar-beet fields that extend over the surrounding country. Beet fields are cultivated with the aid of horses, but the weeding is done carefully by hand. Mexicans, because they will work for low wages, are employed to do a large part of this tedious weeding; they form a fairly large colony that seems strangely out of place in this north country. Many do not settle permanently but come here only for the beet season, and whole families weed in the fields together. Their gayety of manner and dress and their foreign speech are conspicuous in this conservative farming area.

EAST GRAND FORKS, 110.6 m. (835 alt., 2,922 pop.), is at the confluence of the Red Lake River and the Red River. A trading post was established on this site before 1800, but the village's history as a settlement did not begin until about 1880.

A sugar-beet factory in East Grand Forks operates through October, November, and December, and is supplied with beets grown in the surrounding district. When all the beets are harvested, a steam shovel loads them on trucks, and they are dumped through a chute that carries them into the machinery of the plant. There they are washed and chopped, and the sugar is extracted. The syrup is filtered, bleached, concentrated in vacuum pans, reduced to crystals, and then sacked in 10-, 25-, and 100-pound bags. Lump and powdered sugar are also manufactured.

At 113 m. US 2 crosses the Red River (the North Dakota Line) to Grand Forks, N. Dak. (see North Dakota, Tour 6).

<<<<<<<<<<<<<<<<<<<<<<<<✿>>>>>>>>>>>>>>>>>>>>>>>

Tour 8

Junction with US 61—Finland—Ely—Tower—Cook; State 1.
Junction with US 61 to Cook, 111.9 m.

The route is paralleled by Duluth & Iron Range Ry. between Ely and Tower.
Graveled roadbed between Illgen City and Ely, bituminous-treated between Ely and Peyla, and maintained earth between Peyla and junction with US 53. Passable in all seasons.

There are hotels in the larger towns only, but resorts and excellent camp sites are numerous.

This route follows State 1 (the Ely-Finland Trail) into the Superior National Forest, extends through the northeast extremity of the Iron Range, and traverses scenic lake shores of the Arrowhead region, which are dotted with numerous resorts and camp sites, a primeval haven for seasonal sportsmen.

At 0 *m.* State 1 branches northwest from its junction with US 61 *(see Tour 1)*, 0.3 miles northeast of Illgen City, a small resort center on Lake Superior.

The ILLGEN FALLS (L), 2.4 *m.*, of the Baptism River, are typical of many beautiful falls in the North Shore area. The river is one of the most fished of northern trout streams, having several branches and tributaries in its upper reaches; the road recrosses a west branch farther north.

At 5.5 *m.* the trail passes through the little Finnish settlement of FINLAND, where the State forest service has district headquarters. Finland is at the junction with a narrow graveled road, old State 1 *(see Tour 1)*.

At this point on the road several foot trails lead R. toward the upper Baptism River, where trout fishing is usually very fine. Some of these trails follow the course of old logging roads over decaying log bridges and in many places are almost obliterated by encroaching vegetation.

The region, although logged over, is still one of the wildest areas in Minnesota. Deep in the heart of this country are swamps with slender, black spruces as tall as virgin white pines; their green spirelike tops emerge from the lower branches, which are hung with gray, streaming moss.

In this region is found the now rare pink ladyslipper, a dainty wild orchid with the generic name *Cypripedium,* derived from the Greek word meaning *slipper of Venus.* This flower, which grows in the swamp lands among sphagnum moss, decaying logs, and wild cranberries, has few equals for delicate beauty.

At 8.2 *m.* the highway enters the SUPERIOR NATIONAL FOREST *(see SUPERIOR NATIONAL FOREST).*

At 16.2 *m.* is (R) the STATE GAME AND FISH STATION *(open to visitors),* where an old logging railroad makes an overhead crossing.

ISABELLA, 21.9 *m.*, is a small village for which this highway was named Isabella Trail.

At 27.5 *m.* (R) is a privately owned LODGE *(main lodge, cabins).*

At 49 *m.* is the SOUTH KAWISHIWI RIVER. Starting from Ely, canoe trips are made down this river *(see SUPERIOR NATIONAL FOREST: Canoe Trips).* The short portages fulfill one of the first prerequisites of a good canoe country. The carries average less than one-quarter mile. The SOUTH KAWISHIWI CAMP AND PICNIC GROUNDS *(fireplaces, water, tent and trailer sites)* are R., and the DISTRICT HEADQUARTERS OF THE U. S. FOREST SERVICE are L.

The pike fishing is good at BIRCH LAKE DAM CAMP AND PICNIC GROUNDS (R), 51.5 *m.* *(fireplaces, but no water),* maintained by the Minnesota Power & Light Company. Most of these northern lakes are noted for their excellent lake trout, pike, and pickerel. Bass are numerous in some lakes: brook and rainbow trout prefer the spring-fed creeks.

At 60.2 *m.* is the junction with County Rd. 35.

Right on this road to the junction with a dirt road, 0.3 *m.;* L. 0.5 *m.* on the dirt road to the ZENITH IRON MINE *(open by special permission),* which was opened in 1892 and is completely electrified.

At 0.9 *m.* on County Rd. 35 is the junction with County Rd. 88; L. 3 *m.* on this road to the junction with County Rd. 603; R. on County Rd. 603, the ECHO TRAIL, which runs northeast, then swerves north, and finally proceeds northwest, through the wilderness of the Superior National Forest. This is a 12-foot graveled road, much of it built on solid rock and seldom impassable.

Free camp sites and picnic grounds, identified by signs, are maintained by the U. S. Forest Service. All have tent and trailer sites, picnic grounds, and water. Canoe routes in the area include those used by the Hudson's Bay Company, the famed Dawson route, well known to all old fur-traders, and others used for centuries by the Indians and later by the French missionaries. At the time of the first Riel Rebellion (1870), English troops moved through this territory from Port Arthur to Fort Garry in a hundred big canoes.

The NORTH ARM BURNTSIDE LAKE CAMP AND PICNIC GROUNDS, 8 *m. (swimming beach)* are L.

The FENSKE LAKE CAMP AND PICNIC GROUNDS, 11.5 *m. (swimming beach),* are R.

The NELS LAKE CAMPGROUND, 14 *m.,* is R.

The SOUTH HEGMAN LAKE CAMP AND PICNIC GROUNDS, 16 *m. (swimming beach),* are R. Indian rock paintings, or pictographs, recently have been discovered on cliffs at the northeastern end of the lake. These ancient drawings include the figure of a man with five moons over his right shoulder, while below him are figures of moose and other game animals. Below the figures is a connecting line, which would seem to indicate that this is a picture-story type of drawing. Although there are several theories as to the meaning of these drawings, generally attributed to the Chippewa, their interpretation is still undecided.

SPRING CREEK CAMPGROUND, 18 *m.,* is L.

The trail skirts SECOND LAKE, on which is (R) the CAMPGROUND, 19 *m.,* and winds up and around a steep cliff overhanging the lake, a breath-taking drive on this narrow graveled road, with a sharp blind corner at the head of the climb.

At the northern end of Big Lake are (L) the BIG LAKE CAMP AND PICNIC GROUNDS, 23 *m. (swimming beach).*

In some places the highway is cut through stands of virgin timber that could well be called "cathedrals of pine." In the early morning or late afternoon deer are sometimes seen, standing with ears pricked to hear the slightest noise, yet seemingly unafraid.

PORTAGE RIVER CAMPGROUND, 25.5 *m.,* is L.

Overlooking Moose River is the CAMPGROUND, 28.2 *m.*

The MEANDER LAKE CAMP AND PICNIC GROUNDS, 31.2 *m. (swimming beach),* are R.

The trail, winding through fine stands of white, Norway, and jack pine, is probably the most beautiful forest road in Minnesota. Game is abundant throughout the area, particularly deer, moose, bear, and smaller animals.

At 34.8 *m.* is the SIOUX RIVER CAMPGROUND.

At 39.7 *m.* are (R) the LAKE JEANNETTE CAMP AND PICNIC GROUNDS *(swimming beach).*

The HUNTING SHACK RIVER CAMPGROUND, 43.8 *m.,* is (L) on Hunting Shack River; this is the last camp site passed on this trail.

At 52.5 *m.* is the junction of County Rd. 603 and County Rd. 24; L. on County Rd. 24 to BUYCK, 54.5 *m.,* a small settlement, which at one time was the Halfway House for prospectors on their way to the Rainy Lake gold fields.

ELY, 61.6 *m.* (1,417 alt., 6,158 pop.), lying on the shore of LAKE

SHAGAWA *(fishing, canoes, launches, swimming)* in the heart of a great northland wilderness, is a city of iron mines as well as a summer resort. Its summer temperature is pleasantly cool and its air free from the pollens that cause hay fever.

One of the last real frontier towns, Ely is the doorway to the country's most extensive canoeing area *(see SUPERIOR NATIONAL FOREST: Canoe Trips 6-13)*, yet it has all the advantages of civilization. A modern touch, for instance, is fishing from a hydroairplane. A plane *(Scenic Airways, Ely: $5.00 per trip and up)*, equipped with pontoons, takes fishing parties from Shagawa to any other nearby lake, and the passengers fish from the pontoons or are left to fish and camp for a longer time.

Ely has 8 schools—including a junior college, with 80 instructors and a student enrollment of 2,000—6 churches, a municipally owned water and light plant, and a community center.

SHAGAWA COUNTRY CLUB, 700 S. Central Ave., is a privately owned 9-hole golf course *(fees: 9 holes, 25¢; 18 holes, 50¢; $1 per day; $3.50 per week)*. MEMORIAL HIGH SCHOOL, 500 E. Harvey St., is a million-dollar building, thoroughly modern and completely equipped.

Ely is the capital city of the Vermilion Iron Range, northernmost of the iron ranges and the first to become productive *(see INDUSTRIAL DEVELOPMENT: Mining)*. Outcroppings of ore deposits were known to the Indians long before the white man's arrival.

Four iron mines, three of which are being operated, are included within the city limits. The active mines are the Pioneer, Zenith, and Sibley, employing normally 1,500 men and carrying an average monthly payroll of $200,000. All mines are underground and operate winter and summer, which makes Ely an all-year mining town. The ore from these mines is taken by rail to Two Harbors on Lake Superior; from there it is shipped by boat to the lower lakes.

Right from Sheridan St. (State 1) on Central Ave. to the junction with the Chandler Location Rd. 0.1 *m.;* R. on this road, which branches obliquely R. over the railroad tracks to the junction with a narrow dirt road (R), 0.2 *m.,* which leads to the PIONEER MINE (shaft B). The Pioneer *(open by special permission)* has two shafts and is one of the largest underground mines in the State. Fully electrified, it has shipped over a million gross tons of ore in one season.

The same method of obtaining ore is used in all these underground mines. Main shafts, reinforced by permanent wooden sides, are sunk outside the ore body at various points. From these shafts, drifts (tunnels) are driven through the solid rock to the ore deposit. Raises (openings) are bored upward from the main drift and subdrifts are made at convenient intervals, until the ore body is well honeycombed with openings; then the ore between the subdrifts is blasted out and dragged by scrapers or pulled by small air-driven electric hoists. The drifts slope toward the main shaft at an easy hauling grade. When the cars dump the ore, it is hoisted to the surface in steel skips (buckets running on rails or between guides) and emptied into cars for distribution to stock piles.

At 64.7 *m.* on State 1 is the junction with a dirt road, near the ROCK-CRUSHING PLANT of the Emeralite Rock Products Company.

Right on this road to BURNTSIDE LAKE, 2.8 *m. (fishing, swimming, canoes, launches, garage facilities, resorts; reasonable rates),* 7 miles long and 7 miles wide. One of the most popular in the border lakes region, Burntside has numerous islands and an irregular wooded shore.

At 80.1 *m.* JASPER PEAK (1,650 alt.), made up largely of red jasper, is passed. Atop it is a FOREST SERVICE LOOKOUT TOWER *(open to visitors)*, reached by a footpath, from which there is an excellent view of the surrounding country.

SOUDAN, 81.1 *m.* (1,500 alt., 800 pop.), is wholly a mining community. The SOUDAN MINE in the village is the oldest and deepest iron mine in Minnesota and produces the richest ore on the range; it is 65 per cent metallic iron. First exploration of the site was made in 1865, and the first shipment of ore, 62,122 gross tons, was made in 1884. The Soudan Mine, now 1,690 feet deep, was the first on the Vermilion Range to be modernized and electrified. The mechanical modernization was completed in 1924, and today an electric hoist lifts 17 tons of ore at 1,000 feet a minute. In October 1936 the ALASKA SHAFT, idle for 30 years, was reopened here. This mine had been sunk to the tenth level, before the ore crusher, engine house, and head frame were dismantled. The shaft is now served by an electric hoist.

By agreement with the village of Tower, Soudan has no stores of any kind, not even a filling station.

TOWER, 83.3 *m.* (801 pop.), on the shores of beautiful LAKE VERMILION *(swimming, boating, fishing, canoeing, resorts)*, is one of the largest and most popular summer resort lakes in the Arrowhead. Coniferous trees and lofty rolling hills of solid granite surround the lake, which is 35 miles long, has over 1,000 miles of shore line, and contains more than 365 islands. Fishermen are attracted to this lake from all over the United States. Wall-eyed pike, great-northern pike, muskellunge, perch, and rock bass are plentiful.

Lake Vermilion was called Sah-Ga-Ee-Gum-Wah-Ma-Mah-Nee (Ind., *Lake of the Sunset Glow*) by the Chippewa, who lived here for hundreds of years. The history of this region includes repeated battles between the Sioux and Chippewa, both of whom desired the excellent hunting and fishing ground. Later this became a fur-trading area and in 1865–66 was the scene of Minnesota's first gold rush. Finally the region was developed through the iron-mining industry. Tower is the oldest mining town in northern Minnesota, having been founded in 1882.

EAST TWO RIVERS flows into Vermilion Lake through Tower, making it possible for boats to navigate almost to the center of the village.

PEYLA, 87.8 *m.* (30 pop.), is a little settlement at the southernmost tip of Lake Vermilion.

State 1 runs westward along the divide and traverses beautiful country of fast streams and wooded lakes.

In COOK, 111.9 *m.* (1,320 alt., 300 pop.), dairying is the leading industry; a large business is done in the shipping of spruce and balsam for Christmas trees. Two Cook quarries yield a grayish blue granite. One of the two known deposits of green granite is near Cook; the other is in Germany.

Cook is at the junction with US 53 *(see Tour 5).*

◄◄◄◄◄◄◄◄◄◄◄◄◄◄◄◄◄◄◄◄◄◄◄☼►►►►►►►►►►►►►►►►►►►►►►

Tour 9

(Burr Oak, Iowa)—Rochester—Zumbrota—Twin Cities—Anoka—St. Cloud—Alexandria—Fergus Falls—Moorhead—(Fargo, N. Dak.); US 52.
Iowa Line to North Dakota Line, 391.6 m.

The Chicago Great Western R.R. parallels the route between Rochester and Twin Cities, Northern Pacific Ry. between Twin Cities and St. Cloud, and Great Northern Ry. between Twin Cities and Moorhead.
Paved roadbed entire distance, except for 26.8 miles between Evansville and junction with US 59. Open all year.
Adequate accommodations along entire route.

This route crosses the State diagonally from the southeastern corner to the central-western part of Minnesota; traversing the southeastern dairy-farming section it continues through Rochester, known for the Mayo Clinic, to the industrial Twin Cities; then crosses the Mississippi River and passes the granite quarries around St. Cloud; from there into a scenic lake region between Alexandria and Fergus Falls and on to the fertile Red River Valley and the North Dakota Line.

Section a. IOWA LINE to MINNEAPOLIS, 146.6 m. US 52.

US 52 crosses the Iowa Line, 0 *m.,* at a point 119 miles north of Dubuque, Iowa *(see Iowa, Tour 2).*
HARMONY, 9.3 *m.* (1,336 alt., 821 pop.), is L. of the highway.

Left from the northern outskirts of Harmony on State 139 to the junction with a county road, 2.9 *m.;* R. on this road to NIAGARA CAVE, 5.2 *m. (open year around, 7 a.m.-9 p.m.; adm. 55¢; guides).* A feature of the cave is a 60-foot SUBTERRANEAN WATERFALL 200 feet below the earth's surface; it cascades into an underground river. Other interesting formations in the electrically lighted cavern are a small NATURAL CHAPEL with open pews, a WISHING WELL, and 5 miles of passageway through three distinct levels. This cavern was accidentally discovered in 1926 by a farmer who repeatedly lost his pigs in a most mysterious manner. One after another they disappeared, and for a long time the explanation remained unknown. Then one day while walking through his fields he heard almost inaudible grunts and squeals. Following the sound he came to an opening in the earth, and further exploration led him to the vast subterranean caverns. In this labyrinth of tunnels the farmer found his errant pigs, and, more important, Niagara Cave's existence was revealed. It was opened to the public in 1933 and is the largest of a number of caves that have been discovered in this area.

At 17.1 *m.* is the junction (R) with US 16 *(see Tour 13);* between this point and Fountain, US 52 and US 16 are united.
At 19.9 *m.* the road skirts the village of PRESTON *(see Tour 13);* at 20.7 *m.* is (L) the PRESTON GOLF COURSE *(reasonable fee).*
FOUNTAIN, 24.8 *m.* (1,306 alt., 303 pop.), is built on rich, rolling

land underlain with limestone, and is named for its scores of natural springs. At Fountain is the junction (L) with US 16 *(see Tour 13)*.

In this section is rolling farm country. US 52 crosses the winding Root River at about 30 *m.*

CHATFIELD, 33.6 *m.* (976 alt., 1,269 pop.), once the seat of Fillmore County, was named for Judge Andrew Chatfield (1810–1875), who presided over the county's first court. The village has a municipally owned light plant, and a water system supplied by hillside springs. In the center of the village a marker (R) indicates the junction of the territorial road between St. Paul and Dubuque with another from Winona. Between 1856 and 1861 the southern Minnesota land office was here.

There are very few lakes in this section of the State, but streams and rivers—most of which flow into the Mississippi—are numerous. The steep slopes are occasionally crossed by zigzag paths—an indication of sheep grazing. The hilltops are forested with oak, maple, and elm. The valleys are grass-grown pastures for the many small dairy herds—usually Jersey or Guernsey—or fields of corn or wheat; only an occasional pig farm with its miniature gabled huts reminds one of the extensive hog-raising country to the south.

MARION, 45.4 *m.,* was a horse-changing stop on the old St. Paul-Dubuque stagecoach route, and in 1856 was the unsuccessful rival of Rochester for the county seat. Defeated in this ambition and ignored by the railroads, the village gradually declined in population to a few families.

ROCHESTER, 52 *m.* (988 alt., 20,621 pop.) *(see ROCHESTER).*

Points of Interest. Mayo Clinic, Medical Museum, Mayo Park, Pioneer Log Cabin, Soldiers' Memorial Field, Reid-Murdock Cannery.

Rochester is at the junction with US 14 *(see Tour 12)* and US 63 *(see Tour 18)*.

US 52 skirts the city along the south and west and passes a canning factory (L) topped with a huge ear of corn.

At 52.9 *m.* is the junction with 3rd Ave. SE.

Left on 3rd Ave. SE. to the privately owned A-1-A AIRPORT, 0.6 *m.,* with 2,600-foot runways and a 3-million-candlepower beacon. The airport receives day and night passenger and mail planes and operates additional emergency schedules. The well-equipped UNIVERSAL AVIATION SCHOOL offers a complete course in mechanical training and ground work.

At ORONOCO (R), 65 *m.* (1,041 alt., 150 pop.), the highway crosses two branches of the Zumbro River. Between the bridges a marker records the gold rush of 1857–58, when prospectors, hearing of gold flecks in the river, flocked to the town. A short-lived boom began with the formation of a mining company and the construction of sluices for washing out gold. Winter halted the operations; when spring floods swept away the sluices, enthusiasm waned, and the mining venture was abandoned. The town was established in 1854 by settlers who came to develop the water-power resources of the Zumbro. Today the town and its countryside receive their greatest income from herds of dairy cattle, Holsteins for the most part, which get abundant pasturage on the lowlands and on the slopes of the wooded knolls.

PINE ISLAND, 71.4 m. (961 pop.), is to the L. of the highway. Swiss settlers brought the art of cheese-making to Pine Island, which, with 30 factories in its vicinity, is known as the "Cheese Center of Minnesota." In 1914 a 6,000-pound cheese, said to have been the largest ever produced from one day's whey, was made on a flatcar and shipped to the State fair at St. Paul.

ZUMBROTA, 77.5 m. (975 alt., 1,350 pop.), is to the R. of the highway. In the ZUMBROTA FAIRGROUNDS, about 0.5 mile north from the center of town, is Minnesota's only COVERED BRIDGE, which once spanned the Zumbro River. The 116-foot structure, erected about 1863 (architect unknown), is of the latticed wooden-truss type and has a roadway 15 feet wide. Following New England precedent, the bridge resembles a capacious barn.

As the highway ascends the numerous rolling hills, it overlooks wide expanses of corn, wheat, and pasture, varied only by heavy groves of oak and numerous farms. The brick or stone silos, red barns, and white homes of the farmsteads are invariably surrounded by rows of carefully nurtured evergreens.

CANNON FALLS, 99.2 m. (810 alt., 1,358 pop.), is named for the falls of the Cannon River, called by the early French explorers the Canot (canoe) River. English traders who came later thought the Indians were trying to say "cannon" and wrote it that way on their maps. Once a pioneer milling center, the town today is a focal point for farm-produce shipping.

North of Cannon Falls the hills become less prominent until at 110 m. the country is flattened to an immense field of grain.

At 122.1 m. is the first view of the wide Mississippi River Valley (R).

At 132.1 m. is the junction with State 100.

1. Right on State 100 to SOUTH ST. PAUL (705 alt., 10,009 pop.), 2.7 m., an incorporated city (not a part of St. Paul as is commonly thought), now the third largest livestock market in the world.

Its chief industrial plants—the packing houses and tanneries—surround the UNION STOCKYARDS. There are also foundries, railroad shops, gravel plants, a malt house, and a concrete-block factory.

Many inhabitants are the second and third generations of southern European immigrants—Serbians, Montenegrins, Rumanians, Bulgarians, and Poles; there are also a few Negroes and Mexicans.

A. B. Stickney, builder and president of the Chicago Great Western R.R., backed by businessmen of St. Paul, established the Union Stockyards in 1888. Previously it had been merely a watering place for livestock shipments on the way to Chicago, but packing houses were opened when the stockyards were built. The yards employ men night and day to receive, feed, and water all arriving animals. The original 4 acres of scattered wooden pens and unpaved alleys have been replaced by a model plant covering 254 acres, with facilities for testing, vaccinating, dipping, dehorning, and branding, all carried on in compliance with Federal and State laws. The double-decked hog pens on the east side are fitted with sanitary feeding and drinking facilities and a sprinkling system to keep the animals cool in hot weather. Sheep corrals, in the southeastern corner, include complete equipment for feeding, handling, sorting, shearing, and dipping. A show barn is maintained at the north end of the yard.

The ARMOUR PACKING HOUSE *(visitors; 9:30, 10:30, 2:30; Sat. p.m., Sun., and Mon. excepted)* was established in 1919 at a cost of $15,000,000. It comprises 22 buildings grouped around a large red brick central unit. There are 4 miles of railroad tracks within the grounds, and 110 refrigerator cars can be accommodated under sheds at one time.

SWIFT AND COMPANY'S SOUTH ST. PAUL PLANT *(open to visitors daily at 9:10, 10:20, 1:10, 2:30; Sat. p.m., Sun. and Mon. excepted)*, just north of the Union Stockyards, is one of the largest pork-packing plants in the country; it also handles cattle, sheep, and chickens. Its specialty foods and byproduct plants are important units. Many related industries—box, barrel, and carton-making, and feed supply establishments—are grouped around the packing plants. Company buyers purchase hogs, cattle, calves, and sheep in the stockyards from commission men who represent the livestock producers.

Left on State 56, which leaves the downtown section and skirts the bluff on whose summit, in the suburb known as South Park, is the SITE (not marked) OF KAPOSIA, a former Sioux village, which was on the east bank of the Mississippi when white men first came. This band under the leadership of Little Crow, one of a long line of Little Crow chieftains, was at first friendly to the whites; but while under a son, Little Crow V, it played a leading role in the New Ulm uprising *(see Tour 2: LOWER AGENCY)*. Little Crow's band of Sioux set up their tepees here in 1837, when they moved across from the east side of the river. Indian mounds are numerous in the vicinity. It was here that the Rev. Samuel W. Pond (1808–1891) tried to teach the Indians to plow—one of the first of such attempts.

2. Left from US 52 on State 100 (Mendota Rd.) to the junction with State 55, now the route, at 4.6 *m.;* L. from the junction 0.5 *m.* on a graveled road to ACACIA PARK CEMETERY (Masonic), on the highest point of land in the vicinity. This burial ground, known as PILOT KNOB, was the site of an important Indian treaty negotiated in 1851. It commands a view of historic ground and was used by Indians and early settlers for meetings and observations. Formerly an Indian burial ground, this part of the hill was included in the present cemetery in 1923; the Indian remains were disinterred and buried elsewhere.

At 5.1 *m.* on State 55 is the junction with State 13 (Sibley Memorial Highway). Here is a red granite marker (L), in the form of an arrowhead and about 10 feet high, designating this vicinity as the SITE OF TREATY AGREEMENTS (1805, 1837, 1851), which ceded much of the Minnesota Territory to the United States. The first military post in the territory, called New Hope, also known as St. Peter's Cantonment, was established approximately on this site in 1819, but was later removed to the present Fort Snelling.

Right 0.1 *m.* on State 13 to ST. PETER'S ROMAN CATHOLIC CHURCH (L), a small frame structure in which is preserved the cross that surmounted the steeple in 1853. A large part of the congregation today, as in its earlier years, is French. The Easter sunrise services attract many visitors.

At 0.4 *m.* on State 13, on the east bank of the Mississippi at the mouth of the Minnesota River, is MENDOTA (719 alt., 173 pop.), the first permanent white settlement in Minnesota. The name is derived from a Sioux word meaning *meeting of the waters.* The story of this community, which figured most prominently in the history of the State, is interwoven with romance, adventure, and tragedy. There are no records of permanent settlement before 1800, but when the Northwest and Louisiana Territories were acquired, settlers, soldiers, and fur-traders began penetrating this vast Indian-inhabited wilderness and chose the site for settlement *(see HISTORICAL SURVEY)*. In 1805 Lt. Zebulon M. Pike (1779–1813) acquired from the Sioux a tract of land from the mouth of the Minnesota to the Falls of St. Anthony. For him was named PIKE ISLAND, whose heavy woods obscure the Mississippi at this point.

Mendota, then known as St. Peter's (it received its present name in 1837), was the key point for the American, Columbia, and Fort Factory Fur Trading Companies. The settlement became the meeting place for traders and trappers under the guidance of Taliaferro, D. Lamont, Alexis Bailly, Henry H. Sibley, and Jean Baptiste Faribault. Faribault moved his family to this site in 1822, when an ice jam in the Minnesota River threatened to flood his home on the east bank below Pike Island. Duncan Campbell, a half-breed Sioux, is believed to have built a cabin here in 1826.

On Main St. is (L) the SIBLEY TEA HOUSE *(lunches, dinners)*, a brick house built in 1854 by Sibley's secretary, Hypolite Du Puis, on the hill above his employer's home. The brick was shipped from Milwaukee and the building cost $3,500. It was remodeled by the D.A.R. and was opened to the public about 1930. Many old pieces of furniture are preserved in the house.

Left from the highway around a curving road to the HOME OF HENRY HASTINGS SIBLEY, 0.6 *m. (open 10-8, Apr.-Dec., adm. 25¢)*, built in 1835. This was the first stone house in Minnesota. Sibley (1811–1891) came to Mendota in 1834, when 23 years of age, as factor for the American Fur Company. Through his influence the settlement became a pioneer center of business and cultural activities. He married in 1843 and brought his wife to his Mendota home, which for years was open to friends and strangers. John Frémont, George Catlin, Joseph Nicollet, Captain Marryat, Stephen A. Douglas, and many others were guests here. Indians frequently came and went, using the upper floor, which they reached by an outside stairway, as sleeping quarters. Nine children were born to the Sibleys in the same room of this house. In 1860 the Sibleys moved to St. Paul and gave the house to St. Peter's Roman Catholic Parish in Mendota; it was then used as a convent and school. From 1897 to 1899 Burt Harwood used the structure as an art school and studio. A Mendota merchant used the building as a storehouse in 1905, but neglect made it useless, and it became a shelter for tramps.

Members of the D.A.R., on a river excursion in 1909, became interested in its preservation. In addition to restoring the building (an inner wall surface has been removed to show the construction), the society added old furniture either belonging to the Sibley family or of the same period, and opened it as a museum on June 14, 1910. Later the carriage house and the tea house were restored.

Sibley's home, Minnesota's most famous old house, closely resembles the types predominant in the old Western Reserve territory in Ohio—Colonial in design, but simpler in detail. Because of the remoteness from other sources, the stone was brought from the bluffs and the island; willows wrapped with hay made the lath; mud from the river bottom mixed with straw was used for plaster. The roof was of hand-split shakes and the floors were of timbers cut by hand and joined with wooden pegs. There were six rooms in the original house, in addition to the basement and attic. The large basement contained three units, one of which served as a diningroom and kitchen, the other two as cold rooms for storing food. A drain running to the river carried water from the melting ice. On the first floor, the north front room was used by General Sibley to conduct his business as fur agent. This later became the parlor, and an office was added on the east side. In this addition is the only fireplace in the house, except the one in the basement. Also on the first floor a large diningroom ran across the entire building; a library and a large kitchen are at the rear.

Adjoining the Sibley Estate (R) is the JEAN BAPTISTE FARIBAULT HOUSE, built in 1837. Faribault's family lived on the lower floor and the upper story was used for lodgers. Like the Sibley home, its general character is Colonial. The structure is rectangular, of yellow sandstone with symmetrical fenestration. White trim, small-paned windows, green shutters, and a beautiful, plain-white wood cornice give the house its character. Originally there was a wooden addition in the back for a kitchen and diningroom, with bedrooms above. On the first floor were a billiard room, a bar, and living rooms. The basement had an ice vault, storerooms, and an extra kitchen. Fireplaces were used to heat the larger rooms. The second floor had bedrooms and sittingrooms, the third floor a ballroom and a community meeting hall. Long after the Sibley house was restored, this companion piece was used as a warehouse with a railroad spur built to serve it. Its restoration began in 1935, and today it has almost regained its original appearance.

At 5.2 *m.* on State 55 is the MENDOTA BRIDGE, completed in 1926. More massive than other Minnesota River bridges, this span, which crosses the entire river valley, is 4,119 feet long and 120 feet high. The Mendota Bridge has four lanes for motor traffic and two pedestrian lanes. To the L. are miles of hills and lowlands of the Minnesota River Valley; to the R. the Minnesota joins the narrower Mississippi channel; in the distance are the spires and towers of the Minneapolis loop.

At 6 m. on State 55 is FORT SNELLING. *(Obtain permission from adjutant to visit buildings; dress parades on Fri. at 4:30 p.m. in spring and summer; polo on Sun. at 3 p.m. in June-Aug., adm. 50¢; horse shows in Feb., Apr., Sept., adm. 50¢-$2; trapshooting in June, rifle and revolver contests in July.)* Even before it was established as a military post, its strategic site, on the angle formed by the confluent Minnesota and Mississippi, was well known to fur-traders and explorers. Father Hennepin in 1680 and LeSueur in 1700 were probably the earliest white men to arrive at the junction of these two water-courses. Following these explorers came first the French trappers and traders and then the English trading companies, until, after the Treaty of Ghent in 1814, foreign fur-trading activities were prohibited in this and other United States territory. In 1805 title to the land on which the fort stands was acquired for the Government from the Sioux by Lt. Zebulon Pike. The initial price is said to have been 60 gallons of whiskey although the Government later offered the Indians $2,000 in cash.

In 1819 a detachment of infantry under Lt. Col. Henry Leavenworth (1783–1834) was assigned to establish an Army post as a wedge to open up this northwest Indian country. Log cabins and a stockade, called Camp New Hope, were built near the present site of Mendota, but a year later the troops were moved across the Mississippi to Camp Cold Water, beside a large spring just north of the Minnesota's mouth. That same year Col. Josiah Snelling (1782–1828) succeeded Leavenworth in command and immediately began construction of a permanent Fort St. Anthony at the present site on the bluffs overlooking both rivers. The fort was occupied in 1822, though it was not completed until the following year when the Indian council house was finished. In 1825 the name was officially changed to Fort Snelling in honor of its commanding officer.

The influence of the fort upon the Indians was made effective through the quiet work of its agent, Maj. Lawrence Taliaferro (1794–1871), who for 20 years supervised fur trade, issued licenses to traders, and strove constantly to keep peaceful relations between the Sioux and Chippewa. The Indians called Taliaferro "Four Hearts" because of his impartiality.

For more than 30 years Fort Snelling was the farthest northwest post of the Army. After the establishment of other forts, however, Snelling lost much of its importance and was used primarily as a supply station. At present Fort Snelling covers 2,387 acres, has 1,667 men, and 308 buildings. The Third Infantry, organized in 1784, is now stationed here; this regiment's color guard wears copies of the regiment's first uniforms. Today the Third Infantry trains summer encampments of the Citizens' Military Training Corps, Reserve Officers' Training Corps, Organized Reserves, and the National Guard. Every year on September 21 the regiment observes Third Infantry Day, in celebration of its part in the siege, assault, and capture of Monterey in 1846. On this day appropriate military ceremonies are staged and a general reunion of regiment members is held.

Right from State 55 in the center of the fort to a small STONE CHAPEL (L) built of the same material as the old Round Tower and following in several details the same design. In the basement is the FORT LIBRARY *(open Mon., Tues., Thurs., Fri., 1-4:30 p.m., 6-9 p.m.).*

A few rods farther (R) is the old ROUND TOWER, built in 1820 of limestone quarried from nearby bluffs. Although only 20 feet high, it served as a lookout from which Indians as well as returning expeditionists could be watched. In 1841 castellations were added to enhance its military appearance. It was in this tower that the later famous slave, Dred Scott, then a servant of Dr. Emerson, medical attaché, was married to a girl slave in 1837. In 1862 Count Zeppelin (1838–1917), then a 24-year-old German officer and a military attaché to the United States, had his quarters in the tower. Even then Zeppelin was experimenting with his ideas of balloon flight, and in 1864 on a spring night he rose 300 feet above the tower and made a 30-minute flight by means of a canvas bag filled with illuminating gas.

After the Civil War the tower was remodeled and used as a guardhouse until

1880, when the present guardhouse was erected. In 1918 it was taken over as a residence by the fort civilian engineer who occupied it for 19 years.

In 1937 it was agreed by Army officials and the State historical society to convert the tower into a museum of Minnesota history. When all partitions have been removed, portraits, historical material, and war trophies will be assembled and exhibited on the walls.

To the L. are the GENERAL OFFICES of the fort. Right, across the car tracks, are the red brick OFFICERS' BARRACKS, and a few yards beyond, as the road curves back along the river, is the HEXAGONAL TOWER (L), overlooking the Minnesota River just east of the Mendota Bridge. This was originally a blockhouse of stone, three stories high, which commanded the road and causeway from the early ferry landing. The road to the gate of the fort went directly beneath its walls. The tower's bastion-like arrangement, with deep loopholes for rifles, is well preserved, and eastward along the bluff are the remains of the wall that formerly enclosed the old fort. The position of the towers was such that they projected beyond the plane of the walls to permit raking the base of the fort walls with gunfire in case of attack. Both the Hexagonal and Round Towers are strictly utilitarian and military in design, and are the earliest structures of pioneer days still standing in Minnesota.

ST. PAUL, 136.7 *m.* (703 alt., 271,606 pop.) *(see ST. PAUL).*

Points of Interest. Capitol Square, City Hall, Cathedral of St. Paul, Government dam and locks.

St. Paul is at the junctions with US 12 *(see Tour 10)*, US 10 *(see Tour 16)*, US 212 *(see Tour 11)*, and US 61 *(see Tour 1)*.

US 52 follows S. Robert St. in St. Paul, crossing the Mississippi River on the Robert St. Bridge, around Capitol Curve to University Ave.; L. on University Ave. to Washington Ave. in Minneapolis; L. on Washington Ave. to Hennepin Ave.

MINNEAPOLIS, 146.6 *m.* (812 alt., 464,356 pop.) *(see MINNE-APOLIS).*

Points of Interest. Minnehaha Falls, Chain of Lakes, University of Minnesota, flour mills at St. Anthony Falls.

Minneapolis is at the junction with US 8 *(see Tour 19)*, US 12 *(see Tour 10)*, and US 169 *(see Tour 3)*, US 212 *(see Tour 11)*, and US 65 *(see Tour 14)*.

Section b. MINNEAPOLIS *to* NORTH DAKOTA LINE, *245 m. US 52.*

In Minneapolis US 52 follows Washington Ave. through the downtown section to Broadway Ave.; L. on Broadway Ave. past the west city line (Victory Memorial Drive), at 3.7 *m.*

ROBBINSDALE, 5.3 *m.* (979 alt., 4,427 pop.), northwest Minneapolis suburb, was platted in 1887 and named for Andrew B. Robbins, pioneer owner of the present town site.

OSSEO, 12.8 *m.* (888 alt., 561 pop.), a village platted in 1856, occupies a part of BOTTINEAU PRAIRIE, where Pierre Bottineau (1817–1895), a half-breed guide, made his land claim in 1852. The town was named for Osseo, son of the evening star in the *Song of Hiawatha*. Osseo is a poultry-producing center, serving the Twin City market.

From CHAMPLIN, 17.1 *m.* (350 pop.), whose population is predominantly French, northward for more than fifty miles stretches the potato growing belt, one of the most important in Minnesota.

Champlin is at the junction (R) with US 169 *(see Tour 3)*. Between Champlin and Elk River US 52 and US 169 are united.

ANOKA, 18.2 *m.* (904 alt., 4,851 pop.) *(see Tour 16)*, is at the junction with US 10 *(see Tour 16)*. Between Anoka and East St. Cloud, US 52 unites with US 10.

ELK RIVER, 30.1 *m.* (924 alt., 1,026 pop.) *(see Tour 16)*, is at the junction (R) with US 169 *(see Tour 3)*.

At EAST ST. CLOUD, 65.9 *m.*, US 52 crosses the Mississippi.

ST. CLOUD, 66.9 *m.* (1,029 alt., 21,000 pop.) *(see ST. CLOUD)*.

Points of Interest. Granite quarries and finishing plants; River Shore Parks; St. Cloud Teachers' College; Lake George; St. Mary's Church.

Right on 9th Ave. from its junction with US 52 (St. Germain St.) to the junction with 8th St. N., 0.7 *m.;* L. on 8th St. N. to the UNITED STATES VETERANS HOSPITAL, 3.3 *m. (visiting hours 2-4, Tues., Thurs., Sun., and holidays; conducted tours by special arrangement with the hospital)*, opened in 1924. At present there are 47 buildings; the large medical and administrative staff cares for approximately 800 veterans.

At 69.9 *m.* is WAITE PARK (1,318 pop.), at the junction with State 23.

Left on State 23 to ROCKVILLE, 8.4 *m.* (1,075 alt., 294 pop.), a quarrying center where giant derricks and hoists are in operation. The town is built on an ancient mountain of granite whose whole mass has been depressed by geologic action. For almost 30 years the inhabitants of Rockville have obtained their livelihood from granite. In 1935 many quarry workers were unemployed, but at that time, with Federal aid, the town built a new school of pink granite from the adjacent quarries.

On US 52, at about 71.5 *m.*, where the highway crosses the Sauk River, is the FORD USED BY THE RED RIVER OX CARTS. There was an important trading center here in pioneer days; west of this point US 52 closely follows the old ox-cart trail.

ST. JOSEPH, 75.2 *m.* (1,050 alt., 1,009 pop.), is the home of ST. BENEDICT'S CONVENT AND COLLEGE (L). Although classes had been held earlier, the school was officially opened in 1880. It includes both collegiate and preparatory classes. In addition to the convent the sisters maintain a HOSPITAL, two INDIAN SCHOOLS, and two HOMES FOR THE AGED. The interior of the SACRED HEART CHAPEL is in Italian Renaissance style; its altar is of imported marble.

At 78.3 *m.* is the junction with a graveled road.

Left on this road, between the stone pillars, ST. JOHN'S UNIVERSITY and ST. JOHN'S ABBEY, 1.4 *m.*, are set in a thick grove of evergreens. The college and the abbey were begun in 1856, when Bishop Cretin brought a group of Benedictine fathers and lay brothers here from Pennsylvania. The Benedictines established themselves on a farm a short distance below St. Cloud on the banks of the Mississippi and immediately applied for a seminary charter from the Territorial legislature. This was granted in 1857, and the first class, composed of five students, was housed, fed, and taught in a crude frame building. The present buildings were erected in 1911. Today St. John's University is one of the largest of the order; the art and architecture courses are particularly outstanding. Brother Clement Frischauf, distinguished scholar of Beuronese art (founded in the Benedictine abbey of Beuron, Germany, in 777), has painted in the apse of the abbey church a much admired mural of Christ's head on a gold-leaf background.

The school's LIBRARY of 65,000 volumes is equipped for many kinds of reference work and has a large number of interesting folios and quartos. Its collections of incunabula, hand-drawn portions of the Scriptures produced before the 16th century, and other rare volumes are notable. Housed in the same building on the third floor is an interesting MUSEUM containing old and modern Chinese souvenirs, Indian relics, historic silver, church vestments, articles of worship, and many exhibits of marine life. The RELICS OF ST. PERQUINUS, who was martyred by the Romans at the age of 16, are under the main altar in the church basement. They were brought to this country from Germany and placed in St. John's in 1932.

AVON, 82.5 *m.* (1,124 alt., 362 pop.), and ALBANY, 89.2 *m.* (1,201 alt., 851 pop.), are transportation and shopping centers for many surrounding lakes and resorts.

West of Albany US 52 traverses gently rolling agricultural country, where dairying is of primary importance.

At 98.6 *m.* is the junction with an improved road.

Left on this road to NEW MUNICH, 3.3 *m.* (321 pop.), largely populated by Bavarians, where Corpus Christi Day (the Thursday following the eighth Sunday after Easter) is observed with an Old World procession. After the 10-o'clock mass has been celebrated the worshippers leave the church, led by little girls in white who scatter flowers from baskets. Preceded by crossbearers and three servers praying in unison, they follow the priest bearing the Blessed Sacrament to four flower-decked shrines which are about 1 mile apart and form a square. From the church to the first shrine they pass between a double row of poplar trees brought from nearby woods. At each shrine, when the service has been read and the Host held aloft, a shot is fired in a neighboring field, and all kneel in prayer. After the prayer, the procession, singing and carrying ceremonial banners, wends its way onward through the fields.

MELROSE, 101.1 *m.* (1,801 pop.), once a settlement at a ford on the Pembina Trail, is now a point of shipping and distribution on the Great Northern Ry.

SAUK CENTER, 109.8 *m.* (1,248 alt., 2,716 pop.), at the junction with US 71 *(see Tour 2),* is on the southern tip of elongated BIG SAUK LAKE *(municipal tourist camp, 9-hole golf course, picnic grounds).* This was the boyhood home of Sinclair Lewis (1885–   ), who used the town and its surrounding area as the setting for several of his novels. *(See THE ARTS.)*

A boulder at 7th and S. Main marks the SITE OF THE OLD STOCKADE used by early settlers for protection against Indian attacks.

Sauk Center has a COMMUNITY CLUB, 3rd St. E., that furnishes information concerning the numerous fishing lakes and summer resorts in the surrounding country.

Northwest of Sauk Center the country is varied; forests, lakes, hills, and swamps intersperse stretches of level prairie. Many of the swamps have been drained, making excellent meadows; clover and alfalfa are particularly good crops.

OSAKIS, 124.9 *m.* (1,310 alt., 1,155 pop.), on the lake of the same name, has long been a popular fishing and summer resort. Osakis (Ind., *danger)* refers to the many fierce encounters that took place on this former dividing line between Sioux and Chippewa territory.

At 133.9 *m.* is LAKE VICTORIA *(swimming, boating, fishing).*

ALEXANDRIA, 135.4 *m.* (1,400 alt., 3,876 pop.), was organized as a township in 1866 and named for Alexander Kinkaid, one of its first settlers, who with his brother, William, came to the region from St. Peter in 1857 and laid claim to a large tract in what is now Douglas County. In those days the only trails in this heavily wooded region were those followed by the ox carts of the Red River fur-traders.

In 1873 the St. Paul & Pacific Ry. laid its tracks to Alexandria, but the company failed, and the first passenger train into the town (in 1878) was that of its successor, the St. Paul, Minneapolis, & Manitoba. When James J. Hill obtained ownership of the road, he acquired the right-of-way of the present Great Northern Lines.

Alexandria's early prosperity was dependent upon the exceptionally rich surrounding farm lands, which are still its most important asset, but a large income is now derived from the visitors who flock to the extensive lake area. Alexandria sponsors an annual Resorters' Golf Tournament *(first week in August)* on the 18-hole GOLF COURSE. Within the city is a small bass-stocked LAKE.

Knute Nelson (1843–1923) came to Alexandria in 1870 and later became Governor and U. S. Senator. He is the only American of Norwegian birth honored by a statue in Oslo, Norway's capital.

A large ROCK GARDEN *(open)* at 420 Lincoln Ave., with flowers, massive rock formations, ponds, and waterfalls, has been developed by P. J. Noonan.

At the Alexandria Chamber of Commerce, 608 Broadway, the much-discussed KENSINGTON RUNESTONE is on exhibit. The stone was found in 1898 near Kensington, southwest of Alexandria, by Olof Ohman, a Swedish farmer, who dug it out from under the roots of a poplar tree on his farm. The discovery of the stone aroused some local excitement at the time, but as no one could read the inscription, Ohman used it as a doorstop for one of his sheds—fortunately placing the incised side down. When interest in the stone was revived by Hjalmar R. Holand, the inscription was translated: "Eight Goths [Swedes] and 22 Norwegians upon a journey of discovery from Vinland westward. We had a camp by two skerries [islands] one day's journey north of this stone. We were out fishing one day. When we returned home we found ten men red with blood and dead. A V M [Ave Virgo Maria] save us from evil." On the edge of the stone was this inscription: "[We] have ten men by the sea to look after our vessel fourteen days' journey from this island. Year 1362."

The authenticity of this runic writing is still a subject of controversy and, if not yet established, is far from disproved. Sent abroad, the stone has been pored over by many of Europe's leading archeologists, some of whom have been convinced, while others have regarded it with puzzled uncertainty. If, as many believe, the inscription was faked, the jokester had an almost incredible knowledge of runic writing. That it is of no recent date is testified by the age of the tree whose roots surrounded it when found.

1. Right from Alexandria on State 29 past the shores of Lakes L'Homme Dieu (R), 3.5 *m.*, Carlos (L), 5 *m.*, and Miltona (L), 12.5 *m.* to PARKER'S PRAIRIE, 22.6 *m.* (1,425 alt., 631 pop.), which affords fishing and grouse- and pheasant-shooting in season. Fred A. Barker, local taxidermist and student of natural history, has supplied specimens of birds to some of the country's largest museums. His knowledge of ornithology has been of use to several scientists of national repute who have visited his MUSEUM *(open daily)* in the village.

2. Left from Alexandria on State 29 to GLENWOOD, 17 *m.* (1,420 alt., 2,220 pop.), on the shore of beautifully wooded LAKE MINNEWASKA *(tourist camps, summer hotel, and 9-hole golf course)*, largest lake in Pope County. MOUNT LOOKOUT, within the city, is 90 feet high and affords an excellent view of the lake. There is a driveway to the top of the bluffs.

Many INDIAN MOUNDS and BURIAL GROUNDS, containing graves of Chief White Bear, and the Princess Minnewaska, for whom the lake is named, are on the north shore.

Glenwood has one of the state's most productive FISH HATCHERIES, which over a period of 20 years has distributed approximately one and one-fourth billion trout, pike, and bass to Minnesota waters.

The town's several large foreign groups include Bohemians, Norwegians, and Swedes; each maintains to some degree its native language, inherited traditions, and Old World customs.

The people of Glenwood are interested in music, and the Norwegians especially are active in its development; a local LUTHERAN CHURCH has for years specialized in Bach. The Glenwood Symphony Orchestra is made up of volunteers from all occupations. A local high-school teacher, Mrs. W. F. Dougherty, gave free musical instruction for a time when the school failed to include musical courses.

Northwest of Alexandria US 52 traverses a region of fine fishing lakes and natural woodland.

BRANDON, 148.6 *m.* (1,363 alt., 311 pop.), is 2 miles south of the site of a village called Chippewa, which grew up around the old stagecoach station. When in 1879 the Great Northern tracks were extended westward to the spot where Brandon now stands, Mary Griffin, of Minneapolis, laid out a town site, and gradually the village of Chippewa was moved down to the railroad. Brandon, Vt., for which the settlement was named, was the birthplace of Stephen A. Douglas, for whom the county was named. The COMMUNITY BUILDING, one block to the R. of the highway near the center of town, is a combination auditorium and fire hall constructed by the WPA of native field stone and masonry.

EVANSVILLE, 153.5 *m.* (1,354 alt., 397 pop.), an important shipping point for dairy products and livestock, was in 1859 a stage station on the trail from St. Cloud to Fort Abercrombie, N. Dak. The Evansville Business Association furnishes information regarding the surrounding region and lakes.

To the R. of the highway beyond the village of MELBY, 158.9 *m.*, is LAKE CHRISTINA, 162.2 *m. (fishing and duck-shooting);* it is not visible from the highway but lies beyond a low ridge. On the north shore of the lake are the SEVEN SISTERS. These stately hills are a part of the State's terminal-moraine topography and are from 100 to 350 feet high. Their steep slopes are grass covered and sparsely wooded. Lake Christina's shallow waters are filled with wildrice and other foods that attract great flocks of migratory water-fowl.

At 180.3 *m.* is the junction with US 59 *(see Tour 17)*. Between this point and 192.8 *m.*, US 52 and US 59 are one route.

FERGUS FALLS, 186.4 *m.* (1,190 alt., 9,389 pop.), seat of Otter Tail County, is the western gateway of another widely known park region. The OTTER TAIL RIVER, a branch of the Red River, flows directly through the city.

Fergus Falls was staked off by Joseph Whitford, blacksmith, engineer, and frontiersman, who led an expedition here in 1857 to lay out a new town site. Platted in 1870 and incorporated as a village in 1872, the town was named in honor of James Fergus, who financed Whitford's expedition. Fergus (1813–1902), a Scot who came to the State in 1854, was prominent in the Territorial activities of both Minnesota and Montana.

The first post office was in a log cabin; the postmaster was a German who, it is said, could not read English, but fulfilled the duties of his office by emptying the mail pouch in the middle of the floor and allowing villagers to look through the pile for their letters.

In the city are 17 factories and 2 flour mills, supplied with power from the Red River Falls by the Otter Tail Power Company, which furnishes 175 cities and villages of Minnesota and North and South Dakota with power and light.

Fergus Falls has the largest co-operative creamery in the Northwest, with 37 additional co-operative creameries in the trade area. In 1928, a boom year, Fergus Falls co-operatives paid their farmer members over $22,500,000 net returns.

The CITY HALL AND COURTHOUSE, Washington Ave. and Mill St., a reproduction of Independence Hall in Philadelphia, is built on the riverbank; its grounds are beautifully landscaped and terraced down to the water's edge. In the basement is a MUSEUM *(open 9-5 weekdays, Sat. 9-1)* of pioneer utensils and other relics. Nearly 150 photographs of early scenes and events in and around Fergus Falls have been collected by the Otter Tail Historical Society and have been arranged as a permanent exhibit in the entrance hall.

Across the bridge from the city hall is a hotel, its diningroom almost overhanging the river; below it are TERRACED ROCK GARDENS descending to the water line.

At the northern city line (R), on a hill overlooking the city, is the FERGUS FALLS STATE HOSPITAL (for mental cases), second largest in the State, with an average of nearly 2,000 patients. The hospital consists of an administration building with 22 adjoining wards, a psychopathic unit, a hospital for patients with contagious diseases, two buildings for tubercular patients, one for convalescents, facilities for occupational activities, a nurses' home, and a dormitory for male attendants. The institution's farm and garden division maintains about 260 cattle and 20 horses. A weekly news publication, talking pictures, "amateur nights," and a library of more than 4,000 volumes provide leisure activities for the patients. Local radio station KGDE broadcasts on a wave length of 1200 kc.

In June 1919 a tornado destroyed Fergus Falls, killing nearly 60 people; but the State hospital and the two local hospitals were among the few buildings unharmed. Freaks of this storm include a shingle driven through a fence post, a flock of chickens picked clean, and the walls of a house carried away bodily, leaving a cupboard full of unbroken china.

After the tornado the city was rebuilt with many civic improvements. Wooded parks, beautiful hills, the river with its several dams and many fine bridges, all added to the city's attractiveness.

The hill road around LAKE ALICE provides a pleasant short drive. In February a Winter Carnival and in July a Summer Carnival, featuring seasonal sports, are held at Lake Alice in the north residential section.

Fergus Falls has a 9-hole golf course and a municipal tourist camp.

Right from Fergus Falls on State 3 to the village of BATTLE LAKE, **18.2** *m.* (552 pop.), on the shore of WEST BATTLE LAKE. This spot was the scene of a desperate battle in 1795 between the Chippewa and Sioux for the possession of the hunting and fishing grounds of this area. The Chippewa from the vicinity of Cass Lake were led by Ukkewaus, an old warrior who, with his four sons and a party of braves, came upon a small band of the enemy fleeing along the lake shore. The Chippewa braves pursued them, running through the woods to head them off, but the Sioux reached their camp in time to avoid capture. The invaders, now greatly outnumbered and too exhausted from the pursuit to retreat, chose a strategic position for defense. After keeping up a hopeless battle for some time, Ukkewaus determined to save some of his followers and ordered the survivors to flee. While they retreated the old warrior and his sons held off the attackers until their ammunition gave out, when the Sioux killed and scalped them.

West Battle Lake, with its clear water and sandy beaches, is a quiet resort region; its groves, woodlands, and farms lend variety to the scenery.

At **22.6** *m.* on State 3 is CLITHERALL (1,369 alt., 151 pop.), on Clitherall Lake, noted for its fine fishing. At Clitherall a Mormon colony was founded in 1865 by 30 families who came by ox cart from Manti, Iowa.

Right from Clitherall on a country road to the small village of LEAF MOUNTAIN, **31.1** *m.,* where three moraines converge. At **32** *m.* is INSPIRATION PEAK STATE PARK, a high, rough, wooded area of 84 acres, whose peaks provide an exceptional view of the surrounding country.

In the vicinity oak, maple, ash, birch, and elms thrive; ironwood is the common underbrush. On the cut-over lands are sumac, bittersweet, dwarf buckthorn, and dogwood. Both woodland and prairie flowers grow in profusion on hillsides and bottom lands.

West of Fergus Falls the wooded areas become increasingly interspersed with brush-land vegetation, and the rolling hills gradually level out into the true prairie, almost all of it now cultivated farm land.

BARNESVILLE, 220.2 *m.* (1,024 alt., 1,279 pop.), a shipping center for wheat, potatoes, and livestock, has five large elevators, a flour mill, and a co-operative creamery. Repair shops of the Great Northern Ry. are here.

Barnesville is on the Tintah beach level of the prehistoric Lake Agassiz. That this huge lake replaced large stretches of forest is obvious from the remnants of trees that are constantly being recovered from beneath the lake deposit. The topography of this ancient lake bed presents a seemingly limitless expanse. The prairie winds sweep across its level surface, turning the propellers of generators that provide electric power for rural homes; in dry seasons these winds carry tons of fine topsoil to the surrounding States.

Northwest of Barnesville, US 52 descends into the vast Red River valley prairie-land, known for its potato and grain crops. The treeless plains abound with white-tailed jackrabbits, which are extensively hunted.

MOORHEAD, 244 m. (904 alt., 7,651 pop.) *(see Tour 16)*, is at the junction with US 10 *(see Tour 16)* and US 75 *(see Tour 4)*.

At 245 m. US 52 crosses the Red River (the North Dakota Line, and enters Fargo, N. Dak. *(see North Dakota, Tour 8.)*

◄◄◄◄◄◄◄◄◄◄◄◄◄◄◄◄◄ ☼ ►►►►►►►►►►►►►►►►►►►

Tour 10

(Hudson, Wis.)—Twin Cities—Delano—Litchfield—Willmar—Benson —Ortonville—(Aberdeen, S. Dak.); US 12.
Wisconsin Line to South Dakota Line, 196.1 m.

Route is paralleled by Great Northern Ry. between Twin Cities and Benson.
Roadbed is paved between Wisconsin Line and Benson, bituminous-treated between Benson and junction US 59, and graveled between US 59 and Ortonville. Passable in all seasons.
Usual accommodations.

Beginning at the beautiful and historic St. Croix River on the eastern boundary of Minnesota, US 12 passes through the industrial Twin Cities and enters the picturesque lake region in the south-central part of the State; in the west it traverses farming country of broad till-plain broken by occasional low hills.

At 0 m. US 12 crosses the St. Croix River on a TOLL BRIDGE *(15¢ for driver and car, 5¢ for each additional passenger)* from Hudson, Wis. *(see Wisconsin, Tour 19)*.

At 0.3 m. is the junction with State 95.

Left on State 95 the St. Croix Scenic Highway follows the route of the old Point Douglas Rd., the first military road (1851) in Minnesota. The river is hidden from view by the bluffs, back of which the road winds across Bolles Creek, 3.3 m., on whose bank in 1845 Lemuel Bolles built the first Minnesota flour mill.

AFTON, 4 m. (693 alt., 148 pop.), a picturesque little village on the west shore of LAKE ST. CROIX *(small-mouth bass fly-fishing)* and at the base of a wooded bluff, was named for Robert Burns' poem *Afton Water*. It was settled by the French in the late 1830's, but was not platted until 1855. Among the early settlers in Afton was Joseph Haskell, one of the State's first farmers. Several lumber mills were formerly operated here.

The OCTAGON HOUSE (L), 4.8 m., was built in the 1860's and is said to have been used as a refuge by settlers during Indian scares.

The design of the Octagon House was unquestionably inspired by O. S. Fowler's

A Home for All, or the Octagon Mode of Building, published in 1854. That this books was circulated in Minnesota is obvious, for there are several similar structures in the State. The two-story frame house is covered with wide, battened vertical boarding. Though it conforms to no specific style, its mass is pleasing. Through a cupola at the apex of the pyramidal roof extends a thin, square chimney. In all of the cupola walls are windows that overlook the St. Croix River Valley. Each side of the octagon is about 14 feet 2 inches. Although most of the rooms are triangular or trapezoidal, there are two rectangular rooms, the parlor on the first floor and the bedroom immediately above it. At the rear is an L-shaped wing, the kitchen and woodshed.

Beyond the Octagon House on the opposite side of the street is the ANDREW MACKEY HOUSE, a rambling one-story structure designed in the New England manner and built in 1855. There is a long porch of the Connecticut type built into the angle of the house. The details of the doorway and porch columns are of the Greek Revival style. The house has a plain cornice with returning eaves. The grounds are enclosed by a pine picket fence with a paneled gate of Gothic design.

West of the junction with State 95, US 12 passes through gently rolling farm land varied by occasional lakes and clumps of hardwood.

US 12 enters St. Paul on Hudson Road (Hastings Ave.) to Kellogg Blvd.; L. on Kellogg Blvd. to Robert St.

ST. PAUL, 16.9 *m.* (703 alt., 271,606 pop.) *(see ST. PAUL).*

Points of Interest. Capitol Square, City Hall, Cathedral, Government Dam and Locks.

St. Paul is at the junctions with US 61 *(see Tour 1),* US 52 *(see Tour 9),* US 10 *(see Tour 16),* and US 212 *(see Tour 11).*

In St. Paul US 12 follows Robert St. to University Ave.; L. on University Ave. to Washington Ave. in Minneapolis; L. on Washington Ave. to Hennepin Ave.

MINNEAPOLIS, 26.8 *m.* (812 alt., 464,356 pop.) *(see MINNEAPOLIS).*

Points of Interest. Minnehaha Falls, Chain of Lakes, University of Minnesota, flour mills at St. Anthony Falls.

Minneapolis is at the junctions with US 8 *(see Tour 19),* US 52 *(see Tour 9),* US 169 *(see Tour 3),* US 212 *(see Tour 11),* and US 14 *(see Tour 14).*

US 12 follows Hennepin Ave. to Wayzata Ave.; R. on Wayzata Ave.

At 39.3 *m.* is the junction with State 101, at which point the highway nears the shore of LAKE MINNETONKA *(see Tour 11).* In this region are wooded hills and numerous lakes.

At 55.1 *m.* is DELANO (737 alt., 914 pop.), named for Francis R. Delano, pioneer Minnesota lumberman and railroad superintendent. The town contains a large pickling plant, a printing establishment, and a granite-monument works—one of the largest retail memorial manufactories in the Northwest.

At 60.4 *m.* is the junction with State 25.

Right on State 25 to BUFFALO, 7.1 *m.* (981 alt., 1,409 pop.), seat of Wright County, named for the numerous buffalo fish in adjoining BUFFALO LAKE. Here at one time was an abundance of ginseng, a plant in constant demand by the Chinese, who attribute to it a high medicinal value. The cash received for it relieved the hardships of the settlers in the early days. In 1877 a new courthouse was built at an estimated cost of $26,000, but the panic of that year delayed the payment, and by the time the debt was cleared the accrued interest increased the cost to $105,000.

Margaret Culkin Banning, prominent Minnesota writer, was born in Buffalo in 1891.

Numerous surrounding lakes offer opportunities for fishing and hunting wild fowl.

At Buffalo is the junction with State 55.

Left on State 55 to ANNANDALE, 22.7 m. (1,066 alt., 663 pop.), hub of the summer resort region of Wright County, with 16 lakes within a 6-mile radius. Many local historians insist that the town was named by a visiting politician for an actress, Lizzie Annandale, posters of whose appearance had been put up on the town site. Others say the village was named for the Annan River and a seaport in southern Scotland.

The Rev. Frank E. Higgins, the "lumberjack sky pilot," served his first pastorate in the Methodist Episcopal church of Annandale in the early 1890's.

Left from Annandale on an improved road to the junction with another improved road, 26.8 m.; R. on this road to FRENCH LAKE, 30.5 m., whose population is predominantly Finnish; L. from French Lake on an improved road to the junction with US 12 at 39.5 m.

HOWARD LAKE, 70.5 m. (1,078 alt., 763 pop.), has a large SEED FARM AND NURSERY, established in 1879, and is the scene of the annual Wright County Fair. The village and the adjoining lake were named for John Howard, English philanthropist and exponent of prison reform.

This area was badly damaged during the locust scourge that reached its climax in 1878. In that year the pests ate every green plant in the region and even attacked clothing. The farmers, in desperation, joined in a State-wide day of prayer for deliverance from the plague. Soon afterwards the grasshoppers disappeared.

A TOURIST CAMP (*free camping, running water*) is at the northeastern end of the village.

In the early settlement of COKATO, 76.7 m. (1,044 alt., 1,125 pop.), Swedish settlers predominated, but today Finns outnumber them. Cokato (Ind., *at the middle* or *stopping place*) has a large canning factory, and a produce company annually ships more than 100 carloads of poultry and eggs.

Pastures give way to corn and wheat around Cokato, and rolling plains of grain extend almost the entire length of the route.

DASSEL, 82.4 m. (1,087 alt., 785 pop.), surrounded by beautiful lakes (*recreational facilities, municipal tourist camps*), was named for Bernard Dassel, secretary of the St. Paul & Pacific Ry. in 1869.

Left from Dassel on State 15 to HUTCHINSON, 15 m., (1,042 alt., 3,406 pop.), at the junction of several improved roads that run through the lake district. The town was founded in 1855 by the brothers Asa, Judson, and John Hutchinson, members of a family of singers, who gave concerts of popular and abolitionist songs throughout the United States from 1841 until the close of the Civil War. When Hutchinson was incorporated in 1881 the village charter allowed women to vote on all local questions. The influence of these advanced-thinking pioneers and their early support of abolition, temperance, and woman-suffrage legislation, is evident in this village today, music and education being considered particularly important in Hutchinson. In addition to commercial enterprises usual to a town of this size,

Hutchinson supports eight churches, a seminary, library, community hospital, and a number of co-operative undertakings among which are two fire-insurance companies and a store. In the Sioux uprising of 1862 (*see Tour 2: LOWER AGENCY*) several important encounters centered around Hutchinson, and only by heroic effort were villagers able to prevent the entire settlement from being wiped out. A considerable portion of the town was burned, including Pendergast Academy, one of the earliest schools in Minnesota. When word of the uprising reached the Upper Agency, John Other Day, a Christian Indian whose wife was white, aided by a half-breed, gathered 62 persons into the brick warehouse; they were guarded by some friendly Wahpeton Sioux. In the morning Other Day guided his charges to safety at Hutchinson.

It was near Hutchinson that Little Crow, leader of the Indians in the outbreak, was killed. He and his 16-year-old son were evidently engaged in picking berries when they were seen by Nathan Lamson and his son Chauncey, who were hunting deer in the same brush land. In an exchange of shots the older Lamson and Little Crow both were wounded slightly; after considerable reconnoitering, Chauncey finally fired the fatal shot.

Hutchinson early became the nucleus of the game-conservation organization. Among its well-known game conservationists were Carlos Avery for whom a large game preserve is named, and Sam Anderson, who made his farm a haven for wild fowl of all kinds. The Minnesota Game Protective League, which started here, is acquiring the farm, which will become a permanent refuge.

LITCHFIELD, 93.8 *m.* (1,123 alt., 2,880 pop.), seat of Meeker County, platted in 1869 on ground from which wheat was harvested that same year, was named in honor of three Litchfield brothers who aided in the construction and financing of the St. Paul & Pacific R.R., then being built through to the site of the town. Litchfield, an industrial and trading center, has creameries, a powdered-buttermilk plant, and a woolen mill, and ships stock and poultry.

The resort area around Litchfield has so many lakes that the statement, "every road from Litchfield leads to a lake," is almost literally true.

The TOURIST PARK (*camping, running water*) is on the north end of LAKE RIPLEY (*fishing, swimming*), which adjoins the town on the south.

The city is the center of a Federal Farm Security Administration project, which (October 1937) has purchased 93 farms. This permits the re-establishment of 116 families, formerly living in less productive areas, to whom the units are resold on a 40-year amortization basis. The applicants for these resettlement farms are carefully investigated, and only those are accepted whose records give reasonable assurance of managerial ability. The infiltration plan of scattering the farms over a fairly large area has been used. The necessary houses and barns are built by the construction branch of the project; in some cases the smaller buildings are hauled intact to their destination.

ATWATER, 107.6 *m.* (1,120 alt., 694 pop.), holds an annual Watermelon Festival (*first week in August*) at which watermelon is served free.

WILLMAR, 121 *m.* (1,123 alt.; 6,173 pop.), the seat of lake-dotted Kandiyohi County, is on the southern shores of FOOT LAKE and in the center of a well-stocked game region, for many years a disputed hunting ground of the Sioux and Chippewa.

The first settlement in Kandiyohi County was made in 1856 by Elijah

Woodcock, but most of the early population was frightened away by the Indian uprising in 1862.

The city of Willmar was founded in 1869 and was platted on company land by a railroad engineer employed by the newly arrived St. Paul & Pacific R.R. Company. In the early days of the town the company owned the land and the only grain elevator; even the village council meetings were held in the railroad depot.

Willmar was named for Leon Willmar, railroad agent who represented London bond-holders. To his son, Paul, he presented a section of land on the lake, also called Willmar, on which elaborate buildings were erected and improvements made, but within 10 years it was abandoned by the adventurous son, who returned to Europe.

Today Willmar has several factories and is a shipping center for grain and livestock; it is also a division point of the Great Northern Ry.

The WILLMAR PUBLIC LIBRARY displays curios and books collected by the late Col. Cushman Rice, philanthropist and soldier of fortune, who provided funds for the construction of the local hospital. Willmar's orchestra and choral society of 200 voices make frequent concert tours.

The WILLMAR MEMORIAL AUDITORIUM is a brick structure with concrete trim, erected through Federal aid. It is the largest assembly hall within a 70-mile radius. Over the entrance are 3 bas-relief panels 6 by 18 feet in size. Executed by the Federal Art Project in cast stone, the panels depict Agriculture, Government, and Railroad Transportation. The paneling of the oak doors in the lobby also was done by WPA artists.

THE TOURIST CAMP *(running water, free camping)* is on 7th St., about 0.5 mile north of US 12.

Willmar is at the junction with US 71 *(see Tour 2)*.

West of Willmar US 12 crosses a flat plain, dotted with farms and small groves of trees, and then enters the prairie region where early settlers lived a very primitive life. Because trees were scarce, the dwellings were often dugouts built into the side of a hill. They had dirt floors, their roofs of hay and sod often sprouted a luxuriant growth of grass, and the walls, made of stakes and latticed willow branches, were reinforced with mud. Their furniture was almost entirely home-made, and cooking was done over open fires. Added to the hardships of everyday life were severe winter snowstorms, prairie fires, and raids by hostile Indians.

In this region, just west of Willmar and at a point near US 12, 13 Swedish settlers were murdered during the Sioux uprising in 1862 *(see Tour 2: LOWER AGENCY)*. One family in the neighborhood was saved by hiding in the cellar; when the plundering Indians entered the cabin, they accidentally pushed a trunk over the trapdoor and the trembling group was spared.

BENSON, 152.7 m. (1,040 alt., 2,095 pop.), was for 2 years the western terminus of James J. Hill's Great Northern Ry. At that time scores of ox carts on the old Pembina Trail waited here to unload supplies that were being relayed from the East to Manitoba, the Dakotas, and the Sisseton Agency on Lake Traverse.

At this spot a century ago the women and children of a party of Sioux on a hunting expedition from Lac qui Parle, with the missionary, Gideon Pond (1810–1878), were attacked and scalped by Chippewa. The battle of Rum River several years later was fought to avenge this attack.

Settled in 1870, Benson had grown to 300 by 1875. Promoters' rosy pic-tures of fertile, wealth-producing fields had stimulated immigration, but the lack of timber forced the newcomers to live in floorless sod huts, and a 2-year grasshopper plague devastated the crops. In spite of difficulties, claim-stakers plunged into wheat-farming, and the village soon became the shipping point for a 200-mile area that exported 260,000 bushels in 1875.

Land business was stimulated in 1876 by the removal of the U.S. Land Office from Litchfield to Benson. In that same year agitation began for the construction of a direct railroad to Duluth that would carry Benson's wheat to the port and return cheap lumber and fuel. But no such road was ever built. A disastrous fire in 1880 caused severe losses, but resulted in the erection of more substantial structures. In the early 1880's Benson at-tempted to establish a flour-milling industry, but lost this business to larger centers with more advantageous locations.

Today Benson is still dependent upon agriculture and dairying; it has four grain elevators, a co-operative creamery, and two livestock-shipping associations.

The TOURIST CAMP *(running water)* is in the southwestern part of town, across the railroad tracks.

Right from Benson on State 9 to CLONTARF, 6 *m.* (180 pop.). In a widely circulated pamphlet entitled *Invitation to the Land* (1876), the site of Clontarf was described by Archbishop Ireland as "wide open opportunity-waiting spaces of the west." Oratory, advertising, and brochures in the "poverty stricken and demoralized crowded centers of the East" brought an Irish-Catholic "prohibition colony" from Pennsylvania to Benson. Thence they proceeded north by ox cart to the 117,000 acres that were under the jurisdiction of Archbishop Ireland. They named their settlement Clontarf, for.an Irish watering place near Dublin, scene of Brian Boru's victory over the Danes. Churchmen of the colony protested against killing the grass-hoppers that devoured their crops the first year, believing the pests were "heaven's punishment for the people's sins."

About 2 miles northwest of the village Clontarf Industrial School was estab-lished by Archbishop Ireland to instruct Indian boys in the Roman Catholic faith and to teach them the arts of husbandry. The several buildings had a capacity of 80 pupils, although the average attendance at first did not exceed 40. The school was taken over by the Federal Government in 1897; in 1898 it was closed and the students were transferred to the Morris Industrial School nearby.

At 169 *m.* is the junction with US 59 *(see Tour 17).*

Prominent granite formations are visible near Ortonville.

ORTONVILLE, 195.1 *m.* (985 alt., 2,017 pop.), is on the southern shore of BIG STONE LAKE, the source of the Minnesota River. In this area the streams are well stocked with fish, and game birds are abundant. The country surrounding Big Stone Lake was a favorite camping and hunting ground for the Sioux; the many INDIAN MOUNDS along its shores yield interesting artifacts.

C. K. Orton, for whom Ortonville was named, settled here in the sum-mer of 1872. In the fall of 1873 he laid out the town site and established a trading post with the Sioux Indians. As the settlers filtered into the country and took up homesteads, Ortonville began to flourish as a western outpost, despite the fact that the closest rail connection was 50 miles away. As the region developed, the town became one of the principal outlets for agricultural produce; grain was shipped down the lake to Ortonville on steam-driven barges.

Today the town is known for its granite-quarrying and canning industries. Large quantities of ruby-red granite, valued for its beauty and texture, are quarried here and shipped to other sections of the State to be polished. Seven large quarries operate throughout the year and provide an income to hundreds of families.

The Big Stone Canning Company in Ortonville has one of the largest corn canneries in the United States. This company, originator and patent holder of equipment used in canning whole kernels, ships each year about 150,000 cases of sweet corn to wholesalers.

A Sweet Corn Festival, sponsored by the Town and Farm Club, is held every August and has drawn as many as 20,000 persons to Ortonville. Visitors are given a free sweet-corn dinner and a program of entertainment.

Ortonville is an attractive, unusually clean town, with several parks; almost all of its streets are paved or bituminous-treated.

In the western outskirts of Ortonville, US 12 crosses the Minnesota River where (R) about one-quarter mile upstream is the BIG STONE LAKE DAM, constructed by the WPA. A dike, a short distance to the west, diverts the Whetstone River from South Dakota into the lake. The dam and the dike raise the level of Big Stone Lake 3 to 6 feet. They are but two units of the Upper Minnesota River Water Conservation Program, which is further carried out in the Lac qui Parle Lake region *(see Tour 17)*.

Ortonville is at the junction with US 75 *(see Tour 4)*.

At 196.1 *m.* US 12 crosses the South Dakota Line, 66 miles east of Aberdeen, S. Dak. *(see South Dakota, Tour 2)*.

<<<<<<<<<<<<<<<<<<<<❀>>>>>>>>>>>>>>>>>>>>

Tour 11

Twin Cities—Chaska—Granite Falls—Montevideo—Dawson—(Watertown, S. Dak.); US 212.
Twin Cities to South Dakota Line, 179.6 m.

The Chicago, Milwaukee, St. Paul & Pacific R.R. parallels route between Twin Cities and Montevideo.
Roadbed paved except few miles in extreme west. Open all year.
Usual accommodations at short intervals.

The eastern end of this route is in the Twin Cities; from there US 212 traverses part of the Minnesota River Valley and then passes through a dairying and diversified farming area. Between Granite Falls and Montevideo the route is again in the valley of the Minnesota River and finally runs due west in a long straight course across great fertile prairies to the North Dakota Line.

ST. PAUL, 0 *m.* (703 alt., 271,606 pop.) *(see ST. PAUL).*

Points of Interest. Capitol Square, City Hall, Cathedral of St. Paul, Government dam and locks.

St. Paul is at the junction with US 10 *(see Tour 16),* US 12 *(see Tour 10),* US 52 *(see Tour 9),* and US 61 *(see Tour 1).*

West on Kellogg Blvd. in St. Paul from its junction with Robert St. to Marshall Ave.; L. on Marshall Ave. across the INTERCITY BRIDGE over the Mississippi River to Lake St. in Minneapolis.

MINNEAPOLIS, 9.5 *m.* (812 alt., 464,356 pop.) *(see MINNEAPOLIS).*

Points of Interest. Minnehaha Falls, Chain of Lakes, University of Minnesota, flour mills at St. Anthony Falls.

Minneapolis is at the junction with US 65 *(see Tour 14),* US 169 *(see Tour 3),* US 52 *(see Tour 9),* US 12 *(see Tour 10),* and US 8 *(see Tour 19).*

Straight ahead on Lake St. in Minneapolis, around the north shore of Lake Calhoun to Excelsior Ave.; L. on Excelsior Ave.

At 11.1 *m.* (W. Lake St. and Excelsior Ave.) is the junction with State 7.

Right on State 7, an excellent wide parkway, to ST. LOUIS VILLAGE, 2.4 *m.*, whose warehouses and depot adjoin the road.

MINNEHAHA CREEK, 3.9 *m.*, outlet of Minnetonka, links the chain of Minneapolis lakes with the Mississippi River below Minnehaha Falls.

At 4.6 *m.* is the intersection with an improved road; L. on this road to HOPKINS, 1.9 *m.* (920 alt., 3,834 pop.). This community is on the western edge of a flat outwash plain well suited to truck-farming; the produce finds a ready market in the Twin Cities. Famed for the abundance of its raspberry crop, the village annually holds a raspberry festival following the berry-picking season. Named for Harley H. Hopkins (1824–1882), an early postmaster, the town numbers among its industries a plant of the Minneapolis-Moline Power Implement Company, 130 9th Ave. S. *(open to visitors),* a large manufacturer of farm implements.

The Hennepin County Fair is held on the 22-acre exhibition grounds annually during the latter part of August.

BLAKE SCHOOL, Mendelsohn Rd., is a private preparatory and elementary school for boys. It was founded in 1907 by William Blake; the present location was acquired in 1911. A series of 13 MURAL PANELS in the library representing *Boy Heroes* were painted by H. W. Rubins.

At 6.8 *m.* is the junction with a paved road; L. on this road to the GLEN LAKE TUBERCULOSIS SANATORIUM, 1 *m.*

State 7 continues through a district of wooded knolls and tamarack swamps, varied by truck farms and cornfields. At 9.8 *m.* is the intersection with State 101, and at 11 *m.* is the paved road (R) to Deephaven and other points on the east shore of Lake Minnetonka. At 11.7 *m.* CHRISTMAS LAKE is visible to the L., and at ST. ALBAN'S BAY, 11.8 *m.*, is the first view (R) of LAKE MINNETONKA, which, although only 12 miles long, has 250 miles of scalloped, wooded shore line.

The lake is still as popular with vacationers as it was in the eighties and nineties, although the scene has greatly changed.

Speedboats and sailboats nose among the numerous bays and islands, where once steamers plied. Large hotels have been replaced by summer homes—varying from crude cabins to palatial mansions—that line the irregular shores and overlook the lake from its profusion of capes, straits, bays, arms, and points.

A romantic background enhances picturesque Minnetonka. Here the Sioux and Chippewa worshipped the Great Spirit, Manitou, ruler of the waters of Me-ne-a-ton-ka.

Governor Ramsey, with a party including Col. John H. Stevens (1820–1900), pushed up Minnehaha Creek to the lake in 1852 and officially gave it the English version of its Indian name. Thirty years before, Joseph R. Brown (1805–1870), then a Fort Snelling drummer boy, had come up the same route, and recorded his explorations of Minnetonka.

Travelers to Minnesota in the middle 19th century often mentioned Minnetonka in glowing accounts, some referring to it as the "most beautiful lake in the State." It afforded exceptionally fine fishing in those days, and game was abundant in the adjoining "big woods."

Once a picturesque sight on Minnetonka's waters, the luxurious, many-decked steamers that supplied transportation between the various points of the lake have long since made their last excursions. The first of these, the *Governor Ramsey,* built in 1860 for the Rev. Charles Galpin of Excelsior, was a 50-foot, flat-bottomed, side-wheeler driven by a nonreversible engine. The boat was rechristened *Lady of the Lake* in 1867; later it was renovated, lengthened 8 feet, and renamed *Minnetonka.*

The largest of the steamers that enlivened Minnetonka's waters was the *Belle of Minnetonka,* equipped to carry 3,500 persons. As the *Phil Sheridan* it had steadily plied the Ohio and the Mississippi since 1866, bringing new settlers, businessmen, and tourists to the prosperous Middle West. In 1882 the boat was dismantled, shipped to Minnetonka, and launched on a colorful lake career under its new name. But the *Belle of Minnetonka's* usefulness, like that of the *Minnetonka* and all the other boats in the lake service, finally came to an end; only six steamboats were left in 1926. Now there are none, since modern travelers prefer the motorboat or automobile.

The lake has been publicized by Lieurance's *By the Waters of Minnetonka* and Cadman's *Land of the Sky Blue Water.*

Lake Minnetonka offers opportunity for such aquatic sports as sailing, motorboating, aquaplaning, swimming, and fishing. There are also facilities for golf and tennis.

At 12.8 *m.* is the junction with a side road; R. 0.2 *m.* here to EXCELSIOR AMUSEMENT PARK *(recreational concessions, picnic grounds).*

EXCELSIOR, 0.5 *m.* (917 alt., 1,072 pop.), was organized in 1858 and owes its name and settlement to a colony, the Excelsior Pioneer Association, which was formed in New York City, November 12, 1852. The CITY BATHING BEACH AND PARK adjoin the lake shore west of the business district.

TRINITY CHAPEL, on 3rd St., was erected through the efforts of Arthur Vickers, an Englishman, who solicited financial aid for it in England. The chapel, built in 1862, is of concrete made from lime and pit-run gravel, poured into forms of 15-inch boards that were raised at each pouring. The architect is unknown. The first congregation assembled in 1862, and that year services were held inside a stockade to insure protection against hostile Indians. The chapel was moved to its present site in 1907, the guild hall added in 1928, and the pulpit designed and built by a parishioner in 1930.

At 13.3 *m.* on State 7 is the junction with State 41; L. on State 41 at 2.9 *m.* is the junction with State 5; R. on State 5 to the ZUMBRO HEIGHTS EXPERIMENTAL FARM at 5.8 *m.* Here, on the south shore of LAKE MINNEWASHTA, 237 acres are devoted to the development of hardy fruits. Among the 40 or more varieties so far developed is the Latham raspberry, now planted locally as extensively as all other varieties combined. This and a raspberry known as the "Chief" bring to the State each year a return exceeding the total purchase and maintenance cost of the experimental farm. Most widely planted of all northern Great Plains apples is the "Haralson," also a product of this farm. Here also American varieties of plums have been crossed with Japanese species to produce hardy fruits that can be grown in the upper Great Plains and Canada. At 6 *m.* on State 5 is a junction with a dirt road; R. on this road between TAMARACK LAKE and SCHULTZ LAKE to the junction with State 7 at 7.1 *m.*

At 13.6 *m.* on State 7 is GIDEON BAY, named for Peter Gideon, who developed the "Wealthy" apple while operating the State Fruit Farm, established here in 1879.

At 14.1 *m.* is the junction (R) with a paved road, an alternate and shorter (by 22 miles) route between this point and the north shore of the lake.

Right on this road, across the Narrows connecting the upper and lower lakes, to the junction with the main side tour at 3 *m.*

At 14.8 *m.* State 7 passes through the village of EUREKA and winds around SMITHTOWN BAY, southernmost point of the lake.

At 22.1 *m.* is ZUMBRO HEIGHTS, and at 24.6 *m.* is a junction with a paved road that leads R. between Halsted Bay and Priests Bay to join the main route on the north side of the lake at 2.2 *m.*, thus shortening the loop tour by 6.6 miles.

At 23.8 *m.* is the junction with a dirt road; R. through the Vogelgesang farm to the large bed of yellow LOTUS LILIES on Halsted Bay, 0.5 *m. (adm. 10¢),* in bloom about the middle of July. The blossoms of this plant, which here is found far north of its usual habitat, often measure 8 to 10 inches in diameter. Theories as to their presence here vary; the most plausible explanation seems to be that they were brought on the rough bottoms of early river boats.

State 7 continues westward through rolling, heavily wooded hills interspersed with small, cultivated plots to ST. BONIFACIUS, 29 *m.* (941 alt., 336 pop.). This small village was the early center of bee-keeping in Minnesota. The industry was established by Father Jaeger, formerly a priest of St. Bonifacius Church, which, like the town, takes its name from the German St. Boniface.

At St. Bonifacius is the junction with State 110.

Right on State 110 the route traverses a thriving farm region interspersed with groups of resort cottages dotting the lake shore. MOUND, 33.8 *m.* (668 pop.), is a village on the north shore of the upper lake.

At 34.6 *m.* is the junction (just south of the railroad station) with a hard-surfaced road; R. on this road at 34.9 *m.* is the junction with the road leading R. across the Narrows *(see above).*

At 35.1 *m.* (R) is the MOUND PUBLIC GOLF COURSE *(9 holes, reasonable fee).*

At 36 *m.* is SETON.

At 37.1 *m.* is SPRING PARK and the HOTEL DEL OTERO *(restaurant, bathing beach, dancing pavilion).*

From here to Wayzata the road follows the irregular shore line and dips back occasionally into the wooded hill country. Numerous side roads lead both R. and L. to summer homes or colonies.

MINNETONKA BEACH, 38.9 *m.,* is a village of homes and summer resorts on LAFAYETTE BAY. Here stood the Lafayette Hotel, built in 1882. It showed a combination of architectural designs and was the largest hotel during the lake's heyday.

Excellent views of the lake are numerous on this stretch of road. At night the lights of Excelsior, with its roller coaster and ferris wheel, move like fireflies across the water's surface.

At 41.8 *m.* is the junction with a side road; L. to ORONO ORCHARDS GOLF CLUB *(9 holes, small fee),* 0.7 *m.,* which maintains a sporty course with rolling fairways and well-kept grass greens.

WAYZATA (Ind., *at the pines, the north*), 43.4 *m.* (936 alt., 1,100 pop.), the largest town on Lake Minnetonka, is the trading center for the entire north-shore summer population.

The route (the right fork) leads east to the junction with State 101, 44 *m.*

Right on State 101 at 46.6 *m.* is the junction with a paved road; R. on this road to NORTHOME, 0.8 *m.,* on ST. LOUIS BAY, where the Hotel St. Louis, built in 1879 and torn down in 1907, once stood.

At 48.6 *m.* the junction with State 7 completes the loop tour of the lake.

Southwest of Minneapolis US 212 follows a winding course to the deep broad valley of the Minnesota River. It borders small lakes and stream beds and climbs over the rounded hills, once covered with the dense stands of hardwood known as the Big Woods. Near the remaining heavily wooded knolls are summer homes and farmsteads.

At 13.9 m. US 212 crosses Minnehaha Creek, which follows an ancient glacial river bed. In the small valleys are numerous drying lakes and muck deposits.

At 23.6 m. the Minnesota River is visible to the L. Here the outwash plain—contrasting so sharply with the hilly moraine—was named Eden Prairie. Morainic hills crowd close to the broad terraces of the Minnesota Valley.

At 26.9 m. the SHAKOPEE LIMESTONE LEDGES, through which the waters now cut a gorge, are visible on the opposite shore of the Minnesota River near the town of Shakopee (see Tour 3).

At 27.3 m. is the junction (L) with US 169 (see Tour 3).

CHASKA, 31.2 m. (721 alt., 1,901 pop.), seat of Carver County, is predominantly German. Chaska (Ind., first) was the name of two successive Sioux chiefs of an Indian village near the town. Three INDIAN MOUNDS are in the CITY PARK.

Sugar beets are the leading crop in this vicinity; there is a refinery, as well as a brickyard and canning factories, in the town. Chaska serves as a shipping and marketing center for the prosperous farming and dairying area surrounding it. Local MINERAL SPRINGS have been commercialized as mud baths for the treatment of various diseases.

The annual Homecoming and Sugar Day is celebrated here (2nd week in June).

Chaska once unknowingly entertained the James-Younger gang for a few days before the Northfield raid. The gang attracted considerable attention when it rode into town on fine mounts, but the men were not recognized and were invited to sit in on a poker game with Sheriff Du Toit, the local newspaper editor, and other prominent citizens.

West of Chaska US 212 leaves the broad valley of the Minnesota River and proceeds through a region of gently rolling hills.

At 32.2 m. is the junction with an improved road.

Left on this road to EAST UNION, 3 m. (30 pop.), one of the earliest Swedish communities in Minnesota, where Lutherans built a CHURCH and PARSONAGE about 1859. The church is a very plain stone structure with pitch roof and rectangular high windows along the sides. Over the entrance is a square tower with an arched doorway, lancet windows, corner buttresses, and a wooden spire; the belfry has lancet openings; the whole is freely designed.

The interior has a coved wood ceiling. Dividing the chancel from the nave is a pair of columns with elaborate brackets of wood, carved in a winding, interlaced design.

In back of a small altar of white wood is a large painting of the scene on Calvary, a feature found in many country churches in Sweden. Left of the altar is a baptismal font, and a white wooden balustrade defines the sanctuary. The pulpit, of pedestal type, is attached to the left column. The whole architectural scheme is simple and unaffected.

COLOGNE, 40 *m.* (947 alt., 355 pop.), is a German community named for the ancient city on the Rhine.

NORWOOD, 47.8 *m.* (990 alt., 607 pop.), is in a region of hills, lakes, sloughs, and clayey plains; on the latter are produced excellent fruit, vegetables, and grass for pasturage.

GLENCOE, 59.1 *m.* (1,001 alt., 1,925 pop.), the seat of McLeod County, is a cattle-shipping point in an area of dairy and fur farms. It has a PICNIC GROUNDS AND TOURIST PARK *(free camping, running water, stove).*

Right from Glencoe on State 22 to a junction with a country road at 1.8 *m.;* R.' on this road to SILVER LAKE, 8 *m.* (1,052 alt., 477 pop.); here Czechs settled in 1874 and established their own churches and library. In Silver Lake small boys still go from house to house early Easter Monday, in Czech called *Dyngus,* with whip and baskets to collect Easter eggs from the girls and threaten to switch those lying abed. The ancient significance of this as a fertility rite has apparently been forgotten. The women make apple strudels and potato dumplings and grow their own poppies—to insure plenty of seed for their *kolacky* buns. This town, small as it is, has given the State several noted scholars and has a fine group of women singers.

BROWNTON, 70 *m.* (1,018 alt., 632 pop.), is on Buffalo Creek. In the Sioux uprising of 1862 one of the first massacres of white settlers occurred here. The TOURIST PARK *(free camping, fireplace, running water)* is two blocks (R) from the highway.

At 76.9 *m.* is STEWART (1,063 alt., 541 pop.), on the eastern edge of a 50-mile undulating plain covered with rich glacial drift. West of the lakes scattered in the eastern part of this expanse, the horizon is broken by moraines.

BUFFALO LAKE, 83.7 *m.* (1,073 alt., 545 pop.), named for a small lake in the vicinity, is in a dairying area where the principal crops are corn and hay.

HECTOR, 88.4 *m.* (1,018 alt., 864 pop.), is in a region formerly known for excellent water-fowl shooting. While extensive drainage eliminated much of the game, Mongolian pheasants, recently introduced into the locality, are now quite numerous. An annual Summer Festival is held on July 19. A free TOURIST PARK *(camping, running water, tennis courts),* is at the R. of US 212.

BIRD ISLAND, 97.4 *m.* (1,089 alt., 1,004 pop.), was named by the Indians for an isolated grove of trees inhabited by numerous birds. The shade and firewood made it a favorite camping ground of the Indians and early traders.

OLIVIA, 102.5 *m.* (1,082 alt., 1,475 pop.) *(see Tour 2),* is at the junction with US 71 *(see Tour 2),* which unites with US 212 for 2 miles.

DANUBE, 107.7 *m.* (1,083 alt., 332 pop.), was named for the European river. A small moraine 3 miles long and less than 1 mile wide lies south of the city and provides a landmark in the otherwise unvaried till-plain. To the north are similar ridges.

At SACRED HEART, 120.2 *m.* (1,056 alt., 685 pop.), Charles Patterson, a fur-trader, established a trading post about 1783. Because Patterson constantly wore a bearskin hat, the Indians called him "sacred hat man," for to them the bear was sacred. With usage, "sacred hat" became "sacred heart," and thus the town was named. In the Sacred Heart GRANITE OUT-CROPS considerable quarrying has been done.

Left from Sacred Heart on an improved road to the junction with a dirt road, 6 *m.*; L. on this road, along the Minnesota River flats, to the RUINS OF FARTHER AND GAY CASTLE at 7 *m.* This 19-room granite mansion was erected in 1861 by Joseph R. Brown and destroyed by the Sioux during the outbreak of 1862. Carter Drew, a Scottish surveyor and a guest of Brown's, suggested naming the house Farther and Gay Castle, as a pun on the Fotheringay Castle in England, where Mary, Queen of Scots, spent her last days. During its short existence the mansion was the scene of many elaborate parties; Brown took great pride in his hospitality and dispensed it in a lavish manner. Today only a portion of the walls remains.

At 124.2 *m.* Hawk Creek has cut a deep bed into the soft drift plain. After crossing a mile-wide moraine US 212 descends again into the valley of the Minnesota River.

GRANITE FALLS, 130.2 *m.* (922 alt., 1,791 pop.), is on a boulder-strewn bluff overlooking the Minnesota Valley. In the valley Archean granites are exposed; these rocks belong to the oldest era of geological history. Although agriculture is the important industry today, the founders of the town were attracted by the power possibilities of the falls. Here one of the largest power plants of the Northern States Power Company supplies electricity to all the surrounding towns. Since the severe droughts in the last decade, however, the company has supplemented power from the falls with that from other stations.

The town has a new SPORTS FIELD with floodlights, and a SWIMMING POOL at MEMORIAL PARK.

Granite Falls was the home of Andrew J. Volstead, author of the "Volstead Act" for Federal prohibition.

Left from Granite Falls on State 67 to the marked SITE OF THE UPPER SIOUX INDIAN AGENCY *(see Tour 2: LOWER AGENCY)*, at about 6 *m.* The agency was established in 1854 and occupied until 1862, when many white people from here and nearby missions were escorted to safety by friendly Indians at the time of the Sioux uprising. The agency became a place of considerable importance and was one of the two Indian capitals. Near here also are the marked SITES OF THE RIGGS AND WILLIAMSON MISSIONS, established in the early 1850's. These missions supervised the activities of the Sioux who became Christians and established homes and farms in the white man's fashion, but who were exiled from the State after the uprising. The missions were first moved to South Dakota in 1863 and then to the Santee Reservation in northeastern Nebraska in 1866.

Northwest of Granite Falls US 212 follows the Minnesota River, where at one time the rushing waters of the prehistoric River Warren cut into the stony bed; most of the rocks in the vicinity are gray granite, with a scattering of red and black.

MONTEVIDEO, 143.5 *m.* (922 alt., 4,319 pop.), seat of Chippewa County, was named for the capital of Uruguay; the mayor of the South American city presented the Uruguayan flag to this municipality in 1905. SMITH PARK, on the western edge of town, is a 35-acre TOURIST CAMP *(free kitchen facilities)*. At the CHIPPEWA FAIRGROUNDS, on the outskirts of Montevideo, are a race track and a baseball diamond.

The bluffs of the city offer a remarkable panorama of the merging valleys of the Minnesota and Chippewa Rivers.

Montevideo is at the junction with US 59 *(see Tour 17)*.

West of Montevideo a great mass of rock is visible from the highway. Many students are convinced that this is a recently fallen meteor, for explorers who visited the area a few years ago did not report it.

At 144.5 *m.* is the entrance to CAMP RELEASE STATE PARK. A granite MONUMENT, 51 feet high, commemorates the release September 26, 1862, of 269 prisoners, mostly women and children, from captivity among the Sioux Indians. In this vicinity stood the friendly Sioux village of Chief Red Iron; the OUTLINE OF ONE OF THE DEFENSE TRENCHES is still visible across the top of the hill. The park, comprising 14 acres, has been planted with coniferous and hardwood trees and is ideal for campers and picnickers.

In this region is still found the *Psoralea* or Indian breadroot, a plant with great blue spikes and edible tubers used as food by early voyageurs and frontiersmen; although now quite scarce it is consumed locally. Here are few lakes; the swamps, once numerous, have been drained or have been dried by droughts. Agriculture and dairying are the principal occupations, and corn and hay the major crops. The prosperous farms with their comfortable houses and substantial farm buildings lie in the valleys or in the lee of hills, surrounded by wooded patches that serve as windbreaks and add to the attractiveness of the home sites.

Although most of the farmers here are of Scandinavian or German extraction, less than one-fifth descending from pioneer American stock, there are no bilingual districts. These people, interested in making permanent homes in rich farming land, were all quickly Americanized.

This land is so level that before the erection of modern wire fences snow-sailing was a popular and very exciting sport. Sail-sleighs, resembling ice boats and with room for supplies, shot across the snow with amazing speed, covering distances as great as 100 miles in a single day. Snowsailing is still popular in some localities, but the long trips of former days are no longer possible.

DAWSON, 160.1 *m.* (1,054 alt., 1,386 pop.), is the home of Theodore Christianson (1883–   ), thrice Governor of and later Senator from Minnesota.

A new religious sect has spread rapidly among the farms and small villages in this area. Its members, called the Followers of Christ, do not use church buildings, preferring to congregate in the open to listen to their preachers, who always go about in pairs. They believe in immersion and in a literal acceptance of the New Testament.

At 167.1 *m.* is the junction with US 75 *(see Tour 4)*.

At 179.6 *m.* US 212 crosses the South Dakota Line, 34 miles east of Watertown, S. Dak. *(see South Dakota, Tour 3)*.

⇽⇽⇽⇽⇽⇽⇽⇽⇽⇽⇽⇽⇽⇽⇽⇽⇽❂⇾⇾⇾⇾⇾⇾⇾⇾⇾⇾⇾⇾⇾⇾⇾⇾⇾

Tour 12

(La Crosse, Wis.)—La Crescent—Winona—Rochester—Owatonna—Mankato—New Ulm—Tracy—Lake Benton—(Huron, S. Dak.); US 14. Wisconsin Line to South Dakota Line, 286.2 m.

Chicago & North Western Ry. parallels route all the way.
Paved roadbed almost the entire distance. Open all year.
Usual accommodations; hotels in cities.

This east-west route across the entire State borders the broad Mississippi from La Crescent to Winona, traverses the southeastern farming district between Owatonna and New Ulm, skirts the beautiful lake district near Mankato, and crosses the fertile southwestern portion of the State to South Dakota.

West of La Crosse, Wis. *(see Wisconsin, Tour 20)*, US 14 crosses the Mississippi River on a free bridge at 0 *m.* and follows a shaded road across the island-studded river bottoms.

LA CRESCENT, 1.9 *m.* (647 alt., 250 pop.), at the confluence of several Mississippi tributaries, has little to suggest its boom days of the early 1850's. Rivalry with La Crosse influenced the settlers to change the town's name from Manton to La Crescent, the Mohammedan emblem, under the mistaken conviction that La Crosse was named for the crusaders' symbol.

The town's earliest settler, Peter Cameron, a fur-trader, arrived in 1851 and, visioning a metropolis here, dug a canal to the Mississippi hoping to drain the lowlands. Parts of his abandoned project are still visible.

For several miles along the productive south slope overlooking the town, where the frost is usually light, are orchards planted in Territorial days. Although the hillsides seemed well suited to apple growing, it was not until species were imported from Russia and other northern countries that crops were entirely satisfactory. At present the region grows 50 kinds of apples and 30 varieties of plums.

La Crescent is at the junction with US 16 *(see Tour 13)* and US 61 *(see Tour 1)*; between La Crescent and Winona US 14 and US 61 are one route *(see Tour 1)*.

WINONA, 27.5 *m.* (666 alt., 20,850 pop.) *(see WINONA)*.

Points of Interest. Sugar Loaf, Garvin Heights State Park, Winona Teachers' College, College of St. Teresa.

At 29.1 *m.* US 14 leaves US 61 and swings L. around the buildings of St. Mary's College (L), 30.3 *m. (open to visitors)*, which stand on the heights overlooking the northwestern part of Winona. Its establishment as a Roman Catholic institution in 1913 was a realization of the hopes of a former college professor and theological seminary rector, Rt. Rev. Patrick R. Heffron, second bishop of Winona, who first dreamed of a classical institution to be erected at the diocesan seat here. For 20 years after its opening the college was conducted by the diocesan clergy, first as a junior college and academy, and since 1925 as a 4-year college of liberal arts. In 1933 St. Mary's passed to the control of the Brothers of the Christian Schools. The main buildings of the college are designed in the neo-classic style with Corinthian porticos.

At 30.7 *m.* US 14 enters the soil-erosion-control demonstration area *(see Tour 1)* and mounts steadily through deep-walled ravines to the upland from the river valley. Widenings in the valley floor are patched with wheat fields and corn fields; grapevine and Virginia creeper hold back the crumbling yellow bluffs bordering the road.

This is a butter-making area, although only a few years ago a railroad official refused to send a refrigerated car here because, he said, there wasn't enough butter in the area to grease its wheels.

STOCKTON, 35.1 *m.* (175 pop.), is one of many old gristmill towns strung along the creeks that flow to the Mississippi.

At 37.5 *m.* is FARMERS' COMMUNITY PARK (R), with picnic grounds in a wide, shaded, grassy glen.

The ARCHES, 39.1 *m.* *(adm. 10¢-15¢, May-Oct.; no fee in winter)*, a private resort (R), is open during the entire year. The resort has camping and picnic grounds, an outdoor swimming pool, and a zoo.

At 40.6 *m.* the highway reaches the level tableland with its wide stretches of corn and wheat broken only by farmsteads and their fringes of poplar and hardwood.

LEWISTON, 41.4 *m.* (656 pop.), which lies 0.5 mile (L) from the highway, was the first stagecoach stop on the Winona-Rochester line. RAMER'S TAVERN, now a private dwelling, is a relic of those robust days. Weary travelers broke their journeys here and took full advantage of the excellent food and good cheer for which the old tavern was famous.

When the site of ST. CHARLES, 51.4 *m.* (1,300 alt., 1,311 pop.), was surveyed in 1854, the founders offered an acre lot to every Christian Democrat who would settle here.

Right from St. Charles on State 74 to WHITEWATER STATE PARK, 6 *m.* *(fishing, golf course, fireplaces, campgrounds, bathing beach)*, a 60-acre park named for the Whitewater River, called Minnieska (Ind., *white water*) because it is churned in a tortuous rock-bound channel. In the park State 74 descends along a wooded valley whose walls are of lichen-covered limestone. Deer, once almost exterminated, are being reintroduced, and small wild animals are fed in winter at the forest reservation; beavers are being brought back to the streams.

At 52 *m.* is (R) a MUNICIPAL CAMPGROUND *(picnic facilities)*; the fairgrounds are to the L.

An event in this district is Gopher Count Day. Fifty years ago frontier youngsters set aside one day for trapping these destructive rodents, choosing sides for the contest and agreeing that those bringing in the finest tails would be provided with candy by the others. Many enthusiastic young trappers still compete for sweets and other refreshments.

At 61 *m.* the country is typical of the dairy regions—pastures, roadside meadows, acres of corn whose shining leaves contrast with the feathery cream color of ripening wheat, fields of peas, and neglected lots, yellow with mustard. The countryside near Rochester becomes more rolling, the trees heavier and varied by an occasional orchard.

ROCHESTER, 70.9 *m.* (988 alt., 20,621 pop.) *(see ROCHESTER)*.

Points of Interest. Mayo Clinic, Mayo Park and Pioneer Log Cabin, Soldiers' Memorial Field, Reid-Murdock Cannery.

Rochester is at the junction with US 52 *(see Tour 9)* and US 63 *(see Tour 18)*.

KASSON, 87.1 *m.* (1,252 alt., 1,200 pop.), is a typically prosperous commercial village in a fertile dairy section. It maintains a SWIMMING POOL *(free)*, a good GOLF COURSE *(9 holes, reasonable fee)*, and a 7-acre RECREATION GROUND with rock garden and waterfall.

Right from Kasson on State 57 to MANTORVILLE, 3 *m.* (387 pop.), with rather primitively operated quarries. St. Mary's Hospital and many of the better buildings of Rochester are constructed of solid slabs from these hills. Many buildings in Mantorville—including the old courthouse, churches, the brewery built into the hillside, the HUBBLE HOUSE, and a three-story pioneer hotel near the TOURIST PARK—were built in the 1850's of Mantorville stone and are still in good condition. The 13-foot slab of native stone that has been used as a porch at the entrance to the Congregational church for 80 years shows no signs of age. Farmers of the neighborhood still attend the meetings of Minnesota's oldest farmers' organization, the Dodge County Agricultural Society, organized in Mantorville in 1857.

Frank B. Kellogg (1856–1937) and Rear Admiral F. E. Beatty spent boyhood days in this village.

When the railroad builders of the 1880's ignored the town, most of the 600 New England settlers took their movable possessions to the new Great Western Ry. station at Kasson, leaving their stone dwellings and newly planted English oaks, now nearly 6 feet in diameter, as relics of their industry.

On the east side of Main St., one block south of the courthouse, is an 80-year-old frame TAVERN built by one of Minnesota's first wildcat promoters. Returning from the California gold rush with his pocket full of nuggets, the founder of this now-deserted settlement is said to have bought up land on the Zumbro River, sprinkled gold dust along the river bed, suggestively named his town site Sacramento, and let it be gossiped that he was panning gold. Although his real-estate boom was short, this stage stop and tavern on the old Dubuque-St. Paul Trail is still called Sacramento.

Left from Mantorville on an improved road to the ruined walls of one of Minnesota's earliest colleges, the METHODIST SEMINARY, 2 *m.*, built before the Civil War. This and parts of an ABANDONED MILL of native limestone are all that remain of the vanished village of WASIOJA. In 1861 Peter Mantor enlisted Company C here, to join Minnesota's Second Regiment. Nearly all were killed in action and Wasioja's widows and orphans abandoned the town.

At 9 *m.* on State 57 is BERNE, a small Swiss colony. Cold springs, rocky caves, and even a cheese factory give Alpine color to this 75-year-old settlement.

Left from Berne on an improved road to CONCORD, 15 *m.*, settled by New Englanders. It was abandoned for the new settlement at West Concord when the Great Western Ry. laid its track 3 miles west of the town.

WEST CONCORD, 18 *m.* (613 pop.), on the improved road at the junction with State 56, is one of many villages suddenly transplanted during the 1880's to the newly laid Great Western tracks. West Concord was long nicknamed "Webfoot" because of its muddy, almost impassable streets.

DODGE CENTER, 92.7 *m.* (1,288 alt., 850 pop.), ships garden produce, butterfat, and cattle to eastern markets. Excellent crops of peas and corn supply a local canning factory.

CLAREMONT, 100 *m.* (1,280 alt., 350 pop.), was settled during the 1850's by New Englanders who built a road to the village of Wasioja, planted elms on both sides, and called it Claremont St. This once beautiful drive, however, is now treeless and overgrown with weeds.

West of Claremont US 14 runs in practically a straight line through level farm land and pastures.

ANDERSON, 104 *m.*, is a small village.

Right from Anderson on a country road to RICE LAKE *(fishing, swimming, duck shooting)*, 2 *m.*, where a century ago nomadic Dakota tribes harvested wild rice in the shallow bayous. Relics are still unearthed from their camp sites and are collected by property-owners near the lake shore.

To the site of OWATONNA, 111.2 *m.* (1,129 alt., 7,654 pop.), Chief Wadena is said to have moved his entire village, that his frail daughter might drink daily from its MINERAL SPRING, thus making Owatonna the first Minnesota health resort. The water, rich in iron and sulphur, is described as similar to that of the Vichy springs in France. This spring, on the northeastern side of the town, is now within a TOURIST CAMPGROUND *(fireplaces, cabins)*.

Owatonna, seat of Steele County, is on a winding little river, ironically named by the Indians "Owatonna" *(straight)*.

In addition to the usual symbols for crossroads, stores, and churches found on rural maps, this district, with an average of 20 dairy cows to each farm, adds a circled C for "creamery." The county has 17 co-operative creameries and produces more butter than any other county of comparable size in the United States.

For an experiment in art education, the Carnegie Foundation and the University of Minnesota selected Owatonna as the typical American town; it is not within commuting distance of a large city, nor is it dominated—although it has a fairly large Czechoslovakian colony that still commemorates its national memorial day on the second Sunday in June—by a single religion, race, or industry. This project, begun in 1933, is an attempt to determine how art can be incorporated into education so that it becomes an integral part of every citizen's existence. Instructors from the East introduced in the schools an art curriculum and service department, offering townspeople free guidance in home decoration, landscape gardening, merchandising, dressmaking, and civic planning. As a permanent gift to the town, the foundation has placed on the second floor of the PUBLIC LIBRARY *(open weekdays, 9 a.m.-9 p.m.)*, Broadway and Elm Sts., an ART COLLECTION of 2,000 prints, many unframed reproductions, and several hundred volumes of art literature. Despite its short existence the project has become such a vital part of the community life that its sponsors have agreed to extend the 5-year appropriation until the city shall be able to support it unaided.

PILLSBURY MILITARY ACADEMY, S. Grove St., originally called Minnesota Academy, is a boys' preparatory school. Founded September 10, 1877, the school was renamed Pillsbury in 1886 in recognition of George A. Pillsbury's (1816–1898) "unusually generous interest in the school." Boys are admitted to the sixth grade and carried through to the college level. Its 1936–37 enrollment was 92.

The NATIONAL FARMERS' BANK BUILDING, Main St., erected in 1908, was designed by Louis Sullivan (1856–1924). Impressed by Sullivan's avowed revolt against the Revival architecture of the late 19th century, the local bankers promised him a free hand with the plans and, though collectively dubious about his finished design, they nevertheless accepted it. The following description of the building is from *Louis Sullivan, Prophet of Modern Architecture,* written by Hugh Morrison and published by W. W. Norton and The Museum of Modern Art.

"Only a partial impression of the beauty of both interior and exterior can be obtained from photographs, since the effect of the original depends so largely on color. The exterior of the bank has a base of reddish brown sandstone ashlar, laid in courses of different heights, and penetrated by simple rectangular door and window openings. Above this the wall is faced by tough shale brick in soft variegated colors, the general effect being rich dark red. The walls of red Roman brick are opened by two great arched windows thirty-six feet in span, and are capped by a heavy cornice of unique design, consisting simply of corbelled courses of brick bounded above and below by bands of brown terra cotta. The total effect is very rich with the colors blending softly from a distance, but strongly individual at close range.

"The interior is a large square room rich in decorative detail and glowing in color, although the total effect of light spaciousness absorbs the detail so that it is never obtrusive or over-brilliant.

"The room is amply lighted by the great arch windows on two sides and a skylight overhead, and there is a curious quality to the light—a greenish tinge, like sunlight passed through sea water.

"Noteworthy details are the green terra cotta enframement of the clock, the decorative panel over the entrance door, and the lighting fixtures, the shades of which are miniatures of the whole building. The furniture, including the check desk, was all especially designed."

Owatonna is at the junction (L) with US 65 *(see Tour 14)* and US 218 *(see Tour 14).*

WASECA, 127.3 *m.* (1,153 alt., 3,815 pop.), sprang up in the midst of a wheatfield when the railroad reached this point in 1867. As a terminus of the road, Waseca (Ind., *rich or fertile in provisions)* soon outstripped other settlements in the county which had begun as early as 1854. In less than a year the community numbered 129 buildings and 700 persons and became important as a shipping point for wheat.

The Waseca County Anti-Horse Thief Detective Society, organized in 1864 when settlers suspected horse thieves among them, was only recently disbanded. The organization was highly successful, recovering all but one stolen animal during its vigilance. In 1870 lynching of two of the town's residents, alleged members of an Iowa gang, was narrowly averted. When the automobile began to supersede the horse, the society, while still clinging to its name, included the new motor-driven vehicles within the scope of its guardianship.

There is a public TOURIST CAMP on the western shore of CLEAR LAKE *(boats, fishing, cabins, cottages)* adjoining the town on the northeast; on the lake are several summer resorts and a large BOY SCOUT CAMP *(visitors welcome).* Fishing is good, catches including bluegill, crappie, bass, and pickerel.

A large cannery processing corn and peas, a produce plant, a co-operative creamery, three poultry hatcheries, and a flour mill are here.

Adjoining the town on the west is a 246-acre unit of the State experimental farm known as the Southeast Station. When purchased in 1911, the section was almost entirely swamp land, but drought and drainage have made it tillable. Most unusual of the valuable studies in corn-, swine- and cattle-breeding are the continual brother-sister matings of Poland China swine to determine most favorable methods of animal improvement.

Right from Waseca on State 13 to WATERVILLE, 12.1 *m.* (1,007 alt., 1,419 pop.), a popular resort center. At Waterville is the junction with State 60.

Left on State 60 to ELYSIAN, 18.1 *m.* (1,047 alt., 388 pop.), a focal point for a group of fishing and resort lakes extending north and west.

Left from Elysian on a graveled road that skirts the eastern Shore of LAKE ELYSIAN, the largest and one of the most beautiful lakes in this group. At 25.9 *m.* is the junction with US 14.

MANKATO, 152.7 *m.* (785 alt., 14,038 pop.), is the Sioux name for the blue earth found in the vicinity, which Le Sueur shipped to France in 1701 under the impression that it was copper-bearing *(see HISTORICAL SURVEY).*

Mankato, on the great bend of the Minnesota River where it turns sharply north and is joined by the Blue Earth River from the south, is in a valley 1.5 miles wide and from 150 to 200 feet deep. The torrent that cut the deep valley also dictated the future plan of Mankato, whose streets run from northeast to southwest, paralleling the principal terraces of the river valley; the side streets are steeply graded.

It was a cold day in January 1852 when three St. Paul men, Henry Jackson, Parsons K. Johnson, and Daniel Williams, set out for the great bend of the Minnesota River to found a city there, now Mankato. Six days were required to complete the journey, the party traveling by sleigh over the open prairie. As they neared their destination the men encountered a band of Sioux Indians led by Chief Sleepy Eye. The chief, mindful of a treaty, refused to let them settle on his domain until the Government had paid him. An offer of a barrel of pork and other choice provisions caused him to abandon his stand, and the party was permitted to proceed with its plans. On February 6, 1852, these men selected the site for the new city and began work on its first building. Built of logs, it was a low one-story shanty about 12 feet square, with neither windows nor floor.

From this primitive beginning Mankato developed rapidly into a frontier settlement. The settlers were beset by difficulties on every hand, but the Indian menace took front rank.

At the conclusion of the Sioux uprising in 1862 *(see Tour 2: LOWER AGENCY),* over 400 Indians were tried; the 303 condemned to death were brought to Mankato and held at Camp Lincoln (now Sibley Park) to await President Lincoln's approval of the verdict. Lincoln commuted the sentences of all but 39.

The day of the execution, December 26, was bitterly cold. Large throngs of people, among them many armed men, milled through the streets of Mankato. Every vantage point for the hanging had been appropriated hours before. Two thousand Minnesota troops had been moved to the scene to prevent disorder, but no violence was attempted.

A last-minute occurrence was the reprieve of one of the condemned Indians. Thirty-eight Indians were hanged simultaneously from a single gallows. They asked that the chains, by which they were bound in pairs, be removed so they might walk to the platform in single file. This was done, and, singing an Indian war song, each placed the rope around his own neck and continued singing while the cap was adjusted over his eyes. At the appointed time, W. H. Dooley, whose entire family had been massacred at Lake Shetek, cut the 2-inch scaffolding rope, and the entire number dropped to their death.

With this multiple hanging, the largest legal wholesale execution that has ever taken place in the United States, came the end of Indian worries to the residents of Mankato. A granite marker commemorating the hanging stands on the site of the execution, on the northwest corner of Front and Main Sts.

Mankato is southwestern Minnesota's leading metropolis. Industry here merges with agriculture and both are reflected in the prosperous atmosphere of Mankato's business district, for its geographical location has made Mankato a natural trade center for all southwestern Minnesota, northern Iowa, and eastern South Dakota. Its natural resources include quarries of high-quality limestone products (see INDUSTRIAL DEVELOPMENT: Mining). Its factories, of which there are 42, produce brick and cement, flour and foods, clothing and leather goods, boxes and brooms, and sundry other items. Agriculture of the area finds a market here; Mankato's hog market is the third largest in the State. The poultry industry combined with creamery products is a big factor in industrial importance, while railroad and trucking facilities provide excellent service for shippers and jobbers.

Beautiful tree-lined residential districts, scenic drives, and charmingly landscaped parks combine to give Mankato a gracious and homelike aspect. SIBLEY PARK, in the southernmost section, has 152 wooded acres, and contains a ZOO and a BOTANICAL GARDEN.

Adjacent to Sibley Park at the confluence of the Blue Earth and Minnesota Rivers are two DAMS reaching out from each bank and joined in the middle by a dike. Partially financed by Federal funds, these have an overall length of approximately 1,000 feet and play an important part in the flood-control project of the Minnesota Valley.

The Blue Earth County Historical Society sponsors two MUSEUMS in Mankato, one (free: open 3-5 weekdays) in the basement of the Public Library, 120 S. Broad St., and the other (free: open in summer) in Sibley Park. These two collections include relics of the Indian, Mexican, and World Wars, as well as objects of local historical interest—such as the first pencil-sharpener used in the county, weapons, old pictures, and costumes.

The MANKATO STATE TEACHERS COLLEGE, founded 1868, is on S. 5th St.; the BETHANY LUTHERAN COLLEGE stands on a hill in the southern part of town.

Mankato has many musical organizations and was the home of both Florence Macbeth and Mayme Schippel, who sang in American and European concerts.

Mankato is at the junction with US 169 *(see Tour 3)*.

West of Mankato the rugged hills and ravines extend in all directions; the scenery along the deep-cut, limestone-ledged valley of the Minnesota River is magnificent. In pioneer times this region was on the western margin of the Big Woods, but today only a wooded ravine or an occasional elm grove remains.

Wild-fowl shooting is excellent on the prairies, and on the uplands pheasants are abundant.

At 179.8 *m.* is a famous outcrop of rock that has endured tremendous changes since the continent was born. This formation, known as Old Redstone, is a conspicuous hill of about 2 square miles uplifted into the wide valley of the Minnesota. Older than the glaciers, this mass of pink quartzite, one of the hardest and oldest of rocks, survived the weathering of the Paleozoic era and stood out—a lone island in the Cretaceous seas that leveled the land and deposited a thick layer of what is now limestone. The oncoming glaciers buried it under deep drift, but their melting waters, merging into the prehistoric River Warren, removed the covering. Unable to cut through Old Redstone's hard foundation, the torrent swerved around the ledge, cutting the 200-foot valley with its numerous terraces.

NEW ULM, 182.9 *m.* (837 alt., 7,837 pop.), seat of Brown County and a thriving, up-to-date city, stands on high land that was once an island in the glacial River Warren. The village occupies three terraces at the confluence of two rivers, the Minnesota and the Cottonwood; the business district lies below the residential section and at a still lower level is the railway station.

Unlike many pioneer settlements, New Ulm was not a haphazard, opportunity-seeking venture. In the fall of 1854 representatives of a German land society in Chicago came to the site and officially named it for the cathedral city of Ulm in Württemberg, Germany. A year later, agents of the Turner Colonization Society of Cincinnati arrived and, finding the settlement in financial difficulties, arranged for the purchase of the town site and a merger of the two societies under the name of the German Land Association of Minnesota. The community was developed and managed under a socialistic plan.

At New Ulm occurred one of the important battles of the Sioux uprising *(see Tour 2: LOWER AGENCY)*. Into the town at the outset of the conflict poured refugees until the population had swelled to more than 1,200. Preparations were at once made for its defense, and an early attack was repulsed. Another seemed certain. In this crisis Judge Charles E. Flandrau, former Indian agent, assembled a force of volunteers at St. Peter and hastened to the relief of the village. A breastwork was thrown up around the outskirts, but the main defense was concentrated on the central part of the town.

The expected attack came from the west. Yelling, whooping, and singing war songs, the Indians came in on ponies, riding not straight ahead but back and forth, as they gradually decreased the distance between themselves and the defenders. This method of attack not only made them difficult targets but also allowed them to shoot from the protected side of their ponies, firing from under the animals' necks.

The soldiers on the outer breastworks were so terrified by these unfamiliar tactics that they fled in panic to the center of the city. The obvious strength of the inner defense led the Indians to try a new strategy. About 500 of them began advancing toward a protective thicket of oak brush from which they hoped to set fire to the town. Colonel Flandrau sensed this move and led a sortie of a hundred well-armed men against them and after desperate hand-to-hand fighting the Indians were routed.

In preparation for the next day's attack the fortifications were strengthened still further and, trusting to the Indians' terror of cannon, imitations made of stove pipe were constructed along the breastworks. Anvils, struck simultaneously, contributed a realistic boom, and when the Indians were successfully repulsed in their second major attack, much credit was given to inventors of this improvised artillery.

After their defeat the Sioux held a council, ceased the attack, and soon disappeared. Behind them they left 26 dead soldiers, many wounded, and the smoking ruins of 190 houses. Only 25 houses were left standing to shelter 1,200 people. Colonel Flandrau decided to evacuate the town, and the dreary procession of refugees and defenders set out for Mankato, 30 miles away. Luckily they were met by a fresh company of 100 soldiers who were coming to their relief, and with this additional strength as a rear guard they reached their destination in safety. It was many weeks, however, before the refugees could face their devastated town and begin the task of rebuilding. Today, adjacent to the courthouse square, a bronze monument commemorates the heroism of the town's defenders.

More than any other group the Germans have been responsible for the early and sustained interest in music that has characterized the town. German is still spoken in the streets, but with less and less frequency. The Turnverein, a well-known German gymnastic organization, has a branch here that frequently gives public exhibitions.

New Ulm was among the early milling centers of the state and today counts flour production among its most important industries.

The New Ulm LIBRARY AND HISTORICAL MUSEUM, 25 N. Broadway St., contains many exhibits, including historical displays and a collection of signed photographs of famous persons. Funds for financing this building, erected in 1936, came from the profits of the municipally owned heating system, established in 1916, which New Ulm operates in addition to its water, sewerage, and electric light plants.

The predominating Roman Catholic element in New Ulm is responsible for the locally famous WAY OF THE CROSS, a hillside pathway near LORETTO HOSPITAL on N. 5th St. At short distances along this winding path are small houses sheltering the Stations of the Cross, with figures sculptured in full relief.

The RUINS OF THE OLD WARAJU DISTILLERY are in HERMANN MONUMENT PARK, Broadway and Center Sts.

HERMANN MONUMENT, on a bluff in a park of the same name, was erected about 1898 by the Sons of Hermann, a fraternal organization of Germans. A free TOURIST CAMP *(running water, swimming)* is maintained near the monument.

Left from New Ulm on State 15 to the COTTONWOOD RIVER STATE PARK, 2 *m.*, whose 840 acres include a large area in the valley of the Cottonwood River.

West of New Ulm US 14 leaves the river valley and crosses the undulating moraines whose clayey soil is excellent for farming.

ESSIG, 190 *m.* (24 pop.).

Right from Essig (on a road to the R. of the village creamery) to the MILFORD MONUMENT, 2.5 *m.*, in memory of 50 settlers who were slain in the Sioux uprising. Right from the Milford Monument on an improved road to the marked SITE OF A BATTLE BETWEEN THE PIONEERS AND INDIANS, 3.5 *m.*

SLEEPY EYE, 197.3 *m.* (1,034 alt., 2,576 pop.), is named for the friendly Indian chief, Isk-Irk-Ha-Ba *(sleepy eye)*, who is believed to have been buried beneath the monument near the railroad station. The 40-acre SLEEPY EYE LAKE STATE PARK *(free camping and picnic grounds)*, on the site of this Indian chief's village, lies within the town.

Right from Sleepy Eye on State 4 to FORT RIDGELY STATE PARK (L), 10.4 *m.* *(camping, picnicking, golf)*. This 155-acre tract includes the SITE OF OLD FORT RIDGELY, built in 1853, a flourishing post in Territorial days. Here occurred a critical encounter during the Sioux uprising of 1862 *(see Tour 2: LOWER AGENCY)*, when many of the settler refugees sought shelter within its buildings. At this time Fort Ridgely was merely a military fort whose few detached and unfortified buildings had not even the protection of a stockade. Three ravines a short distance away provided protection for attackers and added to the difficulty of defense.

Against this post, the Indians—some say 1,000 shared in the attack—made two successive onslaughts on August 20 and 22. (The intervening day of respite was caused by a heavy rain.) Huddled in a two-story stone building were 300 noncombatants. The defending force consisted of 180 poorly armed men; the soldiers, for the most part, had been recruited only a few days before. Twice the Indians gained access to the outlying log buildings and twice they were dislodged. When the last desperate charge was repulsed with a blast of canister, the siege was over; 3 of the garrison had been killed, 13 wounded, and among the number saved was a baby born during the battle. The loss among the Indians has been estimated at about 100.

The payment due the Indians ($72,000 in gold), which might easily have appeased the braves, had arrived at the fort only a few hours after the uprising had gotten under way. Had Little Crow succeeded in his attack and secured the gold, he planned to sweep down upon all the settlements farther down the valley. The Government later presented each of the gallant defenders with a medal on which was inscribed, "Tee-yo-pa nah-tah-ka-pee" *(They kept the door shut.)*.

All historic spots within the park are marked. An annual music festival *(during May)* is given by the combined musical organizations of a dozen southern Minnesota counties.

In SPRINGFIELD, 211.2 *m.* (1,028 alt., 2,050 pop.), Sauerkraut Festivals are held each September. Eating contests, followed by dancing and other amusements, are the main attraction.

Springfield, platted in 1877 and first called Burns, is said to have been named for a large SPRING between the town and the Cottonwood River.

At 218.9 *m.* is the junction with US 71 *(see Tour 2)*.

In LAMBERTON, 226 *m.* (1,264 alt., 728 pop.) is KUHAR PARK

(picnic grounds, bathing beach, illuminated baseball park), consisting of 23 wooded acres on the Big Cottonwood River.

At one time there were gold-mining activities in this area, and in some places gold was found, but the supply was limited and operations were soon abandoned.

TRACY, 243.5 *m.* (1,395 alt., 2,575 pop.), named for a former president of the Chicago & North Western Ry., is known throughout Minnesota for its Box Car Day, which attracts about 30,000 people. This annual celebration is held the first week in September and is sponsored by the Tracy Civic and Commerce Association. There are parades, pageants, a queen coronation, carnival dancing and free acts, sports exhibitions, games, and musical selections by the community band. The event is an expression of good will toward the people of this territory.

There are modern tourist cabins here.

At 250.7 *m.* is the junction with US 59 *(see Tour 17)*.

BALATON, 256.4 *m.* (1,528 alt., 600 pop.), was named for a lake in Hungary. It has a TOURIST CAMP *(tables, running water, fireplaces)*.

At 260.7 *m.* is the junction with State 91.

Right on this graveled road to CAMDEN STATE PARK, 8 *m.* *(camping facilities, trails, swimming pool)*.

TYLER, 269.8 *m.* (1,750 alt., 905 pop.), a Danish settlement, was colonized in the early 1870's by Grundtvigians, followers of Nikolai Frederik Severin Grundtvig. The town was platted and named for C. B. Tyler, a pioneer of southwestern Minnesota. In 1884 the organization secured an option on 35,000 acres of land purchasable by Danes only. The following year, when the quota of 100 new settlers had arrived, the achievement was marked by a celebration.

Danes still predominate in this village and the Danish language is used in church services. Old World customs and folkways *(see IMMIGRATION AND RACIAL ELEMENTS)* are retained by the older generation, and native foods are served. Tyler supports a Danish weekly newspaper.

Grundtvig (1783–1872) was a Danish theologian and poet. His strong belief that patriotism should be one of the predominate principles of religion and his desire to make possible education of the masses led him to established a system of "folk high schools." Grundtvig's innovation evoked widespread interest in various countries and brought about the establishment of five such schools in the United States. One of these is the DANEBOD FOLK SCHOOL in Tyler. Opened in 1888 and named in honor of a Danish queen, the school is locally known as the People's College. The students are almost entirely from farms and small communities; its motto is "enlightenment must be our delight." A typical day's program includes morning devotion and Bible hour, literature, music lectures, and craft and hobby hour. The evening entertainment is often centered around Danish "sanglege" *(singing-games)*.

In Tyler there is a co-operative creamery, a co-operative butter and stock produce plant, and a cement and tile company.

An EXHIBITION OF HISTORICAL RELICS is shown at the Lincoln County Fair *(usually last week-end in Aug.)*.

The town of LAKE BENTON, 277.5 *m.* (1,755 alt., 903 pop.), is on the southern shore of Lake Benton, at one time the largest lake in south-western Minnesota. Lake Benton, like many other of Minnesota's glacial lakes, is now almost completely dry. Here, as throughout the older glacial area, the process of evaporation and seepage has gone on for centuries; hundreds of lakes had already disappeared when the settlers arrived. Others, among them Lake Benton, were still in existence. This drying up of glacial lakes, although normally a gradual one, has in some instances been hastened by drainage, removal of plant cover, and continued drought. Conservation methods will restore some of the lakes and retard the dis-appearace of many others. The lake and town were named for Thomas H. Benton of Missouri by his son-in-law, John C. Frémont (1813–1890), who came here in 1838 with Joseph Nicollet.

Lake Benton is at the junction with US 75 *(see Tour 4)*.

West of Lake Benton, US 14 runs through a fertile valley and at 286.2 *m.* crosses the South Dakota Line, 41 miles east of Huron, S. Dak. *(see South Dakota, Tour 4)*.

◄◄◄◄◄◄◄◄◄◄◄◄◄◄◄◄◄◄◄ ✿ ►►►►►►►►►►►►►►►►►►►►

Tour 13

(La Crosse, Wis.)—La Crescent—Preston—Austin—Albert Lea—Blue Earth—Fairmont—Worthington—Luverne—(Sioux Falls, S. Dak.); US 16.

Wisconsin Line to South Dakota Line, 291.4 m.

The Chicago, Milwaukee, St. Paul & Pacific R. R. parallels this route between La Crescent and Jackson; and the Chicago, St. Paul, Minneapolis & Omaha Ry. be-tween Worthington and South Dakota Line.

Paved roadbed between La Crescent and Hokah, bituminous-treated between Hokah and junction with US 52, paved between junction US 52 and Fountain, graveled between Fountain and Spring Valley, paved between Spring Valley and Alden, graveled between Alden and Blue Earth, and paved between Blue Earth and South Dakota Line. Open all year.

Usual accommodations.

This route parallels the southern boundary of the State through a fertile, gently rolling farm region, crosses many rivers and tributary brooks, and, near Albert Lea and Fairmont, passes a few scattered lakes before enter-ing the true prairie country.

US 16 crosses the Mississippi River on a free bridge from La Crosse, Wis. *(see Wisconsin, Tour 21)*, and follows a tree-shaded road across the wide river bottoms. Acres of white and yellow waterlilies and patches of water-hyacinth separate the numerous islands, whose entire surface is a mass of swamp and forest cover.

LA CRESCENT, 1.9 *m.* (647 alt., 520 pop.) *(see Tour 12)*, is at the junction with US 14 *(see Tour 12)* and US 61 *(see Tour 1)*.

West of La Crescent the route traverses the Driftless Area, a 10,000-square-mile triangular section that the continental glacier failed to cover; it spreads over the eastern halves of Winona and Houston Counties and extends into Iowa and Wisconsin—once a small island in a sea of ice. The deeply eroded valleys are lined with hardwoods or low bushes, and the hills are covered with a deep, fine soil called loess. The underlying bed of limestone is visible in the high bluffs along the larger streams.

At 4.5 *m.* is the junction with State 26.

Left on State 26 to BROWNSVILLE, 7 *m.* (639 alt., 274 pop.), on the shores of the Mississippi. Under the ledge of a high bluff is an OLD STEAMBOAT LANDING of the 1840's, known for years as Wildcat Bluff. Here three trappers, the first settlers in Houston County, mounted a stuffed wildcat on a pole over the levee to identify their landing for steamboat skippers.

HOKAH, 7.7 *m.* (654 alt., 452 pop.), is a picturesque dairy community on a widening of the Root River. The village is in a deep ravine and is the site of one of 20 flour or lumber mills that once throve along the Root River and its tributary creeks.

Left from Hokah on State 44 to CALEDONIA, 13 *m.* (1,179 alt., 1,554 pop.), the seat of Houston County. Founded and named in 1852 by Sam McPhail (1828–1902), Caledonia still has the extremely narrow streets laid out in the original McPhail town plat. A Mormon colony under the leadership of one of the Youngs camped here for a time in rude huts. Local residents blame Jacob Webster, who came to Caledonia in 1854, for the abundance of dandelions in Minnesota. Webster, hungering for greens, they say, sent to New England for dandelion seed, which grew all too prolifically in the Minnesota soil.

A large section of land in the Caledonia district has been given over to a Federal soil-conservation project. The soil-improvement plan, by which the farms affected benefit materially, is entirely under the direction of the Federal Government and consists of dam-building, crop control, terracing, reversion to timber, and the like. *(Guides available at Caledonia Soil Conservation Project office on Main St.)*

At 24 *m.* on State 44 is SPRING GROVE (1,322 alt., 867 pop.).

When the election contest between Houston, Caledonia, and Brownsville for the determination of the seat of Houston County was held here in 1855, Houston voters brought posters representing Brownsville buried by rock avalanches under Wildcat Bluff. Brownsville citizens displayed cartoons of Houston flooded under spring freshets. Caledonians more wisely brought hard-boiled eggs and jars of a rare pioneer delicacy—butter. Assembled voters contentedly gorged themselves on fresh butter and made Caledonia the county seat. Spring Grove's first store still displays its original trade-mark, "The Sign of the Lion."

West of Hokah US 16 follows a deeply eroded, boulderless valley, with exposures of Cambrian rocks and isolated pinnacles of Ordovician limestone. Wild flowers thrive in this soil, and in May masses of bluebells, sweet-william, cowslips, and violets cover the river lowlands. Later, shrubs blanket the hillsides, sumac and huckleberry hiding the less sturdy flowers.

In HOUSTON, 19.8 *m.* (684 alt., 794 pop.), are hundreds of SPRINGS that attracted settlers. Once a steamboat port on the navigable Root River, Houston is today a dairy and poultry center. Many of its present houses, churches, and bridges were built in the earliest days of the town. The counters, walls, and ceilings of a candy store on Main St. are overgrown with English ivy planted there some 50 years ago.

Left from Houston on State 76 past a STONE CHURCH (L) to the first road branching R. at approximately 1.5 *m.;* R. on this road to YUCATAN, 9.2 *m.,* where Indian heads and arrow signs indicate the entrance to the YUCATAN CATACOMBS which, like the many caves in the area, are a honeycomb of fantastic crystal domes, stalactites, chandelier rocks, and bizarrely colored underground chambers. Once the tombs and dwelling places of Winnebago tribes, the Yucatan Catacombs are now popular recreation spots for sightseers and campers. The entrance to the catacombs overlooks the prosperous Beaver Valley, Crystal Creek, and the surrounding dairy country.

At 21 *m.* the route winds through an open valley with meadows and cultivated fields, but soon circles the eroded hills and at 29 *m.* passes the FERNDALE COUNTRY CLUB GOLF COURSE *(reasonable fee).* The hills over which the road winds become smoothed off as the nonglaciated region is left behind. At 30 *m.* the road descends the valley along its smoothly wooded wall. The bluffs become less pointed and their valleys wider.

RUSHFORD, 32.1 *m.* (727 alt., 1,125 pop.), to the R. of the highway, is in the deep valleys of the Root River and Rush Creek. This area was covered by the earliest glaciers, so long ago, however, that the lakes have drained or dried and a fine silt or loess has covered the hills and washed into the lowland. The route follows the winding course of the Root River, which at 44 *m.* is buried in a grove of elm, walnut, and cottonwood matted with wild grape.

At 48.4 *m.* is the spot (unmarked) where Buffalo Bill (1846–1917), rehearsed one of his Wild West Shows; the bluff above the site of his dugout is called BUFFALO BILL'S PEAK. The road descends a beautifully wooded stretch where a heavy growth of conifers—far from their usual habitat— is mixed with the more characteristic hardwoods.

At 48.6 *m.* US 16 winds past sharp bluffs and limestone hills.

At 49.7 *m.* is LANESBORO (846 alt., 1,014 pop.), in a valley of almost unbelievable charm where the south branch of the Root River has cut a deep gorge. Fifty years ago, in the comparative obscurity of Lanesboro, Dr. John C. Hvoslef, Norwegian naturalist, carried on his important work in ornithology. Several churches built of native stone more than 50 years ago are still in use.

The highway skirts the village along the east and, three blocks after turning R. across its southern edge, passes a road (L) leading up a steep hill to a GOLF COURSE *(9 holes, reasonable fee)* that overlooks the whole valley.

At 51 *m.* is the STATE FISH HATCHERY (L), fed by an enormous spring said to flow at the rate of 10,000 gallons a minute. A small LAKE and the 20-acre SYLVAN PARK add to the beauty of the view as the road leaves the valley and ascends the rugged hillside, where (R) are PICNIC

GROUNDS at 52 *m.* The Dawson brothers, inventors of the Dawson flour-mill rollers *(see INDUSTRIAL DEVELOPMENT: Milling),* had a foundry here in pioneer days.

At 55.5 *m.* is the junction with US 52 *(see Tour 9),* and for 7.7 miles US 16 and US 52 are one route.

At 57.1 *m.* is the junction with State 80.

Left on State 80 along the valley of a branch of the Root River, one of the most beautiful but least known parts of the State. Here flow many streams of clear, cold water. Some of them gush from tunnel-like caverns, flow for a short distance in the open, and then disappear between towering rock walls.

FORESTVILLE, 8.4 *m.,* was depleted in population by the Civil War and later, when the railroad was laid elsewhere, the citizens abandoned their old mill.

At the east end of a 1,500-acre tract of virgin hardwood forest stands the old MEIGHEN STORE, built before the town was founded in 1855 *(permission to enter obtainable at First National Bank in Preston).* Tom Meighen's hospitality, both at his store and his home, has become a legend. There seemed to be no limit to his readiness to serve others, and he offered an unfailing welcome to friends and strangers alike. His store drew customers from many miles around, and Indians often vied with settlers for places to hitch their ponies when they came into town to trade furs for flour and other supplies. Meighen's relationship with the Indians was always friendly, and he was often invited to participate in their hunting expeditions.

The old stagecoach station was just beyond the store; customers sitting on the porch had an excellent view of the stage's approach. Announced by blasts from the coachman's horn, it would dash around a clump of trees, slosh through the stream, and come to a jerky, sudden stop accompanied by the shrieking of its ungreased axles. From the same porch today the RUINS OF AN OLD DISTRICT SCHOOL, built of native hand-pressed brick, the DRILL GROUND of Union soldiers, and the RUINS OF A GRISTMILL AND DAM are visible.

On the store shelves are paper collars, oxhide shoes, bustles, sidesaddles, early issues of *Blackwood's* and *Harper's* magazines, and many objects that were already curios in most parts of the country at the time this store closed 30 years ago.

PRESTON, 58.3 *m.* (925 alt., 1,214 pop.), seat of Fillmore County, has two newspapers, a large co-operative creamery, a livestock-shipping association, a chicken hatchery, and the old Minnesota Hotel and Tibbets House, reminders of stagecoach days. The old COURTHOUSE, built in 1863 of hand-pressed brick, is still in use and stands (L) at the main intersection of town.

At 60 *m.* (L) is the PRESTON GOLF COURSE *(reasonable fee).*

At FOUNTAIN, 63.2 *m.* (1,306 alt., 303 pop.) *(see Tour 9),* US 52 branches R. from US 16.

The area west of Fountain is agricultural, specializing in dairying; well-built farmhouses and barns adjoin the highway.

SPRING VALLEY, 79.4 *m.* (1,371 alt., 1,712 pop.), is named for the many springs in this area; underground rivers and caves are numerous.

A large portion of land in the Spring Valley region is included in a Federal soil-conservation project. Sponsored by the Federal Government—neither the State nor county participates—this soil-improvement work includes terracing, dam-building, crop control, and other conservation measures. *(Guides available at Soil Conservation Project office.)*

Spring Valley is at the junction (L) with US 63 *(see Tour 18);* between here and 84.4 *m.* US 16 and US 63 are one route.

Right from Spring Valley on State 74 to the TUNNEL MILL (L), 4.9 *m. (tunnel open to visitors)*, interesting for its old-fashioned construction and the millrace that was tunneled for more than 0.25 mile through a hill of solid rock. The mill and tunnel were begun in 1869. Four men required more than a year's time and 3 tons of dynamite to build the tunnel.

Beautiful picnic grounds in Masonic Park adjoin this site and offer a fine view of the surrounding valley. The Root River at this point makes a horseshoe bend around the promontory through which the millstream tunnel was dug.

West of Spring Valley the more gently rolling terrain, slower streams, outwash plains, and boulders indicate that here the highway is traversing the typical glaciated region *(see NATURAL SETTING: Geology and Paleontology)*.

At 103.1 *m.* is the junction with State 56.

Left on State 56 to ROSE CREEK, 5 *m.* (210 pop.), named for the small stream that winds through it, twisting and turning between level fields of grain.

TAOPI, 17.8 *m.* (102 pop.), was named for a well-known chief of a band of Santee Sioux. Taopi (Ind., *wounded man*) was converted to Christianity, and aided the whites during the Sioux uprising. He is commemorated in a book, *Taopi and His Friends*. Today, in dramatic contrast with Indian tribal customs, all of the municipal officials are women, women own two of the three principal stores, a woman serves as postmistress, and the village's most illustrious citizen is Mrs. Thomas Cahill, 88-year-old pioneer.

The AUSTIN COUNTRY CLUB *(9 holes, reasonable fee)* is (R) at 108.8 *m.*

AUSTIN, 110.9 *m.* (1,195 alt., 12,276 pop.), seat of Mower County, lies on both banks of the beautiful Cedar River, which is spanned in the town by several bridges. Platted in 1856 it was named for its first settler, Austin R. Nicholas (1814–1914).

Austin did not win its right to the courthouse without a struggle, for it has not always been the largest town in the county. The first meeting of the county commissioners appointed by Governor Gorman (1816–1876) in 1856 was held at Frankfort. Frankfort was declared by this body to be the seat of county government. No official building was erected, however, and a portable tin box served as file, vault, and safe.

Two members of the commission were from the Austin vicinity. They reasoned that "wherever the box was, there was the county seat." Gaining possession of the box they rode for Austin pursued by the Frankforters in whose band rode the sheriff.

At the hotel in High Forest, a halfway station, they were overhauled and arrested, but not until they had bribed the bartender to hide the box in a snowbank. These events aroused the voters to the full import of the problem and in a county-wide election in 1857 Austin was named the county seat.

Austin has outgrown other towns of the county. The growth, which has been continuous even through the depression years, is due in large part to the continued expansion of the HORMEL PACKING AND FOOD PRODUCTS PLANT here. The Hormel Company's annual gross sales amount to millions of dollars, and it turns out 315 food products, 37 of which are canned. The plant occupies more than 33 acres and draws its raw materials—livestock, grain, and vegetables—from a territory that extends 50 miles to the north and east, 100 miles to the south, and 400 miles to the west. The company employs 3,000 workers. The tallest building in town is the nine-story cannery unit.

The shops and roundhouse of the Milwaukee Road constitute Austin's other main industrial plants.

A NATURAL SPRING delivers 2,250,000 gallons daily, through a municipally owned waterworks that began operation in 1887. In 1900 the light and power plant was taken over by the city, central heating for the downtown district was begun in 1927, and the natural gas distributing system of the Interstate Power Company was taken over in 1935. The administrative office and the machinery of these municipally owned public services are housed in the MUNICIPAL UTILITIES PLANT, which each year reports earnings in excess of $100,000.

At the head of Main Street is HORACE AUSTIN STATE PARK. Its 50 acres of heavily wooded islands and river bank occupy historic land. Before 1841 several companies of United States soldiers had camped on this site, a Fort Snelling officer and party, including Dred Scott, then a slave, had pitched tents here on a hunting expedition, and General Sibley of the American Fur Company had established a hunting shack. Game was so plentiful in the region that in 1840 Sibley's party shot 2,000 deer, 50 elk, 50 bear, and some buffalo during a winter.

Austin is at the junction with US 218 *(see alternate end of Tour 14).*

HAYWARD, 128.2 *m.* (158 pop.), has a large co-operative creamery —one of the Land O'Lakes chain—and a grain-elevator association of 146 members. On the northern outskirts of the town is a STATE GAME REFUGE that shelters many thousands of ducks, pheasants, and other wild fowl.

In this district US 16 enters a region that is distinguished by noticeable glaciation. The usual glacial topography is evident, and lakes, absent in the better-drained eastern section, are numerous; old river valleys, although somewhat obscured by the accumulated drift, are still visible and usually contain lakes or chains of lakes.

At about 126.8 *m.* is the SITE OF AN OLD INDIAN CAMP, where many arrowheads and other Indian relics have been found.

At 129.1 *m.* is the junction (R) with US 65 *(see Tour 14).*

ALBERT LEA, 131 *m.* (1,229 alt., 10,169 pop.), seat of Freeborn County, built on the low hills near Fountain and Albert Lea Lakes, was named by Joseph N. Nicollet for Col. Albert Lea (1808–1891), who surveyed the area in 1835. For years the hunting ground of hostile Indian tribes, this land surrounding the two lakes was dangerous ground for both pioneers and Indians. Today the place is an industrial center at the junction of four railroads. The town has two large gas-stove factories, a meat-packing plant, and a fish hatchery; it does a million dollar business annually through its dairy and oil co-operatives.

Horse racing, popular sport of pioneer days, figured prominently in the history of the city. In 1859 Albert Lea was a straggly little town of log houses and frame shacks. Its main street, Broadway, flanked by a few stores whose home-made "shingles" announced their wares, was the home stretch of a race course that brought fame to the little community. The track crossed the prairie, carefully avoiding surveyors' stakes, to a wagon bridge over the river a mile away.

One afternoon the loungers in front of Gray's saloon taunted Sheriff Heath into running his horse, Old Tom, against Red Eye, one of the fleetest geldings in the community. Old Tom was not much to look at. He had hauled the sheriff's shay around town for some time without arousing noticeable enthusiasm. A bet of $25 was put up, and the horses were led to the bridge. To the surprise of everyone, including Sheriff Heath, Old Tom breezed in, an easy winner. When he won subsequent races handily from such local favorites as Crazy Frank, Selan, Sleepy Kate, and Bay Lady, all the town was convinced that they had a great horse.

Itasca *(see below)*, later a ghost town, in 1859 looked not unlike Albert Lea and was a fighting rival for the coveted prize—the county courthouse. The Itasca town-site promoters, having been assured that Itasca Fly, owned by an Iowa stable, was the "fastest horse in the Northwest," now bought him and challenged Albert Lea to a race. The occasion warranted desperate measures. One night several Albert Lea residents went secretly to Itasca and spirited Itasca Fly from his home paddock. Out on the open prairie they ran him in a trial heat against Old Tom, who pounded across the starlit prairie to win.

A lot of Albert Lea money was in evidence on the day of the race and the Itascans covered it with their cash, their real estate, and their personal property. Old Tom once again rose nobly to the challenge and outstripped the Itasca entry by 40 feet. After this defeat the Itascans, unable to recoup their losses in time for a successful courthouse fight, threw their support to Albert Lea.

Motorcycle hill-climbing events, held in the summer on the steep hill in the section northwest of town, attract many contestants. On Albert Lea Lake is a large GAME REFUGE *(visitors admitted)*; around Fountain Lake is a scenic drive; parts of both lakes are within the city.

Albert Lea is at the junction (L) with US 65 *(see Tour 14)*.

1. Left from the southern end of Albert Lea on a county road skirting the southern shore of Albert Lea Lake is a marker and plate, 1 *m.*, indicating the SITE OF ST. NICHOLAS, a vanished town that was the first village in Freeborn County. St. Nicholas, a town with a sawmill in addition to the usual enterprises, was another and one of the strongest of the courthouse competitors. In the county-wide elections, however, Albert Lea emerged the victor *(see above)*.

2. Right from Albert Lea on State 13 through Paradise Prairie, named for its unusual fertility, to the ITASCA SCHOOL, 2.2 *m.* This is the site of Itasca, once Albert Lea's rival for the county seat *(see above)*.

West of Albert Lea, where a chain of terminal moraines marks the eastern margin of the great Keewatin glacier, US 16 traverses the broad glacial till plain that extends from the Minnesota River southward into Iowa. Moraines and lakes are less frequent than along the glacial margins, and the country is largely prairie, covered for the greater part by rich black loam.

The village of ALDEN, 141.5 *m.* (1,266 alt., 532 pop.), was established in 1869 and is said to have had the first Grange organization

(1873) in this part of the State. An ALFALFA MILL here *(open to visitors)*, one of the very few in the country, has a daily output of 24 tons. Most of the green-colored meal it produces is shipped to the Twin Cities to be used as poultry feed.

BLUE EARTH, 168.1 *m.* (1,085 alt., 2,884 pop.), seat of Faribault County, is on the river of the same name, a tributary of the Minnesota. River and town are named for the blue-green clay that was dug from the rocks of the river gorge by the Indians.

The city has brightly lighted streets, a portion of the profits from the municipally owned light plant being used for street lighting. Arched standards are used with colored bulbs in clusters to make designs and pictures, the most ambitious of which is the Stars and Stripes.

Blue Earth is the busy trading center of a productive diversified-farming district. It has one of the largest corn- and pea-packing plants in the country, an ice cream factory, which operates its own creamery, and the Blue Earth Co-operative Creamery, which processes a large portion of the dairy products from the surrounding farms.

Sugar-beet raising and truck gardening have recently been introduced into the farming picture. Migratory Mexican workers are employed for the hard labor of weeding, hoeing, and topping the beets, wage scales being too low to attract local labor.

After the Sioux uprising of 1862, Civil War Capt. P. B. Davy "gentled" the local renegades and organized them into the Blue Earth Wild West Show which played in several southern Minnesota towns.

In the BLUE EARTH PROTESTANT CEMETERY is a MONUMENT TO MOSES SAILOR, first settler. It is carved in stone in the shape of a log cabin about 2½ by 4 feet and has stained-glass windows and old tapestries.

The CHURCH OF SAINTS PETER AND PAUL, a beautiful building in the English Gothic style, is an object of community pride.

In the Blue Earth PUBLIC LIBRARY several MURALS, reproductions of Greek and Roman friezes, adorn the walls.

Blue Earth is at the junction with US 169 *(see Tour 3)*.

In Clifford's MINIATURE PARK *(open to visitors)*, 185.7 *m.*, are trees, hills, and valleys molded in cement.

FAIRMONT, 185.9 *m.* (1,195 alt., 5,521 pop.), seat of Martin County, is on 4 of a north-south chain of 18 lakes *(launch excursions through 4 lakes)*. The regular serial arrangement of this and two other nearby chains is interesting. The distribution indicates the preglacial existence of a stream bed whose course was stopped, but not completely obliterated, when the glaciers covered the land with drift. Some of the lakes are connected by streams, but a complete drainage has not been established.

In the COURTHOUSE, built on the site of an old stockade erected during the Sioux uprising of 1862, is a COLLECTION OF LOCAL RELICS of the days when the town's several fur-trading posts were flourishing.

In the 1870's the community was devastated by a 4-year grasshopper plague and was saved from complete extinction only by the persistent efforts of a newly arrived colony of English farmers. This extraordinary group, most of whom were Oxford and Cambridge graduates—several of them titled—came here at the instigation of a Yankee promoter. Despite their crop failures caused by locust ravages, many of these Englishmen were able to survive. They became known throughout the State and surrounding areas as the "Fairmont Sportsmen," and are credited with introducing fox-hunting in southern Minnesota. Attired in hunting coats, made by the village tailoress, they rode to hounds over hill and stream, in quest of any quarry that appeared. A story is told of "one run of thirty miles in three hours, where the dead-beaten wolf swam the Watonwan River—the huntsman after him, swimming with one arm, and steering his jaded mare with the other." At the State fair of 1878 the Britishers, clad in their red coats and high boots, rode "genuine hurdle races, flying amid clouds of blinding dust over four-foot hurdles." So spectacular was their exhibition on this occasion that they "divided the honors with President Hayes and the celebrated trotter Rarus."

The town has pea and corn canneries, chicken hatcheries, packing plants, creameries, a modern airport (1 mile southeast of the business district), and a large TOURIST CAMP (free camping, running water) in INTERLAKEN PARK in the northern section of town.

There is excellent pheasant and water-fowl hunting in the vicinity.

West of Fairmont US 16 enters gently rolling country where dairying and general farming are the chief occupations. The soil is exceptionally fertile.

The village of WELCOME, 194.6 m. (519 pop.), lies in a beautiful valley containing several lakes. The citizens, eager to justify the town's name, are unusually hospitable to strangers.

SHERBURN, 200.6 m. (860 pop.), has, as its recreational center, FOX LAKE PARK (9-hole golf course, baseball diamond, dance pavilion). Bass, pickerel, pike, and crappie are abundant in nearby lakes.

At 213.7 m. is the junction with US 71 (see Tour 2). US 16 and US 71 are united between this point and Jackson, where US 16 turns R. The JACKSON MUNICIPAL TOURIST PARK is at this junction, the spot where an outlaw Sioux band under Inkpaduta attacked the town, then called Springfield. Seven settlers were killed, but the Indians were driven away. A State MONUMENT TO THE SLAIN SETTLERS stands in the park. In a semicircular INDIAN MOUND have been found the leg bones of a man, and a stone ball about 2 inches in diameter, apparently rounded with primitive tools.

JACKSON, 216 m. (1,485 alt., 2,206 pop.), in the fertile valley of the Des Moines River, which winds through the town, is surrounded by high, heavily timbered hills. Twice the scene of violent Indian uprisings (see Tour 2: LOWER AGENCY), Jackson has commemorated its victims by a historic marker near its eastern edge.

Surrounding flax farms supplied the State's first tow mill, opened here in 1861. Tow rope in commercial quantities is still shipped from the town.

Here is a modern TOURIST CAMP (cabins, hot and cold water, tables and benches; moderate rates).

Right from Jackson on a dirt road to a MODEL DAIRY FARM (visitors welcome), 2 m., with concrete buildings, rock-paved cattle yards and lanes, and landscaped gardens. A profusion of signs explains to the urbanite some of the intricacies of

modern agriculture and stock-breeding. The owner has a COLLECTION OF SCIEN-
TIFIC AND PRIMITIVE RELICS on display.

At 225.2 *m.* is the junction with State 86.

Right on State 86 to LAKEFIELD, 4 *m.* (1,349 pop.), on slightly rolling wooded
land traversed by a creek. Lakefield *(9-hole golf course, two public tennis courts)*
has a well-equipped TOURIST CAMP *(no fee for first, small charge succeeding
nights; tents may be pitched; cabin for cooking).*

West of Jackson US 16 crosses level prairie land that stretches far to
the north and south. In the vicinity of Worthington another series of terminal moraines and north-south valleys and ridges mark the western extension of the Keewatin glacier. The most westerly of the ridges follows
the Coteau des Prairies, a long highland that resisted further westward
glacial extension.

WORTHINGTON, 247.3 *m.* (1,585 alt., 3,878 pop.), seat of Nobles
County, when established in 1871, was a prohibition colony called Okabena (Ind., *the nesting place of herons).* Original deeds to downtown
property forbade the sale of liquor on the premises, and even today local
ordinances prohibit the sale of drinks stronger than 3.2 per cent beer.

It is not true that Worthington citizens were completely weaned away
from spirituous liquors, although a local pioneer story so relates. In 1871
a Worthington storekeeper smuggled in a crock of whisky and surrep-
titiously dispensed it as a side line to his regular business. Two of his
patrons, knowing that there were only 5 gallons to begin with, decided to
check up on the amount left for their future enjoyment. Throughout the
winter they recorded their intake. When a compilation showed that they
had already consumed more than 40 gallons, they indignantly confronted
the storekeeper, and in fairness to him (fearing that their sense of taste
might have been dulled by regular libation), they asked a friend to sample the strong drink. He testified that it bore no trace of whisky whatso-
ever, although the cork from the jug did smell faintly of it. The storekeeper then admitted that he had made a practice of replacing each drink
sold with a like amount of rainwater. In this manner his customers had
been "educated to get a kick out of water."

Profiting by the sales tax in nearby Iowa towns, Worthington's Main
St. each Saturday night is lined with shoppers' cars, four abreast.

Here one of the region's largest creameries and produce companies pays
local farmers about $4,000,000 annually for their products. There are also
several other co-operative industries.

The Okabena apple was developed in orchards on the southern shore of
Lake Okabena, adjoining the town.

Unusual for so small a town is the local well-mounted polo team that
has an excellent rating among both civilian and Army teams. Half of the
15 or 20 games each season are on the home field. Worthington has a
9-hole GOLF COURSE *(small fee);* on the shores of Lake Okabena are
BATHING BEACHES; air shows are occasionally held at the city's airport.
In the CITY PARK on Lake Ave. is a PUBLIC TOURIST CAMP *(electric
lights, water, fireplaces).* A bathhouse, pavilion, and recreational equip-

ment including horseshoe courts are in the park. Pheasant, duck, and rabbit shooting are excellent in the vicinity.

Worthington is at the junction with US 59 *(see Tour 17)*.

West of the city US 16 traverses the Rock River Valley, a region particularly adapted to agriculture. In midsummer the fields are blanketed with wheat, interspersed with large fields of corn. The several streams crossing the highway are the only variation in this flat plain extending westward from the highland.

At 278 *m*. US 16 crosses the Rock River.

LUVERNE, 278.3 *m*. (1,451 alt., 2,644 pop.), is in an area explored first by the scientist, Joseph N. Nicollet, in 1839, but hostile Indians kept settlers from this territory for 30 years thereafter. When they finally ventured back, they were plagued by the 4-year grasshopper invasion and by frequent brush fires.

Made prosperous by creamery, livestock, and grain co-operatives, Luverne today has a large fire-truck manufacturing company; its quarries supplied the beautiful red granite for the ROCK COUNTY COURTHOUSE here and for many other buildings that add color to the town. The JAIL, adjacent to the courthouse, and the CARNEGIE PUBLIC LIBRARY with its impressive Greek columns are built of red granite, as are a church, a school and a hotel. Even some residences are enclosed by low, red-stone fences.

The TOURIST PARK *(camping, running water, playground equipment)* is at the eastern edge of town.

Luverne is at the junction with US 75 *(see Tour 4)*.

Southwest of Luverne the soil is old, gray drift, covered in many places by the wind-deposited loess. In this area the rainfall is lighter than in southeastern Minnesota, but the soil is exceedingly fertile.

At 291.4 *m*. US 16 crosses the South Dakota Line, 15 miles east of Sioux Falls, S. Dak. *(see South Dakota, Tour 5)*.

‹‹‹‹‹‹‹‹‹‹‹‹‹‹‹‹‹‹‹☼›››››››››››››››››››››

Tour 14

Minneapolis—Farmington—Northfield—Faribault—Owatonna—Albert Lea—(Northwood, Iowa) ; US 65.
Minneapolis to Iowa Line, 120.6 m.

The Chicago, Rock Island & Pacific R.R. parallels the whole route; the Chicago, Milwaukee, St. Paul & Pacific R.R. between the Twin Cities and Owatonna.
Paved roadbed entire distance; open all year.
Usual accommodations.

This route traverses a prosperous, diversified dairying and agricultural section of southern Minnesota, winds through livestock-breeding and trading centers, and crosses a highly productive truck-farming region.

MINNEAPOLIS, 0 *m.* (812 alt., 464,356 pop.) *(see MINNEAPOLIS).*

Points of Interest. Minnehaha Falls, Chain of Lakes, University of Minnesota, flour mills of St. Anthony Falls.

Minneapolis is at the junction with US 169 *(see Tour 3)*, US 52 *(see Tour 9)*, US 12 *(see Tour 10)*, US 212 *(see Tour 11)*, and US 8 *(see Tour 19)*.

South from Lake St. US 65 follows Lyndale Ave.

At 7 *m.* is the junction with State 5.

Right on State 5 to the junction with a dirt road, 2.7 *m.;* L. on this road to the BUSH LAKE SKI SLIDE, 4.7 *m.* *(adm. to ski meets, 50¢)*, on the highest point in Hennepin County. It was built in 1935 by Twin City sportsmen and is the largest ski slide in Minnesota (1937). The 100-foot steel scaffold, modeled after the slide at Lake Placid, makes possible jumps of more than 200 feet. The hill on which it stands has an upper curve of 38 degrees and a lower curve of 35 degrees. The Northwest Ski Meet and other tournaments are held here *(Jan. and Feb.);* about 30,000 spectators can be accommodated. The Minneapolis, Northfield & Southern Ry. runs excursions to Bush Lake on tournament days. Slalom and practice courses have been laid out on nearby hills; a cross-country course starts at the slide and leads across the lake.

At 7.5 *m.* is the junction with a graveled road.

Right on this road to BLOOMINGTON, 1.5 *m.*, a small village. The GIDEON POND HOUSE, of dignified and almost formal design, was built in 1855 by Gideon Pond, one of the early missionaries, on a bluff overlooking the Minnesota River. A symmetrical design has been carried out in salmon-colored brick made locally by hand; the building is rectangular (25 by 32 feet) and has two stories. A recessed doorway with sidelights is placed squarely in the middle of the façade without further embellishment, and the divided windows have shutters. The brick cornice is quite plain and is carried around the house; it is formed by projecting first one row and then two rows of brick. A brick frieze occurs only at the eastern and western elevations. The general detail of the old house is classic in character and the molding profiles are simple. The trim is pine, probably made of local material.

US 65 crosses the Minnesota River at 11.2 *m.*

ANTLERS PARK, 21.7 *m.*, on the shore of LAKE MARION, is a resort *(bathing beach, picnic grounds, refectory, 18-hole golf course)*.

FARMINGTON, 28.2 *m.* (903 alt., 1,342 pop.), is a retailing center for a diversified farming community. The Twin City Milk Producers' Association, a co-operative with a membership of 8,105 farmers, has its largest plant here; it has a daily capacity of 225,000 pounds of milk.

At Farmington is the junction with an improved road, called the Hastings Rd.

Left on this road to WESTWOOD, 3 *m.*, and the WESTWOOD FARM *(open to visitors)*, known for its dairy products and modern equipment.

Between Farmington and Faribault the highway follows the eastern boundary of the area once covered by a hardwood forest that was known to explorers and early settlers as the Big Woods. Remnant groves of this

heavy stand of timber add beauty to the smoothly cultivated acres and
broad pasture lands. These groves include maple, basswood, white and red
elm, and red oak. Along the bottom lands of the Cannon River are great
drooping willows; higher up, giant cottonwoods fringe the banks of the
stream.

CASTLE ROCK, 31.9 *m*. (945 alt.), was named for a towering sandstone bluff that lies east of the highway but within the town limits. This
rock, now greatly reduced by erosion, was noted on Nicollet's map of
1844. It had served as a landmark for Indians and early traders.

Between 41.3 *m*. and Northfield, US 65 follows the high bank of the
Cannon River; both sides of the stream in this vicinity are maintained as
an arboretum by Carleton College.

NORTHFIELD, 42.8 *m*. (915 alt., 4,153 pop.). In the early 1900's
Northfield's champion butterfat producers earned for the town the title,
"Holstein Capital of America." Rice County farmers organized America's
first Holstein breeders' club in 1903. From the Schilling and Miller farms
have come the dams of many of the large Holstein herds of the Northwest. Spring Brooke Bess Burke, a Miller cow, was several times national
butterfat champion. Northfield daily handles over 50,000 pounds of cream
and is an important source of the Twin City milk supply; its "contented
cows" also supply the Northfield evaporating plant, a branch of the Car-
nation Company.

Northfield was the site of one of the 3 flour mills of the old Cannon
River combine, which produced 3,000 barrels of flour a day, won inter-
national prizes, and received $2 a barrel premium in eastern markets *(see
INDUSTRIAL DEVELOPMENT: Milling)*.

The town was once a center of Grange activities, which included the
successful operation of two flour mills in Rice County. Thrifty New Englanders settling here sought to give permanent form to the co-operative
practices they had known in the East—collective buying, husking bees, and
house-building, but owing to internal strife, the Grange ceased to be an
influence in this region after 1876.

In addition to the dairy industry, Northfield also has factories producing farm machinery and breakfast foods.

The I.O.O.F. HOME FOR THE AGED, for Minnesota and surrounding
States, is here.

Many residents still remember "the seven minutes that shook Northfield," on September 7, 1876, when Jesse James, Missouri badman, and
his bandit gang attempted to hold up the FIRST NATIONAL BANK on
Bridge Square. Failing to open the bank safe, the eight desperadoes emptied their guns time after time to terrorize the town, killing two citizens
and wounding another. Merchants near the bank hastily armed themselves
and fired through open windows, inflicting equal casualties on the bandits.
Clel Miller and Bill Stiles were killed and Bob Younger was wounded.

Within seven minutes of the time they appeared in Northfield the
mounted gunmen were galloping out of town to the southwest, pursued
by a posse. By night 200 men had joined the chase and a few days later,
when the manhunt was at its height, more than 1,000 pursuers were in

the field. Jesse and Frank James ran the gantlet and got away on stolen horses. On September 21 the remainder of the outlaw gang was rounded up in Hanska Slough, Brown County. Charlie Pitts was killed outright and the three Younger brothers were shot, captured, and sentenced to prison for life.

Approximately 1,500 Indian mounds are in scattered groups within 10 miles of Northfield.

The town has two colleges and an exceptionally fine student choir *(see THE ARTS: Music)*.

The campus of ST. OLAF COLLEGE, covering 170 acres of a wooded hillside called Manitou Heights (130 feet above the town), is on St. Olaf Ave., a mile west of the business district.

In 1874 a group of Norwegian Lutherans, desiring "to keep their young people in contact with the church, while giving them a liberal arts education," raised $6,000 and organized St. Olaf's School. By 1886 the school had expanded into a college, and by 1935 the original investment of $6,000 had grown into an estimated corporate holding of $2,750,000. The college buildings—Halle Steensland Library, Ytterboe Hall, and Mohn Hall, the latter named for the Rev. Thornbjorn Mohn, first president of the school—were all constructed of native stone. The gray limestone administration building on the brow of the hill, built in the style of a Norman castle, was the gift of Harold Thorson, St. Olaf's chief benefactor.

Below the campus is the VALE OF TAWASENTHA, a natural amphitheater where a play, usually one of Shakespeare's, is presented each spring by student actors. Steep paths lead down into the ravine, thickly wooded with Norway pines.

St. Olaf is supported in part by the $46,000 annual appropriation of the Norwegian Lutheran Church of America and by donations from patrons of the Norwegian arts. The annual enrollment of about 1,000 students continues to be 75 percent Norwegian, 86 percent Lutheran. One year's study of the Norse language is required of students of Norwegian extraction, and 3 years' study of religion is required of all.

St. Olaf's Student Choir toured the United States and Europe under the direction of Professor F. Melius Christiansen (1876–1931); it specializes in interpretations of Bach and the old Lutheran choirmasters. This choir has influenced not only the music of the Lutheran Church in Minnesota, but also choral singing in many other States. The annual St. Olaf Music Festival, held the third week in May, includes concerts by the choir, the college band, and a chorus of 500 to 1,000 singers, many of them from the Twin Cities and surrounding towns.

O. E. Rölvaag, scholar and novelist, who taught literature at St. Olaf, is the author of *Giants in the Earth,* popular in America as well as in his native country *(see THE ARTS: Literature)*.

CARLETON COLLEGE, on high ground L. of US 65, has an enrollment of 800 students. The school exchanges professorships with eastern and European universities. Its musical and dramatic activities, culminating in the annual May Fete *(3rd week in May)* held since 1911, attract large audiences. The scene of the festival is the ISLAND in the HUNTINGTON MEMORIAL PARK, where the audience is seated in a natural amphitheater.

The college grounds comprise 800 acres adjoining the Cannon River and include part of a picturesque valley containing the George Huntington Lyman Memorial Lakes.

The CARLETON ARBORETUM, 300 acres on both sides of the Cannon River, has shelters and feeding stations for birds and a 6 mile nature trail, carefully marked *(mimeographed guides of plants along trail obtainable in wooden racks along the route).*

Thorstein Veblen (1857–1929), the economist and philosopher, was brought by his Norwegian immigrant parents from Wisconsin to Minnesota when he was 8 years old. Despite his Norwegian parentage, he chose Carleton rather than St. Olaf for his education. His sharp wit and iconoclastic attitude earned him constant criticism, but his brilliance was recognized by many of the students and a few of his professors. However, the 7 years he spent at home in apparent inactivity, after he received his Ph.D. from Yale, stamped him in local minds as an utter failure. His subsequent fame as author of *Theory of the Leisure Class,* as translator of the Icelandic *Laxdela Saga,* and as the writer of numerous economic and philosophic works did much to dispel this regional prejudice.

Between Northfield and Faribault, US 65 passes 16 abandoned mill sites of Civil War days.

At DUNDAS, 46.3 *m.* (958 alt., 377 pop.), about 75 years ago, were the flour mills of the Archibald brothers, who had established a wide reputation when the mills of Minneapolis were still in their infancy. The Archibalds were pioneers in a new method, making flour by a secret process developed by a French family named La Croix, who were brought to Dundas in the 1860's. Sifters, blowers, and an intricate system of silk sieves produced flour that brought envious millers from the entire Northwest to watch the rollers, feel the machinery, and experiment with the mysteries of Rice County wheat. Farmers, after traveling 200 miles to see the long rows of vibrating sifters, dubbed the Archibalds the "shaking millers." When the younger La Croix took the secret of Dundas flour to the Washburns of Minneapolis, an obscure sifter-scraper in the Minneapolis plant grasped the opportunity to patent the process. The local mills were soon displaced by the new plants at the Falls of St. Anthony, and Dundas became one of southern Minnesota's typical crossroad villages built around a creamery and a church or two.

The Cannon River land boom of 1856, the collapse of which left a string of deserted villages along the valley, was described by Edward Eggleston (1837–1902) in 1873 in a novel entitled the *Mystery of Metropolisville.* The preface says:

"Metropolisville is only a memory now, but the wild excitement of '56 is a tradition hardly credible to those who did not feel its fever. The last time I saw the place the grass grew green where once stood the city hall, the corn stalks waved their banners at the very site of the old store (I ask pardon, the 'Emporium') and what had been a square, staring white courthouse—not a temple but a barn of justice—had long since fallen to base uses. It had grown as hundreds of other frontier villages had grown in the flush times; it died as so many others did, of the financial crash which was the inevitable sequel of speculative madness. The main street is now a county road where the dogfennel blooms, and the plowshare turns over the earth in places where corner lots once sold for $100 the front foot. The lot once sacredly set apart on the map as 'depot ground' is now a potato patch. Gone are the land sharks, claim speculators, town proprietors, trappers, stage drivers, since the railroads missed Metropolisville and the land bubble collapsed."

At BRIDGEWATER, 51.3 *m.*, the road crosses a long 5-mile ridge of gravel known as the BRIDGEWATER ESKER, which in some places is 75 feet high. The rounded pebbles of this gravel layer indicate its deposition by a channel of water beneath glacial ice. The Cannon River now cuts through the ridge.

At 56.6 *m.* is the junction with State 21.

Right on this road to FRENCH LAKE (*fishing, duck shooting*), about 8 *m.*, one of the last lakes in Minnesota to freeze in the fall. Lining its shores is one of the largest tracts of virgin hardwood in the State. Included in this beautiful forest are hard maples and giant oaks, nearly 200 years old. French Lake, deep and sandy-beached, is well stocked with black bass, pike, and crappie.

FARIBAULT, 58 *m.* (971 alt., 12,767 pop.), seat of Rice County, lies on a low alluvial terrace in the valleys of the Cannon and Straight Rivers. The city spreads over the slopes to the summit of the 200-foot bluffs.

Here in 1826 the shrewd trader, Alexander Faribault (1806–1882), built the largest of his six trading posts. For a quarter of a century before the stampede of settlers in the 1850's, Faribault fur carts, creaking across the grass-grown trails of Minnesota's southern triangle, represented the only commerce of these prairies.

French-Canadian trappers and traders joined Faribault at his trading post, and were followed by New Englanders who dominated the period of early settlement. Later they were outnumbered by northern European immigrants, but the city retains a characteristic New England flavor.

The first frame dwelling put up in Faribault was the home of Alexander Faribault, built at a cost of $4,000. The lumber was brought from St. Paul, but difficulty in traversing the highway made it necessary to leave part of the supplies by the roadside; the lumber so left was burned in a prairie fire. The FARIBAULT HOUSE, which still stands near the center of town, and the Whipple House, built in 1871 (now razed), long dominated the architecture as well as the social life of the city.

When in 1859 Henry Benjamin Whipple (1822–1901), Episcopal clergyman and friend of the Indians, was consecrated the first Bishop of Minnesota, Faribault became the nucleus of his Indian missions and the see of the Episcopal Church. Born in upper New York State, Whipple studied at Oberlin Institute, then a stronghold of abolitionist thought. He married at 20, and for the next 7 years varied his activities by being in turn a "rational abolitionist," a conservative Democrat, a politician and a businessman. At the age of 27 he was persuaded by his wife to take holy orders and embarked upon an energetic career that was to keep him in the public eye until the time of his death.

Coming to Faribault in the spring of 1860, Bishop Whipple held his first services in the little frame chapel of the Episcopal mission. Besides the chapel, in which the parish school was kept on weekdays, the mission consisted of two frame houses and a shanty in which lived a few young men studying for the ministry and supporting themselves by farming a few acres of land donated by Alexander Faribault.

On this site, the shaded ground of the terrace above the valley, now stand the vine-covered buildings of the three schools founded by Bishop Whipple: SEABURY DIVINITY SCHOOL, SHATTUCK SCHOOL, now Shattuck Military Academy, and ST. MARY'S HALL, a school for girls.

When Bishop Whipple arrived in Minnesota there were 15 or 16 small frame or log churches in the diocese with 4 clergymen and a dozen missionary clerics. He went immediately to the task of building the church, but the Indian problem occupied much of his attention.

He attributed the degradation and squalor of the red men to the indifference and rascality of the whites. He proposed as a remedy that the Government assume the character of a guardian for its Indian wards. This view later became the principle of Indian policy administration, but not until after he had been roundly denounced by high Government officials for his defense of the Sioux after the outbreak of 1862.

In his 40 years as the Episcopal Bishop of Minnesota the hard-working ecclesiastical leader became an important public figure. His counsel was sought by Queen Victoria as well as by the Presidents of this country, and during his career he preached in many of the cathedrals here and in England.

Adding to the academic atmosphere of Faribault are ST. JAMES MILITARY ACADEMY and the STATE SCHOOLS FOR THE BLIND, DEAF, AND FEEBLE-MINDED. The Faribault school for the deaf and dumb was established by the legislature in 1858 and the school for the blind in 1864 as regular departments of the Minnesota Institute for the Deaf, Dumb, and Blind. The school for the feeble-minded began in 1879 as an experimental division. A small class of 15 children was organized, and the therapeutic results were so encouraging that in 1881 it was connected permanently with the other three divisions.

Consistent with stories of Faribault's cultured pioneers who left behind their plowshares to load their wagons with books, is the new BUCKHAM MEMORIAL LIBRARY, southeast corner of Division and Central Aves. This modern structure, set against a hill and stepped up in ascending rectangles against the incline, has an auditorium and a gallery of historical exhibits and relics.

Faribault horticulturists, winners of the peony prize at Chicago's Century of Progress Exposition, proclaim their city the "Nation's Peony Capital," and each year have 20,000 of these flowers in bloom for a mid-June peony show.

Many acres of land in the vicinity of Faribault have been included in a Federal soil-conservation project. This soil-improvement work, consisting of dam-building, terracing, reversion to timber, crop control, and so on, is under the supervision of the Federal Government (*guides available at Faribault Soil Conservation office in the Federal Bldg.*).

MEDFORD, 67 *m.*, became the first settlement in Steele County (1853), when five men erected houses on the east bank of the Straight River.

OWATONNA, 73.9 *m.* (1,154 alt., 7,654 pop.) *(see Tour 12)*, is at the junction with US 14 *(see Tour 12)*.

At Owatonna is the junction with US 218, an alternate and shorter route between this point and the Iowa Line.

Left from Owatonna on US 218, a straight paved road paralleling the Red Cedar River for more than 25 miles to AUSTIN, 32.9 *m.* (1,195 alt., 12,276 pop.) *(see Tour 13)*, at the junction with US 16 *(see Tour 13)*.

At 45.5 *m.* US 218 crosses the Iowa Line, 93 miles north of Waterloo, Iowa *(see Iowa, Tour 3)*.

At 74.8 *m.*, at the southern edge of the city, is KAPLAN WOODS STATE PARK (R), comprising 180 acres and adjacent to Owatonna's fairgrounds. This area was recently purchased by the State and contains a remnant of virgin timber; persistent effort will doubtless keep it a wilderness area.

At CLARK'S GROVE, 99.1 *m.* (1,260 alt., 180 pop.), Minnesota's first permanent co-operative creamery was organized in 1890, only a short time after the State's first attempt at co-operative dairying. Used as a basis for study and as an example by Professor Haecker (1846–1938), dairy expert, in his long campaign to organize Minnesota dairymen, this co-operative was the forerunner of Minnesota's State-wide Land O' Lakes Association.

Left from Clark's Grove on an improved road to HOLLANDALE, 5 *m.*, a small village where 200 families form a colorful community, predominantly Dutch. In spring and summer Hollandale is like a bit of old Holland transplanted. The quiet industrious families live in brightly painted cottages, built in a 2-mile square about the center of an old lake bed. The gardens are neatly arranged, proclaiming the characteristic precision of their owners, and flowers add to the color and attractiveness of the scene. Over the gateways of some homes are mottoes—"Nothing without God's blessing," "Work and Prosper," and others indicative of their owners' faith.

Once a rice swamp, this 17,000-acre peat lowland was improved by a land promotion company at a cost of approximately $3,000,000. The original cost of the land was less than one-twentieth of this amount, but drainage and ditch liens against the land and other improvements used up the balance. The main drainage ditch flows into the Cedar River, just over the line in Mower County.

The promotion company's first plan was to sell the land only to persons of Dutch descent, but for lack of a sufficient number of applicants it was found necessary to make the offer to anyone who had the necessary funds. The land was sold from $100 to $500 per acre, and much of it still has an outstanding indebtedness, but many of these farmers are sound financially and are doing well. A total of 3,200 carloads of potatoes, onions, and other vegetables are marketed annually, about two-thirds of which are handled through the Hollandale Marketing Association.

At 106.3 *m.* is the junction with US 16 *(see Tour 13)*, which unites with US 65 between this point and Albert Lea.

ALBERT LEA, 108.2 *m.* (1,229 alt., 10,169 pop.) *(see Tour 13)*, is at the junction with US 16 *(see Tour 13)*.

South of Albert Lea the country becomes more like a prairie; its low, slightly rolling hills are infrequently interspersed with groves of trees.

GORDONSVILLE, 119.6 *m.* (200 pop.), is the site of the first settlement in Freeborn County. In this vicinity old-fashioned square dances are held in barns. At the Dutch and Norwegian weddings, celebrated with native dances and foods *(see IMMIGRATION AND RACIAL ELEMENTS),* the guests come from miles around, often numbering from 100 to 150 persons.

Indian relics, including arrowheads, stone hatchets, and hammers have been unearthed in mounds nearby.

At 120.6 *m.* US 65 crosses the Iowa Line, 159 miles north of Des Moines, Iowa *(see Iowa, Tour 4).*

<<<<<<<<<<<<<<<<<<<<<☼>>>>>>>>>>>>>>>>>>>>>>

Tour 15

Junction with US 61—Aitkin—Crosby—Brainerd—Motley; US 210.
Junction with US 61 to Motley, 118.3 m.

The Northern Pacific Ry. parallels the entire route.
Roadbed paved between junction with US 61 and Brainerd, and bituminous-treated between Brainerd and Motley. Open all year.
Tourist camps at short intervals; hotels in larger towns.

This east-west route crosses the ore-shipping district west of Duluth, the comparatively high area west of Lake Superior, the vacation area of concentrated lakes, and roughly follows the historic Crow Wing River.

US 210 branches west from its junction with US 61, 0 *m. (see Tour 1),* 2.3 miles west of CARLTON.

West of the junction the soil is very stony loam, but many of the valleys contain heavy clay that becomes muddy during the rainy season. Farther west and south the peat bogs make much of the land untillable; nevertheless many areas have been developed into profitable farms by the hard-working Finns who came to the area to work in the mines, developed respiratory diseases or became dissatisfied with underground and seasonal work, and turned to farming. They cleared the heavy forest growths, worked and reworked the soil, and finally forced it to yield sufficient crops to give them and their families a living.

CROMWELL, 21.5 *m.* (1,330 alt., 207 pop.), is on ISLAND LAKE.

Left from Cromwell on State 73 to the NORTH STAR COUNCIL BOY SCOUT CAMP *(open to visitors),* 1 *m.,* an exceptionally good camp for honor scouts.

At 22 *m.* US 210 crosses the Cromwell terminal moraine, extending for approximately 6 miles through the partly swampy bed of a former glacial lake.

TAMARACK, 34 *m.* (1,290 alt., 145 pop.), is a small hamlet near the eastern entrance to the Paul Bunyan resort and lake country.

Right from Tamarack on an improved road to the junction with another improved road, 4 *m.;* L. on this road to LAKE MINNEWAWA, 8 *m.,* on whose beautiful, wooded shore is a municipal TOURIST CAMP *(free camping, running water).*

MC GREGOR, 43.9 *m.* (1,254 alt., 216 pop.).

Right from McGregor on State 65 to a GOVERNMENT DAM, 12.8 *m.,* at the outlet of BIG SANDY LAKE, which helps control the Mississippi River flood waters.

LIBBY, 13 *m.,* on Big Sandy Lake, was an important point on the trade route between the Mississippi and the East under both French and British rule. This region today is the lake and resort area of north-central Minnesota's vast vacation land.

For years professors of universities and colleges in Minnesota and surrounding states have studied the large INDIAN VILLAGE-SITE here to obtain first-hand information for their classes. Most of the interesting relics found are now in the possession of Minnesota and Iowa Universities. There are no longer any wigwams on this location; the Indians dress very much like white people and speak English. Very few, however, have much education; they live in a rather shiftless manner in small shacks and gather berries and wildrice for a meager existence. They add to their income by selling hand-made souvenirs to tourists.

These Indians sometimes don their tribal costumes and dance at entertainments, such as the annual midwinter carnival sponsored by the local American Legion post. Indian missions were established at Big Sandy as early as 1832. INDIAN MOUNDS are numerous in the vicinity.

At BROWN'S POINT, 13.6 *m.,* the Northwest Company built one of its largest trading posts in 1794. Thirty-four years later a similar post was established by the American Fur Company and managed by William Aitkin (1785–1851), for whom Aitkin County and the county seat are named.

At 22 *m.* is the junction with an improved road; R. on this road to BOOT LAKE *(fishing, swimming, duck shooting),* 24 *m.,* crystal clear and surrounded by beautiful woods.

At 58 *m.* is the junction (R) with US 169 *(see Tour 3),* which for 7.9 miles is united with US 210.

HASSMAN, 59 *m.,* is a small village.

AITKIN, 65.9 *m.* (1,216 alt., 1,545 pop.), seat of Aitkin County, is an attractive farming village and a shipping center for large quantities of dairy products, turkeys, and small fruits. It stands on the sandy part of the plain of prehistoric Lake Aitkin *(see Tour 3),* whose beach was 1 mile south of town. Aitkin and much of the country was inundated by disastrous floods in the spring of 1938.

Francis Lee Jacques, noted bird illustrator now (1938) on the staff of the American Museum of Natural History in New York City, had a taxidermy shop here in his youth.

A fête celebrated regularly in this vicinity is the Swedish Midsummer-Day Festival, held on one of the large farms each year. All the Swedish residents gather on this day to renew acquaintances, play games, sing folk songs, and eat Swedish foods. Different farms and picnic grounds are chosen each year for the event.

Every fall, members of the Aitkin Turkey Growers' Association make a "turkey tour," traveling to the various farms that belong to the association and, at noon, feasting on a turkey banquet. Speeches are given at the farms by representative turkey-growers and by poultry specialists from the State university.

West of Aitkin US 210 traverses unusually beautiful country, enriched during the spring and summer by the vivid coloring of wild flowers. White trillium, blue violets, arbutus, gentian, ladyslippers, and waterlilies grow in profusion beside the highway or in the swamps. In the autumn bittersweet berries add their brilliant yellow-red to the crimson of the hardwoods interspersed among the evergreens.

Among the wild edible fruits are blueberries, high- and low-bush cranberries, pin cherries, raspberries, chokecherries, and grapes. Here are found 46 varieties of edible mushrooms. The hazelnut is abundant and the butternut is occasionally found in this area, considerably north of its usual habitat.

DEERWOOD, 76.8 *m.* 1(1,310 alt., 552 pop.), is surrounded by 30 lakes that afford varied recreation. Several acres of virgin pine lie directly south of the village, and at the northern end is a BEAVER DAM.

The DEERWOOD SANATORIUM for tuberculosis patients has 24 beds and is supported jointly by Crow Wing and Aitkin Counties.

Deerwod was the home of Cuyler Adams, who discovered iron in the Cuyuna Range (1904) and named the range with a combination of the first syllable of his own name and that of his dog, Una.

Left from Deerwood on State 6 to ECHO LAKE, 2.6 *m.*, where Vogt Bros. have landscaped their grounds and laid out beautiful FORMAL GARDENS *(open; nominal fee)*.

CROSBY, 80.4 *m.* (1,200 alt., 3,451 pop.), is at the eastern end of the Cuyuna Iron Range, where manganiferous ore is extensively mined. The Cuyuna, southernmost of the Minnesota iron ranges, is the most recently developed. Embracing an area that includes Deerwood, Crosby, Ironton, and Brainerd, it has no outstanding topographic features. The surface is fairly even and consists of a heavy mantle of glacial drift containing few boulders. Since there are no ore outcroppings or other indications of the presence of iron, the deposits were discovered only by the use of a dip needle. The distribution of the bed is now determined by drilling *(see INDUSTRIAL DEVELOPMENT: Mining)*.

The first iron ore was shipped from the Cuyuna in 1911. At the beginning of the World War the foreign supply of manganese used in making steel was shut off, and local mining operations almost ceased until it was found that the Cuyuna manganese ores could be successfully mixed with the oxide ores.

The mines add tremendously to the municipal tax income of the Cuyuna Range towns, permitting many civic improvements that small towns cannot usually afford. Their schools are exceptionally fine and the Americanization of the many resident nationalities is expedited by their progressive methods.

In addition to mining there is considerable activity in pulpwood and lumber.

In this area are 365 lakes, with good black bass, crappie, pike, and pickerel fishing *(resorts and other tourist accommodations generally available)*.

1. Right from Crosby on a country road to one of the world's few SINTERING

PLANTS, 1.5 *m.*, owned by the Evergreen Mine Company *(open to visitors; guides obtained at company office).*

The sintering process converts ore dust into lumps by means of heat, so that the iron will be adaptable to blast-furnace treatment. At the plant the pulverized ore is mixed with coke and the mixture run over traveling grates, on which the coke burns out and the ore drops in glowing masses into steel cars. The sintering machine is 240 feet long and has a capacity of 1,400 long tons in 24 hours.

2. Right from Crosby on State 6 to the MILFORD MINE, 6 *m.* On February 5, 1924, underground water flooded the mine and 42 men were drowned. Although the mine was pumped out, not a body was found for months; a year elapsed before the last victim was recovered. Out of this tragedy a ghost story has developed around the figure of Harley Harris, hero of the disaster. When the water burst into the mine, Harris, who was within the mine, twice sounded the siren warning and then tied a rope around his waist so that the weight of his body would keep the siren shrieking. He died in his efforts to save his companions. Later, when work was resumed, many of the men left because they believed they could hear the siren and could see Harris with the rope tied around him. The day following the disaster, a woman whose husband had been trapped hurled herself into the dark waters; the miners thought they heard her voice, too, shrieking and moaning in the dark.

IRONTON, 81.7 *m.* (1,260 alt., 1,033 pop.), like Crosby, bounds the Cuyuna Iron Range district on the east.

Right from Ironton on an improved road to RIVERTON, 4 *m.* Here is the ORE-DRYING PLANT *(open to visitors)* of the Pickands-Mather Company. This is the largest ore-drying plant in the United States. After being pulverized, the ore is run into huge cylindrical tubes that rotate over coal fires; there are three tubes, capable of drying 80 tons of ore an hour.

BRAINERD, 95.7 *m.* (1,231 alt., 10,221 pop.), is one of the most important northern gateways to thousands of lakes and resorts, and is known as the "Capital of the Paul Bunyan playground." In 1935 the annual Paul Bunyan Carnival *(the 4th week in June),* which honors the great legendary logger, drew 200,000 persons. An annual winter carnival is held in February.

This once active metropolis of the timber country was established in 1870 with the coming of the Northern Pacific Ry. and named for the railroad president's wife, Ann Eliza Brainerd Smith, who received the commission of lieutenant colonel during the Civil War for her "gallant and efficient service."

Brainerd was then a town of shacks and tents, of unpaved streets and wooden walls. Eight thousand lumberjacks quenched their thirst in its thirty-six saloons, while company officials foregathered at the town's famed hotel, the Headquarters House, whose proud distinction was that it had over six hundred joints of stovepipe. Despite the traditional fighting, drinking, and gambling, Brainerd believed in chivalry and boasted that women were safe on the streets at any hour of the day or night.

At the height of its boom, Brainerd and the county government bonded themselves heavily to induce a lumber company to establish a mill in the city. This brought a rush of business until the timber was depleted; then the mill shut down and the county was left stripped and in debt. A difficult period followed while the cut-over country was being converted into farm land; eventually iron ore was discovered in the vicinity, and prosperity was restored.

Brainerd still plays an important role in the lumbering industry. The Northern Pacific maintains shops in the town, and the only wallpaper factory in the State is here. Brainerd has also become a prominent shipping point for the dairy products of Crow Wing County.

The WPA has erected a $90,000 ARMORY at 5th and Laurel Aves., which provides one of the largest assembly halls in this part·of the State.

The CROW WING COUNTY HISTORICAL MUSEUM in the courthouse *(open weekdays 9-5, Sat. 9-12;* free) exhibits historical objects, such as Indian and pioneer relics. The County Garden and Flower Society holds annual spring and fall exhibits here.

Col. Freeman Thorp, painter of noted personages, whose portrait of President Lincoln hangs in the Capitol in Washington, lived near this town from 1895 until his death in 1922.

Brainerd is the headquarters of State Ranger District No. 4, comprising 2 million acres and divided into 6 patrol districts, with a single ranger assigned to each. With only 6 men covering 2 million acres, adequate fire prevention is impossible; but a special effort is being made to give Crow Wing County better than average protection, so that it may serve as a model for the district. Seven observation towers, each with a visibility of about 15 miles, facilitate fire-fighting activities.

The forestry department is also endeavoring to preserve these north woods as a recreational area. In addition to regular forest-conservation work, this department has laid out campgrounds and made bathing beaches available. The five State forests in the district are being extended by acquisition of tax-delinquent land.

Brainerd is at the junction (L) with US 371 *(see Tour 20)*.

At 97.8 *m.* is the junction (R) with US 371 *(see Tour 20)*.

PILLAGER, 108.9 *m.* (1,236 alt., 296 pop.), the approximate geographic center of Minnesota, is named for a band of Chippewa who had a village on the town site.

MOTLEY, 118.3 *m.* (1,227 alt., 397 pop.), a village formed in 1874, is at the junction with US 10 *(see Tour 16)*.

◄◄◄◄◄◄◄◄◄◄◄◄◄◄◄◄◄◄◄◄❂❭❭❭❭❭❭❭❭❭❭❭❭❭❭❭❭❭❭❭❭❭

Tour 16

(Prescott, Wis.)—St. Paul—East St. Cloud—Little Falls—Staples—Detroit Lakes—Moorhead—(Fargo, N. Dak.) ; US 10.
Wisconsin Line to North Dakota Line, 275.8 m.

Route paralleled by Chicago, Milwaukee, St. Paul & Pacific R.R. and Chicago, Burlington & Quincy R.R. between Point Douglas and St. Paul; by Great Northern Ry.

between St. Paul and East St. Cloud; and by Northern Pacific Ry. between St. Paul and Moorhead.
Roadbed paved, except for bituminous-treated stretch between Little Falls and Detroit Lakes; passable in all seasons.
Good accommodations.

This route passes through metropolitan St. Paul and traverses the heart of Minnesota's dairy and agricultural belt, following the winding course of the Mississippi in a northwesterly direction. The highway penetrates deep into the Paul Bunyan region, the scene of annual lumberjack carnivals, and then turns west after leaving Detroit Lakes. From this vacation playground, the route leads directly into the Red River Valley, whose rich soil produces a tremendous potato and wheat crop, and finally crosses the Red River, the western boundary of northern Minnesota.

At 0 *m.* US 10 crosses the St. Croix River on a toll bridge *(25¢ for driver and car; 5¢ each additional passenger)*, 16 miles west of Ellsworth, Wis. *(see Wisconsin, Tour 18).*

POINT DOUGLAS, at the junction of the Mississippi and St. Croix Rivers, is the site of a pioneer Minnesota town, now abandoned. In 1805 Lt. Zebulon M. Pike purchased a tract here as part of a military acquisition. The Government ultimately established the post on the site of the present Fort Snelling. At Point Douglas, which was founded and named by Levi Hertzell and Oscar Burris in 1839, Woodruff & Sons built a mill in 1851, but it was afterward removed to Prescott, Wis. Point Douglas was the starting place of the old Douglas Rd., the first military road in Minnesota, which was laid out by U. S. Army engineers in 1851.

In this lower St. Croix Valley, widened by the rush of glacial waters, animal and plant life differ considerably from that of the adjoining uplands. Here the conifers, usually restricted to the northern woods, survive in sheltered ravines, as do many plants from regions far to the south. The river valley also marks the northwestern limit of the brilliantly colored cardinal.

At 3.1 *m.* is the junction with US 61 *(see Tour 1),* which between this point and St. Paul coincides with US 10.

This area has a typical glacial topography with irregular rolling hills interspersed with glacial "kettles," small depressions filled with richer soil washed into them from the surrounding "knobs."

At 11.3 *m.* is NEWPORT (750 alt., 541 pop.).

US 10 follows Point Douglas Rd. in St. Paul to Hastings Ave.; L. on Hastings Ave. to Kellogg Blvd.; L. on Kellogg Blvd. to Robert St.; R. on Robert St. to University Ave.

ST. PAUL, 20.4 *m.* (703 alt., 271,606 pop.) *(see ST. PAUL).*

Points of Interest. Capitol Square, City Hall, Cathedral of St. Paul, Government dam and locks.

St. Paul is at the junction with US 12 *(see Tour 10),* US 52 *(see Tour 9),* US 212 *(see Tour 11),* and US 61 *(see Tour 1).*

Leaving St. Paul, US 10 follows University Ave. to Rice St.; R. on Rice St. to Como Ave.; L. on Como Ave. to Lexington Ave.; R. on Lexington Ave.

At 33.7 *m.* is the junction with US 8 *(see Tour 19)*.

Through this region are miles of peat bogs, which sometimes smolder for months. Although their inaccessibility makes it difficult to quench the fires, they rarely break into flame and are seldom a menace. The burning peat gives off an acrid, heavy odor that hangs low in summer over miles of the surrounding area.

ANOKA, 46.6 *m.* (904 alt., 4,851 pop.), formerly an important set-tlement on the old Red River Trail, is at the junction with US 52 *(see Tour 9)* and US 169 *(see Tour 3)*, which become one route with US 10 from this point to Elk River.

Anoka's annual Hallowe'en Party was instituted in 1920 by a group of businessmen to do away with destructive Hallowe'en pranks. The festival was so successful that it was repeated, and each celebration has been more elaborate than the preceding one. A large parade is held; prizes are given for the best costumes and floats; boxing and wrestling matches and other contests are the order of the evening.

In the city's cemetery is a MONUMENT TO JONATHAN EMERSON, an old settler, erected by himself a year before his death. Engraved upon the stone in more than 2,500 words are verses from the Bible and his philos-ophy of life, ending with the once popular epitaph that begins, "Remem-ber me as you pass by for as you are now, so once was I."

One block north of the Champlin-Anoka Bridge is the WOODBURY HOUSE *(not open to public but visible from road at 1632 S. Ferry St.)*, built in 1854 by Dr. Edward P. Shaw, who helped to plat the township of Anoka. The house is a relatively simple two-story frame structure with wood siding and a one-story kitchen and diningroom wing at right angles with the main section. In the angle thus formed is a porch. While the general effect suggests New England, there are certain elements of the Greek Revival—in the detail of the doorway—and a suggestion of the Vic-torian—in the jigsawed brackets that support the cornice along the sides and on the gable ends of the house. The doorway is simple; its moldings show exaggerated and decadent forms of the cyma (waved) curve, as do those on the main cornice. There is evidence that the house originally had blinds on all the windows.

All of the early Governors were entertained in the Woodbury House, and more than a score of people were given refuge in it during the Sioux uprising of 1862.

Residents believe the LARGE STONE near the mouth of the Rum River with its inscription "Father Louis Hennepin—1680" was carved by the Franciscan himself.

Sixty-five or seventy years ago it was thought that Anoka and not Min-neapolis would become the metropolitan center of the State, its position on the two rivers, the Rum and the Mississippi, making an ideal location for a milling center. However, with the development of electrical power at Minneapolis and the increasing importance of automotive and rail trans-portation, the value of the site diminished.

The municipal STADIUM, built in 1915, stands on the hill bordering the Rum River; it has been used more as a park than as the outdoor theater for which it was intended. Anoka has a number of parks and playgrounds, all of which are within easy walking distance of the downtown section. RIVERSIDE PARK *(camping facilities)* is on the banks of the Rum River across from the stadium, with which it is connected by a rustic bridge.

Recreational facilities, especially for the summer months, are numerous. A municipal golf course, and a recreation building and clubhouse, are on 102 acres of ground in the northwest section of town. There is a supervised SWIMMING BEACH on the Mississippi at the foot of Rice St., where free instruction is provided by the Red Cross; the beach is equipped with a bathhouse, dock, and lifeboat. North of Anoka there is good small-mouth bass fishing in the Mississippi.

This area is interspersed with groves of native timber and is traversed by the Rum and Sunrise Rivers, tributaries of the Mississippi. The RUM RIVER is one of Minnesota's most famous streams. Father Hennepin, Jonathan Carver, and Sieur du Luth traversed its water, and many others followed them. It was a favorite highway for the fur-traders and bore the first pine logs cut in the State.

The woods and pastures are full of wild flowers. In the spring the purple crocus and blue wood violet are contrasted with white and yellow violets. The low or pasture rose is common along the highways and in the fields, together with the bright yellow butter-and-eggs, wild pea, intertwined with wild morning-glory, or great bindweed.

DAYTON STATION, 51.3 *m.,* an abandoned railroad-junction town, formerly an Indian trading post, was platted in 1852 as Itasca but was later overshadowed by Dayton across the river. Near Dayton Station the Crow River flows into the Mississippi. Geologists have ascertained that the Crow once was the bed of the preglacial St. Croix, which proceeded from its upper reaches through the vicinity of Pine City, Dayton, and Rockford to the Mississippi. During an interglacial period, the river in this bed flowed southwest, but a lobe of ice pushing into the valley changed the direction and shunted the river into its present course far to the east.

Pond lilies grow thickly in the shallow water along the slow-moving streams and in stagnant ponds beside the highway. Ginseng, a medicinal herb found in the woods, became a source of income and tided over many a settler's family through bad years.

ELK RIVER, 58.5 *m.* (924 alt., 1,026 pop.), is the seat of Sherburne County. The town and the river, which enters the Mississippi at this point, were both named for the herds of elk found here by Pike. The first house in Elk River, a trading post, was erected in 1848 by the French trader and guide, Pierre Bottineau. It stood on a bluff just east of the bridge across the Elk on US 10. Bottineau also built a hotel in 1850 on the bank of the Mississippi about a half mile below the mouth of the Elk.

The village of Elk River was platted in 1865, replatted in 1868, and when incorporated in the winter of 1880–81, included both Orono and Elk River. A large number of early settlers came here from Maine and nearly all of them were experts in lumbering. Early in the 1900's, however, when the lumbering industry began to decline here, as elsewhere in

Minnesota, dairying became and has continued to be the financial mainstay.
Elk River is at the junction (R) with US 169 *(see Tour 3)*.

Visible to the north and east of the Mississippi is the triangular area
known as the Anoka Sand Plain, covering about 858 square miles. This
plain probably was produced by the lowering of the water table which resulted from the down-cutting of the river. When the plant cover disappeared, it left the dry surface sand exposed to the erosive southwest wind.
In many places the fine sand has been blown into well-defined dunes, some
of which reach a height of 20 feet.

BIG LAKE, 68.1 (960 alt., 417 pop.), was settled in 1848 as Humboldt, but its name was changed in 1867 with the coming of the railroad.
The village is popular as a summer resort, and has many cottages, an
AMUSEMENT PARK, and a PAVILION. The adjoining lake of the same
name is a favorite picnic site.

Left from Big Lake on State 25 to MONTICELLO, 3.3 *m.* (933 alt., 924 pop.).
A Hungarian nobleman, Baron Moritzius Weissberger, a follower of Kossuth,
got title to 700 acres near this place. He left for 18 months and returned to find his
land "jumped" by a town site company. Weissberger was forced to leave and the
town was reincorporated here in 1861.

Monticello, once the seat of Wright County, was the scene of a notorious murder in 1859. H. A. Wallace was killed and a neighbor, Oscar F. Johnson, was
accused of the crime. He was tried and acquitted, whereupon he was promptly
lynched. Emery Moore, prominent among the lynchers, was arrested but quickly
released by an armed mob. Troops were dispatched to the scene; all lynchers and
rescuers were arrested and turned over to the civil authorities.

Right from Monticello on a graveled road to SILVER CREEK, 14.2 *m.* (477
pop.). It was first settled by New Englanders; then in 1854 came 31 Hollanders
from Amsterdam who purchased 80 acres of land and built a house 50 by 70 feet
in which the whole group lived. All but 10 had left within 2 years, but others
came, and there is still a preponderance of Dutch in the community. The original
house, however, is gone.

Right from Silver Creek on a graveled road to HASTY, 18.7 *m.*, on the Mississippi. The only LIMBURGER CHEESE FACTORY in the State is here.

Left from Hasty on State 152 to CLEARWATER, 24.2 *m.* (212 pop.); R. from
Clearwater a free bridge crosses the Mississippi River and US 10 is regained at
29.1 *m.*

BECKER, 76 *m.* (966 alt., 214 pop.), was founded in 1867 with the
coming of the railroad.

CLEAR LAKE, 83 *m.* (1,016 alt., 242 pop.), was founded at the same
time and had the same origin as Becker. It was named for the nearby lake.

A decidedly modern adaptation of the old prison rock-pile idea has been
made at the MINNESOTA STATE REFORMATORY, 92.7 *m.*, on extensive
grounds embracing one of the finest quarries in the State. Its 55 acres are
enclosed by a massive granite wall and the buildings are of the same material; the quarrying, cutting, and placing of the stone have all been done
by inmates. Opened in 1889 as a penal institution for young men between
16 and 30, it is now the classification point for all criminal male adults
sentenced to a State institution. After a thorough examination and observation covering several weeks, men listed as hopelessly incorrigible are
sent to other institutions, while those believed capable of rehabilitation are

retained and given vocational and educational training and moral guidance.

EAST ST. CLOUD, 94.2 m. (1,040 alt., 625 pop.), is at the junction with US 52 (see Tour 9).

This is a region of famous granite quarries and rock outcroppings (see INDUSTRIAL DEVELOPMENT: Quarrying). Machinery used in the excavation stands at various points along the road.

SAUK RAPIDS, 96.1 m. (1,008 alt., 2,656 pop.), is on the site chosen by the Sac Indians as a refuge after they had been driven from Wisconsin for their raids on the white settlers. They were a source of much trouble in this new territory.

When Sauk Rapids became the northern terminal of the Northern Pacific and Great Northern Rys., it assumed importance as the junction of rail and ox-cart traffic. The FOUNDATION OF AN OLD SAWMILL on the river front is all that is left of the town's boom days, for the cyclone of 1886 leveled the entire city. Flour-milling is now the principal industry.

Various kinds of pink granite were formerly quarried in the immediate vicinity, but now the local finishing plants are engaged in fabricating stock from other quarries. A large supply of high-grade rock is still available in the area, however. Sauk Rapids granite has been used in the Civic Opera Building, Chicago; Angell Hall, University of Michigan; and in many other prominent buildings.

A RETREAT of the Roman Catholic order of Poor Clares of Saint Francis, one of 10 in the United States, is built on a hill (R). Founded by Saint Clara, at Assisi, Italy, in 1212, on the ideals of Saint Francis, the order of nuns adheres to extreme poverty and devotes itself chiefly to the education and care of young girls. It has been represented in this country since 1875. The habit is of gray frieze with a linen rope belt.

At 97.1 m. a signboard on the highway points (L) to the SITE OF RUSSELL TRADING POST, marked by a granite stone. Less than 50 feet north of this spot is the unmarked point where Red River carts crossed the Mississippi.

At SARTELL, 98.8 m. (1,044 alt., 521 pop.), the Indian boundary established by the Prairie du Chien Treaty of 1825 crosses the Mississippi River. By this treaty Sioux Indians were restricted to the territory south of this mythical line, while that north of it was designated as Chippewa country. The boundary site is marked by a signboard.

The Mississippi at this point is spanned by a 22-foot DAM, which has widened the river for some distance above it.

A PAPER MILL (open to visitors), engaged in the manufacture of ground wood-pulp and high-grade paper, is on the river and is operated by a hydro-electric power plant of 7,000 horsepower. The daily capacity of the mill is 80 tons of finished product. The village also has a sawmill and a planing mill. Surrounded by an extensive farming and dairy country, Sartell is a shipping point for livestock and grains.

WATAB, 101.8 m. (1,080 alt.), was organized in 1858, and, like the Indian trading post on the same site, which antedated it 10 years, is named for the Watab River. Watab is the Chippewa word for the long slender roots of both the tamarack and jack pine, which were dug, split, and used as threads by the Indians in sewing their birchbark canoes. Both trees grow on or near the lower part of the Watab River.

The first bridge to be attempted across the Mississippi above St. Anthony Falls was that built at Watab in 1855; when the bridge was practically completed, a high wind lifted the superstructure from its supports and it collapsed into the river.

The highway passes (R) LITTLE ROCK LAKE *(fishing, swimming)* at 105.2 *m.*

RICE, 108.9 *m.* (1,086 alt., 314 pop.), was named for an early tavern proprietor.

At 126.9 *m.* (L) is the LITTLE FALLS TOWN AND COUNTRY CLUB *(9-hole golf course, reasonable fee),* on the eastern bank of the Mississippi.

LITTLE FALLS, 127.2 *m.* (1,134 alt., 5,014 pop.), built on both shores of the Mississippi, is the seat of Morrison County. The rapids for which the town is named were first called "Painted Rocks" by French voyageurs and were explored in 1805 by Zebulon M. Pike. Here, where the river descends 11 feet in 0.25 mile, a dam was built in 1890, and lumber, flour, and paper mills thrived. An excessively high flood stage in June 1853 raised the Minneapolis steamboat *North Star* over these falls on the only known northward passage to Itasca.

About 1895 a village school teacher discovered artificially flaked quartz fragments in the valley drift of this vicinity, thus establishing the possibility of an early postglacial culture, a theory recently corroborated by the discovery of the "Browns Valley Man" *(see Tour 4).*

The most important park in Little Falls, the LINDBERGH STATE PARK *(picnic grounds)* of 100 acres, is on the west bank of the Mississippi and surrounds the home of Col. Charles A. Lindbergh. Pike's Creek runs through the park.

The story-and-a-half house is set on a high stone basement; the frame construction is covered by clapboard siding. A small porch shelters the front entrance. Restoration was begun in 1935 as a WPA project, the sum of $2,500 being used to make what repairs were necessary and to replace, insofar as possible, the missing furniture. In the entrance room is a decorative map of Colonel Lindbergh's solo flight, painted in oil on masonite by Bertrand Old of the Federal Art Project.

Charles A. Lindbergh, Jr., lived with his mother and father in this house while he was a very small child. Little Falls was his home until he was graduated from high school. At this time he entered the University of Wisconsin.

Charles A. Lindbergh, Sr., began to practice at Little Falls after he was graduated from the law department of the University of Michigan in 1883. He distinguished himself as a Progressive Republican in the U. S. House of Representatives from 1907 to 1917. His persistent and courageous denunciation of war propaganda and profiteering not only caused him to be extremely unpopular but undoubtedly contributed to his defeat for the office of U. S. Senator in 1917 and for the Governorship of Minnesota in 1918. In 1924 he was again nominated for the office of Governor of Minnesota, but died before the primary.

PINE GROVE PARK *(picnic grounds)*, at the western boundary of the city, harbors one of the few remaining stands of white pine trees in the State. In the park are herds of deer, elk, and buffalo.

At the northern edge of the town is a RECREATIONAL AND PARK AREA. Financed by the Federal Government, this improvement also includes a water-softening plant. Its exterior is constructed of waste white granite, and the plant softens the extremely hard local water so that it is suitable for household use.

HOLE-IN-THE-DAY'S BLUFF rises 40 feet above the surrounding low morainic hills northeast of town and is named for an Ojibway chief, who was slain by his own people and buried on its summit.

A city-owned TOURIST CAMP *(free)* is at the north city entrance on US 371.

Little Falls is at the junction (R) with US 371 *(see Tour 20)*.

North of Little Falls the vegetation becomes more dense; the hills are wooded; pines and ground shrubs are abundant.

RANDALL, 137.8 *m.* (1,201 alt., 302 pop.), was incorporated in 1900 and named in honor of John H. Randall, a Northern Pacific Ry. executive.

CUSHING, 142.8 *m.* (1,288 alt., 175 pop.), was platted in December 1907 and was probably named for Caleb Cushing, eminent jurist, Congressman, and diplomat.

LINCOLN, 148.3 *m.* (1,304 alt., 75 pop.). This vicinity has a fine group of lakes with hilly and wooded shores, numerous points, bays, and islands, and abounds with fish and waterfowl.

MOTLEY, 157.4 *m.* (1,250 alt., 397 pop.) *(see Tour 15)*, is at the junction with US 210 *(see Tour 15)*.

STAPLES, 164.6 *m.* (1,298 alt., 2,667 pop.), is a division point on the Northern Pacific Ry. and claims to be the exact center of the State. Years ago the old Leaf Lake Trail, north of Staples, followed the Leaf River. Today Staples is the center of a good farming district; its creameries and cheese factories annually yield large returns.

VERNDALE, 175.5 *m.* (1,367 alt., 424 pop.). Wheat buying was formerly important to the villages in this section, and Verndale enjoyed a monopoly of the trade from the northern prairies. From 1873, when the county was organized, there was no regular courthouse. In 1887 the Verndale citizens made a strong bid for the county seat, built a courthouse, and offered it to the county. At the same time, however, a structure proffered by the Wadena citizens was accepted in preference to Verndale's. The quarrel between these two towns is an example of the bitter feuds, so common in the early days, for the privilege of being designated the county seat. Here the fight that started in 1879 did not culminate until 1886. Both villages hired men for "residents," who practically ran the town until after election. It was considered unsafe for women to go into the streets. Wadena won the election, but Verndale carried the case to court, and not until 1887 was the final decision rendered.

The highway here passes through a farming region of comparatively flat land. Rivers and streams are plentiful but lakes are rare.

WADENA, (Ind., *a little round hill*), 182.2 *m.* (1,372 alt., 2,512 pop.), probably was named for the rounded outlines of the Crow Wing River bluffs at the original Wadena trading post. Wadena is also a common Indian name. The town became a distributing center, and while it has lost some of its early industries it has added others. Today it supports a number of wholesale houses, a canning factory, and an ice-cream manufacturing plant, and ships livestock. WESLEY METHODIST HOSPITAL, under the supervision of the Northern Minnesota Conference of the Methodist Episcopal Church, completed in 1924 at a cost of $100,000, is on the eastern outskirts of town. Besides well-equipped, thoroughly modern facilities, it offers a 3-year nurses' training course that meets the requirements for registration in Minnesota. Wadena is at the junction with US 71 *(see Tour 2)*.

At 190.7 *m.* US 10 crosses the Leaf River.

NEW YORK MILLS, 198.6 *m.* (1,433 alt., 668 pop.), is a Finnish community that has retained many of the Old Country customs. The Finns still use their native bathhouse, the *sauna,* in which they douse water on a heated rock fireplace, loll in the steamy atmosphere, and beat their bodies with twigs to induce perspiration. They then dash cold water on themselves and apparently enjoy the invigorating effect. The *Minnesotan Uutiset,* a Finnish newspaper published in New York Mills, is loyally supported.

More than 200 species of wild birds nest in this territory or rest on their migratory flight.

The winding Otter Tail River is at 207.7 *m.,* where (R) is a CAMPGROUND *(free).*

At PERHAM, 209.8 *m.* (1,390 alt., 1,411 pop.), US 10 enters Minnesota's Park region, a district renowned as a vacation playground, offering a variety of outdoor sports. Otter Tail County, in which Perham lies, contains more than 1,000 of Minnesota's 10,000 lakes; known as the fisherman's paradise, the region is amply provided with resorts and tourist accommodations.

Left from Perham on State 78 to a bridge over the Red River at 8.8. *m.* On the L. is RUSH LAKE *(fishing, swimming, boating),* one of the large lakes of the region. The Indians of this area used more than 40 species of plants as food. Wild ginger was an appetizer; berries and leaves of the bearberry served as flour to thicken gravy; dried cornsilk in broth took the place of salt; aster leaves were boiled like spinach and eaten with fish; stalks of woodvine were eaten in the manner of corn on the cob and also boiled down to a syrup. Wild "potatoes," celery, pumpkin, squash, flowers of milkweed, bulbs from the roots of bulrushes, the sap of basswood and aspen, mosses from white pines, and dried berries provided sustenance for the Indians long before the white man saw America.

The SITE OF OTTER TAIL CITY, a vanished village, is on the extreme northeastern end of OTTER TAIL LAKE (R) adjoining the mouth of the river. The town was an important trading post (1850–60) on the route from the flourishing town of Crow Wing to Pembina and the Selkirk settlements. It contained the U. S. land office for the district and one of the two post offices in the county, and was the county seat. The land office was removed to Alexandria in 1862, and the county seat to Fergus Falls in 1872, and as a result the "city" was soon depopulated. All the buildings have long since disappeared and only the cellars remain. The site of this once flourishing trading center and seat of government is now a field of waving grain.

Otter Tail Lake is the largest of 1,000 lakes in Otter Tail County; it is 3 miles wide and 11 miles long. Recognized as one of the finest fishing spots in the State, it is heavily patronized by devotees of rod and reel. The shores of Otter Tail Lake resounded to the creaking of the Red River carts, when this mode of transportation was at its height. The "woods trail" of the Pembina-St. Paul cart route skirted the northeast corner of the lake.

At 20.3 *m.* is the junction with a country road; R. on this road to a junction at 22.5 *m.;* R. here along the shore line of Otter Tail. This route provides a beautiful view of the lake surrounded by birch and pine. In this region in the late 1880's the Rocky Mountain locust destroyed acres of wheat. The plague did much to diversify agriculture in Otter Tail and surrounding counties.

At 41.3 *m.* this country road joins State 78; L. here to the junction with US 10 at 47.1 *m.*

FRAZEE, 221.4 *m.* (1,410 alt., 1,041 pop.), in the heart of the park region, has many summer resorts centered about convenient lakes. The pioneering visitor can find isolated nooks, seemingly as remote from civilization as when the prehistoric tribes roamed this area. Here are hunting grounds and fish-filled streams.

In the tamarack swamps near Detroit Lakes grows the pitcher plant or side-saddle flower whose leaves hold a gill of water; here also blooms the rare pink ladyslipper and the more common yellow variety.

HAMILTON'S AQUATIC FARM (L), 229.6 *m.,* was established in 1920 and today supplies a wide demand for aquatic seed and nursery stock. Before orders are filled, a personal survey is made of the waters where planting is contemplated, and the natural condition of the water is determined, so that suitable plants may be selected. Among the species most commonly sold are wildrice, wildcelery, duck potatoes, muskgrass, lilies, flags, and rushes.

DETROIT LAKES, 230.9 *m.* (1,386 alt., 3,675 pop.), is the seat of Becker County; the name of the town was derived from a word spoken by a French priest over 200 years ago. This missionary, standing on the shore of the lake with his French companions and Chippewa guides, commented on the distinct *detroit* (a strait or narrows). Henceforth, the Indians and white fur-traders employed that name for the immediate vicinity; "Lakes" was added in 1927 as being characteristic of the district.

Detroit Lakes is known as the capital of the park region, not only for its 500 adjacent lakes, but also for the numerous city and resort hotels and lake cabin groups which cater to thousands of summer visitors.

The MUNICIPAL TOURIST CAMP *(50¢ a day with special rates for longer stays; showers, gas, recreation hall)* comprises 30 acres on the north shore of Detroit Lake to the R. of US 59 and about 0.25 mile from the point where it turns to circle the lake.

A CITY PARK (in addition to the tourist park) is also on the north shore of Detroit Lake, where US 59 turns R. This park covers 25 wooded acres and has a large pavilion for dancing and other amusements. Orchestras, usually of radio fame, furnish music for summer dancing. Other equipment in the park includes tables, benches, and playground apparatus. Baseball and softball diamonds and tennis courts are available. At the

FAIR GROUNDS, on the lake just before the tourist park, is an amphitheater for outdoor concerts and other entertainments; there is also a football field lighted for night games.

The CARNEGIE PUBLIC LIBRARY *(open daily 2-5 p.m., 7-9 p.m.)*, at the junction of US 10 and Washington Ave. S., contains 9,400 volumes and houses the International Mind Alcove, a Carnegie endowment for the promotion of international peace and good will. The library clubrooms are in the lower part of the building. The rural distribution of books is under the direction of the local library.

Besides the CHURCH OF THE MOST HOLY REDEEMER of St. Benedict's Mission on Washington Ave., commonly regarded as one of the best in the entire Indian Service, Detroit Lakes has a number of fine church edifices of various denominations and architectural styles.

The BECKER COUNTY INFIRMARY, adjoining the fairgrounds, is an asylum for the aged. Local facilities include a MODERN PRIVATE HOSPITAL, 115 E. Frazee St., and the COMMUNITY HOSPITAL on Lincoln Ave.

The Summer Carnival *(July)* is under the direction of the Junior Chamber of Commerce. This entertainment includes a parade of decorated floats, a bathing-beauty contest, swimming and diving competitions, waterball games, speedboat racing, canoe tilting and racing, surfboard riding, logrolling, and fly casting.

The Junior Chamber of Commerce and the Detroit Lakes Ski Club also stage a yearly Winter Carnival and Ski Meet in February. The progam includes an ice pageant, parade, ball, skating races, figure skating, hockey games, tobogganing on Water Tank Hill, a dog derby, and wood-chopping and sawing contests.

The large summer-tourist business helps to determine the principal imports, which include oil, automobiles, garage supplies, creamery and packing necessities, and many other finished products. Exports include butter and turkeys, which command special prices in eastern markets, eggs, poultry, potatoes, beef cattle, sheep, and wool. Spring water is supplied to the entire Northern Pacific Ry. system and to other buyers. Hundreds of carloads of ice are sent annually to western points and thousands of tons of sand and gravel are transported to points east and west.

Detroit Lakes is at the junction with US 59 *(see Tour 17)*. From Detroit Lakes the route traverses a rolling morainic region that becomes more tillable as it progresses westward.

AUDUBON, 238.1 *m.* (1,332 alt., 278 pop.), was named for the great ornithologist, John James Audubon (1780–1851), at the suggestion of his niece who, with a party of tourists, once camped in the vicinity.

LAKE PARK, 243.7 *m.* (1,174 alt., 624 pop.), was settled in 1870.

Left from Lake Park on a county road to BIG CORMORANT LAKE, 10.6 *m.*
The so-called ANCHOR STONES, on the northwestern shore of Big Cormorant Lake, are three large granite boulders, each with a drilled hole 9 inches deep and 1 inch wide; they are about 300 feet from the present lake on an earlier shore line. It is believed that they were used about 1362 by a small party of Norse explorers. In defense of this opinion, it is pointed out that today, as for centuries past, Norwegian boatmen tie up their skiffs with a rope run through a hole drilled in a rock on the shore.

Skeptics have propounded a variety of theories to explain the drilling of these stones. Some debaters hold that pioneer loggers made them to anchor booms. But no logging was ever carried on here. Others insist that some farmer drilled the rocks preparatory to clearing the land by dynamiting; but it seems improbable that a farmer would have dynamite in this backwoods 75 years ago.

Whatever their origin, the anchor stones and the Kensington Runestone *(see Tour 9)*, which have been attributed to the same early Norse exploring party, continue to be a source of discussion.

HAWLEY, 254 *m.* (1,174 alt., 958 pop.), was settled by an English colony in 1871.

At about 260 *m.* US 10 skirts the southern boundary of a STATE GAME REFUGE consisting of 26,880 acres, established in 1924.

Here the highway gradually descends almost 200 feet to the prairie of the Red River Valley, an excellent farming area and the bed of the ancient glacial Lake Agassiz. The terrace from which the highway descends was formed by a rock escarpment that caused the deposit of glacial drift. West of this point the country is largely given over to wheat and potato production. Very few trees and shrubs mark the area except along the river banks, where are willows, scattered poplars, and oaks. The region, however, is rich prairie and abounds with roses, poppies, goldenrod, bell-flowers, daisies, sunflowers, morning glories, painted-cups, and clover.

The last herds of bison seen in Minnesota roamed the Red River country 75 years ago. In 1801 Alexander Henry, resident general manager of the Northwest Company, wrote in his journal that buffalo, attempting to cross the thin ice of the Red River, drowned and drifted by in great herds, from March 30 to April 25.

This treeless plain is a habitat of the white-tail jackrabbit, which is extensively hunted. Varieties of field mice, moles, shrews, and ground squirrels are also found. Mink, muskrat, and skunk are trapped along the streams and prairie sloughs. Deer and coyotes are infrequent visitors; both prefer the brush and timber districts farther east and north.

GLYNDON, 266.5 *m.* (946 alt., 388 pop.), was platted as a railway village in 1872.

US 10 crosses the south branch of the Buffalo River at 269.2 *m.* Along the highway, despite the lack of trees, there are numerous birds: phoebes, pewees, and larks; the western meadow chickadees are found throughout the winter; nut-hatches, wrens, and thrushes are common summer residents.

DILWORTH, 272.5 *m.* (983 pop.), is a division point on the Northern Pacific Ry.

The site of MOORHEAD, 274.9 *m.* (929 alt., 7,651 pop.), was selected because it was a natural terminus for all forms of transportation. The ox trains of Red River carts found it so, as did the barges of the early 19th century, and later the steamboats, railroads, and automobiles.

The muddy frontier settlement, growing with the railroad, was christened Moorhead on September 22, 1871, in honor of Dr. William G. Moorhead, a director of the Northern Pacific. The original store in the village handled everything from dry goods to machinery; flour sold for $15 a barrel and molasses and kerosene for $2 a gallon. Buildings of two stories had a ground structure of logs and a second story of canvas. When a shooting occurred, the dwellers in the upper part dropped down behind the logs, escaping with no more serious injuries than bruises and bumps, as the bullets whistled through the canvas.

Early visitors to this fertile Red River region did not recognize the possibilities of farming the land. The belief was then prevalent that the treeless prairie country was of no agricultural value. In fact, General Sibley, after a western campaign, wrote of the territory, "It is fit only for the Indians and the Devil"—an opinion not supported by an incident in Moorhead's early history. A farmer came into the barroom of a local hotel and proudly exhibited a sack full of fresh vegetables. He had raised them, he said, on his farm a few miles away. The reaction of the assembled company—mostly strangers to the district—ranged from polite to pugnacious disbelief. One man flatly called the farmer a liar. At this point the vegetable grower, presumably more outraged by the slur upon his soil than upon his veracity, produced a gun from among the carrots and peas and shot his accuser.

The license to run a ferry to the "lawless" hamlet of Fargo across the river cost $15 in the early days. The tolls were: vehicles drawn by two animals, 25¢, additional animals 5¢ each; loose stock, not more than 10 head, 10¢ each, and, above that number, 5¢ a head; foot passengers, 5¢ each. An early financial notice was a bill for $12 submitted to the county commissioners on January 24, 1875, by Sheriff J. B. Blanchard, for notifying the Indians to leave Clay County.

In 1882 Moorhead had become one of the most famed centers of the State, with 14 hotels and restaurants. Outstanding among these was the Grand Pacific Hotel, "the pride of Moorhead," constructed at a cost of $165,000. The hotel had 140 rooms with connecting baths and included steam heat and gas in its service. The interior decorations won the admiration of its patrons, as did the handsome bar with its full stock of "invigorating beverages." Too "grand" to pay, the hotel subsequently was ordered razed by James J. Hill, its mortgagee.

Before the citizenry exercised county option and ousted the saloon industry, the town was a mecca for the thirsty from across the river in dry North Dakota. The liquor trade had grown to such tremendous proportions in the little city's saloons that it had achieved a degree of notoriety not to the liking of many of its inhabitants.

With the passing years Moorhead developed into one of Minnesota's leading educational centers. CONCORDIA, a college at 809 7th Ave. S., was established in 1891 and has an average enrollment of 420 students from nine states. It has an excellent conservatory of music, which sponsors its fine mixed choirs, bands, and orchestra. The property of Concordia is valued at $385,000; its endowment fund totals $600,000. The college offers its graduates the bachelor of arts degree. MOORHEAD STATE TEACHERS' COLLEGE, 1104 7th Ave. S., formerly Moorhead Normal School, was the fourth normal college organized in the State. S. G. Comstock, a resident of the city, donated 6 acres of land for the original campus. He was a member of the State senate and was instrumental in bringing the school to the town.

St. Ansgar's Hospital, 715 N. 10th, and the Nurses' Training School are operated by the Franciscan order of Roman Catholic nuns (Poor Clares). The hospital has 30 beds, 8 registered and 20 student nurses, and 8 staff physicians.

Moorhead's organized park system includes Holes Park, a wooded 5-acre tract fronting the Red River, with equipped playgrounds and stoves for picnickers, all under the supervision of a caretaker, and the well-furnished Tourist Park, 1st and Center Sts., of 6 acres, which has a beautiful situation on the Red River close to the business district.

In addition to being the leading potato center in the Northwest, the town manufactures many products that depend upon the raw materials of agriculture; they include butter, ice cream, and bakery goods. The million-dollar Fairmont Creamery, 101 N. 8th St., handles $3,000,000 worth of dairy products and poultry a year. The annual poultry show in the armory is the second largest in Minnesota. Tent and awning manufacture and metal-working are likewise active industries. It is estimated that the value of Moorhead's manufactured products amounts to $4,000,000 each year.

Moorhead is at the junction with US 52 *(see Tour 9)* and US 75 *(see Tour 4).*

At 275.8 *m.* US 10 crosses the Red River (the North Dakota Line), and enters Fargo, N. Dak. *(see North Dakota, Tour 8).*

Tour 17

St. Vincent—Thief River Falls—Detroit Lakes—Fergus Falls—Montevideo—Marshall—Worthington—(Cherokee, Iowa); US 59.
St. Vincent to Iowa Line, 468.5 m.

The Minneapolis, St. Paul & Sault Ste. Marie Ry. parallels the route between St. Vincent and Detroit Lakes; Great Northern Ry. between Pelican Rapids and Fergus Falls; Chicago, Milwaukee, St. Paul & Pacific R.R. between Appleton and Montevideo.
Graveled roadbed between St. Vincent and junction with State 32; bitumen and graveled between junction with State 32 and Erskine; paved between Erskine and Detroit Lakes; bitumen and paved between Detroit Lakes and Elbow Lake; and in the 200 miles between Elbow Lake and Iowa Line the highway is paved for only 18 miles. Open all year.
Usual accommodations.

This route across the western part of the State traverses in the north typical Red River prairie land for approximately 45 miles and crosses several beaches and sandy shore lines of glacial Lake Agassiz; in the central section it skirts the western limits of the famous park region, the vacation playground between Detroit Lakes and Elbow Lake; in the south it winds through diversified dairying and agricultural sections, then through an area that increases in ruggedness toward the Iowa Line.

Section a. ST. VINCENT *to* DETROIT LAKES, *200.6 m. US 59.*

The residents of ST. VINCENT, 0 *m.,* (788 alt., 304 pop.), stroll informally across the Canadian Border and back to visit friends and relatives. In many cases some members of a family live in St. Vincent and others in the nearby Canadian town of Emerson.

St. Vincent, peaceful and serene, the oldest village in Kittson County, seems little changed from its pioneer days. A trading post was established on or near the site in the 1790's. The town was named for St. Vincent de Paul, renowned for his work among the poor; in the early part of the 17th century he organized charities in France and established religious orders to care for the needy. Many of the early settlers migrated from Prince Edward Island, and endured almost unbelievable hardships as they traveled the frozen trail across Canada in subzero temperatures. Many of these sturdy pioneers later intermarried with the Chippewa Indians; their descendants were known for their remarkable feats of endurance.

At 2 *m.* is the junction with US 75 *(see Tour 4),* which is united with US 59 for 4.3 miles.

LANCASTER, 25.3 *m.* (908 alt., 456 pop.), is the largest Kittson County village on the Soo Line. In the early 1880's when this section, then a rough and rugged hinterland, was first being settled, the railroad was a number of miles to the west and Indians were numerous and sometimes troublesome. Lancaster was incorporated in 1905 and today is a thriving village, with a large creamery serving the ever-growing dairy industry of the region.

BRONSON, 39.3 *m.* (959 alt., 239 pop.), was named for Giles Bronson, a farmer who in 1882 built a log cabin 3 miles to the east and later became well known for his hospitality to sportsmen and homesteaders. His cabin served as the community post office.

The village, on a prominent glacial moraine that stretches for a long distance north and south, is between the middle and south forks of the stream called Two Rivers.

Bronson's fine CONSOLIDATED SCHOOL has been given a "class A" rating by the State Board of Education. Dairying is a major industry; there are many herds of purebred and high-grade cattle in the vicinity. The Bronson creamery, now a member of the state-wide Land O' Lakes Association, was established in 1905 and by 1926 had attained a production of 122,000 pounds of butter per year. Wheat and other grains are important products, but the potato crop is so large that shipments have frequently totaled 500 carloads annually.

At 39.8 *m.* is the junction with a county road.

Left on this road to TWO RIVERS STATE PARK, 1 *m.*, 2,000 acres of which are now developed.

Right from Two Rivers State Park on a dirt road to the BRONSON DAM, 1.5 *m.*, built with Federal aid on the south fork of the Two Rivers River. The dam is 85 feet long and impounds a 30-foot head of water, forming a lake about 330 acres in area. The primary purpose of the dam is to raise the water table in this region.

HALMA, 47.3 *m.* (998 alt., 129 pop.), is in a fine agricultural section, particularly adapted to diversified farming. It is not definitely known· how the name Halma originated, but it may be a variation of Holm, the name selected by the town to honor a merchant and postmaster, but rejected by the Post Office Department to avoid duplication.

At 53.3 *m.* is the junction with State 11 *(see Tour 6).* Between this point and KARLSTAD, 57.3 *m.* (1,048 alt., 304 pop.) *(see Tour 6),* US 59 and State 11 are united.

STRANDQUIST, 66 *m.* (1,064 alt., 139 pop.), was named for a Swedish merchant, the first storekeeper and postmaster of the community.

In 1914 the neighboring rural districts were merged into Strandquist Consolidated School District No. 65, and a modern brick high school was erected in the village the following year. The number of pupils enrolled is approximately 150.

The Strandquist COMMUNITY HALL, erected in 1931, serves as an auditorium and gymnasium.

The surrounding territory, an excellent haven for game birds and deer, is visited by many hunters.

At 74.9 *m.* is the junction (R) with a dirt road.

Right on this road to MIDDLE RIVER STATE PARK, 6.7 *m.* *(picnic facilities, swimming hole),* 220 acres.

NEWFOLDEN, 80.2 *m.* (1,097 alt., 244 pop.), was named for a seaport in northern Norway. The winding Middle River almost completely encircles the town, adding to the beauty of the landscape and affording fine fishing and boating. Newfolden is also a center for deer hunters.

Prior to 1882 the entire territory around Newfolden was a wilderness inhabited only by Indians. In 1882 began the influx of Scandinavian settlers, who were the founders of this prosperous modernized farm community and whose descendants compose almost the entire present population. The first homes were built of logs, with an occasional roofing of sod. Many of the barns were built entirely of sod. The most traveled route to the nearest grain market at Argyle, one day's journey west by wagon, was the roundabout trail along the south side of Middle River. There were no roads or bridges and these early settlers had to find the easiest way to market.

Newfolden's chief industry is its co-operative creamery; several other local co-operatives also function successfully. One of these underwrites fire and lightning insurance on a large scale for the surrounding territory. The town has a hotel, a garage, and a lumberyard. Its high school offers a regular accredited course including commercial studies.

HOLT, 91.6 *m.* (1,161 alt., 193 pop.), was named in honor of Dr.

Halvor Holte of Crookston, who not only ministered to the early settlers but also was active in establishing hospitals and organizing public health societies, including the Minnesota Public Health Association of which he served as a director.

The village's small creamery has 280 farm patrons, and in 1935 manufactured 310,000 pounds of butter.

For many years the Holt 4-H Club has been the largest in Marshall County and has taken the greatest number of prizes in competition. In addition, this small village has a 20-piece band that plays at fairs and on other occasions. Potato and grain fields adjoin the highway leading into Thief River Falls.

THIEF RIVER FALLS, 103.6 m. (1,136 alt., 4,268 pop.), formerly called Rockstad, was at one time the site of a camp used by Dakota Indians who held the territory only by escaping the notice of Chippewa war parties. Unwilling to leave their rich hunting ground and living in constant fear of attack, they built a high embankment of earth around their lodges for defense and took every means in their power to escape notice—even hunting with bows and arrows instead of guns, to eliminate noise. Nevertheless they were discovered by the Chippewa and after a brave stand were annihilated. From the earthworks, the Chippewa gave the stream its early name, Secret Earth River. Through some error in pronunciation, the French and English fur-traders changed it to Stealing Earth River, then to Thief Lake, and finally to Thief River Falls.

Today this city, the seat of Pennington County, is the center of an immense area that had been drained for agriculture. A large tonnage of hay and forage, baled for market, is shipped from here annually.

Along Red Lake River (boating, bathing), its name suggested by the reddish tinge of the swamps in the vicinity, is a CITY PARK. RUINS OF AN OLD INDIAN SETTLEMENT are at Squaw Point, where Thief and Red Lake Rivers join. In early days steamboats plied Red Lake River from Red Lake to Thief River Falls, but large rocks prevented navigation south of the city. The winding river, still abounding with pike, pickerel, catfish, whitefish, and suckers, lost much of its beauty when the vast stands of timber that lined its banks were removed by lumber companies.

Thief River Falls is the focal point for one of the Federal Farm Security Administration's infiltration projects. Within a radius of about 25 miles, this agency his purchased tracts of land without buildings, or farms of large acreage, on which to resettle families moved from submarginal lands; houses and barns of standard size and type have been erected. In moving families to more productive areas, the local office rigorously investigates the background, initiative, and managerial ability of the many applicants. The resettlement sites are established near schools, markets, and other developments. At present (1938) the Thief River Falls Farms project has completed 92 farms and expected to have 111 by August of this year.

South of Thief River Falls the route traverses a territory settled chiefly by French immigrants.

ERSKINE, 139.6 m. (1,192 alt., 511 pop.) (see Tour 7), is at the junction with US 2 (see Tour 7).

WINGER, 149.9 *m.* (1,231 alt., 258 pop.), was named for a group of farms in the Gudbransdel Valley district in central Norway.

At 156.3 *m.* is BEJOU (Chippewa, *hello*) (1,226 alt., 99 pop.).

MAHNOMEN, 164.4 *m.* (1,213 alt., 989 pop.), is the seat of Mahnomen (Chippewa, *wildrice*) County. There are Indian settlements in the vicinity. Farms in this region have co-operative associations for marketing livestock, poultry, and dairy products.

At OGEMA, 179.9 *m.* (1,266 alt., 253 pop.), is the junction with a graveled road.

Left on this road to WHITE EARTH, 6.1 *m.,* the agency for the WHITE EARTH INDIAN RESERVATION. According to the terms of the White Earth Treaty, the first group of 150 Indians was moved from Crow Wing to the reservation on June 14, 1868, accompanied by Maj. J. B. Bassett. The present population of the reservation is about 8,000 and its area 1,200 square miles.

At one time this land provided millions of feet of pine, and today the cut-over district furnishes large quantities of cordwood for building purposes, fuel, pulpwood, and railroad ties. The Indians make sugar from the sap of the numerous maple trees and collect the wildrice that thrives in the swamps. Fishing, hunting, and trapping are common on the reservation.

Although commonly called a reservation, the Indian holdings in the region have been tremendously reduced since many individuals have sold their allotments. Indian Affairs authorities, aware of the poverty following loss of land, have long sought to repurchase farms, but their first opportunity came when the Federal Emergency Relief Administration's land program—which later was made a part of the Farm Security Administration—purchased 27,000 acres of submarginal land in Mahnomen County in 1934. Indian officials requested the area for Indian families and, by additional purchases from their own funds of a more fertile region to the north, acquired practically all of Little Elbow and Twin Lakes Townships. The lands are not transferable as were the old reservation farms, and their occupants are chosen by tribal council. Well-trained Indians are responsible for entire farms; less experienced men are able to work in forests or to labor on large farms. An all-Indian CCC force works in cooperation with the Forest Service. In the meantime roads and schools are being built in areas where farms, although productive, were submarginal because of their isolation.

White owners in the resettlement area were transferred to other farming areas, usually the Thief River Falls region *(see above).* Owners of the more productive lands sold their farms readily, most of them acquiring land in less isolated areas.

Rehabilitation of the Indians who will make use of this area has already begun on a 640-acre tract at the reservation headquarters. Three hundred and thirty acres have been divided into 6-acre plots, upon which one- or two-story shingle or clapboard houses have been built. Of the 216 persons engaged in the construction of these homes and their surrounding farm buildings, all but 10 were Indians.

All of the reservation Indians originally came from various parts of northern Minnesota and from three principal bands: the Mississippi Band, from Crow Wing and Gull Lake; the Pembina Band, from the upper Red River Valley; and the Otter Tail Pillagers, from Otter Tail Lake. All three groups are of the Algonkian stock. The number of full-blooded Indians has decreased alarmingly, and intermarriage threatens to obliterate the distinctive language, culture, and traditions of the Chippewa civilization.

A well-equipped HOSPITAL, operated at the White Earth Agency with Chippewa funds, serves the Indians as efficiently as their distrust of the white man's medicine will permit. Many of the older generation still refuse to reveal intimate problems to strangers.

The native Chippewa shelter is a birchbark wigwam, constructed on a framework of poles to form a domed top. The tepee is rarely seen. These wigwams, however, are used only in summer during the wildrice harvesting. When the weather turns cold, most of the Indians move to small log cabins or tar-papered board shacks.

The Chippewa handiwork is of excellent quality. Their products of tanned buckskin are soft and pliable with a chamois-like texture and a rich, dark brown color that is obtained by a smoking process. The odor of Chippewa leather products, pungent but agreeable, is a distinctive feature of the beaded moccasins, the much-sought buckskin jackets, and other garments. Probably the finest examples of Chippewa workmanship are their birchbark canoes, now, however, rarely made. They are remarkably seaworthy and their lightness is an important feature on long-portage journeys.

St. Benedict's Mission, adjacent to the village of White Earth, one of the finest schools in the Indian Service, was established in 1868 by Archbishop John Ireland, at that time a young Army chaplain. The mission was first composed of log buildings, constructed by the Indians to serve as schools and churches. At the same time the site of the present Calvary Cemetery, where Chief White Cloud is buried, was marked. In 1881 two brick-veneered structures, which now serve as the church and rectory, were erected on the wooded shore of Mission Lake. Supplementing the day school, an orphanage for 30 children was opened in connection with the mission. In 1892 the school was further enlarged by means of a grant from the Federal Government. This provided for 100 more children, allotting $100 a year from the Indian Tribal Education Fund for each child. Preference is given to orphans, children from broken homes, or those who are not conveniently near a day school. St. Benedict's farm of 150 acres, with a garden and an orchard, produces most of the required food. This mission represents the first religious and educational effort to benefit the Indians in the surrounding region.

The Chippewa hold an annual festival in White Earth Village *(June 14)* in commemoration of the arrival of their first band of 150 at the reservation in 1868. The program is of unusual interest to visitors, for it includes public councils, or pow-wows, in formal tribal costumes, with speeches, songs, several types of native dances, a sham battle between the Chippewa and Sioux, canoe, foot, and pony races that display the Indians' remarkable athletic ability, and many games, including lacrosse.

DETROIT LAKES, 200.6 *m.* (1,301 alt., 3,675 pop.) *(see Tour 16),* is at the junction with US 10 *(see Tour 16).*

Section b. DETROIT LAKES *to the* IOWA LINE, *267.9 m.* US 59.

Southwest of Detroit Lakes US 59 runs through an area of many lakes.

A group of 28 Indian Mounds, 14.4 *m.,* is between PELICAN LAKE (R) and LIZZIE LAKE (L); the largest of these mounds is 68 feet long and 9 feet wide.

At about 21.4 *m.* on US 59, while the highway was being constructed in 1932, was found a prehistoric skeleton that is estimated by some anthropologists to be at least 20,000 years old. It was found 20 feet below the surface in an ancient lake bed that probably existed before the last glacial period. The skeleton, now called the "Minnesota Man," is actually that of a young girl of about 16. A small dagger, fashioned from the antler of some animal, lay beside her. It is believed that the girl met death by drowning *(see FIRST AMERICANS: Archeology).*

PELICAN RAPIDS, 24.7 *m.* (1,302 alt., 1,365 pop.), is a prosperous town on the Pelican River, surrounded by numerous lakes and resorts. As a shipping point for grain and livestock, the community serves a wide trade area.

At 41.3 *m.* is the junction (R) with US 52 *(see Tour 9);* between this point and 53.8 *m.* US 59 and US 52 are united *(see Tour 9).*

FERGUS FALLS, 46.4 *m.* (1,196 alt., 9,389 pop.) *(see Tour 9).*

ELBOW LAKE, 68.6 *m.* (1,199 alt., 903 pop.), in the center of a substantial farming region, began with a courthouse around which the village grew. A plebiscite, won under dubious circumstances, transferred the county seat to a neighboring town, whose citizens seized the county records and carried them to their new courthouse. The voting fraud was exposed, however, and a judgment was returned in favor of Elbow Lake, whereupon a posse of its citizens made a night raid and recaptured the official records, thus ending the dispute.

Elbow Lake *(9-hole golf course, tennis courts)* has a fine MUNICIPAL AUDITORIUM and LIBRARY, erected in 1934. In winter nearby hills provide runways for skiing, and skating rinks are cleared on some of the lakes. The village maintains a neat, quiet TOURIST CAMP *(stoves, fuel, good water; free)*.

South of Elbow Lake US 59 traverses the beautiful Pomme de Terre Lake country and then crosses an ancient glacial moraine, an area of rugged hills and winding valleys.

At 82.3 *m.* is the junction with State 27.

Right on State 27 to HERMAN, 12 *m.* (1,172 alt., 518 pop.), chosen in 1914 because of its civic merit as the model town in Minnesota. One of the oldest towns in the county, Herman was first settled in 1871. Several lakes in the vicinity afford excellent wild-fowl shooting.

This town is near the margin of prehistoric glacial Lake Agassiz, which is believed to have covered 5,000 square miles. Its gravelly ridge, known to geologists as Herman Beach, is clearly defined *(see NATURAL SETTING: Geology)*.

In 1926 a mastodon tooth 10½ inches long was unearthed in a gravel pit near Herman. It is one of the upper molars of the prehistoric animal.

MORRIS, 99.8 *m.* (1,140 alt., 2,474 pop.), is the seat of Stevens County. The WEST CENTRAL AGRICULTURAL COLLEGE, at the southeastern boundary of the city, was originally an Indian mission school operated by Roman Catholic nuns. Under the supervision and jurisdiction of the Federal Government, it has gradually evolved to its present status. On the campus are 14 buildings, including administrative offices, dormitories and classrooms, an experimental station, a weather station, and farm buildings.

The NATIONAL GUARD ARMORY has a display of WAR RELICS *(open to public)* from the Civil, Spanish-American, and World Wars. This collection is said to be one of the best in Minnesota.

In the surrounding lakes fishing and wild-fowl shooting are excellent; pheasants are particularly abundant.

At 120 *m.* is the junction with US 12 *(see Tour 10)*.

APPLETON, 127.3 *m.* (1,040 alt., 1,625 pop.), a former Indian camp site, is on the Pomme de Terre River, named for an edible root with "eyes" like a potato, which was used by the Indians for food.

The OTTER TAIL POWER PLANT on the river serves a large district and has two 1,760-horsepower Diesel engines. The thoroughly modern local FLOUR MILL *(visitors welcome)*, on the river bank at the north end of Main St., has a capacity of 180,000 bushels. It has an output of 1,000 barrels of flour in 24 hours.

A large GRAVEL PIT at the northwestern outskirts of the city is owned by the Chicago, Milwaukee, St. Paul and Pacific R.R. and the State Highway Department.

Appleton has one of the finest modern MUNICIPAL WELLS and PUMP STATIONS in the State. Pure water is pumped into the 100,000-gallon tank from a depth of 180 feet at the rate of 500 gallons a minute.

A large ARMORY, the home of a machine-gun unit of the 135th Infantry, is in the center of the town; the 135th is a direct successor of the old First Minnesota, one of the first regiments offered to President Lincoln at the beginning of the Civil War.

Bordering the river in the northeastern section of Appleton is a beautiful park, formerly a slum district. It was recently laid out and constructed as part of a Federal relief program that also beautified US 59 along its route through the city.

The PUBLIC LIBRARY on Main St. *(open Mon., Wed., and Sat. afternoons and evenings)* contains 8,000 volumes.

The APPLETON GOLF CLUB is a rolling 9-hole course. The city also has two fine TENNIS COURTS and a BATHING BEACH with a lifeguard and instructor.

Between Appleton and Montevideo US 59 parallels the Minnesota River; at one point the river broadens to form the elongated Lac qui Parle Lake.

Whether the town of MILAN, 136.7 *m.* (1,010 alt., 548 pop.), 95 per cent of whose citizens are Norwegian, was named for the Italian city, is not known. An unusual gala event, the Lefse Fete, is held in Milan in August. On the second day of the fete, Norwegian potato flatcakes, called "lefse," and coffee are served free of charge.

At 145.7 *m.* on US 59 is the junction with a graveled road.

Right on this road to CHIPPEWA LAC QUI PARLE STATE PARK *(picnic grounds)*, 2.8 *m.* This 17-acre tract along the Minnesota River includes the site of one of the earliest Protestant Indian missions in Minnesota, established in 1835. It manufactured the first cloth in the State, but was burned in 1854.

Joseph Renville (1779–1846), a picturesque *coureur de bois* who had been a captain with the British forces in the War of 1812, erected a stockade overlooking the foot of Lac qui Parle Lake shortly after 1826. Here he lived on a feudal scale with many retainers about him. The Rev. Thomas S. Williamson (1800–1879) established a mission in this stockade in 1835. With the assistance of Renville and the Rev. Gideon H. Pond, he here translated the Gospels and several hymns into the Dakota language, using a phonetic system based upon an adaptation of the English alphabet devised by Gideon H. and Samuel W. Pond. Here, with the assistance of Williamson and the Ponds, the Rev. Stephen R. Riggs (1812–1883) compiled the first grammar and dictionary of the Dakota language, published by the Smithsonian Institution in 1852. The site of the mission is indicated by a marker overlooking the picnic grounds. The exact site of the stockade is unknown.

The 300-foot DAM at this site is a unit in one of the major water-conservation programs carried out by Federal aid in Minnesota. The dam not only controls the flow from Lac qui Parle Lake into the Minnesota River, but also impounds waters of the Lac qui Parle River. Diversion of the Chippewa River, approximately 4 miles directly east, further augments Lac qui Parle Lake. Dam construction backs up high waters of the Chippewa River through Watson Sag into the lake, raising its level about 10 feet and flooding much of the Minnesota River Valley floor. Approximately 17 miles above the Lac qui Parle dam is the confluence of the Pomme de

Terre River with the Minnesota River. Here another dam, 112 feet long, creates Marsh Lake by water covering the Minnesota River bottoms. This lake is expected to have an average depth of 6 feet and to prove valuable as a nesting area for water-fowl.

MONTEVIDEO, 153 m. (922 alt., 4,319 pop.) *(see Tour 11)*, is at the junction with US 212 *(see Tour 11)*.

MARSHALL, 191.5 m. (1,165 alt., 3,250 pop.), seat of Lyon County, on a branch of the Redwood River and in country studded with lakes, streams, and waterfalls, is the center of a prosperous farming district.

Marshall has a roller mill, three hatcheries, a produce plant and creamery, a wholesale fruit company, a large wholesale grocery company, and several smaller industries.

The Minnesota Highway Department has district headquarters and shops near the courthouse. A fine modern high school was erected in 1932, and there is also a parochial school.

The AMERICAN LEGION FIELD has a swimming pool, tennis courts, a baseball diamond and other recreational facilities. The local GOLF COURSE *(nominal fee)* has 9 holes.

An annual Zinnia Day exhibit is held in July.

Right from Marshall on State 39 to CAMDEN STATE PARK, 8.8 m. *(shelter, refectory, bathing pool)*, consisting of 469 acres of wooded valley along the Redwood River, an otherwise sparsely timbered country. Hiking trails wind through the densely wooded areas and along the crest above the valley, affording exceptional views.

At 207.6 m. is the junction with US 14 *(see Tour 12)*.

At 219.7 m. is the junction (L) with State 47, which is united with US 59 for 6 miles.

Left on State 47 to the junction with a graveled road, 6 m.; L. on this road to LAKE SHETEK STATE PARK, 10.5 m., 175 acres, on Lake Shetek, one of the largest lakes in southwestern Minnesota, on whose shores are three summer resorts. The site of the park was the scene of a massacre during the Sioux outbreak of 1862 *(see Tour 2: LOWER AGENCY)*; a monument commemorating the battle and an old LOG CABIN are here.

South of the junction with State 47, US 59 traverses a region of high, rolling prairie, well drained by rivers and streams.

SLAYTON, 225.7 m. (1,511 alt., 1,102 pop.), seat of Murray County has a municipal TOURIST CAMP *(free camping, running water)* beside the water tower.

AVOCA, 231.9 m. (285 pop.), founded in 1878 by Roman Catholics, was named for a river in Ireland.

FULDA, 239.8 m. (1,532 alt., 818 pop.), in an excellent farming territory, is predominantly German, and was named for the ancient city in central Europe. The coming of the railroad and the settlement in the early 1870's by Bishop Ireland's colonists started the growth and development of this community.

A co-operative creamery producing butter, cheese, and related products, and a co-operative oil company for petroleum products distribution, are in Fulda *(visitors welcome at both plants)*.

Fulda has a Tourist Camp *(9-hole golf course)*. There are two LAKES *(swimming, fishing)* within the village limits.

South of Fulda the gently undulating prairie land is excellent farming country. Black loam with clay subsoil predominates, and there are very few outcroppings of rock.

WORTHINGTON, 257.3 *m.* (1,585 alt., 3,475 pop.) *(see Tour 13)*, is at the junction with US 16 *(see Tour 13)*.

At 267.9 *m.* US 59 crosses the Iowa Line, 65 miles north of Cherokee, Iowa *(see Iowa, Tour 8)*.

◄◄◄◄◄◄◄◄◄◄◄◄◄◄◄◄◄✿►►►►►►►►►►►►►►►►►►►►►►→

Tour 18

(Ellsworth, Wis.)—Red Wing—Lake City—Zumbro Falls—Rochester—Spring Valley—(Waterloo, Iowa); US 63.
Wisconsin Line to Iowa Line, 93 m.

The Chicago, Milwaukee, St. Paul & Pacific R.R. parallels the highway between Red Wing and Lake City; the Chicago Great Western R.R. between Rochester and Iowa Line.
Roadbed paved between Red Wing and Lake City, graveled between Lake City and Rochester, and paved between Rochester and the Iowa Line. Open all year.
Usual accommodations.

This north-south route through southeastern Minnesota traverses a productive dairy and farming section that has very few lakes but many streams flowing through deep-wooded valleys.

US 63 crosses the Mississippi at Red Wing on a free bridge, 15 miles south of Ellsworth, Wis. *(see Wisconsin, Tour 9)*.

At RED WING, 0.2 *m.* (712 alt., 9,629 pop.) *(see Tour 1)* is the junction (R) with US 61 *(see Tour 1)*. Between Red Wing and Lake City US 63 and US 61 are united *(see Tour 1)*.

LAKE CITY, 17.5 *m.* (713 alt., 3,210 pop.) *(see Tour 1)*, is at the junction (L) with US 61 *(see Tour 1)*.

Southwest of Lake City US 63 crosses a region where the hills (R) are capped with wind-blown dust called loess. This fine soil that absorbs water slowly is readily eroded into deep ravines; thus it needs careful manipulation to prevent its being washed away. The road ascends a river valley whose limestone walls are a mass of sumac and grapevine, and whose bluffs are tunnelled with the nests of swallows. At 22 *m.* the valley narrows until only an attenuated patch of corn interrupts the extent of brush in the ravine. Farther on there is an occasional glimpse from a hilltop of the flat upland.

ZUMBRO FALLS, 32.6 *m.* (836 alt., 186 pop.), is a railway village at the falls of the Zumbro River, whose name is a corruption of Riviere des Embarras, meaning *river of difficulties;* the name was chosen by the French settlers because of the quantity of driftwood in the stream. When the English came to the region and questioned the Indians as to the river's name, they entered it in their journals as Zumbro—the closest phonetic spelling of the Indians' French at which they could arrive. The broad expanding branches and short trunk of the Zumbro were called by the Dakota Indians the "Wasi Oju," or *the place of the pine tree.* Today only a few white pines are found on islands and in sheltered places on its higher tributaries.

At 37 *m.* is a junction with a graveled road.

Right on this road across a bridge at 0.4 *m.* and along the river to the ZUMBRO HYDROELECTRIC DAM, 3 *m.,* a part of the Rochester municipal light and power system. A small park has been built on the shores of the 14-mile-long artificial lake.

The route between Zumbro Falls and Rochester passes between fields of corn, grain, and occasional acres of peas. Pea-vining machines are at several places along the road, but are in operation only a short time in early summer.

ROCHESTER, 52.7 *m.* (988 alt., 20,261 pop.) *(see ROCHESTER).*

Points of Interest. Mayo Clinic, Mayo Park and Pioneer Log Cabin, Soldiers' Memorial Field, Reid-Murdock Pea Cannery.

Rochester is at the junctions with US 14 *(see Tour 12)* and US 52 *(see Tour 9).*

STEWARTVILLE, 64.4 *m.* (1,240 alt., 793 pop.), on the banks of the Root River, was named for Charles N. Stewart, who established a mill here in 1858. At this point the Root River flows through a valley 100 feet below the plain. Although the valley is beautifully wooded, the vegetation is definitely prairie-like.

At 65.4 *m.* is the junction with an improved road.

Right on this road to the SITE OF HIGH FOREST, 2 *m.,* once a thriving village. Today it is marked only by a FLAGSTAFF carrying a banner presented to the community after the Civil War by Rear Admiral Andrew Hull Foote (1806–1863), who was an opponent of the slave trade and such an ardent temperance reformer that he is credited with abolishing the alcohol ration in the Navy. The significance of this flag is not known, but presumably it honored the war heroes of this town.

South of Stewartville are many streams, fed by countless springs that rise in rocky dells.

RACINE (Fr., *root*), 70.1 *m.* (1,296 alt., 275 pop.), is named for Root River nearby.

South of Racine the topography is gently undulating and is covered with the gray drift characteristic of this region. The soil is fertile, clayey loam, merging with the loess-covered area of the extreme southeast. The limestone underlying the glaciated cover soil is visible along the partially wooded ravines.

US 63 crosses Bear Creek at 72.3 *m.* and Deer Creek at 74.4 *m.,* both tributaries of the Root River.

At 74.6 *m.* is the junction with US 16 *(see Tour 13)*. Between this point and SPRING VALLEY, 79.6 *m.* (1,317 alt., 1,712 pop.), US 63 and US 16 are one route.

Here the limestone is only thinly covered by soil; sink holes, remnants of preglacial valleys, are common. Many surface streams disappear into these holes and form fantastic caverns.

At 84.8 *m.* is the junction with an improved road.

Right on this road to OSTRANDER, 1.5 *m.* (151 pop.), settled by Norwegians in 1854. Cultivation of flax and timothy, which replaced the wheat and oat crops destroyed by chinchbugs many years ago, has been very successful.

The first church in this vicinity, built in 1867, has been remodeled and enlarged and still stands in the village. When first built, it had only a part-time pastor, Dr. Koren of Decorah, Iowa. The building was of logs that had to be hauled many miles from the deep timber, and the frame, hewn with a broadax, was sided and shingled. The interior was left unfinished for many years.

At 93 *m.* US 63 crosses the Iowa Line, 74 miles north of Waterloo, Iowa *(see Iowa, Tour 3)*.

◄◄◄◄◄◄◄◄◄◄◄◄◄◄◄◄◄◄◄◄◄❁►►►►►►►►►►►►►►►►►►►►►►

Tour 19

(St. Croix Falls, Wis.)—Taylors Falls—Center City—Forest Lake—Minneapolis; US 8.
Wisconsin Line to Minneapolis, 53.5 m.

The Northern Pacific Ry. parallels the route between Taylors Falls and Forest Lake. Paved roadbed. Open all year.
Usual hotel and tourist-camp accommodations.

This route crosses the deep, narrow, rock gorge of the St. Croix River, winds around the high bluffs directly west of Taylors Falls, enters the popular resort region of the Chisago Lakes, and, traversing fine farming lands, passes west of the Centerville chain of lakes just north of Minneapolis.

US 8 crosses the ST. CROIX RIVER, that forms part of the boundary between Wisconsin and Minnesota, on a free bridge from St. Croix Falls, Wis. *(see Wisconsin, Tour 16)*.

TAYLORS FALLS, 0 *m.* (795 alt., 527 pop.) *(launch trips in summer)*, was named for Jesse Taylor, who came here in 1838 to establish timber claims. First called Taylor's Place and later Taylors Falls (the apostrophe was removed by legislative act), this town is in an area of special interest to geologists.

In INTERSTATE PARK (L), which extends along both sides of the river, are the DALLES OF THE ST. CROIX—examples of the eroding power of ice and rock-filled streams on the basaltic lava flows that covered the Cambrian rocks and blocked the river course before glacial floods cut the gorge.

The formation is porphyritic trap, an igneous rock forced upward, while still in a fluid state, through crevices in the earth's crust. When it cooled, the rock solidified. The rocky ledges are crowned with pine trees and a dense undergrowth of bushes and vines. The rocks are mostly gray in color but occasionally reveal patches of brilliant red, yellow, and green.

Interesting to layman and geologist alike are the POT HOLES, varying in diameter from a few inches to 30 feet. Outjutting formations have been given descriptive names: the Devil's Chair is 80 feet high; nearby is a smaller rock called the Devil's Pulpit; on the Wisconsin side stands the Old Man of the River.

The name Dalles (Fr. *flagstone* or *slab of rock*) was given by the early French *voyageurs* to the rock-walled gorge, but is also used as a descriptive term for several other river ledges. Du Luth descended the river about 1680, and later Frenchmen are believed to have built a fort on the lowlands at the foot of the dalles. In the 19th century lumbermen found the territory in the possession of Chippewa Indians.

Legends recount bloody battles between the Sioux and Chippewa in this area. The Chippewa are said to have once tumbled huge boulders off LOOKOUT MOUNTAIN (opposite the present boat landing) upon the attacking Sioux, who came up the river in canoes. Because of these conflicts the valley was known to the Indians as the "Valley of Bones."

The St. Croix River, connected by portage from its upper waters with a stream draining into Lake Superior, was once the line of communication between the Mississippi and the Great Lakes. In those days a busy transportation waterway for timber and furs, the St. Croix is now a quiet stream, beloved by fishermen, canoeists, and summer residents, whose cabins are hidden by the trees that line its banks. So swift is the river's current in this upper stretch that one can drift in a canoe the 30 miles from the falls to Stillwater in a day.

Both the upper dalles at Taylors Falls and the lower dalles, 2 miles farther down the river, rise in almost perpendicular palisades above the rushing stream. The broad outer valley wall is more than 200 feet high; the downcutting stream flows in a narrowed but much sharper channel.

The first steamer to navigate the St. Croix River was the *Palmyra,* about 1838. It came from St. Louis loaded with sawmill equipment and a crew of 36 mill hands, and docked at St. Croix Falls, but its arrival so excited the Indians that the venture nearly came to grief. When the little sternwheeler reached the head of navigation at the dalles, the bluffs were crowded with Chippewa tribesmen who watched with awe as it was eased up to the bank. The Indians danced and screamed, working themselves into a frenzy; suddenly one of them accidentally dislodged a rock that went rolling down the bank. The suggestion of this act moved his fellows to a concerted attack, and in no time boulders were hurtling down the cliffs, and the steamer was in grave danger of complete destruction. In this emergency the *Palymyra's* captain pulled the whistle open, and the engineer loosed a roaring cloud of steam which so terrified the Indians that they fled pell-mell into the woods, not to return for days.

One of the large houses remaining from the lumber-boom era of the St. Croix Valley is the RESIDENCE OF WILLIAM H. C. FOLSOM at Taylors Falls, which was built of locally sawed lumber in 1854 by Folsom and carpenters from Maine. There have been no alterations of any consequence since the house was built; it is still occupied by descendants of the first owner.

The plan was derived from the New England central-hall type, with a parlor and sittingroom to the L. of the entrance and a diningroom to the R. At the left side of the house is a pedimented portico, two stories in height. While the general appearance suggests the Georgian Colonial style, the trim and detail of windows are typically Greek Revival. A well-proportioned full cornice is carried completely around the house, forming pediments at the gable ends. The detail is freely executed; the graceful curves of the classic moldings are here reduced to flat-sided sections—perhaps due to the lack of proper tools for shaping. The double-hung windows, which have the customary shutters, are divided into 12 panes to each sash. The long windows on the porch that have a Greek enframement are slightly tapered at the sides.

The buildings surrounding the old house form a typical New England farm group. The stable, wagon shed, wellhouse, and outbuildings fit perfectly into the picture of what Seymour in his *Sketches of Minnesota* called the "New England of the West."

Taylors Falls marks the southern limits of the white-pine area, except for isolated groves that have survived along the streams feeding the St. Croix and Mississippi.

Thick grass covers part of the lower islands of the St. Croix, but in the spring they are submerged by the swollen river and become catch-alls for a tangled mass of floating trees and driftwood.

Near Taylors Falls in the St. Croix Valley wild flowers, trees, and shrubs abound. Pine, spruce, balsam, and juniper are found throughout the region; hardwoods that ordinarily thrive farther south grow in these sheltered valleys. The rare moccasin-flower *(picking prohibited by State law)*, State flower of Minnesota, is occasionally found along the banks of the river, rooted in shallow pockets between rocks that are covered with pine needles and leaf mold. This wild orchid, *Cypripedium reginae*, commonly called the Indian-shoe or ladyslipper because of its shape, blooms from May to July.

US 8 climbs the steep hill at the base of which the village lies, revealing a beautiful view of the river and its small wooded islands, and follows the valley past a TOURIST CAMP, 1.2 *m.* (L), and around high rocky cliffs.

At 3.1 *m.* is the junction with State 95, a surfaced road known as the St. Croix Scenic Highway.

Left on State 95 to the junction with a dirt road at 0.8 *m.;* L. on this road through a narrow wooded ravine to the deserted village of FRANCONIA, 0.9 *m.* Ansel Smith, first settler, came in 1852 and named the town for his former home in the White Mountains of New Hampshire. The first white pine logged on the St.

Croix was cut here, made into rafts, and towed down the river. By 1890 the town had a population of 252, and was growing, but with the passing of lumbering its residents left. Today many of its cottages stand vacant, and the river flat where logs were rafted is frequented by stray sheep and goats. A footpath (L) follows the river's edge to the rocky dalles a half mile upstream. Winding south along the upper level of the St. Croix River Valley and spanning several small creeks, State 95 is fringed with woods of maple, oak, willow, and sumac, or bordered with fields of wheat, corn, and alfalfa. The well-kept farms are hedged with windbreaks of evergreen, oak, and maple.

At 14.5 m.. is MARINE-ON-ST. CROIX (927 alt., 297 pop.), formerly Marine Mills. This is the second oldest town in the State, and, since Minnesota's first settlement (Mendota) was founded by Government-employed persons, Marine is actually the oldest civilian settlement. The first white men here were Lewis S. Judd and David Hone who, on May 8, 1838, came up the St. Croix from the Mississippi on the steamer *Palmyra* and founded the Marine Lumber Company. They named the settlement for a village in Illinois that had been founded by several sea captains from the East. The first mill started operations in 1839. Only a small water-power mill, it nevertheless ran for 50 years during which it sawed 197,000,000 board feet of lumber. A flour mill and two hotels were erected soon after lumbering was established, and the town was early the scene of bustling activity. The hotel register of the old Marine House has been preserved and contains the signatures of many distinguished visitors, among them Ulysses S. Grant and John Jacob Astor. Celebration of the town's centennial starting June 11, 1938, and continuing throughout the 4 following months.

Today the tree-shaded village has a quiet charm beloved alike by the descendants of its pioneers and by the group of city folk who have built homes along the river bank. One block north of the center of the village are TWO HOUSES (R) in New England style, built in the early days by lumber magnates, and now all but hidden from view by trees and shrubs. Both are white frame Colonial structures with green shutters; one is topped with a cupola.

The MEETING HOUSE AND JAIL in Marine was built in 1872 to serve a dual purpose during the rowdy days of lumbering on the St. Croix. The work was done by Gust Carlson, builder, who undoubtedly was the architect as well. It is a rectangular structure about 44 feet long and 26 feet wide, of local limestone. The doors and windows are designed with segmental heads and protected by batten shutters. The masonry walls, formed of rough-faced stone (ashlar), are accented at the corners by bevel-edged quoins. The interior is of plaster, with a wooden wainscot and molding profiles that still retain their classic character—though the features of the structure are wholly Victorian Romanesque.

At the foot of a winding, marked, dirt road leading from the center of the village is the TOLL FERRY *(35¢ one way, 50¢ round trip, for cars; 5¢ one way for pedestrians)*, which crosses the river from Marine to Wisconsin.

State 95 continues south, skirting the St. Croix, cutting back occasionally into the fields of grain and corn. Here and there wooded hills cut off the river view. At 23.4 m. is the ST. CROIX BOOM-SITE MARKER (L), noting that at this point the millions of logs cut along the upper St. Croix and its tributaries were stopped, sorted, rafted, and then floated down to the sawmills.

At 25 m. the road follows the steep bluffs, in the walls of which are numerous caves used by nearby residents for storage purposes.

At 25.6 m. is the INDIAN BATTLEGROUND MARKER (R) opposite the old State prison ravine, where a bloody skirmish took place July 3, 1839. A Chippewa band, en route from Fort Snelling to its home hunting grounds, camped at "battle hollow," and at dawn were attacked by a Sioux war party; Chippewa dead totaled 50. Across the road is the old FOUNDRY.

STILLWATER, 26.4 m. (688 alt., 7,173 pop.), is the site of a tamarack cabin plastered with mud, built in 1839 by Joseph Renshaw Brown, who was influential in the early history of the State. Local historians agree that the cabin was near the present railroad viaduct crossing at the north end of town, near Brown Creek. The Wisconsin Territorial Assembly in 1840 placed the county seat on "Joe Brown's claim" at the head of Lake St. Croix. In 1844 the town of Stillwater was incorporated. Four years later a convention held here undertook the organization of Minnesota as a Territory *(see HISTORICAL SURVEY)*.

The present town has a well-planned system of parks, playgrounds, and boulevards. Its river bank has been landscaped and converted into a public park. Stillwater also has a municipal 9-hole golf course.

Included in the town's educational facilities, which are used by a large portion of the population, is the CARNEGIE PUBLIC LIBRARY. On exhibit in the library is a bottle of wine over 50 years old, and the minutes of the annual meetings of a veterans' organization, the Last Man's Club of Company B, First Minnesota Volunteer Infantry, formed here on July 1, 1884, by 34 veterans of the Civil War. At that time they set aside the bottle of wine, to be drunk by the last surviving member of the club. This proved to be Charles Lockwood, but he never drank the wine, because of its sentimental associations with his dead comrades. Lockwood died in 1935.

In the auditorium of the HIGH SCHOOL, corner of 3rd and Pine Sts., is a MURAL painted in fresco-secco by Miriam Ibling of the Federal Art Project. Entitled *Youth and the Modern World,* the mural symbolizes the development of the knowledge of science and the arts, and the growth of the community.

Stillwater was formerly the center of the logging industry that began in 1836 when the first timber was cut with the permission of the Chippewa Indians but not of the Federal Government. In 1837, after a formal treaty had been made with the Chippewa, large-scale operations were started that antedated commercial cutting on the Mississippi and Rum Rivers by about 10 years. The first commercial sawmill was built on the St. Croix some distance above Stillwater, and soon thousands of logs were floating down the river to finishing mills at points along the Mississippi as far south as St. Louis.

The rafts, of 8 to 10 strings of logs tied together and steered by a long sweep at each end, are said to have been inspired by an accident. When a boom at one of the mills broke and released hundreds of logs, the men sent along the banks to guide the escaped logs to their destination, found they could successfully ride several that were impacted and direct them with their poles. Thence the idea of a raft. Rafting was always a hazardous and laborious occupation. The river was uncharted, the rafts were unwieldy, and Lakes St. Croix and Pepin, on the route, were subject to sudden and dangerous squalls. But the pilots were expert, fearless, and proud of their ability. Raft pilots received from $300 to $500 a month, a wage that allowed them to dress for ceremonial occasions in French calf boots, black cassimere trousers, red flannel shirts, flowing black silk neckties, wide-brimmed felt hats, and, for lady visitors, white kid gloves.

Perhaps the most famous raftsman on the upper Mississippi was Capt. Stephen B. Hanks, a cousin of Abraham Lincoln, who in 1843 took the first raft of logs from the St. Croix to St. Louis. Hanks, a familiar figure in Mississippi towns, became almost a legendary figure when in 1857 he won the $1,000 prize for the first boat to reach St. Paul and open the navigation season. Twenty boats starting from Galena competed in the race. Several were crushed and sunk, trapped by shifting ice floes on Lake Pepin; but Hanks, guiding his vessel through the narrow path of open water between the ice pack and the shore, outdistanced his rivals, and drew up at St. Paul's landing to be greeted by wild plaudits from the cheering city.

Stillwater, like other little river towns, received a generous share of the lumbermen's wages. Food, drink, and entertainment brought extravagant prices. Many tales are told of Stillwater in these lumberjack days. One relates that in the spring of 1886 the completion of a log drive coincided with the opening of a district court, an event that drew all the prominent lawyers from the surrounding territory on both sides of the river. The lawyers came first and reserved every bed at the Sawyer House before the lumberjacks arrived. Infuriated at finding no beds available, the loggers, led by a giant Scandinavian, yanked the astonished barristers from their beds and drove them, clad in their nightshirts, into the barroom, where the frightened lawyers were set on the 50-foot bar and nailed down by the tails of their old-fashioned nightshirts. Thus pinioned they were commanded, when the foreman fired his gun, to leap to the floor 5 feet below. If they negotiated the distance awkwardly, they were ordered to buy drinks for the company. The lumbermen were severe critics but finally permitted the half-frozen lawyers to consume a few drinks also, and the revelry lasted into the early morning. The Lumberjack Festival, held here annually in September or October, recalls this vanished industry with costume parades and log-rollings.

At Stillwater a free bridge connects State 95 with Wisconsin 35 *(see Wisconsin, Tour 12)*.

South of Stillwater State 95 follows the shore line of LAKE ST. CROIX *(small-mouth bass fly-fishing)*; the river here has widened and taken on the characteristics of a lake.

At BAYPORT, 28.9 *m.* (688 alt., 2,590 pop.), is the MINNESOTA STATE PRISON *(open daily at 10:30 and 2:30 except Sun.; adm. 25¢)*. The prison includes 22 enclosed acres and a farm of 1,000 acres west and south of the walls. Farm machinery and twine are manufactured here and sold in the open market. The industry is managed so efficiently that the prison is self-supporting. All net profit accrues to the State treasury. The larger tower inside the walls is the reservoir for the water supply.

There is a large sash and door factory in Bayport; the brick smokestacks along the river mark former mills.

South of Bayport State 95 follows the old Point Douglas Rd., constructed by U. S. Army engineers in 1851; this was the first improved road in Minnesota. Paralleling Lake St. Croix the highway offers a fine panorama of the mile-wide lake, with its unusually clear water and sandy beaches. Across the lake the bluffs rise precipitously. Resorts and summer homes are numerous along the shore; some of the finer estates have hanging gardens built on terraces. Old, nearly submerged floating logs, called deadheads, remnants of lumbering days, are frequent in the water.

Here the vegetation typical of the far north country is intermixed with the trees and shrubs usually found in the middle western States. Pine, spruce, and balsam are interspersed with the hardwoods. Second-growth timber and eroded hillsides are sad reminders of the days when dense forests covered the valley and the St. Croix was one of the leading lumbering centers of the United States.

Large game animals are now extremely rare in this area; deer and bear are never seen. There are very few foxes, but game birds and small animals are still common.

The scenic highway continues southward to AFTON, 37.6 *m. (see Tour 10)*.

At CENTER CITY, 9.8 *m.* (929 alt., 285 pop.), on CHISAGO LAKES, more than 8,000 Scandinavians from the surrounding country in 1929 celebrated the 75th anniversary of the founding of the village.

Swedish families of the area also celebrate the Midsummer-Day Festival on June 24 and 25 of each year. During this period, according to an old Swedish belief, young girls who pick the solitary blooms from nine different flowers and proceed home without being distracted from their paths, will be able to vision their future husbands when they press the flowers beneath their pillows at night. Very few of the present generation seek this nocturnal revelation, however. The church is the center of this festival, which in Sweden marks the beginning of summer.

LINDSTROM, 11.5 *m.* (561 pop.), is the largest of the three Swedish villages on the Chisago Lakes.

The region around CHISAGO CITY, 14.4 *m.* (945 alt., 416 pop.), is well known for its summer resorts and excellent fishing.

Chisago City, Center City, and Lindstrom were the center of Swedish culture and religion in Minnesota. Settlement of the region began in 1850 at the invitation of the surveyor, Norberg. Many families left Sweden in 1851 to follow the first settlers who came here from Illinois and St. Louis, but the cholera epidemic of 1853–54 brought death to many before they could reach their destination, and to others in the new land who were infected by the survivors. The remaining settlers determined to strengthen the Swedish Lutheran Church, hoping it would keep them together. Although the first service was held in 1851, it was not until Dr. Carlson (who had come from Scandinavia to fill a Chicago pulpit) visited the Chisago colony that the church became a strong force in the vicinity. He organized the Minnesota Conference of the Swedish Lutheran Church on May 12, 1854, with approximately 100 members. The site of the barn in which the meeting was held is a few yards east of the Chisago cemetery.

WYOMING, 21.4 m. (905 alt., 214 pop.) *(see Tour 1)*, is at the junction with US 61 *(see Tour 1)*. Between Wyoming and FOREST LAKE, 25.9 m. (937 alt., 916 pop.) *(see Tour 1)*, US 8 and US 61 are united. US 61 branches L. at 26.8 m.

At 44.5 m. on US 8 is the junction with US 10 *(see Tour 16)*.

At 45.2 m. is the junction with State 96.

Left from the junction on State 96 to TWIN OAK HILL FARM *(open to visitors till 9 p.m.)*, 4 m., the modern farm home of Louis W. Hill, son of the late James J. Hill. On this estate the railroad builder and pioneer is buried beside his wife. The farm contains modern scientific farming laboratories and equipment. A chalet of the Swiss type of architecture is on the premises.

NEW BRIGHTON, 46.5 m. (920 alt., 500 pop.), calls itself the squash center of Minnesota.

Left from New Brighton on the paved New Brighton Rd. to the second junction with County D, 2.3 m. L. to State 51, 2.8 m. on State 51 to the junction with a dirt road; L. on this road 2.3 m. to NAZARETH HALL, on a 90-acre tract at LAKE JOHANNA. The seminary was built in 1923 at an approximate cost of $500,000. The architecture, with the exception of the chapel, which is Romanesque, is similar to that found in Lombardy. The seminary is in six connected sections; especially beautiful is the reception room with its arched ceiling and tiled floor. Wine-red seats and benches of Roman design contrast vividly with the austere simplicity of the chapel. This educational center is financed by the Archbishop Ireland Educational Fund.

South of New Brighton on US 8 (New Brighton Blvd.), at 50.9 m., is the junction with Lowry Ave. in Minneapolis; R. on Lowry to Central Ave. NE.; L. on Central Ave.

MINNEAPOLIS, 53.5 m. (812 alt., 464,356 pop.) *(see MINNEAPOLIS)*.

Points of Interest. Minnehaha Falls, Chain of Lakes, University of Minnesota, flour mills at St. Anthony Falls.

Minneapolis is at the junction with US 169 *(see Tour 3)*, US 52 *(see Tour 9)*, US 12 *(see Tour 10)*, US 212 *(see Tour 11)*, and US 65 *(see Tour 14)*.

◄◄◄◄◄◄◄◄◄◄◄◄◄◄◄◄◄◄◄◄◄◄◄ ☒ ►►►►►►►►►►►►►►►►►►►►►►►

Tour 20

Bemidji—Cass Lake—Walker—Brainerd—Little Falls; US 371.
Bemidji to Little Falls, 133.4 m.

The route parallels the Great Northern and the Minneapolis, St. Paul & Sioux
Ste. Marie Rys. between Bemidji and Cass Lake; Great Northern Ry. between Cass
Lake and Walker; the Minnesota & International Ry. between Walker and Brainerd;
and the Northern Pacific Ry. between Brainerd and Little Falls.
Bituminous-treated roadbed between Bemidji and Brainerd, paved between Brainerd
and Little Falls. Open all year.
Usual accommodations.

This north-south route from Bemidji, near the western entrance to the
Chippewa National Forest, borders the western extremity of the Arrowhead region, touches Leech Lake, crosses the Paul Bunyan resort area, and
parallels the Mississippi through historic Indian country between Brainerd
and the industrial city of Little Falls.

BEMIDJI, 0 *m.* (1,351 alt., 7,202 pop.) *(see Tour 7)*, is at the junction with US 2 *(see Tour 7)* and US 71 *(see Tour 2)*. Between Bemidji
and Cass Lake *(see below)*, US 371 and US 2 are united.

CASS LAKE, 18.4 *m.* (1,323 alt., 1,409 pop.), was called "Ga-mi-
squawakokag sagaiigun" *(the place of red cedars)* by the Chippewa, because of the many cedars growing on an island in the adjacent lake of the
same name. It was renamed by the explorer, Schoolcraft, to commemorate
Lewis Cass, who led an expedition through the region in 1820.

David Thompson, surveyor and geographer, records that in 1798 there
was a fur-trading post here under John Sayer of the Northwest Company. On the lake shore Bishop Whipple, the first Episcopal bishop of
Minnesota, founded a mission (about 1860) for the Chippewa. It is said
that on the bishop's first visit to this wilderness he asked a chief whether
he might safely leave his valise for a time in the Indian village. "Oh, yes,"
replied the chief, "there is no other white man in this part of the country."

STAR ISLAND *(reached by motor launch)*, the largest island in Cass
Lake, was so named because of its shape. In 1832 it was mapped and described by Schoolcraft as Grand Island or Colcaspi, a name coined in honor
of three of its explorers, Pike, Cass, and Schoolcraft. The island was formerly the domain of Chief Yellow Head, who ruled a band of about 160
Indians. They lived along the shores of Windigo, a small lake 0.25 mile
long at the very center of the island, in the heart of a forest of virgin Norway pine, much of which still stands. Today Star Island is a summer resort. Its extensive sandy beaches are excellent for swimming and boating,
and the entire island has been kept in a primitive state by the summer residents whose cottages line the shores. It can be reached only by boat.

The shores of Cass Lake and the surrounding country to the north, south, and east are now included in the Chippewa National Forest *(see Tour 7)*.

The town has two nurseries: the LYDICK NURSERY, comprising about 75 acres, one of the largest in the State; and the CASS LAKE NURSERY, of about 10 acres, which supplies 64 million seedlings to the Chippewa Indian Agency, whose jurisdiction extends over the Chippewa (Ojibway) of Minnesota, and the reservations at White Earth, Mille Lacs, Leech Lake, Nett Lake, Grand Portage, and Cass Lake *(see FIRST AMERICANS: Indians)*. An annual Midwinter Indian Fair, with displays of Indian handicraft, is held here in late February or early March.

Industrial units in the town include a sawmill, a crating factory, and a pickle-salting station.

At NORWAY BEACH on Cass Lake is a PUBLIC CAMPGROUND *(fine swimming; tables, fireplaces, pumps)*.

At 24.4 *m.* US 371 skirts PIKE BAY, the southern portion of Cass Lake where the LAKE STATES FOREST EXPERIMENT STATION maintains an experimental forest for the intensive study of tree growth. OJIBWAY BEACH *(well-equipped public campground)* is on Pike Bay.

South of Pike Bay US 371 passes many small lakes and beautiful winding streams.

The little village of LEECH LAKE, 34 *m.* (1,333 alt., 20 pop.), and the adjacent lake were named for a huge leech that, according to legend, the Indians once beheld swimming in the water here. Leech Lake, the third largest in the State, is 40 miles across and has 640 miles of shore line; it is famous for its wall-eyed and great-northern pike, muskie, bass, and bluegill.

In the early days three distinct stream beds were traced at the bottom of the narrows (directly east of Leech Lake Station) by Capt. Nate Dally, who believed that the basin of Leech Lake once held six or seven separate lakes. As a glacial drainage stream, the Mississippi is thought to have flowed through this basin. The remains of an oak forest still existed in the white sand of the lake bottom until 1897, when the ice loosened the stumps and forced them to the shore.

The land surrounding Leech Lake is almost entirely cut over; its groves are of Norway and white pine with an intermixture of poplar and a few hardwoods.

Minnesota's most recent Indian battle took place in 1898 at Sugar Point on the east shore of Leech Lake. A United States marshal, who had been sent out to bring back an Indian named Bug-ah-na-ghe-shig to testify in a Federal case against illicit liquor dealers, met with resistance. "Bug" refused to go, saying that the previous year he had been taken to Duluth as a witness in a similar case and after testifying had been turned loose to walk home, a distance of over 100 miles.

The marshal immediately ordered the agency police to arrest the Indian, but 17 of his friends subsequently rescued him. Federal troops were then called out to take the whole group of Indians into custody. General Bacon, who had recently returned from service in Cuba, crossed the lake from Walker to Sugar Point with a detachment of the regular Army. When the soldiers landed, the Indians fired a volley and then shoved the boats from the beach as the detachment ran for cover. Major Wilkinson (1835–1898) and six privates were killed in the battle that followed, while the Indians, though subdued, registered no casualties.

At about 37 *m.* is KABEKONA BAY (R), an inlet of Leech Lake; here is a STATE CAMP concerned with highway development, which is under the supervision of the U.S. Department of the Interior.

WALKER, 39.4 *m.* (1,336 alt., 618 pop.), seat of Cass County, was named for Thomas Barlow Walker (1840–1928), pioneer lumberman and landowner in Minnesota. Coming to Minnesota in 1862, Walker was surveyor for sections of the St. Paul & Duluth R.R. and later purchased great tracts of pine land in Cass County. He sold the land on which the present town stands to the Leech Lake Land Company, but reserved the right to the standing timber. When he sent men to cut the trees, the settlers attempted to drive them away, and the ensuing resentment lasted for some time.

In Walker is a MUSEUM established in 1894 to house collections of animals and birds native to the district. The annual Flower Show *(2nd week in Aug.)* displays exhibits from several counties.

Partly within the village limits are the TIANNA FARMS *(open to visitors),* covering more than 1,000 acres that are cultivated entirely by motor machinery. Its cattle are purebred Aberdeen Angus. State and national dairying records have been set for years by the Tianna Farms. In the herds are 24 cows whose average production is 11,940.5 pounds of milk and 641.7 pounds of butterfat a year. In 1932 the entire milking herd averaged 510 pounds of butterfat, highest herd average for the Minnesota, Wisconsin, and Michigan districts.

Right from Walker on State 34 to the junction with State 64, 10.4 *m.;* L. on State 64 to the junction with State 87, 23 *m.;* R. on State 87 to BADOURA, 24.7 *m.*

Minnesota's first NURSERY for the production of evergreens was established here in 1931 in newly created Badoura State Forest. By 1936 it had been expanded until 20 million seedlings could be grown on its numerous plots. A modern sprinkler system supplies water for the tiny seedlings, and windbreaks of cedar trees control the drifting sand. Visitors during the autumn planting season can watch the interesting tree-digging machine, which can be operated either by tractor or capstan. A peat-grinding machine pulverizes this fertilizer for use on the seed beds. An office building and laboratory, a machine shed, and a seed extraction plant complete the physical equipment. The collection of pine cones for seed extraction is carried on by the forest and Federal employees as well as by local residents. Each forest-ranger reports the size of cone crop expected from his area, but one year's supply is kept on hand for use in case of cone-crop failure. Cones are purchased only from supervised areas, for careless pickers collect immature or unhealthy seeds, and often cut down or injure trees while taking the cones. The price paid for pine cones varies; 75¢ is the usual price for a bushel of jack-pine cones, although Norway pines are worth twice this amount.

At AH-GWAH-CHING (Chippewa, *out-of-doors*), 42.4 *m.* (50 pop.), is the MINNESOTA STATE SANATORIUM for tubercular patients. This institution, consisting of 35 buildings on 886 acres of rolling timber land overlooking the west shore of Leech Lake, serves the 47 counties that do not support separate sanitariums. Patients are eligible for admission only if they have been residents of Minnesota for one year prior to the date of their application. The sanitarium's staff of 190 employees includes 5 physicians and 60 registered nurses; it maintains its own dairy herd of registered Holstein cattle.

TEN MILE LAKE, 49.9 *m.*, was the site in 1895 of the town of Lothrop, then a railroad terminal with a population of 2,000. When the Minnesota & International Ry. was routed to the north, Lothrop was moved to another point. Today there is nothing to indicate the old village site.

HACKENSACK, 52.5 *m.* (256 pop.), is a small village named for the city in New Jersey by James Curo, ranchman, merchant, and first postmaster.

BACKUS, 60.8 *m.* (314 pop.), another railroad village, was named for Edward W. Backus (1860–1934), pioneer Minnesota lumberman.

The little town of PINE RIVER, 69.8 *m.* (1,319 alt., 422 pop.), platted in 1901, was at one time a rival of Walker for the county seat.

During the lumbering era of the 1880's, logs were floated down Pine River, through Whitefish and Cross Lakes to the east, and thence into the Mississippi.

At 70.4 *m.* US 371 crosses the Pine River.

At 77.8 *m.* is the junction with a county road.

Left on this road to UPPER HAY LAKE, 2.5 *m.* At 8 *m.* is WHITEFISH LAKE *(excellent fishing)*, with beautifully wooded shores, clear water, and inviting sandy beaches.

JENKINS, 78 *m.* (148 pop.), is a small hamlet platted by and named for George W. Jenkins, a lumberman.

At 78.5 *m.* is the junction with a country road.

Left 0.1 *m.* on this road to a group of INDIAN MOUNDS and elongated embankments. All are from 3 to 4 feet high; the largest is 700 feet long. It is estimated that they contain 10,000 tons of black soil.

PEQUOT, 82.3 *m.* (1,303 alt., 488 pop.), is now a resort town, although it had its origin in the lumber industry.

Left from Pequot on a country road, through dense pine woods dotted with groves of maple and oak, to BIG PELICAN LAKE *(fishing, golf, bowling, riding, games)*, 4.6 *m.*, one of the most popular resort lakes in north-central Minnesota. It offers a wide variety of vacation activities in a beautiful natural setting.

At 88.1 *m.* on US 371 is NISSWA, a small village in the heart of the resort region.

At 89.1 *m.* is an improved road known as Gull Lake Drive.

Right on this road to GULL LAKE, 1.3 *m.*, one of the most popular resort lakes in the entire Paul Bunyan playground. Through a screen of pines and graceful birches, patches of clear blue water are visible. Many homes and lodges have been built around Gull Lake, and 30 resorts dot its shores. One resort occupies the site of an ancient burial ground of the Pillager, Gull Lake, and Gull River Indians.
At 2.3 *m.* is LAKE MARGARET (R). At 6.3 *m.* is AGATE LAKE (R).
At 13.6 *m.* is the junction with a country road; R. on this road to the junction with another dirt road, 14 *m.;* L. on this road past LAKE SYLVAN, 14.6 *m.* (R), and the southern tip of Gull Lake (L) to PILLSBURY FOREST, the first forest reserve in Minnesota. Established in 1899, with a grant of 990 acres from the Pillsbury estate, it now includes 1,261 acres.
At 16 *m.* is STEPHENS LAKE (L). RED SAND LAKE (R) is at 18.2 *m.*
At 19.2 *m.* is the junction with US 371.

At 92.1 *m.* on US 371 is (R) the marked SITE OF THE ST. COLUMBA MISSION (1852).

At 100.9 *m.* is the junction (L) with US 210 *(see Tour 15)*.

BRAINERD, 103 *m.* (1,231 alt., 10,221 pop.) *(see Tour 15)*, is at the junction (R) with US 210 *(see Tour 15)*.

At 110.6 *m.* is CROW WING, site of an early Indian village and trading post of this name.

At 112.6 *m.* a STATE EXPERIMENTAL FARM *(open to visitors)* is making land tests on the sandy soil.

On the Mississippi at 120 *m.* is FORT RIPLEY, a railway village.

Right from this village on a dirt road, across the bridge, to the SITE OF OLD FORT RIPLEY, 2 *m.*, built in 1849–50 and occupied until July 1878. This military post, established as a buffer against the Indians, was used as a shelter for the settlers in the uprising of 1862. Of the old fort nothing remains today except the ruins of the powder magazine, the only building of stone.

This site is now included in the 20,000 acres comprising CAMP RIPLEY *(Sun. evening band concerts; parade, guard mount)*, the National Guard camp for Minnesota troops. The land varies from sandy plains to wooded hills, making an ideal area for training; it is used by Army, Navy, and Marine aerial squadrons. In a level area approximately a mile in length and a half mile in width are the main parade ground, infantry brigade area, field artillery brigade, aviation field, and utility area; each unit has its own living quarters. The infantry brigade has a headquarters building, mess hall, bathhouses, warehouse, and tents to accommodate 3,000 men. The utility area, south of the parade ground, has shops, arsenals, warehouses, and storage facilities. Although training is confined to the months of June, July, and August, the utility unit operates the year around, maintaining supplies for the entire Minnesota National Guard.

The reservation has already over 100 buildings; it is being steadily developed and, when completed, will have facilities for training an infantry division of approximately 9,000 men in two weeks. Half of Camp Ripley's 52 miles of roadway *(open to visitors except during maneuvers or gun-firing)* are beautiful scenic drives.

LITTLE FALLS, 133.4 *m.* (1,134 alt., 5,014 pop.) *(see Tour 16)*, is at the junction with US 10 *(see Tour 16)*.

Superior National Forest and Canoe Trips

THE Superior National Forest is one of the great wilderness areas of the United States. Lying in the northeastern corner of the State, entirely within the borders of Minnesota's Arrowhead region, this area covers a total of nearly 3 million acres, of which over 1,700,000 acres are Federal property. On the north the forest parallels for 150 miles the Canadian boundary and adjoins a similar Canadian territory, a portion of which is known as the Quetico Provincial Park. Together the Superior and the Quetico form a picturesque wilderness, a matchless canoe country where cold, crystal waters, teeming with fish, sparkle in long, narrow, winding basins separated by mere strips of land or by tumbling rapids. Though partly Canadian, this region is most easily accessible by railway or motor-car from the south. To the north it becomes a primeval forest, almost impenetrable except from American waters.

Through a maze of lakes and rivers, the northern part of the forest area drains into Hudson Bay through the Rainy River, the southern portion through numerous swift streams into Lake Superior. Its woodlands protect the headwaters of navigable streams of both the United States and Canada.

Within the Superior National Forest is a so-called "primitive area," whose virgin timber and interweaving lakes and streams form a sportsman's paradise. Only by canoe, on foot, or by hydro-airplane, can the fisherman and camper traverse this area; on its waters and short portages can be seen beaver, muskrat, grouse, porcupine, bear, deer, and moose, but never a road, resort, or permanent camp. Hunting is prohibited within the greater portion of its boundaries, but all manner of game fish, from salmon trout to muskie, can be taken.

All fish and game in the forest are State property, and State licenses must be secured to take them. Nearly 1,250,000 acres of the forest, including the largest portion of the primitive area, lie within a State game refuge.

Thrice in the path of great glaciers which carved its countless valleys and ridges, the Superior National Forest contains over 5,000 lakes, ranging in size from a few acres to 70 square miles. For centuries the Indians knifed the quiet lake waters in their birch canoes and shot the treacherous river rapids between the shores of Lake Superior and the international boundary. Here they hunted and fished, picked berries, harvested wildrice, wore deep the short portages with the tread of moccasined feet. First of the white men to explore its wilds were the Jesuit fathers, who came to the region more than 200 years ago. After them the traders, the *bois-brulés,* and the *voyageurs* blazed their portages between its waters, shouldering their burdens of two 90-pound packets of fur per man; here the Hudson's Bay Company and the Northwest Company fought for trade supremacy. Originally the Sioux knew it as their domain, but the Chippewa, armed with the white man's muskets, succeeded in driving the Sioux from their hunting grounds.

When the fur trade languished, lumbering sprang up as Minnesota's chief industry; the wasteful logging practice plus the devastating fires that followed destroyed a vast acreage of productive timber. Today the southern part of the forest, with its sections of inferior growth, is evidence of the havoc wrought by human greed; the northern portion, however, is still a mighty tree-covered wilderness.

The Superior National Forest has grown around a nucleus of 36,000 acres established in February 1909. Since then its area has been increased by frequent acquisitions.

Since the United States Forest Service instituted its program of protection and reforesting, the management policy has been one of annual timber-cutting on a sustained yield basis. In an attempt to prevent serious fires, 25 lookout stations are maintained; each CCC and work camp has been organized as a fire-fighting unit, and hydro-airplanes are available for patrol duty in emergencies. Ever alert for telltale smoke in this vast area, the forest-ranger experiences extreme difficulty and hardship in his daily job, which often involves camping out in below-zero weather and snowshoeing long distances over frozen trails. Especially dreaded are the isolated fires in the inaccessible primitive district where discovery depends upon airplane patrols. In the intensively managed portions, 200 miles of road have been built, 101 miles of portage constructed, and 81 miles of trails added. With increasing use of the forest as a recreational area, however, fire prevention has become more and more a public responsibility. More than half of the fires, it is estimated, are caused by careless campers.

Another important phase of conservation is the protection of the forest's animal and plant life. Game and fish specialists have cooperated with recreational engineers to make hunting and fishing resources unexcelled. Each year waters are restocked with fish. Dams, deflectors, and shelters are built in the trout streams, and the banks and bottoms are improved; tons of birch and cedar slashings are fed to the deer at their yarding areas.

Houses for wood ducks have been erected; variations in timber types will facilitate an increase in ruffed grouse. Wildrice and duck potatoes have been planted in many lakes. Game censuses have been taken, stream and lake surveys made. The water table created by beaver dams is to be preserved, where necessary, by man-made structures.

While the fundamental purpose of the Superior National Forest (to protect and utilize its timber resources) remains unchanged, increasing emphasis is being placed upon its recreational value. In 1925 the "Primitive Plan" for the area was adopted. Nearly 1,200 square miles were set aside to be preserved in their pristine state; logging is to be confined to interior areas and prohibited on lake shores; portages, rivers, and streams preserved as nearly as possible in their natural condition. Almost 90 per cent of the forest's lakes are concentrated in the primitive area, where they form the nucleus of the canoe transportation system. The balance of the region, nearly 2 million acres, is dotted with lakes not sufficiently connected to form a transportation unit.

Future recreation development will be centered about the lakes. To many of the more isolated waters, roads are to be constructed, and on their shores will be built public campgrounds, picnic facilities, resorts, summer homes, and boys' and girls' camps. The Government owns approximately 1,500 miles of lake frontage and thousands of miles of frontage on rivers and streams. The primitive area will remain accessible only by boat, canoe, or hydro-airplane, though some foot trails will be built into portions of the area not accessible by water. The road-building program, however, will be held to a minimum. Such roads as the Ely-Buyck, the Ely-Finland, the Stony, the Temperance, and the Gunflint wind through an enchanting forest land. These roads are suitable only for slow, light traffic.

No roads penetrate the primitive area. Here, like the Indian and fur-trader of a bygone day, the modern vacationer must paddle his canoe through the long, narrow lakes, past picturesque shores lined with muskeg and virgin pine, boulders and rock ledges and sandy beaches, packing his boat and duffle over the short, frequent portages. While many routes and side trips can be taken, canoeists have developed a number of well-marked passages through the region. A two-day jaunt or an extended journey, a lazy fishing tour or a back-bending voyage of exploration—the modern adventurer can attempt any of these in the Superior National Forest.

◄◄◄◄◄◄◄◄◄◄◄◄◄◄◄◄◄◄◄❋►►►►►►►►►►►►►►►►►►►►

General Information for Canoe Trips

Headquarters: Federal Building, Duluth, Minnesota.

Seasons: Lakes are usually ice-free by May 10 in the Superior National Forest. The freeze-up period begins as early as October 10, and most of the lakes are covered with ice by November 1. The best months for fishing are May, June, September, and October. Camping conditions are especially ideal during July and August, during which time the fishing is also good.

Transportation: All trips can be reached either from HOVLAND, TOFTE, GRAND MARAIS *(see Motor Tour 1)*, ELY, or TOWER *(see Motor Tour 8)*. Grand Marais, Tofte, Ely, and Tower are served by the Northland-Greyhound Lines, Inc., and Ely and Tower by the Duluth & Iron Range Ry.

Accommodations: Except for resorts and lodges on land that was privately owned before the area was set aside as a national forest, there are no accommodations whatever in the primitive area. The remaining portion has lodges, camp sites, and tourist camps at convenient intervals.

Climate, Equipment, Clothing: (See GENERAL INFORMATION ON MINNE-SOTA.)

Maps and Detailed Information: The descriptions of canoe tours are not adequate for the use of the canoeist. They are intended merely as directional aids. Complete information regarding the tours, as well as all other canoe trips, portages, and camps in the area, can be obtained from the Federal and State Forest Service, the Duluth Chamber of Commerce, the Minnesota Arrowhead Association in Duluth, other chambers of commerce throughout the district, and resorts in areas traveled.

Portages: All American portages in the Superior National Forest are well built, with good trails and frequent canoe rests. The foot of most portages is marked by the Forest Service with a sign so placed that it can be seen at reasonable distances.

Each sign gives the name of the portage, its length, and the lake or river to which it leads. Portages in Canadian waters are usually marked only by a blaze on a tree, or a Forest Service sign, warning the camper to put out his fires. For convenience in estimating distance traveled, the canoeist should estimate the rate of travel, with two men paddling, at approximately 3 miles per hour.

Special Warning: Rapids in strange waters should not be run, since they may lead to falls or impassable water.

Canoe Trip 1: *International Boundary Route from Gunflint Area*

McFarland Lake—Mountain Lake—Rose Lake—Gunflint Lake—Saganaga Lake—Cypress Lake—Big Knife Lake—Prairie Portage—Upper Basswood Falls—Table Rock or Skull and Crossbones Camp sites—Crooked Lake— Iron Lake—Shortiss Island (Lac La Croix)—Near Coleman Island (Lac La Croix)—Group of islands (on northwest end of Lac La Croix)— south end of Lac La Croix—Loon Lake—Vermilion Narrows.

17 days: 235 miles of paddling, 9 miles of portaging.

Excellent fishing of all kinds.
Guides available at McFarland Lake, Crane Lake, and at various points of entry.
Most of the portages are marked by signs showing names of lakes and distances.
Portages around rapids are noted.
Current varies with different sections of the route, especially rapid and treacherous at lower end of Basswood River.

Following the International Boundary, this route is one of picturesque scenery, many primitive portages, all kinds of fishing, a variation in size and current of streams, numerous rapids, falls, and narrows. The picture rocks on Lac La Croix are interesting. The pictures, of unknown origin, painted with dull-red ocher, about 5 feet above the water's edge, and each from 6 to 8 inches in length, represent a moose, goat, hands, bear paws, deer, a circle, and a man holding a spear.

Points of entry to this route are cross-referred.

MC FARLAND LAKE *(resort and undeveloped camp site)* is 36 miles northeast of Grand Marais *(see Tour 1, sec. a)* on Arrowhead Trail, where motor transportation to McFarland Lake is available.

North across McFarland Lake *(see Canoe Trip #2)* and paddle into LITTLE JOHN LAKE; north on Little John into JOHN LAKE; north on John and portage 80 *rods* to EAST PIKE LAKE; north across East Pike and portage about 1 mile to MOOSE LAKE; west across Moose and portage about 172 *rods* to LILY PONDS; west across Lily Ponds and portage about 26 *rods* to MOUNTAIN LAKE *(end of first day's trip; partially developed camp site).*

West across Mountain and portage about 85 *rods* to WATAP LAKE; west across Watap and paddle into ROVE LAKE *(Canoe Trip #2 can be reached south via Daniels Lake);* west on Rove and portage northwest about 560 *rods* to ROSE LAKE *(end of second day's trip; partially developed camp site; landlocked salmon fishing; Canoe Trip #2 can be reached south via Stairway Portage).*

South on Rose and portage 1 *rod* to RAT LAKE; west on Rat and portage 80 *rods* to SOUTH LAKE: northwest on South Lake and portage north about 80 *rods* to NORTH LAKE *(entry north into Canadian interior)*; north and west on North Lake and portage about 5 *rods* to LITTLE GUNFLINT LAKE; paddle west into GUNFLINT LAKE *(end of third day's trip; resort; partially developed camp site; landlocked salmon fishing)*.

Northwest on Gunflint and paddle into MAGNETIC LAKE; north on Magnetic and paddle into GRANITE RIVER *(downstream)*; portage about 6 *rods* *(rapids)* from Granite River to Granite River; north on Granite River and portage about 80 *rods* *(rapids)* to COVE LAKE; northwest on Cove and portage about 240 *rods* *(rapids)* to Granite River; portage around three rapids from Granite River to GNEISS LAKE; paddle west and north on Gneiss into MARABOEUF LAKE; north across Maraboeuf and portage 12 *rods* *(rapids)* into Granite River; 2½-*rod* portage *(rapids)* from Granite River to SAGANAGA LAKE *(end of fourth day's trip; partially developed camp site; land-locked salmon and wall-eyed pike fishing; see Canoe Trip #5; entry north into Canadian interior)*.

Southwest on Saganaga and portage 5 *rods* to SWAMP LAKE; 93-*rod* portage from southwest end of Swamp to CYPRESS LAKE *(end of fifth day's trip; partially developed camp site)*.

Portage 3 *rods* from west end of Cypress to LITTLE KNIFE LAKE; paddle west into and to the west end of KNIFE or BIG KNIFE LAKE *(end of sixth day's trip; partially developed camp site; good fishing for wall-eyed pike; see Canoe Trip #13)*.

Portage 74 *rods* *(rapids)* from Knife Lake to KNIFE RIVER *(downstream)*; 4-*rod* portage *(rapids)* from Knife River to SEED LAKE; 24-*rod* portage *(rapids)* from Seed Lake to Knife River; 12-*rod* portage *(rapids)* from Knife River to CARP LAKE *(entry into Canadian interior)*; 44-*rod* portage *(rapids)* from Carp to BIRCH LAKE *(see Canoe Trip #13)*; west across Birch and into SUCKER LAKE; west skirting north end of Sucker to PRAIRIE PORTAGE *(end of seventh day's trip; partially developed camp site; falls)*.

Portage 33 *rods* *(around falls)* to BASSWOOD LAKE *(good fishing for landlocked salmon and wall-eyed and northern pike; entry north into Canadian interior)*; north and west across Basswood to UPPER BASSWOOD FALLS *(end of eighth day's trip; partially developed camp site)*.

Portage 275 *rods* around falls to BASSWOOD RIVER *(downstream; fast current, treacherous rapids)*; 24-*rod* portage *(rapids)* from Basswood River to Basswood River; 40-*rod* portage *(rapids)* from Basswood River to Basswood River; 12-*rod* portage *(around LOWER BASSWOOD FALLS)* to CROOKED LAKE *(Indian picture rocks; Forest Service cabin; end of ninth day's trip; partially developed TABLE OF ROCK or SKULL AND CROSSBONES camp sites; see Canoe Trip #10; entry into Canadian interior)*.

Paddle 5 or 6 miles from east end of Crooked Lake to a point 3 miles east of CURTAIN FALLS on west end of lake *(end of 10th day's trip; partially developed camp site)*.

Portage 116 *rods (around CURTAIN FALLS)* to IRON LAKE *(end of 11th day's trip; partially developed camp sites on islands; ample time to enjoy scenery of REBECCA FALLS and wall-eyed pike fishing).*

West across Iron and short liftover *(rapids)* to BOTTLE LAKE; west across Bottle and portage 90 *rods* to LAC LA CROIX *(Indian picture rocks, excellent fishing, 861 islands; see Canoe Trips #11, #12, and #14; entry into Canadian interior);* paddle north to SHORTISS ISLAND *(end of twelfth day's trip; partially developed camp site on northwest end of island).*

Paddle north around east side to north end of COLEMAN ISLAND *(end of thirteenth day's trip; partially developed camp sites on several islands in this vicinity).*

Paddle due west about 12 miles to group of islands on northwest corner of Lac La Croix *(end of fourteenth day's trip; partially developed camp sites on some islands).*

South on Lac La Croix to 30-*rod* portage to LOON LAKE *(end of fifteenth day's trip; partially developed camp site).*

West across Loon to 50-*rod portage (canoe and luggage are conveyed on small-railed narrow-gage flatcar)* around LOON DAM FALLS to LOON RIVER; northwest *(downstream)* on Loon River to LITTLE VERMILION LAKE; north across Little Vermilion and through LITTLE VERMILION NARROWS *(end of sixteenth day's trip; partially developed camp site).*

Paddle into SAND POINT LAKE; north and south across Sand Point; south through KING WILLIAM'S NARROWS into CRANE LAKE; paddle across to south shore *(resorts, cabins; outfitting; fishing, swimming, boating; motor transportation; see Canoe Trip #15).* Retrace to starting point *(17 days)* or take motor transportation.

Canoe Trip 2: *From Gunflint Area*

East Bearskin Lake—Clearwater Lake—McFarland Lake—East Bearskin Lake.
3 days: 38 miles of paddling, 5 miles of portaging.

Average fishing for pike and trout.
Guides available at East Bearskin Lake, Clearwater Lake, and Grand Marais.
Portages marked by signs showing names of lakes and portage distances; no portages to avoid rapids.

This route passes through excellent scenery with rugged shores and high cliffs. Camp sites are undeveloped.

EAST BEARSKIN LAKE *(lodges, store, housekeeping cabins, campground, summer home sites, boating, fishing, outfitting)* is 26.5 miles north of Grand Marais *(see Tour 1; Sec. a)* on side road 1 mile off the Gunflint Trail, where motor transportation to East Bearskin Lake is available.

From west end of East Bearskin Lake portage 104 *rods* to SEED LAKE; north across middle of lake and portage 112 *rods* to FLOUR LAKE; across west end of Flour and portage 155 *rods* to west arm of HUNGRY

JACK LAKE; paddle north to 8-*rod* portage to WEST BEARSKIN LAKE *(Canoe Trip #1 can be reached north by either Daniels Lake, or Duncan Lake and Stairway Portage)*; portage 1 *mile (motor transportation)* to CLEARWATER LAKE *(end of first day's trip; lodging, meals, swimming, boating, outfitting, excellent trout fishing)*, on Gunflint Trail *(see Tour 1, Sec. a)*.

Paddle to east end of Clearwater and make 214-*rod* portage to WEST PIKE LAKE; from east end of West Pike 122-*rod* portage to EAST PIKE LAKE; from southwest end of East Pike portage 160 *rods* to MC FAR-LAND LAKE *(end of second day's trip; resort; unimproved public camp site)*.

Cross west end of McFarland and, if water is low, portage 5 *rods* south to PINE LAKE *(if high, channel is passable; submerged rocks)*; from southwest end of Pine portage 240 *rods* to CANOE LAKE; from southwest end of Canoe portage 22 *rods* to ALDER LAKE *(submerged rocks)*; portage from northwest end of Alder 48 *rods* to East Bearskin; paddle west to starting point.

Canoe Trip 3: *From Gunflint Area*

Poplar Lake—Winchell Lake—Brule Lake—Cherokee Lake—Long Island Lake—Henson Lake—Poplar Lake.
6 days: 47 miles of paddling, 5 miles of portaging.

Good fishing for pike and trout.
Guides available at Poplar Lake and Grand Marais.
Portages marked by signs showing names of lakes and portage distances; portages around rapids are noted.
Current in Long Island River negligible.

This route passes through several burned-over and logged areas which do not mar the scenic effect, for the lakes are interesting and beautiful. Camp sites are undeveloped.

POPLAR LAKE *(lodges, boating, swimming, complete outfitting)* is 30 miles northwest of Grand Marais on Gunflint Trail *(see Tour 1, Sec. a)*, where motor transportation to Poplar Lake is available.

South across Poplar Lake to 50-*rod* portage to LIZZ LAKE; south on Lizz to 75-*rod* portage to CARIBOU LAKE and through narrows *(submerged rocks)*; south on Caribou and 23-*rod* portage to HORSESHOE LAKE *(submerged rocks in narrows)*; 92-*rod* portage from southwest end of Horseshoe to GASKIN LAKE; 51-*rod* portage from southwest end of Gaskin to WINCHELL LAKE *(end of first day's trip; undeveloped public camp site; excellent trout fishing)*.

Portage 15 *rods* from southwest end of Winchell to TRAP LAKE; 325-*rod* portage from south end of Trap to MULLIGAN LAKE; 32-*rod* portage to LILY LAKE; 60-*rod* portage from south end of Lily to BRULE LAKE *(end of second day's trip; undeveloped public camp site; good landlocked salmon fishing)*.

Paddle west across Brule and portage 6 *rods* from west shore to SOUTH

TEMPERANCE LAKE; 52-rod portage from north end of South Temperance to NORTH TEMPERANCE LAKE; 103-rod portage northwest to SITKA LAKE; 130-rod portage northwest to CHEROKEE LAKE *(end of third day's trip, undeveloped public camp site)*.

Portage 14 *rods* north end of Cherokee to GORDON LAKE; 25-rod portage north end of Gordon to LONG ISLAND RIVER; paddle north *(downstream)* and two short portages *(rapids)* to LONG ISLAND LAKE *(end of fourth day's trip; undeveloped public camp site)*.

Portage 17 *rods* from east end of Long Island Lake to MUSKEG LAKE; cross Muskeg east and portage 187 *rods* to KISKADINNA LAKE; 37-rod portage from the east end of Kiskadinna to ONEGA LAKE; 32-rod portage from east end of Onega to HENSON LAKE *(end of fifth day's trip; undeveloped public camp site)*.

Portage 40 *rods* from the east end of Henson to PILLSBURY LAKE; short portage east to a small lake; 96-rod portage north to MEADS LAKE; 300-rod portage from east end of Meads to POPLAR LAKE; paddle northeast to starting point.

Canoe Trip 4: *From Gunflint Area*

Round Lake or Cross River—Tuscarora Lake—Little Saganaga Lake—Frazer Lake—Kekekabic Lake—Sea Gull Lake.
5 days: 56 miles of padding, 6 miles of portaging.

Fair fishing for landlocked salmon, speckled trout, wall-eyed pike, and black bass. Guides available at Round Lake, Sea Gull Lake, and Grand Marais.
Portages are unmarked except between starting point and Little Saganaga Lake and Ogishkemuncie and Sea Gull Lakes, where names and distances a^re given.
Portages around rapids are noted.
Current in rivers sluggish.

This route passes through a very wild and scenically splendid region. Its camp sites are few and undeveloped.

ROUND LAKE or CROSS RIVER *(lodges, housekeeping cabins, boating, fishing, swimming, outfitting)* on a 2-mile spur road off Gunflint Trail *(see Tour 1, Sec. a.)*, reached by motor transportation from Grand Marais.

Northeast *(upstream)* on Cross River and portage 96 *rods (rapids)* from Cross River to Cross River; follow Cross River *(upstream)* paddling through several small PONDS and portage 30 *rods* to HAM LAKE; southeast on Ham and portage 30 *rods* to Cross River; liftover *(around beaver dam)* from Cross River to Cross River; paddle south on Cross River and take small STREAM to the R.; upstream on stream at point shown on map as Cross Bay and portage about 60 *rods (rapids)* to SNIP LAKE; south on Snip and portage about 60 *rods* to COPPER LAKE; 160-rod portage from the extreme west end of Copper to TUSCARORA LAKE *(end of first day's trip; undeveloped public camp site; excellent landlocked salmon fishing)*.

From west end of Tuscarora portage twice and cross two small PONDS to OWL LAKE; short portage from west end of Owl to CROOKED

LAKE; southwest across Crooked and portage about 80 *rods* to MORA
LAKE; west across Mora and portage 30 *rods* to LITTLE SAGANAGA
LAKE *(end of second day's trip; undeveloped public camp site; good
wall-eyed pike fishing; numerous islands delightful for camping; see
Branch Route to Ogishkemuncie Lake).*

Portage 18 *rods* from southwest end of Little Saganaga to BEAVER
POND; south on Beaver Pond and portage 9 *rods* to ELTON LAKE;
1-*rod* liftover (around rapids) from south end of Elton to BEAR LAKE
(mountain-trout fishing); 70-rod portage from west end of Bear to HOE
LAKE; west across Hoe and portage 60 *rods* to a SMALL LAKE; west
across small lake and portage 40 *rods* to V LAKE; 152-*rod* portage from
west end of V to LEDGE LAKE; west across Ledge and portage 202 *rods*
to CAP LAKE; 72-*rod* portage from west end of Cap to ROE LAKE;
west across Roe and portage 33 *rods* to LITTLE SAGUS LAKE; 65-*rod*
portage from west end of Little Sagus to FRAZER LAKE *(end of third
day's trip; undeveloped public camp site; good wall-eyed pike fishing).*

Portage 16 *rods* from north end of Frazer to GERUND LAKE; 30-*rod*
portage from north end of Gerund to AHMAKOSE LAKE; 97-*rod*
portage from north end of Ahmakose to WISINI LAKE; 10-*rod* portage
from north end of Wisini to STRUP LAKE *(black-bass fishing);* 86-*rod*
portage from north end of Strup to KEKEKABIC LAKE; cross to eastern
shore of lake *(end of fourth day's trip; undeveloped public camp site;
excellent landlocked salmon fishing; to reach Canoe Trip # 1 see Canoe
Trip #13).*

Northeast on Kekekabic and make a short portage to EDDY LAKE *(to
reach Canoe Trip #1 portage 37 rods from northwest end of Eddy to Knife
Lake);* east on Eddy and portage about 32 *rods* to POND; east across
pond and portage about 10 *rods* to second POND; 50-*rod* portage from
east end of second pond to OGISHKEMUNCIE LAKE *(see Branch Route
to Little Saganaga Lake);* northwest across Ogishkemuncie and portage 50
rods to POND; northeast across pond and portage 50 *rods* to JASPER
LAKE; 37-*rod* portage from northeast end of Jasper to ALPINE LAKE;
60-*rod* portage from east end of Alpine to ROG LAKE; east across Rog
and portage 17 *rods* to SEA GULL LAKE *(wall-eyed and northern pike
fishing);* paddle northeast across Sea Gull *(resorts, cabins, outfitting, boating, fishing, swimming; motor transportation back to starting point available).*

Retrace to starting point *(5 days);* or retrace to Ogishkemuncie Lake
(see Branch Route), thence to starting point *(3 days).*

BRANCH ROUTE FROM LITTLE SAGANAGA LAKE TO OGISHKE-
MUNCIE LAKE *(via Little Saganaga Lake; 5.5 miles of paddling, 0.5 of portag-
ing; 1 day one way; good landlocked salmon fishing).*
Paddle to north end of LITTLE SAGANAGA LAKE; short portage into RAT-
TLE LAKE; north across Rattle and portage about 40 rods into GABIMICHI-
GAMI LAKE *(good fishing for landlocked salmon);* northwest across Gabimichi-
gami and portage about 30 *rods* into AGAMOK LAKE; paddle west across
Agamok and portage about 60 *rods* to POND; northwest across pond and portage
about 50 *rods* into Ogishkemuncie Lake. Retrace to Little Saganaga Lake *(1 day);*
or follow main route.

Canoe Trip 5: *From Gunflint Area*

Sea Gull Lake—Red Rock Lake—Sea Gull Lake.
2 days: 23 miles of paddling, 0.5 miles of portaging.

Good fishing for pike and lake trout.
Guides available at Sea Gull Lake.
Portages marked by signs showing names of lakes and portage distances; portages around rapids are noted.
Current in Sea Gull River sluggish.

This route is one of the finest of the scenic routes, with many beautiful islands and rugged shores. Camp sites are few and undeveloped.

SEA GULL LAKE *(lodge, meals, houskeeping cabins, boating, fishing, swimming, outfitting)* is 56 miles north of Grand Marais on Gunflint Trail *(see Tour 1, Sec. a)*, where motor transportation to Sea Gull Lake is available.

Southwest across Sea Gull Lake and portage 17 *rods* to ROG LAKE; 60-*rod* portage from west end of Rog to ALPINE LAKE; north across Alpine and portage 51 *rods* to RED ROCK LAKE *(end of first day's trip; undeveloped public camp sites)*.

Portage 8 rods from north end of Rog Lake to BIG SAGANAGA LAKE *(see Canoe Trip #1)*; paddle along south shore of Big Saganaga Lake to extreme southeast end and south into SEA GULL RIVER; south *(upstream)* on Sea Gull River, portaging twice *(rapids)* to Sea Gull Lake; east to starting point.

Canoe Trip 6: *From Gunflint Area*

Sawbill Lake—Polly Lake—Little Saganaga Lake—Snip Lake—Cherokee Lake—Sawbill Lake.
5 days: 62 miles of paddling, 5 miles of portaging.

Good fishing for wall-eyed and northern pike.
Guides available at Sawbill Lake.
Portages are marked by signs showing names of lakes and portage distances; portages around rapids are noted.
River currents are sluggish, except for that in the Kawishiwi River.

This route offers beautiful and interesting scenery, with many beaver dams. It has numerous camp sites, but they are unimproved.

SAWBILL LAKE *(lodge, campground, excellent fishing for wall-eyed and northern pike, boating, swimming, and outfitting)* is at the end of Temperance River Road, 24 miles north of Tofte ˉ*(see Tour 1, Sec. a)*, where motor transportation to Sawbill Lake is available.

West across Sawbill Lake to 27-*rod* portage to ALDON LAKE; from southwest end of Aldon portage 144 *rods* to BETH LAKE; west end of Beth portage 232 *rods* to GRACE LAKE; south arm of Grace west to 14-*rod* portage to GRACE RIVER *(downstream; jagged submerged rocks)*; two short portages *(rapids)* to 76-*rod* portage *(rapids)* to east side of PHOEBE LAKE; west across upper half of Phoebe to PHOEBE RIVER *(downstream);* 120-*rod* portage *(rapids)* to HAZEL LAKE; northwest across Hazel to 51-*rod* portage *(falls)* to Phoebe River *(submerged rocks);* three portages *(rapids)* on river to 108-*rod* portage to POLLY LAKE *(end of first day's trip; undeveloped public camp site).*

Northwest across Polly and portage 17 *rods* to KAWISHIWI RIVER *(downstream);* 50-*rod* portage *(rapids)* and then 157-*rod* portage *(rapids)* to KOMA LAKE; north across Koma to 20-*rod* portage *(rapids)* to Kawishiwi River; portage 40 *rods* to KAVENDEBA LAKE; portage between and cross two PONDS to 26-*rod* portage to PAN LAKE; north across Pan portaging between two PONDS to 43-*rod* portage to south shore of BEAR LAKE *(mountain-trout fishing);* north across Bear to 1-*rod* portage to ELTON LAKE; north to 9-*rod* portage to BEAVER POND; across Beaver Pond to 18-*rod* portage to LITTLE SAGANAGA LAKE *(end of second day's trip; undeveloped public camp site; good fishing for wall-eyed pike and lake trout; see alternate return to Sawbill Lake).*

Paddle to southeast end of Little Saganaga and portage 30 *rods* to MORA LAKE; east then curve northwest in Mora to about 80-*rod* portage to CROOKED LAKE; east by northeast across widest part of Crooked and short portage to OWL LAKE; across two small PONDS and short portage to TUSCARORA LAKE; east across Tuscarora to 160-*rod* portage to COPPER LAKE; northeast on Copper and portage about 60 *rods* to SNIP LAKE *(end of third day's trip; undeveloped public camp site).*

Cross length of Snip east and portage about 180 *rods* to CROSS BAY LAKE; south on Cross Bay and portage 50 *rods* to RIB LAKE; south on Rib and portage 30 *rods* to KARL LAKE, which narrows into LONG ISLAND LAKE; southwest on Long Island into LONG ISLAND RIVER *(upstream);* two portages *(rapids)* south on Long Island River to 25-*rod* portage to GORDON LAKE; 14-*rod* portage south from Gordon to CHEROKEE LAKE *(end of fourth day's trip; undeveloped public camp site; landlocked salmon fishing).*

Across to southwest end of Cherokee Lake and west into CHEROKEE RIVER *(upstream)* for short distance; south bank of river 192-*rod* portage to SKOOP LAKE; south across Skoop and 12-*rod* portage to ADA LAKE; west on Ada Lake and portage 75 *rods* to ADA CREEK *(downstream);* portage 75 *rods* to north end of Sawbill Lake, and paddle south to starting point.

ALTERNATE RETURN TO SAWBILL LAKE *(via Little Sag Route: 15 miles of paddling, 4 of portaging; 2 days; rigorous traveling over divide; fair pike fishing; docks at some portages).*

Portage 30 *rods* from southeast end of LITTLE SAGANAGA to MORA LAKE; from south end of Mora portage 96 *rods* to HUB RIVER; south *(upstream)* on Hub River and portage 13 *rods (rapids)* from Hub River; 301-*rod* portage *(rapids)* Hub River to HUB LAKE; at south end of Hub Lake portage 12 *rods* to MESABA LAKE *(end of first day's trip; unimproved camp site).*

Southeast across Mesaba and portage 109 *rods* to HUG LAKE; south across Hug and portage 2 *rods* to DUCK LAKE; portage 80 *rods* from south end of Duck to ZENITH LAKE; southwest across Zenith and portage 270 *rods* to KELSO RIVER *(downstream);* 84-*rod* portage *(rapids)* from Kelso River to Kelso River; liftover *(around dam and rapids)* from Kelso River to Kelso River; south into KELSO

LAKE; south and east on Kelso Lake into Kelso River; portage 17 *rods* from Kelso River to SAWBILL LAKE; southeast on Sawbill to starting point.

Canoe Trip 7: *From Ely Area*

Lake One—Lake Three—Hudson Lake—North Kawishiwi River—Polly Lake—Parent Lake—Isabella Lake—Isabella River—Bald Eagle Lake—South Kawishiwi River—Lake One.

11 days: 83 miles of paddling, 9 miles of portaging.

Good fishing for wall-eyed and northern pike.
Guides available at Lake One, Ely, and Winton.
Portages marked by signs showing names of lakes and portage distances; portages around rapids are noted.
Current in sections of the various rivers is rapid.

This route takes the canoeist through a wild and remote country, with beautiful scenery and lakes dotted with numerous islands. Four of the camp sites are developed while the remaining seven are only partially developed.

FERNBERG LANDING or LAKE ONE *(resort, housekeeping cabins, forest lookout station, developed camp site, boating, swimming, outfitting)* is on Fernberg Road 22 miles east of Ely *(see Tour 8)*, where motor transportation to Fernberg Landing or Lake One is available.

Southeast across LAKE ONE; portage 36 *rods* to POND; from Pond portage 89 *rods* to LAKE TWO; east and south across Lake Two through narrows into LAKE THREE *(end of first day's trip; developed camp site)*.

Paddle east across Lake Three through narrows into LAKE FOUR; paddle east and north across Lake Four into NORTH KAWISHIWI RIVER *(upstream)*; portage 17 *rods* *(rapids)* from N. Kawishiwi River to N. Kawishiwi River; portage 23 *rods* *(rapids)* from N. Kawishiwi River to N. Kawishiwi River; portage 5 *rods* *(rapids)* from N. Kawishiwi to HUDSON LAKE *(end of second day's trip; developed camp site)*.

From the east end of Hudson Lake portage 90 *rods* to *INSULA LAKE;* paddle to the east end of Insula *(end of third day's trip; developed camp site)*.

Paddle into the N. Kawishiwi River for about 1 mile, then portage 17 *rods* *(rapids)* from the N. Kawishiwi River to the N. Kawishiwi River; paddle into and skirt the south end of LAKE ALICE and again into the N. Kawishiwi River; 17-*rod* portage *(rapids)* from the N. Kawishiwi River to the N. Kawishiwi River; 81-*rod* portage *(rapids)* from the N. Kawishiwi River to N. Kawishiwi River; 19-*rod* portage *(rapids)* from N. Kawishiwi River to N. Kawishiwi River *(end of fourth day's trip; partially developed camp site)*.

Portage 71 *rods* *(rapids)* from N. Kawishiwi River to MULBERG LAKE; southeast across Mulberg and into N. Kawishiwi River; 24-*rod* portage *(rapids)* from N. Kawishiwi River to KOMA LAKE; south across Koma Lake and portage 157 *rods* *(rapids)* into N. Kawishiwi River; 50-*rod* portage *(rapids)* from N. Kawishiwi River to N. Kawishiwi River; 17-*rod* portage *(rapids)* from N. Kawishiwi River to POLLY LAKE *(end of fifth day's trip; partially developed camp site)*.

South across Polly and portage 82 *rods* to TOWNLINE LAKE; south across Townline and portage 179 *rods* to KAWASACHONG; south across Kawasachong and liftover *(beaver dam)* into N. Kawishiwi River; liftover *(beaver dam)* from N. Kawishiwi River to N. Kawishiwi River; paddle into SQUARE LAKE; liftover *(rapids)* from Square Lake to N. Kawishiwi River; paddle into KAWISHIWI LAKE; portage 582 *rods* to PARENT LAKE *(end of sixth day's trip; partially developed camp site).*

West across Parent Lake and portage 57 *rods (rapids)* to PARENT RIVER *(downstream);* 24-rod portage *(rapids)* from Parent River to Parent River; 32-rod portage *(rapids)* from Parent River to Parent River; 39-rod portage *(rapids)* from Parent River to Parent River; 22-rod portage *(rapids)* from Parent River to Parent River; 39-rod portage *(rapids)* from Parent River to Parent River; 26-rod portage *(rapids)* from Parent River to Parent River; 19-rod portage *(rapids)* from Parent River to Parent River; 40-rod portage *(rapids)* from Parent River to Parent River; 22-rod portage *(rapids)* from Parent River to Parent River; 15-rod portage *(rapids)* from Parent River to Parent River; 26-rod portage *(rapids)* from Parent River to Parent River; 15-rod portage from Parent River to Parent River; 27-rod portage from Parent River to ISABELLA LAKE *(end of seventh day's trip; partially developed camp site).*

West across Isabella Lake and portage 22 *rods (rapids)* to ISABELLA RIVER *(downstream);* 12-rod portage *(rapids)* from Isabella River to Isabella River; 106-rod portage *(rapids)* from Isabella River to Isabella River; 27-rod portage *(rapids)* from Isabella River to Isabella River; 15-rod portage *(rapids)* from Isabella River to Isabella River *(end of eighth day's trip; partially developed camp site near Island River Junction).*

Portage 40 *rods (rapids)* from Isabella River to Isabella River *(Forest Service cabin);* 36-rod portage *(rapids)* from Isabella River to Isabella River; 16-rod portage *(rapids)* from Isabella River to Isabella River; 156-rod portage *(rapids)* from Isabella River to Isabella River *(Forest Service cabin);* 158-rod portage *(rapids)* to BALD EAGLE LAKE *(end of ninth day's trip; partially developed camp site).*

Paddle northwest across Bald Eagle into GABBRO LAKE *(in low water it is necessary to make a short portage between these two lakes because of rapids);* 148-rod portage *(rapids)* from the northwest end of Gabbro Lake to the SOUTH KAWISHIWI RIVER *(downstream);* paddle on S. Kawishiwi River for about a mile and turn northeast and upstream portaging 27 *rods (rapids)* from S. Kawishiwi River to the S. Kawishiwi River *(end of the tenth day's trip; partially developed camp site).*

Portage 22 *rods (rapids)* from S. Kawishiwi River to S. Kawishiwi River; 7-rod portage from S. Kawishiwi to S. Kawishiwi River; paddle into NORTH KAWISHIWI RIVER *(upstream);* 8-rod portage *(rapids)* from N. Kawishiwi River to N. Kawishiwi River; 24-rod portage *(rapids)* from N. Kawishiwi River to N. Kawishiwi River; 16-rod portage *(rapids)* from N. Kawishiwi River to N. Kawishiwi River; 12-rod portage *(rapids)* from N. Kawishiwi to LAKE ONE; paddle northeast to starting point.

Canoe Trip 8: *From Ely Area*

White Iron Lake or Silver Rapids—Clear Lake—Birch Lake—White Iron Lake or Silver Rapids.

3 days: 30 miles of paddling, 1 mile of portaging.

Good fishing for wall-eyed pike.
Guides available at Ely.
Portages marked by signs showing names of lakes and portage distances; portages around rapids are noted.
Current in North and South Kawishiwi Rivers sluggish, rapids fast.

This route has excellent scenery along the rivers and many fair though undeveloped camp sites.

WHITE IRON LAKE or SILVER RAPIDS *(lodges, meals, housekeeping cabins, boating, swimming, fishing, outfitting)* is 8 miles east of Ely *(see Tour 8)*, where motor transportation to White Iron Lake or Silver Rapids is available.

East from White Iron Lake and Silver Rapids on North Kawishiwi River *(upstream)* into FARM LAKE; east across Farm into NORTH KAWISHIWI RIVER *(upstream)*; 132-rod portage from south bank of N. Kawishiwi River to CLEAR LAKE *(end of first day's trip; undeveloped public camp site)*.

South across Clear to 224-rod portage to S. KAWISHIWI RIVER; south and west *(downstream)* on S. Kawishiwi; several portages *(swift rapids)* on S. Kawishiwi River into BIRCH LAKE *(end of second day's trip; excellent developed public campground, community building, and ranger station at east end of Birch Lake)*.

Paddle west across Birch and turn north to portage into WHITE IRON RIVER; downstream *(few portages; swift rapids)* on river to WHITE IRON LAKE; paddle north to starting point.

Canoe Trip 9: *From Ely Area*

Fall Lake or Winton—Basswood Lake.

1 day: 13 miles of paddling, 4 miles of portaging.

Good fishing for pike.
Guides available at Ely, Winton, or Fall Lake.
There are no portage signs.

This route is a quick entry to international waters and has no developed camp sites.

FALL LAKE *(lodge, meals, housekeeping cabins, boating, fishing, swimming, outfitting)* is 5 miles east of Ely *(see Tour 8)*, where motor transportation to Fall Lake is available.

Paddle to northeast end of Fall Lake; portage 4 m. *(motor transportation)* to BASSWOOD LAKE. Retrace to starting point *(1 day)* or paddle northeast 5 m. *(see Canoe Trip #1)*.

BRANCH ROUTE TO BASSWOOD LAKE *(via Pipestone Bay; 15 miles of paddling, 0.25 miles of portaging; 1 day one way; interesting falls and rapids; good pike fishing; topography very rugged, not much timber)*.

Paddle to northwest arm of Fall Lake and portage *10 rods (falls)* to NEWTON LAKE; north on Newton and portage *61 rods (falls)* to PIPESTONE BAY, a part of Basswood Lake *(see Canoe Trip #1)*. Retrace to starting point *(1 day)*.

Canoe Trip 10: *From Ely Area*

Burntside Lake—Fenske Lake—Grassy Lake—Murphy Lake.
3 days: 20 miles of paddling; 4.5 miles of portaging.

Excellent fishing for bass and wall-eyed pike.
Guides available at Burntside Lake or Ely.
Portages marked by signs showing names of lakes and portage distances; portages around rapids are noted.
Current in rivers is negligible.

This is an interesting route to international waters. Except for the Fenske Lake Camp and Picnic Grounds, its camp sites are undeveloped.

BURNTSIDE LAKE *(lodges, housekeeping cabins, fishing, swimming, outfitting)* is 8 miles northwest of Ely *(see Tour 8)*, where motor transportation to Burntside Lake is available.

North on Burntside Lake, upstream on DEAD RIVER and along eastern tip of WEST TWIN LAKE into EAST TWIN LAKE; *13-rod* portage from north end of East Twin to EVERETT LAKE; north across west end of Everett and portage *120 rods*, crossing the ELY-BUYCK TRAIL to FENSKE LAKE *(end of first day's trip; well-developed camp and picnic grounds; excellent bass fishing; an alternate starting point; see Tour 8)*.

East across Fenske and portage *10 rods* to LITTLE SLETTEN LAKE *(excellent bass fishing)*; north across Little Sletten and portage *70 rods* to BIG SLETTEN LAKE *(excellent bass fishing)*; north across Big Sletten and portage *122 rods* to T LAKE *(excellent bass fishing)*; north across T Lake and portage *45 rods* to GRASSY LAKE *(end of second day's trip; undeveloped camp site; excellent bass fishing)*.

East across Grassy into RANGE RIVER *(downstream)*; *26-rod* portage *(rapids)* Range River to Range River; *141-rod* portage *(rapids)* from Range River to Range River, and then RANGE LAKE; *160-rod* portage from north end of Range Lake to SANDPIT LAKE; north across Sandpit to MURPHY LAKE *(end of third day's trip; undeveloped public camp site)*.

Retrace to starting point *(3 days)* or paddle west across Murphy and portage 1.25 *m.* to JACKFISH BAY of BASSWOOD LAKE *(see Canoe Trip #1)*. Or follow either of two branch routes *(see Branch Routes)*.

1. BRANCH ROUTE TO CROOKED LAKE *(via Gun Lake; 17 miles of paddling, 1.3 miles of portaging; 2 days; partly logged-over area but beautiful scenery; excellent bass and pike fishing)*.
Portage *80 rods* from north end of MURPHY LAKE into HORSE LAKE; skirt southwest end of Horse and portage *40 rods* into small POND; then *15 rods* to FOURTOWN LAKE; from west end of Fourtown portage *50 rods* to BOOT LAKE; west and north on Boot and portage *56 rods* to FAIRY LAKE; *70-rod* portage from north end of Fairy into GUN LAKE *(end of first day's trip; undeveloped public camp site)*. Portage *300 rods* from northeast end of Gun to WAGOSH LAKE *(excellent bass fishing)*; *33-rod* portage from north end of Wagosh to NIKI LAKE *(excellent bass fishing)*; from Niki paddle into CHIP-

PEWA RIVER *(downstream)*; one short portage *(rapids)* on river and paddle to CHIPPEWA LAKE; from west end of Chippewa paddle into TURTLE RIVER *(downstream)*; with 2 or 3 short liftovers *(portages)* around beaver dams follow Turtle River into PAPOOSE LAKE; north on Papoose into Turtle River *(downstream)* and portage *80 rods* to FRIDAY BAY of CROOKED LAKE *(end of second day's trip; undeveloped public camp site)*. Retrace to Murphy Lake *(2 days, also see Canoe Trip 1)*.

2. BRANCH ROUTE TO CROOKED LAKE *(via Horse River; 6 miles of paddling, 1 mile of portaging; 1 day; submerged rocks in river; good wall-eyed pike fishing; game plentiful)*.

Portage *80 rods* from north end of MURPHY LAKE into HORSE LAKE *(excellent wall-eyed pike fishing)*; paddle from east side of Horse Lake into HORSE RIVER *(downstream)*; *42-rod* portage *(rapids)* from Horse River to Horse River; *51-rod* portage from Horse River to Horse River *(rapids)*; *234-rod* portage *(rapids)* from Horse River to Horse River; paddle into BASSWOOD RIVER *(downstream)*, then into CROOKED LAKE *(undeveloped public camp site)*. Retrace to Murphy Lake *(1 day, also see Canoe Trip 1)*.

Canoe Trip 11: *From Ely Area*

Burntside Lake—Big Lake—Stuart Lake—Boulder River.
3 days: 34 miles of paddling; 6 miles of portaging.

Average fishing for bass.
Guides available at Burntside Lake or Ely.
Portages are marked by signs showing names of lakes and portage distances; portages around rapids are noted.
Currents in Stuart, Dahlgren, and Boulder Rivers very slow where paddling is done.

This route passes through an interesting area with numerous beaver dams, moose, deer, and bear. Camp sites are well developed.

BURNTSIDE LAKE *(lodges, housekeeping cabins, boating, fishing, swimming, outfitting)* is 8 miles northwest of Ely *(see Tour 8)*, where motor transportation to Burntside Lake is available.

North across Burntside Lake into NORTH ARM of lake; *240-rod* portage northwest from North Arm to SLIM LAKE; *2-mile* portage from Slim Lake to Big Lake *(end of first day's trip; developed public campground at north end)*.

Portage *77 rods* to ELY-BUYCK ROAD *(another starting point)*; *1.3-mile* portage north from Ely-Buyck Road to STUART RIVER; north *(downstream)* on Stuart River; *96-rod* portage *(rapids)* from Stuart River to Stuart River; *54-rod* portage *(rapids)* from Stuart River to Stuart River; *64-rod* portage *(rapids)* from Stuart River to Stuart River; *74-rod* portage *(rapids)* from Stuart River to STUART LAKE *(end of second day's trip; developed public campground; good bass fishing)*.

North and west across lower half of Stuart Lake; *128-rod* portage from west end of Stuart Lake to DAHLGREN RIVER; north *(downstream)* on Dahlgren River *(submerged rocks, but passable)*; *122-rod* portage *(rapids)* from Dahlgren River to Boulder River. Retrace to starting point *(3 days)*.

For alternate return *(see Canoe Trip #12)* or paddle northeast *(downstream)* into LAC LA CROIX *(see Canoe Trip #1)*.

Canoe Trip 12: *From Ely Area*

Burntside Lake—Cummings Lake—Moose Lake—Nina Moose Lake—
Lake Agnes.
4 days: 31 miles of paddling; 4.75 miles of portaging.

Good fishing for bass and wall-eyed pike.
Guides available at Burntside Lake and Ely.
Portages marked by signs showing names of lakes and portage distances; portages
around rapids are noted.
Current in river is negligible.

This route passes through wild rugged country and affords excellent opportunities to see moose and deer. Its camp sites are only partially developed.

BURNTSIDE LAKE *(lodges, housekeeping cabins, boating, fishing,
swimming, outfitting)* is 8 miles northwest of Ely *(see Tour 8)*, where
motor transportation to Burntside Lake is available.

West across Burntside Lake and portage 1.4 *m.* to CRAB LAKE; northwest across Crab and portage 16 *rods* into LITTLE CRAB LAKE *(good
bass fishing)*; paddle north *(downstream)* into KORB RIVER and portage
north 24 *rods* to KORB LAKE *(good bass fishing)*; across Korb Lake
east into Korb River *(downstream)*; 60-*rod* portage *(rapids)* west from
Korb River to eastern shore of CUMMINGS LAKE *(end of first day's
trip; partially developed camp site; good bass fishing)*.

North across Cummings; portage 2 *miles* to northern shore of MOOSE
LAKE *(end of second day's trip; partially developed camp site; good bass
fishing)*.

Northwest across Moose Lake and portage 71 *rods (rapids)* to MOOSE
RIVER; 137-*rod* portage *(rapids)* from Moose River to Moose River;
130-*rod* portage *(rapids)* from Moose River to Moose River; 77-*rod*
portage *(rapids)* from Moose River to Moose River; 60-*rod* portage
(rapids) from Moose River to Moose River; 117-*rod* portage *(rapids)*
from Moose River to Moose River; follow Moose River to ELY-BUYCK
ROAD *(developed public campground; another starting point)*; portage
177 *rods* across Ely-Buyck Road and past rapids to Moose River; two short
portages *(rapids)* on Moose River to NINA MOOSE LAKE *(end of third
day's trip; partially developed camp site; excellent pike fishing)*.

Cross Nina Moose Lake north into NINA MOOSE RIVER *(downstream)* two 0.3-*mile* portages *(rapids)* on Nina Moose River to LAKE
AGNES *(end of fourth day's trip; partially developed public camp site;
good wall-eyed pike fishing)*.

Retrace to starting point *(4 days)*; or cross Lake Agnes northeast and
portage 116 *rods* to BOULDER RIVER *(see Canoe Trip #11; ½ day)*;
or follow Branch Route to Lac La Croix *(see Branch Route)*.

BRANCH ROUTE TO LAC LA CROIX *(via Oyster Lake, 15 miles of paddling; 1.25 miles of portaging, 2 days; moose and deer; good landlocked salmon
and wall-eyed pike fishing; rigorous traveling)*.
Portage 190 *rods* from LAKE AGNES to OYSTER RIVER; upstream on Oyster

River with short portage *(rapids)* from Oyster River into OYSTER LAKE *(end of first day's trip; partially developed public camp site; landlocked-salmon fishing)*.

West across Oyster Lake and portage *64 rods* to ROCKY LAKE; north on Rocky Lake and portage *87 rods* to GREEN LAKE; north on Green and portage *122 rods* to GE-BE-ON-E-QUET LAKE; north on Ge-be-on-e-quet Lake and portage *35 rods (small falls)* to GE-BE-ON-E-QUET CREEK and paddle *(downstream)* into POCKET CREEK; paddle west *(downstream)* and portage *24 rods (rapids)* from Pocket Creek to Pocket Creek; paddle into POCKET RIVER and west *(downstream)* into LAC LA CROIX *(see Canoe Trip 1)*.

Retrace to Lake Agnes *(2 days)*, or follow Canoe Trip 1.

Canoe Trip 13: *From Ely Area*

Moose Lake—Ensign Lake—Thomas Lake—Kekekabic Lake—Knife Lake.

4 days: 35 miles of paddling; 2 miles of portaging.

Variety of fishing.
Guides available at Moose Lake, Ely, and Winton.
There are no portage signs on this route; but the portages are good, some with docks.
Portages around rapids are noted in text.
Current in Thomas River is very sluggish.

This route offers a convenient entry into international waters. Its camp sites are only partially developed.

MOOSE LAKE *(meals, lodging, housekeeping cabins, boating, swimming, fishing, outfitting)* is 18 miles east of Ely *(see Tour 8)*, where motor transportation to Moose Lake is available.

North across Moose Lake and into NEWFOUND LAKE *(to reach Canoe Trip #1 paddle north across Newfound to Sucker Lake; north across Sucker into Carp; north across Carp into Birch Lake)*; 36-rod portage *(rapids)* from extreme northeast end of Newfound to ENSIGN LAKE and paddle to southeast shore *(end of first day's trip; partially developed camp site)*.

Portage 56 *rods* south to BASS LAKE; south across Bass and portage 177 *rods* to FLY LAKE; south across Fly and portage 25 *rods* to MARSH LAKE; south across Marsh and portage 45 *rods* to JORDEN LAKE; 10-*rod* portage from east end of Jorden to IMA LAKE; southeast across Ima and portage 50 *rods* to THOMAS RIVER; south *(upstream)* on Thomas River portaging 17 *rods (rapids)* from Thomas River to Thomas River; 29-*rod* portage from Thomas River to POND; south across Pond and portage 8 *rods* to THOMAS LAKE *(end of second day's trip; partially developed camp site)*.

East on Thomas and paddle through channel into FRAZER LAKE; 16-*rod* portage from north end of Frazer to GERUND LAKE; 30-*rod* portage from north end of Gerund to AHMAKOSE LAKE; 96-*rod* portage from north end of Ahmakose to WISINI LAKE; 10-*rod* portage from north end of Wisini to STRUP LAKE; 86-*rod* portage from northwest end of Strup to KEKEKABIC LAKE *(end of third day's trip; partially developed camp site)*.

Portage 86 *rods* from north end of Kekekabic to PICKLE LAKE; 28-*rod* portage from north shore of Pickle to SPOON LAKE; north across middle of Spoon and portage 31 *rods* to BONNIE LAKE; northeast across Bonnie and portage 42 *rods* to KNIFE LAKE and paddle to western shore *(end of fourth day's trip; partially developed camp site).*

To return: Follow Canoe Trip #1, then through Sucker, Newfound, Moose Lakes *(1 day)*; or retrace *(4 days).*

Canoe Trip 14: *From Tower Area*

Vermilion Lake—Little Trout Lake—Little Indian Sioux River camp site —East Bay of Loon Lake—Lac La Croix.
4 days: 57 miles of paddling; 5.5 miles of portaging.

Good fishing for wall-eyed pike, bass, and landlocked salmon.
Portages on Little Indian Sioux River from Little Trout Lake to Lac La Croix are only ones marked; portages around rapids are noted in text.
Guides available at Tower (Vermilion Lake).
Current in rivers is sluggish.

This route, through scenic country, is an early Indian route. Portages are good and moose are plentiful. The Little Indian Sioux Campgrounds are the only ones developed.

Starting point is at VERMILION LAKE *(resorts, meals, lodging, public campgrounds, housekeeping cabins, excursion trips, marine mail service, complete outfitting)* at Tower.

North across Vermilion Lake around east end of PINE ISLAND, turn west around north side of island, then north through NARROWS; 80-*rod* portage *(motor transportation)* from north end of Narrows to TROUT LAKE *(see branch route to Burntside Lake via Pine Lake)*; paddle from northeast end of Trout into LITTLE TROUT LAKE *(end of first day's trip; undeveloped camp site; sand beach).*

Portage 1.3 *m. (submerged rocks)* from northeast end of Little Trout to LITTLE INDIAN SIOUX RIVER *(see branch route to Burntside Lake via Little Indian Sioux River)*; north *(downstream)* on Little Indian Sioux River and make a 24-*rod* portage *(rapids)* from Little Indian Sioux River to Little Indian Sioux River; 90-*rod* portage *(rapids)* from Little Indian Sioux River to Little Indian Sioux River; 15-*rod* portage *(Sioux Falls)* from Little Indian Sioux River to Little Indian Sioux River; portage 80 *rods* around rapids and across ELY-BUYCK ROAD *(end of second day's trip; developed public campground).*

Portage 125 *rods* from Little Indian Sioux River to Little Indian Sioux River and paddle into UPPER PAUNESS LAKE; east across Upper Pauness and portage 42 *rods* east to LOWER PAUNESS LAKE; north on Lower Pauness and portage 110 *rods* to LOON LAKE *(forest lookout station; interesting canyon called Devil's Cascade)*; paddle to EAST BAY in Loon *(end of third day's trip: undeveloped public camp site; sand beach; see Canoe Trip #1).*

Portage 174 *rods* from northeast arm of Loon to SLIM LAKE; 47-*rod* portage from north end of Slim to CREEK; paddle north *(downstream)* on Creek into POND and portage north 74 *rods* to SOUTH LAKE; southeast on South and portage 125 *rods (very steep portage)* to STEEP LAKE *(excellent bass fishing);* 46-*rod* portage from north end of Steep to EU-GENE LAKE; 86-*rod* portage from north end of Eugene to GUN LAKE *(good fishing for landlocked salmon);* 55-*rod* portage from north end of Gun to LAC LA CROIX *(undeveloped public camp site; see Canoe Trip #1).*

Retrace to starting point *(4 days).*

1. BRANCH ROUTE TO BURNTSIDE LAKE *(via Pine Lake; 24 miles of paddling, 6 miles of portaging; 2 days; good bass fishing and beautiful scenery).*

From east shore of TROUT LAKE portage 240 *rods* to PINE LAKE; 1.8-*mile* portage from north end of Pine to BUCK LAKE *(black-bass fishing);* 99-*rod* portage from southeast end of Buck to WESTERN LAKE *(end of first day's trip; undeveloped public camp site; black-bass fishing).*

Portage 199 *rods* from east end of Western to GLENMORE LAKE *(good bass fishing);* 189-*rod* portage from southeast end of Glenmore to SCHLAMN LAKE *(good bass fishing);* 80-*rod* portage from extreme east end of Schlamn to LUNNETTA LAKE *(good bass fishing);* 80-*rod* portage *(rapids)* from northeast end of Lunnetta to LUNNETTA RIVER; east *(downstream)* on Lunnetta into LITTLE CRAB LAKE; south on Little Crab and portage 16 *rods* to CRAB LAKE; 1.3-*mile* portage from southeast end of Crab to BURNTSIDE LAKE; east across Burntside to lodges and road, where motor transportation is available at Tower.

2. BRANCH ROUTE TO BURNTSIDE LAKE *(via Little Indian Sioux River; 24 miles of paddling; 2.5 miles of portaging; 3 days; route very crooked and traveling slow; good bass fishing).*

South and east on LITTLE INDIAN SIOUX RIVER *(upstream)* and portage 21 *rods (rapids)* from Little Indian Sioux River to Little Indian Sioux River; southeast and portage 32 *rods (rapids)* from Little Indian Sioux River to Little Indian Sioux River; 10-*rod* portage *(rapids)* from Little Indian Sioux River to Little Indian Sioux River; 74-*rod* portage *(rapids)* from Little Indian Sioux River to Little Indian Sioux River; 27-*rod* portage *(rapids)* from Little Indian Sioux River to Little Indian Sioux River; 39-*rod* portage *(rapids)* from Little Indian Sioux River to Little Indian Sioux River; 24-*rod* portage *(rapids)* from Little Indian Sioux River to Little Indian Sioux River; 99-*rod* portage *(rapids)* from Little Indian Sioux River to OTTER LAKE *(end of first day's trip; undeveloped public camp site).* East across Otter and portage 4 rods to CUMMINGS LAKE; paddle across to eastern shore *(end of second day's trip; undeveloped public camp site; good bass fishing).*

Portage 80 *rods* to KORB LAKE *(good black-bass fishing);* paddle west across Korb and into KORB RIVER *(upstream);* 24-*rod* portage *(rapids)* from Korb River to Korb River and paddle into LITTLE CRAB LAKE; south on Little Crab and portage 16 *rods* to CRAB LAKE; 1.3-*mile* portage from southeast end of Crab to BURNTSIDE LAKE; east across Burntside to lodges and road, where motor transportation is available to Tower.

Canoe Trip 15: *From Tower Area*

Vermilion Lake—Vermilion Dam—Vermilion River—Crane Lake.
4 days: 59 miles of paddling; 2 miles of portaging.

Average fishing for wall-eyed and northern pike.
Guides available at Tower, Vermilion Dam, Crane Lake.
Portages are unmarked.
River current is not rapid.

This route, used by the Indians and early explorers, passes many small farms along the riverbank and goes through several wild-rice beds where wild ducks feed. Wildrice beds, which resemble large grain fields in shallow water, usually along the lake shore, are feeding places for wild fowl at certain times of the year.

Starting point is at VERMILION LAKE *(resorts, meals, lodging, public undeveloped campgrounds, housekeeping cabins, excursion trips, marine mail service, fishing, swimming, boating, complete outfitting)* at Tower.

North and northwest on Vermilion Lake and north through NILES BAY; north to VERMILION DAM *(end of first day's trip; resorts, meals, lodging, housekeeping cabins, excursion trips, fishing, boating, swimming, outfitting, undeveloped camp site).*

100-*rod* portage *(around falls and dam)*; northeast into VERMILION RIVER; downstream on river and portage 80 *rods (rapids)* from Vermilion River to Vermilion River; 60-*rod* portage *(rapids)* from Vermilion River to Vermilion River; 40-*rod* portage *(rapids)* from Vermilion River to Vermilion River; 50-*rod* portage *(rapids)* from Vermilion River to Vermilion River; 30-*rod* portage *(rapids)* from Vermilion River to Vermilion River *(end of second day's trip; undeveloped camp site).*

Portage 40 *rods (rapids)* from Vermilion River to Vermilion River; 40-*rod* portage *(rapids)* from Vermilion River to Vermilion River; 60-*rod* portage *(rapids)* from Vermilion River to Vermilion River *(end of third day's trip; undeveloped camp site).*

Portage 40 *rods (rapids)* from Vermilion River to Vermilion River; 30-*rod* portage *(rapids)* from Vermilion River to Vermilion River; 0.8-*mile* portage *(around falls and gorge)* from *Vermilion River to* CRANE LAKE *(end of the fourth day's trip; several campgrounds; meals, lodging, housekeeping cabins; swimming; boating, outfitting; good wall-eyed pike fishing; see Canoe Trip #1).*

PART IV

Appendices

Chronology

1654–60   Radisson and Groseilliers, French traders, make two journeys into the "upper country," possibly Minnesota, and demonstrate possibilities of a remunerative fur trade.

1665   Father Claude Allouez establishes a Jesuit mission at La Pointe, near Ashland, Wisconsin, and finds hostile Sioux at the mouth of the St. Louis River at the head of Lake Superior.

1670–71   Jesuit cartographers map Lac Tracy or Supérieur (Lake Superior), with a river, presumably the St. Louis, at the western end.

1679   Daniel Greysolon, Sieur du Luth (DuLhut) plants the banner of France in the vicinity of Duluth, and "in the principal village of the Sioux tribe, known as the Issati" near Mille Lacs.

1680   Father Louis Hennepin, Recollet missionary, and his companions, Accault and Auguelle, are sent by La Salle to explore the upper Mississippi which they reach after a journey down the Illinois. The three are captured by the Sioux and taken to the Indian village at Mille Lacs. Hennepin and Auguelle on their descent of the Mississippi discover and name the Falls of St. Anthony.

1689   May 8, at Fort St. Antoine, near the foot of Lake Pepin, Nicholas Perrot, who reached the upper Mississippi several years before, lays formal claim to all the upper river for France.

1695   Pierre Charles le Sueur builds a fort on Isle Pele (Prairie Island) above Red Wing.

1700   Le Sueur establishes Fort L'Huillier on the Blue Earth River near Mankato.

1727   Sieur de la Perriere and Jesuits establish Fort Beauharnois at Frontenac on Lake Pepin and open first mission in Minnesota.

1731   Sieur de la Vérendrye, his sons, and his nephew, La Jemeraye, begin exploring waterways on northern border and extend operations far northwest into Canada. One of the many forts erected along this route is St. Charles, on the Lake of the Woods, within the present area of Minnesota.

1756   Joseph Marin and his son abandon the Frontenac post, last French fort on the upper Mississippi.

1763   France cedes to Great Britain the Minnesota country east of the Mississippi, the area west of the river having been secretly relinquished to Spain the previous year. British traders take over the fur traffic.

1766–67   Jonathan Carver, New Englander, exploring under British auspices, spends the winter on the upper Mississippi, ascends the Minnesota River, and visits the Sioux at a cave in the St. Paul river bluffs.

1783   Land east of the Mississippi is ceded to the United States by Great Britain.

1784   The Northwest Company secures control of the Minnesota fur trade.

1789   Wabasha mobilizes a thousand Sioux warriors to help the British quell the Revolution.

1796   Laws of the Ordinance of 1787 are extended over the Northwest Territory, including the northeastern third of Minnesota, east of the Mississippi River.

1800   Spanish possessions west of the Mississippi are retroceded to France.

1803   The Louisiana Purchase gives the United States a vast region west of the Mississippi, including western Minnesota.

1805   Lt. Zebulon M. Pike visits upper Mississippi, secures from Sioux the land cessions at the mouths of the Minnesota and St. Croix Rivers for United States military posts.

1806   The Rev. Samuel Peters alleges, in a petition to Congress, that he has purchased from Carver's American heirs their right to the grant made in 1767.

1812   British military occupancy is reestablished on upper Mississippi. Indians of Minnesota region join the British in the war.
        Lord Selkirk establishes a colony of Irish and Scotch at the present site of Winnipeg, Manitoba, in the lower Red River Valley.

1815   The last British garrison on upper Mississippi evacuates Prairie du Chien.

1816   Control of the fur trade south of the international boundary passes from the Northwest Company to John Jacob Astor's American Fur Company.

1819   United States troops establish a cantonment, forerunner of Fort St. Anthony, on the south shore of the mouth of Minnesota River.

1820   September 10, soldiers lay the cornerstone of Fort St. Anthony (forerunner of Fort Snelling), at mouth of the Minnesota River, on opposite shore from cantonment at Mendota.
        Gen. Lewis Cass, Governor of Michigan Territory, visits Minnesota with an exploring party, reaches the Mississippi by way of Sandy Lake, ascends to Cass Lake, and descending to Fort St. Anthony attempts mediation between the Sioux and Chippewa.

1821   On the west bank of the Falls of St. Anthony the garrison starts building the first sawmill in the Minnesota region.
        Five Swiss families from Selkirk colony in Red River Valley seek refuge at Fort Snelling and start farming.

1823   May 10, the *Virginia*, first steamboat to navigate the Mississippi from St. Louis to the Minnesota River, reaches Fort St. Anthony.
        Near the sawmill on west bank of the Falls of St. Anthony the gar-

rison at Fort St. Anthony starts operating the first grist and flour mill of the Minnesota region.

Maj. Stephen H. Long explores the Minnesota and Red River Valleys and the northern frontier.

An Italian, Giacomo C. Beltrami, explores near the source of the Mississippi.

1825   The dividing line between the Sioux and Chippewa is agreed upon at Prairie du Chien.

Name of Fort St. Anthony changed to Fort Snelling.

1826   The Red River overflows, driving many of Selkirk's Swiss colonists to the refugee settlement at Fort Snelling, where they arrive the following year.

1832   Henry R. Schoolcraft, previously a member of the Cass expedition, reaches the upper Mississippi River by way of Fond du Lac (Duluth), the Savanna portage, and Sandy Lake, and locates the source of the Mississippi in a lake which he names Itasca, July 13.

1833   October, the Rev. W. T. Boutwell at Leech Lake establishes the first Protestant mission among Minnesota Indians west of the Mississippi.

1834   Henry H. Sibley settles at the mouth of the Minnesota River, near the fort, as an agent for the American Fur Company.

The Pond brothers, missionaries to the Sioux, arrive at Fort Snelling. During the summer they build a cabin on Lake Calhoun.

1835   A Presbyterian church, the first church for white people in Minnesota, is organized at Fort Snelling.

George Catlin, famous painter of Indian subjects, visits Minnesota; the following year he examines the red pipestone quarries in the southwestern part of the State.

George W. Featherstonhaugh makes a geological survey of the southwestern part of the State.

The Lac qui Parle mission is founded by the Rev. Thomas Smith Williamson.

1836   Commercial logging begins on the St. Croix.

Joseph N. Nicollet establishes headquarters at Fort Snelling and begins Minnesota explorations. His careful scientific investigations indicate that a rivulet feeding Lake Itasca is the source of the Mississippi.

Wisconsin Territory organized. Minnesota East becomes part of Crawford County, Wisconsin.

1837   Governor Henry Dodge of the Wisconsin Territory meets the Chippewa at Fort Snelling and obtains cession of all their pine lands on the St. Croix and its tributaries.

The Sioux cede their land east of the Mississippi to the United States, opening great areas for settlement.

1838   Franklin Steele takes squatter's claim and builds shanty on east bank of the Falls of St. Anthony; this is the nucleus of Minneapolis. Pierre Parrant builds shanty on present site of St. Paul.

1839   First commercial sawmill in the State begins operation at Marine-on-the-St. Croix.

Joseph Renshaw Brown takes a claim at Dakota, addition to Stillwater.

1840   January 9, St. Croix County, including all of Minnesota east of the Mississippi, is established by Wisconsin Territory.

May 6, by order of the Secretary of War, Swiss squatters are expelled from Fort Snelling and, moving down the river, establish the village first known as Pig's Eye, later St. Paul.

1841   November, a log chapel erected by Father Lucian Galtier on the present site of St. Paul, is dedicated to St. Paul, the Apostle.

First post office in Minnesota opens at Point Douglas, at the mouth of the St. Croix River.

1843   A sawmill is built in the village of Stillwater, which is rapidly absorbing Dakota.

1847   St. Paul town site is platted, and within its limits the first school in the State for children of all races and sects is opened.

Construction of a sawmill starts on the east bank of the Falls of St. Anthony.

1848   May 29, Wisconsin becomes a State, but without jurisdiction over the part of its territory in the Minnesota region.

June 12, Minnesota settlers hold a meeting at St. Paul to consider a demand for Territorial status.

August 26, a settlers convention meets at Stillwater and resolves to ask that a new Territory be created and named Minnesota.

October 20, Henry H. Sibley, of Mendota, is elected delegate to Congress from that part of the Wisconsin Territory not included in the new State.

Land east of the Mississippi is placed on sale by Government.

St. Anthony Village is platted.

1849   January 15, Delegate Sibley is admitted to Congress.

March 3, Congress creates the Minnesota Territory.

March 15, nominations for Territorial officers are submitted to the Senate by President Taylor. Alexander Ramsey of Pennsylvania is commissioned Governor on April 2.

April 28, *The Minnesota Pioneer,* the first newspaper to be printed in Minnesota, is issued at St. Paul, with James Goodhue as editor.

June 1, Governor Ramsey declares the Territory organized.

September 3, the first Territorial Legislature convenes at St. Paul and adjourns November 1.

November 1, St. Paul is incorporated.

November 15, the Minnesota Historical Society, oldest cultural institution in the State, is organized.

1850   The census records 6,077 inhabitants.

1851   The capitol, university, and penitentiary are located at St. Paul, St. Anthony (Minneapolis), and Stillwater respectively.
November 26, the preparatory department of the State university opens at St. Anthony.
The Sioux treaties of Traverse des Sioux and Mendota open the territory west of the Mississippi for settlement.

1852   A prohibitory liquor law is passed and although ratified by the people April 5 is declared void by a Territorial court.
Minneapolis is proposed as the name for a village on south side of the Falls of St. Anthony.

1853   A great tide of immigration to the Sioux cessions begins.
The first capitol is completed at St. Paul.
Baldwin School, later Macalester College, is opened at St. Paul.

1854   March 4, St. Paul is given a city charter.
Hamline University is established at Red Wing by the Methodists.
St. Anthony Falls commercial flour mills begin operation.
Opening of the Rock Island Railroad, the first line to reach the Mississippi, is celebrated in Minnesota.
Minneapolis is surveyed.

1855   The extravagant land boom and inflation period commences.
April 13, the City of St. Anthony is organized.
August 2, the Minneapolis plat is filed.

1856   March 1, Minneapolis is incorporated a "town with council."
May 26, the original plat of Duluth is filed.

1857   February 26, Congress passes the Minnesota Enabling Act.
July 13, the Minnesota Constitutional Convention assembles.
August 27, the boom is checked by financial panic.
October 13, a constitution is adopted and State officers elected, headed by Sibley as Governor.
The census shows 150,037 population.
St. John's College near St. Cloud is opened by Benedictines.

1858   May 11, Minnesota is admitted to the Union as a State.
May 24, State officers are sworn in.
The State authorizes a $5,000,000 loan to railroads; grading begins.

1859   October 11, at first election after Minnesota's admission to the Union, Ramsey is elected Governor.
Hard times continue; railroad construction ceases.
The State forecloses mortage loan bonds on land-grant railroads.
First wheat is exported.

1860   Federal census numbers 172,023 Minnesotans.
Telegraphic communication is established.
First normal school west of Mississippi is opened by the State at Winona.

1861   April 14, Governor Ramsey, at Washington, makes the first proffer of Civil War troops by offering a thousand men from Minnesota.

June 22, First Minnesota Regiment, vanguard of Minnesota's contribution of 21,982 troops, leaves Fort Snelling.

1862 July 2, first railroad in Minnesota begins operations between St. Paul and St. Anthony (Minneapolis).

August 18, Minnesota Sioux revolt; more than 400 whites are killed within a few days.

September 23, Indians are defeated at Battle of Wood Lake and the white captives released.

December 26, thirty-eight of the 306 condemned Indians are hanged at Mankato.

1863 The State School for the Deaf opens at Faribault.

1866 December 6, State Hospital, the asylum for the insane, opens at St. Peter.

A department for the blind is added to the State school at Faribault.

1867 Regular railroad communication is established with Chicago.

A new period of prosperity brings heavy immigration, railroad building, and real estate inflation.

State Reform School (forerunner of State Training School at Red Wing) opens at St. Paul.

Minneapolis is given a city charter.

1868 A State Normal School opens at Mankato.

1869 Collegiate department of University of Minnesota opens with William W. Folwell as chancellor.

The Grange movement, originated by a Minnesotan, Oliver H. Kelley, centers in Minnesota. Forty of the 49 chapters are organized here.

A State Normal School opens at St. Cloud.

1870 The population reaches 439,706.

Duluth and St. Paul are connected by a railroad.

A process invented by Edmond N. La Croix revolutionizes wheat milling.

1871 Railroads reach Red River Valley from St. Paul and Duluth.

First Granger Acts are passed by legislature.

1872 The State Board of Health, third in the Union, is created by the legislature.

Minneapolis and St. Anthony merge as City of Minneapolis.

1873 January 7, 8, 9, blizzard kills 70 persons and cripples many others. The five-year grasshopper invasion begins.

Following the eastern financial failures, Jay Cooke's projected railroad and steamboat center of Duluth is almost wiped out.

1874 Chilled rollers, perfected after European models, are introduced in the Washburn "A" Mill, Minneapolis.

1875 A Constitutional amendment authorizes women to hold office and vote in school affairs.

1877   An amendment providing for biennial instead of annual sessions of State Legislature is adopted.

1878   May 2, three flour mills at Minneapolis explode and 18 lives are lost. Railroads are extended into the extreme northwestern part of the State, carrying many settlers to the Red River Valley.

1879   A State hospital for the insane opens at Rochester.
A department for the feeble-minded is added to the State school at Faribault.
December 10, President Hayes appoints Alexander Ramsey Secretary of War.

1880   The population reaches 780,773.

1881   First biennial session of legislature opens.
Provision is made for payment of repudiated railroad bonds of 1858.
March 1, the State Capitol is destroyed by fire but a second capitol is planned to occupy the same site.
March 5, President Garfield appoints William Windom Secretary of the Treasury.

1884   The first iron ore is shipped from Vermilion Range.

1885   Million population mark is passed; the State census records 1,117,798 residents.

1886   A State Public School for Dependent Children opens at Owatonna.

1887   The State school tax is adopted.
The Merritt brothers discover iron ore on the Mesabi Range.

1888   A State Normal School opens at Moorhead.

1889   The Minnesota State Reformatory opens at St. Cloud.
Work begins on the first electric railroad in State, at Stillwater.
The first co-operative cheese factory and creamery is organized, in McLeod County.
St. Mary's Hospital is opened at Rochester, with Dr. William W. Mayo and his two sons as members of the staff.

1890   A State hospital for the insane opens quarters at Fergus Falls.
Federal census lists the population at 1,301,826.
The State Training School moves to Red Wing.

1892   October 17, first iron ore is shipped from the Mesabi Range.
June 7, Republican National Convention opens at Minneapolis.

1893   Financial panic checks the rapid growth of lumbering and milling, railroad expansion, and settlement.
Merritt mining interests are pledged to John D. Rockefeller.

1894   Forest fires wipe out the towns of Hinckley and Sandstone, sweep over 400 square miles, cause the death of more than 400 persons, and leave 2,200 homeless. Property loss exceeds $1,000,000.

1896   Large tracts of timber and farm lands in the northern part of State are opened to settlement by the reduction of Red Lake Chippewa Indian Reservation.

1898   July 27, cornerstone for new capitol is laid.

Minnesota, first State to respond to the President's call, supplies four regiments for the Spanish-American War.

1899   John Lind, first non-Republican Governor since 1860, is inaugurated.

1900   Population reaches 1,751,394, with rural settlement almost entirely confined to southern and western part of State.

Anoka and Hastings State Asylums open.

1901   Minnesota's exhibits at the Pan-American Exposition identify her as the "Bread and Butter State".

1902   A State Normal School opens at Duluth.

1903   A new tide of immigration centers in the northern and western portions.

1905   The legislature convenes for first time in the new $8,000,000 capitol.

1907   A State-wide tax is levied for support of highways.

1908   The fiftieth anniversary of Minnesota's admission to the Union is celebrated at State Fair, with an attendance of 326,753 for the week.

A State Sanatorium for tubercular patients opens at Ah-gwah-ching (on Leech Lake).

1910   The population passes two million mark; total is 2,075,708.

1911   The first iron ore is shipped from Cuyuna Range.

State Home School for Girls opens at Sauk Center.

Gilette State Hospital for Crippled Children opens at St. Paul.

The first air mail flight is completed from Minneapolis to Rock Island; Hugh Robinson is pilot.

1912   A new primary law and "corrupt practices" act is passed by legislature in special session.

State hospital for inebriates opens at Willmar.

1915   The Mayo Foundation inaugurates medical instruction and research at Rochester, as part of the State University Graduate School.

1916   Iron, steel, and Portland cement plants for large scale production open at Duluth.

Four regiments of Minnesota militia serve on Mexican border.

July 19, National Prohibition Convention opens at St. Paul.

1917   Minnesota mobilizes war resources, contributes 123,325 for national service, and enrolls an additional 20,000 men in the "Home Guards."

1918   Forest fires sweep large areas in Carlton and St. Louis Counties; the death toll is 432.

The Minnesota Non-Partisan League is organized.

May 11, a new building for Minnesota Historical Society is dedicated.

1919   The State Normal School at Bemidji opens.

1920   Population reaches 2,287,125.

A State Reformatory for Women opens at Shakopee.

1923   Farmer-Laborites secure both seats in the United States Senate.

1925   General reorganization of State government is effected. A Commission of Administration and Finance is established.

A colony for epileptics opens at Cambridge.

1927   The Inland Waterways Corporation inaugurates barge service to St. Louis.

1930   Population reaches 2,563,953.

1931   Floyd B. Olson, first Farmer-Laborite Governor, takes office.

1932   Minnesota casts its first Democratic majority in a national election.

1933   The State trunk highway system is increased to 11,500 miles.

1937   Farmer-Laborites dominate State offices, lower house of the legislature, Minnesota Congressional delegation, and hold both U. S. senatorial seats.

≪≪≪≪≪≪≪≪≪≪≪≪≪≪≪≪≪≪☿≫≫≫≫≫≫≫≫≫≫≫≫≫≫≫≫≫≫

Suggestions for Further Reading

THIS bibliographic note focuses on books by and about the Federal Writers' Project in Minnesota, major historical works on general topics, and recent guidebooks that may be of interest to readers of *The WPA Guide to Minnesota*. Hundreds of publications on more specific subjects and on the state's communities are listed in Michael Brook, comp., *Reference Guide to Minnesota History: A Subject Bibliography of Books, Pamphlets, and Articles in English* (St. Paul: Minnesota Historical Society, 1974), and Brook and Sarah P. Rubinstein, comps., *A Supplement to Reference Guide to Minnesota History: A Subject Bibliography, 1970–80* (St. Paul: Minnesota Historical Society Press, 1983). In addition, a wealth of articles on various subjects have been published in *Minnesota History*, the quarterly journal of the Minnesota Historical Society, since the magazine's inception in 1915.

For reviews of *The WPA Guide to Minnesota*, first published in 1938 as *Minnesota: A State Guide*, see *Minnesota History* 20 (Mar. 1939): 64–66; *Saturday Review of Literature*, Dec. 24, 1938, p. 22; *Minneapolis Tribune*, Dec. 4, 1938, sec. 2, p. 6; and *St. Paul Pioneer Press*, Nov. 27, 1938, sec. 2, p. 6.

An excellent book on the Federal Writers' Project by Jerre Mangione, its former national coordinating editor, is *The Dream and the Deal: The Federal Writers' Project, 1935–1943* (New York: Little, Brown and Company, 1972). An excellent study that places the Project in the context of 1930s culture is William Stott, *Documentary Expression and Thirties America* (New York: Oxford University Press, 1973). Mabel Ulrich, director of the Minnesota Writers' Project, wrote "Salvaging Culture for the WPA," *Harper's Monthly* 178 (May 1939): 653–664, which describes the goals and frustrations of those who produced this volume.

The Minnesota Writers' Project produced several other works, including *St. Cloud Guide* (St. Cloud: n.p., 1936); *Minneapolis, Story of a City* (Minneapolis: n.p., 1940); *Minnesota*, Recreation Series (Northport, N.Y.: n.p., 1941); *Bohemian Flats* (Minneapolis: University of Minnesota Press, [1941]); *The Minnesota Arrowhead Country*, American Guide Series (Chicago: Albert Whitman, 1941); *Kittson County (A School History)* ([St. Paul]: n.p., 1940); *Logging Town: The Story of Grand Rapids, Minnesota* (Grand Rapids: [Village?], 1941); *The Mayors of St. Paul, 1850–1940*, *including the First Three Town Presidents* (St. Paul: [City Council?], 1940); and *Wabasha County*, by Franklyn Curtiss-Wedge; Minnesota County Histories Series ([Minneapolis: n.p., 1938]). "Achievements of the Minnesota Writers' Project of W.P.A." ([1942]), a typescript, is in the Minnesota Historical Society's reference library.

On the WPA in Minnesota, see Minnesota Works Projects Administration, *Works Progress Administration Accomplishments: Minnesota, 1935–1939* ([St. Paul?, 1939?]); Nancy A. Johnson, *Accomplishments: Minnesota Art Projects in the Depression Years* (Duluth: Tweed Museum of Art, University of Minnesota, 1976); Karal Ann Marling, *Wall-to-Wall America: A Cultural History of Post-Office Murals in the Great Depression* (Minneapolis: University of Minnesota Press, 1982). The Minnesota Historical Society holds the papers of the Minnesota WPA, many photographs taken by its photographers, and a microfiche catalog of photographs (available from the Library of Congress) that were taken in Minnesota and seven other midwestern states by the Farm Security Administratin and the Office of War Information.

The standard works on Minnesota history are William Watts Folwell, *A History of Minnesota*, 4 vols. (St. Paul: Minnesota Historical Society, 1921–30; corrected eds. 1956–69) and Theodore C. Blegen, *Minnesota: A History of the State* (Minneapolis: University of Minnesota Press, 1963). A brief and readable history is William E. Lass, *Minnesota: A Bicentennial History*, States and the Nation Series (New York: Norton, 1977).

Several books give an added dimension to Minnesota's history and people by emphasizing pictorial sources. See, for example, Bertha L. Heilbron, *The Thirty-Second State: A Pictorial History of Minnesota* (St. Paul: Minnesota Historical Society, 1966); John Szarkowski, *The Face of Minnesota* (Minneapolis: University of Minnesota Press, 1958); and Peter Seitz, *A Minnesota Mosaic: The Bicentennial in Photographs* (Minneapolis: Minnesota American Revolution Bicentennial Commission, 1977).

More recent guides to Minnesota are Richard Olsenius, *Minnesota Travel Companion: A Unique Guide to the History along Minnesota's Highways* (Wayzata: Bluestem Productions, 1982); *Minnesota Travel and Recreation Guide* (Rockford, Ill.: Rockford Map Publishers, Inc., 1984); and Priscilla Clayton, comp., and Vicki Stavig, ed., *Minnesota Guide* (Minneapolis: Dorn Books, 1983). Other books that give information helpful to travelers are David Gebhard and Tom Martinson, *A Guide to the Architecture of Minnesota* (Minneapolis: University of Minnesota Press, 1977); June D. Holmquist and Jean A. Brookins, *Minnesota's Major Historic Sites*, rev. 2d ed. (St. Paul: Minnesota Historical Society, 1972); June D. Holmquist and others, *History along the Highways: An Official Guide to Minnesota State Markers and Monuments*, Minnesota Historic Sites Pamphlet 3 (St. Paul: Minnesota Historical Society, 1967); Dorothy P. Kidder and Cynthia A. Matson, comps., *A Supplement to History along the Highways: An Official Guide to Minnesota Markers and Monuments, 1967–72*, Minnesota Historic Sites Pamphlet 6 (St. Paul: Minnesota Historical Society, 1973); Ron Hunt and Nancy Eubank, *A Living Past: 15 Historic Places in Minnesota*, Minnesota Historic Sites Pamphlet 7 (St. Paul: Minnesota Historical Society, 1973); Grover Singley, *Tracing Minnesota's Old Government Roads*, Minnesota Historic Sites Pamphlet 10 (St. Paul: Minnesota Historical Society, 1974); and Warren Upham, *Minnesota Geographic Names: Their Origin and Historic Significance*, rev. 2d ed. (St. Paul: Minnesota Historical Society, 1969).

Several books offer tours of specific regions of the state, including Margaret B. Bogue and Virginia A. Palmer, *Around the Shores of Lake Superior: A Guide to Historic Sites, Including a Color Tour Map Showing Lake Superior's Historic Sites* (Madison: University of Wisconsin Sea Grant College Program, 1979); Cotton Mather and Ruth Hale, *Prairie Border Country: Twin Cities to Rochester* (Prescott, Wis.: Trimbelle Press, 1980); Harry Swain and Mather, *St. Croix Border Country* (Prescott, Wis.: Trimbelle Press, 1968); Cheryl Heide et al., *Along the Mississippi: The Great River Road in Southeastern Minnesota* ([St. Paul]: Minnesota Department of Transportation, 1984); and Rhoda Gilman, Carolyn Gilman, and Deborah M. Stultz, *The Red River Trails: Oxcart Routes Between St. Paul and the Selkirk Settlement, 1820–1870* (St. Paul: Minnesota Historical Society, 1979). On the state's parks, see pamphlets in the Minnesota State Parks Heritage Series.

On Duluth, see Glenn N. Sandvik, *Duluth: An Illustrated History of the Zenith City* (Woodland Hills, Calif.: Windsor Publications, 1983); Ryck Lydecker and Lawrence J. Sommer, *Duluth Sketches of the Past: A Bicentennial Collection* (Duluth: American Revolution Bicentennial Commission, 1976); and James Allen Scott, *Duluth's Legacy: Architecture*, vol. 1 (Duluth: The City, 1974).

Recent books on the Twin Cities include Lucile M. Kane and Alan Ominsky, *Twin Cities: A Pictorial History of St. Paul and Minneapolis* (St. Paul: Minnesota Historical Society Press, 1983); Ronald Abler, John S. Adams, and John R. Borchert, *The Twin Cities of St. Paul and Minneapolis* (Cambridge, Mass.: Ballinger Publishing Company, 1976); Lucile M. Kane, *The Waterfall that Built a City: The Falls of St. Anthony in Minneapolis* (St. Paul: Minnesota Historical Society, 1966); Joseph Stipanovich, *City of Lakes: An Illustrated History of Minneapolis* (Woodland Hills, Calif.: Windsor Publications, 1982); Virginia B. Kunz, *St. Paul: Saga of an American City* (Woodland Hills, Calif.: Windsor Publications, 1977); and J. Fletcher

Williams, *A History of the City of St. Paul to 1875* (St. Paul: Minnesota Historical Society, 1876; Borealis Books, 1983).

Helpful information about specific areas in the Twin Cities is contained in Judith A. Martin and David A. Lanegran, *Where We Live: The Residential Districts of Minneapolis and St. Paul* (Minneapolis: University of Minnesota Press and Center for Urban and Regional Affairs, University of Minnesota, 1983); Sue E. Holbert and June D. Holmquist, *A History Tour of 50 Twin City Landmarks*, Minnesota Historic Sites Pamphlet 2 (St. Paul: Minnesota Historical Society, 1966); Karen Mason and Carol Lacey, *Women's History Tour of the Twin Cities* (Minneapolis: Nodin Press, 1982); Bernard Jacob and Carol Morphew, *Pocket Architecture* (Minneapolis: Minnesota Society, American Institute of Architects, 1984); Donald Empson, *The Street Where You Live: A Guide to the Street Names of St. Paul* (St. Paul: Witsend Press, 1975); Sister Joan Kain, *Rocky Roots: Three Geology Walking Tours of Downtown St. Paul* (St. Paul: Ramsey County Historical Society, 1978); John J. Koblas, *F. Scott Fitzgerald in Minnesota: His Homes and Haunts*, Minnesota Historic Sites Pamphlet 18 (St. Paul: Minnesota Historical Society, 1978); Ernest R. Sandeen, *St. Paul's Historic Summit Avenue* (St. Paul: Living Historical Museum, 1978); Lanegran and Sandeen, *The Lakes District of Minneapolis: A History of the Calhoun-Isles Community* (St. Paul: Living Historical Museum, 1979); John R. Borchert et al., *Legacy of Minneapolis: Preservation Amid Change* (St. Paul: Voyageur Press, 1983); James Berman, ed., *Saint Anthony Falls Rediscovered* (Minneapolis: Minneapolis Riverfront Development Coordination Board, 1980); Nicholas Westbrook, ed., *Guide to the Industrial Archeology of the Twin Cities* (St. Paul: Society for Industrial Archeology, 1983).

Minnesota's land and its resources are featured in John R. Borchert and Neil C. Gustafson, *Atlas of Minnesota Resources and Settlement*, rev. 3d ed. (Minneapolis: Center for Urban and Regional Affairs, University of Minnesota, 1980). On geology, see Richard W. Ojakangas and Charles L. Matsch, *Minnesota's Geology* (Minneapolis: University of Minnesota Press, 1982); Constance J. Sansome, *Minnesota Underfoot: A Field Guide to the State's Outstanding Geologic Features* (Bloomington: Voyageur Press, 1983); Edmund C. Bray, *Billions of Years in Minnesota: The Geological Story of the State* (St. Paul: Science Museum, 1977). On the state's waters, see Thomas F. Waters, *The Streams and Rivers of Minnesota* (Minneapolis: University of Minnesota Press, 1977) and R. Newell Searle, *Saving Quetico-Superior: A Land Set Apart* (St. Paul: Minnesota Historical Society Press, 1979).

The residents of the state have been studied in several comprehensive works. For Minnesota's Indian people, see Roy W. Meyer, *History of the*

Santee Sioux: United States Indian Policy on Trial (Lincoln: University of Nebraska Press, 1967); Kenneth Carley, *The Sioux Uprising of 1862*, rev. 2d ed. (St. Paul: Minnesota Historical Society, 1976); Carolyn Gilman, *Where Two Worlds Meet: The Great Lakes Fur Trade* (St. Paul: Minnesota Historical Society, 1982); William W. Warren, *A History of the Ojibway People* (St. Paul: Minnesota Historical Society, 1885; Borealis Books, 1984); and Gerald Vizenor, *A People Called the Chippewa* (Minneapolis: University of Minnesota Press, 1984). Indians and immigrants to the state are covered in June D. Holmquist, ed., *They Chose Minnesota: A Survey of the State's Ethnic Groups* (St. Paul: Minnesota Historical Society Press, 1981). Noteworthy women are the subjects of Barbara Stuhler and Gretchen Kreuter, eds., *Women of Minnesota: Selected Biographical Essays* (St. Paul: Minnesota Historical Society Press, 1977). The exploits of several lesser-known Minnesotans are described in Helen M. White, *The Tale of a Comet and Other Stories* (St. Paul: Minnesota Historical Society Press, 1984).

The state's politics, including Minnesota's notable third parties, are surveyed in Carl H. Chrislock, *The Progressive Era in Minnesota, 1899–1918* (St. Paul: Minnesota Historical Society, 1971); Millard L. Gieske, *Minnesota Farmer-Laborism: The Third Party Alternative* (Minneapolis: University of Minnesota Press, 1979); John E. Haynes, *Dubious Alliance: The Making of Minnesota's DFL Party* (Minneapolis: University of Minnesota Press, 1984); and G. Theodore Mitau, *Politics in Minnesota*, rev. ed. (Minneapolis: University of Minnesota Press, 1970).

Minnesota's industries and agriculture have been discussed in Don W. Larson, *Land of the Giants: A History of Minnesota Business* (Minneapolis: Dorn Books, 1979); Carol Pine and Susan Mundale, *Self-Made: The Stories of 12 Minnesota Entrepreneurs* (Minneapolis: Dorn Books, 1982); Dan Morgan, *Merchants of Grain* (New York: Viking Press, 1979); Hiram Drache, *The Day of the Bonanza: A History of Bonanza Farming in the Red River Valley of the North* (Fargo: N.Dak. Institute for Regional Studies, 1964); Agnes M. Larson, *History of the White Pine Industry in Minnesota* (Minneapolis: University of Minnesota Press, 1949); Albro Martin, *James J. Hill and the Opening of the Northwest* (New York: Oxford University Press, 1976); Edward W. Davis, *Pioneering with Taconite* (St. Paul: Minnesota Historical Society, 1964); and David A. Walker, *Iron Frontier: The Discovery and Early Development of Minnesota's Three Ranges* (St. Paul: Minnesota Historical Society Press, 1979).

Minnesota's cultural life is featured in Rena N. Coen, *Painting and Sculpture in Minnesota, 1820–1914* (Minneapolis: University of Minnesota Press, 1976) and Karal Ann Marling, *Colossus of Roads: Myth and Symbol along the American Highway* (Minneapolis: University of Minnesota Press, 1984).

For personal narratives that give interesting views on living in Minnesota, see Chester G. Anderson, ed., *Growing Up in Minnesota: Ten Writers Remember Their Childhoods* (Minneapolis: University of Minnesota Press, 1976); Ignatia Broker, *Night Flying Woman: An Ojibway Narrative* (St. Paul: Minnesota Historical Society Press, 1983); Lucy Leavenworth Wilder Morris, *Old Rail Fence Corners: Frontier Tales Told by Minnesota Pioneers* (St. Paul: Daughters of the American Revolution, 1914; Minnesota Historical Society, 1976); Peg Meier, ed., *Bring Warm Clothes: Letters and Photos from Minnesota's Past* (Minneapolis: Minneapolis Star and Tribune Company, 1981); Walter O'Meara, *We Made It Through the Winter: A Memoir of Northern Minnesota Boyhood* (St. Paul: Minnesota Historical Society, 1974); and, from a slightly different perspective, Walter N. Trenerry, *Murder in Minnesota: A Collection of True Cases* (St. Paul: Minnesota Historical Society, 1962).

Index

Key to Maps of Minnesota, 1938

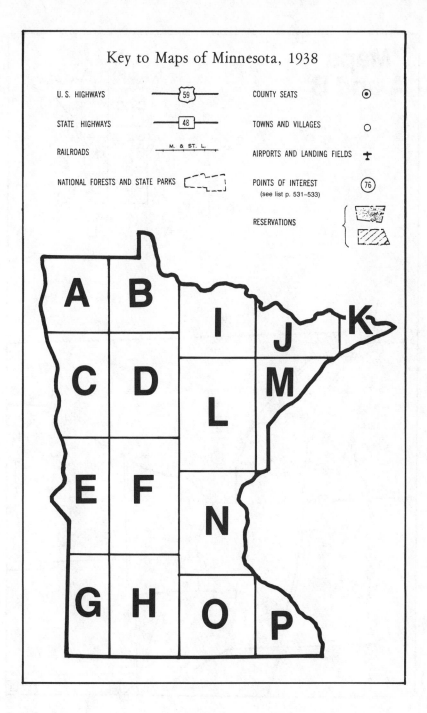

U. S. HIGHWAYS

STATE HIGHWAYS

RAILROADS   M. & ST. L.

NATIONAL FORESTS AND STATE PARKS

COUNTY SEATS

TOWNS AND VILLAGES

AIRPORTS AND LANDING FIELDS

POINTS OF INTEREST
(see list p. 531–533)

RESERVATIONS

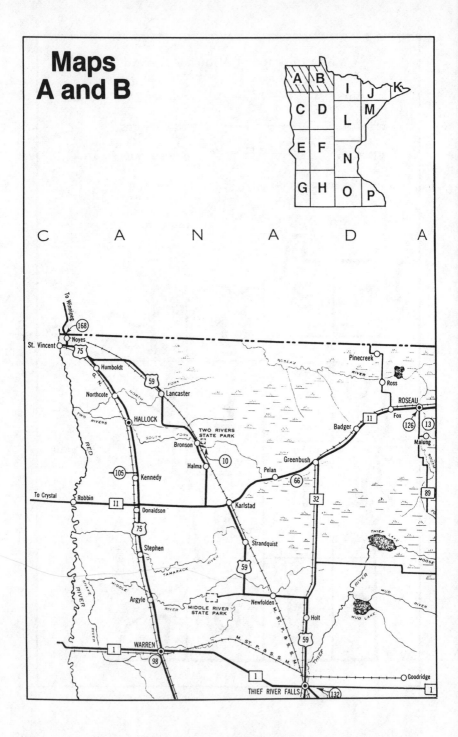

Maps
A and B

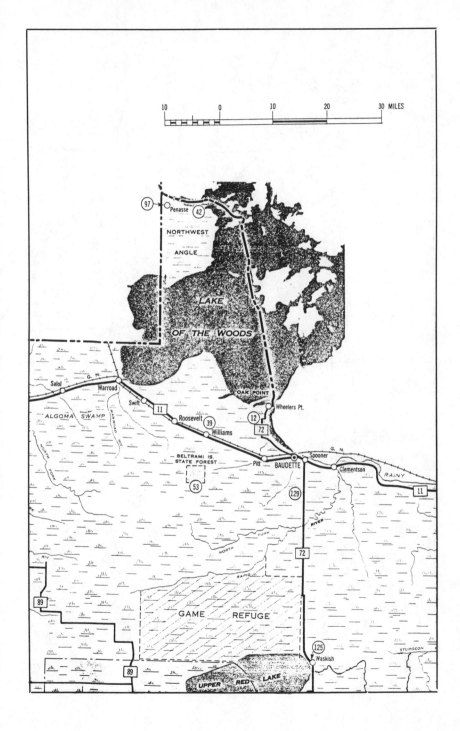

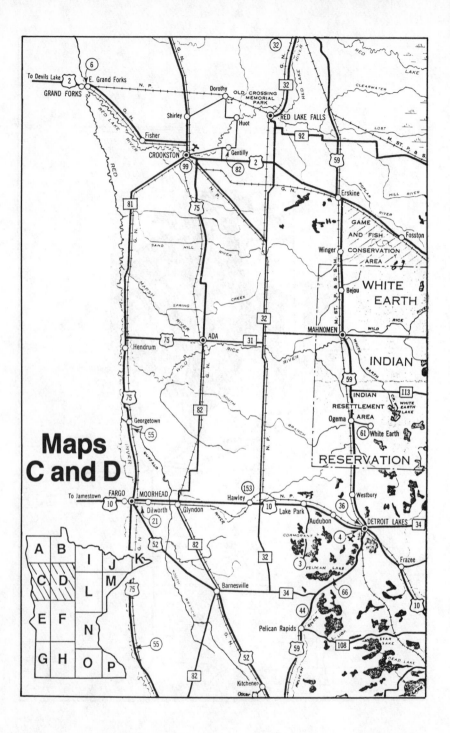

Maps C and D

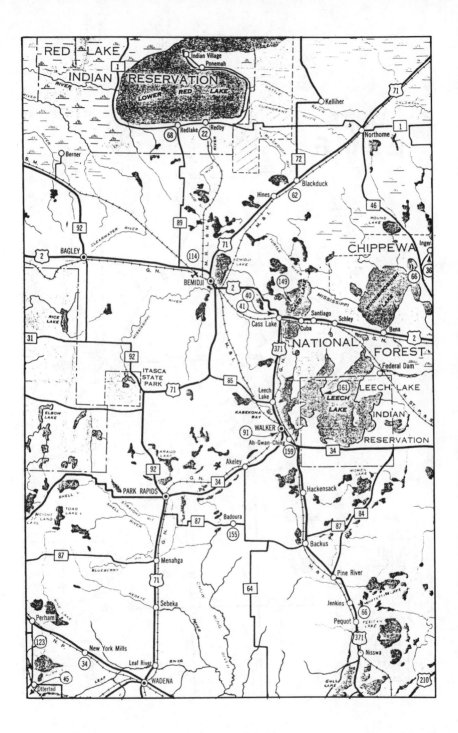

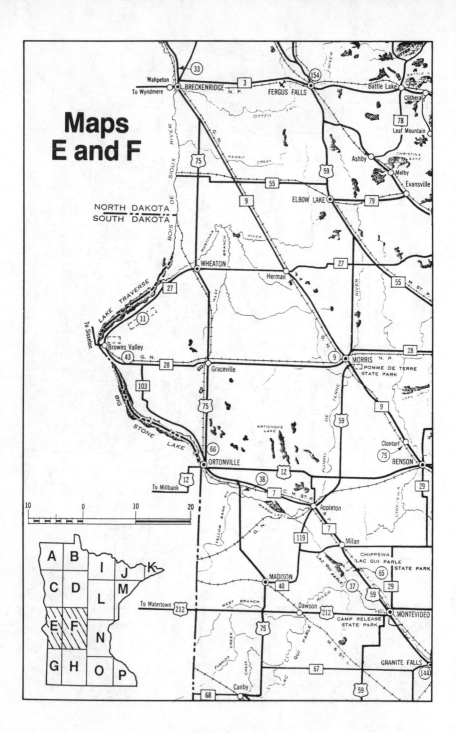

Maps
E and F

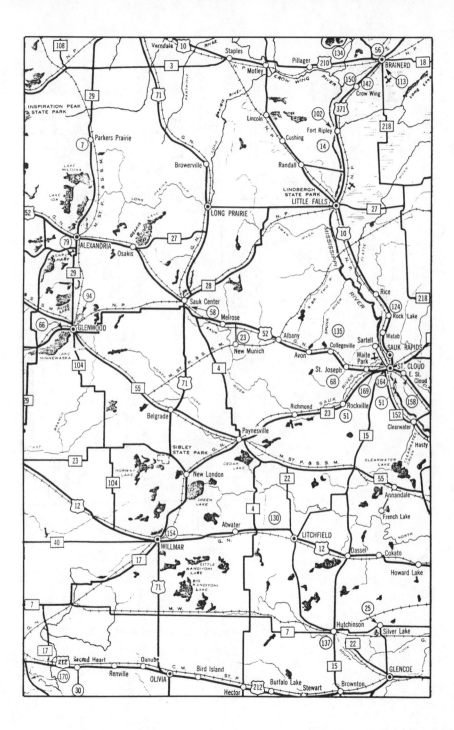

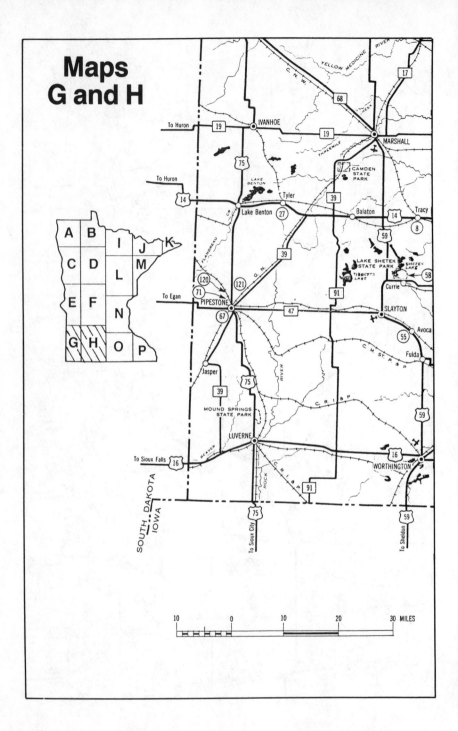

Maps
G and H

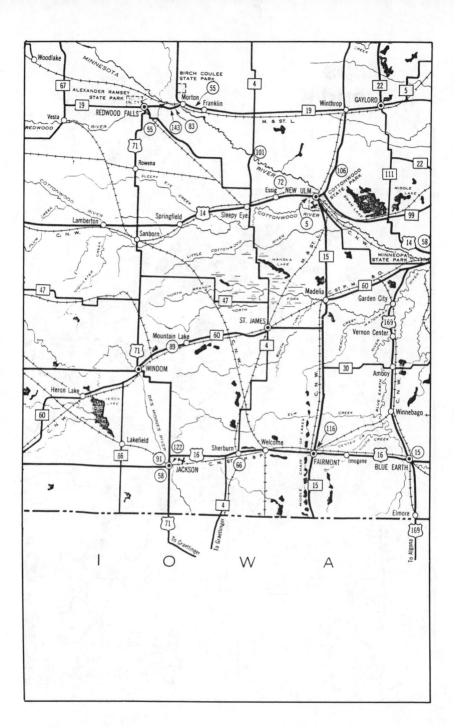

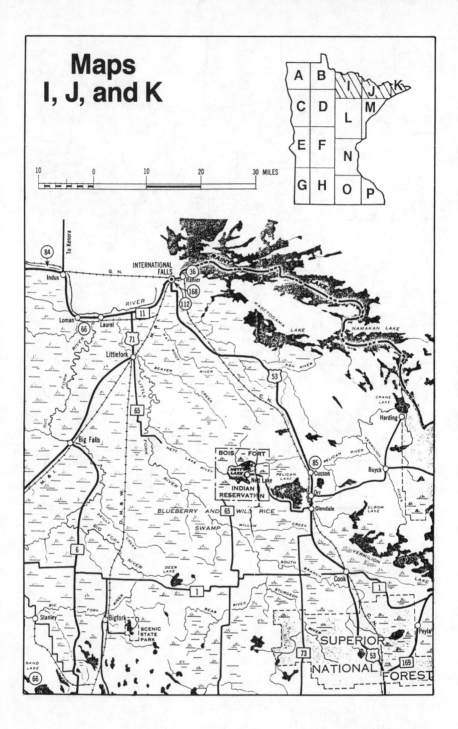

Maps
I, J, and K

A	B		I		J	K
C	D			L	M	
E	F			N		
G	H		O	P		

10   0   10   20   30 MILES

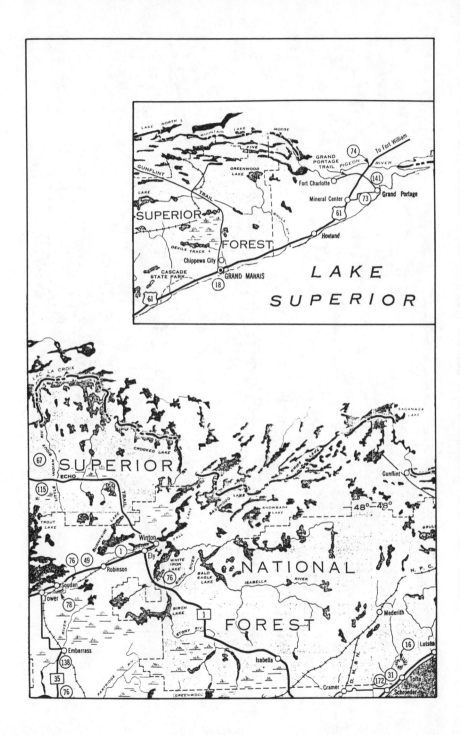

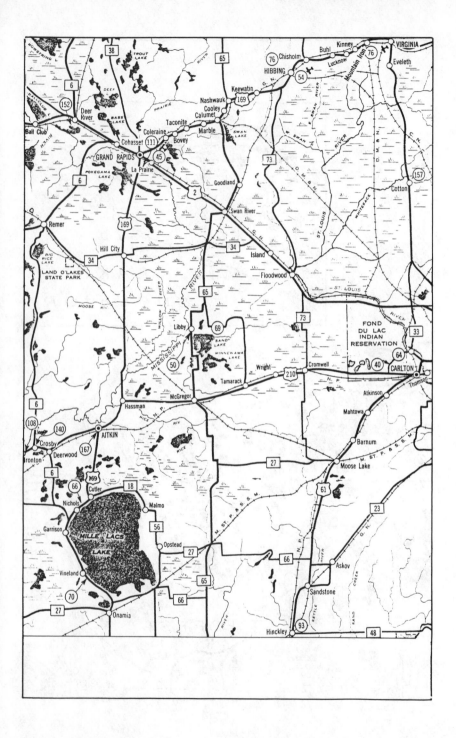

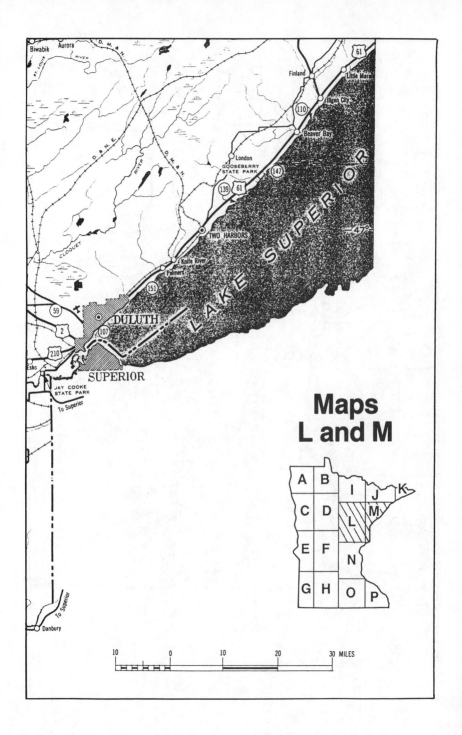

**Maps
L and M**

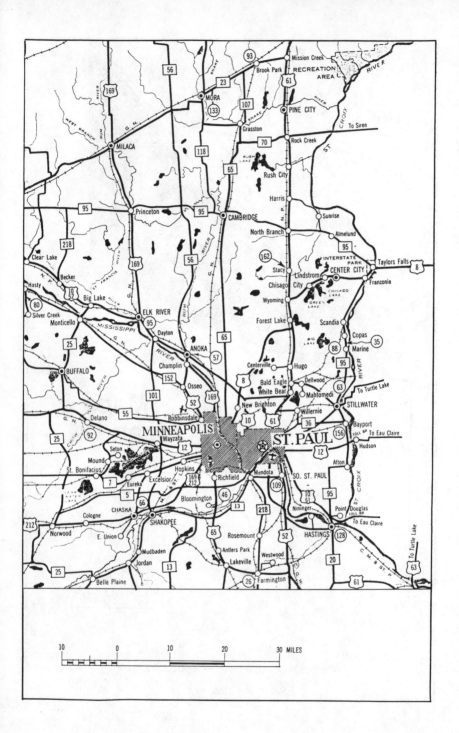

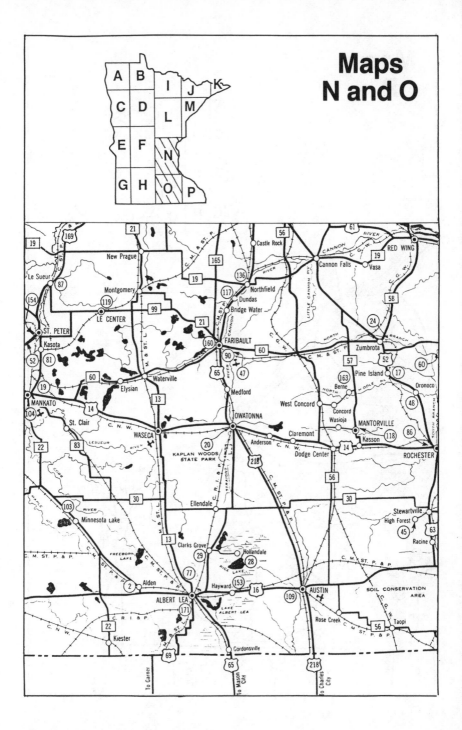

Maps
N and O

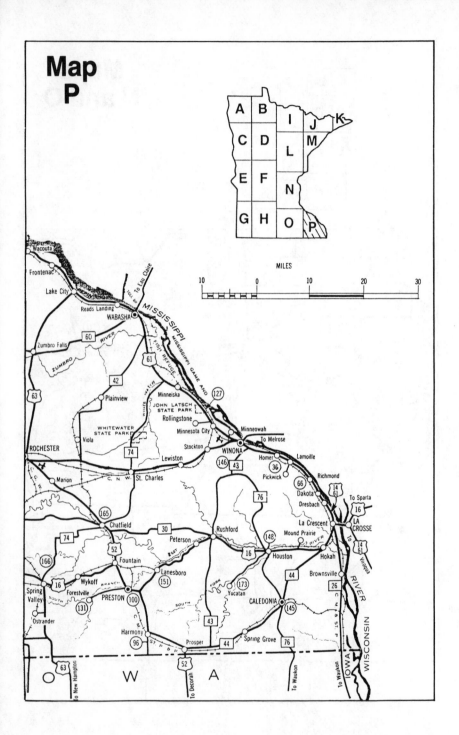

Map
P

List of Points of Interest

1. Airplane fishing trips, J
2. Alfalfa mill, O
3. Anchor stones, C
4. Aquatic plant nursery, C
5. Battle of New Ulm, 1862, H
6. Beet sugar factory, C
7. Bird museum, F
8. Box Car Day, G
9. Branch Agricultural College, E
10. Bronson Dam, A
11. Browns Valley, E
12. Burbot oil extracting plant, B
13. Campbell Beach, A
14. Camp Ripley, F
15. Canning factory, G
16. Carlton Peak, J
17. Cheese factory, O
18. Coast Guard Station, K
19. Colleges, O
20. Community Art Experiment, O
21. Concordia and State Teachers College, C
22. Cooperative fishery, D
23. Corpus Christi Day service, F
24. Covered bridge, O
25. Czech colony, F
26. Dairy, N
27. Danebod Folk School, G
28. Dutch colony, O
29. Early creamery cooperative, O
30. Farther and Gay Castle, F
31. Father Baraga's Cross, J
32. Federal Resettlement Area, C
33. Femco Farms, E
34. Finnish community, D
35. First commercial saw mill, N
36. Fish hatchery, C, D, I, P
37. Flood control dam, E
38. Flood Control Project, E
39. Flowing wells, B
40. Forest Experiment Station, D, L
41. Forest tree nurseries, D
42. Fort St. Charles, B
43. Fossil Man, E
44. Fossil Minnesota Man, C
45. Ghost town, C, L, O
46. Gideon Pond House, N
47. Girls' School, O
48. Gold Rush of 1857, O
49. Gold Rush of 1865, J
50. Government Dam, L
51. Granite quarries, F
52. Gustavus Adolphus College, O
53. Herd of caribou, B
54. Hibbing High School, L
55. Historical markers, C, G, H
56. Historical museum, F
57. Historic house, N
58. Historic site, F, G, H
59. Homestead Project, M
60. Hydroelectric dam, O
61. Indian agency, C
62. Indian battlefield, D
63. Indian battleground marker, N
64. Indian hospital, L
65. Indian mission, E
66. Indian mounds and burial grounds, A, C, D, E, F, I, L, N, P
67. Indian relics, G, J
68. Indian school, D, F,
69. Indian site, L
70. Indian trading post, L
71. Indian training school, G
72. Indian and pioneers battlefield, H
73. Indian village, K
74. International Bridge, K
75. Irish settlement, E
76. Iron mines, J, L

Index to Maps of Minnesota, 1938